NEW POLITICAL PARTIES OF EASTERN EUROPE AND THE SOVIET UNION

Other recent current affairs and economics titles from Longman Group UK Limited include the following:

The World Trade System, edited by Robert Fraser (1991)

Directory of Pressure Groups in the European Community, edited by Alan Butt Philip (1991)

The World's News Media, edited by Harry Drost for CIRCA Ltd (1991)

Revolutionary and Dissident Movements: An International Guide (3rd edition), (1991)

Federal Systems of the World, edited by Daniel J. Elazar and compiled by the Jerusalem Institute for Federal Studies (1991)

Gulf Crisis Chronology, compiled by the BBC World Service (1991)

Political and Economic Encyclopaedia of South America and the Caribbean, edited by Peter Calvert (1991)

Trade Unions of the World 1992–93 (3rd edition), edited by Martin Upham (1991)

OPEC and the World Energy Market: A Comprehensive Reference Guide (2nd edition), edited by Gavin Brown (1991)

Maritime Affairs: A World Handbook (2nd edition), edited by Edgar Gold and compiled by the Associates of the Oceans Institute of Canada (1991)

Handbook of Reconstruction in Eastern Europe and the Soviet Union, edited by Stephen White (1991)

BBC World Service Glossary of Current Affairs, compiled by BBC Monitoring (1991)

Political Scandals and Causes Célèbres since 1945: An International Reference Compendium (1990)

Political and Economic Encyclopaedia of Western Europe, edited by CIRCA Ltd (1990)

Treaties and Alliances of the World (5th edition), edited by Nicholas Rengger (1990)

World Guide to Environmental Issues and Organizations, edited by Peter Brackley (1990)

Communist and Marxist Parties of the World (2nd edition), edited by Roger East (1990)

Youth Movements of The World, by William D. Angel (1990)

Political and Economic Encyclopaedia of the Soviet Union and Eastern Europe, edited by Stephen White (1990)

The European Parliament, by Francis Jacobs and Richard Corbett, with Michael Shackleton (1990)

Anti-Nuclear Movements: A World Survey of Opposition to Nuclear Energy, by Wolfgang Rüdig (1990)

The Broken Mirror: China after Tiananmen, edited by George Hicks (1990)

The British Trade Union Directory, edited and compiled by Wolodymyr Maksymiw (1990)

NEW POLITICAL PARTIES OF EASTERN EUROPE AND THE SOVIET UNION

Edited by
BOGDAN SZAJKOWSKI

With Contributions by

John B. Allcock, Marko Milivojević, Jonathan Osmond, George Sanford,
Nigel Swain, Bogdan Szajkowski, Stephen White, Gordon Wightman

NEW POLITICAL PARTIES OF EASTERN EUROPE AND THE SOVIET UNION

Published by Longman Group UK Ltd, Westgate House,
The High, Harlow, Essex, CM20 1YR, United Kingdom
Telephone (0279) 442601
Telex 81491 Padlog
Facsimile (0279) 444501

DPA
DIRECTORY PUBLISHERS
ASSOCIATION

Distributed exclusively in the USA and Canada by Gale Research Inc., 835 Penobscot Building, Detroit, Michigan 48226, USA.

ISBN 0582 085756 (Longman)

© Longman Group UK Ltd 1991

All rights reserved; no part of this publication may be reproduced, stored in a retrieval system, or transmitted in any form or by any means, electronic, mechanical, photocopying, recording, or otherwise without either the prior written permission of the Publishers or a licence permitting restricted copying issued by the Copyright Licensing Agency Ltd., 90 Tottenham Court Road, London W1P 9HE.

A catalogue record for this book is available from the British Library.

Printed and bound in Great Britain by Bookcraft (Bath) Ltd

To Professor Jean Blondel

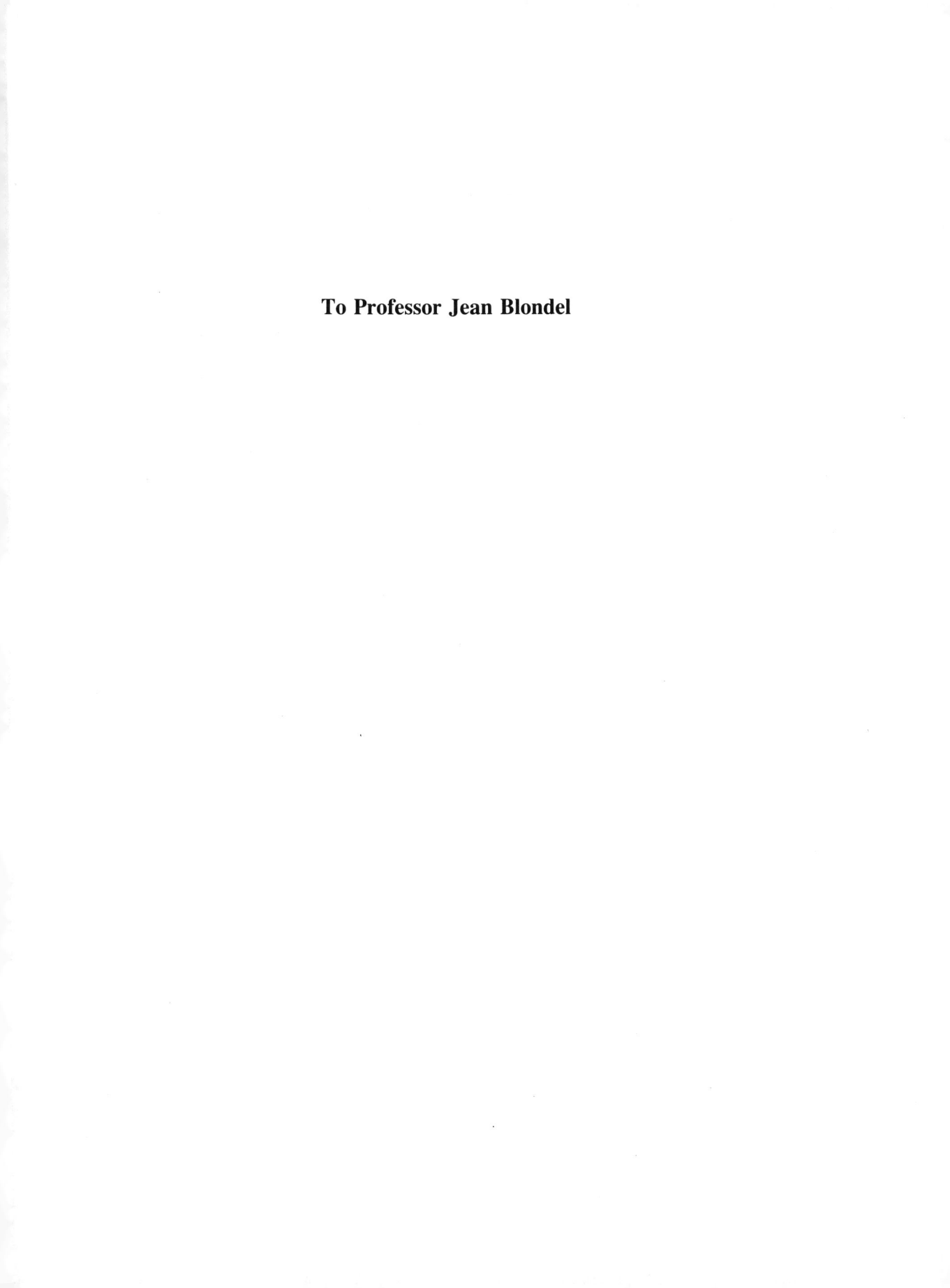

CONTENTS

Preface viii

List of abbreviations of party names x

Albania *Marko Milivojević* 1

Bulgaria *Bogdan Szajkowski* 19

Czechoslovakia *Gordon Wightman* 53

Estonia *Stephen White* 93

Germany *Jonathan Osmond* 95

Hungary *Nigel Swain* 129

Latvia *Stephen White* 169

Lithuania *Stephen White* 171

Poland *George Sanford* 175

Romania *Bogdan Szajkowski* 219

Union of Soviet Socialist Republics *Stephen White* 251

Yugoslavia *John B. Allcock* 293

Index 369

PREFACE

The communist political system this century to all intents and purposes eradicated and marginalized party politics. Starting with the Bolshevik revolution in 1917, the experience of communist practice during the past seven decades led to the eradication of the working party system and a consequent centralization and strict administration of party politics. The ruling communist party became the Ministry of Politics, beyond reproach and beyond reform.

The popular revolutions which took place at an astonishing speed in Central and Eastern Europe in 1989 and in Albania a year later, and which are still continuing in the Soviet Union, resulted in the proliferation of political parties and an explosion of popular support for party politics, the abandonment of restrictions and controls and the flowering of new ideas and formulas, together with the airing of old concepts which under communist rule had existed only below the surface.

A cursory glance at the list of political parties included in this book which have emerged in Central and Eastern Europe and the Soviet Union suggests the following six broad categories. Firstly, parties of nostalgia; historical parties that existed before the communist takeovers and have re-emerged with the support of their old members. With few exceptions these have avoided major internal splits but they appear to have been unable to increase their membership and popular appeal. The second category of parties, initially based on mass popular movements such as Solidarity and Civic Forum, has shown the biggest proliferation, splits and divisions as parties readjust to the realities of power. Civic Forum and Solidarity have been useful and convenient umbrellas for many diverse views and ideologies, united while in opposition to communist rule, but where subsequent personality clashes have led to disunity and discord. The third group of nationalist parties has encapsulated the nationalist aspirations of diverse ethnic groups long denied by the communist rulers. These parties represent homogeneous and often vociferous constituencies and as such present a considerable challenge to the new political authorities in these countries. The fourth category includes parties inspired by their western counterparts such as the Green and Feminist Movements and other less serious equivalents like Friends of the Beer Party and the Monster Loony Party. In the fifth category are included the religious parties devoted specifically to the advancement of religious views and the social, political and moral teaching of various denominations. The final category includes the remnants of the communist parties, now under revised names and with extremely small memberships. As they have lost their grip on power they have been subject to often acrimonious divisions and quarrels.

This book presents a comprehensive picture of the development and current state of political parties and party politics in the Soviet Union and Eastern Europe. Every effort has been made to give accurate and up-to-date information and analysis wherever possible. In the overwhelming number of cases contributors to this volume have been able to obtain

PREFACE

a complete set of data on history, membership, programme, structure and affiliations and electoral behaviour. However, in some cases it has proved to be impossible to obtain this information. Fortunately the gaps are only in respect to small parties which were reluctant to disclose such information for reasons of their own.

The list of abbreviations on p. x and a comprehensive index will help to guide the reader through the labyrinth of organizations and associations. The parties themselves are listed alphabetically within each country or republic section.

The Editor and authors wish to acknowledge the following publications which have been helpful: RFE/RL Research Institute Report on Eastern Europe; Keesings Record of World Events (Longman, Harlow); BBC Summary of World Broadcasts; East European Reporter; *Izvestiya Tsk KPSS*; V. N. Berezovsky and N. I. Krotov (eds), *Neformal'naya Rossiya* (Moscow, *Molodaya gvardiya*, 1990).

Professor Stephen White wishes to acknowledge the assistance of Peter Lentini of the Institute of Soviet and East European Studies, University of Glasgow.

The Editor began working on this book while at the European University Institute in Florence and is grateful to the President and the Council of the Institute for the award of a Jean Monnet Fellowship. He would also like to acknowledge the help of the Institute Library and in particular the Social Science Librarian Peter Kennealy.

The Editor gratefully acknowledges the co-operation of the publishers for the speed with which this book has been produced; thanks are due in particular to Dr John Harper and Nicola Greenwood of Longman for their advice and patient hard work on the project.

Bogdan Szajkowski
University of Exeter

October 1991

Abbreviations of names of party officers in this book are the following:

cent.	=	central
ch.	=	chairman/chairwoman
dep.	=	deputy
g.s.	=	general secretary
hon.	=	honorary
l.	=	leader
nat.	=	national
perm.	=	permanent
pres.	=	president
sec.	=	secretary
sec.-gen	=	secretary-general

ABBREVIATIONS OF PARTY NAMES

AAP	Albanian Agrarian Party
ACDP	Albanian Christian-Democratic Party
ACP	Albanian Communist Party
ADF	Albanian Democratic Front
ADP	Albanian Democratic Party
AEP	Albanian Ecology Party
AFD	Alliance of Free Democrats
AJL	Alternative Jugendliste
AJL	Alternative Youth List
ANP	Albanian National Unity Party
APA	Albanian People's Army
APDP	Albanian Party of Democratic Prosperity
APL	Albanian Party of Labour
ARF	Alliance of Reform Forces
ARFM	Alliance of Reform Forces of Macedonia
ARFM	Alliance of Reform Forces of Montenegro
ARFV	Alliance of Reform Forces of Vojvodina
ARFY	Alliance of Reform Forces of Yugoslavia
ARFYBH	Alliance of Reform Forces of Yugoslavia for Bosnia and Hercegovina
ARFYC	Alliance of Reform Forces of Yugoslavia for Croatia
ARP	Albanian Republican Party
ASA	Alternative Socialist Association
ASDO	Associated Serbian Democratic Opposition
ASO	Alternative Socialist Organization
ASO	Alternativo Sotsialistichesko Obedinenie
ASP	Albanian Socialist Party
ASP	Alternative Socialist Party
ASZ	Agraszovetseg
AVNOJ	Anti-fascist Council for the National Liberation of Yugoslavia
AWP	Albanian Workers' Party
AYDI	Association for a Yugoslav Democratic Initiative
BANU	Bulgarian Agrarian National Union
BANU-NP	Bulgarian Agrarian National Union — Nikola Petkov
BBB	Bulgarian Business Bloc
BBWR	Non-Party Bloc for Collaboration with Government
BCP	Bulgarian Communist Party
BDU	Byelorussian Democratic Union
BFD	Bund Freier Demokraten

ABBREVIATIONS

BFD	League of Free Democrats
BH	Bosnia and Hercegovina
BSA	Bund Sozialistischer Arbeiter
BSA	League of Socialist Workers
BSPS	Bashkimi i Sindikatave te Paravura Shqiperise
BZD	Bialoruskie Zjednoczenie Demokratyczne
CA	Centre Agreement
CADP	Civic Agreement for Democracy and Pluralism
CAS	Confederation of Anarcho-Syndicalists
CC	Civic Committee
CCATU	Central Council of Albanian Trade Unions
CCDP	Croatian Christian Democratic Party
CD	Centrum Demokratyczne
CD	Christian Democracy
CDLP	Christian Democratic Labour Party
CDP	Croatian Democratic Party
CDPP	Christian Democratic People's Party
CDSU	Christian Democratic Social Union
CDSU	Christlich-Demokratische Soziale Union
CDU	Christian Democratic Union (Germany)
CDU	Christian Democratic Union (Romania)
CDU	Christlich-Demokratische Union Deutschlands
CDU	Croatian Democratic Union
CDUBH	Croatian Democratic Union of Bosnia and Hercegovina
CDUR	Christian-Democratic Union of Russia
CENTERN	Centre Group of the Nordic Council
ChD	Chrzescijanska Demokracja
ChDSP	Chrzescijansko-Demokratyczne Stronnictwo Pracy
ChPP	Chrzescijanska Partia Pracy
ChRO	Christian Civic Movement
ChSU	Christian Social Union
CI	Citizens' Initiative
CIP	Confederation for an Independent Poland
CL	Confederation of Labour
CLP	Christian Labour Party
CMC	Conservative-Monarchist Club
CMDP	Croatian Muslim Democratic Party
CNU	Christian National Union
CP	Communist Party
CP	Conservative Party
CPP	Communist Party of Poland
CPP	Croatian Peasant Party
CPP	Croatian People's Party
CPR	Croatian Party of Rights
CPSU	Communist Party of the Soviet Union
CPY	Communist Party of Yugoslavia
CRP	Christian Republican Party

CSCE	Conference on Security and Co-operation in Europe
CSLP	Croatian Social-Liberal Party
CSPD	Christian Social Party of Germany
CSPD	Christlich-Soziale Partei Deutschlands
CSU	Christian Social Union
CSU	Christlich-Soziale Union
DA	Democratic Departure
DA	Democraticher Aufbruch
DACM-DSM	Democratic Action Civic Movement — Democratic Social Movement
DBD	Democratic Farmers' Party of Germany
DBD	Demokratische Bauernpartei Deutschlands
DBU	Deutsche Forumpartei
DBU	German Beer Drinkers' Union
DC	Democratic Centre
DC	Democratic Coalition (Montenegro)
DCMV	Democratic Community of Magyars of Vojvodina
DEMOS	Democratic Opposition
DFD	Democratic Women's League of Germany
DFD	Demokratischer Frauenbund Deutschlands
DF M	Democratic Forum Mazowia
DFP	German Forum Party
DJ	Democracy Now
DJ	Demokratie Jetzt
DK	Demokratska Koalicja
DKP	German Communist Party
DLAC	Democratic League of Albanians of Croatia
DLCV	Democratic League of Croats in the Vojvodina
DLG-EKO	Democratic League of Greens — EKO
DLK	Democratic League of Kosovo
DMP	Democratic Monarchist Party
DP	Democratic Party (Bulgaria)
DP	Democratic Party (Poland)
DP	Democratic Party (Croatia)
DP	Democratic Party (Montenegro)
DP	Democratic Party (Soviet Union)
DPR	Democratic Party of Russia
DPS	Democratic Party of Socialists
DPS	Dvizhenie za Prava i Svobodi
DPU	Democratic Unity Party
DRPM	Democratic Reform Party of Muslims
DRSM	Demokratska Reformska Stranka Muslimana
DS	Demokratska Stranka
DS	Demokratska Stranka (Croatia)
DSAH	Demokratski Savez Albanaca Hrvatske
DSHV	Demokratski Savez Hrvata u Vojvodini
DSS	Demokratska Stranka Socijalista
DSS BiH	Demokratski Socijalisticki Saves Bosne i Hercegovine

ABBREVIATIONS

DSU	Deutsche Soziale Union
DSU	German Social Union
DSZ-EKO	Demokratski Savez Zelena — EKO
DU	Democratic Union (Poland)
DU	Democratic Union (Soviet Union)
DVU	German People's Union
DZVM	Demokratska Zajednica Vojvodanskih Madara
EPCG	Ekoloski Pokret Crne Gore
EWA	Erster Weiblicher Aufbruch
EWA	First Female Departure
F & P	Freedom and Peace
FDJ	Freie Deutsche Jugend
FD M	Forum Demokratyczne Mazowsze
FDP	Free Democratic Party
FDP	Freie Demokratische Partei
FDR	Forum of the Democratic Right
FDUD	Free Democratic Union of Germany
FDUD	Freie Demokratische Union Deutschlands
FIDESZ	Alliance of Young Democrats
FIDESZ	Fiatal Demokratak Szovetsege
FKgP	Fuggetlen Kissgazda, Foldmunkas es Polgari Part
FMDP	Fuggetlen Magyar Demokrata Part
FMDP	Independent Hungarian Democratic Party
FP	Freedom Party (Poland)
FPD	Forum Prawicy Demokratycznej
FPDUD	Faction of the Democratic Right Within the Democratic Union
FVP	Fortschrittliche Volkspartei
FVP	Progressive People's Party
GA-S	Green Action — Split
GDR	German Democratic Republic
GI	Grazhdanska Initsiativa
GKMN	Gibanje za Kulturu Mira i Nenasilja
GP	Grey Panthers — Pensioners' Party of Slovenia
GS	Greens of Slovenia
GU	Green Union
HDF	Hungarian Democratic Forum
HDS	Hvatska Demokratska Stranka
HDUR	Hungarian Democratic Union of Romania
HDZ	Hrvatska Demokratska Zajednica
HDZ BiH	Hrvatska Demokratska Zajednica Bosne i Hercegovine
HKDS	Hrvatska Krscanska Demokratska Stranka
HMDS	Hrvatska Muslimanska Demokratska Stranka
HNS	Hrvatska Narodna Stranka
HPP	Hungarian People's Party
HRF	Human Rights Forum (Albania)
HRP	Hristiyan-Republikanska Partiya
HSDP	Hungary's Social Democratic Party

NEW POLITICAL PARTIES OF EASTERN EUROPE AND THE SOVIET UNION

HSLS	Hrvatska Socijalno-Liberalna Stranka
HSP	Hrvatska Stranka Prava
HSP	Hungarian Socialist Party
HSS	Hrvatska Seljacka Stranka
HSWP	Hungarian Socialist Workers' Party
HVK	Hazafias Valasztasi Koalicio
IFM	Peace and Human Rights Initiative
IFM	Initiative Frieden und Menschenrechte
IMF	International Monetary Fund
IMRO	Internal Macedonian Revolutionary Organization
IMRO-DPMNU	Internal Macedonian Revolutionary Organization — Democratic Party for Macedonian National Unity
IMU	Independent Miners' Union
IRP	Italian Republican Party
ISP	Independent Smallholder, Land Labourer and Citizens' Party; Smallholders' Party
JU	Junge Union
JU	Young Union
KDA	Kosovo Democratic Association
KDNP	Keresztenydemokrata Neppart
KGB	Committee for State Security
KIK	Klub Inteligiencji Katolickiej
KLD	Kongres Liberalno-Demokratyczny
KNL	Klub Nowoczesnego Liberalizmu
KPD	Communist Party of Germany
KPD	Kommunistiche Partei Deutschlands
KPN	Konfederacja Polski Niepodleglej
KPP	Komunistyczna Partia Polski
KQQBSP	Keshilli Qendror i Bashkimeve Profesionale te Shqiperise
KUL	Catholic University of Lublin
KZ-M	Klub Zachowawczo-Monarchistyczny
KZRKiOR	National Union of Agricultural Circles
LCBH-PDC	League of Communists of Bosnia and Hercegovina — Party of Democratic Changes
LC-MY	League of Communists — Movement for Yugoslavia
LCM	League of Communists of Montenegro
LCTP	Slovene Craftsmen's and Tradesmen's Party
LCY	League of the Communists of Yugoslavia
LDC	Liberal-Democratic Congress (Poland)
LDK	Lidhja Demokratike e Kosoves
LDP	Liberal Democratic Party (Bulgaria)
LDP	Liberal Democratic Party (Slovenia)
LDP	Liberal Democratic Party of Germany
LDP	Liberal-Democratic Party (Soviet Union)
LDP	Liberal-Demokratische Partei
LDPD	Liberal Democratic Party of Germany
LDP I	Liberal-Democratic Party Independence

ABBREVIATIONS

LDP N	Liberalno-Demokratyczna Partia Niepodleglosc
LDS	Liberalna Demokraticna Stranka
LILO	Lila offensive
LILO	Lilac Offensive
LP	Liberal Party (Bosnia and Hercegovina)
LP	Liberal Party (Slovenia)
LPK	Liberal Party of Kosovo
LS	Liberalna Stranka (Bosnia and Hercegovina)
LS	Liberalna Stranka (Slovenia)
LSCG	Liberalni Savez Crne Gore
LSYC	League of Socialist Youth of Croatia
MAAK	Dvizenje za Semakedonska Akcija
MAAK	Movement for Pan-Macedonian Action
MASPOK	Masovni Pokret — Mass Movement
MBO	Muslim-Bosnian Organization
MBO	Muslim-Bosnian Organization
MBO	Muslimanska-Bosnjacka Organizacija
MChD	Young Christian Democrats
MCPN	Movement for a Culture of Peace and Non- violence
MDF	Magyar Demokrata Forum
MDPSM	Mlada Demokratsko-Progresivna Stranka na Makedonija
MDS	Hrvatska Muslimanska Demokratska Stranka
MFT	Munnich Ferenc Tarsasag
MLC	Modern Liberalism Club
MLIN	Mlada Inicijativa
MNP	Magyar Neppart
MRF	Movement for Rights and Freedoms
MSP	Magyar Szocialista Part
MSZDP	Magyarorszagi Socialdemokrata Part
MSZMP	Magyar Szocialista Munkaspart
MVD	Ministry of Internal Affairs (Soviet Union)
MWP	Movement of the Working People
NAM	Non-Aligned Movement
NAP	NepAkarat Part
NATO	North Atlantic Treaty Organization
ND	Narodowa Demokracja
ND	New Democracy-Movement for Serbia
ND	Nova Demokratija-Pokret za Srbiju
NDP	National Democratic Party (Georgia)
NDP	National Democratic Party (Macedonia)
NDP	National Democratic Party (Poland)
NDP	National Democratic Party (Romania)
NDPD	National Democratic Party of Germany
NDPD	National-Demokratische Partei Deutschlands
NF	Neues Forum
NF	New Forum
NIK	Supreme Control Chamber

NEW POLITICAL PARTIES OF EASTERN EUROPE AND THE SOVIET UNION

NLF	National Liberation Front
NLP	National Liberal Party
NOP	Narodowe Odrodzenie Polski
NP	National Party (Montenegro)
NP	National Party (Poland)
NPD	National Democratic Party of Germany
NPP	National Peasant Party (Croatia)
NPR	Narodowa Parta Robotnicza
NRPP	National Rebirth of Poland Party
NS	Narodna Stranka (Montenegro)
NSF	National Salvation Front
NSS	Narodna Seljacka Stranaka
NVC	National Veterans' Committee
OKP	Solidarity Civic Parliamentary Club
OMONIA	Democratic Union of the Greek Minority
OWP	Camp of Greater Poland
OZON	Camp on National Unity
PAPS	Party of the Alliance of Peasants of Serbia
PAS	Partie Agrar Shqiperise
PBKS	Partia Bashkimi Kombetarwe Shqiperise
PC	Partia Centrum
PC	Porozumienie Centrum
PCE	Party of Citizens' Equality
PChDF	Polish Christian Democratic Forum
PCR	Polish Christian Right
PCSU	Polish Catholic Social Union
PDA	Muslim Party of Democratic Action
PDA	Party of Democratic Action
PDC	Party of Democratic Changes
PDD	Partija Demokratsko Delovanje
PDP	Partija za Demokratski Prosperitet vo Makedonija
PDP	Partis Demokratis Populore
PDP	Party for Democratic Prosperity in Macedonia
PDR	Party of Democratic Renewal
PDS	Partei des Demokratischen Sozialismus
PDS	Partia Demokratike Shgiperise
PDS	Partia Shqiptare Demokristiane
PDS	Partia Socialdemokrate (Kosovo)
PDS	Party of Democratic Socialism
PEP	Polish Economic Party
PES	Partia Ecologia Shuiperise
PFN	Polski Front Narodowy
PGP	Polish Green Party
PHP	Polish Handicrafts Party
PK	Partia Konserwatywna
PKR	Polski Klub Republikanski
PKUD	Parliamentary Klub Unia Demokratyczna

ABBREVIATIONS

PNF	Polish National Front
POB	Political Opposition Block
POFOSZ	Alliance of Hungarian Political Prisoners
POFOSZ	Magyar Politikai Foglyok Szovetsege
PORDiP-CADP	Porozumienie Obywatelskie na Rzecz Demokracji i Pluralizmu
PPCh	Polska Prawica Chrzescijanska
PPFB	Polish Party of the Friends of Beer
PPG	Polska Partia Gospodarcza
PPK	Parliamentary Party of Kosovo
PPOS	Polska Partia Obywateli Swiata
PPP	Polish Peasant Party
PPP-Bak	Polish Peasant Party (Bak Faction)
PPPC	Progressive People's Party of the Centre
PPPP	Polska Partia Przyjaciol Piwa
PPPW	Polish Party of Friends of Whisky
PPR	Polska Partia Robotnicza
PPR	Polish Workers' Party
PPS	Polska Partia Socjalistyczna
PPS-DR	Polish Socialist Party — Democratic Revolution
PPSiNS	Powszechna Partia Slowian i Narodow Sprzymierzonych
PPS-N	Polska Partia Socjalistyczna (Nezalezna)
PPS-O	Polska Partia Socjalistyczna (Odrodzona)
PPS-RD	Polska Partia Socjalistyczna — Rewolucja Demokratyczna
PPS-TKK	Polska Partia Socjalistyczna (Tymczasowy Komitet Krajowy)
PPZ	Polska Partia Zielonych
PRON	Patriotic Front of National Rebirth
PRP	Partia Rzemiosla Polskiego
PRS	Partia Republikanska Shqiperise
PR-TRP	Partia Republikanska — Towarzystwo Republikanskie Polskie
PSCG	Partija Socijalista Crne Gore
PSDS	Partia Socialdemokratike e Shqiperise
PSDU	Polish Social Democratic Union
PSL	Polskie Stronnictwo Ludowe
PSL-Bak	Polskie Stronnictwo Ludowe (Grupa Henryka Baka)
PSL-Odrodzenie	
PSL-Rebirth	
PSL-S	Polskie Stronnictwo Ludowe Solidarnosc
PSL-Solidarity	
PSL-Wilanow	
PSL-Wilanowskie	
PSP	Polish Socialist Party
PSPP	Polska Socjalistyczna Partia Pracy
PSP-PNC	Polish Socialist Party (Provisional National Committee)
PSP-R	Polish Socialist Party (Rebirth)
PSS	Partia Socialiste Shqiperise
PSU	Polska Unia Socjaldemokratyczna
PUS	Polish Social Democratic Union

NEW POLITICAL PARTIES OF EASTERN EUROPE AND THE SOVIET UNION

PUWP	Polish United Workers' Party
PW	Partia Wolnosci
PWP	Polish Workers' Party
PY	Party of Yugoslavs
PYM	Party of Yugoslavs in Macedonia
PZKS	Polski Zwiazek Katolicko-Spoleczny
PZPR	Polska Zjednoczona Partia Robotnicza
RCDM	Russian Christian-Democratic Movement
RDP	Radical Democratic Party
RDS	Democratic Social Movement
RDS	Ruch Demokratyczno Spoleczny
REPs	Die Republikaner
REPs	The Republicans
RLP	Ruch Ludzi Pracy
ROAD	Democratic Action Movement
ROAD	Ruch Obywatelski Akcja Demokratyczna
RP	Republican Party (Bulgaria)
RP-PRS	Republican Party — Polish Republican Society
RSFSR	Russian Soviet Federal Socialist Republic
RWD	Ruch Wolnych Demokratow
SA	Socialist Alliance (Croatia)
SA	Socialist Alliance (Slovenia)
SA	Socialist Alliance (Yugoslavia)
SAWPY	Socialist Alliance of Working People of Yugoslavia
SCD	Slovene Christian Democrats
SD	Stronnictwo Demokratyczne
SDA	Social Democratic Association
SDA	Stranka Demokratske Akcije
SDF	Serbian Democratic Forum of Kosovo and Metohija
SDF	Srpski Demokratski Forum Kosova i Metohije
SDL	Slovene Democratic League
SDLM	Social-Democratic League of Macedonia
SDMP	Socijaldemokratska Partija na Makedonija
SDP	Romanian Social Democratic Party
SDP	Serbian Democratic Party
SDP	Social Democratic Party (Romania)
SDP	Social-Democratic Party (Kosovo)
SDP	Stranka Demokraticne Prenove
SDP	Stranka Demokratskih Promjena
SDPA	Social Democratic Party of Albania
SDPBH	Serbian Democratic Party of Bosnia and Hercegovina
SDPC	Social-Democratic Party of Croatia
SDPM	Social-Democratic Party of Macedonia
SDPR	Social Democracy of the Polish Republic
SDPR	Social Democratic Party of the Russian Federation
SDPS	Social-Democratic Party of Slovenia
SdRP	Socialdemokracja Rzeczypospoliitej Polskiej

ABBREVIATIONS

SDS	Sayuz na Demokratichni Sili
SDS	Srpska Demokratska Stranka
SDS BiH	Srpska Demokratska Stranka Bosne i Hercegovine
SDSCG	Socijaldemokratska Stranka Crne Gore
SDSH	Socijaldemokratska Stranka Hrvatske
SDSM	Socijaldemokratski Sojuz na Makedonija
SDSS	Socialdemokraticna Stranka Slovenije
SDZ	Slovenska Demokraticna Zveza
SED	Socialist Unity Party
SED	Sozialistische Einheitspartei Deutschlands
SEO	Stranka za Enakopravnost Obcanov
SFRY	Socialist Federal Republic of Yugoslavia
SJ	Stranka Jugoslovena
SJM	Stranka na Jugosloveni vo Makedonija
SKBiH-SPD	Savez Komunista Bosne i Hercegovine — Stranka Demokratskih Promjena
SKCG	Savez Komunista Crne Gore
SKD	Slovenska Krscanski Demokrati
SK-PJ	Savez Komunista — Pokret za Jugoslaviju
SKZ	Slovenska Kmecka Zveza
SLP	Serbian Liberal Party
SLP	Socialist Labour Party
SLS	Srpska Liberalna Stranka
SMR	Serbian Movement for Renewal
SN	Stronnictwo Narodowe
SOFI	Socialist Women's Initiative
SOFI	Sozialistische Frauen-Initiative
SOS	Slovenska Obrinopodjetniska Stranka
SP	Labour Party (Poland)
SP	Sijedi Panteri — Stranka Upokjencev Slovenije
SP	Solidarnosc Pracy
SP	Stronnictwo Pracy
SpAD	Spartacist Workers' Party of Germany
SpAD	Spatakist-Arbeiterpartei Deutschlands
SPC	Socialist Party of Croatia
SPD	Social Democratic Party of Germany
SPD	Sozialdemokratische Partei Deutschlands
SPL	Slovene Peasant League
SPM	Socialist Party of Macedonia
SPM	Socijalisticka Partija na Makedonija
SPO	Srpski Pokret Obnove
SPPiS	Stowarzyszenie Polityczne "Prawda i Sprawiedliwosc"
SPS	Socialist Party of Serbia
SPS	Socijalisticka Partija Srbije
SRP	Serbian Radical Party
SRS	Srpska Radikalna Stranka
SRSCG	Savez Reformskih Snaga za Crnu Guru

NEW POLITICAL PARTIES OF EASTERN EUROPE AND THE SOVIET UNION

SRSJ	Savez Reformskih Snaga Jugoslavije
SRSJ BiH	Savez Reformskih Snaga Jugoslavi je za Bosnu i Hercegovinu
SRSJH	Savez Reformskih Snaga Jugoslavije za Hrvatsku
SRSM	Sojuz na Reformskite Sili na Makedonija
SRSV	Savez Reformskih Snaga Vojvodina
SSH	Socijalisticka Stranka Hrvatske
SSO-DSBiH	Savez Socijalisticih Omladina-Demokratski Savez Bosne i Hercegovine
SSOH	Savez Socijalistickih Omladina Hrvatske
SSP	Serbian Socialist Party
SSS	Socialist Party of Slovenia
SSS	Socialisticna Stranka Slovenije
StSSljS	Stranka Saveza Seljaka Srbije
SZDSZ	Szabad Demokratak Szovetsege
UCD	Union of Constitutional Democrats
UChS	Unia Chrzescijansko-Spoleczna
UCPR-P	Union of Communists of the Polish Republic Proletariat
UD	Unia Demokratyczna
UDF	Union of Democratic Forces
UFC	Union of Free Co-operatives
UFV	Unabhangiger Frauenverband
UFV	Independent Women's Association
UFW	United Front of Workers of the USSR
UITUA	Union of Independent Trade Unions of Albania
UJDI	Udruzenje za Jugoslovensku Demokratsku Inicjativu
ULYA	Union of Labour Youth of Albania
UPP	United Peasant Party
UPR	Unia Polityki Realnej
UPSAN	Universal Party of Slavs and Allied Nations
URP	Union of Real Politics
USDO	Udruzena Srpska Demokratska Opozicija
USPD	Independent Social Democratic Party of Germany
USPD	Unabhangige Sozialdemokratische Partei Deutschlands
UVP	Independent People's Party
UVP	Unabhangige Volkspartei
UWS	Unia Wolnych Spoldzielcow
UZ	Unia Zielonych
VAA	Association of Working Groups for Employee Politics and Democracy
VAA	Vereinigung der Arbeitskreise fur Arbeitnehmerpolitik und Demokratie
VdgB	Union of Mutual Peasant Aid
VdgB	Vereinigung der gegenseitigen Bauernhilfe
VKSP	Vserossiiskii komitet Sotsialisticheskoi partii
VL	United Left
VL	Vereinigte Linke
VMRO-DPMNE	Vnatresna Makedonska Revolucionerna Organizacija — Demokratska Partija za Makedonsko Nacionalno Edinstvo
VR	Vatra Romaneasca Union
WiP	Wolnosc i Pokoj

ABBREVIATIONS

WU	Women's Union (Albania)
YCP	Yugoslav Communist Party
YDPPM	Young Democratic Progressive Party of Macedonia
YNA	Yugoslav National Army
ZA-S	Zelena Akcija
ZCh-N	Zjednoczenie Chrzescijansko-Narodowe
ZKP-Proletariat	Zwiazek Komunistow Polskich
ZMW	League of Rural Youth
ZS	Zeleni Slovenije
ZSL	United Peasant Party
ZSL	Zjednoczone Stronnictwo Ludowe
ZUR	Zakon o Udruzenom Radu

ALBANIA

Marko Milivojević

In June 1991, the regime of the communist Albanian Party of Labour (APL), also referred to as the Albanian Workers' Party, ended abruptly and unceremoniously, following a 25-day nationwide general strike organized by the Union of Independent Trade Unions of Albania (UITUA). On June 4, President Ramiz Alia accepted the resignation of the government of Prime Minister Fatos Nano, which immediately followed the signing of a six-point agreement by the leaders of the APL, the UITUA, and the Albanian Democratic, Social Democratic, Republican and Agrarian Parties (respectively, the ADP, SDPA, ARP, AAP), plus the Democratic Union of the Greek Minority (OMONIA). The following day, Alia directed Ylli Bufi, formerly Minister of Nutrition in the Nano government, to form a new administration after intensive consultations with the country's main opposition parties. Formally approved by Alia on June 11, this coalition "government of national stability" consisted of 24 portfolios, of which half went to the APL (eight party appointments, including the portfolios of Prime Minister and Foreign Affairs; four non-party appointments proposed by the party, including one of the Deputy Premierships and Public Order); seven to the ADP (five party, including the other Deputy Premiership and the Economy; two non-party, including Defence); two apiece to the SDPA and ARP; and one to the AAP.

Concomitantly, the 10th APL Congress took place in Tiranë's Palace of Congresses, where Xhelil Gjoni, then still a member of the Politburo and Secretary of the Central Committee, delivered the keynote opening speech. Formerly the Tiranë First Secretary, and one of the outstanding Hoxharite-Stalinist hard-liners in the APL leadership, the newly "reformed" Gjoni delivered a scathing indictment of the practice, if not the idea, of "socialism" in Albania since 1944, when the communists seized absolute power in the country and maintained a brutal and unreconstructed Stalinism implemented by the country's late dictator, Enver Hoxha (1908–85). For the majority of the APL's apparatchiks, Hoxha remains as dominant in death as he was in life. This was clearly demonstrated at the 10th Congress, when Gjoni's speech was received in stunned silence by the 1,400 delegates, who responded to it by loud and prolonged cheering for Hoxha. Though unlikely to deter the APL's reformist-opportunist leadership, now led by Party Chairman Nano (also briefly Minister of Foreign Economic Relations in the Bufi government), these widespread pro-Hoxha sympathies were nevertheless profoundly embarrassing, bearing in mind that "the mission of the 10th Congress was to be a boundary marker, closing one epoch and opening the first page of a new era".

Symbolized by a change of name, from the APL to the Albanian Socialist Party (ASP), this apparent political metamorphosis was sceptically received by the parliamentary and trade union opponents of the communists. The main opposition party, the ADP, is strongly anti-communist, but will have to wait until the summer of 1992 at the earliest before being able to challenge the ASP in an election, according to the fifth point of the June 3 agreement. The powerful UITUA, with a membership of 350,000, though ultimately responsible for the creation of the Bufi government, is not part of it, nor beholden to any of its political parties. Its leaders may well have extreme difficulty in delivering the sixth point of the June 3 agreement in which the UITUA "agreed, in co-operation with the new government, to guarantee social peace and not stage strikes during the functioning of this government". Worsening economic conditions alone are already raising serious doubts about this no-strike pledge. The general strike, basically political in its objectives, was also obviously fuelled by deep economic and social grievances, which the June 3 agreement did not actually address, and which have yet to be resolved. The most contentious of these, that is, pay rises of anywhere between 50 per cent and 150 per cent and improved working conditions, are in themselves guarantors of future conflict in a collapsing economy, where GDP *per capita* could fall as low as US$500 in 1991 (by far the lowest in Europe). During the first quarter of 1991, agricultural and industrial output declined by 33 to 50 per cent on the previous year, while virtually nothing was produced by the urban working class during the later general strike of May–June. In such a situation mass hunger and poverty are matters of real concern to the average Albanian, whose primary problem is sheer physical survival. In this regard, Albania, with both the highest population growth rate (2.1 per cent p.a.) and the youngest population (50 per cent of which is below the age of 20 years) in Europe, is more akin to Bangladesh than to any other poor European country, which is in fact "rich" by Albania's incredibly low living standards.

Socially, Albania's urban areas are gripped by growing lawlessness, with large numbers of people either fleeing abroad (with over 50,000 having already fled to Italy, Yugoslavia and Greece since the summer of 1990) or turning to criminal violence. The volatile situation in nearby Kosovo in Yugoslavia also contains the potential for serious violence which cannot but affect Albanian political life, whose recent democratization has reactivated the issue of the possible reunification of the divided Albanian nation into a reconstituted Greater Albania in the Balkans. In this regard, all the country's main political parties, including the previously lukewarm APL, are now publicly committed to bringing this about as soon as wider circumstances in Albania and Yugoslavia permit, although the end result of that could well be a war with Serbia, the nominal overlord of Kosovo.

Though its leaders publicly pretended otherwise, the APL regime was profoundly affected by the Year of Revolutions in Central-Eastern Europe, which ended dramatically with the violent overthrow of the Ceauşescu regime in Romania. In Albania, the Hoxharite *Sigurimi* secret police dominated the APL apparatus and society in a fashion similar to that of Ceauşescu's *Securitate* in Romania. Thanks to Italian and Yugoslav television coverage of the Romanian revolution, the end of Ceauşescu was to serve as the trigger for Albania's Year of Revolutions in 1990.

The Albanian anti-communist revolution began in Shkodër in northern Albania in December 1989, spreading to Durrës, Fier, Vlorë and Tiranë the following month. Following further violent disturbances in Kavajë in March, and the first recorded political strike in Berat in April, 5,000 demonstrators in Tiranë successfully sought refuge in a number of foreign embassies in the city in July. All these people were allowed to leave the country under UN supervision. In the same month, Alia's first Politburo personnel changes took place. A more extensive reshuffle of the APL leadership was effected in

December, when large demonstrations, riots and strikes were the daily norm throughout all the major urban areas of Albania, and in Tiranë in particular.

During this momentous month, nationwide popular pressure forced Alia's APL leadership to authorise a multi-party system of government, and to schedule the country's first free elections for the spring of the following year. An amended constitution was also promised, so as to legalize opposition political parties. The first of these, the ADP, was founded at this time in Tiranë by two prominent members of the country's dissident intelligentsia: Sali Berisha, a physician, and Gramoz Pashko, an economist, both based at the University of Tiranë and both former communists. This was to propel them, and their new party, to national prominence in 1991, when the ADP became the only real and credible political opposition to the APL. A related ADP initiative at this time was the Human Rights Forum (HRF), whose primary objective was the freeing of all political prisoners in the country. In southern Albania, home to an ethnic Greek minority population, the OMONIA was founded to protect its interests. In 1991, the OMONIA became the third most important parliamentary party after the APL and the ADP.

During the first quarter of 1991, a number of less important political parties were formed in January (ARP and AEP), February (AAP), March (SDPA) and April (ANUP). Apart from the ANUP and the SDPA, all these parties contested the March–April elections, but failed to win any parliamentary seats. However, all these parties were involved in the consultations that led to the formation of the Bufi government in June, with the SDPA, the ARP and the AAP all gaining portfolios in it. This gave them a political importance out of all proportion to their otherwise slender resources. The AEP, the political mouthpiece of the socially influential Albanian Greens, is similarly more important than it appears, as is the émigré-financed ANUP. The latter, which is the only one of the new parties to operate formally in nearby Kosovo, now expects to translate its lavish finances into large numbers of votes in the 1992 election. More generally, all the minor parties expect to do well in 1992, if only because the ADP could well become as unpopular as the ASP by then.

The UITUA, though not a conventional political party, is nevertheless an autonomous mass force that is arguably more politically and socially significant than any of the country's political parties, including the ASP and the ADP. Created out of the constituent unions of the former Central Council of Albanian Trade Unions, which freed itself of all APL control in December 1990, the UITUA has been very careful to preserve its hard-won autonomy. As the only legitimate representative of the urban working class, the UITUA was and remains the most implacable opponent of the communists, but this did not mean accepting the orders of the ADP. Thus, when the ADP leadership called for a general strike in April 1991, following post-election *Sigurimi*-instigated violence in Shkodër, the UITUA did not oblige. Instead, it started its own general strike for its own reasons in mid-May, and kept it going solidly until the APL capitulated completely in early June.

Far more than the disturbances of December 1990 and February 1991 (when Alia asked Nano to form his first government), or even the historic elections of March–April, it was this general strike that finally broke the power of the old APL once and for all; a fact not likely to be forgotten by the country's new political parties which could well suffer a similar fate should they cross the UITUA in the future.

Having formerly described itself in its constitution of 1976 as "the sole directing political power in state and society", and "the state of the dictatorship of the proletariat", the APL regime found it extremely difficult to concede the principle of multi-party politics (only formally proscribed in Albania). It was truly the last bastion in Central-Eastern

Europe. Thus, it was only in November 1990 that the People's Assembly promulgated a new electoral law to allow secret ballots and multi-candidate contests in any future elections. Even at this eleventh hour, however, multi-candidate did not mean multi-party for Alia's APL leadership, although the historic 13th Plenum of the APL Central Committee the following month was forced to accept formally that it did mean just that in practical political terms. Later the same month, an important move was made towards an amended constitution, with the publication of a first draft which, *inter alia*, described the renamed Republic of Albania as a "democratic state", and omitted any reference to Marxism-Leninism as an ideology or a system of government. However, this draft was never actually debated in the People's Assembly owing to the postponement of the country's first multi-party elections from February to March–April of the following year.

Consequently, the new opposition political parties were not actually formally legalized by the time of the spring elections. It was only after the new People's Assembly was elected that a APL–ADP parliamentary compromise allowed the unanimous passing, on April 30, of a Law on the Main Constitutional Provisions, which will remain in effect until a new constitution is promulgated later in 1991. Though entirely transitional in nature, the Law nevertheless symbolically represented Albania's break with its Stalinist past, although this was more on paper rather than in terms of actual practice as far as the pro-Hoxha majority of the APL apparatus was concerned.

Article 6 of the Law, concerned with the depoliticization "by law" of the entire government, declared that political pluralism was "one of the fundamental conditions of democracy" in Albania. Articles 24 and 26 turned the Presidency into a non-party office, thereby forcing Alia to resign all his major party positions in May. With 46 articles, the new Law covered many other crucial issues, such as human, trade union and religious rights, thereby effectively disposing of the worst clauses of the country's notorious Criminal Code. As regards religion, Article 7 of the Law guaranteed "freedom of religious belief", thereby ending a 23-year legal ban on all religious activity by the country's Muslims, Orthodox Christians and Catholics (respectively 70 per cent, 20 per cent and 10 per cent of the population prior to 1967). Finally, Article 33, which governs the President's powers as regards the formation or resignation of the Council of Ministers, allowed the Bufi government to take up office in June 1991.

Thus 79 years after it gained its independence from the Ottoman Empire in 1912, and 67 years after its first and only experience of parliamentary government under Orthodox Bishop Fan Noli in 1923–24, Albania held its first multi-party elections in March–April 1991. Initially scheduled for February 1991, the elections were postponed under opposition pressure until the following month, following the ADP's first big rally in December 1990, when over 10,000 people demonstrated in Kavajë. This gave the new political parties time to organize themselves and to campaign. However, the election campaign was extremely short at just under three months (for the APL and the ADP; less for the rest), which was obviously to the advantage of the incumbent APL regime.

At stake were the 250 seats of the unicameral People's Assembly, itself last "elected" by the old APL apparatus in February 1987. At that time, and throughout the post-1945 period, there was a single list of candidates proposed by, and standing for, the APL-controlled Albanian Democratic Front (ADF), whose chairperson until December 1990 was Hoxha's influential widow, Nexhmije Hoxha, the symbolic leader of the APL hard-liners since 1985. By the time of her removal from power, however, the ADF had become relatively more independent of the APL, having in fact served as a cover for much opposition and dissent in the country since 1989, when Ismail Kadare, Albania's foremost living writer and a radical critic of the APL regime (who later defected to France in October 1990), became ADF vice-chairperson. This greater autonomy was also achieved by the Women's Union (WU), the National Veterans' Committee (NVC), and, above all the rest, the radical Union of Labour Youth of Albania (ULYA), which in fact completely broke away from APL control in December 1990.

Thus, according to a March 1991 list published by the recently created Central Electoral Commission, the APL and its four nominal "fronts" (ADF, WU, NVC, ULYA) fielded 644 of the 1,074 registered candidates. With each parliamentary seat representing one electoral constituency, the APL put up candidates in 243 constituencies; the ADF in 122; the WU in 94; the ULYA in 94; and the NVC in seven. Of the opposition parties, the ADP put up candidates in every electoral constituency (250); the ARP in 165; the AAP in 37; the AEP in 10; and, the OMONIA in five, with 17 independents running in 16 electoral constituencies. Thus, while over 60 per cent of the candidates were communist, the ADP was able to challenge them in every constituency, which indicated that it was a nominally nationwide political organization three months after its foundation, although in fact virtually all its resources were concentrated on organizing and campaigning in the country's major urban areas. These resources came variously from the APL regime, Kosovo and, most important of all, wealthy Albanian diaspora émigré sources in Western Europe and the United States, who also largely financed the ARP, the only other remotely nationwide opposition party. Of the others, they were either too young (AAP), too poorly resourced (AEP), or too regional (OMONIA) to make much impact, although the well organized and financed OMONIA did very well in its ethnic Greek heartland in southern Albania, winning each of the five constituencies in which it put up candidates.

Publicly validated as being technically free by a team of international observers, which was not the same as being completely fair, the March–April elections were nevertheless reasonably representative of Albanian public opinion. The elections (see Table 1) were held in two rounds, and first-past-the-post (a simple majority ensured victory in the first round, with a second where no candidate won an absolute majority). The voter turnout

Table 1: Elections to the People's Assembly, March–April 1991

	1st Round (March 31)	2nd Round (April 7 & 14)	Total
Albanian Party of Labour	162	7	169
Democratic Party	65	10	75
Republican Party	0	–	0
Ecology Party	0	–	0
Agrarian Party	0	–	0
OMONIA	3	2	5
National Veterans' Committee	1	–	1
TOTAL	231	19	250

Source: Keesing's Record of World Events Vol. 37, No. 4, p.38160 (Longman, Harlow).

was 98.9 per cent, with nearly two million voting in 5,450 polling stations nationwide. With the notable exception of the OMONIA, the lack of any element of proportional representation wiped out the minor opposition parties in the first round, leaving only the APL and the ADP in what was always very much a two-party electoral race.

With around 60 per cent of the popular vote, the APL won enough seats to give it a two-thirds majority in the People's Assembly, but this was entirely due to its victories in the rural areas, where two-thirds of the country's population of 3.2 million people live. Virtually all the major urban areas, and Tiranë in particular, voted solidly for the ADP. This was a political disaster for the APL regime, with Alia polling a mere 32 per cent of the vote in electoral constituency number 218 in Tiranë.

Having failed to gain an electoral mandate, Alia remained President only because of the APL majority in the People's Assembly. His Prime Minister, Nano, did a little better, with a second round victory in one of the very few Tiranë constituencies held by the ADF–APL. Nano then asked the ADP to enter into a coalition government, but this was refused on account of killings by the *Sigurimi* on April 2 in Shkodër, where the local ADP leader, Arben Broxhi, was shot in the back while trying to calm a rioting crowd.

These killings indicated that the elections had only exacerbated Albania's political instability and its bitterly polarized society. In this regard, the ADP could not defeat the APL outright, but the APL could not hope to rule without the co-operation of the ADP and the UITUA. In the rural areas, where communist influence and propaganda were strongest (particularly in the Tosk south, birthplace of the APL), the farmers were rewarded for their loyalty in April, when the entire system of collectivized agriculture was allowed effectively to collapse, which in turn had the effect of worsening urban–rural differences and conflicts, as the countryside cut food deliveries to the already hungry towns. In addition, the linguistic-cultural-political Tosk-Gheg conflict became much worse, with the strongly anti-communist Gheg north (where a third of the population lives) turning against the historically pro-communist rural south, and looking towards the two million Ghegs of nearby Yugoslavia. With a reconstituted Greater Albania in the Balkans, the Ghegs might once again dominate the country, which would itself push the Tosk south further away from its northern rival, leaving Tiranë — only a centralized source of power under the APL regime — in a no-man's land. In the extreme south, the resurgence of Greater Albanian nationalism to the north greatly alarmed the ethnic Greek minority population, whose sights are now firmly set on ever closer links with Greece.

Directory of Parties

Albanian Agrarian Party (AAP)
Partie Agrar Shqipërisë (PAS)

Address. Tiranë,

Foundation. February 1991.

Membership. Reportedly the fastest growing party in Albania, which is to be expected given the essentially rural nature of the country. The AAP is also the only party to be specifically and exclusively concerned with the country's rural areas and their problems. As of June 1991, its membership was reportedly in the region of 30,000, although it has yet to publish exact figures. Could well be as large as the ADP by the end of 1991, which would make it a serious contender for winning the 1992 elections.

Leadership. A managing commission; Meno Gjoleka (ch.); Llambo Billa (dep. ch.). These two figures also founded the party. The other key figure is Resmi Osmani, who joined the Bufi government in June 1991 as Secretary of State for Agriculture, an important though secondary portfolio, with the crucial Agriculture and Food ministerial portfolios going to the ASP.

History. Though the sudden appearance of the AAP led some to suggest that it was yet another communist stalking horse, this seemed highly improbable given the considerable power and influence of the APL in the rural areas at that time. It was a genuine party, but like the ARP was often too respectful towards Alia and Nano, which was curious bearing in mind that they were ultimately responsible for the disaster that befell the Albanian countryside under the communists.

Organization. Uniquely among Albania's new political parties, the AAP is concentrating all its resources on building an organization in the countryside, where it has made remarkable progress since its foundation. However, its chief problem is a very slender resource base, which can only be resolved by looking to outside sources for financial assistance. Some such funds have already been obtained, especially for the AAP's influential newspaper, *Progresi Agrar* (Agrarian Progress).

Programme. Against a background of chaos in the rural areas (caused by the APL in April), the AAP issued a "Declaration" in May 1991. A detailed and highly specific party programme of great political potential in its essentials, it demanded new laws to, *inter alia*, regulate the privatization of former collectivized property and land; set up new Agricultural Bank credit arrangements for farmers; establish the right to form new and voluntary communal arrangements (such as co-operatives); and create new jobs for those left unemployed by the collapse of collectivized agriculture in April, which has drastically reduced food output and increased hunger in the towns.

Albanian Democratic Party (ADP)
Partia Demokratike Shqipërisë (PDS)

Contact name. Genc Pollo.

Address. Rruga Konferenca e Pezes, Tiranë.

Telephone. 214 63.

Foundation. December 1990.

Membership. As of Feb. 1, 1991, the ADP leadership claimed a membership of 60,000, which was plausible, given the popularity of the party in the country's urban areas, and particularly among the younger generation, and the exodus of people out of the APL. As of June 1991, its rapidly increasing membership is thought to have exceeded 80,000, and it may well reach a 100,000 by the end of 1991.

Leadership. A six-person executive, variously referred to as an initiating or managing commission, which is dominated by its Chairman, Sali Berisha, and its Deputy Chairman, Gramoz Pashko, who is also a Deputy Premier and Minister of the Economy in the Bufi government. The other key figure in the commission is its Secretary, Eduard Selami, who was the chief ADP negotiator in the talks that led to the formation of the Bufi government in June 1991.

History. Part of a dissident intelligentsia largely made up of disillusioned ex-communists, the founders of the ADP followed their unofficial leader, Kadare, in his use of the APL's institutions — notably the ADF and the ULYA — to undermine the party from within in 1989–90. Thus, in March 1990, *Zëri i Rinisë* (Voice of the Youth), the ULYA newspaper, published an outspoken and extremely influential interview with Kadare, who openly called for the overthrow of the APL regime. This is now generally taken to be the beginning of the revolt of the intellectuals in Albania. In May 1990, *Drita*, the weekly newspaper of the Union of Albanian Writers and Artists of the Albanian Academy of Sciences (itself another pro-Kadare stronghold), published Berisha's first major interview, significantly entitled "The Intellectual Faces the Tasks of the Times", which called for an autonomous and intellectually honest intelligentsia, whose major social role at that time was to act as an embryonic opposition movement in a country destroyed by communist totalitarianism.

The movement was led by Kadare until his defection to France in October 1990, and depended on the country's radicalized university and high school students to use mass street politics to force the APL regime to make major concessions in December 1990, when the ADP was founded immediately after the student demonstrations of the 9th in Tiranë. The ADP newspaper, *Rilindja Demokratike*, was also launched at this time with an initial print-run of 60,000 copies, as was the ADP off-shoot, the HRF, led by the intellectual Arben Puto. Thereafter, Puto's HRF became the local monitoring group of the influential International Helsinki Federation for Human Rights. The following month, the HRF was involved in the creation of the Association of the Former Political Prisoners and Detainees, all of which was strongly supported by the ADP, whose historic Kavajë rally in December 1990 was specifically organized to demand the freeing of all the country's remaining (around 8,000) political prisoners. This was achieved by the time of the spring elections, following further pressure by the ADP-HRF on this crucial issue. As a result, Albania's formerly poor human rights record was judged good enough for it to be accepted as a full member of the Conference on Security and Co-operation in Europe (CSCE) in June 1991, following a seven-month probationary period as an observer at the CSCE. Further international respectability came in the same month with the visit of the US Secretary of State, James Baker, who was welcomed by a crowd of over 200,000 people in Tiranë, where he met the main ADP leaders.

Organization. In contrast to the highly centralized APL, the ADP was organized on a quasi-federal basis from its very inception, with considerable autonomy being given to local party branches in all the country's major urban areas. Other than Tiranë, the ADP was and remains very strong in Shkodër, Tropoja (Berisha's birthplace on the border with Kosovo), Lac, Durrës and Kavajë in northern and central Albania; and, in Elbasan, Lushnja, Fier, Berat, Vlorë and Korcë in the south. Its leaders, Berisha (a Gheg) and Pashko (a Tosk) appealed to the entire country, often mentioning the largely Tosk nature of the APL, whose late dictator, Hoxha, was born in Gjirokastër in the extreme south.

The ADP's greatest organizational strength (in the urban areas), however, was paradoxically also a great weakness, as it had little real presence in the countryside, where the APL won the spring elections. In May, therefore, the well financed ADP began a major organizational drive into the rural areas, with the campaign beginning in the southern Fier district.

Programme. First published on Feb. 1, 1991, to mark the beginning of its electoral campaign, the ADP programme was defined by strong anti-communism and pan-Albanian nationalism, with the latter being the particular concern of Berisha, while the party's commitment to democratic politics and free market economics was the responsibility of Pashko, a trained economist. In addition, the ADP stressed its commitment to constitutional reform, human rights, opening up the country to the outside world, and welcoming ever closer contacts with the Albanian diaspora émigré communities in Western Europe, North America and the Middle East. Such contacts yielded substantial outside financial assistance, without which the ADP could not have mounted a national electoral campaign and later rural organizational drive in 1991.

Affiliations. The key external political alliance of the ADP is with the mass Kosovo Democratic Association (KDA) and its various member political parties, in Priština. Well organized and financed, and led by the intellectual Ibrahim Rugova, the KDA reportedly played a major, though often covert, role in the gestation, formation and subsequent development of the ADP in 1990–91. Itself financed by a number of very wealthy Albanian émigrés, such as the Kosovar financier Hajdin Sejdija in Zürich, the KDA reportedly introduced the ADP to such key outside sources of finance. The result of all this was a *de facto* ADP-KDA alliance, which was reportedly signed in Zürich in February 1991, when Pashko met Rugova. Sejdija is also thought to have made a pledge to increase his financial support to both parties, which are both closely allied to the ethnic Albanian Party of Democratic Prosperity (PDP) in western Macedonia, and to the ruling slavic Muslim Party of Democratic Action (PDA) in Bosnia-Hercegovina, in Yugoslavia.

During the same European tour, Pashko also met Kadare in Paris and received the public backing of this influential writer. The following month, the two ADP leaders visited the United States, where there is an Albanian community of 250,000 people. During the visit, they were received at the US State Department, which they chose to interpret as being *de facto* American government recognition of their claim to being the only worthy recipients of US humanitarian and other assistance to Albania. The Bush Administration did not publicly respond to this, nor to the ADP's prediction that it would win the elections of the same month.

Albanian Ecology Party (AEP)
Partia Ecologia Shquipërisë (PES)

Address: Tiranë.

Foundation. January 1991.

Membership. The smallest of the new parties, the AEP had no more than 1,000 members as of March 1991. This is thought not to have changed in the second quarter of the year.

Leadership. Founded and thereafter led by Alban Rado and Namik Huti, two Tiranë intellectuals.

History. Although "Green" issues have always been important to Albania's largely rural population, the idea of a modern "Green Movement" was entirely the creation of a small number of Tiranë intellectuals influenced by similar trends at work in the rest of Europe during the 1980s. Motivated to act by the poor ecological record of the APL regime, this group of committed people was nevertheless very uncertain about actually founding a political party (an ambiguity about traditional politics that is common to all the European Green Parties). Once founded, the AEP did not act like a conventional party, but more like a social pressure group, as was reflected in the very small number of candidates it fielded in the spring elections.

Organization. Basically confined to Tiranë, with some supporters in the other major towns, where the AEP is run on a shoestring basis.

Programme. Rather than campaigning for traditional political and social issues in 1991, the AEP issued various statements pleading for social peace and ecological health, but without suggesting how these goals might be brought about in the future.

Albanian National Unity Party (ANUP)
Partia Bashkimi Kombëtare Shqipërisë (PBKS)

Addresses. Tiranë, Albania and Priština, Kosovo, Yugoslavia.

Foundation. April 1991.

Membership. As the youngest of the new political parties, the émigré-financed ANUP has rapidly increased its membership in both Albania and Kosovo to a reported 10,000, as of June 1991. Its lavish finances, plus the growing strength of extreme pan-Albanian nationalist sentiments in Albania and even more in Kosovo, explain this success, which could well place the ANUP into the serious contender league for winning the 1992 elections.

ALBANIA

Leadership. Exact details unknown, but founded and thereafter led by Iaajet Beqiri, a jurist, and Pal Delia, both Bektashi (a Sufi sect of nominal Sunni Muslims) believers. Led in Priština by Halil Alidema.

History. Founded to take advantage of the radicalization of pan-Albanian nationalism in 1991, the ANUP had its roots in a number of earlier extreme pan-Albanian political and cultural organizations, such as the Political Patriotic Association *Cameria* (Maternal Hearth), whose newspaper, *Cameria-Vatra Amtare*, was to attack the OMONIA's involvement in the formation of the Bufi government in June 1991. The other key influence, which now partly defines the very identity of the ANUP, was the influential Bektashi sect, whose World Council of Elders, led by Reshat Baba Bardhi, is based in Tiranë. Though rooted in the south, this sect transcends the Tosk-Gheg division of Albania, which explains the crucial ANUP presence in Kosovo, where there are also many Bektashis.

Organization. Uniquely among Albania's new political parties, the ANUP also formally operates in Kosovo, which has set an important precedent for the others to follow, given the increasingly porous nature of the border between Albania and Kosovo, and also the border between the country and the predominantly ethnic Albanian area of western Macedonia in Yugoslavia. In Albania, the ANUP is now in the process of creating a nationwide organization, being particularly strong in Tiranë and Shkodër.

Programme. An extreme pan-Albanian nationalist party, whose Priština branch basically wants immediate reunification with Albania or war with Serbia, the ANUP is also the nearest thing to an "Islamic" party in Albania's otherwise highly secular politics, although its Bektashism is still regarded with suspicion by many orthodox Sunni Muslims, who are themselves led by the Grand Mufti of Albania, Hafiz Salih Terhat Hoxha, based at the Elem Bay mosque in Tiranë (reopened in January 1991).

Affiliations. More than any other Albanian political party, the ANUP is a creature of Albanian diaspora émigré organizations, and particularly those based in the Middle East and Turkey, where there is a large ethnic Albanian community, although local pressures often forced such people to take on Turkish identity. Some of these "organizations" are very dubious, being fronts of the Albanian mafia, which is now very active in Kosovo and, according to some reports, even Albania, where crime and lawlessness is a growing social problem. Involved in international narco-terrorism, this mafia is extremely rich, with various "respectable" frontmen in e.g. Switzerland. The Albanian mafia is now determined to buy itself political power in Kosovo or Albania.

Albanian Republican Party (ARP)
Partia Republikana Shqipërisë (PRS)

Address. Bulevardi Deshmoret e Kombit, Tiranë.

Telephone. 271 70.

Foundation. January 1991.

Membership. Although the ARP was the third largest party in terms of the number of candidates put forward in the March–April 1991 elections, it has yet to become a large membership party in the way that the ADP did in 1991. This perhaps explains why it has not yet published any membership figures, which were thought to be no more than 8,000 as of April 1991.

Leadership. A steering commission, whose Chairman is Sabri Godo, a minor novelist, and whose Secretary is Vangjush Gambeta, formerly the deputy editor-in-chief of the APL newspaper, *Zëri i Popullit*. These two dominant figures also founded the ARP, which is socially similar to the ADP, as both are clearly political groups of the intelligentsia and the managerial technocracy. Its two negotiators in the June 1991 talks that led to the formation of the Bufi government were Hysen Cobani and Teodor Kareco, who are reportedly the second echelon of the ARP leadership.

History. One of the minor opposition parties that emerged suddenly in the political slipstream of the rising ADP in 1991, the ARP's social origins were not so much concerned with principled opposition and dissent (largely true of the ADP leadership), but with opportunism. Gambeta, formerly of the APL, is a prime example of this type, who "opposed" the APL, but were often remarkably deferential towards Alia and Nano. This led some to suspect that the ARP was one of the stalking horses of the communists.

Organization. Like the ADP, the ARP is largely an urban phenomenon, with branches in many major towns, including Durrës, Burrel, Berat, and Gjirokastër. Unlike the ADP, however, the ARP is very much oriented to the Tosk south, with no real presence to date in the north, and particularly the key city of Shkodër. Despite its claims, the ARP is not a genuinely nationwide party. In the rural areas, it has virtually no presence whatsoever.

Programme. With a platform very similar to that of the ADP, the ARP has had a problem creating a distinct identity for itself and its programme. It is, however, a far more conservative party than the ADP, advocating a gradual approach on issues like the transition to a free market economy (the ADP believes in doing this very quickly). The ARP is also the only party to pay any sort of attention to the exiled Monarchist Movement of the self-styled "King Leka I of the Albanians" (son of King Zog, who ruled Albania from 1924 to 1939). The ARP is bitterly hostile to Leka, whom it regularly abuses, although he is an irrelevance in current Albanian politics.

Affiliations. As with the ADP, the ARP was largely financed by foreign sources, and especially Italy, where an old Albanian community of some 50,000 people lives in the south. The ARP is also one of the few Albanian parties to obtain the support of a foreign non-Albanian source, which was the Italian Republican Party (IRP), whose leader, Giorgio La Malfa, briefly visited Durrës in March 1991. The IRP is the only Italian party to have taken any real interest in the welfare of the 25,000 Albanian refugees in Italy, whose government threatens forcibly to repatriate them to Albania later in 1991.

Albanian Socialist Party (ASP)
Partia Socialiste Shqipërisë (PSS)

formerly **Albanian Party of Labour (APL — Partia ë Punës e Shqipërisë — PPS)**

Contact names. Fatos Nano; Shkelqin Begari.

Address. Bulevardi Deshmoret et Kombit. Tiranë.

Foundation. June 1991 (ASP); November 1941 (APL).

ALBANIA

Membership. Claimed to be 160,000 at the 10th Congress (June 1991), but this was pure propaganda, given the rise of the ADP in 1990–91, and numerous reports of large-scale resignations and expulsions over the same period. Though still probably the largest party in Albania, the discredited and declining APL reportedly had no more than 100,000 members as of February 1991, which was a third fewer than its official membership of 150,000 at the 9th Congress (1986). As of June 1991, its falling membership was thought to be less than that of the expanding ADP and the other opposition parties, all of which are now thriving as regards the growth of their respective memberships.

Leadership. 81-person steering committee led by a presidency of 15 people. Fatos Nano, former Prime Minister and then briefly Minister of Foreign Economic Relations, became chairman of the presidency of the ASP at the 10th Congress (June 1991) of the former APL, thereby replacing the already defunct position of party first secretary, formerly held by Ramiz Alia since 1985. Divested of all his APL offices in May 1991, Alia is now a "non-party", though unelected, President, but much doubt remains whether he can act in the politically neutral manner that his office demands. Ylli Bufi, Chairman of the Council of Ministers or Prime Minister as of June 1991, is of the ASP, but is effectively regarded as non-party by the ADP and the other opposition parties, whose leaders approved his appointment as part of a wider compromise deal with the APL and the UITUA. Of the old APL Central Committee Secretariat and Politburo, including Xhelil Gjoni, the former hard-liner turned "reformer", not one person remained, following a thorough purge at the 10th Congress, when most of the Hoxharite old guard at the highest levels of the party were either expelled from the new ASP or removed from their steering committee. All the people on this committee and its presidency are relatively unknown outside Albania, with the exception of Nano, whose relative youth, advanced education, pragmatism and willingness to change are representative of the élite group he now leads, though not the larger mass below them, who mainly comprise the old APL.

History. Created in November 1941 by Comintern Yugoslav Communist Party (YCP) agents, the "Albanian" Communist Party (ACP), renamed the APL in 1948, was in fact no more than an off-shoot of the YCP throughout the period 1941–45, when YCP-ACP dual party membership was the norm for all the ACP's leaders, including Hoxha, who helped found a National Liberation Front (NLF; later renamed as the ADF) under the "guidance" of Tito's representatives in September 1942. In 1943–44, the exit of the Italian and then German occupiers of the country, coupled with substantial Allied military assistance, enabled the NLF to hijack, and then completely dominate, the country's nationalist movement, so as to seize absolute power in November 1944, following a brief civil war with its right-wing rivals. A typically Stalinist "election" took place in December 1945, when the ACP was the only party allowed. In January 1946, the new People's Assembly formally proclaimed the People's Republic of Albania (later the People's Socialist Republic of Albania), and promulgated its first constitution, which was based on Stalin's of 1936, and which was operative until its 1976 replacement.

Thereafter, Hoxha's party was to be defined by the most hard-line Stalinism, while leading to ideologically inspired quarrels of great bitterness with Yugoslavia(1948), the Soviet Union (1961), and, finally, the People's Republic of China (1978). All of these former allies were to be labelled as "revisionist" by Hoxha, who regarded himself as the only true Marxist-Leninist in the world. The end result of such dogmas was complete international isolation. Internally, the APL was characterized by extreme instability at the top, involving frequent and violent purges by Hoxha and his *Sigurimi* henchmen. Beginning with a bloody purge of alleged "Titoists" in 1948, and ending with the murder of Prime Minister Mehmet Shehu and many of his followers in 1981, Hoxha carried out at least seven major purges of the APL and its Albanian People's Army (APA). Nobody was able to moderate Hoxha's ideologically inspired fantasies, which reduced his country to complete ruin long before he died in 1985, when his chosen successor, Alia, took over under the watchful eye of his widow. Until events forced change upon him in 1990, Alia had only wanted to preserve the essential elements, if not the violent excesses (which were moderated as regards other members of the APL élite), of the rigid Stalinist system that he had helped build since joining the Politburo in 1961. In this, Albania was unique in Central-Eastern Europe, with the notable exception of Romania under Ceauşescu. The result of this aversion to any sort of change was a backward, brutal and deeply flawed political system that proved very difficult to change in 1990–91.

Organization. Formerly a classically Stalinist party in organizational matters, where the APL Central Committee Secretariat and Politburo exercised total control of the party committees in the country's 26 districts (Tiranë being the most important) and all its major institutions (notably the collective farms, enterprises, trade unions, armed forces, and the secret police), the ASP is now in a state of possibly terminal organizational and political collapse. Never a mass party (only 5 per cent of the population in 1986), mass resignations and expulsions in 1990–91 have severely depleted its ranks, especially at the lower and middle levels. This also reduced its income, as did the depoliticization of the executive in April 1991, when the APL's stranglehold on the state and all its resources was fatally undermined. Among other things, the party's daily newspaper, *Zëri i Popullit* (Voice of the People), will not long survive this worsening cash squeeze.

During the same month, the system of collectivized agriculture was allowed to collapse, thereby breaking the power of the local communists, often hardcore Hoxharites. In the urban areas, the ADP completely replaced the APL as a credible political force with any sort of real organization, which was virtually non-existent for the APL in towns such as Shkodër and Kavajë. Within the declining and contracting party, political confusion and demoralization — graphically revealed during the 10th Congress — reactivated the APL's old tendency towards internal feuding and chronic instability. The result of that was that many districts, particularly in the south, broke from the Alia-Nano reformist clique in Tiranë, while the more radical social democratic elements broke with the party completely, as with the ULYA in December 1990, and the formation of the SDPA in March 1991.

Programme. In its election campaign of early 1991, and during its strange 10th Congress in June of the same year, the discredited APL showed a complete inability to present a credible programme to the country. The "new" ASP, like the "new" APL that fought the spring election, espoused positions (multi-party democracy, the replacement of the centrally planned economy with a free market system ending Albania's international isolation, greater support for the Albanians of Yugoslavia) that not only completely contradicted its entire Stalinist past, but, more significantly, attracted the vocal disapproval of most of its still largely Hoxharite membership. In this regard, its reformist-opportunist leadership became seriously out of touch with its dwindling membership, which is most unlikely to be replaced by new blood in the future. The ASP is thus clearly a party of the past, despite its reformist leadership and its change of name and organization.

Affiliations. Completely isolated by choice in the communist world following Hoxha's split with the Chinese in 1978, the APL was left to "affiliate" only with its own creations, the supposedly "autonomous" political fronts. With the notable exception of the genuinely independent ULYA, whose most recent First Secretary, Isen Bashkurti, dramatically left the APL in March 1991, the ADF, the WU and the NVC are all now in varying stages of political and economic decline. All were perceived as APL creations and failures. The NVC, which has one seat in the People's Assembly, was also closely allied to the APA, the *Sigurimi*, and a number of the latter's own "fronts", such as the so-called Movement for the Defence of the Interest of the People and Homeland, which appeared in February 1991 under the leadership of a suspected *Sigurimi* agent, Agim Bajraktari.

Democratic Union of the Greek Minority (OMONIA)
also known as **OMONIA Socio-Political Organization**

Address. Gjirokastër.

Foundation: December 1990.

Membership. As the only legitimate representative of Albania's ethnic Greek minority population, the OMONIA is the third largest political party, with a reported membership of anywhere between 50,000–60,000 as of June 1991. The exact figure is not available, as the OMONIA has chosen not to publicize it, given the extreme political sensitivity over the number of ethnic Greeks in the country (60,000 according to the former APL regime; 400,000 according to successive governments in Athens; probably between 150,000–200,000 in actuality), and the borderland areas they live in.

Leadership. Exact details unknown, but founded and thereafter led by Jani Jani and Panajat Barka, two ethnic Greeks from Gjirokastër.

History: Repressed by Hoxha's xenophobic regime, the Orthodox Christian ethnic Greek community of southern Albania (or northern Epirus, according to the Greeks of Greece proper) is now thought to have begun covert opposition and dissent against the local Tosk communist authorities as early as December 1989, when the Greek government also chose to make a public issue of the brutal *Sigurimi* murder of four brothers of the ethnic Greek Prassos family, who had attempted to flee from Albania the previous October. In January 1990, large demonstrations took place in Athens to protest against the mistreatment of the ethnic Greeks in Albania.

In 1990 in Albania, where ethnic Greeks are to be found throughout the south but concentrated near the border with Greece, Greek anti-communists are believed to have participated in demonstrations, riots and strikes in all the area's major towns, including Fier, Vlorë, Berat, Korcë, Tepelene, Përnet, Erseke, Saranda and Gjirokastër, a key town in both Albanian and Greek history. The local communist repression is believed to have been particularly severe, which explains why anywhere between 10,000–15,000 Greeks (6,000 from December 1990 to January 1991 alone) fled to Greece in 1990–91, which was also an important destination for many Albanian refugees.

Having been founded at the same time as the ADP and the UITUA, the OMONIA attempted to stem this exodus in 1991, but was unable to do so. Its leaders strongly suspected that this movement of Greeks out of Albania was being "encouraged" by local pan-Albanian nationalists, communist and otherwise, who wished forcibly to rid the country of its Greek minority "problem" once and for all.

Organization: A strongly regional organization, the OMINIA is very strong in the extreme south, but also has branches in all the area's major towns as far north as Fier, where a branch was founded in March 1991.

Programme: Exclusively concerned with protecting the previously neglected interests of the country's ethnic Greek minority, the OMONIA has proved to be the most successful of the new political parties, winning every one of the five constituencies it stood in during the spring elections. It is, however, a purely ethnic Greek party that is of no interest to Albanian voters. Though publicly committed to a further strengthening of a largely non-existent "friendship" between the Albanian and Greek peoples, the OMONIA also looks to ever closer links with Greece. This has led some extreme pan-Albanian nationalists to accuse its leaders openly of convert secessionist sympathies,

Affiliations. Not publicly advertised for obvious reasons, but believed to include strong links with various political parties in Greece (notably New Democracy), Greek diaspora émigré organizations and the powerful Greek Orthodox Church. External Greek finance was certainly made available to the OMONIA in 1991.

Social Democratic Party of Albania (SDPA)
Partia Socialdemokratike ë Shqipërisë (PSDS)

Contact names. Skendir Gjanushi; Teodor Laso.

Address. Bulevardi Deshmoret e Kombit, Tiranë.

Foundation. March 1991.

Membership: Largely made up of those apparatchiks who left the APL in the first quarter of 1991, the initial organizing group of the SDPA consisted of around 50 people, including 20 parliamentary deputies. At the time of its first national congress in June, the SDPA reportedly had around 3,000 members. It is one of the smallest new parties.

Leadership. A managing commission with a presidium; Skender Gjinushi (ch.), a former Minister of Education; Teodor Laco (dep. ch.), a writer and film director. These two figures were also the leading lights in the initial organizing group of the party. Other leading personalities in the SDPA include Haxhi Aleko, Ruzhdi Pullaha and Gaqo Apostoli.

History. Though the rigidly Stalinist APL of the Hoxha years never had any genuine social democratic tradition, such forces did begin to appear under Alia, and especially during the political confusion of 1990–91, when the APL in fact split internally, with a reformist faction battling the Hoxharite-Stalinist hard-liners. Though small in terms of numbers, this group was more important than it looked, as it reportedly enjoyed the covert encouragement of both Nano and Alia. Once it split from the APL, however, it was just another minor party, whose very formation indicated that the APL could not then be reformed in a genuinely social democratic direction, despite its change of name at the 10th Congress in June 1991. For the anti-communists, for whom the very word "socialism" is an anathema, it was no more than a APL stalking horse.

Organization. Though it was no more than a "paper" party initially, the SDPA had established branches in Korcë, Gjirokastër, Tepelene, Vlorë, Fier, Berat and Durrës as of May 1991. Like the ARP, it is very much a party of the south, although its leaders often expressed strongly pan-Albanian sentiments in a bid to gain a presence in the Gheg north, where the problem of Kosovo is a major issue. In this regard, a SDPA delegation visited Rugova's KDA in Priština in June 1991.

Programme. Given the fact that the very idea of "socialism" was discredited by Hoxha's APL, the SDPA has found it very difficult to make any sort of credible case for a true democratic socialism. Instead, it has opportunistically jumped on the pan-Albanian bandwagon in a bid to win greater popular support. Its first national congress, for example, was largely dominated by the Kosovo issue.

Affiliations. Though still connected to the ASP — itself a supposedly social democratic party — the SDPA was accepted into the Confederation of Social Democratic Parties of Central and Eastern Europe at its second conference in Slovenia, Yugoslavia, in May 1991. Teodor Laco, Haxhi Aleko and Isen Bashkurti (of ULYA fame) attended these proceedings on behalf of the SDPA, which has also established close relations with its equivalent party in nearby Kosovo.

Union of Independent Trade Unions of Albania (UITUA)
Bashkimi i Sindikatavë të Pavarura Shqipërisë (BSPS)

Address. Tiranë.

Foundation. December 1990.

Membership. With an estimated 350,000 members as of June 1991, the UITUA is considerably larger than all of the country's political parties combined. The only true mass grouping in the country, the UITUA has organized 50–60 per cent of the urban working class, and aims to have a membership of 750,000–800,000 by the end of 1991.

Leadership. As of June 1991, when the UITUA held its first formal national conference in Tiranë, its managing council and its presidium was chaired by Kastrict Muco. During the historic 25-day general strike that ended on June 10, the general strike central commission was chaired by Valer Xheka, the single most important figure in the UITUA since its foundation. In Tiranë, the two key strike leaders were Hyqmet Melazi and Hysen Bardhi. The single most important union or federation, the radical Independent Miners' Union (IMU), is chaired by Shyqri Xibri.

History. Formerly no more than "transmission belts" of the APL, and rigidly controlled by it through the Central Council of Albanian Trade Unions (CCATU; Këshilli Qëndror i Bashkimeve Profesionale të Shqipërisë — KQBPS), Albania's trade unions were reviled by the very urban working class that they and the APL claimed to represent. Led by a veteran APL leader, Sotir Koçollari ("elected" at the CCATU's 10th Congress in June 1987), the CCATU claimed to have 750,000 members in 1990. This represented the entire urban working class.

The working class in Albania did not actually begin the Year of Revolutions (this was done by Shkodër's students in December 1989), but played an absolutely decisive role in the destruction of the APL's regime in 1991, as a result of the first recorded political strike which took place in Berat, in the south, in April 1990. Later, politically motivated strikes broke out all over Albania, but such actions lacked any sort of centralized co-ordination and leadership, which the pro-APL leadership of the old CCATU could not provide by definition. In December 1990, when things came to a head politically in Albania, the constituent unions of the old CCATU finally broke free of all APL control, creating the UITUA shortly after doing so.

Organization. As its name suggests, the UITUA is a union of 14 separate independent unions or federations, which were and are loosely bound together by a Tiranë-based leadership. Of these unions, the IMU was and remains the most important, both as regards its size (30,000 members in a strategic sector of the economy) and militancy, which was dramatically demonstrated by the mass hunger strikes of the miners at Valias near Tiranë in May 1991. The other key unions included the Independent Trade Union of Oil Workers (30,000 members in another vital sector of the economy), plus those controlling the railways/road transport, iron and steel production, the country's ports and major utilities, and particularly electrical production and distribution.

Programme. First presented to the Nano government in April 1991, and then forcibly demanded of it by means of a general strike the following month and into June, the UITUA's famous 17 points were, in fact, mostly to do with pay (rises of 50–150 per cent immediately), working conditions, the social wage and trade union rights, and particularly the right to strike. However, since the UITUA leadership ended its general strike without actually achieving these economic demands, it was clear to all that the strike, from first to last, was political in intent, as a strongly anti-communist and historically abused urban working class organized itself to break the power of the communists. It did just that, thereby creating an entirely new political order in the country in June 1991. Politics will thus define the UITUA in the future, which may well see the emergence of a new political party, or parties, entirely beholden to, and created by, the UITUA, whose distrust of the country's present political parties is intense. If this happens, Albania's political landscape will be radically changed again, thereby raising the possibility of a UITUA-controlled government coming to power after the 1992 elections.

Affiliations. None that are known about, although the UITUA, which described itself "as an up-to-date organization in tune with the European trade union movement" at its first national conference in June 1991, is clearly now keen to establish ever closer links with its counterparts in the rest of Europe, beginning no doubt with the Kosovar trade unions in nearby Yugoslavia. In this regard, it is known that substantial financial assistance was made available to the UITUA in 1991 from Kosovar and Albanian diaspora émigré sources in Western Europe, North America and the Middle East. Without it, it is most unlikely that the UITUA's general strike would have lasted as long as it did.

BULGARIA

Bogdan Szajkowski

Bulgarian party politics since the end of World War II followed a similar pattern to that of other Central and Eastern European countries. Communist control was established initially through the Bulgarian Communist Party's (BCP) dominance of the Fatherland Front government, formed after a bloodless coup on Sept. 9, 1944. The communists filled the key positions in the new government including the crucially important Interior and Justice Ministries. Gradually other political groups within the Front were purged of incompatible individuals which led to increasing dominance of the Front by the communists. The Front's successes in the first postwar elections on Nov. 18, 1945 when it won 88.2 per cent of the vote, led to another victory on Sept. 8, 1946 in the referendum on the abolition of the monarchy. This allowed for the proclamation of the People's Republic on Sept. 15, 1946. Attempts to resist the slide into communist totalitarianism by a group within the Bulgarian Agrarian National Union (BANU) which participated in the Fatherland Front, came to an end in 1947. On July 7, 1947, Nikola Petkov, an outstanding leader of BANU and principal opponent of the communists, was arrested on trumped-up charges of conspiracy together with 23 other Agrarian deputies in the Grand National Assembly. He was expelled from the parliament, tried and inevitably found guilty. The execution of Petkov on Sept. 23, 1947 marked the effective end of resistance to the BCP-dominated Fatherland Front. The arrest and trial of Petkov and his associates formed part of a much larger process of the so-called war crimes trials which began in 1945, which in effect was a particularly ruthless and bloody consolidation of power, perhaps the most brutal in postwar Eastern Europe. Between 180,000–200,000 people were repressed, about 18,0000 were killed without trial and 2,500 were executed under death sentences. Almost one million people were forced to join co-operative farms.

The BCP established its total domination within the Fatherland Front in the elections of Oct. 27, 1946. Thereafter all political groups and parties were absorbed within the Front. The only exception was BANU which was allowed to function as a separate political party but within the Front and as an appendix to the BCP.

For the rest of the postwar period the Fatherland Front changed from its initial function as an antifascist umbrella coalition and became a major organ, mobilizing, controlling and monitoring social and political development at neighbourhood, district, town and city level. It encompassed BANU, the Communist Youth League (*Komsomol*), the Trade Unions, the Women's Organization and, theoretically, the BCP. In practice, however, the Communist Party controlled the activities of the Front which were in essence and scope determined by the party.

The BCP faithfully carried out the Soviet model of development, nationalization of industry and banking, industrialization, collectivization of agriculture, central control of the economy, emasculation of any forms of dissenting trends, and in terms of external relations complete subjugation to Soviet foreign policy. Similarly, the development of political structures to a large extent followed closely that of the USSR.

The death of Stalin in March 1953 was followed in Bulgaria by the adoption of a "New Course" which incorporated many of the political and economic features of the de-Stalinization process in the Soviet Union. In keeping with the developments in Moscow the government and party leadership in Sofia was divided in 1954 and Todor Zhivkov was appointed the Secretary-General of BCP. Initially portrayed as a reformer, Zhivkov consolidated his position over the next six years and in 1962 also became the Prime Minister. In 1971 he gave up this position to become the President of the newly created Council of State and continued to unite the chief government and party posts until 1987.

Zhivkov ruled Bulgaria for 35 years in an increasingly sycophantic way. He even proposed to the Soviet Union that Bulgaria should be incorporated into the USSR as a constituent republic. In an attempt to silence Bulgarian exiles and frightened opponents inside the country, he ordered the use of the secret police in assassinations carried out in Britain and France. The Bulgarian Secret Service was also implicated in the attempted assassination of Pope John Paul II in 1981. All this caused immeasurable damage to Bulgaria's international reputation. Moreover, from 1984 the Turkish minority was subjected to what was officially called "regeneration process".

In order to enforce the ethnic homogeneity of the country, the regime embarked on the policy of "promotion and consolidation of an emphatic Bulgarian self-consciousness" by declaring that the 1.5 million ethnic Turks in Bulgaria were not Turks at all but Turkicized Bulgarians. They were forced to renounce their Islamic names and adopt new Bulgarian ones. The use of the Turkish language in public and on the telephone was forbidden. The regime imposed new lay burial rituals to eliminate any vestiges of tradition and faith and a representative was instructed to follow the funeral to ensure that it was carried out correctly. Furthermore, Turkish cemeteries were closed down and the circumcision of infants as required by the Muslim faith punishable by law. Zhivkov and his regime paid lip service to *perestroika* but his version amounted merely to tinkering with the system rather than genuine reforms. Over the years he became increasingly out of touch with reality and the regime was paralysed within its own straightjacket.

The fast-deteriorating economic situation coupled with the regime's massive abuses of human rights — particularly against the Turkish minority — and the worsening environmental situation, all results of BCP policies, gave impetus to the fledgling dissident movement. Various groups began to appear between 1988 and 1989. The Independent Association for Human Rights formed in January 1988; the Club for the Support of Perestroika and Glasnost organized at Sofia University in November 1988; the Citizens' Initiative formed in December 1988; *Podkrepa* (Support) Independent Trade Union organised in February 1989; the Committee for Religious Rights, Freedom of Conscience and Spiritual Values, established in March 1989; and *Ecoglasnost*, formed in April 1989, all played an important role in mobilizing public opinion and articulating demands for change. They also laid the foundations for the subsequent working party system in Bulgaria.

At the beginning of May 1989 four ethnic Turks began a hunger strike to protest against the compulsory changing of Muslim names. At the end of the month thousands demonstrated in Sofia and other parts of the country against the regime's national assimilation policy. Zhivkov responded by announcing that the law allowing Bulgarians to travel abroad, which was to come into force in September 1989, applied with immediate effect to the Turkish minority. On May 20, the regime began to expel the leaders of the ethnic Turks' hunger strikes and demonstrations. Several waves of expulsions followed later. The flood of refugees forced the Turkish authorities to close its borders with Bulgaria on Aug. 22. By then some 310,000 people had left Bulgaria. The regime's sponsored exodus of ethnic Turks not only substantially undermined Bulgaria's international reputation because of its appalling human rights record, but also had a devastating effect on the depopulation of the rural areas since most of the ethnic Turks worked on the land and consequently in agricultural production.

The regime suffered a further dent in its already bad international standing when demonstrations organized by *Ecoglasnost* during the CSCE conference on the environment in Sofia in October were brutally suppressed by the police.

On Nov. 10, 1989, a communiqué from the Central committee plenum announced that Todor Zhivkov had resigned from all his posts. The fiction of his resignation became apparent within a few days. What had brought about Zhivkov's departure was not a popular revolution, as elsewhere in Eastern Europe, but a carefully staged coup. The crucial factors in the conspirator's calculations were clearly the disintegration of the communist regimes in Poland, Hungary and the GDR in particular, Gorbachev's abandonment of the old guard and their support for change, the worsening economic situation of the country and Bulgaria's increasing international isolation because of its human rights record. Moreover Zhivkov's attempts to promote his playboy son Vladimir (in July he was appointed head of the Central Committee's Department of Culture) further eroded support among his colleagues. In the tidal wave sweeping across Eastern Europe, Bulgaria's communist leaders tried to save themselves and their party.

The coup, which was in the making for some three months, was organized by the then Prime Minister Georgi Atanasov, Foreign Minister Petur Mladenov, who visited Moscow just before the Central Committee meeting, and the Minister of Foreign Economic Relations, Andrei Lukanov. A crucial role was also played by the Minister of Defence, Gen. Dobri Dzurov, an old supporter of Zhivkov who at the critical stage of the Central Committee's deliberations refused to back him up.

Mladenov replaced Zhivkov as a state and party leader. Together with the purged Politburo and government he pledged to promote political pluralism and respect the rule of law. On Dec. 29, the government repudiated the "Bulgarisation" campaign and invited the ethnic Turks who had fled the country to return. However, the decision was greeted with protests, particularly in the region of Khaskovo with the largest Muslim and Turkish speaking population. The protests reflected deep divisions over ethnic issues in Bulgarian society.

At the end of November 1989 the contours of a working multi-party system began to emerge with foundation of the Union of Democratic Forces (UDF). The Union was launched on Nov. 23, during a meeting at Sofia University. It initially consisted of 10 parties and organizations connected with the struggle against the totalitarian regime: the Bulgarian Social Democratic Party; the Bulgarian Agrarian National Union — Nikola Petkov; *Ecoglasnost*; the Federation of Clubs for Glasnost and Democracy; the Committee for Religious Rights, Freedom of Conscience and Spiritual Values; the Club for the Victims of Repression after 1945; Citizens' Initiative; the Federation of Independent Students' Societies; the Independent Association for the Defence of Human Rights; and the Independent Labour Federation, *Podkrepa*. Dr Zhelyu Zhelev, the country's most prominent dissident, was elected chairman of the UDF Co-ordinating Council.

The Union began to press the BCP to enter into round-table negotiations, similar to those that took place in Poland and Hungary, in order to determine the future shape of the country's political institutions and its pluralistic framework. The communists prevaricated. It took the threat of a general strike in December before the BCP agreed on the composition of the parties in the negotiations and general procedures.

The democratization process moved a step further when on Jan. 15, 1990 the Grand National Assembly removed parts of Article 1 of the Bulgarian constitution which defined the BCP as the leading force in society and state. There followed a decision by the BCP Politburo on Jan. 24 to disband the party and *Komsomol* organizations in the armed forces.

Between Jan. 30 and Feb. 2, 1990 the BCP held its 14th "Congress of Renewal" which became a scene of a bitter inner-party disputes and periodic turmoil. It revealed the deep divisions among Bulgaria's communists and younger reformers. Radicals organized into three principal factions – the Bulgarian Road to Europe, the Alternative Socialist Organization and the Movement for Democratic Socialism – threatened to split the party until the last moments of the Congress proceedings. They claimed that some 37 per cent of the party members had showed interest and sympathy with their ideas. The delegates produced few innovations, none of particular significance. The Congress accepted the resignation of Petur Mladenov from his party post and elected Aleksandur Lilov, Politburo member under Zhivkov who fell out of favour in 1983, as the chairman of the party's new Presidium. The Manifesto on Democratic Socialism adopted by the Congress described the party as Marxist and not Marxist-Leninist. This alarmed a large proportion of the delegates who thought that it represented too much of a concession to social democracy. In the new statute the principle of democratic unity was substituted for the Leninist principle of democratic centralism. The Central Committee was replaced by a Supreme Council and the Politburo by a Presidium composed of 11 persons and headed by a chairman and two deputies, rather than the secretary-general as in the past. Some of the most bitter exchanges among the delegates were made when the results of the secret elections to the Supreme Council were made public. It excluded the reformers. Subsequently, in order to avoid "the unhappy experience of the communist parties in the other socialist countries", the membership of the Council was increased by 22 (from 131 to 153) to include representatives of the BCP factions. It was an obvious attempt at a compromise between the reformists and hard-liners and a frantic attempt to preserve the organizational unity of the party. The Congress also decided to hold a referendum among its members on changing the party's name. Some 64 per cent of the total membership (86 per cent of those who participated in the referendum) voted to rename the BCP as the Bulgarian Socialist Party (BSP), which became its official name on April 3, 1990.

The round-table negotiations conducted intermittently since the middle of January until May resulted in the signing of several separate agreements over the period of five months. On March 12 the first three documents were signed setting out preliminary agreements on the introduction of a multi-party system, "free and competitive" parliamentary elections, to take place by the end of June, and equality of all forms of ownership. On March 30 a further package of documents on political reforms was signed. These included agreement on amendments to the constitution, Law on Political Parties and Electoral Law, all subsequently approved by the Grand National Assembly. The Constitutional

Amendment Law abolished the Council of State and replace it by the post of President as a head of state (not to be a member of leadership of any party), whose extensive prerogatives included also that of the Commander-in-Chief of the Armed Forces. The participants of the round table agreed that Petur Mladenov should be elected as the President of the Republic. Other amendments stipulated that the Grand National Assembly was to operate as a permanent working legislature and consist of 400 deputies.

Some of the most tedious and difficult debates of the round table concerned the provisions of the Electoral Law passed by parliament on April 3. The compromise reached provided for elections of half of the 400 deputies by majority vote in 200 single-seat constituencies, while the other half of the chamber would be elected by proportional representation from party lists in 28 multi-seat constituencies. Each voter had the right to two votes, one to elect a candidate in a one-mandate election region and another to make a choice from party lists. Political parties, political blocks and coalitions of at least 500 voters had the right to nominate their candidates for the elections. The Law on Political Parties legalized political pluralism and guaranteed the citizen's right to form political parties. However, it prohibited the creation of political organizations on religious or ethnic basis, those that incite racial, national, ethnic or religious hatred and/or seek to achieve their ends through violence. Meeting one of the constant demands of the opposition, which was the eradication of the intimidating influence of communist party cells in places of work, the law also stipulated that political parties and other organizations and movements were forbidden to carry out organized political activity at workplaces. These included rallies, demonstrations, meetings, canvassing and other forms of public campaigns. Moreover, the Law stipulated that political parties would have equal rights to state support in terms of premises and other basic infrastructure necessary for its proper functioning. But they could not be financed by state bodies, institutions, other organizations, economic enterprises and anonymous sources at home and abroad. Foreign citizens were allowed to make private or collective donations to the maximum of $500. The acquisition and management of party property would be scrutinized by special parliamentary committee.

All parties entered the election campaign with a high level of confidence. The UDF emphasized that the elections were a referendum on communist rule during the past 46 years, while the BSP campaigned as a party of "responsible conservative change".

The first round of voting took place on June 10. The results (see Table 1) gave the BSP twice as many seats as the UDF in the single-seat constituencies, while the difference narrowed significantly in the multi-seat constituencies where the proportional system was used. The proportional system also benefited BANU through which it won their only seats in the parliament. The other beneficiary of the proportional system turned out to be the MRF which emerged with the third largest number of seats.

The second round of elections in 81 single-seat constituencies in which no candidate had won an absolute majority took place on June 17 (see Table 2). The trend established during the first round was followed with a considerable degree of consistency with the BSP, UDF and MRF receiving roughly a similar number of votes to those of the first round.

The results were disappointing for almost all the parties. Although the BSP, largely because of the mixed electoral system, emerged with an absolute majority in the Grand National Assembly, it received less than 50 per cent of all the votes. The UDF captured a large number of votes in the cities but it trailed rather badly in the countryside. The results placed BANU with only 16 seats in fourth place in terms of parliamentary representation and thus undermined its claims to be a significant political force in the country. The unexpected winner of the electoral process was the Movement for Rights and Freedoms which surprisingly won 23 seats.

Although the elections were free, there was considerable evidence of intimidation of voters and manipulation of public resources by the BSP. Foreign observers catalogued threats against UDF members and said some opposition activists were dismissed or warned that they would lose their jobs if they did not support the BSP. Army conscripts were disciplined for expressing support for the UDF and the country's one million Gypsies were told that they would lose their homes and jobs under a UDF government.

Accusations of bully-boy tactics, intimidation and manipulation by the BSP focused in particular on rural areas, where diehard communists exercised a substantial amount of control over villagers. The peasants were told by government officials that they would lose their jobs and pensions and that they would have to pay for hospitals and education if the UDF came to power and brought in a market economy.

The results of the June elections, instead of stimulating the process of transition in Bulgaria, in fact produced a prolonged political stalemate which despite several attempts has not been resolved at the time of writing. Since the elections, the BSP has adopted an increasingly obstructive attitude to political and economic reforms while the UDF on the other hand has refused to be drawn into coalition. The result has been an ever-deepening mistrust between the two principal political blocks and prolonged delays in the enactment of major legislation required for the fundamental restructuring of Bulgaria's political, social and economic institutions.

The political impasse has been punctuated by the resurfacing of ethnic conflict. Demonstrators met the MRF deputies when the Grand National Assembly conveyed its meeting in Veliko Turnovo, the historical seat of the Bulgarian governments, in July 1990. Further mass protests and strikes took place in the regions of Kurdzhali, Khaskovo, Razgrad, Shumen, Aytos and other areas the same month. Although ostensibly against the formation of parliamentary groups on an ethnic principle, in fact these protests were against the existence of MRF and the Jan. 15, 1990 Act rescinding the policies of the "Bulgarisation" process and allowing Bulgarian ethnic Turks to return from Turkey and reclaim their property.

In July 1990 Petur Mladenov was forced to resign the Presidency of the Republic over a videotape showing that in December 1989 he advocated the use of tanks against demonstrators. In the Grand National Assembly, five ballots of three candidates, Chavdov Kyuranov (BSP), Petur Dertliev (UDF) and Viktor Vulkov (BANU), failed to elect a successor. Finally the impasse was broken when Dr Zhelyu Zhelev, the chairman of the Co-ordinating Council of the UDF, was accepted as the sole candidate and elected by 284 votes on Aug. 1. As the position of President requires that he may not be affiliated with a political party or group, Zhelev officially left the UDF. The choice of Zhelev was interpreted as the beginning of a breakthrough in the long political impasse.

On the insistence of the new President the hotly disputed Depolitization Act demanded by the UDF was finally approved by the Parliament on Oct. 24, 1990. Under the Act, members of the Armed Forces, paramilitary employees of the Ministry of Internal Affairs, the Security Protection Service, the Intelligence Service, judges, public prosecutors, investigation magistrates, diplomats and the staff members of the Presidency may not be members of political parties, organizations, movements and coalitions with political purposes. They had to relinquish party membership within a month of the Act coming into force and declare themselves to have done so in writing. Failure to do this would result in dismissal from individual posts.

During 1990, three successive governments, consisting of BSP members and two or three figures unaffiliated with any political party or group, tried without success to tackle the country's increasing political, social and economic problems. In the autumn the rising tide of discontent culminated in a general strike organized by university students and trade union organizations. The strike coincided with the presentation in parliament of an economic reform programme by Prime Minister Andrei Lukanov. The programme was voted down by the Grand National Assembly, despite the socialist majority, and consequently forced Lukanov's resignation on Nov. 29. His resignation was generally interpreted as a sign of the final demise of one-party BSP-dominated governments.

On Nov. 29 President Zhelev convened a meeting of representatives of the main political parties and groups, which led on Dec. 7 to the appointment of Dimitur Popov (non-party) as Prime Minister and to the initialling on Dec. 14 of an Agreement Guaranteeing a Peaceful Transition to Democratic Society. (The signing of the Agreement took place only on Jan. 3, 1991.) With the Agreement, political forces resolved to guarantee further peaceful transition to a democratic society based on political pluralism. They declared that all contradictions connected with the transition were to be resolved on the basis of the law and through the institution of parliamentary democracy. The Agreement contained a detailed legislative programme and timetable for the Grand National Assembly. It envisaged that by the end of 1990 seven bills, including legislation on local government and territorial organization, and a bill on the election of local government organs, were to be submitted to the parliament. This package of legislation would enable local government elections in February or March 1991. In January 1991 another set of bills was to be considered by the Assembly, including one on the sale, privatization and transformation of state and municipal enterprises. Finally, by March 1991, a new constitution was to be adopted and a new general election held by the end of May or the first days of June 1991. The Agreement also included the consent of the political forces to the composition of the government with a limited term of office until new parliamentary elections, as well as a guarantee of a moratorium on political actions, including strikes.

The intention of the Agreement was to give a certain degree of impetus to the processes of change and to identify a much needed wider common framework for all political actors. When it came to the signing, seven of the political groups gave their signatures with reservations, while the *Podkrepa* Independent Trade Union refused to sign it altogether. Moreover, the extremely ambitious legislative programme fell behind virtually from the day the Agreement was signed.

On Dec. 19, 1990, after 12 days of extensive consultations, Dimitur Popov presented at the last moment before the expiry of the already extended parliamentary dateline, the composition of the new interim government. The cabinet included for the first time since 1944 three representatives of the opposition Union of Democratic Forces. The UDF was given the key economic ministries of Finance and Industry, Trade and Services and the post of one of the Deputy Prime Ministers. Seven posts, including that of Defence Minister, were allocated to the Bulgarian Socialist Party, two including the Ministry for Foreign Affairs to the Bulgarian Agrarian National Union, while five posts, including that of the Minister of Interior, were allocated to non-party members.

An indication of the precarious nature of the Bulgarian politics of transition is the fact that the three UDF members of the government were within days of its formation expelled from the respective political parties, despite the consent for their participation that had been given by the party leaders during the negotiations on the cabinet composition.

The issue of acceptance of political responsibilities during the postwar history of Bulgaria, which has dominated the country's politics since the overthrow of Zhivkov, was at least partially resolved by the declaration of the BSP. The Supreme Council of the BSP issued on March 27, 1991, a declaration extending sympathy and apologies to all communists, members of other political parties and non-party people who had suffered unlawful and unfair physical, moral and professional harassment under totalitarianism. The declaration pointed out that political responsibility and guilt could not be confined to a handful of people, however great their guilt may be. The party's collective bodies, such as the Politburo and the Secretariat of the Central Committee, as well as the leaderships of other party bodies, the former government, the Council of State, parliament and the top apparat, had played an important part in the decision-making and in the actual exercise of power. The BSP also accepted its responsibility for the grave mistakes and setbacks in the economic policy which had led to the present acute economic crisis in the country. Furthermore, the declaration also stated that in the ideological sphere, the most serious abuses were connected with the establishment of Marxism-Leninism as the monopoly ideology and of dogmatism in the theory and treatment of Marxism. Accordingly, the BSP found the roots of the crisis in the Stalin-style political system imposed and accepted in Bulgaria. The formulations of the dictatorship of the proletariat, democratic centralism, the absolutization of class struggle, the party's ideological and political monopoly, the total state control and centralization of economic management, were seen to underlie the grave abuses of the socialist ideal. The declaration clearly stated that these formulations were incompatible with democracy under the new conditions.

The BSP's admission of responsibility for the country's economic and political problems has improved somewhat the prospect for the acceleration of the transition process. The ambitious legislative programme contained in the Agreement on Peaceful Transition to Democratic Society, which has substantially fallen behind schedule, was revived again when on April 4, 1991 the Grand National Assembly approved its revision. The new Agreement accelerated the modified legislative process. On July 12 the new constitution was finally approved by the parliament. By the middle of August, the long-drawn-out discussion in the Assembly on new electoral law was also coming to a conclusion, making possible its adoption. The long awaited and hotly discussed new parliamentary election has been set for Oct. 13, 1991.

BULGARIA

Table 1: Distribution of seats among political parties after the first round of parliamentary elections

	Single seat constituencies	*Multiple seat constituencies*	*Total*
Bulgarian Socialist Party	75	97	172
Union of Democratic Forces	32	75	107
Bulgarian Agrarian National Union		16	16
Party of Rights and Freedoms	9	12	21
Fatherland Front	1		1
Social Democrats	1		1
Independent	1		1
TOTAL	119	200	319

Source. Duma, June 14, 1990.

Table 2: Election results, 1990

	Votes	*Percentage*	*Seats*
Bulgarian Socialist Party	2,886,363	47.15	211
Union of Democratic Forces	2,216,127	36.20	144
Bulgarian Agrarian National Union	491,500	8.03	16
Party of Rights and Freedoms	368,929	6.03	23
Others	1,588,279	2.59	6
TOTAL	6,121,198	100.0	400

Source. Author's calculation from various editions of *Duma* between June 12 and June 22, 1990.

Directory of Parties

Agrarian Youth League
Zemedelski Mladezhki Sayuz

Foundation. December 1989.

Membership. Unknown.

Leadership. Minchev Plamen (ch.)

History. The League is a youth section of the Bulgarian Agrarian National Union — Nikola Petkov. The original League was banned in 1947.

Alternative Social-Liberal Party (ASP)
Alternativna Sotsialiberlna Partiya

Contact name. Ilian Shotlekov.

Address. 1000 Sofia, Blvd. V. Levski 10A.

Telephone. 44 19 31, 44 21 98.

Foundation. Feb. 11, 1990.

Leadership. Prof. Nikolay Vasilev (ch. of Political Council).

Membership. Unknown.

History. The party was founded by a group which left the BCP in February 1990 at the time of the second conference of the Alternative Socialist Association, a reformist faction within the former BCP, now the Bulgarian Socialist Party.

Programme. The ASP supports the struggle of the UDF for the immediate dismantling of the totalitarian social, political and economic structures and for the persistent democratization of society. The party supports the radical reforming forces in the BSP and BANU.

Affiliation. Member of the Union of Democratic Forces since October 1990.

Alternative Socialist Association
Alternativo Socialistichesko Obedinienie

Address. 1000 Sofia, ul. Gurko 66.

Leadership. Manol Manolov (pres.)

Membership. 5,000.

History. The Association was originally created in the spring of 1990 as a faction within the BSP.

BULGARIA

Programme. The establishment of a left-wing democratic centre in Bulgaria. The Association sees the Bulgarian Social Democratic Party as its natural ally.

Bulgarian Agrarian National Union (BANU)
Bulgarski Zemedelski Naroden Sayuz (BZNS)

Contact name. Konstantin Yanchev.

Address. 1000 Sofia, ul. Yanko Zabunov 1.

Telephone. 88 19 51.

Foundation. 1900.

Membership. 120,000.

Leadership. Viktor Vulkov (ch.)

History. Since the beginning of the 1950s it has been effectively controlled by the BCP, which virtually vetted new members recruited from the *Komsomol* and put the membership ceiling to 120,000. Throughout the postwar period it participated in communist-dominated governments which allowed the BCP to maintain the fiction that Bulgaria was a two-party state. After the overthrow of Zhivkov in November 1989 the BANU decided to act as an independent opposition party. It refused to take part in the Lukanov administration formed on Feb. 1, 1990. It did, however, agree to take part in the Popov interim government named on Dec. 19, 1990. One of the unresolved problems for the party is its merger with BANU-NP. On Aug. 27, 1990, the BANU Standing Committee stated that the unification of the two Agrarian Parties is possible. It suggested that after the merger the new Agrarian Party should be an independent political organization in alliance with all democratic forces and working with the UDF in united opposition for the complete dismantling of the totalitarian system. However, despite several attempts to negotiate the merger, no progress has been made on this issue principally because of the distrust and contempt with which the party is viewed by the BANU-NP.

Publication. Zemedelsko Zname (Agrarian Banner).

Bulgarian Agrarian National Union — Nikola Petkov (BANU-NP)
Bulgarski Zemedelski Naroden Sayuz — Nikola Petkov (BZNS-NP)

Address. 1000 Sofia, Blvd. Dondukov 39.

Telephone. 39 01 94, 39 02 08.

Foundation. November 1989. (Revival of the original BZNS, established in the late 1940s.)

Leadership. Milan Drenchev (sec.-gen.); Nikodim Popov, Vielin Kirimov, Krum Nevrokopski, Mihail Mihailov (members of the secretariat).

Membership. 500,000.

History. The BANU-NP is distinguished from the Bulgarian Agrarian National Union which, since 1947, has been compromised by its association with the communists. The Union is named after Nikola Petkov, its outstanding leader in the 1940s and principal opponent of the communists, who was hung on Sept. 23, 1947. The party's 26th regular congress (the first in 58 years) was held in Sofia from April 19–25, 1991. The party has repeatedly stated that the unification of both of the Agrarian Parties can and should take place only within the framework of the UDF.

Programme. To provide a democratic Agrarian alternative to the official Bulgarian Agrarian National Union; to win the rehabilitation of Petkov and other members of the union persecuted during the 1940s and 1950s; and to campaign for democracy and a market economy, based on private agriculture.

Affiliation. Member of an opposition alliance, the Union of Democratic Forces, since its foundation in December 1989.

Publication. *Naradno Zemedelsko Zname* (National Agrarian Banner).

Bulgarian Business Bloc
Bulgarski Biznes Blok

Foundation. Nov. 5, 1990.

Leadership. George Ganchev (pres.)

History and programme. Founded by Valentin Mollov, a leading private businessman, the Bloc describes itself as a right-wing Anglo-Saxon and Thatcherite-type political formation which seeks to attract Bulgaria's best economic and intellectual brains. The Bloc aims at turning Bulgaria into a free-trade zone. It argues that its geographical proximity with the USSR makes Bulgaria a natural bridgehead for the invasion of West European and North American capital into the "boundless" Soviet market.

Bulgarian Business Party
Bulgarska Biznes Partiya

Address. 1000 Sofia, "Sredec", Blvd. Al., Stambolinski 2A.

Leadership. Aleksandur Cherpokov (pres.)

Bulgarian Communist Party (BCP)
Bulgarska Komunisticheska Partiya (BKP)

Foundation. 1891.

Membership. 1,000,000 (January 1990).

History. The BCP had its origins in the Bulgarian Social Democratic Party which split in 1903, the result of which was the formation of the Workers' Social Democratic Party. This group renamed itself the Bulgarian Communist Party in 1919. Ordered by the courts to be disbanded in 1924, it reappeared as the legal Workers' Party in 1927. After the dissolution of all political parties by the Military League-Zveno government in 1934 it continued its activities underground as the Bulgarian Workers' Party (Communist), its policies being directed from Moscow. After the seizure of power in 1944 it changed its name to Bulgarian Communist Party in 1948. The BCP ruled Bulgaria with the support of the Bulgarian Agrarian National Union until Dec. 19, 1990. In 1954 Todor Zhivkov became the party's Secretary-General, a post he combined with that of Prime Minister between 1962 and 1971, and since 1971 President of the Council of State. He was overthrown by an internal coup on Nov. 10, 1989. The BCP held its 14th "Congress of Renewal" between Jan. 30 and Feb. 1, 1990. In September 1990 the BCP changed its name to the Bulgarian Socialist Party.

Bulgarian Communist Party
Bulgarska Komunisticheska Partiya

Address. 1404 Sofia, Blvd. Mladezhki prohod bl. 5, B.

Telephone. 59 16 73.

Leadership. Ivan Spasov.

History. Originally formed as the Party of the Working People on April 25, 1990. It adapted its present name on June 21, 1990, and was formally re-founded in September 1990.

Bulgarian Communist Party (Marxist)
Bulgarska Komunisticheska Partiya (Marksismu)

Address. 1000 Sofia, p. k. 21 ul. Pozitano 20, et. II.

Telephone. 85 141 (ext. 299).

Leadership. Boris Petkov.

History. The party held its 15th Congress in Panagyurishte on Nov. 4, 1990, which elected the First Secretary and the Central Committee. The party, consisting of orthodox communists, considers itself the only party based on Marxist-Leninist ideas and the legal successor to BCP property including the buildings in Sofia. It has initiated legal proceedings against the BSP for material and financial assets. The re-founded BCP had split into two groups on March 27, 1991.

Bulgarian Communist Party (Revolutionary)
Bulgarska Komunisticheska Partiya (Revoliucionna)

Address. 9000 Varna, Beloslav, ul. Sava 39.

Telephone. 52 42 36.

Foundation. March 8, 1991.

Leadership. Angel Tsonev.

Formerly known as the Bulgarian Revolutionary Youth Party, the party was founded in Varna and registered in April 1990. It claims that "there is no other party in Bulgaria based on true Marxism-Leninism" but itself. The party decided to "accept the communist Todor Zhivkov as one of its members on account of the great merit he has earned in serving the International Workers' and Communist Movement if he wishes to join the party".

Bulgarian Democratic Forum
Bulgarski Demokraticheski Forum

Address. 1505 Sofia, ul. G.S. Rakovski 82.

Telephone. 89 02 85, 75 64 50.

Leadership. Vasil Zlatarov, (pres.); Nikola Yanachkov, Hristo Yonov, Ivan Evlogiev (vice-pres.)

History. A right-wing organization, the successor to the Union of Bulgarian National Legions disbanded in 1944. The Forum has an observer status with the Union of Democratic Forces.

Bulgarian Democratic Party
Bulgarska Demokraticheska Partiya

Address. 1528 Sofia, Druzhba 1, bl. 42, vh. 5, et. 3.

Telephone. 79 66 18.

Bulgarian Democratic-Constitutional Party
Bulgarska Demokrat-Konstucionna Partiya

Address. 4000 Plovdiv, ul. Chataldzha 6.
Telephone. 43 79 1, 55 61 35.

Leadership. Ivan Ambarev (l.); Aleksandur Dolev, Nikolai Buchkov.

Bulgarian Democratic Youth Federation
Bulgarska Demokratichna Mladezh

Address. 1000 Sofia, Blvd. Al Stamboliski 11.

Telephone. 87 26 89.

Foundation. Feb. 27, 1990.

Leadership. Rosen Karadimov (ch.)

The Federation emerged as a result of the dissolution of the Dimitrov Youth Communist League.

BULGARIA

Bulgarian Labour Social-Democratic Party
Bulgarska Rabotnicheska Sotsialdemokraticheska Partiya

Address. 1373 Sofia, Zapaden Park, ul. Suhodolska 2, bl. 32, ap. 5.

Telephone. 22 81 58.

Leadership. Mahol Dimitrov (sec.)

Bulgarian Liberal Party
Bulgarska Liberalna Partiya

Address. 1000 Sofia, p.k. 819, ul. Haidushka gora 4, bl. 35 A, vh. A, et. 9, ap. 29.

Telephone. 58 51 19.

Leadership. Vlkan Vergev (pres.); Ekaterina Zahareva (sec.-gen.)

Bulgarian National Democratic Union (BNDU)
Bulgarski Natsionalen Demokraticheski Sayuz (BNDS)

Foundation. Dec. 8, 1989.

Leadership. Nikolay Genchev (ch.); Ventsislav Nachev, Luko Zahariev, Mincho Minchev, Georgi Genov, Licho Gogov, Mariya Yankova.

Bulgarian National Party
Bulgarska Narodna Partiya

Address. 1000 Sofia, ul. Tsar Samuil 115.

Telephone. 80 21 16.

Leadership. Dimitur Brankov (pres.); Stroimir Minkov (sec.)

Bulgarian National Democratic Party
Bulgarska Nasionalna Demokraticheska Partiya

Address. 1000 Sofia, Blvd. Vitosha 25.

Telephone. 80 15 10.

Leadership. Lchezar Stoyanov (pres.)

Bulgarian National Radical Party
Bulgarska Natsionalna Radikalna Partiya

Address. 1000 Sofia, ul. Alen mak 6.

Telephone. 65 51 19, 88 46 52.

Leadership. Ivan Georgiev (pres.); Zdravko Bakalov, Ivan Krctev (secretaries).

Programme and organization. Small group with extreme nationalist platform. It supports Bulgarian territorial claims against its neighbours and Turkey in particular, revision of international agreements and the emigration to Turkey of Bulgaria's Turkish minority. The party is suspected of having strong links with the *nomenklatura* of the BSP. It publishes *Bulgarski Glas* (Bulgarian Voice).

Bulgarian People's Party (BPP)
Bulgarska Narodna Partiya (BNP)

Address. 1343 Sofia, Ljulin, Bloc 214.

Foundation. Feb. 5, 1990.

Programme. To support the ideals of equal opportunities, equal rights, freedom, and a just, humane and cohesive society, as well as a federal Europe.

Affiliation. Union of Democratic Forces.

Bulgarian Social Democratic Party
Bulgarska Sotsialdemokraticheska Partiya

Address. 1303 Sofia, Blvd. Al Stambolinski 87.

Telephone. 39 01 12.

Leadership. Atanas Moskov (pres.)

Bulgarian Social Democratic Party (BSDP)
Bulgarska Sotsial-demokraticheska Partiya (BSDP)

Contact name. Rumen Krumov.

Address. 1000 Sofia, 51 Tzar Assen Street.

Foundation. 1891, re-founded Jan. 10, 1990.

Leadership. Dr Peter Dertliev (ch.)

Membership. 84,000.

History. The party was suppressed after 1948 but never actually banned. It held its first congress since its revival (38th in its history) between 23–25 March 1991. The congress approved the party's programme and a political statement.

Programme. The party categorically distances itself from Marxism-Leninism and its relapses; it opposes communism, eastern socialism and all other forms of totalitarianism and extremism; it sees the democratic state committed to the rule of law as the only form of political system of Bulgarian society. The BSDP campaigns for democracy, for a welfare market economy, for the equitability of three types of ownership (private, co-operative and state). Co-operatives are viewed as the most suitable form of privatization for Bulgaria.

BULGARIA

Organization. Rules approved by the 38th congress give the central leadership an imposing presence in the work of the party's branches.

Affiliation. Member of the Union of Democratic Forces since its foundation in December 1989; the Socialist International.

Publication. The BSPD has its own newspaper *Svoboden Narod* (Free People) which resumed publication after a break of 43 years on Feb. 1, 1990.

Bulgarian Socialist Party (BSP)
Bulgarska Sotsialisticheska Partiya (BSP)

Foundation. Dec. 31, 1989.

Leadership. Ivan Velkov (ch.)

Membership. 10,000.

History. The BSP emerged from a political circle formed at the end of 1988. It disputes the BCP's right to rename itself as the Bulgarian Socialist Party in April 1990.

Programme. To promote democracy and end the "Stalinist and Brezhnevist political, ideological, and economic system" of socialism. The BSP renounces class-based politics and defends the rights of the individual.

Bulgarian Socialist Party (BSP)
Bulgarska Sotsialisticheska Partiya (BSP)

Contact name. Klara Marinova.

Address. 1000 Sofia, 1 Dondoukov Blvd.

Telephone. 84 01.

Leadership. Aleksandur Lilov (ch. of the Presidium); Aleksandur Tomov (dep. ch.); Andrei Lukanov (dep. ch.); Apostol Dimitrov (dep. ch.)

Membership. 250,000 (declining).

History. The BSP is a continuation of the BCP which changed its name in April 1990 as a result of a referendum conducted amongst its members in the spring of 1990. The change of name was officially approved by the 15th Congress of the BCP which became the 39th consecutive Congress of the BSP. The claim of the BCP to assume the name of the Bulgarian Socialist Party is disputed by the Bulgarian Socialist Party, founded on Dec. 31, 1989.

Programme. The party's programme adopted at its 39th Congress held between Sept. 22–25, 1990 stipulates that the BSP is a mass parliamentary party which expresses the interests of the working people and which attains its goals by democratic means and in compliance with the constitution and the law of the land. Its activities are based on the values of Marxism, of the experience and traditions of the socialist movement and the contemporary left democratic parties and movements. As a party of democratic socialism it is a part of the world socialist left.

Organization. Several prominent factions have emerged within the party since November 1989. The most vocal and vociferous include:

Alternative Socialist Association (ASA), led by Prof. Ivan Nikolov, was established on Jan. 12, 1990, and has 100 clubs throughout the country. It aims to promote democracy by campaigning for the radical democratization of the BSP. The ASA objects to the results of the extraordinary congress of BCP held between Jan. 30 and Feb. 1, 1990.

Alternative Socialist Organization, led by Valentin Vatsev. This faction is highly critical of the BSP leadership, claiming that genuine reformers have been systematically removed from responsible positions in the party.

Bulgarian Road to Europe, led by Rumen Georgiev, who is the chairman of a 12-person Co-ordinating Committee. It was formed on Jan. 4, 1990, at Sofia University as an anti-Stalinist wing of the BCP. At the extraordinary BCP congress (Jan. 30–Feb. 1, 1990) the group won a significant representation in the party's leadership. Its platform claims to have co-ordinating committees in 52 towns throughout the country. It supports the democratic understanding of socialism, pluralism of property, de-Stalinization of the BCP/BSP, the eradication of Zhivkovism, the separation of the BSP from the state and the establishment of a multi-party system, transition to a market economy, and the promotion of Bulgaria's interaction within the European Communities.

Democratic Forum, a small faction formed in the spring of 1990.

Marxist Alternative Movement, led by Prof. Mitryu Yankov and claims several thousand members.

Movement for Democratic Socialism, which is the most significant faction within the BSP. It claims to have 13,000 members in Sofia and over 9,000 members in the provinces. It is headed by Aleksandur Tomov who became deputy Prime Minister in the interim government formed in December 1990. The Movement aims to rally broad social circles around a platform of democratic socialism based on the principle of market economy, political pluralism, the people's self-government, social justice, and freedom of the individual.

Movement for Radical Changes in the Socialist Party, which is a small but very active faction demanding fundamental restructuring of the BSP.

Christian Democratic Front
Hristiyan-Demokraticheska Fronta

Leadership. Nikolai Vasilev.

Membership. Predominantly intellectuals, former members of the BCP, vehement anti-communists today.

Affiliation. Member of the Union of Democratic Forces since October 1990.

BULGARIA

Christian Republican Party (CRP)
Hristiyan-Republikanska Partiya (HRP)

Address. 1066 Sofia, p.k. 113.

Telephone. 52 24 06.

Foundation. Nov. 24, 1989, in Plovdiv.

Leadership. Konstantin Adzharov (ch.); Dimitar Petkanov (sec.); Elisaveta Adzharov, Ekaterina Petkanova.

Membership. Several thousands.

Programme. To combine the virtues of Christianity with republican principles. In February 1990 the party proposed the holding of a referendum on whether Bulgaria should be a republic or a monarchy.

Organisation. 24 branches and a youth league.

Affiliation. Member of the Political Opposition Block.

Citizens' Initiative (CI)
Grazhdanska Initsiativa (GI)

Address. 1000 Sofia, Blvd. Dondukov 39.

Telephone. 39 01 93.

Foundation. Dec. 25, 1988, in Ruse, relaunched on Nov. 27, 1989 in Sofia.

Leadership. Lyubomir Sobadjiev (ch.); Dimitar Todorov Angelov, Totyu Totov, Hristo Peev, Emil Stumbov.

Membership. 8,500.

History. The CI has its roots in two earlier organizations; the Ruse section of the Independent Association for the Defence of Human Rights, and the Committee 273 (named after an article in the penal code used to imprison opponents of the regime). A year later it became a national organization.

Programme. Defence of human rights and the promotion of public debate and political awareness. Support for *glasnost* and the speedy end of the command administrative system. The movement supports the socially weak and homeless and is also involved in investigating communist crimes.

Affiliation. Member of the Union of Democratic Forces since its foundation in December 1989.

Club for the Victims of Repression after 1945
Klub na Represiranite sled 1945 Godina

Address. 4000 Plovdiv.

Telephone. 22 700 71.

Foundation. September 1989.

Leadership. Dimitur Bakalov (ch.); Vangel Gorev, Todor Kavaldzhiev, Tako Karaivanov, Ivan Nevrokopski.

History. Set up by ex-political prisoners, most of them Agrarian Union activists, it was responsible for the discovery of mass graves of opponents of communism killed in the 1940s. The Club's national conference took place on April 1, 1990 in Plovdiv.

Programme. The gradual rehabilitation of all democrats, socialists, agrarians, and non-party people who suffered repression after 1945; to win constitutional guarantees of freedom of research and publication on Bulgaria's postwar history; to construct a memorial to the victims of communist persecution; to win indemnities for surviving relatives.

Affiliation. Member of the Union of Democratic Forces since its foundation in December 1989.

Committee for Religious Rights, Freedom of Conscience, and Spiritual Values
Komitet za Zashtita na Religioznite Prava Svobodata na Savestta i Duhovnite Tsenosti

Foundation. March 9, 1989 in Veliko Turnovo.

Leadership. Rev Hristofor Subev (ch.); Petar Kanev Petrov (sec.)

Programme. To campaign for an end to political interference in Church affairs and religious life; to promote religious education, publishing, and broadcasting; to campaign for the legalization of religious charitable work; to promote religious tolerance in Bulgaria.

Organization. Although the Committee was established by an Orthodox priest, both clergy and lay people are its members. It is a more political than religious organization, characterized by extreme anti-communism.

Affiliation. Member of the Union of Democratic Forces.

Conservative Party
Konservativna Partiya

Address. 1505 Sofia, kv. Reduta, ul Ribarica 22, bl. 4.

Telephone. 72 02 82.

Leadership. Ivan Edisonov, (pres.); Stefan Kospartov (dep. pres.)

Constitutional Alliance
Konstitucionen Sayuz

Address. 4000 Plovdiv, ul. Oplchenska 10-A.

Foundation. Jan. 5, 1991, in Plovdiv.

Leadership. Manol Zhurnalov (pres.)

BULGARIA

History. The Constitutionalists had one of the longest battles of any party in Bulgaria over their registration. The Sofia City Court refused to register the party in January objecting to its programme, which challenges the republican framework of the state system. The party appeals against the decision eventually went to the Supreme Court which, on May 7, reversed the decision of the lower courts and thus allowed the party's registration.

Programme. The party challenges the validity of the 1946 referendum on the abolition of monarchy. It considers the referendum as an "unlawful, coercive and unprecedented act in the history of democratic states".

Democratic Forum
Demokratichen Forum

Foundation. January 1990.

Leadership. Dragomir Draganov.

Programme. To revive the BCP and the Bulgarian economy, essentially by promoting austerity and efficiency and eliminating the power of the *nomenklatura*; to create a democratic civil society and to separate the party from the state.

Organization. The Forum is a radical-left group within the BCP.

Democratic League for the Defence of Human Rights
Demokratichnata Liga za Zashtita na Pravata na Choveka

Foundation. November 1988 in the village of Drashan, near Vratsa.

Leadership. Mustafa Yumerov (ch.); Sabri Iskenderov, Ali Ormanliev.

Membership. Over 10,000.

Programme. To campaign for human rights in Bulgaria; to restore democratic principles in public life.

Organization. The League's membership consists largely, but not exclusively, of ethnic Turks. Its leadership was expelled to Turkey after the formation of the organization.

Democratic Movement for Constitutional Monarchy
Demokratichno Dvizhenie za Konstytucjonalna Monarhia

Contact name. Nikola Zheliavski.

Address. 1463 Sofia, ul. Tsar Asen 55, vh. 5.

Telephone. 89 75 45.

Foundation. Jan. 17, 1990.

Leadership. Bozhnka Milusheva, Konstantin Halachev, Hristo Metaniev.

Programme. The party campaigns for the restoration of civil rights of Simeon II of Turnovo (the last king of the Bulgarians, currently living in Madrid) and for the establishment of a democratic state based on the principles of constitutional monarchy.

Democratic Party (DP)
Demokraticheska Partiya (DP)

Contact name. Vasil Iliev.

Address. 1000 Sofia, Blvd. Dondukov 34, et. IV, st. 8.

Telephone. 80 01 87, 88 20 46.

Foundation. 1886, re-founded January 1990.

Leadership. Stefan Savon (ch.); Georgi Markov (dep. ch.)

History. Traditional right-wing party. Held power several times prior to the communist takeover in 1944. The DP never entered into any agreements with the communists. It was banned by the communist regime in 1947 and at the end of 1948 liquidated altogether.

Programme. Political and economic pluralism.

Affiliation. Member of the Union of Democratic Forces since February 1990.

Democratic Party in Bulgaria
Demokraticheska Partiya v Bulgaria

Address. 1000 Sofia, Mladost 2, bl. 226, vh G.
Telephone. 74 48 22.

Leadership. Konstantin Georgiev (ch.); Bogdana Zhelyazka (sec.)

Democratic Women's Movement
Demokratichen Sayuz Zhenite

Address. 1463 Sofia, Blvd. Patriarch Evtimin 82.

Telephone. 52 53 18.

Leadership. Emilia Maclarova, Nora Ananieva, Rumiana Modeva.

Programme. The Movement, established on March 17, 1990, aims to protect women's rights.

Dimitrov Communist Youth Union
Dimitrovski Komunisticheski Mladezhki Sayuz

Foundation. 1947.

Membership. 750,000 (early 1990, rapidly declining).

BULGARIA

History. The union has been known previously as the People's Youth Union (*Sayuz na Narodna Mladezh*) and the Proletarian Youth Union (*Rabotnicheski Mladezhki Sayuz*) before adopting the current name in 1958. Its membership has been steadily declining since 1987. After the overthrow of Todor Zhivkov in November 1989 the Union became increasingly independent and critical of the BCP leadership. Its Congress in February 1990 severed all institutional links with the BCP and adopted the name of the Bulgarian Democratic Youth Federation.

Programme. To organize youth activities.

Ecoglasnost

Address. 1504 Sofia, 28 Marin Drinov Str.

Foundation. April 13, 1989.

Leadership. Peter Slabakov (ch. of National Council); Georgi Avramov (sec. of National Council).

Membership. Over 50 clubs and organizations throughout the country.

History. The roots of the group lie in the so-called Committee of Ruse, Bulgaria's first dissident formation, a spontaneous movement of intellectuals — predominantly film-makers and writers — for ecological preservation of the town of Ruse. In October 1989 *Ecoglasnost* organized demonstrations in Sofia, during the Conference on Security and Co-operation in Europe conference on the environment, which were brutally suppressed by the police. These events precipitated Zhivkov's downfall and marked the beginning of the democratization process. After the February 1990 congress of the BCP, many of the communist party members withdrew from *Ecoglasnost* and the alliance became a politically anti-communist movement defined by environmentalism. The first national conference of the movement took place on April 1, 1990, in Sofia.

Programme. To campaign for the implementation of ecological laws; to promote *glasnost* and educate the public on ecological issues. The priority of the movement is the socio-ecological self-protection of the population and control over management decisions on which the people's health and state of their living environment depends.

Organization. A nationwide environmental pressure group with branches throughout the country, many of which have announced that they are autonomous and some of which have taken different names, such as Eco-Voice in Plovdiv.

Affiliation. Member of the Union of Democratic Forces since its foundation in December 1989.

Federation of Christian Parties and Movements

Formed on Dec. 30, 1990, as a grouping of three small parties; the Christian Democrats, the Christian Radicals and the New Christian Democrats.

Fatherland Party of Labour

Leadership. Dimitur Arnandov (ch.)

Extreme nationalist party, an off-shoot of the People's Committee for Defending National Interests. It stresses Bulgaria's role as a barrier against Islam.

Federation of Clubs for Glasnost and Democracy
Federatsiya na Klubove za Glasnost i Demokratsiya

Address. 1000 Sofia, 134 Rakovski Street.

Foundation. Jan. 20, 1990.

Membership. 67 clubs around the country.

Leadership. Prof. Ivan Dzhadzhev (ch.)

History. Originally founded on Nov. 30, 1988, as a discussion club at Sofia University by 120 leading writers, poets, film-makers, philosophers, sociologists and scientists under the name Club to Support Glasnost and Perestroika. They suffered harassment from the authorities and several were sacked from their jobs. Many of the Club's founders were prominent members of the BCP, and were expelled from the party. Its first chairman was Dr Zhelyu Zhelev. On Jan. 20, 1990, 19 clubs from Sofia and other parts of the country formed the Federation. A split within the leadership of the organization in early 1990 led to the departure of a number of its BCP members.

Programme. To conduct a free public debate on the major problems facing Bulgaria and to promote *glasnost* and democracy.

Organization. Some 20 provincial branches including Plovdiv, Bourgas, Pazardzhik and Smolyn.

Affiliation. Member of the Union of Democratic Forces since its foundation in December 1989.

Federation of Independent Students' Societies
Federatsiya na Nezavisimi Studentski Druzhestva

Address. 1000 Sofia, Blvd. Dondukov 39.

Telephone. 39 00 18.

Foundation. January 1990.

Leadership. Stlian Stoichev (pres.) Zahari Nikolov (sec.)

History. The Federation emerged from the Independent Students' Society founded in Sofia University on Nov. 15, 1989. The students organized two occupational strikes in the universities. The first, in June and July 1990, proved to be instrumental in bringing about the fall of President Petar Mladenov. The second strike in the autumn of 1990 contributed significantly to the bringing down of the government of Andrei Lukanov and his government.

Programme. To encourage free expression and democratization in higher education, to campaign for the freedom of association for young people and the removal of ideological constraints on academic life.

Affiliation. Member of the Union of Democratic Forces since its foundation in December 1989.

Green Party
Zelena Partiya

Address. 1000 Sofia, Blvd. Yanko Saksov 30.

Telephone. 44 21 85.

Foundation. Dec. 28, 1989.

Leadership. Aleksander Karakachanov (ch.); Dimitri Novakov, (dep. ch.); Lyubomir Ivanov, (dep. ch.)

Membership. 1,000 in Sofia alone.

History. Formed by a group of former *Ecoglasnost* members of whom Aleksander Karakachanov, the mayor of Sofia, is the most prominent member.

Programme. To establish a pluralistic democracy in which legislative and executive power are decentralized to the maximum extent possible; to base the economy on ecological principles and to promote local and private initiative.

Organization. 15 branches in Sofia and eight branches in the provinces. The party lacks a specific social base.

Affiliation. Member of the Union of Democratic Forces since January 1990.

Independent Association for the Defence of Human Rights in Bulgaria
Nezavisimo Druzhestvo za Zashtita na Choveshkite Prava v Bulgariya

Foundation. Jan. 16, 1988.

Leadership. Ilya Minev (ch.); Stefan Vulkov (dep. ch.)

Membership. Over 1,000 in early 1990.

History. The Association, the oldest dissident group in the country, was established after six Bulgarian dissidents sent an appeal to a Conference on Security and Co-operation in Europe follow-up conference in Vienna, in which they protested against human rights violations by the communist regime. Its members were subjected to some of the harshest persecution of any dissident groups and several were forced into exile. Many of its initial members were ethnic Turks joining the Association in protest against the communist regime's process of "Bulgarisation". The membership of the group fell after June 1989 when some 310,000 of the ethnic Turks left Bulgaria. The issue of the Turkish minority was a source of major divisions within the Association, with some members advocating strongly that this should not be a subject of concern for its activities. During 1990 the Association has more or less disintegrated due to the controversial behaviour of Rumen Vodenicharov, who left the parliamentary group of the UDF and declared himself independent.

Programme. To collect information on political prisoners and other cases of abuse of human rights; to campaign for legal reforms; to protect minority rights.

Affiliation. Founding member of the Union of Democratic Forces.

Independent Trade Union Federation Podkrepa
Nezavisima Federatsiya na Truda Podkrepa

Foundation. Feb. 11, 1989, in Plovdiv.

Address. 1000 Sofia, 134 Rakovski Street.

Leadership. Dr Konstantin Trenchev (ch.); Todor Gagalov (dep. ch.); Plamen Darakchiev (sec.)

Membership. Over 500,000.

History. Originally conceived as a trade union for scientific, technical, educational, and cultural professions, the Federation later broadened its scope of membership and activities. *Podkrepa*'s foundation congress (March 17–24, 1990) approved the Federation's statute and political resolution. *Podkrepa* has subsequently emerged as a powerful organization and has played an increasingly important role in Bulgarian politics, in some respects comparable to that of Solidarity in Poland. The general strike organized by the Federation in November 1990 helped to bring down the Lukanov cabinet and made it possible for the key economic ministries to be given to UDF experts.

Programme. To defend workers' rights.

Affiliation. Member of the Union of Democratic Forces from December 1989 till the autumn of 1990. Since then, it has an observer status only. International Confederation of Trade Unions and the World Confederation of Labour.

Liberal Congress Party
Partyia Liberalen Kongres

Contact name. Dimitur Tomov.

Address. 1000 Sofia, Blvd. Dondukov 39.

Telephone. 39 00 18.

Leadership. Yanko Yankov (pres.); Bozhidar Palyushev, (dep. pres.); Lyulian Kocev, (dep. pres.)

History. Formerly known as the Social Democratic Party (Non-Marxist), the party was re-named on Jan. 12, 1991.

BULGARIA

Liberal Democratic Party (LDP)
Liberalno-Demokraticheska Partiya (LDP)

Address. Stara Zagora, 26A Karadsha Str.

Foundation. Nov. 27, 1989.

Leadership. Hristo Santulov (ch.)

History. The party was founded in Stara Zagora as the Union of Free Democrats, and adopted the current name in January 1990.

Programme. To work for a democratic society based on the rule of law. The state President should be elected directly by the population.

Affiliation. Political Opposition Block.

Liberal-Democratic Party in Bulgaria
Liberalno-Demokraticheska Partiya v Bulgaria

Address. 1113 Sofia, ul. Chehov 10.

Telephone. 70 60 40.

Liberal Party
Liberalna Partiya

Address. 2300 Piernik, ul Radomir 1.

Telephone. 2 34 98, 7 59 64.

Liberal Union
Liberalnyi Sayuz

Foundation. April 1990.

History. Originally formed on Jan. 11, 1990, as the Political Opposition Block, it adopted its present name in order to attract wider popular support during the June 1990 parliamentary elections.

Organization. Opposition alliance of six political parties and groups, including the Christian Republican Party and Liberal Democratic Party.

Monarchic-Conservative Union
Monarhichsko-Konservativen Sayuz

Address. Veliko Turnovo. p.k. 334.

Telephone. 3 13 04.

Movement for Rights and Freedoms (MRF)
Dvizhenie za Prava i Svobodi (DPS)

Contact name. Osman Oktay.

Address. 1408 Sofia, Ivan Vazov ul., Petar Topalov Shmid bl., 50, vh. B, ap. 55.

Telephone. 51 98 22, 65 8 32.

Foundation. Jan. 4, 1990.

Leadership. Ahmed Dogan (pres. of the Co-ordinating Council); Osman Oktay (organizational sec. of the Co-ordinating Council).

Membership. 100,000.

History. The Movement has its roots in the resistance of the Turkish minority to the "Bulgarisation" process conducted with particular ferocity by the communist regime between 1985 and 1989. The MRF began its activities in the underground in the spring of 1985. Uncovered in June 1986, its leadership, including Ahmed Dogan, was sentenced to long prison terms. Between 1986 and December 1989 its activities were planned and directed from prison. Originally formed in December 1989 as the Movement for the Rights and Freedoms of the Turks and Muslims in Bulgaria, the MRF Co-ordinating Council resolved that the Movement should undertake to protect the universal rights and freedoms of individuals and communities as a whole, rather than just those of local Turks and Muslims. Officially registered on April 26, 1990, the MRF conducted an extremely well organized electoral campaign prior to the June 1990 parliamentary elections and won 23 seats in the Grand National Assembly, thus becoming the third largest political force in the country. The first national conference of the MRF was held between March 26–27, in Sofia.

Programme. The Movement calls for respect for all civil rights and freedoms of individuals and that of communities as enshrined in the Bulgarian constitution and international instruments. It opposes all forms of segregation in education, the economy or culture. It rejects any form of separatism, nationalism or fundamentalism, as well as attempts to fuel ethnic hatred and calls for hostility.

Organization. Membership of the Movement is open to all Bulgarian citizens regardless of their language, ethnic identity and party affiliation. Some 80 per cent of the MRF's members are Bulgarian Turks. Members of the BSP are eligible for membership but cannot hold senior posts in the organization.

Publication. Weekly newspaper *Prava i Svobodi* (Rights and Freedoms).

National Committee for the Defence of National Interests
Obshtonaroden Komitet za Zashtita na Natsionalnite Interesi

Foundation. January 1990.

Leadership. Dimitar Arnaudov (ch.;) Mincho Minchev (spokesman); Kiril Haramiev, Kamen Garelov.

BULGARIA

History. The Committee was formed as an alliance of provincial nationalist groups in the wake of the Dec. 29, 1989, decision of the BCP Politburo condemning the "Bulgarisation" process of the Turkish minority by the Zhivkov regime. The decision to restore the names and rights of this minority was, however, greeted by rallies, strikes and street violence across the country.

Programme. To represent the interests of the ethnic Bulgarian community in areas of mixed population; to promote public discussion of national questions; to oppose separatist and autonomous movements among ethnic minorities.

National Liberal Party "Stefan Stambolov"
Narodnoliberalna Partyia "Stefan Stambolov"

Address. 5000 Veliko Turnovo.

Telephone. 2 73 98.

Leadership. Zafir Vielinov.

National Union "Zveno"
Naroden Sayuz "Zveno"

Telephone. Sofia 89 13 40.

Leadership. Vera Peicheva (sec.)

National Youth Union

Foundation. May 5, 1991.

Organization. This is an umbrella organization of most of the youth sections of parties and groups that comprise the UDF. The founding members of the Union include: Union of Young Social Democrats; Union of Macedonian Associations; Internal Macedonian Revolutionary Organization; Nikola Petkov Agrarian Youth Union; Club of Friends of Jesus Christ; Union of the Democratic Party; and Federation of Independent Students' Associations.

New Social Democratic Party
Nova Sotsialdemokraticheska Partyia

Address. 1504 Sofia, p.k. 14.

Telephone. 44 99 47, 22 24 40.

Leadership. Vasil Mihailov (pres.); Petar Atanasov (dep. pres.)

Radical Democratic Party (RDP)
Radikalna Demokraticheska Partiya (RDP)

Address. 1000 Sofia, Blvd. Dondukov 34, et. III, st. 6–8.

Telephone. 80 02 69, 80 03 45, 80 02 91, 80 02 99.

Foundation. 1902, re-founded Dec. 4, 1989.

Leadership. Elka Konstantinova (pres.); Aleksander Yordanov, Mikhail Nedelchev (co-pres.). Other prominent members of the leadership include: Boycho Petrov, Asen Kolushki, Aleksandar Tarkalanov.

History. The RDP is a successor of a small centrist party which existed until 1944.

Programme. To establish a secular, democratic republic with a mixed economy.

Organization. A powerful right-wing party with a strong influence among the educated urban population.

Affiliation. Member of the Union of Democratic Forces since December 1989.

Publication. The party publishes and influential paper *Bek XXI* (21st Century).

Republican Party (RP)
Republikanska Partiya (RP)

Address. 1606 Sofia, Blvd. Gen. Ckobelev 46.

Telephone. 54 25 91.

Foundation. Jan. 22, 1990.

Leadership. Lenko Roussanov (pres.); Ivan Sotirov (sec.)

Programme. To establish Bulgaria as a democratic parliamentary and law-governed republic with a mixed economy. The RP advocates the separation of party and state and the depoliticization of the ministries of Internal Affairs, Defence, the courts, the Chief Prosecutor's Office, radio and television organizations and the official news agency.

Affiliation. Observer status with the Union of Democratic Forces.

Republican Party in Bulgaria
Republikanska Partiya v Bulgaria

Address. 1000 Sofia, ul. Graf Ignatiev 2.

Telephone. 88 22 35, 87 47 64.

Leadership. Aleksandur Popov (pres.); Olga Ivanovna (dep. pres.)

BULGARIA

6 September Forum
Forum "6 Septemvri"

Foundation. Jan. 22, 1990.

Membership. Nine opposition groups.

Leadership. Unknown.

Organization. The Forum is an umbrella alliance for small opposition organizations in southern Bulgaria.

Socialist Youth Union
Socialisticheski Mladezhki Sayuz

Address. 1000 Sofia, Blvd. Al. Stambolinski 11.

Telephone. 87 25 26.

Svoboda
Freedom

Also known as the Coalition for the Turnovo Constitution (referring to the constitution of 1879), it was formed on Dec. 30, 1990. It consists of 13 small political parties that had been members of the Liberal Union, the National Democratic Forum, and the Christian Social Union.

Union for Civic Economic Initiative
Sayuz za Grazhdanska Stopanska Initsiativa

Foundation. Dec. 22, 1989.

Leadership. Prof. Zahari Staykov.

Programme. The union's founding document is based on the statutes of the British and Belgian chambers of commerce. Its aims are to support private enterprise; to oppose state monopolies in the economy; to provide legal assistance to members and represent them in discussions with the government.

Union of Democratic Forces (UDF)
Sayuz na Demokratichni Sili (SDS)

Contact name. Mikhail Nadelchev.

Address. 1000 Sofia, 134 Rakovski Street.

Telephone. 88 25 01.

Foundation. Nov. 23, 1989.

Leadership. Filip Dimitrov (ch. of Co-ordinating Council); Mihan Drenchev (dep. ch.); Hristofor Sbev (dep. ch.)

History. The UDF was established by 10 groups and organizations connected with the struggle against the totalitarian regime. The following were its founding members: Bulgarian Social Democratic Party; Bulgarian Agrarian National Union — Nikola Petkov; *Ecoglasnost*; the Federation of Clubs for Glasnost and Democracy; the Committee for Religious Rights, Freedom of Conscience, and Spiritual Values; the Club for the Victims of Repression after 1945; Citizens' Initiative; the Federation of Independent Students' Societies; the Independent Association for the Defence of Human Rights; and the Independent Labour Federation *Podkrepa*. The latter withdrew from the UDF in autumn 1990. The first chairman of the Union was Dr Zhelyu Zhelev. He resigned the chairmanship after being elected President of Bulgaria on Aug. 1, 1990.

In December 1989 the Radical Democratic party joined the UDF, followed by the Green Party in February 1990, the Christian Democratic Front in October 1990, and the Alternative Socialist Party in October 1990. Three organizations have observer status: the Independent Labour Federation *Podkrepa*, the Bulgarian Democratic Forum, and the Republican Party.

Organization. In August 1991 the UDF consisted of 16 political parties and organizations and three others having an observer status. The union is a coalition that cuts across almost the entire political spectrum of Bulgarian party politics with the exclusion of left-wing or pro-communist parties and those associated with the Zhivkov regime. The backbone of the UDF are opposition movements and organizations formed in 1988 and 1989 as well as political parties outlawed by the communists and restored after the fall of Zhivkov. There have been two basic trends since the formation of the Union. The first is the coalition of spontaneously formed organizations which were not interconnected under the totalitarian regime. This perhaps explains their number. The other is the movement trend — people joining the organizations not so much because of a doctrinaire allegiance, but because they were accessible.

Structurally, the UDF has a broad network of organizations throughout the country. At the central level power appears to be dispersed across the Co-ordinating Commission, the parliamentary group and the Presidency of the Republic. Perhaps the single most important factor in the survival of the UDF as an umbrella organization comprising members very diverse in strength as well as political outlook, is the shared opposition to the communists. The cohesivenes of the Union, however, is unlikely to continue after the next parliamentary election scheduled for October 1991, which would give the UDF a majority in the Grand National Assembly and necessitate the formation of a governing administration.

Programme. To establish a democratic political system and a market economy; to unite the democratic opposition. The Union is defined, however, not by a programme or policy statement but by the common opposition of its constituent organizations and their members to the Bulgarian Socialist Party.

Publication. Daily newspaper *Demokratsija* (Democracy).

BULGARIA

Union of Democratic Muslims
Sayuz na Demokratichni Myusyulmani

Foundation. 1989.

Leadership. Dimitar Chaushev, Yuli Mladenov Bakardzhiev.

Programme. To involve the Muslim minorities in creating democracy in Bulgaria.

United Democratic Centre

Leadership. Lyubomir Pavlov and Stoyan Ganev (co-pres.)

Membership. The Party has practically no rank-and-file members. It was formed by a group of UDF economists and lawyers who were instrumental in developing the UDF's programme.

Affiliation. Member of the Union of Democratic Forces since February 1990.

United Front for the Restructuring and Defence of Socialism
Edinen Front za Preustroistvo i Zashtita na Sotzialisma

Foundation. Jan. 18, 1990.

Leadership. Prof. Vasil Ivanov, Prof. Asen Katov, Col. Mitriu Yanchev, Gen. Stoyan Kutsarov.

Programme. To foster a revival of the moral and political strength of the BCP in order to prevent a capitalist restoration in Bulgaria and to resist the challenge of the Union of Democratic Forces; to promote democratization and political pluralism.

Organization. The Front is a conglomerate of four main BCP factions: Alternative Forum (*Alternativen Forum*) founded on Jan. 4, 1990; the Movement for Developing Marxism and Renewing Socialism (*Dvizhenie za Razvitie na Marksizma i Obnovlenie na Sotsializma*) founded in January 1990; the Public Forum (*Obshtestven Forum*) founded in January 1990; and Unity-Movement for a Socialist Revival (*Edinstvo-Dvizhenie za Sotsialistichesko Vazrazhdane*), founded in January 1990.

The following minor parties and political groups have also been registered:

Alev, an organization of Bulgaria's Muslims which aims for the preservation and promotion of cultural and religious traditions and values of the Turkish and Muslim population.

Christian Democratic Community established in Veliko Turnovo on April 2, 1991 led by Rev. Hristofor Suber.

Confederation of Independent Syndicates in Bulgaria.

Confederation of Independent Trade Unions, led by Krustyn Petkov.

Dobrudzka All-Bulgarian Union founded on Sept. 24, 1990 which seeks to reawaken, preserve and promote the Bulgarian national spirit.

Ecoforum for Peace Association, led by Pavel Georgiev.

General Assembly of the Union of Economic Leaders, chaired by Stoyan Drundarov. Its programme supports market economy but not the "shock therapy" which it considers to be socially to costly.

Ilinden, the Alternative Movement of Those Resettled from Aegean, Vardar and Pirin Macedonias, founded on Nov. 14, 1989, is devoted to the protection of the rights of Macedonians in Bulgaria. It was originally accepted as a member of the Union of Democratic Forces but after strife broke out in January 1990 it was ejected from the UDF as an organization set up along purely ethnic divisions. The leader of the UDF at that time, Dr Zhelyu Zhelev, declared on Jan. 21, 1990, that there was no Macedonian minority in Bulgaria.

Independent 19 November Club, a left-wing organization established in the city of Burgas.

Movement for Civic Peace founded on June 29, 1990, which comprises representatives of several political parties and public organizations, the Orthodox Church and the Chief Mufti's Office. It aims to enrol all public and political forces and all people who are striving for the building up of a democratic, humane and law-abiding state in Bulgaria.

Movement for the Promotion of Marxism and the Renewal of Socialism, which declares itself in favour of Marxism free of Stalinist dogmas and upgraded to a modern level. It held its national conference in Sofia on Jan. 22, 1990.

Progressive People's Party, founded in Sofia on March 2, 1990. It seeks to continue the establishment of an economically stable, intellectually free, law-governed and democratic civil society with equal opportunities for all.

Union of Free Democrats, co-founded by the Forum of Free Democrats, the Free Democratic Party and the Union for Civil Society on Feb. 9, 1990. It declares itself in favour of total privatization, monetary reform, the confiscation of misappropriated property and the fair distribution of the burdens of market economy. The Union also advocates that the BSP, which succeeded the BCP, should repay the country's foreign and public debt.

CZECHOSLOVAKIA

Gordon Wightman

The "velvet revolution" of November 1989 brought an end to almost 42 years of communist rule in Czechoslovakia and almost 45 years during which the Communist Party was the decisive force in Czechoslovak politics. Its representatives were included in the provisional government set up in 1945, at the end of World War II and, following the party's success in the May 1946 parliamentary elections, when it won 38 per cent of the vote and became the largest party in the Constituent National Assembly, its leader, Klement Gottwald, was appointed Prime Minister. Nevertheless, at that point in time, Czechoslovakia retained a coalition government in which the Communists shared ministerial posts with four democratic parties — Czechoslovak Social Democracy, the Czechoslovak Socialist Party, the Czechoslovak People's Party, all three despite their names active only in the Czech provinces of Bohemia and Moravia, and the Democratic Party, which operated only in Slovakia (see Table 1).

It was only after February 25, 1948 that the Communists established effective one-party rule when, following the resignation of 12 non-communist ministers, Gottwald formed a new government, which continued to include members of other parties, but which was dominated by the Communists. From then until 1968, in fact, and even after the enforced absorption of the Social Democrats into the Communist Party in July 1948, members of surviving parties were given ministerial posts (usually those of Health and Justice) as part of the fiction that Czechoslovakia retained a multi-party system. None of those parties was in reality independent of the Communists. The Socialist and People's Parties remained nominally independent but were purged of members who might resist their party's subjection to Communist control. In Slovakia, the Democratic Party which had won 62 per cent of that region's vote as against 30 per cent for the Communists, was simply dissolved, leaving a small splinter group, the Party of Slovak Renewal, and the small Freedom Party to maintain a pluralist image there.

For most of its period in power, the Communist Party enforced policies that were among the most repressive in Eastern Europe. The years immediately after 1948 brought a shift to a Soviet-type political system in which parliamentary institutions were no more than a facade and real power lay in the hands of the Communist Party leadership. The wholesale nationalization of industry (some of which had already come into state ownership before 1948), the collectivization of agriculture and the switch in economic policy to a Stalinist emphasis on heavy industry and armaments production that followed the February 1948 coup were accompanied by a period of terror that was the most severe in Eastern Europe and affected not only the Communists' opponents but also the Communist Party itself.

NEW POLITICAL PARTIES OF EASTERN EUROPE AND THE SOVIET UNION

Table 1: Elections to the Constituent National Assembly, May 26, 1946

	% Votes	Seats
Bohemia and Moravia		
Communist Party of Czechoslovakia	40.17	93
Czechoslovak Social Democracy	15.58	37
Czechoslovak Socialist Party	23.66	55
Czechoslovak People's Party	20.24	46
Blank voting papers	0.35	–
TOTAL	100.00	231
Slovakia		
Communist Party of Slovakia	30.37	21
Labour Party	3.11	2
Freedom Party	3.73	3
Democratic Party	62.00	43
Blank voting papers	0.79	–
TOTAL	100.00	69

Source: *Dějiny Československa v datech* (Prague, 1968), p. 468.

The height of the terror came in November 1952, when 14 senior party and government officials, including the Communist General Secretary Rudolf Slánský, were found guilty on charges of conspiring against the state and 11 of their number, including Slánský, executed.

Although Gottwald's death on March 14, 1953 — only a week after Stalin — enabled a collective leadership to be established in Czechoslovakia under Antonín Zápotocký, who became the country's President, and Antonín Novotný, who was appointed First Secretary of the Communist Party's Central Committee in September, the thaw experienced elsewhere in the communist bloc largely passed Czechoslovakia by. Political trials continued for a time and included one in 1954 directed against alleged Slovak "bourgeois nationalists", among whom was the later party leader and Czechoslovak President, Gustáv Husák.

Destalinization only reached Czechoslovakia after Khrushchev's renewed attack on Stalin at the 1961 congress of the Soviet Communist Party when Novotný (who had assumed the presidency on Zápotocký's death in 1957 in addition to his post as party leader) finally accepted, at a meeting of the Communist Party Central Committee in April 1963, that Czechoslovakia, like its neighbours, had suffered from "a personality cult". That change of course opened the way for tentative changes in economic and political life, but Novotný's continued half-hearted concessions to the reform movement which then emerged within the Communist Party was to end in his removal from his party post on January 5, 1968.

Novotný's successor as First Secretary, Alexander Dubček, ushered in a short-lived period of reform communism popularly known as the Prague Spring. This attempt to marry a form of market socialism with democratization in the political sphere proved, however, unacceptable to the leaders in the Kremlin, who, despite Czechoslovak protestations of loyalty to its alliance with the Soviet Union, feared on the one hand that this "socialism with a human face" would undermine Communist Party control in Czechoslovakia and thus threaten Soviet security interests, and on the other hand that it would prove contagious elsewhere in the *bloc*.

The intervention by Warsaw Pact military forces on the night of Aug. 20–21, 1968 (in which only Romania did not take part) brought a halt to the Prague Spring reforms but it took another eight months for the Soviet leadership to engineer Dubček's removal as party leader. His replacement on April 17, 1969, by Gustáv Husák, set in train the programme of "normalization" that Moscow had demanded and the eradication of the last vestiges of reformism from Czechoslovak public life.

Throughout the 1970s and for most of the 1980s, Czechoslovakia was ruled by a Communist Party leadership which saw emulation of Soviet policy as its primary principle. In practice, the regime in Prague was much harsher than its Soviet counterpart at that time and attempts to challenge official policies and practices were generally dealt with extremely severely. It was only in January 1977 with the appearance of the Charter 77 manifesto that opposition in Czechoslovakia found a method of expressing its dissent that survived the repressive responses of the authorities. Even so, signatories of the document, which focused on violations of civil and political rights, were subjected to very harsh treatment indeed, including constant police surveillance, arrest, imprisonment and pressure to emigrate. They were also dismissed from their jobs and their children prevented from acquiring university education.

Charter 77 may have brought little improvement to the observation of civil and political rights in Czechoslovakia in the 1970s and 1980s but it had a number of other positive effects. It kept alive the spirit of democracy that had been briefly revived in 1968, brought violation of rights to the attention of the international community and sponsored critical and well-informed studies on a range of related issues from education to the environment, which contrasted with the complacent stance of the regime in those areas. It also established a tradition of co-operation and trust between individuals of diverse political views — ex-communists, liberals, members of the Catholic opposition — that had not been evident earlier in the 1970s and that was to help give a cohesion to the opposition during the "velvet revolution" in November 1989 when the public challenge to communist rule finally came. Moreover, victimization by the regime, whether through imprisonment or denigration in the mass media, gave the Charter's spokespersons, like the playwright Václav Havel and the journalist Jiří Dienstbier (both unable to carry on their professions after 1969), a prominence that was to propel them into high office after the "velvet revolution" (the former as President; the latter as Foreign Minister).

Gorbachev's election as the General Secretary of the Soviet Communist Party in March 1985 and his adoption thereafter of reform policies that were not too dissimilar to those of the Prague Spring presented the Czechoslovak leadership with an unpalatable dilemma in the late 1980s. They faced the choice of maintaining their hardline course and abandoning their traditional emulation of Soviet policy, or of continuing to follow Moscow's line and jettisoning the hostility to reform that had, for many, been their main qualification for office during the Brezhnev years.

Almost inevitably, they preferred a compromise that involved a Czechoslovak version of *perestroika* that embraced features of the Soviet economic reform proposals of the time, but they were not prepared to go beyond some token gestures in the direction of political democratization that would not threaten their survival in power. At the same time, they continued to condemn the Prague Spring which, unlike Gorbachev's policies, they alleged, had been an attempt to undermine rather than improve socialism. Even Husák's retirement as Communist Party General Secretary in December 1987 brought little prospect of more substantial changes, since his replacement, Miloš Jakeš, was known to have been hostile to the Prague Spring, and moreover had been responsible for the wholesale purge of reformists from the Communist Party after 1969.

If the Communist Party leadership appeared to remain firmly entrenched, its fate was largely determined by two factors beyond its control. Firstly, while Gorbachev had made it clear that the Soviet Union would not intervene directly in Eastern Europe, he was equally unprepared to protect unpopular governments in the region. Moscow's acquiescence in the appointment of a non-communist Prime Minister and acceptance of minority Communist participation in government in Poland in the summer of 1989 was a major departure from traditional Soviet policy towards the region, and if that did not alarm the leadership in Prague, the fall of Erich Honecker in East Germany in October must have rammed home the message that they could no longer rely on the Soviet Union to come to their aid if challenged by domestic forces.

Secondly, those changes in Moscow's policy came at a time when the public mood in Czechoslovakia had already begun to change. Starting in 1988, increasing numbers of the population began to join in public demonstrations against the Communist regime. A candle-lit vigil in Bratislava in March 1988, involving several thousand Catholics prepared to demand religious freedom and civil rights, was one indication that readiness to protest had extended beyond the small groups associated with Charter 77. It was, however, the 20th anniversary of the invasion, on Aug. 21 that year, that proved a real turning-point when thousands marked the event in Prague's Wenceslas Square.

Not even police brutality inhibited a repetition of similar demonstrations on Oct. 28, the 70th anniversary of the foundation of Czechoslovakia, and on Dec. 10, UN Human Rights Day, when a meeting addressed by Havel was for once permitted by the authorities. The anniversary of the suicide in January 1969 of the student Jan Palach, who had set himself on fire in protest at the concessions the Dubček leadership were making to Moscow's demands for a reversal of the 1968 reforms, provided the occasion for a week of demonstrations in Prague. Despite police brutality, the arrest of Havel and other leading Chartists, his subsequent nine-month sentence on charges of incitement, and new legislation to curb public protests, demonstrations took place once more on May Day, Aug. 21 and Oct. 28.

Another indication of changing public attitudes was seen in the number of people prepared to sign a petition which was circulated on June 29, 1989 under the title *A Few Words*, and which called *inter alia* for greater political freedom, the release of political prisoners, an end to censorship and the oppression of independent civic initiatives. Whereas initially Charter 77 had only attracted 242 signatures and even by the late 1980s only around 2,000 had added their names to that document, the number who signed *A Few Words* is reported to have reached 37,000 by November 1989.

The collapse of communist rule was, nevertheless, sudden and unexpected. What sparked it off was police brutality against a student march on Nov. 17, 1989 which had been sanctioned by the authorities to commemorate the execution by the Nazis of Jan

CZECHOSLOVAKIA

Opletal and other Czech students 50 years before, followed by a rumour, later shown to be untrue, that a student had been killed during the attack. Protests spread, firstly among Prague's student population, then to its theatrical community, and gradually, as it embraced wider sections of the capital's population, to Brno, Bratislava and other Czech and Slovak towns and cities.

Only a week after the student march, on Nov. 24, the entire Communist Party leadership resigned and left the federal Prime Minister, Ladislav Adamec, to try and reach an agreement with representatives of the two new political movements that had been formed to co-ordinate the campaign for an end to one-party rule: Civic Forum in Prague, set up on Nov. 19, and the Public Against Violence, which had been formed a few days later in Bratislava. Aware, thanks to a general strike on Nov. 27, that even workers backed the opposition, Adamec resigned on Dec. 4 when the new coalition government he proposed, in which the Communists would have retained a majority of the seats, was rejected by the representatives of the new political movements.

Six days after that, on Dec. 10, in his last act as Czechoslovak President, Husák swore in a new Government of National Understanding, led by Adamec's deputy, Marián Čalfa, in which the Communists held only 10 of the 21 seats (and two of those, the economists Valtr Komárek and Vladimir Dlouhý, were nominated by Civic Forum). The two new political movements shared another seven seats and the remaining four were divided between the Czechoslovak Socialist Party and the Czechoslovak People's Party which had ended their subordination to the Communist Party after the November revolution.

If it appeared at first that the Communist Party were to play a kind of caretaker role in Czechoslovakia's transition to parliamentary democracy, it quickly became clear that power had effectively shifted to its opponents when Dubček, who had been expelled from the party in 1970, was elected Chairman of the Federal Assembly on Dec. 28, and Havel who had emerged as Civic Forum's leading spokesman, was elected President the following day. By the end of January 1990, the Communists' remaining influence had declined even further when Čalfa, Komárek and Dlouhý all resigned their party membership and one of the few survivors of the old leadership, František Pitra, gave up his post as Prime Minister in the Czech Republic and Deputy Prime Minister in the federal government (he was replaced in February by Civic Forum's spokesman, Petr Pithart).

Between late December 1989 and the end of February 1990, the Communists' domination of the country's three parliaments — the Federal Assembly and the Czech and Slovak National Councils — was brought to an end through the co-option primarily of non-party people nominated by Civic Forum or the Public Against Violence to replace deputies who were expelled or persuaded to step down. As of Feb. 20, only 138 of the 350 seats in the bicameral Federal Assembly were filled by members of the Communist Party and similar non-Communist majorities were established in the Czech and Slovak parliaments.

Both President Havel and the new Government of National Understanding had committed themselves to free parliamentary elections and early in 1990 it was announced they would be held over two days, on June 8 and 9, both for the federal parliament and the National Councils in the two republics. A round-table meeting on Jan. 11 of representatives of the two new political movements and the "traditional" parties (the Communists, Socialists, People's Party, Slovak Freedom Party and the Democratic Party, as the Party of Slovak Renewal had been renamed in December 1989) agreed that the elections should be conducted by the list system of proportional representation which had been used in Czechoslovakia in the interwar period and again in the 1946 elections.

Other systems were considered and rejected. A majority system was seen as undesirable at a time when it would be likely to produce a two-party contest between Civic Forum and the Public Against Violence on the one side and the Communist Party on the other — a polarization which would have conflicted with the goals of re-establishing a democratic and pluralist polity reflecting the true state of public opinion. Alternatives like the West German additional member system were favoured by some experts, but would have required a radical reform of the parliamentary system that would have provoked long arguments and further delayed the elections.

As a result, Czechoslovakia approached the elections with its pre-communist electoral system and only a minor modification to its parliamentary structure. The number of deputies in the first chamber of the Federal Assembly, the House of the People, which is elected in proportion to the electorate throughout the country, was to be reduced from 200 to 150. The second chamber, in which 75 deputies are elected from each of the two republics, was unchanged as were both National Councils, the Czech parliament comprising 200 deputies to represent the 7.5 million voters in that republic, the Slovak 150 deputies to represent its smaller electorate of 3.6 million.

Publication of the Law on the Elections to the Federal Assembly, which received that body's approval on Feb. 27, 1990, revealed that there were to be a number of departures from the traditional "pure" list system. One particular concern was the proliferation of small parties that had won parliamentary representation in the pre-war republic and, to inhibit that process, two obstacles were introduced in the new law. The contenders in the elections could only be political parties, political movements or coalitions of parties which could show that they had at least 10,000 members or which submitted a petition with sufficient signatures to make up for any shortfall in their membership. Secondly, to win seats in each chamber of the Federal Assembly, the contenders would have to obtain 5 per cent of the vote in at least one of the two republics. (Separate legislation provided for the same threshold to apply in the elections to the Czech National Council and a lower, 3 per cent threshold in those for the Slovak parliament.)

A further departure from traditional practice, reflecting firstly a desire to avoid giving party leaderships too much control over parliamentary deputies and secondly a belief, strong within Civic Forum, that the elections would be about personalities rather than parties, was a provision that voters could express four preferences among the candidates on any particular party list. Where at least 10 per cent of voters for that list availed themselves of the opportunity to cast preferential votes, those candidates who received more than half would be moved to the top of the list (the order being decided by the total number of votes given to each candidate).

For the purpose of the elections, the country was to be divided into 12 constituencies, coinciding with the existing administrative regions (*kraj*) — eight in the Czech Republic and four in Slovakia. Apportionment of seats was, however, to be a more complex matter. Where the law specified that 75 seats in the House of the Nations would go to each of the two republics, the new legislation stipulated that, in the case of the House of the People, the 150 places were to be divided between the two republics in proportion to the size of the electorate in the year of the election. (This was to result in the allocation of 101 seats to the Czech Republic and 49 to Slovakia.) Thereafter seats in both chambers were to be allocated to constituencies by identical procedures, in proportion to the turnout in the election in each constituency. Once the number of seats allotted to each constituency had been determined, they would be allocated to parties in proportion to their share of the vote in that constituency (after eliminating those contenders which had failed to reach the 5 per cent threshold). Any unfilled seats would then be allocated, within each of the two republics, by the principle of the greater remainder, to parties with surplus votes and, for that purpose, those parties would be invited to provide new lists of candidates from among those who had not been elected within a constituency.

A new Law on Political Parties, approved on Jan. 23, 1990, had firstly accorded specific recognition to the two new political movements, Civic Forum and the Public Against Violence, and the parties that had survived communist rule: the Communist Party of Czechoslovakia, the Czechoslovak People's Party, the Czechoslovak Socialist Party and, in Slovakia, the Freedom Party and the Democratic Party. Secondly, it set out rules governing the registration of new parties with the Ministry of the Interior by which they were required to have a membership of at least 1,000 and to submit copies of their statutes and aims, along with a list of officers and the address of their headquarters.

The law attempted to bring order to what might have become a somewhat chaotic situation. The end of communist rule had brought a rapid increase in the number of parties but, even before the November 1989 revolution, it should be noted, attempts had been made to establish new political groupings. In February 1989, former reform communists had founded *Obroda* (Reawakening), Club for Socialist Restructuring, through which they hoped to exert pressure for reform on the Jakeš regime, and on Nov. 11 a new party, the Czechoslovak Democratic Initiative, was set up, committed to liberal democratic reforms. By the end of December, parties had begun to proliferate and included a resuscitated Social Democratic Party; a Green Party; a Farmers' Party, founded at the Congress of Co-operative Farmers; a new Christian Democratic Party, set up by the Charter 77 signatory and its one-time spokesman, Václav Benda, and in Slovakia a new Christian Democratic Movement, formed by members of the Catholic opposition.

A report in June revealed that as many as 66 organizations had met the legal requirements for registration as political parties and most of those appear to have taken part in the June parliamentary elections in one form or another. Only 23 contenders were recognized by the Central Electoral Commission as having met the conditions for participation in the contest (and one of those, the Organization of Independent Romanians, dropped out before the poll), but many smaller parties found places on the lists of candidates presented to the electorate by Civic Forum and the Public Against Violence or within coalitions such as the Christian and Democratic Union and the right-wing Free Bloc (see Table 2).

One criticism made of the contenders in the elections was the similarity of their manifestos, and indeed all parties seemed to favour the same goals of pluralism, democracy and a market economy, if with some variation in their degree of enthusiasm for privatization. Nevertheless, there were some other obvious distinctions between them.

The most striking feature was the emergence of parties with a national or regional programme. Nationalism was at its most extreme in the case of the separatist Slovak National Party, which was often more hostile to the Hungarian minority in Southern Slovakia than it was to the Czechs. Regionalism on the other hand was evident in the programme of a contender which favoured greater devolution to Moravia and Silesia, two provinces in the eastern half of the Czech republic; the Movement for Self-Governing Democracy — the Society for Moravia and Silesia. Two other parties, on the other hand, sought to appeal for ethnic harmony. Coexistence attempted to attract support from all groups in the population but its association with the Hungarian Christian Democratic

Table 2: Parties, movements and coalitions standing in the Czech Republic, the Slovak Republic and throughout Czechoslovakia in the June 1990 parliamentary elections

Czech Republic	*Slovak Republic*	*Both Republics*
Civic Forum	**Christian Democratic Movement**	Alliances of Farmers and the Countryside
Christian and Democratic Union	Democratic Party	**Coexistence and Hungarian Christian Democratic Movement**
Electoral Grouping of Interest Associations in the Czech Republic	Freedom Party	
	Gypsies	**Communist Party of Czechoslovakia**
Friends of Beer Party	**Public Against Violence**	Czechoslovak Democratic Forum
Movement for Self-Governing Democracy — Society for Moravia and Silesia	**Slovak National Party**	Czechoslovak Socialist Party
		Democratic-Republican Coalition
		Free Bloc
		Green Party
		Movement for Civic Freedom
		Movement for Czechoslovak Understanding
		Social Democrats

Parties in bold won seats in the Federal Assembly.
Source: Czechoslovak press reports.

Movement identified it in the public mind as a coalition for which the interests of that minority were a high priority. The Movement for Czechoslovak Understanding on the other hand was set up precisely to encourage harmony between Czechs and Slovaks.

The Czech-Slovak division also affected parties for which nationalism was far from a central issue. Only 11 of the contenders in the elections were standing throughout Czechoslovakia and, if social and cultural factors explain the presence of parties like the Gypsies only in Slovakia and of the Friends of Beer Party only in the Czech Republic, the presentation of separate lists in the two republics by the Christian Democrats on the one hand and by Civic Forum and the Public Against Violence on the other emphasized the degree to which parties that otherwise had much in common politically saw a need to address two distinctive national communities.

Despite similarities between the parties' manifestos, it would be wrong to suggest there was no differentiation on left–right lines, at least in terms of self-identification. Civic Forum and the Public Against Violence embraced individuals, clubs and parties from all parts of the political spectrum — the former including on its lists of candidates the Czechoslovak Democratic Initiative and the Civic Democratic Alliance on the right, the Trotskyist Left Alternative and the Club of Social Democrats on the left. Other contenders had a somewhat narrower focus. The Free Bloc, a coalition of four parties, of which the most important was the Republican Union, drew inspiration from the American

CZECHOSLOVAKIA

Republican Party and stressed individualism. The Coalition of the All-People's Democratic Party and the Union for the Republic — Republican Party of Czechoslovakia (listed in the tables as the Democratic-Republican Coalition) stressed privatization, patriotism, law and order and a hostility to immigrants that placed it firmly on the extreme right. The left was represented, the Communist Party apart, by Czechoslovak Democratic Forum, Eurocommunists who had broken with the Communists but were wary of the new enthusiasm for the free market. The Czechoslovak Socialists and Czechoslovak Social Democracy placed themselves in the centre and left-of-centre of the political spectrum; the Christian and Democratic Union, which embraced the Czechoslovak People's Party, the new Christian Democratic Party and nominally the Christian Democratic Movement in Slovakia (which, however, presented its own, separate list of candidates in that republic) on the centre-right.

The outcome of the elections on June 8–9, 1990, was a clear vote for parliamentary democracy (see Tables 3 and 4). Turnout was 96 per cent and, although the Communists retained the support of around 13 per cent of the electorate, spread fairly evenly throughout the country, the size of the vote for the two political movements most clearly associated with the restoration of parliamentary democracy, Civic Forum and the Public Against Violence, was much higher than had been expected before the polls. Civic Forum won roughly half the vote in the elections to both houses of the Federal Assembly and those to the Czech National Council. The Public Against Violence attracted a minority of the electorate both in the contests for the Federal Assembly and the Slovak parliament, but nevertheless managed to push the Christian Democratic Movement, which had earlier been expected to come top in Slovakia, into second place.

Although Civic Forum and the Public Against Violence could have formed a new federal government on their own, they chose to go into coalition with the Slovak Christian Democratic Movement. One reason for that was the requirement that changes to the constitution and major legislation need the support of a three-fifths majority in the House of the People and among Czech and Slovak deputies, voting separately, in the House of the Nations. A second was the desirability of a broad consensus when that government was faced with the difficult tasks of legislating for radical and economic reform. A third was probably a desire to ensure political compatibility between the federal government and its counterpart in Slovakia, where the Public Against Violence could only form an effective government in coalition with the Christian Democratic Movement (and which also involved, as it turned out, the Democratic Party). The desire for a broad consensus was also reflected in Czech Prime Minister Petr Pithart's decision to form a government in that republic in coalition with the Movement for Self-Governing Democracy — the Society for Moravia and Silesia and the Czechoslovak People's Party, despite Civic Forum's two-thirds majority in the Czech National Council.

The outcome of the elections, therefore, appeared to provide the basis for stable and effective government. They did not, on the other hand, as was to become clearer in the months ahead, contribute as much to the development of a more durable party system. Only eight of the 22 contenders competing for seats in the Federal Assembly passed the 5 per cent threshold and only two more (the Democratic Party and the Greens) were elected to the Slovak National Council, thanks to the lower threshold that applied in that case.

The success of Civic Forum and the Public Against Violence, positive though it was in confirming the survival of democratic values among Czechs and Slovaks, came at the expense of more conventional parties comparable to those found in Western democracies

Table 3: Elections to the Federal Assembly of the Czech and Slovak Federative Republic, June 8–9, 1990

House of the People

Czech Republic	% Votes	Seats
Civic Forum	53.1	68
Communist Party of Czechoslovakia	13.5	15
Christian and Democratic Union	8.7	9
Society for Moravia and Silesia	7.9	9
Others	16.8	–
TOTAL	100.0	101

Slovak Republic	% Votes	Seats
The Public Against Violence	32.5	19
Christian Democratic Movement	19.0	11
Communist Party of Czechoslovakia	13.8	8
Slovak National Party	11.0	6
Coexistence	8.6	5
Others	15.1	–
TOTAL	100.0	49

House of the Nations

Czech Republic	% Votes	Seats
Civic Forum	50.0	50
Communist Party of Czechoslovakia	13.8	12
Christian and Democratic Union	8.7	6
Society for Moravia and Silesia	9.1	7
Others	18.4	–
TOTAL	100.0	75

Slovak Republic	% Votes	Seats
The Public Against Violence	37.3	33
Christian Democratic Movement	16.7	14
Communist Party of Czechoslovakia	13.4	12
Slovak National Party	11.4	9
Coexistence	8.5	7
Others	12.7	–
TOTAL	100.0	75

Source: Lidové noviny and Rudé právo, June 11 and 14, 1990.

CZECHOSLOVAKIA

Table 4: Elections to the Czech and Slovak National Councils, June 8–9 1990

Czech National Council	% Votes	Seats
Civic Forum	49.5	127
Communist Party of Czechoslovakia	13.3	32
Society for Moravia and Silesia	10.0	22
Christian and Democratic Union	8.4	19
Others	18.8	–
TOTAL	100.0	200
Slovak National Council		
The Public Against Violence	29.3	48
Christian Democratic Movement	19.2	31
Slovak National Party	13.9	22
Communist Party of Czechoslovakia	13.3	22
Coexistence	8.7	14
Democratic Party	4.4	7
Green Party	3.5	6
Others	7.7	–
TOTAL	100.0	150

Source: *Lidové noviny* and *Rudé právo*, June 11 and 14, 1990.

(with the notable exception of the Christian Democrats) and in other respects the elections produced "victories" for what were regarded by some Czech commentators as "non-constructive" forces as far as the maintenance of a Czechoslovak state and its transition to a stable democracy were concerned: the Slovak National Party, the Movement for Self-Governing Democracy — the Society for Moravia and Silesia, and of course the Communists. (Coexistence, the eighth successful party, though it drew its support primarily from the Hungarian minority in southern Slovakia, does not belong to this negative category.) In the eyes of some Czech commentators, the preference of so many voters for regional or nationalist parties and for the Communists, rather than for new parties like the Free Bloc and historical parties like the Socialists and the Social Democrats, was particularly ominous.

There was little evidence of a significant shift in public support for such parties when local elections were held in the autumn, on Nov. 24 in the Czech Republic and over two days, Nov. 23 and 24, in Slovakia (see Table 5). A lower turnout of 73 per cent in the former suggests that the 3.5 per cent rise in the vote recorded by the Communists did not signify an increase in their support in absolute terms. Nevertheless, if there was a dramatic shift away from the Moravian autonomists in the Movement for Self-Governing Democracy (from around 9 per cent in June to 4 per cent in November) and the Slovak National Party (from 10–13 per cent in June to 3.2 per cent in November), there was also a significant decline in support for both Civic Forum and the Public Against Violence.

Table 5: Local elections in the Czech and Slovak Republics, 23–24 November 1990

Czech Republic	% Seats	% Votes
Civic Forum	31.7	35.6
Independent candidates	27.7	10.6
Communist Party of Czechoslovakia	14.4	17.2
Czechoslovak People's Party	12.1	11.5
Movement for Self-governing Democracy — Society for Moravia and Silesia	2.6	4.2
Czechoslovak Farmers' Party	2.5	1.5
Co-operative Farmer's Political Movement	2.1	0.9
Czechoslovak Socialist Party	1.6	3.5
Czechoslovak Social Democracy	1.6	5.0
Greens	1.3	3.2
Christian Democratic Party	0.4	1.3
TOTAL	98.0	94.5

Slovak Republic	% Seats	% Votes
Christian Democratic Movement	27.4	10,564
Public Against Violence	20.4	7,844
Communist Party of Slovakia	13.6	5,252
Non-party	8.4	3,236
Coexistence	6.3	2,416
Independent candidates	4.4	1,702
Slovak National Party	3.2	n/a
Farmers' Movement	3.1	n/a
Hungarian Christian Democratic Movement	3.0	n/a
Democratic Party	2.3	n/a
Greens	1.2	452
Romany Civic Initiative	n/a	63
Independent Erotic Initiative	n/a	1
TOTAL		38,489

Sources: *Lidové noviny* and *Rudé právo*, Nov. 26 and 28, 1990; *Svobodné slovo*, Dec. 6, 1990.

Nevertheless, by the late autumn of 1990, there were indications that the bases for a new, potentially more stable party system were beginning to be laid as a process of differentiation that had begun within Civic Forum after the June elections, intensified.

Few had expected Civic Forum to survive as a major actor in post-communist Czechoslovakia. It had been conceived as a transitional mechanism uniting all forces opposed to the Communist regime and had been expected to break up well before the June elections. In early July 1990, some of its parliamentary deputies, in what had been the

CZECHOSLOVAKIA

Czechoslovak Democratic Initiative and was renamed the Liberal Democratic Party, hived themselves off and joined other right-wing representatives in an Interparliamentary Club of the Democratic Right.

The emergence of a strong right-of-centre grouping within Civic Forum itself became apparent in October when Václav Klaus, the federal Finance Minister identified with a radical shift to a free market economy, was elected Civic Forum's first chairman. A meeting of officials and delegates from local Civic Forum branches throughout the Czech Republic, held on Dec. 8–9 in Olomouc, indicated extensive support for Klaus's policies and his proposals that Civic Forum should cease to be a broadly based movement and be transformed into a more conventional, but right-of-centre, political party based on individual membership — thus excluding clubs like *Obroda* and parties like Left Alternative.

That was not an attitude universally shared by the movement's adherents and its political representatives. A centrist Civic Forum Liberal Club was set up on Dec. 13 which elected as its spokespersons Jiří Dienstbier, the Foreign Minister, Pavel Rychetský, a federal Deputy Prime Minister, and Dagmar Burešová, chair of the Czech National Council. In contrast to Klaus and his supporters, they took the view that, until the next parliamentary elections in 1992, Civic Forum should remain the broadly based coalition which it had been since November 1989 and which the electorate had voted into power in June 1990.

Although Klaus's proposals that Civic Forum be transformed into a right-wing party carried the day at a Republican Assembly of that movement on Jan. 12, 1991, it proved to be something of a Pyrrhic victory. Provisions in the February 1990 Law on political parties allowed for Civic Forum's abolition, but not for its transformation into a political party, and in the end it was agreed that new parties would be formed — a right-of-centre Civic Democratic Party, and a centrist Civic Movement based on the Liberal Club.

Three months later both parties had been created. A founding congress of the Civic Democratic Party was held in Olomouc on April 20–21, 1991, at which Klaus was elected chairman; a week after that, on April 27, in Prague, the Civic Movement held its founding assembly at which Dienstbier was elected chairman of its republican council. As of June 1991, the former appeared to have the greater popular support and an opinion poll carried out by the independent research organization AISA indicated that 19 per cent of the Czech electorate would vote for the Civic Democratic Party. The Civic Movement, despite the presence within its ranks of prominent personalities like Dienstbier and Petr Pithart, the Czech Prime Minister, was attracting the support of only 6 per cent.

Other parties, however, also benefited from the breakup of Civic Forum. The Social Democrats, who had no representation in parliament, suddenly acquired deputies in the Federal Assembly, when Civic Forum representatives switched their allegiance to that party. The Civic Democratic Alliance, a small right-wing party which had fought the elections as part of Civic Forum, gained nine fairly prominent recruits, including the federal Minister for the Economy, Vladimír Dlouhý, and deputy chair of the Czech National Council, Jan Kalvoda, as a result of the split.

While the breakup of Civic Forum did not seem likely to threaten the survival of the federal government, since the movement's deputies made clear their intention of maintaining it in power until the 1992 elections, greater uncertainty was created by developments within the Public Against Violence, which also underwent a split in the spring of 1991. Although that movement had appeared more cohesive than Civic Forum, it too was rent by internal divisions that came to a head in April 1991. Where the crisis in Civic Forum had to some degree involved disagreements over personality as well as policy (insofar as attitudes to Klaus were a far from irrelevant factor), that was even more true in the Slovak case. The aggressive "poker-playing" and populist style of leadership of Vladimír Mečiar, who had been appointed Slovak Prime Minister in June 1990, had not only alienated many Czechs but also disconcerted many in the Public Against Violence. Mečiar's attempts to obtain as much devolved power as possible for the government in Bratislava, and to protect Slovakia from the worst effects of the liberal economic reform through preservation of a greater role for the state than was deemed consistent with the liberalization planned in Prague, highlighted differences between his policy preferences and those not only of the federal government and most Czech politicians, but also those of the Public Against Violence's elected officers and some members of Mečiar's own government.

The confrontation between Mečiar and his opponents in the Public Against Violence who were more sympathetic to the economic reform advocated in Prague and feared that Mečiar's more nationalist policies would damage relationships between Czechs and Slovaks began at a Republican Assembly of the movement in late February, when Mečiar's attempts to become leader of the Public Against Violence were thwarted. His subsequent formation of a separate platform "For Democratic Slovakia" within that movement was only the forerunner for his formation of a breakaway party, the Movement for a Democratic Slovakia, which held its founding congress on June 22, two months after his dismissal as Prime Minister on April 23.

Mečiar's popularity among Slovak voters, however, was such that that new movement looked as though it might well cast the Public Against Violence into the shade, and also displace the Christian Democratic Movement for the largest share of the Slovak vote. In June 1991, the Movement for a Democratic Slovakia was reported in the AISA poll to have the support of 29 per cent of the Slovak electorate, while the Christian Democrats' share had fallen to 10 per cent.

The emergence from within Civic Forum and the Public Against Violence during 1991 of parties with more precisely defined programmes and reasonable levels of public support suggests that a more stable party system was beginning to take shape in Czechoslovakia. Nevertheless, that process appeared to be more strongly developed to the right-of-centre than on the left of the political spectrum. Negotiations under way in the summer of 1991 between the right-wing Free Bloc (which since the elections had acquired the appendage "Conservative Party" to highlight its place on the political spectrum) and the Civic Democratic Party seemed likely to lead to a merger in the autumn and a further strengthening of the latter party in terms of organization, membership and indeed political personalities. (The Free Bloc's chairman, J.V. Kotas, was a particularly impressive campaigner in the 1990 elections, despite that party's lack of success.) Moreover, the prospects seemed high for an electoral alliance between the Civic Democratic Party and another party close to it on the political spectrum — the Civic Democratic Alliance.

Developments on the left and in the political centre were less predictable. The Communist Party, effectively two organizations since late 1990 — a Communist Party of Bohemia and Moravia and, in Slovakia, a Party of the Democratic Left, with an elected federal council as a weak co-ordinating agency — recorded only slightly lower support in the AISA opinion poll in June 1991 than its share of the vote a year earlier — 10 per cent in the Czech Republic and 11 per cent in Slovakia, but it remained an unattractive prospect as a political ally for most other parties in that part of the spectrum.

CZECHOSLOVAKIA

The prospects for centre and centre-left Czech parties seemed likely to depend, firstly on some regrouping of existing forces that might strengthen the attractiveness of the Socialists or Social Democrats, and secondly, on an eventual swing in at least a moderately leftward direction among voters once the more negative effects of the economic reform made themselves felt. In that respect, these Czech parties were at a disadvantage compared with their counterparts in Slovakia, where the harsher consequences of economic liberalization were more immediate than in the Czech Republic, and the leftist policies of the Movement for a Democratic Slovakia, combined with its nationalist stance, found an early response among the voters which had yet to find any echo in the Czech Republic.

Yet, two observations about the likely development of the party system in Czechoslovakia seem appropriate. Firstly, unless there is a switch before the next elections to a voting system that effectively inhibits a proliferation of parties in parliament, the multi-party tradition that dates back to the foundation of Czechoslovakia, and in the Czech case to the last decades of the Austrian Empire, will continue to apply. Even then, a change of electoral system could not be guaranteed to overcome the cleavages — regional, religious and ethnic, and no doubt soon also economic — that underpinned party diversification in 1990 and 1991. Secondly, a year after the 1990 parliamentary elections, the division of parties along Czech-Slovak lines was even more evident than before, since even the Communist Party — the sole party to compete successfully in both republics — had by then transformed itself into two republic-based organizations. The splits within Civic Forum and the Public Against Violence moreover brought out into the open a fundamental divergence in public opinion between the two republics, with a rightward swing in the Czech case that contrasted with strong support for the left in Slovakia.

Some Czech parties, such as the Socialists, have sought with little success to extend their activities to Slovakia, and even the Civic Democratic Party regarded an extension of its organization into Slovakia as desirable. One possible development might be a merger between the latter and what remains of the Public Against Violence which, by the summer of 1991, saw that party as its closest potential partner in the Czech Republic. Nevertheless, whatever the advantages creation of a right-of-centre federal party of that kind might bring, there would be no certainty that it would find as much support within Slovakia as would the Public Against Violence, if it were to remain independent and committed to no more than a parliamentary alliance with a Czech partner.

New constitutions for Czechoslovakia as a whole were to be prepared in time for approval by the three parliaments before the elections in mid-1992. What they create seems likely to influence not only the nature of Czechoslovakia itself but also the party system. A move towards a confederation of two sovereign republics was a possible option and one that would be likely to reinforce a party system based on the republics and weaken the prospects for parties seeking countrywide support. Maintenance of a federal system on the other hand, whether, as at present comprising the two republics, or on a *Länder* principle similar to that of Germany, would imply a need to encourage the formation of federal parties which could play an integrative role in a polity that would remain in many respects sharply divided.

The creation of Czechoslovakia on Oct. 18, 1918 brought together in one state the historical Czech kingdom of Bohemia and Moravia, which had been an important political and cultural power in mediaeval Europe but had come under Austrian rule early in the 17th century, and the Slovak provinces of Hungary that had been governed by the Magyars since the ninth century. In the interwar period, Czechs and Slovaks together made up only three-quarters of the population and, although the expulsion after World War II of the second largest ethnic group in the country — the 3.5 million Germans — simplified the country's ethnic structure, it did not eliminate the problem of national minorities altogether. The most recent census, in March 1991, indicated that, while the 9.8 million Czechs and 4.8 million Slovaks together constituted 94.1 per cent of its population of 15.5 million, they continued to share their territory with a sizeable Hungarian population of 586,000 (mostly resident in southern Slovakia), 61,500 Poles, 53,400 Germans, 20,600 Ukrainians and 18,600 Ruthenians. (Of the country's estimated half-million Gypsies only 114,000 declared themselves as such in the census.)

Accommodating the interests of those minorities is, however, a matter of minor significance compared with the issue of relations between Czechs and Slovaks. Throughout the interwar period Czechoslovakia remained a unitary state and it was only in 1945 that Slovakia acquired its own parliament, the Slovak National Council, and a quasi-governmental Board of Commissioners. Both in practice lacked the degree of autonomy from the central authorities in Prague that had been initially envisaged and Slovak demands for a greater degree of self-government resurfaced in the mid-1960s. In response to those demands, on Jan. 1, 1969, Czechoslovakia was transformed into a federation comprising two republics, known until early 1990 as the Czech Socialist Republic and the Slovak Socialist Republic, each with its own National Council and government, and with a bicameral Federal Assembly and federal government in Prague. Real power, nevertheless, continued to lie in the hands of a Communist Party that remained unitary and highly centralized, and there was little scope, if any, during the 1970s and 1980s for independent initiative in either of the constituent republics.

In that context it was hardly surprising that Czech-Slovak relations should become a critical issue in post-communist Czechoslovakia. The first indication of the severity of the problem came in March 1990, following President Havel's suggestion that the country should no longer be known as the Czechoslovak *Socialist* Republic (a designation adopted in 1960). After almost two months of arguments, it was renamed the Czech and Slovak Federative Republic on April 20, a choice which satisfied Slovak demands that their individuality be expressed clearly in the country's name (a factor which also led them to prefer the form Czecho-Slovakia to the unhyphenated Czechoslovakia used by Czechs).

A much more serious issue was the constitutional question it was hoped would be resolved before the parliamentary elections which were due to take place in June 1992. Despite the emergence in 1990 of a vociferous pro-independence lobby in Slovakia (most evident in the Slovak National Party and the cultural organization *Matica slovenská*), the majority of both Czechs and Slovaks favoured maintenance of a common state. There was little agreement beyond that and, while most politicians supported some devolution of power from the central authorities to the governments and parliaments of the two republics, opinion among the Czechs seemed to prefer a strong federal government or a switch to a more complex federal structure on the West German *Länder* model in which, for example, Bohemia on the one hand and Moravia and Silesia on the other would form constituent provinces and Slovakia would form a third or itself be divided into two units. Slovaks, by contrast, more often favoured a weaker federal system at times verging on confederation — a step which appeared to many Czechs as potentially too close to the creation of two independent states.

CZECHOSLOVAKIA

That Czech-Slovak division tended to be reflected in the party system that emerged after 1989. Eleven of the 22 contenders in the June 1990 parliamentary elections stood throughout Czechoslovakia and three obtained some representation. Only one — the Communist Party — won seats in both republics. A second, Coexistence, was successful only in Slovakia thanks to its appeal to the Hungarian minority. A third, the Greens, failed to win any seats in the Federal Assembly and the Czech National Council but won six in the Slovak National Council.

The successful parties were, therefore, predominantly those which appealed to a particular constituency within one or other republic. In large part this may be attributed to a need for contenders in Slovakia to portray a national, though not necessarily nationalist, dimension that prevented their alignment with parallel organizations in the Czech Republic. (The creation by the November 1989 "revolutionaries" of two different movements — Civic Forum and the Public Against Violence — and the separate Christian Democratic parties are cases in point.) It is worth noting that a number of unsuccessful federal parties which lacked that Slovak dimension (for example, the Czechoslovak Socialist Party and the Free Bloc) made a markedly worse showing in Slovakia than in the Czech Republic (see Table 6). In part, however, it also reflects a greater allegiance among voters in Slovakia to parties based on national, ethnic or religious affiliation than to those adopting a position on a more conventional left-right political spectrum.

Nevertheless, despite the failure of most federal parties in 1990, a number of parties continue to aspire to support throughout the country and at least one, the Civic Democratic Alliance, which contested the 1990 elections only in the Czech Republic, as part of Civic Forum, subsequently began to look for members in Slovakia. It is not impossible that other parties may follow suit and, as a result, classification of parties as federal, Czech or Slovak must be treated as provisional.

Directory of Parties (Federal)

Association for the Republic — the Republican Party of Czechoslovakia
Sdružení pro republiku — republikánská strana Československa (SPR-RSČ)

Address. U zeměpisného ústavu 1, 160 00 Praha 6.

Foundation. February 1990.

Leadership. Miroslav Sládek (ch.)

History. An extreme right-wing party, the Association for the Republic, failed to reach the 5 per cent threshold required to win seats in the Federal Assembly and the Czech National Council, or even the 3 per cent threshold for the Slovak parliament, in the June 1990 elections. Since then its popularity has grown to around 5 per cent of the Czech electorate, perhaps as the result of the publicity-seeking statements of its leader which often focus on issues that appeal to popular prejudices. The party has gained some notoriety as the result of demonstrations, often involving large numbers of skinhead followers, through which it has attempted to disrupt public meetings such as the welcome for President Bush during his visit to Prague in November 1990.

NEW POLITICAL PARTIES OF EASTERN EUROPE AND THE SOVIET UNION

Table 6: Elections to the Federal Assembly of the Czech and Slovak Federative Republic, June 8–9, 1990 (Parties in order of overall popular vote)

House of the People	Czech Republic %	Votes	Slovak Republic %	Votes	Czechoslovakia Total votes
Civic Forum	53.15	3,851,172	–	–	3,851,172
Communist Party of Czechoslovakia	13.48	976,996	13.81	468,411	1,445,407
The Public Against Violence	–	–	32.54	1,104,125	1,104,125
Christian Democratic Movement	–	–	18.96	644,008	644,008
Christian and Democratic Union	8.69	629,996	–	–	629,996
Movement for Self-Governing Democracy — Society for Moravia and Silesia	7.89	572,015	–	–	572,015
Slovak National Party	–	–	10.96	372,025	372,025
Alliance of Farmers and the Countryside	3.77	273,175	2.58	87,604	360,779
Social Democracy	3.84	278,280	1.89	64,175	342,455
Green Party	3.10	224,432	3.20	108,542	332,974
Coexistence and Hungarian Christian Democratic Movement	0.08	5,472	8.58	291,287	296,759
Czechoslovak Socialist Party	2.75	199,466	0.06	2,086	201,552
Democratic Party	–	–	4.40	149,310	149,310
Democratic-Republican Coalition	0.94	67,781	0.25	8,557	76,338
Free Bloc	0.80	57,925	0.18	6,145	64,070
Freedom Party	–	–	1.44	49,012	49,012
Electoral Grouping of Interest Associations in the Czech Republic	0.66	47,971	–	–	47,971
Czechoslovak Democratic Forum	0.32	22,866	0.02	562	23,428
Gypsies	–	–	0.67	22,670	22,670
Movement for Civic Freedom	0.30	21,585	0.02	580	22,165
Movement for Czechoslovak Understanding	0.11	8,032	0.41	13,947	21,979
Friends of Beer Party	0.12	8,943	–	–	8,943

House of the Nations					
Civic Forum	49.96	3,613,513	–	–	3,613,513
Communist Party of Czechoslovakia	13.80	997,919	13.43	454,740	1,452,659
The Public Against Violence	–	–	37.28	1,262,278	1,262,278
Movement for Self-Governing Democracy — Society for Moravia and Silesia	9.10	658,477	–	–	658,477
Christian and Democratic Union	8.75	633,053	–	–	633,053
Christian Democratic Movement	–	–	16.66	564,172	564,172
Slovak National Party	–	–	11.44	387,387	387,387
Alliance of Farmers and the Countryside	3.99	288,270	2.10	71,204	359,474
Social Democracy	4.17	301,445	1.51	51,233	352,678
Green Party	3.44	248,944	2.58	87,366	336,310

CZECHOSLOVAKIA

Table 6: Cont.

House of the Nations	Czech Republic %	Votes	Slovak Republic %	Votes	Czechoslovakia Total votes
Coexistence and Hungarian Christian Democratic Movement			8.49	287,426	287,426
Czechoslovak Socialist Party	2.89	208,662	0.06	2,073	210,735
Democratic Party	–	–	3.68	124,561	124,561
Free Bloc	1.09	78,910	0.17	5,643	84,553
Democratic-Republican Coalition	1.00	72,155	0.21	7,169	79,324
Electoral Grouping of Interest Associations in the Czech Republic	0.76	54,916	–	–	54,916
Freedom Party	–	–	1.24	42,111	42,111
Czechoslovak Democratic Forum	0.44	32,044	0.01	499	32,543
Movement for Czechoslovak Understanding	0.12	8,738	0.50	16,934	25,672
Movement for Civic Freedom	0.29	21,210	0.03	914	22,124
Gypsies	–	–	0.60	20,445	20,445
Friends of Beer Party	0.19	13,869	–	–	13,869

Source: *Lidové noviny* and *Rudé právo*, June 11 and 14, 1990.

Programme. Its 1990 election leaflet highlighted "Fatherland, Democracy, Prosperity, Strength, Law and Order" while listing a range of populist policies that included reducing the size of the army, a guaranteed minimum wage, treating the family as the foundation of the state and giving maternity leave until children are of school age. Its demand that "unqualified foreign workers" (notably Vietnamese) should leave Czechoslovakia is one feature of its campaigns that have led to accusations of racism.

Club of Committed Non-Party Members (KAN)
Klub angažovaných nestraníků (KAN)

Foundation. March 31, 1990.

Membership. Around 10,000.

Leadership. Bohdan Dvořák (ch.)

History. Formed originally in 1968, KAN was banned in September that year. It was re-established in 1990 and stood in the June parliamentary elections as part of Civic Forum. Based on local clubs, it is firmly on the right of the political spectrum and emphasizes the need to de-Bolshevize Czechoslovak society and complete a rapid transition to a privately owned market economy. It regards the Civic Democratic Alliance, Civic Democratic Party and Republican Union as among its closest political allies. In April 1991, an Assembly (*sněm*) of KAN in Slovakia (*KAN na Slovensku*), representing 1,500 members of the Club in that republic, elected its own Council and chairman, Vratislav Joachymstál.

Coexistence
Együttélés; Spolužitie; Wspólnota; Súžitie

Foundation. Early 1990.

Membership. Around 20,000 (spring 1990).

Leadership. Miklos Duray (ch.)

History. Formed to advance the interests of the several national minorities in Czechoslovakia, including Poles, Ruthenians and Ukrainians, Coexistence's success in the June 1990 parliamentary elections may be attributed primarily to its appeal to the half-million Hungarian minority in southern Slovakia. Although it put up candidates throughout Czechoslovakia, it won little support in the Czech Republic and the 12 seats it obtained in the Federal Assembly were all from constituencies in Slovakia. In the November 1990 local elections in Slovakia, Coexistence on its own won over 6 per cent of the vote.

Affiliations. Coexistence has been most closely associated with the Hungarian Christian Democratic Movement in coalition with whom it put up candidates in the June 1990 parliamentary elections.

Programme. Although it pursues a policy of fair treatment for all national groups in Czechoslovakia, its primary concern has been the Hungarian minority in southern Slovakia. It regards the frontiers of Czechoslovakia as inviolable and in its election campaign advocated that greater control be given Hungarians over their own affairs, that Hungarian and Slovak be recognized as official languages in ethnically mixed areas and that a Hungarian university be established in Komárno.

Communist Party of Czechoslovakia (CPCS or CPCz)
Komunistická strana Československa (KSČS, formerly KSČ)

(*See also* Communist Party of Bohemia and Moravia and Party of the Democratic Left)

Foundation. May 1921.

Membership. 750,000 (November 1990).

Leadership. Pavol Kanis (ch. of federal council); Miroslav Grebenčik (1st dep. ch.)

History. Although the Communist Party was a far from negligible political force during the period between the two world wars, its share of the vote in parliamentary elections at that time (between 10 and 13.2 per cent) provided little indication of the upsurge in its popularity that was to come later. Its commitment after World War II to "a specific Czechoslovak road to socialism" contributed to its success in obtaining the support of 38 per cent of the electorate in the May 1946 elections and its emergence as the largest party in the new parliament.

Its adherence to Czechoslovakia's democratic parliamentary traditions was, however, shortlived and in February 1948 it introduced a system of effective one-party rule that was to last until December 1989. Emulation of Soviet policy and practices was to be the watchword for the party throughout that 41-year period with the exception of the shortlived experiment in "socialism with a human face" during the 1968 Prague Spring. The resumption of repressive policies seven months after the Warsaw Pact intervention in August 1968 and the maintenance of that hard line right up until the November 1989 revolution lost it any prospect of retaining extensive popular support.

After that revolution, the party expelled most of the leaders associated with the post-1968 regime and professed a policy of "national understanding" by which it indicated its readiness to work with the new democratic forces. The more radical policies pursued by the new government after the June 1990 elections led, however, to a shift towards a less conciliatory stance by which it retained its new commitment to reform, but emphasized the need to defend those adversely affected by economic liberalization through adequate social provision, maintenance of the right to work, and workers' ownership of industry alongside the private sector.

The party managed to win around 13.5 per cent of the vote throughout Czechoslovakia in the June 1990 parliamentary elections. In the November 1990 local elections its vote remained unchanged in percentage terms in Slovakia, but rose in the Czech Republic to 17 per cent, an increase that may be better explained by the much lower turnout than as a rise in the party's support in absolute terms. By then, its membership had dropped dramatically from around 1.8 million in 1989 to well under half that number.

Organization. In the course of 1990, important changes were made to the party's organization. Its 18th congress on Nov. 3–4, 1991, recognized that, with the establishment in the Czech Republic of the Communist Party of Bohemia and Moravia on March 31 that year, alongside the Communist Party of Slovakia, the CPCS had become a federal organization. The congress elected a 24-member Federal Council, a chairman for one year — the Slovak Pavol Kanis — and a first deputy chairman — the Czech Miroslav Grebenčík, who was to replace Kanis at the end of his term in office.

Conservative Party — the Free Bloc
Konzervativní strana — Svobodný blok (KS SB)

Leadership. Jiří V. Kotas (ch.)

History. This party was originally known as the Free Bloc, a coalition of right-wing parties which included the Party of Constitutional Democracy (*Strana ústavní demokracie*), the Party of Free Democrats (*Strana svobodných demokrátů*), the Party of Czechoslovak Neutrality (*Strana československé neutrality*) and the Republican Union (*Republikánská unie*) and which contested the June 1990 parliamentary elections unsuccessfully. It transformed itself into a political party in July 1990 and added the title of Conservative Party in March 1991. Influenced by neo-liberal strands of British conservatism, it supports the maximum possible reduction in the role of the state and, though supporting the government's economic reform programme, is critical of some elements in its strategy, such as delays in modernizing the tax system. It advocates either a strong federal system or Czechoslovakia's transformation into two independent states with close economic ties on the Benelux model.

Affiliations. As of the summer of 1991, it seemed likely that the Conservative Party — Free Bloc would merge with the Civic Democratic Party.

NEW POLITICAL PARTIES OF EASTERN EUROPE AND THE SOVIET UNION

Czechoslovak Democratic Forum
Československé demokratické fórum (ČSDF)

Address. Mánesova 44, Praha 2.

Telephone. (02) 25 28 29.

Leadership. Pavel Smutný (ch.)

History. A party formed early in 1990 by pro-reform members of the Communist Party who left its ranks after the November 1989 revolution, unpersuaded of its readiness to adapt to conditions in post-communist Czechoslovakia, it stood unsuccessfully in the June 1990 parliamentary elections. It claims to have about 2,000 members and sympathizers.

Czechoslovak Socialist Party
Československá strana socialistická (ČSS)

Address. nám. Republiky 7, Praha 1.

Telephone. (02) 23 13 051.

Foundation. 1897.

Leadership. Ladislav Dvořák (ch.)

History. Although the party can trace its origins to the foundation in 1897 of the National Socialist Party (*Národně socialistická strana*), it faces a challenge for that mantle in the National Social Party (*Národně sociální strana*), formed in September 1990, which regards the Socialists' emasculation by the Communists after February 1948 and its satellite role during the 41 years of communist rule as an irreparable break with that party's traditions.

The Socialist Party's failure to make much of a mark in post-communist Czechoslovakia may be attributed to its long period of subordination to the Communist Party and its continuing association in the public mind with a "socialism" that was wholly discredited in whatever form. It failed to win any seats in the June 1990 parliamentary elections and its 3.5 per cent share of the vote in the November 1990 local elections in the Czech Republic was only a marginal improvement over the 2.8 per cent it obtained five months before. It attracted even lower levels of support in Slovakia on both occasions.

Programme. In its manifesto for the June 1990 elections, the party appeared close to the centre of the political spectrum, supporting a mixed economy and a gradual transition to a market system.

Affiliations. In the spring of 1991, the Socialist Party attempted to improve its prospects by forming a coalition, the Liberal Social Union (*Liberálně sociální unie*) with the Czechoslovak Farmers' Party.

CZECHOSLOVAKIA

Green Party
Strana zelených (SZ)

Address. TJ Helis, Rooseveltova 31, Praha 6.

Leningradská 1, Bratislava.

Telephone. (Prague) (02) 32 46 44; (Bratislava) (07) 33 13 90 or (07) 33 26 04.

Foundation. December 1989.

Leadership. Miloslav Kejval (Czech Republic); Peter Sabo (Slovak Republic).

History. Despite 11 per cent support in opinion polls early in 1990, the Green Party failed to reach the 5 per cent threshold needed for seats in the Federal Assembly, but its 3.5 per cent share of the vote for the Slovak National Council won it six places in that parliament. In November 1990, it won 898 seats in local councils in the Czech Republic and 452 in Slovakia.

Programme. The Green Party shares goals and policies with ecological movements in other European countries. In its manifesto for the June 1990 parliamentary elections, it stressed it was a party neither of the left nor of the right, and argued that "in contrast with other political parties the Green Party considers protection and renewal of the environment, health and life as the most important interest, to which all other interests must be subjected". In the context of Czechoslovakia's transition to a market economy, its support for demonopolization and privatization of industrial, agricultural and other enterprises and for foreign participation (except in the case of extractive renewable resources and farming land) may be singled out as of particular interest.

Movement for Czechoslovak Understanding
Hnutí československého porozumění (HČP)

Address. Vansovej 5, 811 03 Bratislava.

Leadership. Dr Vladimír Čech (ch.)

History. Formed in February 1990, the movement sought to promote the common interests of Czechs and Slovaks. It favours a unitary state with a single constitution, government and parliament. It contested the June 1990 parliamentary elections unsuccessfully throughout Czechoslovakia, although seven of its candidates won local council seats in November that year — five in the Czech Republic and two in Slovakia.

Obroda (Reawakening), Club for Socialist Restructuring
Obroda, Klub pro socialistickou přestavbu

Formed in February 1989 by former reform communists in an attempt to press for democratic changes, the *Obroda* Club was never accorded legal recognition by the communist authorities. In the June 1990 elections it stood as part of Civic Forum in the Czech Republic and on the Public Against Violence's list in Slovakia. In spring 1991 it merged with Czechoslovak Social Democracy.

NEW POLITICAL PARTIES OF EASTERN EUROPE AND THE SOVIET UNION

Republican Party
Republikánská strana (RS)

Address. Pionerská 2, 831 01 Bratislava.

Leadership. Ivan Ďuriš (ch.)

A neo-conservative party, formed in December 1989, which contested the June 1990 elections as part of Civic Forum in the Czech Republic.

Republican Union
Republikánská unie (RU)

Leadership. Igor Klimovič (ch.)

Formed in January 1990 through the amalgamation of a number of similar small parties, the Republican Union formed part of the Free Bloc coalition which unsuccessfully contested the June 1990 parliamentary elections (*see* Conservative Party). It strongly supports a more radical and tougher implementation of economic reform and sees itself as a party on the right of the political spectrum. In the political sphere it supports a federal system on the West German model in which Czechoslovakia would be divided into three provinces (Bohemia, Moravia and Silesia, and Slovakia).

Romany Civic Initiative
Romská občanská iniciativa (ROI)

Address. Sněmovní 3, 110 00 Praha 1.

Telephone. (02) 23 69 096.

Leadership. Emil Ščuka (ch.)

Formed in November 1989, the Romany Civic Initiative contested the June 1990 parliamentary elections as part of Civic Forum in the Czech Repuoblic and the Public Against Violence in Slovakia. It won two seats in the Federal Assembly, five in the Czech National Council and one in the Slovak parliament. Since then it has adopted a right-of-centre position supporting in particular the development of small businesses, and wishes to emphasize the rights and duties of the Gypsy population as citizens rather than as members of an ethnic group. It claims about 50,000 adherents.

Romany National Congress
Romský národní kongres (RNK)

Leadership. Dr Vladimír Oláh (sec.)

Created in February 1991 in opposition to the Romany Civic Initiative, the Congress embraces 15 social organizations and clubs. It sees itself as left-of-centre and seeks the inclusion of Romanies as a national group in the Constitution, their representation in official institutions and ministries and a conceptual solution to the Gypsy question.

CZECH REPUBLIC

The westernmost provinces of Bohemia, Moravia and Silesia acquired the status of a republic on Jan. 1, 1969, when a federal system was introduced in Czechoslovakia. Just under 95 per cent of the population, or 9.7 million, are Czechs, and the most numerous other groups recorded in the March 1991 census were 308,000 Slovaks, 58,500 Poles and 47,700 Germans. (The number of Gyspies seems likely to be higher than the 33,400 reported on that occasion.)

If ethnic divisions within the Czech Republic are not an issue, the status of Moravia and Silesia acquired importance as the result of the success of the Movement for Self-Governing Democracy — the Society for Moravia and Silesia, in the June 1990 elections, with its commitment to greater autonomy for a region that had had its own provincial administration until the Communists' takeover. The division of the republic into three provinces — Prague, Bohemia, and Moravia and Silesia — is one option under discussion to meet demands for territorial devolution, but the issue has been complicated by the suggestion that the West German *Länder* model might be adopted for Czechoslovakia as a whole, or that Moravia and Silesia might form a third republic within the Czech and Slovak federation.

The Movement for Self-Governing Democracy was exceptional in the Czech Republic insofar as it was a party pursuing a specifically regional interest (although a number of other, very small Moravian parties such as the Moravian National Party (*Moravská národní strana*) have also surfaced). By and large, Czech parties have tended to form on more conventional left–right lines and, although Civic Forum was an exception to that, its disintegration has led to the emergence of new parties (the Civic Democratic Party and Civic Movement) which conform to that pattern.

Directory of Parties (Czech Republic)

Association of Social Democrats
Asociace sociálních demokrátů (ASD)

Contact. Pavel Bergmann (spokesman).

Foundation. May 25, 1991.

Leadership. Rudolf Battěk (ch.)

History. This association was formed, following the breakup of Civic Forum, by members of the Civic Forum Club of Social Democrats who had broken with the re-founded Social Democratic Party a year before and contested the June 1990 parliamentary elections on Civic Forum's list of candidates.

Organization. Based on a network of local clubs, membership is open to individuals and organizations which seek affiliation.

Christian and Democratic Union
Křesťanská a demokratická unie (KDU)

(*See also* Christian Democratic Party, Christian Democratic Movement and Czechoslovak People's Party)

A coalition formed to contest the June 1990 parliamentary elections which embraced the Czechoslovak People's Party, the Christian Democratic Party and a number of smaller parties and clubs. The Slovak Christian Democratic Movement was nominally also a partner in the coalition, but in practice presented its own separate list of candidates in Slovakia, while the Union contested seats only in the Czech Republic. By the summer of 1991, the coalition had collapsed as a result of disputes between the two main Czech parties.

Christian Democratic Party
Křesťanskodemokratická strana (KDS)

Address. Soukenická 22, Praha 1.

Foundation. 3 Dec. 1989.

Membership. 2–3,000 (March 1990).

Leadership. Václav Benda (ch.)

History. A non-denominational Christian party which traced its origins to dissenting religious circles, it sees itself as somewhere on the centre-right of the political spectrum. In June 1990, it contested the parliamentary elections in the Czech Republic as part of the Christian and Democratic Union. Standing independently in the local elections in the Czech Republic on Nov. 24, 1990, it obtained only 1.3 per cent of the vote and 251 seats.

Programme. In the run-up to the 1990 elections, it advocated equal status for state, co-operative and private sectors of the economy, with the proviso that private endeavour had to be positively encouraged. In its view, the state could not be a guarantor of social justice, and society, whether through charitable organizations or trade unions and self-help co-operatives, should take on the main responsibility in that area.

Affiliations. The party's association with the People's Party within the Christian and Democratic Union came to an end in the summer of 1991 and it seemed likely to look for allies among other right-of-centre parties like the Civic Democratic Party.

CZECHOSLOVAKIA

Civic Democratic Alliance
Občanská demokratická aliance (ODA)

Address. Box 659, 111 21 Praha 1.

Štefánikova 17, 150 00 Praha 5.

Telephone and Fax. (02) 54 80 42.

Foundation. December 1989.

Membership. Around 300.

Leadership. Pavel Bratinka (ch.); Daniel Kroupa (1st dep. ch.)

History. A small right-of-centre party which stood in the June 1990 elections as part of Civic Forum, the Civic Democratic Alliance has seen itself as closest to the British Conservative Party in its philosophy. Notable for the prominence of its parliamentary representatives rather than the size of its membership, its profile was enhanced in the spring of 1991, following the breakup of Civic Forum, when nine of that movement's representatives, including the federal Minister for the Economy, Vladimír Dlouhý, the Czech Minister for Privatization, Tomáš Ježek, and the Czech Minister for Agriculture, Bohumil Kubát, switched their allegiance to it. Although it contested the 1990 elections only in the Czech Republic, the Civic Democratic Alliance is a party which is attempting to extend its activities to Slovakia.

Organization. Members are organized in locally based clubs but may also form groups according to professional and other shared interests. District (*oblastní*) organizations, which hold a conference twice a year as a rule and elect a district committee of up to seven members including a chairman, deputy chairman, agent and treasurer, may be formed by at least six clubs. The party's supreme organ is an annual state-wide conference which elects a chairman and two deputy chairmen of the party and its Central Assembly (*ústřední sněm*), to which the conference also elects a further 12 members. The Central Assembly establishes a Secretariat and an advisory political council (*grémium*) comprising the party's representatives in the federal and republic legislatures and is normally led by its first deputy chairman.

Programme. It advocates the rule of law, citizens' political rights and the establishment of a free market. It believes that the state sector of the economy should be minimal. It places social responsibility above social justice and, while recognizing that the state has an irreplaceable role in guaranteeing social provision, believes as much of this as possible should be transferred to the voluntary sector.

Affiliations. In 1991, the Alliance developed close links with KAN (the Club of Committed Non-party Members) and seems likely to form an electoral alliance with the Civic Democratic Party.

Civic Democratic Party
Občanská demokratická strana (ODS)

Foundation. April 20–21, 1991.

Membership. 17,000 (July 1991).

Leadership. Václav Klaus (ch.); Petr Čermák and Miroslav Macek (dep. ch.)

History. The origins of the Civic Democratic Party date back to the summer and autumn of 1990 when, dissatisfied with the disparate character of Civic Forum and its ineffective political structure, Václav Klaus, Finance Minister in the federal government, and from October that year, Civic Forum's chairman, advocated the movement's transformation into a right-of-centre political party. Although Klaus had the support of a majority of the movement's representatives at a Republican Assembly held on January 12–13, 1991, opposition to his proposals was also strong. It was, however, the provisions of the 1990 Law on political parties which allowed Civic Forum's disbandment, but not its transformation into a party, that forced Klaus and his supporters to create a new organization, the Civic Democratic Party, which held its founding congress in April that year. By the summer of 1991 the Civic Democratic Party was the most popular in the Czech Republic, attracting 17–18 per cent in public opinion polls.

Organization. Its Constituent Congress in April 1991 elected a chairman, two deputy chairmen, an Executive Council comprising six representatives from Bohemia and four from Moravia and Silesia, an arbitration committee, auditing commission and financial board. It plans to employ "non-political managers" to run local party organizations. Membership is individual and exclusive.

Programme. The party fully supports Czechoslovakia's rapid transition to a market economy in which the larger part of state-owned enterprises will be privatized. Its activists, much more so than Klaus himself, have shown themselves hostile to the appointment to high office both within their own party and in public life, of all former members of the Communist Party, including 1968 reformers. Despite that hostility, 3 per cent of the party's membership in July 1991 were reported to be former Communists.

Affiliations. A merger with the small Conservative Party — the Free Bloc and an electoral pact with the Civic Democratic Alliance seem strong possibilities. In Slovakia, it sees the Public Against Violence, following the latter's shift to the right in the summer of 1991, as a suitable partner.

Civic Forum
Občanské fórum (OF)

(*See also* Association of Social Democrats, Civic Democratic Alliance, Civic Democratic Party, Civic Movement and Liberal Democratic Party)

History. Formed on Nov. 19, 1989, Civic Forum brought together, in the tradition of Charter 77, representatives of all pro-democracy forces in the Czech Republic, to co-ordinate the campaign to end communist rule which erupted after the brutal police attack on a student march two days before. It benefited in particular from the presence within its ranks of leading Charter 77 activists, like Václav Havel, whose record as spokesman for that movement and for VONS (the Committee for the Defence of the Unjustly Prosecuted), participation in the demonstrations that occurred with increasing frequency in 1988 and 1989, and long periods of imprisonment under the Communists, ensured him public backing in the negotiations which led to the formation of the coalition Government of National Understanding on Dec. 10, and Havel's subsequent election as President on Dec. 29.

Civic Forum, along with the Public Against Violence in Slovakia, became the dominant force in the transition to parliamentary democracy in 1990. Its broad commitment to pluralism, the market and democracy won it the support of around 50 per cent of Czech voters in the June 1990 elections and, although its share fell in the November local elections, it nevertheless retained, even then, the loyalty of 35 per cent of the voters.

Few, given the broad spectrum of political opinion represented within it, had expected Civic Forum to survive until the elections, but it was not until the autumn of 1990 that internal divisions began to crystallize. The election of federal Finance Minister Václav Klaus as its first chairman in October indicated a preponderance among the movement's activists of support for his programme of radical economic reform and a shift to more right-wing policies.

Klaus's advocacy, at a meeting of local Civic Forum officials in Olomouc on Dec. 8–9, of the movement's transformation into a right-of-centre political party based on individual membership and thus excluding the numerous left- and right-wing parties contained within it, brought matters to a head. At a Republican Assembly on Jan. 12, 1991, his views carried the day, but Civic Forum's transformation into a political party was prevented by the absence from the 1990 law on political parties of any provision for such a move.

As a result, the inevitable breakup of Civic Forum as a political force in April 1991 took a different form, as Klaus and his supporters established the Civic Democratic Party, centrists within it formed the Civic Movement, smaller parties went their own way, and some politicians looked for a new home elsewhere, for example in the Civic Democratic Alliance and the Social Democratic Party.

Organization. Civic Forum was a loosely based movement with no formal membership and embracing individuals and a range of clubs and parties of diverse political opinion. Local Civic Forum clubs were formed throughout Bohemia and Moravia with their own "managers". Until the election of Václav Klaus as its first chairman in October 1990, it had no formal leadership and relied on a Co-ordinating Centre and a series of spokespersons in the tradition of the Charter 77 movement. At the Republican Assembly on Jan. 13, 1991, a 17-member Republican Council was elected embracing the movement's chairman, 10 representatives chosen by district (*okres*) clubs and six parliamentary deputies (three from the Liberal Club and three from the Interparliamentary Club of the Democratic Right).

Civic Forum's list of candidates in the June 1990 parliamentary elections included its own nominees, independent candidates and representatives of a broad range of smaller parties, including Czechoslovak Democratic Initiative (now the Liberal Democratic Party), the *Obroda* (Reawakening) Club, the Left Alternative, the Pan-European Union, the Civic Democratic Alliance and the Civic Forum Club of Social Democrats (now the Association of Social Democrats).

Civic Movement
Občanské hnutí (OH)

Foundation. April 27, 1991.

Membership. 30,000 (July 1991).

Leadership. Jiří Dienstbier (ch.); Pavel Rychetský and Petr Pithart (dep. ch.)

History. The Civic Movement had its origins in the Civic Forum Liberal Club, formed on Dec. 13, 1990, in response to the emergence within that movement of strong support for its transformation into a right-of-centre party, based on individual membership. Members of the Liberal Club, by contrast, believed that until the 1992 parliamentary elections Civic Forum should retain the character of a broad-based movement and the programme with which it had faced the voters in June 1990.

Following Civic Forum's Republican Assembly on Jan. 12–13, 1991 and the decision by Václav Klaus and his supporters to form what became the right-of-centre Civic Democratic Party, the Liberal Club set off down a parallel path. The Civic Movement was formally constituted at a founding assembly on April 27, 1991, when Foreign Minister Jiří Dienstbier, who had been the most outspoken critic of Klaus's views and a defender of the concept of a broadly based movement, was elected chairman.

Despite the presence within its ranks of Dienstbier and a number of other prominent politicians, such as Petr Pithart, the Czech Prime Minister, and Pavel Rychetský, a Deputy Prime Minister in the federal government, the Civic Movement has proved less successful than the Civic Democratic Party in establishing itself with the electorate, of whom only 5–6 per cent expressed support in mid-1991.

Organization. In contrast to the Civic Democratic Party, the Civic Movement sought to retain something closer to the loose structure of Civic Forum and envisaged individual and associate membership. Its Constituent Assembly elected a 40-member Republican Council as well as a chairman and two deputy chairmen.

Programme. While generally supporting the liberal economic programme under way in Czechoslovakia in 1991, the Civic Movement places greater emphasis on social policy than did the Civic Democratic Party. It sees itself in the centre of the political spectrum.

Affiliations. The presence of West German Foreign Minister Hans-Dietrich Genscher at the movement's Constituent Assembly suggested links might be established with the German Free Democrats.

Communist Party of Bohemia and Moravia
Komunistická strana Čech a Moravy (KSČM)

(*See also* Communist Party of Czechoslovakia)

Address. Politických vězňů, Praha 1.

Foundation. March 31, 1990.

Membership. 430,000 (June 1991).

Leadership. Jiří Svoboda (ch.); V. Novák (exec. sec.)

History. The formation of a party organization for Bohemia and Moravia was planned during the Prague Spring but thwarted by the Soviet leadership after the 1968 invasion.

The idea was mooted again in late 1988 by the then Communist General Secretary, Miloš Jakeš, but no action was taken before the November 1989 revolution. The party's founding congress was held in Prague on March 31, 1990 and elected Jiří Machalík as its first chairman. At a subsequent, first congress on Oct. 13, 1990, Machalík was replaced by the film and TV director, Jiří Svoboda.

Organization. Although the leading body in the new party remained a 101-member Central Committee, formally elected by the March congress, in practice 85 of those members were chosen in multi-candidate secret ballots at district (*okres*) conferences and another 15 chosen by the congress from among its parliamentary representatives. The last member was the chairman, also directly elected by the congress. An Executive Committee and three Secretaries were then elected by the new Central Committee.

Programme. A programme approved by the March 1990 congress claimed that the party wished to follow a policy of national understanding and support the development of democracy, and the creation of a humane society in a state based on the rule of law. It continued to regard Marx's humanist message and his methodological legacy as the basis for its policy, but wished to become a party of labour that was internally pluralist in its views. It supported a state regulated market system in a mixed economy.

Czechoslovak People's Party
Československá strana lidová (ČSL)

Address. Revoluční 5, Praha, 1.

Telephone. (02) 23 15 451.

Foundation. October 1918.

Membership. 100,000 (June 1991).

Leadership. Josef Lux (ch.)

History. Founded less than a month before the creation of Czechoslovakia, the People's Party quickly brought in a new leadership after the November 1989 revolution and ended the "satellite" status it had had during communist rule. An allegation on the eve of the June 1990 elections that its new chairman, Josef Bartončík, had collaborated with the secret police, was thought to have adversely affected support for the Christian and Democratic Union coalition within which the party was standing and which obtained just under 9 per cent of the vote. In the November 1990 local elections, when it stood on its own, the People's Party did markedly better than that, with 11 per cent. Opinion polls in mid-1991 provided conflicting evidence on its support, one suggesting only 4 per cent the other 9 per cent. Its nominees were included in the new government of the Czech Republic formed in June 1990.

Programme. As part of the Christian and Democratic Union coalition in the June 1990 parliamentary elections, the party offered a manifesto which rejected socialism in any form and stressed its commitment to a moral and spiritual renewal of society. Traditionally a Christian party, it placed particular weight on religion and improving the position of the churches and the family. In the economy it supported a shift to private enterprise.

Affiliations. The collapse of the Christian Democratic Union coalition in the summer of 1991 brought to an end an uneasy relationship with the Christian Democratic Party. Apart from links with that party and the Christian Democratic Movement in Slovakia, the People's Party included among its list of nominees in the June 1990 parliamentary elections representatives of a number of smaller parties including the Free Peasants' Party (*Svobodná rolnická strana*), the Association of Private Farmers (*Sdružení soukromých zemědělců*), the Association of Czechoslovak Businessmen (*Sdružení československých podnikatelů*), the Moravian Civic Movement (*Moravské občanské hnutí*) and the Masaryk Democratic Movement (*Masarykovo demokratické hnutí*).

Czechoslovak Social Democracy
Československá sociální demokracie (ČSSD)

Address. Lidový dům, Hybernská 7, Praha 1.

Telephone. (02) 26 38 78.

Foundation. 1878; forcibly merged with Communist Party, July 1948; re-founded December 1989.

Membership. 13,200 (spring 1991).

Leadership. Prof. Jiří Horák (ch.); Jozef Wagner (centr. sec.)

History. The Czechoslovak Social Democratic Party proved to be the most popular in the country's first parliamentary elections in 1920, when it won over 25 per cent of the vote. Its support declined dramatically to roughly half that level following the departure of its left wing to form the Communist Party in 1921. In the 1946 elections, it was the second most popular party in Bohemia and Moravia, winning almost 24 per cent of the Czech vote, but in July 1948 the party was forced to amalgamate with the Communists. During the Prague Spring, a preparatory committee was set up with a view to re-establishing the party, but the move was prohibited by Moscow after the August 1968 invasion and it was not until December 1989 that Social Democracy was reborn as an independent party.

The party's failure to reach the 5 per cent threshold required to win seats in the Federal Assembly and the Czech National Council in June 1990 may in part be attributed to general antipathy to any form of socialism in post-communist Czechoslovakia, but it also reflected divisions within its ranks. The election as the party's chairman in March 1990 of Professor Jiří Horák, a political scientist who had spent the previous 40 years in exile in the USA, brought dissension within the membership and persuaded one of the leading figures in the party's rebirth, Rudolf Battěk, a former Charter 77 spokesmen, to stand as a member of a separate Club of Social Democrats within Civic Forum in the June 1990 parliamentary elections. Although the Social Democrats only won 1,052 seats (1.5 per cent) in the November 1990 local elections in the Czech Republic, their 5 per cent share of the vote was a marginal improvement on the less than 4 per cent vote they obtained in June. Although it seemed no nearer to winning greater popular support by mid-1991, it gained some parliamentary representation as a result of the breakup of Civic Forum when six deputies from that movement switched their allegiance to the Social Democrats in March 1991. If the decision by the *Obroda* Club in the spring of 1991 to amalgamate with the Social Democrats seemed to indicate a move to strengthen the party as the basis for a democratic, left-of-centre organization, its prospects were hampered by continuing disputes with Battěk and his Club of Social Democrats who opted to form a separate Association of Social Democrats in May 1991.

Programme. The 1990 manifesto suggested that it was a party slightly to the left of centre, committed to a social market, a mixed economy and individual rights.

Affiliations. Czechoslovak Social Democracy is a member of the Socialist International. In the 1990 elections it formed a coalition with the Social Democratic Party in Slovakia.

Farmers' Party
Zemědělská strana (ZS)

Leadership. František Trnka (ch.)

Founded on Jan. 12, 1990, the Agricultural Party formed the core of a coalition, the Alliance of Farmers and the Countryside (*Spojenectví zemědělců a venkova*) which unsuccessfully contested the June 1990 parliamentary elections throughout Czechoslovakia. The party on its own was more successful in the November local elections in the Czech Republic when it won 1,701 council seats and its members were elected mayors in 136 smaller Czech towns. Although it has been seen as a voice for the powerful co-operative farm lobby, it recognizes the need for economic reform. In June that year, it formed a coalition with the Czechoslovak Socialist party entitled the Liberal Social Union (*Liberálně sociální unie*), and regards parties such as the Social Democrats, Greens and Civic Movement as among its potential allies.

Left Alternative
Levá alternativa (LA)

A small political movement, formed in November 1989, which is committed to democratic, self-governing socialism, whose chairman is Vladimír Říha, but whose best known member is the former dissident, Peter Uhl (appointed head of the Czechoslovak News Agency, ČTK, in 1990). It contested the 1990 parliamentary elections as part of Civic Forum.

Liberal Democratic Party
Liberálně demokratická strana (LDS)

Foundation. Nov. 11, 1989 (as the Czechoslovak Democratic Initiative).

Membership. About 3,600 (April 1990).

Leadership. Emanuel Mandler (ch.)

History. Although the Liberal Democratic Party grew out of a party formed as the Czechoslovak Democratic Initiative just before the "velvet" revolution in November 1989, in practice its origins date back even further to the autumn of 1987 when its founders came together to press for liberal democratic reform in an informal social movement called the Democratic Initiative. Included on Civic Forum's list in the June 1990 parliamentary elections, the Liberal Democratic Party won two seats in the Federal Assembly and five in the Czech National Council. It pronounced itself independent of Civic Forum in July that year and, although 27 of its members were elected to local councils in November 1990 on Civic Forum lists, another 38 won seats as representatives of their own party.

elections, the Liberal Democratic Party won two seats in the Federal Assembly and five in the Czech National Council. It pronounced itself independent of Civic Forum in July that year and, although 27 of its members were elected to local councils in November 1990 on Civic Forum lists, another 38 won seats as representatives of their own party.

Programme. It sees itself as a party of the centre right, committed to radical economic reform, liberal democracy and independent local government. It has reservations over what it regards as "the hegemony of the revolutionary establishment" — the predominance in high office of participants from dissenting circles — and wishes to encourage greater involvement of all citizens in political life.

Affiliations. In 1991 it sought to establish links with the Christian Democratic Party, the Civic Democratic Alliance and the Civic Democratic Party, and has entered into negotiations with the Association of Social Democrats.

Movement for Self-Governing Democracy — the Society for Moravia and Silesia
Hnutí za samosprávnou demokracii — Společnost pro Moravu a Slezsko (HSD-SMS)

Foundation. 1990.

Leadership. Jan Kryčer (ch.)

Greater autonomy for the provinces of Moravia and Silesia that lie in the eastern half of the Czech Republic is the key feature of the Movement for Self-Governing Democracy's programme. In June 1990, it won between 8 and 10 per cent of the vote in the elections to the Federal Assembly and the Czech National Council, and thus well over 20 per cent of the vote in the only two constituencies (North Moravia and South Moravia) where it presented a full list of candidates. In the November 1990 local elections, it did much less well, winning only 4 per cent of the total Czech vote. Its first chairman, Boleslav Bárta, died of a heart attack on May 31, 1991, during all-party talks on constitutional reform called by President Havel. Originally included in the Czech Government formed in June 1990, it quit that coalition in January 1991.

National Social Party
Národně sociální strana (NSS)

Foundation. Sept. 8, 1990.

Leadership. Čestmír Čejka (ch.)

History. A new party formed as the result of a split in the Czechoslovak Socialist Party, it challenges the latter's claims to be the legal and political heir of the Czechoslovak National Socialist Party which was founded in 1897 and was a major political force in pre-communist Czechoslovakia. It favours the establishment of a federal system on the West German model, supports the government's economic reforms and, while stressing the freedom of the individual and free enterprise, wishes to represent the interests of employees and trades unionists. In the November 1990 Czech local elections it won 150 seats and its members were elected mayors in 10 towns including Teplice, Tábor and Žatec. It sees itself as on the left of a *bloc* of right-wing parties including the Civic Democratic Party, the Civic Democratic Alliance, KAN, the Christian Democratic Party and the Liberal Democratic Party.

SLOVAK REPUBLIC

Situated in the easternmost part of Czechoslovakia, Slovakia remains much more ethnically heterogenous than the Czech Republic. Slovaks, of whom there are 4.5 million, form 85.6 per cent of its population according to the March 1991 census, and 566,700 Hungarians another 10.8 per cent. In addition, there are a further 16,900 Ruthenians and 13,800 Ukrainians, while only 80,600 registered as Gypsies (a much lower figure than is believed to be the case in reality).

Unlike the Czechs, the Slovaks have never had their own state, with the exception of the short period between 1939 and 1945 when the Nazis established a puppet regime. The failure of past governments to accommodate continuing demands for self-government meant that issue came to dominate Slovak politics, particularly after the June 1990 elections. Separatism found its champion in the Slovak National Party, but most other Slovak parties were committed to some form of common state with the Czechs, albeit one in which most favoured a substantial transfer of power from the federal level to the republics. It was an issue made more complicated by a belief among many Slovak politicians that only a devolution of this kind to Bratislava would enable the Slovak government to protect its population against the worst effects of economic liberalization in a republic where insolvencies and unemployment were likely to be much higher than in Bohemia and Moravia.

Those two factors were to lie at the heart of the split in the Public Against Violence in the first half of 1991 and the formation of the Movement for a Democratic Slovakia by its former nominee as Slovak Prime Minister, Vladimír Mečiar. The departure of Mečiar and his supporters left a much smaller Public Against Violence as almost the only Slovak party unequivocally committed to a strong federal system and radical economic reform. Although the coalition government it had formed with the Christian Democratic Movement and the Democratic Party in June 1990 survived, it was nevertheless one weakened by Mečiar's departure and by the extensive public support evident for his new movement.

The new party system in Slovakia differed from the one evolving in the Czech Republic not only in the greater focus on the issue of self-government and the less widespread enthusiasm for radical economic reform evident in that republic. Greater religious commitment in Slovakia led to the emergence of a stronger Christian Democratic Movement than was the case in Bohemia and Moravia and ethnic divisions inevitably led to the creation of parties, albeit of minor significance, along ethnic lines — such as the Hungarian Christian Democratic Movement which preferred an electoral alliance with Coexistence to links with its Slovak co-religionists. Ethnic exclusiveness was, however, far from universal and, apart from movements such as Coexistence and the Movement for Czechoslovak Understanding (see above), both of which sought to overcome national barriers, the inclusion within the Public Against Violence of the Hungarian Independent Initiative (*Maďarská nezávislá iniciatíva*) was another attempt to bridge the ethnic divide.

Directory of Parties (Slovak Republic)

Christian Democratic Movement
Kresťanskodemokratické hnutie (KDH)

Foundation. December 1989.

Membership. 300,000 (March 1990).

Leadership. Ján Čarnogurský (ch.); Ján Petrík (centr. sec.)

History. Formed after the November 1989 revolution, the Christian Democratic Movement grew out of the Catholic opposition in Slovakia of the 1970s and 1980s but quickly established a strong base throughout that republic. Though nominally a partner in the Christian and Democratic Union, it preferred to have its own list of candidates in Slovakia in the June 1990 parliamentary elections. On that occasion, it was the second most popular party in Slovakia, winning 19 per cent of the vote for the House of the People and the Slovak National Council respectively and 17 per cent for the House of the Nations. In the local council elections on Nov. 23 and 24, 1990, however, it displaced the Public Against Violence from its first place in Slovakia when it won over 27 per cent of the vote in that republic. The Christian Democratic Movement is a partner in the federal coalition government formed in June 1990, although its chairman, Ján Čarnogurský (who had earlier been a Deputy Prime Minister in the federal Government of National Understanding), chose to move to Bratislava at that point in time and was appointed Deputy Prime Minister in the Slovak government headed by Vladimír Mečiar. In April 1991, following the split in the Public Against Violence and Mečiar's dismissal, he succeeded the latter as Prime Minister of Slovakia.

Programme. Among its original goals were Czechoslovakia's transition to a market economy, based on private ownership, support for the family and help for the less well-off, both from the state and private organizations. There are indications that the movement in general does not share the more nationalist approach adopted since the June 1990 elections by Čarnogurský, who has declared his readiness to support the maintenance of a common state with the Czechs for the immediate future but added that, once Czechoslovakia is admitted to the European Community, Slovakia should have its own representatives there.

Democratic Party
Demokratická strana (DS)

Address. Šafárikovo n. 4, Bratislava.

Telephone. (07) 50 933.

Foundation. 1944.

Leadership. Ján Holčík (ch.)

CZECHOSLOVAKIA

History. Between March 1948 and December 1989, the Democratic Party was known as the Party of Slovak Renewal and had survived as one of the "satellite" parties active in Slovakia throughout the period of communist rule. The change of name was a reversion to that of a party which had won 62 per cent of the vote in Slovakia in the 1946 elections and from which the Party of Slovak Renewal had been a splinter movement encouraged to form its own party by the Communists after the February 1948 coup. The Democratic Party failed to reach the 5 per cent threshold needed for seats in the Federal Assembly in the June 1990 elections, but its 4 per cent of the vote in those for the Slovak National Council won it seven places in that parliament. It participated with the Public Against Violence and the Christian Democratic Movement in the coalition Slovak government formed after the elections, but its popularity fell in the November local elections when it obtained just over 2 per cent of the vote.

Freedom Party
Strana slobody (SS)

Foundation. April 1946.

History. Founded in April 1946, the Freedom Party survived as a satellite party throughout the period of communist rule. It moved towards a separatist programme in 1990 but failed to obtain seats either in the Federal Assembly or the Slovak National Council in the June 1990 elections.

Hungarian Christian Democratic Movement
Slovak name: **Maďarské kresťansko-demokratické hnutie (MKDH)**

A party which stood in coalition with Coexistence in the June 1990 parliamentary elections and independently in the local elections in Slovakia in November that year, when it won 3 per cent of the vote. It was reported to have a membership of around 40,000 in the spring of 1990.

Movement for a Democratic Slovakia
Hnutie za demokratické Slovensko (HZDS)

Foundation. June 22, 1991.

Leadership. Vladimír Mečiar (ch.)

History. The Movement for a Democratic Slovakia was formed as a result of a split within the Public Against Violence that erupted in February and March 1991. It reflected divisions between, on the one hand, the latter's elected officials who supported the radical economic reform proposed by the federal government in Prague and were favourably inclined to maintenance of relatively strong federal authorities and, on the other hand, more nationalist politicians led by the then Slovak Prime Minister, Vladimír Mečiar, who favoured greater protection of the Slovak economy against the effects of economic liberalization and a weaker federal system in which the governments in the Czech and Slovak Republics would have greater powers. Mečiar's personality and an aggressive style of leadership, which was not only directed at securing concessions from the federal authorities and from the Czechs but also at colleagues with whom he disagreed in Slovakia, were another bone of contention. His decision to establish a separate platform "For a Democratic Slovakia" within the Public Against Violence preceded his dismissal as Slovak Prime Minister on April 23, 1991, but soon after that a new Movement for a Democratic Slovakia was set up as a separate organization of which Mečiar was confirmed as chairman at its constituent congress on June 22, 1991. His personal popularity with the Slovak electorate and the Movement's identification as a defender of Slovak interests account for its high rating among the Slovak electorate, 29 per cent of whom were reported to support it in one opinion poll held in June 1991 and 39 per cent in another poll held a month later.

Programme. The Movement claims to be a party of the centre and adheres to the policy associated with Mečiar during his period as Prime Minister of protecting Slovakia against the worst effects of economic liberalization through the retention of a strong role for the state in social policy. On constitutional issues, its founding congress in June 1991 moved towards support for a confederation in which Slovakia would acquire, it argued, international legal status.

Party of the Democratic Left
Strana demokratickej l'avice (SDL')

Formerly the Communist Party of Slovakia (see separate entry)

Membership. 194,000 (October 1990).

Leadership. Peter Weiss (ch.)

History. A separate Communist Party of Slovakia was formed in February 1939 following Slovakia's attainment of autonomy in the preceding autumn. Banned under the puppet Slovak state set up in March 1939, it retained its independence from the Communist Party of Czechoslovakia, based in Prague, between 1945 and September 1948 when it was subsumed once more within the latter party. The policy of destalinization adopted in the 1960s enabled the Slovak Party, which retained its own Central Committee and Presidium, to pursue a slightly more independent course and to press for satisfaction of Slovak grievances. During the Prague Spring its support for the introduction of a federal system ensured its implementation despite the Warsaw Pact intervention. During the 1970s and 1980s, the Slovak party was subordinated once more to the leadership in Prague but was quick to react to the overthrow of communist rule in December 1989 and under its new leader, Peter Weiss, search for a new role in post-communist Czechoslovakia. At its congress on Oct. 20–21, 1990, the party was renamed "The Communist Party of Slovakia — Party of the Democratic Left", but jettisoned its old name altogether at the end of the year.

Organization. The October 1990 congress established a bicameral leadership comprising a 21-member Central Committee elected by the congress and a Council of delegates elected by district (*okres*) organizations.

Programme. Committed broadly to the same goals as its counterpart in the Czech Republic of defending the interests of workers and other less well-off groups and a role for the state in the economy, particularly in Slovakia.

CZECHOSLOVAKIA

Public Against Violence
Verejnosť proti násiliu (VPN)

Address. Jirásková 10, 811 01 Bratislava.

Telephone. (07) 33 17 06 or (07) 33 33 16.

Foundation. November 1989.

Leadership. Jozef Kučerák (ch.)

History. Formed in November 1989 in Bratislava to co-ordinate the campaign for democracy in Slovakia during the "velvet revolution", the Public Against Violence initially played a similar role to Civic Forum in representing a broad spectrum of democratic opinion in that republic. As the 1990 elections approached, it looked as though it would yield second place in a strongly religious region to the Christian Democratic Movement, but in fact came top of the poll with the largest share of the vote for both houses of the Federal Assembly and the Slovak National Council. Among its candidates were Alexander Dubček, First Secretary of the Communist Party of Czechoslovakia during the 1968 Prague Spring and chairman of the Federal Assembly since Dec. 28, 1989, and Marián Čalfa, federal Prime Minister since Dec. 10, 1989.

In the local elections on Nov. 23–24, 1990, it lost first place to the Christian Democrats, but managed to retain the vote of 20 per cent of the electorate. A split in the movement early in 1991 led to the formation by Vladimír Mečiar, Slovak Prime Minister between June 1990 and April 1991, of a breakaway organization, the Movement for a Democratic Slovakia, leaving the Public Against Violence a weaker force in Slovak politics but one that was more united in its commitment to a federal Czechoslovakia and radical economic reform.

Organization. Headed by a Republic Assembly comprising delegates elected by local clubs and by a Slovak Council, elected by that Assembly. The chairman of the movement is elected by that Council.

Programme. The Public Against Violence's election manifesto, similar to that of Civic Forum, placed it in the centre of the political spectrum. With the departure of Mečiar and his supporters in 1991, however, it moved to a position closer to that of the Civic Democratic Party in its emphasis on a radical economic reform. It is unequivocally committed to a relatively strong federal system.

Affiliations. By the summer of 1991, the Public Against Violence had come to regard the Civic Democratic Party as its most likely partner in the Czech Republic.

Slovak National Party
Slovenská národná strana (SNS)

Address. Štefánikova 47, 811 04 Bratislava.

Telephone. (07) 47 004 or (07) 46 460.

Foundation. March 1990.

Leadership. Jozef Prokeš (ch.)

History. The Slovak National Party favours a separate Slovak state and its attitudes to the Hungarian minority in southern Slovakia are often more hostile than those it displays towards the Czechs. It won a much higher share than expected of the Slovak vote in the June 1990 elections — almost 14 per cent in those for the House of the People and the Slovak National Council and 11 per cent for the House of the Nations. Although its support fell to 3.2 per cent in the November 1990 local elections, opinion polls in June and July 1991 suggested it remained the favoured party among 9 per cent and 13 per cent of Slovak voters respectively.

Social Democratic Party in Slovakia
Sociálně demokratická strana na Slovensku (SDSS)

Leadership. Boris Zala (ch.)

A separately organized party which formed a coalition with the Czech-based Czechoslovak Social Democrats to contest the June 1990 parliamentary elections, but won little support from the electorate.

ESTONIA

Stephen White

Socialist rule was briefly established in Estonia in November 1917, but then overthrown in March 1919. The secret protocol of the Nazi-Soviet Pact of 1939 assigned Estonia to the Soviet sphere of influence and in 1940 the republic was incorporated into the USSR. Nationalists secured a majority in the republican parliament in 1990 and declared Estonia independent, the 1940 incorporation being declared without legal force. This declaration was in turn rejected by the Soviet government but, following a decision by the USSR State Council and recognition by most western countries, the republic became an independent state on Sept. 6, 1991.

Estonia has an area of 45,100 sq km and its population (1989 census) is 1,573,000.

Directory of Parties

Christian-Democratic Party of Estonia

Founded in 1988. Its principles include: the common interests of labour and capital; non-violent methods of social change; the rights of private property; the rights of social justice; these are regarded as an integral part of the party's Christian orientation. The party sees itself as "centre-right" or "right-democratic" in the political spectrum.

Communist Party

A split occurred in the republican party organization, although both sections continued to be regarded as part of the CPSU. The CPSU-aligned (mostly Russian-speaking) party and the independent (mostly Estonian-speaking) parties had, in January 1991, six urban and 19 district bodies, together with 1,565 branches. The CPSU-aligned organization was headed by Lembit El'marovich Annus, an Estonian national born in 1941; a member of the CPSU Central Committee since July 1990, he joined the Politburo in January 1991. The independent Communist Party of Estonia was headed by Enn-Arno Augostovich Sillari, an Estonian national born in 1944; First Secretary of the party from March 1990, he joined the CPSU Central Committee and Politburo in July 1990. The activities of the Communist Party were suspended and criminal proceedings initiated against its leadership in August 1991.

Entrepreneurs' Party of Estonia

Founded in March 1990. A "right-of-centre political party which within the limits of the constitution and proceeding from democratic principles conducts a struggle for the establishment of a prosperous Estonian society and to guarantee all the elements of the freedom of the individual".

Party of National Independence of Estonia

Founded in August 1988. Considers contemporary Estonia an "occupied and annexed state" and seeks to restore full independence.

Popular Front

Founded in Tallinn in October 1988 as a body that supported the comprehensive restructuring of socialist society, and the achievement of the "genuine political, economic and cultural independence of the Estonian SSR". From August 1990 the Front sought to re-establish the full independence of Estonia, as it had been proclaimed in 1920. Candidates enjoying the support of the Front won a majority of the seats at republican elections in 1990, and the Front is effectively in government in the republic. Its publications are the bulletin *Vestnik NFE* and *Baba maa* (Free Land).

Social-Democratic Party of Estonia

Founded in September 1990 through a merger of several smaller parties: the Estonian Independent Social-Democratic Party, the Estonian Democratic Labour Party and the Russian Social-Democratic Party of Estonia. Has three seats in the republican parliament; its chairperson is M. Lauristin. Sees itself as a "centrist" party and is a member of the Socialist International. It publishes the information bulletin *Respublika*.

United Republican Party

Founded in September 1990. An explicitly conservative party, whose membership is drawn predominantly from the scientific-technical intelligentsia of Tallinn.

GERMANY

Jonathan Osmond

The German Democratic Republic (GDR) was founded on Oct. 7, 1949, in the territory of the postwar Soviet occupation zone of Germany. It claimed to include the (eastern) Soviet sector of Berlin as its capital, although this was not recognized by the western powers. West Berlin remained an enclave within the GDR, not recognized by the East Berlin regime as part of the Federal Republic of Germany. It had already been the focus of crisis in 1948 (the Berlin blockade), and was so again in 1961 (the building of the Berlin Wall), and in 1989 (the opening of the Wall).

The GDR was not a one-party state, but in practice and then constitutionally it was ruled by the Socialist Unity Party of Germany (SED). This was the result of an amalgamation in 1946 of the Social Democratic Party (SPD) and the Communist Party (KPD), in which the latter soon came to have the dominant role. Although the initial avowed intent of the SED was not to imitate the system in the USSR but to find an appropriate German socialist path, the structures of the GDR faithfully followed a Stalinist model.

At all levels of political and economic life in the GDR the state and the ruling party were intertwined. There was considerable overlap of personnel and also the coexistence of state and party bodies responsible for the same areas, with the party's policy as the overriding factor. The economy was almost entirely socialized and subject to central planning. A vast apparatus of internal security ensured surveillance of the population and the suppression of dissent. Travel opportunities beyond the socialist world were very limited, especially after 1961.

The first leader of the GDR was Walter Ulbricht, who remained as General (then First) Secretary of the SED until his deposition in 1971. He was replaced by his protégé, Erich Honecker, who in 1976 became General Secretary once more and also Chairman of the Council of State (head of state). It was Honecker's dismissal on Oct. 17/18, 1989, which set in train the revolutionary events of the succeeding months. He was replaced briefly by Egon Krenz, who was responsible on Nov. 9, 1989 for opening the Berlin Wall and the remainder of the border with the Federal Republic of Germany.

The founding of political parties had been allowed by the Soviet Military Administration in its decree of June 10, 1945. In 1946 contested elections had been held in the Soviet zone, giving the SED a majority but not an absolute majority of votes, except in Berlin where the SPD stood too. Thereafter there was no free expression of electoral opinion until 1990. Elections to the constitutionally supreme *Volkskammer* (People's Chamber) did involve discussion of candidates at factory and local party level, but the electorate faced only a unified list drawn from the SED itself, from the "mass organizations" (official trade union, women's organization, youth organization etc.), and from the parties of the

Democratic Block (formed 1949). These were the Christian Democratic Union (CDU), Democratic Peasants' Party (DBD), Liberal Democratic Party (LDPD), and National Democratic Party (NDPD). Nominally autonomous, they represented specific sections of GDR society, but they were under the control of the SED and — until 1989 — incapable of truly independent action.

The results of elections reflected the control of the SED. It was difficult and risky to avoid voting or to reject the suggested candidates, so electoral turnout and approval of the united list was almost unanimous. The number of *Volkskammer* seats due to each party was allocated in advance. Even so, the authorities felt the need to fix the published results, and in 1989 the discrepancy between actual and alleged voting behaviour became apparent. Unofficial observers monitored the local elections in May, and challenged the announced results. In the course of 1989–90 it became clear that gross electoral malpractice had been commonplace in the GDR.

The crisis which engulfed the GDR in 1989 had many origins. These included the failure of the economy to satisfy the material needs of the population, the restrictions on travel, the obvious lack of democracy in the system, and the examples of reform to be seen in Poland, Hungary and even the USSR. During the summer of 1989 a mass migration of GDR citizens began via third countries, especially Hungary, which now had an open border with Austria. The SED leadership was meanwhile lamed by the serious illness of Erich Honecker.

Honecker recovered well enough to host the 40th anniversary celebrations of the GDR in October, but the country now faced regular mass demonstrations calling for political reform. Honecker refused to give way, despite the warnings of Mikhail Gorbachev, and faced an internal revolt by his senior party comrades. The *Politbüro* unanimously dismissed him on Oct. 17, 1989.

The months between October 1989 and March 1990 saw the GDR being reshaped into a democratic system. Despite the premiership of Hans Modrow, the SED failed to manage the crisis by itself. Its leading role was excised from the constitution in December by the revitalized *Volkskammer*, and later that month the all-party Round Table debates began. They set much of the agenda of what was to follow. In February Modrow was forced to bring the opposition parties into his "Government of National Responsibility". From that point all cabinet members, including Modrow himself, were theoretically non-party.

Later in February laws were passed on political parties and elections. Parties had to be registered with the *Volkskammer* before they could participate in the March 18 election, and no fascist, militarist or similar organizations were permitted. The electoral law provided for a smaller *Volkskammer* of 400 members (previously 500), chosen by proportional representation under the Hare-Niemeyer procedure, as in the Federal Republic of Germany. However, no 5 per cent hurdle was implemented, so small parties stood a chance of representation. Parties were permitted to present common lists, which allowed the various electoral alliances to function. The country was divided into 15 districts, but voters could cast their ballot at any polling station and the results were counted nationally.

Once the election was over, the drive towards German unity began in earnest. The *Volkskammer*, it is true, continued in its attempts to transform the GDR into a liberal parliamentary democracy with a market economy, but with economic and currency union from July 1, 1990 and political union from Oct. 3, 1990 the real decision-makers were in Bonn.

GERMANY

The GDR underwent the most extreme constitutional change of all the former communist states: it was abolished. Under the terms of the unification treaty between the two Germanies, which came into effect at midnight on Oct. 2/3, 1990, the former GDR became part of the Federal Republic of Germany. The treaty specifies numerous temporary exceptions and transitional arrangements, but the overall impact is to apply the constitutional structures, laws and electoral procedures of the Federal Republic to "the five new federal states" and the entire city of Berlin.

To give the former GDR parliamentary representation in the period pending a new election, the east German parties nominated members of the *Bundestag* in accordance with their proportional strength in the old *Volkskammer*. In all, 144 nominees entered the *Bundestag*, including members of the Party of Democratic Socialism (PDS, formerly SED). Five CDU and FDP delegates, including Lothar de Maizière, joined Chancellor Kohl's government as ministers without portfolio. Meanwhile, *Landtag* elections were held on Oct. 14, 1990 for the newly re-established *Länder* of east Germany. Only the new *Land* and capital of Berlin had to wait until December before electing its own parliament. It had to wait until June 1991 before learning that it is once more to be the seat of parliament and government.

In one very important respect the west German system did not apply immediately in east Germany. After much heated debate and a ruling by the constitutional court in Karlsruhe, it was decided that for the first all-German elections to the *Bundestag* in December 1990 the territories of the two former states should be treated as separate electoral regions. The effect of this was that the normal minimum of 5 per cent of the vote before seats could be taken in the *Bundestag* applied not to Germany as a whole, but to the two separate parts. This allowed those parties which were specifically of the former GDR to gain the parliamentary representation which would have eluded them under a nationwide 5 per cent requirement. They will be vulnerable in the next *Bundestag* elections, however, when the intention is to revert to a standard 5 per cent hurdle.

As the GDR lurched towards a democratic system, there emerged a plethora of new and reformed parties. The details are provided below, but several general trends can be identified. First, the ruling party ousted all its old leadership and shrank rapidly in size and importance. Second, the old block parties attempted to reform from within, but did not have the capacity to do so independently. Only the CDU survived, because of its west German partner. The NDPD was absorbed into the LDP, which was itself absorbed into the west German FDP. The DBD, or what was left of it, joined the CDU. Third, the SPD had precarious beginnings in the GDR. It found it hard to shake off the popular rejection of "socialism" and it survives on only a narrow membership base. In the longer term, however, its future is assured by the existence of the SPD in west Germany. Fourth, the citizens' movements and the various new liberal and centre-right parties could carry the initial revolution, but not the electoral battles against the established west German parties. The overall outcome is that the party political scene of east Germany is now almost a replica of that in west Germany. The CDU, SPD and FDP dominate, with a substantial contribution from the Greens (allied with the remains of the citizens' movements) and the local conservative presence of the DSU in Saxony. This is comparable to, but much weaker than, the Christian Social Union (CSU) in Bavaria. Only the PDS preserves something of the distinctive politics of east Germany, but it is much weakened and beset by internal wrangling.

A problem for all the parties in the east and for politicians deriving from the former GDR is that the past regularly comes back to haunt them. Allegations and scandals abound about the past behaviour of those who have survived the revolution and unification. Stories may be true or false, perhaps deliberately planted by ex-members of the *Stasi* (state security), but they lend an air of fragility to east German politics.

In each of the five separate elections held between March and December 1990 (see Tables 1–5 below) the CDU emerged the clear victor. That it did so was due partly to the mass rejection of the former ruling party and widespread wariness of any party pronouncing itself "socialist", and partly to the grandiose election promises made by Chancellor Kohl and Prime Minister de Maizière. Before the March election Kohl pledged that there would be a 1:1 currency exchange rate for wages, pensions and most savings. Before the December election he and de Maizière assured the east German population that no-one would be worse off through unification. The Bonn government also made a firm undertaking that unity could be financed without raising taxes. The SPD's west German candidate for the chancellorship, Oskar Lafontaine, on the other hand, continually made dire warnings about the way in which unification was being handled. Rightly or wrongly, he awoke the impression in east Germany that the SPD did not wholeheartedly welcome unification. Lafontaine also had the marginal disadvantage of being, like Erich Honecker, a native of the Saarland.

In addition to the main factors there were many others, particularly of a local variety. The DSU built upon Saxon and Thurigian resentment of Berlin; the voters of West Berlin responded to the conduct of the SPD/Alternative List coalition in that part of the city; popular local candidates influenced the vote, such as the west German Foreign Minister, Hans-Dietrich Genscher, in his home town of Halle; and areas such as Berlin and Brandenburg with a larger population of former or actual SED/PDS members understandably returned a stronger-than-average PDS vote. Generally speaking, the CDU and DSU fared better in the south of the GDR's territory, in rural areas, and among blue-collar workers. The age profile of CDU and DSU voters was very broad, while the PDS, the Alliance 90 and the Greens were favoured more by those younger than 40, and the SPD more by those older.

The March 1990 *Volkskammer* elections (Table 1) almost gave the CDU and its Alliance for Germany partners an absolute majority, but it would in any case have needed a two-thirds majority in the chamber for constitutional changes, so coalition talks began with the SPD. The latter had performed well below its showing in the early opinion polls, and was not so very far ahead of a reduced but not humiliated PDS. Outgoing Prime Minister Modrow and new PDS chairman Gregor Gysi had managed to retrieve something from the party's bad image. The liberal League of Free Democrats (BFD) performed moderately well, but the Alliance 90 of the citizens' groups was almost swept out of sight. This was the beginning of the end too for the NDPD and DBD.

The local elections less than two months later (Table 2) displayed already some interesting changes. Turnout fell from the extraordinary 93 per cent in March to 75 per cent, and there were some electoral shifts. All the major parties lost ground, the CDU most of all, and the gainers were the liberal BFD, the farmers' parties and, appropriately for local elections, many independent candidates.

In October elections were held in the reconstituted *Länder* of east Germany (Table 3). They confirmed the strength of the CDU in Saxony and Thuringia and the ongoing decline of its partner, the DSU. The liberals made good progress, especially in Saxony-Anhalt, where Genscher's impact was felt. The SPD could take consolation from the fact that it had stemmed its losses and could lead a coalition in Brandenburg. Elsewhere, however, the CDU took charge. Alliance 90 benefited from its contacts with the growing Green movement, and the PDS fell back, but only slightly.

The later Berlin election (Table 4) also brought victory to the CDU, but it had later to construct a grand coalition with the SPD. The victory was also primarily a West Berlin affair, with the SPD ahead of the CDU in the east, and the PDS not far behind.

The *Bundestag* elections of Dec. 2, 1990 (Table 5) brought Chancellor Kohl the prize of being the elected Chancellor of German unity. The CDU polled 43.4 per cent in the former GDR, which was marginally up on the March election and, together with the sharply diminished vote of the DSU, slightly above the combined result of the CDU and CSU in west Germany. The FDP put in a very strong showing in east Germany: 13.4 per cent, compared to 10.6 per cent in the west. The SPD, dropping back slightly in west Germany, did in the east improve on its March showing (from 21.9 per cent to 23.6 per cent), but this was a poor result. The PDS managed 9.9 per cent in the territory of the former GDR, so comfortably clearing the hurdle into the *Bundestag*, but its overall 2.4 per cent suggests a limited future. The east German Greens, backed by the citizens' movements which spearheaded the revolution, just squeezed in with 5.9 per cent embarrassing their west German counterparts, who this time did not. The far-right Republicans failed to make any impact in east Germany; their 1.3 per cent was less than the 2.3 per cent in west Germany.

After the December 1990 election the CDU suffered electorally and in opinion polls from its handling of the situation in east Germany and its announcement of tax increases from July 1, 1991. It faced severe electoral reverses in west Germany. In April 1991 Chancellor Kohl's home state of Rhineland-Palatinate was lost for the first time to the SPD, and in June the SPD achieved an overall majority in the Hamburg parliament. So far there has been no testing of the electorate in east Germany, where the social and economic problems are most acute, but opinion polls suggest that the loss of confidence in the CDU has been greater there than in west Germany.

An opinion poll published by Infas of Bonn in early June 1991 asked 2,000 electors for which party they would vote if there were a general election held the following Sunday (Table 6). The voting intentions expressed in east Germany showed a dramatic decline in support for the CDU, and a corresponding lift for the SPD. The weak membership base of the latter in east Germany, however, means that it still has a difficult task ahead. The FDP, on the other hand, has a much larger membership to build upon its bedrock of support. It is currently more popular in east than in west Germany. The Greens and citizens' groups have apparently made further recovery since their initial poor showing in March 1990. The PDS continues to shrink, and will on current form not enter the next *Bundestag*, which will be elected with a countrywide minimum requirement of 5 per cent of the vote. Chancellor Kohl's position has been weakened by these recent trends, but the next general election would not normally be held until 1994.

A final disturbing element in east German politics is the growth of right-wing radicalism and neo-Nazism amongst the disaffected youth of the cities. This is a phenomenon which was evident before the fall of the old regime, but is now more in the open. There have been attacks, at least one fatal, on foreigners, and Jewish cemeteries have been desecrated. In Dresden in particular ultra-right groups have been congregating in 1991, including the National Democratic Party of Germany (NPD) and the German People's Union (DVU).

NEW POLITICAL PARTIES OF EASTERN EUROPE AND THE SOVIET UNION

The city has been given by the neo-Nazi fringe the nickname of the new "capital of the movement", the Nazi designation of Munich. The numbers involved are small by European standards — perhaps 2,000 in east Germany plus some 15,000 less-committed supporters — but the violence disturbs a population not used to it and, considering understandable German sensitivity in this area, is most unwelcome to the authorities.

Table 1: Elections to the *Volkskammer*, March 18, 1990 (93.4 per cent turnout)

	Valid votes	%		Seats	
CDU ⎫	4,710,598	40.8 ⎫		163 ⎫	
DSU ⎬ Alliance for Germany	727,730	6.3 ⎬	48.0	25 ⎬	192
DA ⎭	106,146	0.9 ⎭		4 ⎭	
SPD	2,525,534	21.9		88	
PDS	1,892,381	16.4		66	
BFD	608,935	5.3		21	
Alliance 90	336,074	2.9		12	
DBD	251,226	2.2		9	
Green Party & Independent Women's Association	226,932	2.0		8	
NDPD	44,292	0.4		2	
Others	111,307	1.0		2	
TOTAL	11,541,155	100.0		400	

Table 2: Local elections, May 6, 1990 (75 per cent turnout)

	%	Change from March
CDU	34.4	−6.4
SPD	21.3	−0.6
PDS	14.6	−1.8
DSU	3.4	−2.9
BFD	6.7	+1.4
Alliance 90	2.4	−0.5
Farmers' parties (including DBD)	5.7	+3.5
Others	11.5	+7.3
TOTAL	100.0	

GERMANY

Table 3: Elections to the east German *Landtage*, Oct. 14, 1990 (percentage of valid votes cast)

	Brandenburg	Mecklenburg-W. Pomerania	Saxony	Saxony-Anhalt	Thuringia
CDU	29.4	38.3	53.8	39.0	45.4
DSU	1.0	0.8	3.6	1.7	3.3
FDP	6.6	5.5	5.3	13.5	9.3
SPD	38.3	27.0	19.1	26.0	22.8
Alliance 90	6.4	2.2 }	5.6	5.3	6.5
Greens	2.8	4.2 }			
New Forum	–	2.9	–	–	–
PDS	13.4	15.7	10.2	12.0	9.7
Others	2.1	3.4	2.4	2.6	3.0
Turnout	67.4	65.2	73.5	65.6	72.1

Table 4: Elections to the Berlin House of Representatives, Dec. 2 1990

	Berlin %	Seats	West Berlin %	(previous %)	East Berlin %	(previous %)
CDU	40.3	100	48.9	(37.7)	25.0	(18.6)
SPD	30.5	76	29.5	(37.7)	32.1	(34.0)
PDS	9.2	23	1.1	(–)	23.6	(30.0)
FDP	7.1	18	7.9	(3.9)	5.6	(2.2)
GAL[1]	5.0	12	6.9	(11.8)	1.7	(–)
A90/G[2]	4.4	11	1.4	(–)	9.7	(9.9)
Reps[3]	3.1	–	3.7	(7.5)	1.9	(–)

[1] Greens/Alternative List.
[2] Alliance 90/Greens.
[3] Republicans.

Tables 5: Elections to the *Bundestag*, Dec. 2, 1990 (percentage of valid votes cast)

	Germany	West	(1987)	East	(March)	Seats
CDU	36.7	35.0	34.5	43.4	40.8	270
CSU	7.1	9.1	9.8	–	–	49
DSU	0.2	–	–	0.9	6.3	–
SPD	33.5	35.9	37.0	23.6	21.9	239
FDP	11.0	10.6	9.1	13.4	–	79
PDS	2.4	–	–	9.9	16.4	17
Greens	3.9	4.7	8.3	–	–	–
Greens/Alliance 90	1.2	–	–	5.9	–	8
Republicans	2.1	2.3	–	1.3	–	–
Others	1.9	2.4	1.3	1.6	14.6	–
TOTAL	100.0	100.0	100.0	100.0	100.0	662
Turnout	77.8	78.5	84.4	74.5	93.4	–

Table 6: Voting intentions, June 1991, per cent (December 1990 election results in brackets)

	Germany	West	East
SPD	39.5 (33.5)	40.0 (35.9)	37.0 (23.6)
CDU/CSU[1]	38.5 (43.8)	40.0 (44.1)	32.0 (43.4)
FDP	11.5 (11.0)	11.0 (10.6)	14.0 (13.4)
Greens/Alliance 90[2]	5.5 (5.1)	5.0 (4.7)	7.0 (5.9)
PDS	1.5 (2.4)	0.5 (–)	6.5 (9.9)

[1] CDU alone in east Germany.
[2] Greens alone in west Germany.

Directory of Parties

Note: In October 1989 the GDR was still ruled by the Socialist Unity Party of Germany, which also controlled the parties of the "Democratic Block". Since October 1990 the former GDR has been subsumed into a united Germany, and its politics are now dominated by the established parties of the Federal Republic. A strictly-defined list of surviving "new parties" in eastern Germany would, therefore, be a short one indeed. This directory comprises: (i) the "old" parties of the GDR and their adaptation to the new circumstances; (ii) the new, mostly ephemeral, parties of 1989–90; (iii) the parties of the Federal Republic insofar as they were relevant to eastern Germany in 1989–90; and (iv) significant political groupings which were not political parties as such.

Alliance for Germany
Allianz für Deutschland

An electoral alliance formed in February 1990 by the Christian Democratic Union (CDU), German Social Union (DSU) and Democratic Departure (DA) to fight the March election. It proved a means by which the CDU was able to neutralize competing right-of-centre parties. It won 48.0 per cent of the vote and nearly half the seats in the *Volkskammer*, but most of the success belonged to the CDU. After the election the CDU Prime Minister, Lothar de Maizière, kept his promise to include his Alliance partners in government by appointing one DA and two DSU ministers, but they soon left those parties to become independent or join the CDU. DA merged with the CDU in August 1990.

Alliance 90
Bündnis 90

An electoral alliance formed in February 1990 by non-party citizens' groups New Forum, Democracy Now and the Peace and Human Rights Initiative. In the March election it performed disappointingly, with only 2.9 per cent of the vote and 12 seats in the *Volkskammer*. Its share of the vote fell back even further in the local elections in May. Increasingly Alliance 90 co-operated with the east German Greens, and improved upon its early electoral setbacks in the October elections to the east German *Landtage* and in the *Bundestag* election in December 1990. In the latter, in alliance with the Greens, it won 5.9 per cent of the vote and eight seats, and was, like the Party of Democratic Socialism (PDS), accorded "group" but not "fraction" status. It also won 11 seats in the Berlin House of Representatives.

Alternative Youth List
Alternative Jugendliste (AJL)

An electoral alliance of youth groups which stood in the March 1990 election to the *Volkskammer*. It included the Marxist Youth Association, the United Young Left, the Green Youth, and — most importantly — the Free German Youth (*Freie Deutsche Jugend* — FDJ). This last was the youth organization of the ruling Socialist Unity Party, and had been led in the past by both Erich Honecker and Egon Krenz. It had undergone reformist changes during the autumn of 1989 and its leader, Eberhard Aurich, had been replaced by Frank Törkowsky. In the election the AJL achieved 14,615 votes, and it and the FDJ ceased to be of any significance.

Association of Working Groups for Employee Politics and Democracy
Vereinigung der Arbeitskreise für Arbeitnehmerpolitik und Demokratie (VAA)

The party with the longest name and the lowest number of votes (380) in the March 1990 election.

The Carnations
Die Nelken

Foundation. December 1989/January 1990.

Leadership. Brigitte Kahlwald (ch.); Michael Czollek (dep. ch.); Rainer Bartscher (dep. ch.)

History. This small Marxist party came into being in the winter of 1989/90, holding its founding congress on Jan. 13, 1990, in East Berlin. It tried to mobilize communists who had formerly been in the Socialist Unity Party (SED) or not in any party. Having originally been in close contact with the United Left (VL), the Carnations in February joined with it in an alliance to fight the March 1990 election. Between them they won less than 0.2 per cent of the vote and only one seat in the *Volkskammer*.

Programme. Seeing themselves in the political tradition of the murdered early German communists, Rosa Luxemburg and Karl Liebknecht, the Carnations sought a new form of socialism in the GDR. They did countenance a form of market economy, but with worker participation in decision-making and within a socially determined general plan. They rejected a capitalist annexation of the GDR by the Federal Republic, which would bring mass unemployment and poverty.

Affiliations. Action Alliance United Left (from February 1990).

Christian Democratic Social Union
Christlich-Demokratische Soziale Union (CDSU)

One of the 12 groups which formed the German Social Union in January 1990.

Christian Democratic Union of Germany
Christlich-Demokratische Union Deutschlands (CDU)

Contact name. Volker Rühe (g.s.)

Address. Konrad-Adenauer Haus, Friedrich-Ebert-Allee 73–75, D-5300 Bonn 1. (Berlin) Postfach 1316, Jakob-Kaiser-Haus, Charlottenstrasse 53–4, O-1080 Berlin.

GERMANY

Telephone. (0228) 5441; *Telex.* 886804. Berlin: *Telephone.* (0037 2) 2880; *Fax.* (0037 2) 291238; *Telex.* 069 112 240.

Foundation. 1945 (in Soviet occupation zone); 1950 (in Federal Republic of Germany); merged October 1990.

Membership. 760,000 (including 80,000 in east Germany).

Leadership. Dr Helmut Kohl (ch.); Volker Rühe (g.s.). Former GDR leadership: Gerald Götting (ch. 1966–89); Lothar de Maizière (ch. November 1989–October 1990).

History. The CDU in the GDR was one of the Democratic Block or National Front parties in alliance with the ruling Socialist Unity Party (SED). It was founded in July 1945 as a party to represent the Christian middle class, and was broadly equivalent to its West German counterpart. From 1947, however, under the leadership of Otto Nuschke, it entered into political alliance with the SED, and served to organize those career-minded Christians who had not chosen or not been chosen to join the SED itself. In the old GDR parliament the CDU had a number of seats (52) decided in advance by an allocation on the unified election list.

The membership of the CDU in the GDR was at its height at the end of 1947 with 218,000. By the early 1960s only one-third was left (70,000), but after that the party grew steadily to 140,000 in 1987. This was a process encouraged by the SED.

The relationship of the CDU with the churches in the GDR was not always a happy one. Although claiming to represent "socialist state citizens of Christian belief", the CDU came to symbolize compromise with the state rather more than defence of the Christian churches. When in the 1980s dissident groups protesting about militarism, nuclear weapons and pollution centred themselves on the churches, the CDU became even more remote.

In November 1989 Gerald Götting was forced to resign as chairman and he was replaced by the lawyer and musician, Lothar de Maizière, who had not previously been active in the leadership. The party went through a period of crisis as it terminated its membership of the Democratic Block in December but remained in government with the SED. At a special party congress also in December the CDU rejected socialism and professed itself in favour of democratization and German unity. Its position at this stage was precarious, however, because it was open to charges of complicity in the old regime, and it faced electoral competition from both the newly founded Social Democratic Party (SPD) and from other parties on the right. When the German Social Union (DSU) was founded in January 1990 some CDU politicians in west Germany considered allying with the new party rather than with the eastern CDU.

However, a better solution was found with the formation in February 1990 of the Alliance for Germany, comprising the CDU, the DSU and Democratic Departure (DA). With a massive input of west German CDU electoral campaigning and generous promises on the part of Chancellor Kohl, the Alliance scored a remarkable victory in the March elections. The CDU was the principal winner, with 40.8 per cent of the vote and 163 of the 400 seats in the *Volkskammer*. It performed particularly well in the southern parts of the GDR. Lothar de Maizière, who had been deputy prime minister with responsibility for church affairs in the last Modrow cabinet, formed a coalition government on April 9, 1990.

The succeeding months were then dominated by the negotiations towards first economic then political union between the two German republics. De Maizière was often depicted in the press as being under the thumb of Chancellor Kohl, but he did show initiative on occasions. In early August he embarrassed Kohl by revealing their intention (soon thwarted) to bring forward the first all-German elections, and in the middle of the same month he struck out at his coalition partners. He sacked several of his ministers and pushed the SPD out of the coalition.

The CDU had its own problems. In mid-August 1990 the general secretary of the party in the GDR, Martin Kirchner, was removed from office on suspicion of having collaborated with the *Stasi* (state security). There also remained the question of CDU property in the GDR, although in December 1989 the party had handed it over to the Trustee Agency (*Treuhandanstalt*). Meanwhile, despite the accession to the CDU of first the Democratic Farmers' Party (DBD) in June and then DA in August, the membership was falling sharply, bringing the total in mid-1991 down to around 80,000.

On Oct. 1, 1990, the CDU of the GDR joined that of the Federal Republic. Following German unity two days later, de Maizière became a deputy chairman of the federal CDU and a minister without portfolio in the Kohl cabinet. The united party then scored further electoral triumphs in the east German *Landtag* elections, in the elections to the Berlin House of Representatives, and in the elections to the new *Bundestag*. Chancellor Kohl formed a new coalition government in January 1991 of CDU, Christian Social Union (CSU) and Free Democratic Party (FDP). De Maizière was not a member of it, since he had temporarily fallen victim to another alleged *Stasi* scandal, but two other east German CDU politicians were, Günther Krause and Angela Merkel.

If 1990 was a year of triumph for the CDU, 1991 began badly. Kohl's government was forced to announce tax rises to pay for German unification and for the Gulf War, and this contributed to the electoral loss of Kohl's home state Rhineland-Palatinate to the SPD in April and to a poor showing in Hamburg in June. In that same month Günther Krause, Minister of Transport, came under intense pressure to resign because of his alleged role in the granting of motorway services franchises in the month before German unification.

Organization. The CDU of the former GDR has now become part of the existing structure of the CDU in the Federal Republic. This comprises the federal party, the parties in the *Länder*, the district associations, and the local associations. The federal party congress, consisting of delegates from the *Länder* parties, normally meets every two years to decide policy and to elect the party chairman and the federal executive committee. A larger federal committee concerns itself with party matters between party congresses. In addition the CDU has eight associations for youth, women, employees, local government, small business and professional people, the economy, expellees and refugees, and the elderly.

Programme. The 1982 programme of the CDU in the GDR stressed Christian responsibility and democratic obligations. The bases of Christian Democratic thought and action were "loyalty to socialism, confident co-operation with the party of the working class . . . and friendship with the Soviet Union".

The CDU of the Federal Republic, of which the CDU of the former GDR is now a part, describes itself as a "broadly-based classless party amalgamating traditions of Christian social thinking, liberalism and modern conservatism". The CDU is broadly Christian and not tied to any one confession, but the accession of the GDR party has increased its Protestant component. Economically, the CDU is pledged to the social market economy, but has now adopted an ecological perspective as well.

GERMANY

Affiliations. Alliance for Germany (in the GDR from February 1990). Christian Democratic International; European Christian Democratic Union; European People's Party; European Democrat Union; International Democrat Union.

Christian League
Christliche Liga

A small Christian party which gained 10,691 votes (0.09 per cent) in the March 1990 elections to the *Volkskammer*.

Christian Social Association
Christlich-Soziale Vereinigung

One of the 12 groups which formed the German Social Union in January 1990.

Christian Social Party of Germany
Christlich-Soziale Partei Deutschlands (CSPD)

One of the 12 groups which formed the German Social Union in January 1990.

Christian Social Union
Christlich-Soziale Union (CSU)

Founded in Leipzig in January 1990, it was one of the 12 groups which formed the German Social Union later that month. Imitative of, but not to be confused with the CSU in Bavaria, which rules in that state and is part of Chancellor Kohl's government coalition.

Communist Party of Germany
Kommunistische Partei Deutschlands (KPD)

Foundation. 1918. Banned 1933–45. Re-founded 1945. In Soviet occupation zone merged with SPD to form SED 1946. Re-founded January 1990.

Membership. 5,000 (March 1990).

Leadership. Klaus Sbrzesny.

History. The KPD as re-founded in 1945 was the dominant partner in the merger with the Social Democratic Party (SPD) to form the Socialist Unity Party (SED) in 1946. In January 1990 an attempt was made to revitalize the idea of the KPD, in rejection of the SED, now the Party of Democratic Socialism (PDS). The intent was to organize "all honest Communists". The party was refounded in Berlin, and in February held a congress in Frankfurt an der Oder, attended by 100 delegates. Its members were reported to be mainly young people not previously attached to any party.

The KPD explored links with the Carnations, the German Marxist Party and the United Left (but not with the PDS), but stood independently in the March 1990 election. It polled only 8,819 votes, less than 0.1 per cent of the total.

Programme. Humanism, peace and disarmament, social justice, and social ownership as the dominant form of ownership. Opposition to the absorption of the GDR into the Federal Republic, but willingness to countenance unification in a pan-European context.

Democracy Now
Demokratie Jetzt (DJ)

Address. Friedrichstrasse 165, O–1080 Berlin.

Telephone. (0037 2) 291134.

Foundation. September 1989.

Membership. 836 (September 1990).

Leadership. Wolfgang Ullmann (spokesman; b. 1929; minister without portfolio February–March 1990); Konrad Weiss, Hans-Jürgen Fischbek, Ulrike Poppe (spokespersons).

History. DJ, one of the foremost citizens' movements in the GDR during 1989–90, originated in church circles in protest against the falsified election results of May 1989. It began on Sept. 12, 1989 with the declaration of the "theses for a democratic restructuring in the GDR". A total of 15 of its leading members took part in the Round Table debates from December 1989 to March 1990. In February 1990 one of its leaders, the church historian Wolfgang Ullmann, joined Modrow's "Government of National Responsibility" as a minister without portfolio. Konrad Weiss, a film director, joined the government commission responsible for drafting a new media law. Also in February DJ joined with New Forum and the Peace and Human Rights Initiative to form the electoral pact, Alliance 90. This achieved a total vote of 336,074 (2.9 per cent) and 12 seats in the *Volkskammer*.

DJ has never been a large organization. Registered membership has not exceeded 1,000 and the broader circle of activists was at its height in the winter of 1989–90 only 3,000. Since then participation has fallen back significantly. DJ has been dominated by intellectuals in their late 30s and it fulfilled amongst the citizens' movements a theoretical and programmatic role.

In December 1990 the paper *Demokratie Jetzt* was, in collaboration with the Peace and Human Rights Initiative (IFM), retitled *Bündnis 2000*, and in January 1991 DJ formed a loose organizational liaison with IFM. DJ is represented in the *Bundestag* by Wolfgang Ullmann and Konrad Weiss.

Organization. DJ does not see itself as a political party, but as a citizens' movement. It has a central office in Berlin (shared with the Peace and Human Rights Initiative), and offices in the east German *Länder*. It has also formed groups in Bonn, Frankfurt am Main and Cologne.

Programme. A social and ecological market economy; democracy and the rule of law. DJ originally favoured a more gradual, three-stage path to German unity.

GERMANY

Affiliations. Alliance 90 (from February 1990).

Democratic Association GDR 40
Demokratische Vereinigung DDR 40

Foundation. January 1990.

Programme. This "Marxist-Christian" party aimed to maintain the sovereignty of the GDR, on humanitarian, socialist and ecological principles. It called for a new constitution and free elections and the punishment of former *Politbüro* members. The "40" in its title presumably referred to the 40th anniversary of the GDR in 1989.

Democratic Departure/Democratic Awakening
Demokratischer Aufbruch (DA)

Foundation. October/December 1989. Merged with CDU August 1990.

Membership. Nil (55,000 in March 1990).

Leadership. Wolfgang Schnur (ch. 1989–90); Rainer Eppelmann (ch. 1990; b. 1943; Minister for Defence and Disarmament 1990).

History. DA had its origins in church circles in the summer of 1989, before the revolution itself in the GDR. An "initiative group" was formed in July, but a founding meeting was thwarted by the police on Oct. 2. A delegates' meeting on Oct. 29–30 provisionally constituted a party, which was then formally brought into being in Leipzig on Dec. 16–17, 1989. The founders included the Rostock lawyer, Wolfgang Schnur, the Berlin pastor, Rainer Eppelmann, and the Wittenberg pastor, Friedrich Schorlemmer. Schnur acted as chairman from October and was narrowly elected to that post in December. He, Eppelmann, Fred Ebeling and 13 others represented DA at the Round Table debates from December 1989 onwards.

The initial political location of the party was disputed, and — fearing a drift rightward — Schorlemmer took his Wittenberg group and other leading members of the party over to the Social Democratic Party (SPD) on Jan. 18, 1990. Eppelmann became a minister without portfolio in the Modrow government of February 1990, and Schnur in the same month took DA into the Alliance for Germany with the Christian Democratic Union (CDU) and the German Social Union (DSU).

However, on the eve of the March election Schnur was accused in the press of having in the past collaborated with the *Stasi* (state security). He strenuously denied this at first, alleging that he was the victim of a smear campaign. Under continuing pressure, however, he admitted the charge and resigned on March 14, 1990. His successor, Eppelmann, failed in the short time available to undo the huge damage done to the party, and it achieved less than 1 per cent of the vote in the election and only four seats in the *Volkskammer*.

Eppelmann himself was made a minister in the de Maizière government. He insisted in the designation of his post that he was minister not just for defence but also for disarmament, but in a colourful period in office he continued to place arms orders for the National People's Army. The party meanwhile was disintegrating, and Eppelmann resigned from it to become an independent. In August 1990 DA merged with the CDU and by December 1990 Eppelmann was a CDU member of the *Bundestag* for a Brandenburg seat.

Programme. DA brought together a desire for German unity and the market economy with an insistence on social justice and environmental responsibility. It campaigned in the March 1990 election under the title "Democratic Departure: social and ecological".

Affiliations. Alliance for Germany (from February 1990).

Democratic Farmers' Party of Germany
Demokratische Bauernpartei Deutschlands (DBD)

Foundation. 1948. Merged with CDU June 1990.

Membership. Nil (115,000 in 1987).

Leadership. Günter Maleuda (ch. 1987–90; b. 1931; pres. of People's Chamber 1989–90).

History. The DBD was one of the two parties in the GDR (the other being the National Democratic Party) which were set up at the instigation of the Socialist Unity Party (SED) to organize specific social groups. Founded in April 1948, the DBD was intended to draw the small peasantry and rural labourers into the communist sphere, and it played a crucial role in the collectivization of the late 1950s. It was one of the parties of the Democratic Block and the National Front, with 52 seats in the *Volkskammer*. It furnished government ministers, most recently Peter Diederich, who in the restructured Modrow government of February 1990 replaced his party colleague Hans Reichelt as Minister for Environmental Protection. In December 1989 the DBD chairman, Günter Maleuda, was elected president of the *Volkskammer*, narrowly defeating the expected victor, Manfred Gerlach of the Liberal Democratic Party.

The DBD's membership, like that of the other block parties, was rising from the mid-1970s, on SED encouragement. In 1987 it stood at 115,000. At the same time, however, the SED revived its interest in another organization for rural workers, the Union of Mutual Peasant Aid (*Vereinigung der gegenseitigen Bauernhilfe — VdgB*), as a means of infiltrating the SED into the agricultural sector. With about 425,000 members in 1984, the VdgB eclipsed the DBD, but in the revolution of 1989–90 the VdgB suffered a collapse of support because of its SED connections.

In the election of March 1990 the DBD took 251,226 votes (2.2 per cent of the total) and nine seats in the *Volkskammer*. As the economic crisis began to hit GDR agriculture hard in the spring of 1990, the protests of farmers grew and other small agricultural groups and parties were formed. The DBD united with these for the local elections in May and registered a marked improvement on its March result, 5.7 per cent of the vote. The DBD was losing members, however, and failing to find a distinctive new role to play in the transformed system. In June 1990 it merged with the Christian Democratic Union (CDU).

Programme. According to the party statute of 1987 "the DBD sees its most important obligation as being to help develop, advance and consolidate the alliance between the working class and the class of co-operative farmers". By February 1990 the DBD programme favoured democracy, a single statehood of the German nation in the framework of a peaceful Europe, and an ecologically-oriented socially just market economy. It continued to represent all those who worked on the land.

Affiliations. Democratic Block (to December 1989).

Democratic Women's League of Germany
Demokratischer Frauenbund Deutschlands (DFD)

Address. Clara-Zetkin-Strasse 16, O–1080 Berlin.

Telephone. (0037 2) 000952.

Foundation. 1947.

Membership. 1,441,375 (1982).

History. The "mass organization" for women under the old regime in the GDR, and therefore represented in the *Volkskammer*. In the March 1990 election the DFD won over 38,000 votes, 0.33 per cent of the vote, and one seat. It improved its performance in the May local elections to 1.24 per cent, but thereafter was of little significance.

Europe Union of the GDR
Europa-Union der DDR

A party which announced its intentions to stand in the March 1990 election, but then did not.

European Federalist Party — Europe Party
Europäische Föderalistische Partei — Europa Partei

Address. Hopfensack 6, W-2000 Hamburg 11.

A party which won 3,690 votes (0.03 per cent) in the March 1990 *Volkskammer* election.

Forum Party of Thuringia
Forumspartei Thüringen

One of the 12 groups which formed the German Social Union in January 1990.

Free Democratic Party
Freie Demokratische Partei (FDP)

Contact name. Cornelia Schmalz-Jacobsen (g.s.)

Address. Thomas-Dehler-Haus, Baunscheidstrasse 15, D-5300 Bonn 1.
(Berlin) Postfach 1335, Mohrenstrasse 20–22, O–1080 Berlin.

Telephone. (0228) 5470; *Telex.* 886580. Berlin: *Telephone.* (0037 2) 22130; *Telex.* 069 114 806.

Foundation. 1948 (in western occupation zones); December 1989/February 1990 (in GDR). Merged August 1990.

Membership. 171,000 (including 104,000 in east Germany).

Leadership. Dr Otto Graf Lambsdorff (ch., b. 1926); Cornelia Schmalz-Jacobsen (g.s.) Former GDR leadership: Bruno Menzel (ch.); Peter Thietz (ch.); Jurgen Neubert (dep. ch.)

History. An FDP committee was formed in the GDR in December 1989. The party was founded on Feb. 4, 1990. A week later it joined the Liberal Democratic Party (LDP) and the German Forum Party (DFP) in the League of Free Democrats (BFD) electoral alliance. This won 5.3 per cent of the vote and 21 seats in March 1990, and 6.7 per cent of the vote in May. The BFD then provided the basis for organizational amalgamation of the liberal parties in the GDR and then unity with the west German FDP in August 1990.

In the post-unification elections the FDP did particularly well in east Germany, reaching 13.4 per cent of the vote in the *Bundestag* election (10.6 per cent in west Germany). The membership is also currently larger in east than in west Germany, making it the largest party there apart (probably) from the Party of Democratic Socialism (PDS). Rainer Ortleb from the former GDR represents the FDP in Chancellor Kohl's cabinet, as Minister of Education.

Organization. The FDP is organized on *Land* basis, with sub-groups as appropriate. The party congress, which meets annually and which all members are entitled to attend (though only delegates have voting rights), decides policy and elects the party leadership for a period of two years.

Programme. The east German FDP proposed a social market economy, environmental protection, social security, and German economic and political unity. The stance of the long-established FDP in the Federal Republic is of economic and political liberalism, with a strong appeal to businessmen and farmers.

Affiliations. League of Free Democrats (February–August 1990). Liberal International; Federation of Liberal, Democratic and Reform Parties of the European Community.

Free Democratic Union of Germany
Freie Demokratische Union Deutschlands (FDUD)

One of the 12 groups which formed the German Social Union in January 1990.

Free German Union
Freie Deutsche Union (FDU)

One of the 12 groups which formed the German Social Union in January 1990. Originating in the north of the GDR, its chairman was Martin Wisser.

GERMANY

German Beer Drinkers' Union
Deutsche Biertrinker Union (DBU)

A special-interest party which gathered 2,534 votes in the March 1990 *Volkskammer* election. It did not prevent the subsequent closure of numerous breweries in the GDR.

German Forum Party
Deutsche Forumpartei (DFP)

Foundation. January 1990. Merged with west German FDP August 1990.

Leadership. Jürgen Schmieder (ch. 1990); Lothar Ramin (ch. 1990).

History. The DFP, founded in Karl-Marx-Stadt (now Chemnitz) in January 1990, was a breakaway liberal faction of New Forum. Its small membership was concentrated in the south of the GDR. It took part in the negotiations which resulted in the Alliance for Germany, but joined not that electoral pact but the liberal League of Free Democrats (BFD). As part of the BFD the DFP merged in August 1990 with the west German Free Democratic Party (FDP).

Programme. In favour of a social and ecological market economy and of German unity, without an extension of NATO into the territory of the GDR.

Affiliations. League of Free Democrats (February–August 1990).

German Freedom Union
Deutsche Freiheitsunion

One of the 12 groups which formed the German Social Union in January 1990.

German Reunification Party
Deutsche Wiedervereinigungspartei

A small party founded in Berlin in January 1990 to promote the idea of German unity.

German Social Union
Deutsche Soziale Union (DSU)

Address. Merseburger Strasse 82, O–7033 Leipzig.

Telephone. (0037 41) 476051; *radio telephone*. 0161 2811 364.

Foundation. January 1990.

Membership. 12,000 (June 1990).

Leadership. Hans-Wilhelm Ebeling (ch. 1990); Hans-Joachim Walther (ch. 1990); Reinhard Keller (ch. 1991); Theodor Waigel (hon. ch., from CSU).

History. The DSU was founded in Leipzig in mid-January 1990 by Hans-Wilhelm Ebeling, pastor at the Thomaskirche. It drew together 12 small new parties or groups which had emerged since the revolution: the Christian Social Party of Germany; the Free German Union; the Progressive People's Party; the People's Union; the Social Citizens' Union; the German Freedom Union; the Christian Democratic Social Union; the Christian Social Association; the Young Union; the Forum Party of Thuringia; the Free Democratic Union of Germany; and the Christian Social Union.

Being founded later than many of the new parties in the GDR, the DSU was not represented at the Round Table, but it quickly gained support from the Christian Social Union (CSU) in Bavaria, and then helped to form the Alliance for Germany with the Christian Democratic Union (CDU) and Democratic Departure (DA) in February 1990. In the March elections the DSU was overshadowed by the success of the CDU, but scored a respectable 6.3 per cent of the votes and 25 *Volkskammer* seats. The party furnished two ministers in the de Maizière cabinet: Ebeling (economic co-operation) and Peter-Michael Diestel (interior).

Thereafter, however, the DSU began a very sharp electoral decline, ending up with only 0.9 per cent of the east German vote in the December 1990 *Bundestag* election and no seats. One of the main reasons for this was the furious infighting which beset the party. It was evident that it contained incompatible strands, which accused each other of leaning excessively to the right and to the left respectively. In May 1990 Diestel was called upon to resign by his own parliamentary party, on the grounds that he was being too lenient to the former *Stasi* (state security). He resisted this pressure, but resigned from the party in the summer, later to join the CDU. Other leading figures, including the founder Ebeling, also left the party, accusing their rivals of flirting with the far-right Republicans.

In May 1991 the DSU tried to revive itself by drafting a new programme and electing a new leader, Reinhard Keller. The Bavarian CSU welcomed this and said that it was prepared to support the DSU politically and organizationally.

Organization. The DSU is active primarily in Saxony and Thuringia. Its organization was criticized by one of its former leaders: Hans-Joachim Walther complained in the summer of 1990 that the list of members and associations was in such chaos that even he as chairman was not on it.

Programme. The DSU was founded to promote German unity, Christian values, and a restoration of the old *Länder* in the territory of the GDR. It occupies a place on the right of German politics, and has close ties with the Bavarian CSU.

Affiliations. Alliance for Germany (from February 1990).

Green Party/The Greens, Green League
Grüne Partei/Die Grünen, Grüne Liga

Address. Friedrichstrasse 165, O–1080 Berlin.

Telephone. (0037 2) 291657; *Fax.* (0037 2) 291645; *Telex.* 069 114 099.

Foundation. November 1989.

Membership. 6,000 (March 1990).

GERMANY

Leadership. Judith Demba, Friedrich Heilmann, Viktor Liebrenz, Dorrit Nessing-Stranz, Henry G. Schramm, Christine Weiske (all committee members).

History. During the 1980s unofficial ecological groups emerged in the GDR: for instance, the environmentalist library at the Zion church in Berlin, which staged its first exhibition in September 1986. These initiatives faced harassment by the security forces, including the violent entry of the Zion church premises in November 1987, which aroused protest at home and abroad.

By 1988 there were up to 80 small ecological groups in the GDR, primarily in Berlin, Dresden, Erfurt, Halle, Leipzig and Schwerin, but the contact between them was limited. In order to counteract this, the *Netzwerk Arche* (ark network) was founded in January 1988. However, allegations of "centralism" led to a split in the spring of 1988 between the network and the environmentalist library. When later in that year and in 1989 talks did finally take place between the state authorities and the ecology groups, the network was prominently represented.

In the revolutionary circumstances of October–November 1989 there were marked divergences of opinion in the "green" movement. Some activists wanted to represent an ecological standpoint within the other citizens' movements; others, particularly those from the ark network, wanted a separate green party. Out of the arguments emerged in November two new organizations, the Green Party and the avowedly non-political Green League. The Green Party published its first draft programme in December 1989 and held its first congress in Halle in February 1990, shortly after the founding congress of the Green League. At the Round Table debates the Green Party was represented by a total of 17 members and the Green League by 11.

The party contested the March 1990 election together with the Independent Women's Association (UFV), but only received 2.0 per cent of the vote and eight seats. In the autumn, in collaboration with Alliance 90, the position improved, and the *Bundestag* election brought 5.9 per cent and eight seats. This actually exceeded the performance of the longer established west German Greens, who did not reach the 5 per cent barrier.

The east German "Greens" (the Green Party changed its name in September 1990) are now associated with their west German counterparts, but also with what remains of the citizens' movements which carried the revolution of 1989–90. The forms of organization are loose, and in June 1991, for instance, the Greens of Thuringia proposed an amalgamation with the citizens' movements while remaining in the Federal Association of Greens. The political secretary of the west German Greens, Heide Rühle, meanwhile said that unity between them and the citizens' movements was some way off. The Green League still exists separately.

With lignite-mining and burning, old factory plant, intensive agriculture, and the polluted legacy of the Soviet army installations, the environmental damage in the former GDR is of enormous dimensions. Estimates of the cost of repairing it in the coming decades run into DM 100 billions. Green politics can be expected to remain a live issue.

Organization. All party councils must comprise 50 per cent women.

Programme. Environmental measures and disarmament.

Affiliations. Common electoral list with Independent Women's Association (UFV) for March 1990 election. Common list with Alliance 90 in three of five *Länder* elections

October 1990, and in *Bundestag* election December 1990. Contacts with Green League. Membership of Federal Association of Greens (*Bundesverband der Grünen*).

Independent People's Party
Unabhängige Volkspartei (UVP)

Foundation. December 1989.

History. In the election of March 1990 the small UVP won 3,007 votes.

Programme. Social justice, freedom, democracy and peace. All power to the people in a united fatherland.

Independent Social Democratic Party of Germany
Unabhängige Sozialdemokratische Partei Deutschlands (USPD)

Foundation. 1917. Re-founded February 1990.

History. The original USPD was a breakaway from the Social Democratic Party (SPD) during World War I. After some initial success, it had dwindled to insignificance by the mid-1920s. The new version of the party, founded at Fürstenwalde on Feb. 16, 1990, was intended as a resurrection of the principles of the earlier one, but in the election of March 1990 it received only 3,891 votes.

Programme. Radical democratic socialism.

Independent Women's Association
Unabhängiger Frauenverband (UFV)

Address. Friedrichstrasse 165, O-1080 Berlin.

Telephone. (0037 2) 202091 App. 38.

Foundation. February 1990.

Membership. 3,030 (August 1990).

Leadership. Tatjana Böhm, Ina Merkel (spokeswomen).

History. The UFV had origins in the early 1980s, as attempts were made to form a women's movement separate from the official Democratic Women's League of Germany (DFD), although contacts were maintained with the latter. An early group (from 1982) was Women for Peace (*Frauen für den Frieden*).

In the autumn and winter of 1989 various women's initiatives were formed to keep women's issues alive in the course of the revolution. They included LILO (*lila offensive*, Lilac Offensive), SOFI (*Sozialistische Frauen-Initiative*, Socialist Women's Initiative, later renamed *Solidarische Fraueninitiative*, Solidary Women's Initiative), and EWA (*Erster weiblicher Aufbruch*, First Female Departure). Many of the activists involved hoped to bring the various groups into one organization and on Dec. 3, 1989 a "manifesto for an autonomous women's movement" was issued. This was the beginning of the UFV, although the founding congress was not held until Feb. 17, 1990, in East Berlin. The UFV had meanwhile sent a total of 20 representatives to the Round Table and had provided a minister, Tatjana Böhm, in the reconstituted Modrow government. An electoral pact had also been agreed with the Green Party. Between them the parties received 226,932 votes (2.0 per cent) and eight *Volkskammer* seats. In the *Bundestag* election of December 1990 two UFV members, Christina Schenk and Petra Bläss, were elected, but on the lists respectively of the Greens/Alliance 90 and the Left List/PDS.

Organization. Concentrating on women's issues, the UFV does not prohibit simultaneous membership of another party or organization.

Programme. Democracy, women's and environmental issues. Two prominent concerns have been growing female unemployment, and the threat to abortion rights in east Germany from the possible imposition of the less liberal West German legislation.

Affiliations. On united list with the Green Party for March 1990 election.

League of Free Democrats
Bund Freier Demokraten (BFD)

The BFD was originally an electoral alliance formed in February 1990 by the Free Democratic Party (FDP), Liberal Democratic Party (LDP) and German Forum Party (DFP) to fight the March election, when it won 5.3 per cent of the vote and 21 seats. In Lothar de Maizière's cabinet the BFD furnished three cabinet ministers, but two of them had to resign later in some disgrace. The BFD became the basis for a merger of the three liberal parties, which the National Democratic Party (NDPD) also joined. In the May local elections it increased its share of the vote to 6.7 per cent. The BFD merged with the West German FDP in August 1990.

League of Socialist Workers
Bund Sozialistischer Arbeiter (BSA)

Contact name. Ulrich Rippert (nat. sec.)

Address. Postfach 100105, Alfredstrasse 71, W-4300 Essen 1.

Telephone. (0201) 733556.

A small socialist party which gained 374 votes in the March 1990 elections to the *Volkskammer*. Since it is also known as the German Section of the 4th International, it is presumably a Trotskyist party.

Liberal Democratic Party
Liberal-Demokratische Partei (LDP)

Foundation. 1945. Renamed LDPD 1945. Renamed LDP February 1990. Merged with west German FDP August 1990.

Membership. Nil (104,000 in 1987).

Leadership. Manfred Gerlach (ch. 1967–90; b. 1928; acting ch. of Council of State 1989–90); Rainer Ortleb (ch. 1990; b. 1944; Minister for Education 1991).

History. Until the upheaval of 1989–90 the Liberal Democratic Party of Germany (LDPD) was one of the National Front parties allied to the ruling Socialist Unity Party (SED). It was founded in July 1945 as a liberal initiative with a middle-class constituency, but was rapidly pressured into subordinating itself to the SED. After that it was little more than a means by which the SED could organize and discipline white-collar workers, craftsmen, businessmen and professionals. Its membership, at 199,000, was at its height in 1950 and then fell drastically to 67,000 in the early 1960s. From that point, like the other National Front parties, the LDPD grew, as the SED encouraged organization of non-communists in order to bolster the system. In 1987 its membership was 104,000.

The LDPD managed to retain its leader during the early phase of the revolution. Indeed, Manfred Gerlach was the first leader of any of the subordinate parties to speak out in favour of reform. This contrasted with the rhetoric which he had been using for the previous 20-odd years. He came to be seen as a bridge between the SED and those demanding more thorough changes, and after the resignation of Egon Krenz as head of state in December 1989, Gerlach was elected to replace him in a provisional capacity. He resigned as party chairman in February 1990 and declared his intention to retire from politics after the March 1990 elections. Meanwhile three LDP members joined the Modrow government of February 1990. Two of them, Peter Moreth and Kurt Wünsche, had before the revolution been members of the political committee of the LDPD.

For the elections the renamed LDP joined with the Free Democratic Party (FDP) and the German Forum Party (DFP) in an electoral alliance called the League of Free Democrats (BFD), which took 5.3 per cent of the vote and 21 seats. After the election the waning National Democratic Party (NDPD) decided to dissolve itself and join the LDP, which was itself moving closer to the other liberal parties. Under the continuing title of BFD they improved their performance in the May 1990 local elections to 6.7 per cent. The final merger with the west German FDP took place in August 1990. From January 1991 the LDP still had a continuing legacy in the person of Chancellor Kohl's Minister of Education, Rainer Ortleb, who after Gerlach had been the last chairman of the old party.

Programme. In 1987 the party programme declared that "The LDPD is a party working in and for socialism . . . The LDPD directs itself primarily to craftsmen, tradesmen, members of the intelligentsia and white-collar employees . . .". By the autumn of 1989 chairman Gerlach was calling for change in the GDR. By December 1989 the party called for a market economy which guaranteed social and ecological security, a process of German unification, and disarmament in Europe.

Affiliations. Democratic Block (to December 1989). League of Free Democrats (February–August 1990).

National Democratic Party of Germany
National-Demokratische Partei Deutschlands (NDPD)

Foundation. 1948. Merged with LDP March 1990.

GERMANY

Membership. Nil (110,000 in 1987).

Leadership. Heinrich Homann (acting ch. 1967–72; ch. 1972–89); Günter Hartmann (ch. 1989–90); Wolfgang Gläser (ch. 1990); Wolfgang Rauls (ch. 1990).

History. Along with the Democratic Farmers' Party (DBD), the NDPD was founded in the Soviet occupation zone of Germany in April 1948 on the instigation of the Socialist Unity Party (SED), in order to mobilize and control a particular section of society. The NDPD, with its German nationalist aspect, was intended to attract former soldiers, particularly officers, and former members of the NSDAP (Nazi party) who were not implicated in serious crimes. It became part of the National Front and thus little more than a mouthpiece for official ideology. Besides its original membership, however, it did develop a role as representative of small private or semi-private traders and professional people.

The NDPD increased its numbers from the mid-1970s to 110,000 in 1987, as part of an SED policy to build up the allied block parties and draw more people into identification with the system. The events of 1989–90, however, threw the NDPD into great confusion. It's long-serving chairman, Heinrich Homann, resigned from his post in November 1989 and was expelled from the party in December. His successor, Günter Hartmann, lasted only until January 1990, when he was voted out in favour of Wolfgang Gläser. Gläser resigned shortly afterwards, to be replaced by Wolfgang Rauls on Feb. 11, 1990. The party was torn between its record of complicity in the old regime and its potential role as a mobiliser of the nationalist right. On this latter ground it competed with other groups emerging in the GDR, for instance, the German Social Union (DSU). In the March 1990 elections, when it failed in its attempt to ally itself with the League of Free Democrats (BFD), the NDPD performed abysmally (0.4 per cent of the vote and only two seats). Thereupon it decided to merge with the Liberal Democratic Party (LDP), and thus made its way indirectly into the Free Democratic Party (FDP) in August 1990.

Programme. The party programme of 1987 placed the NDPD in the tradition of "nationally-minded petty bourgeois democratic forces" and declared the aim of the party to be "to open up the national question as a class and power question . . . so that the citizens of our country can be conscious of their national identity in and with our republic". By the end of 1989 the NDPD favoured democracy, a market economy and German unification.

Affiliations. Democratic Block (to December 1989).

New Forum
Neues Forum (NF)

Address. Rosa-Luxemburg-Strasse 19, O-1020 Berlin.

Telephone. (0037 2) 806425.

Foundation. September 1989.

Membership. 100,000 (March 1990).

Leadership. Bärbel Bohley, Rolf Heinrich, Sebastian Pflugbeil, Jens Reich, Hans-Jochen Tschiche (founders).

History. Founded in September 1989 and issuing in October a declaration signed by over 200,000 people, New Forum came to be the first major opposition group to make an impact in the GDR. It was not conceived as a political party, but literally as a "forum" for open discussion. It began with an emphasis on socialist and humanitarian values and environmental concerns. It also concerned itself with the necessity for far-reaching economic reform in the GDR; in late November 1989 it held an international economics conference in East Berlin, where matters of currency reform, price subsidies, social ownership, and foreign trade were discussed fully. NF operated at this stage within the context of a GDR still independent in the future.

By January 1990 NF had reached a membership estimated at 150,000 and was publishing its own weekly newspaper, *Die Andere* (The Other One), but it was already falling behind in the political contest. The loose amalgamation found itself competing electorally with new parties linked explicitly with West German counterparts, and falling foul of internal disputes. The issues of German unity and the free market economy forced several of NF's leading figures to renounce the group's new policy. In the elections of March 1990 NF collaborated with Democracy Now and the Peace and Human Rights Initiative in the Alliance 90, but they only reached 2.9 per cent of the vote and 12 seats.

Alliance 90 continued to stand in subsequent elections, with better results. NF itself stood separately in the *Landtag* election in Mecklenburg-West Pomerania in October 1990, but achieved only 2.9 per cent of the vote and split the vote with Alliance 90. NF's loose membership was also falling away rapidly.

Organization. New Forum decided not to become a political party, but to remain a "citizens' movement with a political programme".

Programme. New Forum was principally concerned with humanitarian issues and the democratization of the GDR. From sections of the movement came calls for the re-establishment of the east German *Länder*, for German unity, and for a market economy. Questions of social justice and the environment were very much to the fore.

Affiliations. Alliance 90 (from February 1990).

Party of Central German National Democrats
Partei der Mitteldeutschen Nationaldemokraten

One of several small ultra-right parties reported to be active in east Germany in 1990. The name of the party hints at its affinity to the west German neo-Nazi National Democratic Party of Germany (NPD), and also at the refusal of the extreme right to accept the loss of Germany's eastern territories after 1945. "Central Germany" in this context means the territory of the former GDR.

Party of Democratic Socialism
Partei des Demokratischen Sozialismus (PDS)

Contact name. Wolfgang Gehrcke (g.s.)

Address. Kleine Alexanderstrasse 28, O-1020 Berlin.

GERMANY

Telephone. (0037 2) 2824155; *Fax*. (0037 2) 2071317; *Telex*. 069 112 511.

Foundation. Originally as SED 1946. Renamed SED-PDS December 1989. Renamed PDS February 1990.

Membership. 200,000 (in east Germany); 1,000 (in west Germany).

Leadership. Gregor Gysi (ch.); André Brie (dep. ch.); Marlies Deneke (dep. ch.); Wolfgang Pohl (dep. ch.); Wolfgang Gehrcke (g.s.); Hans Modrow (hon. ch.)

History. The PDS is since Feb. 4, 1990, the successor to the previous ruling party of the GDR. It is a smaller and much altered version. The Socialist Unity Party of Germany (SED) was the Marxist-Leninist political party which ruled the GDR from its inception until the revolutionary changes of 1989–90. It was founded in April 1946 in the Soviet sector of Berlin as an amalgamation of the Communist Party (KPD) and the Social Democratic Party (SPD), and soon came to pursue a Stalinist line. It was led first by Walter Ulbricht and then from 1971 by Erich Honecker.

The SED permeated all facets of life in the GDR, either directly or indirectly, and party adherence became a prerequisite for career advancement in many fields. The party grew to a maximum membership (including candidate members) of 2.3 million. The leading role of the party was enshrined in the constitution of the GDR, and in practice the SED was the decisive organ of government in the state.

By October 1989 the crisis in the GDR was evident to many members of the SED, including some *Politbüro* members. Led by Egon Krenz and Günter Schabowski, they dismissed Honecker. However, even with major concessions, the new leadership of Krenz was unable to halt the challenge to the party. The political suppression, the personal corruption, and the evidence of complete economic mismanagement made it impossible for the SED to continue as before. Krenz was abandoned in December 1989, and the upper echelons and the structures of the old party were swept aside.

A provisional party committee of 100 members was led by the new chairman, Gregor Gysi, who made it his purpose to regenerate the party as the "Party of Democratic Socialism" (SED-PDS, then PDS). Meanwhile, however, the membership base had halved and the sole remaining PDS figure with power, prime minister Hans Modrow, was being moved further and further into coalition agreements and the prospect of German unity. Proposals were made on several occasions to dissolve the party entirely, but in the event, Gysi and Modrow managed to salvage something in the March elections. With 16.4 per cent of the vote and 66 seats, the PDS emerged as the third largest party after the Christian Democratic Union (CDU) and the SPD. It did so on the votes of those loyal to a separate GDR and fearful of a sell-out of its perceived social and socialist achievements. The PDS's stronghold was East Berlin, where it came second to the SPD.

The election result did not mean the end of the PDS, but it did mean the end of its power. Cast into opposition, it failed to find any other party willing to co-operate with it. Attempts were made in 1990 to extend the organization into west Germany, but with scarcely any success. In the *Bundestag* election of December 1990 the PDS vote fell to 9.9 per cent in east Germany, meaning only 2.4 per cent in Germany as a whole. Seventeen PDS members entered the parliament, including Gregor Gysi, who was re-elected chairman in January 1991. However, at that party congress, reconvened in June, internal party disputes raged between an orthodox majority and a radical reformist minority led by presidium members Rainer Börner and Helga Adler. Gysi appealed for dialogue, and made it clear that he was prepared to resign if harmony were not achieved.

The PDS has many problems. Its membership decline is continuing, albeit at a slower rate; that membership is elderly (48 per cent of pensionable age, 9 per cent under 30 years), and far too heterogenous for easy compromise; little progress has been made in west Germany, even with the formerly SED-sponsored German Communist Party (DKP); and there is evidence of great discontent amongst ordinary party members with the party leadership and *Bundestag* members. These last are petitioning the constitutional court for "fraction" not, as at present, "group" status. The former carries political and financial advantages.

The court is also to decide on the PDS's vast financial and property legacy from the SED. In the autumn of 1990 it was revealed that some high-placed PDS members had attempted to spirit large amounts of PDS funds out of the country. In March 1991 the PDS asked for a ruling on whether it could keep 20 per cent of former SED property, disposing of the remainder for social purposes. In June the Trustee Agency (*Treuhandanstalt*) froze the PDS's assets.

Organization. Party congress elects leadership and approves programme.

Programme. Humane socialism in a market economy (although dispute within the party about the latter). Wide-ranging structural help for the new federal states.

Affiliations. PDS candidates often campaign together with the Left List (*Linke Liste*).

Peace and Human Rights Initiative
Initiative Frieden und Menschenrechte (IFM)

Address. Friedrichstrasse 165, O-1080 Berlin.

Telephone. (0037 2) 291190.

Foundation. January 1986.

Leadership. Wolfgang Templin (spokesman); Gerd Poppe (minister without portfolio in Modrow government).

History. An early opposition group, founded by Templin, Poppe and Bärbel Bohley, the IFM derived from the unofficial peace movement of the early 1980s. During the late 1980s it operated illegally and therefore without clear organization, membership or spokespersons. From June 1986 it published the monthly periodical *Grenzfall* ("border incident"). In 1988 five IFM activists, including Bohley and Templin, were expelled from the GDR, later to return after protest. Before the "*Wende*" (turning point) IFM comprised only about 30 people, who were then involved in founding other new citizens' movements (Bohley and New Forum, for instance). From the winter of 1989–90 IFM itself grew and formed regional groups and project groups throughout the GDR. A committee was elected in February 1990.

Poppe, Templin and eight other IFM representatives participated in the Round Table discussions from December 1989 to March 1990. In February 1990 the IFM joined New Forum and Democracy Now in the Alliance 90. Poppe was a member of the Modrow government from February to March 1990, and is now the sole IFM representative in the *Bundestag*.

Organization. IFM has an elected committee, but it has throughout its history endeavoured to avoid all hierarchical forms of organization. Since January 1991 IFM has been collaborating organizationally with Democracy Now (DJ) and they publish jointly *Bündnis 2000*.

Programme. Anti-authoritarian, anti-militarist and pro-disarmament. Anxious to maintain the social achievements of the GDR.

Affiliations. Alliance 90 (from February 1990).

People's Union
Volksunion

One of the 12 groups which formed the German Social Union in January 1990.

Progressive People's Party
Fortschrittliche Volkspartei (FVP)

Foundation. December 1989.

Membership. 200 (December 1989).

Leadership. Bernhard Becher (acting spokesman).

History. One of the 12 groups which formed the German Social Union in January 1990.

Programme. The FVP's main objective was an electoral alliance of all forces in the GDR which rejected a renewed attempt at socialism. It advocated German unity and a market economy.

The Republicans
Die Republikaner (REPs)

Contact name. Franz Schönhuber (ch.)

Address. Sandstrasse 41, D-8000 Munich 2.

Foundation. 1983.

Membership. 25,000 (in west Germany).

Leadership. Franz Schönhuber (ch. intermittently since 1985).

History. The Republicans are a party of the extreme right, often accused of neo-Nazism. They originated in west Germany and scored there some significant electoral successes in

1989: 7.5 per cent of the vote in West Berlin, and 7.1 per cent in the Federal Republic as a whole in the elections to the European parliament. In Bavaria and Baden-Württemberg their advance was even more spectacular, causing fears in Germany and elsewhere of a revival of the extreme right.

The Republicans' appeal was eclipsed by the events of 1989–90 and, partly because their populist chairman Franz Schönhuber was refused entry to the GDR, their hopes of exploiting the situation were dashed. In the December 1990 election to the new *Bundestag* the Republicans' vote was 2.3 per cent in west Germany and even less (1.3 per cent) in east Germany. In the Berlin elections on the same day their vote fell back sharply in west Berlin to 3.7 per cent and they scored only 1.9 per cent in the eastern part of the city. However, with the growing social discontent and radical rightist activity of 1991, the Republicans are trying to assert a presence in the former GDR. They were reported to be organized in Dresden by June 1991, as was a breakaway group calling itself the German Alternative.

Programme. Ultra-nationalist aspirations of recovering Germany's lost territories and encouraging foreign workers to leave Germany.

Social Civic Union
Soziale Bürgerliche Union

One of the 12 groups which formed the German Social Union in January 1990.

Social Democratic Party of Germany
Sozialdemokratische Partei Deutschlands (SPD)

Contact name. Karlheinz Blessing (g.s.)

Address. Ollenhauerstrasse 1, D-5300 Bonn 1.
(Berlin) Rungestrasse 3–6, O-1020 Berlin.

Telephone. (0228) 5321; *Telex* 886306. Berlin: *Telephone.* (0037 2) 2791536.

Foundation. 1875. Banned 1933–45. Re-founded 1945. In Soviet occupation zone merged with KPD 1946 to form SED. In GDR re-founded as SDP October 1989. Renamed SPD January 1990. United with west German SPD September 1990.

Membership. 943,000 (including 22–30,000 in east Germany).

Leadership. Björn Engholm (ch.); Herta Däubler-Gmelin (dep. ch.); Oskar Lafontaine (dep. ch.); Johannes Rau (dep. ch.); Wolfgang Thierse (dep. ch.); Karlheinz Blessing (g.s.); Willy Brandt (hon. ch.)
Former GDR leadership: Ibrahim Böhme (sec. 1989–90; ch. 1990); Markus Meckel (dep. ch. 1990; acting ch. 1990); Wolfgang Thierse (ch. 1990).

History. The original SPD was founded in Gotha in 1875 and adopted a Marxist programme in Erfurt in 1891. By the eve of World War I it was the largest party and had the largest parliamentary fraction in Germany. It survived various splits, only to be banned by the Nazis in 1933. It was re-founded in the Soviet occupation zone in 1945, but was forced to merge with the Communist Party (KPD) in 1946 to form the Socialist Unity Party of Germany (SED). In the Federal Republic the SPD continued, to become one of the major parties of West German politics.

The new form of the SPD in the GDR was founded (originally as the SDP) at Schwante, north-west of Berlin, on Oct. 7, 1989. At this stage it was an illegal organization. The 43 people originally involved had by the end of January 1990 become a membership of 45–50,000. At the party's first national delegates' conference in January 1990 it was decided to change the name from SDP to SPD in order to recognize its commitment to German unity and to facilitate links with the SPD in the Federal Republic. Willy Brandt, honorary chairman of the west German SPD, was asked to assume the same position in the GDR party. He attended an emotional meeting in Gotha early in 1990.

The initial leader of the SPD in the GDR was Ibrahim Böhme. He took the SPD into the March 1990 elections, only to be badly disappointed with 21.9 per cent of the vote and 88 seats. Later that month Böhme fell victim to accusations of collaboration with the *Stasi* (state security). He denied these, but then resigned on grounds of ill health, with the announced intent of clearing his name. Despite several attempts to make a comeback, even after German unification, he failed to free himself entirely of the allegations.

Böhme was succeeded in a provisional capacity by Markus Meckel, who was appointed Foreign Minister in the de Maizière cabinet. The SPD, drawn into the coalition despite its reservations about the German Social Union's (DSU) presence, also furnished five other ministers, including the Minister of Finance, Walter Romberg, who negotiated the treaty on economic and currency union. With Meckel and Romberg in such crucial posts, the SPD might have been expected to make a strong mark on the terms of economic and political union, but their freedom of manoeuvre was much restricted. In August, de Maizière sacked Romberg and drove the SPD out of the coalition. De Maizière himself took over foreign affairs from Meckel.

In June 1990 Wolfgang Thierse was unexpectedly elected the new chairman of the SPD. When the party united with its west German counterpart in September, Thierse became a deputy chairman. He was confirmed in this post at the SPD congress in May 1991.

In the former GDR the SPD has so far suffered at the hands of a buoyant Christian Democratic Union (CDU) and the challenge on the left of the Party of Democratic Socialism (PDS). In December 1990 the SPD could only muster 23.6 per cent of the vote in east Germany, compared to 35.9 per cent in the west. The party's organization in the GDR has proved relatively weak, with a membership well down on its initial promise. After the trials of 1990, however, the west German SPD appears to recovering and this may well have its impact on east Germany.

Organization. The SPD has a large network of local branches. The party congress every two years elects an executive committee, which then elects a presidium.

Programme. The SDP/SPD in the GDR represented a revitalization of social democratic ideals. They are still embodied in the Godesberg programme of the west German SPD, adopted in 1959. According to this, "the Social Democratic Party of Germany is the party of the freedom of the spirit. It is a community of people from different directions of belief and thought". The SPD aims for social justice within a free but properly regulated market economy.

Affiliations. Socialist International; Confederation of Socialist Parties of the European Community.

Socialist Unity Party of Germany
Sozialistische Einheitspartei Deutschlands (SED)

The former communist ruling party of the GDR. *See* Party of Democratic Socialism (PDS).

Spartacist Workers' Party of Germany
Spartakist-Arbeiterpartei Deutschlands (SpAD)

One of several small parties of the left which tried to retrieve socialism from the legacy of the Socialist Unity Party (SED). The SpAD stood in the election of March 1990 and won 2,417 votes.

United Left
Vereinigte Linke (VL)

Contact name. Erhard Weinholz (press spokesman).

Address. Friedrichstrasse 165, O-1080 Berlin.

Telephone. (0037 2) 2202091.

Foundation. October 1989.

Membership. 1,500–2,000 (January 1990); 300–500 (March 1990).

Leadership. Marion Seelig, Thomas Klein (spokespersons).

History. The VL is a socialist group formed in opposition to the old GDR regime. It had various origins, including the groups "Votes against" (*Gegenstimmen*) and "Church from below" (*Kirche von unten*), and the environmental library at the Zion church in East Berlin and the Green "Ark Network", both of which had been harassed by the security forces. In its "Böhlen manifesto" of September 1989 it called for a "left, socialist alternative". From December 1989 the VL was represented at the Round Table debates. In January it temporarily joined an abortive electoral alliance with, among others, the Social Democratic Party, Democratic Departure (DA) and New Forum, and explored links with the Greens and the Independent Women's Association (UFV), but in the following month it switched to a pact with the Carnations, who had previously been a group within VL. In the March election this Action Alliance United Left received 20,340 votes.

The VL subsequently shrank in importance but it did not disappear. In December 1990 Jutta Braband of the VL was elected to the *Bundestag*, but on the Left List/PDS.

Programme. The original aim of the VL was to find a third, socialist path between capitalism and the command socialist economy of the old GDR.

Affiliations. Action Alliance United Left (from February 1990).

GERMANY

Unity Now
Einheit Jetzt

One of several small parties which emerged in early 1990 to promote German unity. It gained only 2,396 votes (0.02 per cent) in March.

Young Union
Junge Union (JU)

One of the 12 groups which formed the German Social Union in January 1990.

Note: Many other small groups and parties emerged in the (former) GDR in the course of 1989–91, but there is little or no information about them and they are not of any individual political significance. Names reported include: Association of Saxon Werewolves*, Combat Sport Group Peipe*, European House Party, German People's Party, Liberal-Socialist People's Party, National Resistance of Germany*, Party of the Centre, Potentialist People's Party, Progressive New Party, and SS-East*. Those marked with an asterisk are of the extreme right.

HUNGARY

Nigel Swain

In the years that followed the 1956 uprising against stalinism, Hungary gained a reputation as the crucible of reform in Eastern Europe. Living standards improved steadily and, after János Kádár (who came to power with the Soviet tanks) had consolidated his personal power in the early 1960s, the stage was set for a series of reforms which culminated in the market socialist New Economic Mechanism of 1968. In the two-and-a-half decades between roughly 1963 and 1988 Kádár successfully achieved a dual compromise with the Soviet Union on the one hand and the Hungarian population on the other. The essence of the Soviet compromise was that Kádár would remain loyal in foreign policy — to the extent of joining the invasion of Czechoslovakia in 1968 — in return for leeway in domestic and especially economic reform. The essence of Kádár's "social compact" with the Hungarian people was that the regime should provide constantly improving living standards in a relaxed ideological climate in return for acceptance of the legitimacy of the Hungarian Socialist Workers' Party (HSWP) regime. Although in the wake of the Czechoslovak invasion neither the economic nor political reforms were as radical as originally conceived, the consumerist compromise continued, and with it Kádár's popularity.

By the mid-1980s, however, both compromises were breaking down. With the advent of Gorbachev, no fine line had to be trod between what was acceptable to the Soviet Union and what was not. More important, living standards had stopped increasing at the end of the 1970s, and the population was tiring of promises that recovery would begin "next year". Public opinion surveys revealed significant increases in the numbers of people who felt that the government was unable to resolve the country's economic problems; economists advised more radical reform including changes in property relations; dissident groups increased in self-confidence; and Kádár proved incapable of going beyond the parameters of his original compromises. From 1985 onwards, when the XIIIth HSWP Congress promised a return to economic growth inconsistent with the realities of Hungary's parlous economic situation, this questioning of government confidence escalated, slowly at first, into a legitimation and, finally, political crisis.

Central moments in the burgeoning crisis were the following. In 1985, at a two-and-a-half day political gathering at Monor in 1985, the "populist" and "urban" (the self-styled "democratic opposition") groupings within the dissident movement came together for the first time. In 1987, four significant events took place. First, radical economists published a document, written the previous year, entitled *Turnabout and Reform*, which, for the first time, brought into the public domain the parlous state of the economy and radical proposals to deal with it. Second, in the summer of 1987 the "urban", "democratic opposition", which had been producing *samizdat* since the mid-1970s (and on a regular basis since 1980) produced a special issue of its magazine *Beszélő* entitled the "Social Contract", calling for political pluralism and a free press. Third, on Sept. 27, the Hungarian Democratic Forum (HDF) was founded in the village of Lakitelek at a gathering attended by writers and critics of the "populist" persuasion and by reform communists such as Imre Pozsgay, with whom many of the former had close links. Finally, the HSWP announced that a special Party Conference would be held in May 1988 to consider how to handle the situation it was reluctant to call a crisis.

In 1988, the pace of political events accelerated. In the first half of the year a series of dissident meetings was held at the Jurta Theatre which, as a Small Co-operative, was independent of government control. In March the "democratic opposition" and other groups established the Network of Free Initiatives, while a younger generation of oppositionists founded the Alliance of Young Democrats (FIDESZ). In April, four prominent reform-minded intellectuals were expelled from the party for attending the Jurta and similar meetings; but at the HSWP special Party Conference in May, it was the hard-liners who were defeated. Kádár was replaced as First Secretary, and a new generation of cadres, who had lived their adult lives under actually existing socialism, came into the leadership.

After a quiet summer, opposition activity began again in the autumn of 1988. The HDF held a second meeting in Lakitelek in September and the Alliance of Free Democrats (AFD) was established as a party in November out of most of the organizations in the Network of Free Initiatives. The Independent Smallholder Party (ISP) re-founded itself, also in November, and Hungary's Social Democratic Party (HSDP) followed suit in January 1989. By February 1989, the HSWP had accepted that Hungary would become a multi-party democracy; in March the opposition groups and parties established an Opposition Round Table and the Christian Democratic People's Party (CDPP) was founded; and in June, as its reformist wing gained in strength, the HSWP agreed to negotiations with the Opposition Round Table on the transformation of the political system. While these talks were under way, on Sept. 11, the government made its historic decision to allow East German "tourists" to cross the border into Austria, so triggering the fall of the Berlin Wall and the other Eastern European regimes.

On Sept. 18, 1989 the talks concluded with an agreement on certain "cardinal laws", such as amending the constitution, establishing a Constitutional Court, and introducing an electoral law to clarify the status of political parties. The AFD and FIDESZ refused to sign the agreement, however, because they rejected the proposal that the direct election of a new President by popular ballot should precede parliamentary elections, and because they were unhappy that the HSWP had not committed itself to disbanding the workers' militia, withdrawing from workplaces and rendering an account of its property. While the HSWP held an extraordinary XIVth Party Congress in October, at which the reformists won the day and the party's name was changed to the Hungarian Socialist Party (HSP), the AFD and FIDESZ collected sufficient signatures to force a referendum on the disputed elements in the September agreement.

Although many viewed the referendum as a distraction since, in the interim (on Oct. 23, 1989) Hungary had become a Republic (as opposed to a People's Republic) and all reference to the "leading role" of the HSWP had been removed from the constitution, it served the purpose of highlighting, at an early date, the differences of opinion within the opposition. While the two new liberal parties (the AFD and FIDESZ), together with the re-founded ISP and HSDP opposed the government, the new nationalist-christian HDF advised its members to abstain. To the HDF's chagrin, however, turnout for the referendum on Nov. 26 exceeded 50 per cent, and the anti-government view narrowly won the day.

Following the referendum, politics changed radically. The AFD gained mass popular support, something it had not thought possible a year earlier. The HDF momentarily lost prestige and accepted that it would have radically to distance itself from the HSP, despite the fact that until then an HDF-dominated parliament and a reform HSP socialist President in the person of Imre Pozsgay had seemed the most probable political outcome. The HSP went into decline, despite a short-term increase in popularity immediately after its change of name. The referendum had proved that it could be defeated; and, when socialist regimes were collapsing around it, its justifiable claim to be truly reformist cut little ice. These radical changes in support for the old and the new parties can be seen in Table 1.

Parliamentary elections finally took place in two rounds in March and April, 1990. As indicated in Table 2, no party gained an absolute majority, but the HDF had most seats and, after a month of negotiating, it formed a coalition government with the two other parties of a nationalist-christian orientation, the ISP and CDPP. The government's first task was further to amend the constitution, and in order to facilitate this the AFD and HDF entered into a pact by which the former would not vote against key measures requiring a 75 per cent majority, provided the latter acceded to having the President appointed by parliament and supporting Árpád Göncz — a member of the AFD — as candidate. Constitutional changes in the summer of 1990 abolished the office of the President of the Council of Ministers, replacing it with a Prime Minister with increased powers, and removed reference in the constitution to "the realization of the values of democratic socialism". Having the President appointed by parliament also required a constitutional amendment, and this was delayed by a last-ditch referendum sponsored by supporters of a directly elected President. Göncz was finally appointed President of the Republic on Aug. 3, 1990.

Despite commitments to rapid privatization, the government's first 100 days achieved little, other than establishing a framework for local elections, and causing a furore by appearing to give churches a free hand for religious education in schools. Elections to the new local authorities took place in two rounds in September and October. Turnout was lower than in the parliamentary elections of the spring: 40.18 per cent in the first round, 28.94 per cent in the second. Forty-two of the 65 registered parties ran candidates, as did 647 social organizations and 12 national minorities; and there were also many more jointly sponsored candidates. The coalition government was severely punished for its inertia in the summer, as Tables 3–5 indicate. In the smaller villages, the winners were the independents, many of whom had previously held office in the HSWP-dominated local government-party structure. In the larger communities, the coalition parties won a majority of seats in only one Budapest district and in only five of Hungary's 19 counties. They fared even worse in the county towns. Only in Kecskemét did the government parties win a clear victory. The local elections constituted a defeat for two of the three coalition parties (the HDF and the ISP — the CDPP maintained its share of the vote). On the other hand, they represented a considerable victory for FIDESZ who had, in Viktor Orbán, a leader of charisma. The behaviour of FIDESZ after the election, however, led some to suspect that popularity and power, rather than the implementation of a political programme, were the party's overriding goals. Despite entering the elections in many towns, including Budapest, in an apparent coalition with the AFD, FIDESZ refused to participate in government after the elections in Budapest and some other towns.

In October 1990, the strength of the political institutions created during the "peaceful revolution" was put to the test by the direct action of a group of workers who, although neither numerous nor particularly underprivileged, manifestly enjoyed popular support. After months of postponing petrol price increases, the government announced an average 65 per cent rise from midnight on Thursday, Oct. 25. Spontaneously, throughout the country, communicating by means of short-wave radio, lorry and taxi drivers blockaded towns, bridges, and border crossings during the course of the Thursday–Friday night.

The blockade lasted until the following Sunday evening. At first, the government stood firm, but the situation then turned to stalemate as the Budapest police chief made it clear he would not use force against the crowds, and the barricades did not come down despite apparent agreement on the Saturday night. Negotiations on the Sunday, broadcast in their entirety live on television, were successful however: the government gave in, withdrawing the price rise until such time as petrol prices were fully liberalized and hence outside the political domain.

Public opinion surveys taken immediately after the negotiations revealed high levels of support for the drivers and criticism of the government, especially for the ministers who had taken the initial tough line. The regime's dramatic decline in popularity after its first six months is further reflected in a public opinion survey taken in November 1990, as indicated in Table 6. After only six months in office, the first democratically elected government in 40 years inspired rather less confidence than the previous undemocratic government that had led Hungary to political crisis and the highest *per capita* foreign debt in Eastern Europe.

Following the taxi blockade, two new political organizations — Imre Pozsgay's Citizens' Movement for the Republic (Pozsgay resigned from the Socialist Party in November) and the Hungarian Centre Alliance — were founded in an attempt to tap the mass of non-voters who had expressed their dissatisfaction with the political choice by supporting the taxi-blockade; but neither have become significant forces. In the first half of 1991, the coalition came increasingly under strain as the ISP insisted on the payment of reparations to those who had lost property, especially land, under the previous regime. A compromise solution, already passed by parliament, was ruled unconstitutional in May on the grounds that land and other forms of property were treated differently. Voices from the ISP subsequently called for full compensation for all, while the HDF, mindful of the needs to attract foreign investors and manage an already sizeable national debt, insisted that this was economically unacceptable.

Although all the major players in Hungarian multi-party politics had been founded or re-founded by April 1989, party formation continued at a mushrooming rate until the parliamentary elections, a process facilitated by the government generously allocating initial party and electoral funds and awarding time slots for radio and television party political broadcasts. Nevertheless, the electoral system which had emerged from the Opposition Round Table negotiations and the subsequent electoral law (an amalgam of first-past-the-post and proportional representation) contained five hurdles to prevent minor parties entering parliament. First, parties had to be registered at the Court of Registration. Second, candidates had to be supported by the signatures of 750 voters within the constituency. Third, in order to figure on any regional (county or Budapest) list (the first proportional representation element in the electoral system), the party had to have candidates in 25 per cent, or at least two, of the constituencies of the region. Fourth, in order to qualify for candidates on the national list (the second proportional representation element in the electoral system), parties had to have candidates on at least seven of the 20 (19 county and Budapest) regional lists. Fifth, candidates elected on either of the lists could only enter parliament if the party's share of the total list vote exceeded 4 per cent. Thus, minor parties might get popular local candidates elected as one of the 176 individually elected constituency members, but they would be unable to supplement them with any of the 152 proportionally allocated list seats unless the 4 per cent barrier were crossed.

These hurdles worked as intended. Although 65 parties were registered at the ime of the parliamentary elections (and over 100 had announced their formation), only 30 organizations (not all registered as parties) succeeded in fielding candidates, only 19 managed to get on one or other of the regional lists, only 12 got onto the national list, and only six crossed the 4 per cent threshold. Since the parliamentary elections, politics has stablized around the six parties in parliament. No new parties entered the local elections, and the majority of the parties outside parliament have faded away, with the exception of the strongly ideological parties of the right and left, and of two of the earliest re-founded parties (the HSDP and the Hungarian People's Party, HPP), both of which took part in the Opposition Round Table negotiations. The disappearance of the extra-parliamentary parties was accelerated by the fact that subsequent state funding has been based on performance in the parliamentary elections. However, since parties are under no obligation to register their dissolution, their names have remained on the register. In many cases the addresses and names in the register give a false impression of solidity; the parties are ethereal in the extreme.

The six parties in parliament can be split into three broad ideological groups: the nationalist-christian persuasion, represented by the coalition government of the HDF, with its origins in the "populist" dissidents, the ISP and the CDPP, both re-founded parties active in the 1940s; the liberal, social-liberal persuasion of the AFD and FIDESZ; and social democracy, represented by the HSP. All six parties support a variant of the "social market economy", and all favour increasing the profile of the Hungarian cultural heritage. They disagree only on the degree of emphasis to accord to that heritage, on priorities in social policy, on the pace of privatization, and on the desirable degree of state intervention in the economy. Most important, they differ on the relative importance given to individual liberties versus collective obligations to family, Church and nation.

Table 1: Support for major parties 1989–90 (Percentage of those who stated which party they would vote for, not of those asked)

Party	Jan	Mar	May	Jun	Jul	Aug	Sept	Oct	Oct-Nov	Nov	Dec	Jan	Mar
HDF	11	17	13	13	14	18	24	20	27	22	23	21	21
AFD	7	12	6	5	3	6	6	7	9	8	14	18	20
ISP	10	10	12	6	11	9	7	6	5	9	12	16	16
HSP	–	–	–	–	–	–	–	35	25	16	16	11	10
HSWP	23	34	32	29	37	32	23	–	6	7	5	4	–
AYD	11	9	16	9	7	7	11	10	8	13	8	7	7
CDPP	–	–	–	5	2	4	4	3	5	4	3	3	5
HSDP	6	11	12	12	10	8	8	6	4	8	6	5	6
HPP*	1	8	5	5	4	3	3	4	2	3	4	2	–

*Peter Veres Association in January 1989.
Source: *HangSúly*, Vol. 1, No. 1, p. 19; No. 4, p. 19; No. 5, p. 18; No. 6–7, p. 35; No. 8–9, p. 35; No. 10, p. 20; *Magyar Nemzet*, 22/11/89, 17/2/90, 14/3/90.

Table 2: Parliamentary elections March–April 1990 (share of vote on Regional List, per cent, and number of seats won)

Party	Regional List	Seats
Hungarian Democratic Forum (HDF)	24.73	165
Alliance of Free Democrats (AFD)	21.39	91
Independent Smallholders (ISP)	11.73	44
Hungarian Socialist Party (HSP)	10.89	32
Alliance of Young Democrats (AYD)	8.95	22
Christian Democratic People's Party (CDPP)	6.46	21
Hungarian Socialist Workers Party (HSWP)	3.68	
Hungary's Social Democratic Party (HSDP)	3.55	
Agrarian Alliance	3.13	1
Entrepreneurs' Party	1.89	
Patriotic Electoral Coalition	1.87	
Hungarian People's Party (HPP)	0.75	
Hungary's Green Party	0.36	
National Smallholders Party	0.20	
Somogy Christian Coalition	0.12	
Hungary's Co-operative and Agrarian Party	0.10	
Independent Hungarian Democratic Party	0.06	
Freedom Party	0.06	
Hungarian Independence Party	0.04	
Alliance for the Village and Countryside		1
Independent		6
Jointly sponsored		3

Source: *Magyar Közlöny* (Hungary's official gazette), 1990, No. 25.

HUNGARY

Table 3: Local Authority elections in 2926 settlements of less than 10,000 (per cent)

	Mayors	"Small list"
Independent	82.9	71.2
ISP	3.7	6.2
HDF	2.3	4.3
AFD	1.9	4.0
CDPP	1.8	2.8
Agrarian Alliance	–	1.3
HSP	–	1.1

Source: *Magyar Közlöny* (Hungary's official gazette), 1990, No. 44.

Table 4: Local Authority elections in 141 settlements of over 10,000 (per cent)

	Individual candidates	List
AFD	17.1	20.7
AFD-AYD joint	17.0	5.0
Independent	14.9	–
HDF	12.0	18.3
AYD	8.4	15.2
ISP	6.0	7.7
CDPP	5.7	8.0
HSP	2.6	10.1
HDF-CDPP joint	2.5	2.5
HDF-ISP-CDPP joint	2.4	2.2
HDF-ISP joint	2.1	–
HSWP	–	–

Source: *Magyar Közlöny* (Hungary's official gazette), 1990, No. 44.

Table 5: Election for Budapest Assembly (per cent)

AFD	34.68
HDF	27.35
AYD	18.16
HSP	7.25
CDPP	4.95
HSWP	3.61
ISP	2.30
Alliance[1]	0.72
Hungary's Social Democratic Party	0.56
National Alliance[2]	0.41

[1]Alliance of Town Defence and Citizen Organizations.
[2]National Alliance of Small Industrialists.
Source: Magyar Közlöny (Hungary's official gazette), 1990, No. 44.

Table 6: Answers to the question: "To what extent do you think the current Hungarian government is directing the country in the right direction?" (per cent)

	November 1990	*November 1989*
"Completely"	6	8
"Mostly"	19	29
"A little"	54	52
"Not at all"	15	7

Source Adapted from Sándor Kurtán et al., *Magyarország Poltikai Evkönyve, 1991*, Budapest, 1991, pp. 639–40.

Directory of Parties

Agrarian Alliance
Agrárszövetség (ASZ)

Address. Budapest V, Arany János utca 10.

Fax. (1) 111 2663.

Foundation. Dec. 3, 1989.

Leadership. Tamás Nagy (pres.); Tibor Nagy-Husszein (dep. pres.)

History. The Alliance was formed out of a merger between the Agrarian Reform Circles Movement (established May 2, 1989) and the Association of Agrarian Reform Circles (established May 16, 1989) which emerged within the HSWP after it acknowledged the right to form party factions in February 1989. It received state support of 10 million forints in 1990, a further 6.6 million for the election, and 42.2 million in 1991 on the basis of its electoral result. It closed 1990 with a surplus of 23 million forints (approximately £168,000).

Although the Alliance did not receive sufficient votes to cross the 4 per cent threshold on the proportional representation part of the parliamentary elections, it figured on the regional and national lists and gained two seats, one in association with the Alliance for the Village and the Countryside. This joint candidate (Dr Wekler) subsequently joined the AFD.

Organization. National Committee, pres. and dep. pres.

Programme. The Alliance focuses on agricultural policy. Reflecting its origins in reform communism, it sees a future for co-operative agriculture, but co-operatives which are genuine owners. It radically opposes the ISP policy of returning land to its pre-collectivization owners. Nevertheless, it advocates returning 50 per cent of agricultural property to co-operative members. It also encourages foreign investment in agriculture and advocates the formation of an Agrarian Bank.

Alliance for the Village and the Countryside
Szövetség a Faluért, Vidékért

Founded in Pécs at the beginning of January 1990 as a continuation of the Village Alliance, it received state support of two million forints in 1990, with a further 100,000 forints specifically for the elections. It participated in the draw for party political broadcast slots, and fielded four candidates, two in Baranya county. Its joint candidate with the Agrarian Alliance was elected, although he subsequently joined the AFD. It closed 1990 with a financial surplus of 1.8 million forints (approximately £13,000). By early 1991 Sándor Kakas had taken over from the original president, Dr Ferenc Csefkó.

Alliance of Christian Democrats
Kereszténydemokraták Szövetsége

The Alliance was founded on Jan. 6, 1990. It received two million forints state support in 1990, with an additional 100,000 for the elections. It took part in the draw for party political broadcast radio and television slots and entered the election campaign as a member of the National Electoral Alliance. It fielded one candidate in the parliamentary elections, but its subsequent activities are unknown. The president is listed as Dr György Szakolczay.

Alliance of Free Democrats (AFD), Free Democrats
Szabad Demokraták Szövetsége (SZDSZ), Szabad Demokraták

Address. Budapest V, Mérleg u. 6.

Telephone. (1) 118 4788, 117 69121, 118 7733.

Foundation. Nov. 13, 1988.

Membership. 33,400 (May 1991).

Leadership. János Kis (pres.). Spokespersons: Gabriella Béki (party organization); Péter Hack, Miklós Hankó Faragó, Miklós Haraszti (press and youth policy); János Kis (foreign affairs); Bálint Magyar, Imre Mécs, Iván Pető (interparty links); László Rajk (cultural policy); Károly Attila Soós (economic policy); Ferenc Wekler (local government, state administration, police). Trade union and interest group policy is handled by László Makkai who does not have the status of spokesperson. Leader in parliament: Iván Pető.

History. Founded on Nov. 13, 1988 out of the majority of the organization which had established the Network of Free Initiatives the previous March. It represents an offshoot of the "urban" rather than "populist" strand in opposition thought (the "democratic opposition"), many of them lapsed marxists, who produced *samizdat* over the preceding one-and-a-half decades and established the unofficial Poor Support Fund. It was the first party to produce an elaborated programme, which is not surprising given the high proportion of economists, sociologists and lawyers in its membership. Indeed, in its first year, it thought of itself as a small party of intellectuals.

By the time of the parliamentary elections, however, as a result of the November 1989 referendum and the party's unearthing of the "Danube-gate" scandal (the continued tapping by the security services of the telephones of opposition party leaders) it had transformed itself into a party with mass support. It received seven million forints state support in 1989, 10 million in 1990 and a further 9.5 million forints for the elections. It fielded 169 candidates in the parliamentary elections and ended up with 91 members of parliament, on the basis of which it was awarded 146.1 million forints (approximately £1,000,000) for 1991. It closed 1990 with a surplus of 10,000,000 forints, thanks to some generous contributions from the German Free Democrats among others. It has also established its own company — Liberty Ltd — and is closely associated with the Foundation for a European Hungary and AB Beszélő kft. Although it was very much the victor of the local authority elections, its share of the vote did not increase as significantly as that of FIDESZ.

Organization. A delegate assembly of delegates from local organizations elects an 80-member National Council and an executive body made up of the spokespersons listed above.

Programme. The party is on the liberal wing of Hungarian politics, and encompasses two major and one minor strands of opinion. The latter is a small liberal-conservative tendency, represented by the philosopher and writer for the *Spectator* Gáspár Miklós Tamás. The two major strands of opinion within the party are the liberal and social-liberal, bordering on social-democratic views. The latter, as exemplified by Ottilia Solt, one of the founders of the Poor Support Fund in 1980, have been somewhat marginalized. Within the party generally, the question of whether members of parliament are delegates or representatives has raised its head. When Péter Tölgyessy (not an active dissident, but supremely influential in the Opposition Round Table negotiations) was replaced as leader of the party in parliament in the autumn of 1990, one of the criticisms levelled at him by the leadership was that he could not behave as a delegate. On the other hand, the leadership itself has been criticized for concluding the May 1990 pact with the HDF behind the backs of the members.

It was the first party with a programme for the "change of system", but much of it was anachronistic by the elections. Its replacement has been promised repeatedly, but was still unavailable in May 1991. The party puts forward a liberal variant of the "social market economy", minimal state intervention, low taxes, an independent central bank, religious freedom, and a health service provided in the main by private companies. On the other hand, it is committed to positive discrimination for ethnic minorities. Its major criticism of the HDF-led coalition is not so much that it is conservative, but that it is trying to return to an out-dated form of conservatism with a strong interventionist state, intolerant of views and behaviour inconsistent with its nationalist-christian, pro-family ideology. It criticizes the government both for intervening too much in, for example, the privatization process, for intervening incompetently when it does, and for endless procrastination.

The party initially opposed all reprivatization and restitution elements in privatization, but in February 1991 changed to a policy of token reparations in the form of vouchers for every Hungarian citizen, since everyone, not just property owners, had suffered under the old regime. This opened them to the accusation that they supported reparations for the torturers as well as the tortured.

Affiliations. It has observer status on the Liberal International and claims links with the socialist parties of Austria, France and Germany.

Alliance of Hungarian Political Prisoners
Magyar Politikai Foglyok Szövetsége (POFOSZ)

Address. Budapest XIV, Kolumbus utca 11.

Telephone. (1) 251 7999.

Leadership. Jenő Fónay (pres.)

The Alliance was founded on Feb. 19, 1989 as a group to defend the interests of former political prisoners. The acting president at the time of registration as a party was Árpád

Göncz, a member of the AFD and subsequent President of the Republic. It received eight million forints state support in 1989, 15 million in 1990 and a further 100,000 forints for the elections, which it entered as part of the National Electoral Alliance. It got no candidates onto the ballot however. Since the elections it has acted more in its original mould as a pressure group, pointing out that the emphasis in 1990 and 1991 on financial restitution for former owners is detracting from the moral suffering of those falsely imprisoned and the need to bring the wrongful imprisoners to justice.

Alliance of Hungarian Revolutionary Socialists, Hungarian Trotskyist Party
Magyar Forradalmi Szocialisták Szövetsége, Magyar Trockista Párt

Reported as having been founded on Oct. 11, 1989. No information is available about its activities or structure. Rumours suggest it has only two members and has already split into two wings.

Alliance of Nature and Society Conservers
Természet és Társadalomvédők Szövetsége

Founded on Jan. 6, 1990 with Dr Tibor Gánti as president of its co-ordinating body. It received two million forints state support in 1990 but has not filed accounts for the year. It managed to get two candidates onto the ballot, but none was elected, and one in Szabolcs-Szatmár-Bereg county received only 206 votes.

Alliance of the Poor and Defenceless
Szegények és Kiszolgáltatottak Szövetsége

The Alliance was registered as a party on Feb. 8, 1990. Nothing more is known of its structure or activities.

Catholic People's Party
Katolikus Néppárt

Founded on Dec. 21, 1989, claiming to be a continuation of the party of the same name established in 1895. Its president is listed as Dr Endre Varga. Its structure and subsequent activities are unknown.

Christian Democratic People's Party (CDPP)
Kereszténydemokrata Néppárt (KDNP)

Address. Budapest XII, Nagy Jenő u. 5.

Telephone. (1) 175 0333, 156 2897.

Foundation. March 17, 1989.

Membership. 15,300, May 1991.

Leadership. László Surján (pres.); Dr László Varga (vice-pres.); Dr Miklós Pálos, Dr Miklós Hasznos, Dr Géza Farkas, Dr Terézia Császár Szilágyiné (dep. pres.); Dr Tibor Füzessy (leader in parliament); Dr Nandor Rott (economic policy committee leader); Dr László Grigási (law and administration committee); Zsuzsa Dobrányi (foreign affairs); Gábor Balogh (social policy); Dr Péter Balász (health); Dr Péter Farkas (environment); Ferenc Inotai (security policy and defence); Dr Miklós Lukács (education policy); Sándor Tóth (press affairs); Gyula Pályi (energy).

History. The party is a continuation of the more progressive Barankovics branch of the Democratic People's Party, founded in October 1944 but not permitted by the allies to operate as a party until Sept. 25, 1945. In the 1947 election it achieved 16.4 per cent of the vote, the second highest share. The party leaders were forced into emigration in 1949. The immediate predecessor of the re-founded party was the Áron Márton Society formed on Dec. 10, 1988. The CDPP was the last of the six parties in parliament to be established, but made up the deficit and ran 105 candidates, winning 21 seats. It received four million forints (approximately £29,000) state support in 1989, a similar figure in 1990 plus 7.1 million forints for the elections. The party finished 1990 with an accumulated deficit of 3,696 forints (approximately £27). On the basis of its electoral performance it received 59.3 million forints (approximately £433,000) in 1991. Like the other major parties, it has a foundation and limited liability company closely associated with it — the Barankovics Foundation and Hunniapack Ltd.

Organization. Has a national committee with representatives from local organizations which appoints a 31-member executive committee and the presidium listed above.

Programme. It sees itself as an ideological, but not denominational party, representing the values of the judeo-christian world view. It sees moral values as more important than policies, and uses the designation "people's" party to show that it does not see itself as representing the interests of a single class. Its electoral programme included supporting private property, a peaceful transition, the development of a market, and a new political culture. Its economic programme placed great emphasis on the need to stop inflation. It also favoured the family wage, family taxation, and the defence of motherhood. It advocated a new family allowance system of 50 per cent of minimum wage for women to stay at home to look after children after the existing maternity grant. It also advocated the creation of more part-time employment opportunities for women, a christian environmental policy, and the permitting of churches to establish church schools. It proved stronger electorally in Budapest, the northern counties and transdanubia than on the Great Plain (which has a stronger Calvinist tradition).

Since the elections it has been the quietest of the coalition parties. Even the decision to bring forward discussion of the restitution of church property in the spring of 1991 does not appear to have been the result of party pressure within the coalition.

Affiliations. Links are claimed with the christian democratic parties of Austria and the Netherlands.

Democratic Pensioners' Party
Demokrata Nyugdíjasok Pártja

The party was registered on Feb. 9, 1990 in the provincial town of Eger. Its structure and subsequent activities are unknown.

Entrepreneurs' Party, Liberal Bourgeois Alliance
Vállalkozók Pártja, Liberális Polgári Szövetség

Address. Kecskemét, Május 1 tér 3, H-6000.

Telephone. (76) 29386. (76) 29473.

Foundation. Oct. 22, 1989.

Leadership. President — vacant; János Wolf (dep. pres., Kecskemét), Imre Oláh (dep. pres., Budapest); executive members: Dr Lajos Kupcsok (Tatabánya), Zoltán Kresz (Balatonföldvár), István Kruzlics (Hódmezővásárhely), Ferenc Heiner (Mándok), Csaba Csikós (Gödöllő).

History. Founded in Debrecen with the name Entrepreneurs' Party as an amalgamation of the Debrecen Democratic Club and the Kapuvár Union of Private Entrepreneurs, it participated in the draw for party political broadcast radio and TV slots and received 10 million forints state support in 1990, together with a further 4.3 million forints for the elections. Prior to the elections it stated that it hoped to win seven to eight seats, but in this it failed. Nevertheless, it got 63 candidates onto the ballot, sufficient to figure on most regional and the national lists, although it achieved only 1.89 per cent of the total vote. This qualified it for a further 9.8 million forint tranche of state support. At its second congress in June 1990 it voted to change its name to the Liberal Bourgeois Alliance and move its headquarters to Kecskemét. It closed 1990 with an 800,000 forint (approximately £6,000) surplus.

Programme. As the name suggests, it is a party of businessmen, in favour of free trade, aid for new small businesses, privatization (but at realistic prices) and lower taxes, especially on businesses. Like other Hungarian parties, it advocates giving support to Hungarians living abroad.

Ferenc Münnich Society, May 1st Society
Münnich Ferenc Társaság (MFT), Május 1 Társaság

Address: Budapest 11, Zsigmond tér 8.

Telephone. (1) 113 4647.

Membership. None disclosed in May 1991, 8–10,000 claimed in 1989.

Leadership. Ferenc Berényi (sec.)

History. The society was founded on Nov. 11, 1988 and registered as a party on Feb. 15, 1990. It received eight million forints state support in 1989, but none subsequently, although it did participate in the draw for party political broadcast radio and TV slots. It closed 1990 with a surplus of 3 million forints (approximately £22,000). In 1991 it changed its name to the May 1st Society.

Programme. In the political turmoil of 1989 the Society was the major representative of the stalinist old guard, with a membership made up of older HSWP members, many currently or previously employed in the police or members of the since disbanded Workers Militia. It insisted on interpreting 1956 as a counter-revolution and viewing capitalism as organically anti-democratic; but it distanced itself from the Workers' Marxist-Leninist Party, and it claimed to oppose stalinism and ultra left-wing factionalism.

FIDESZ, Alliance of Young Democrats
FIDESZ, Fiatal Demokraták Szövetsége

Contact. (UK) Orsolya Pál, Budapest, Hevesi Gyula út 57 I/9, H-1157; (USA) Csaba Dombovári, Budapest, I, utca 23, H-1172.

Address. Budapest VI, Lendvay utca. 28, H-1062.

Telephone. (1) 112 1095, 132 8372; *Fax.* (1) 131 9673.

Foundation. March 30, 1988.

Membership. 14,000 (May 1991).

Leadership. Committee: Andrea Bankós (party organization and internal party affairs); György B. Bencze (enterprise and economic policy); Péter Drahos (education); Gábor Fodor, Balázs Fürjes, Pál Gábor Lippai, Balázs Medgyesy (environment); Márton Módos (foreign affairs); László Ákos Németh (trade unions and interest groups); Zsolt Németh (minority affairs); Viktor Orbán, Tamás Tirts (local government affairs); József Vas. Leader in parliament: Dr Viktor Orbán.

History. One of the first opposition parties to be formed, the HSWP initially disdained to invite it to the Opposition Round Table negotiations. Although it did subsequently participate, like the AFD, it refused to sign the final agreement. It played a prominent role in organizing demonstrations and petitions to make stalinist members of parliament resign in 1989, and its spokespersons made virulently anti-soviet statements in its campaigns for the withdrawal of Soviet troops and at the ceremonial re-burial of Imre Nagy in June 1989.

It received four million forints of state support in 1989, seven million in 1990, plus a further 7.3 million for the elections. For a party aimed at a specific group — young people — it performed well electorally, forwarding 85 candidates of which 22 were elected. On the basis of these results it received 64.4 million forints (£470,000) for 1991. Despite a 1.7 million forint grant from the Soros-Hungarian Academy of Sciences Foundation and a joint income of three million forints from its company and foundation (Fico Ltd and the Democratic Political Cultural Foundation), 1990 closed with a cumulative deficit of 2.8 million forints (approximately £20,000).

The party's popularity increased over the summer of 1990 with the parliamentary performance of Viktor Orban and the party's stand against all displays of nationalism and against all forms of reprivatization. It was even more successful electorally in the local authorities (beating the HSP); but this revealed something of a weakness in depth. In some local authorities it could only field recent school-leavers as committee members.

Organization. An (at least) annual congress of delegates from local organizations appoints a 46-member National Committee.

Programme. FIDESZ is at the liberal end of the political spectrum, with a commitment to radicalism. It favours a broadly liberal nationality and ethnic minority policy, but considers, like most of the other parties, that Hungarian minorities living abroad are part of the Hungarian nation for whom the Hungarian state has a responsibility. Environmental issues also figured prominently in its election programme. Its educational policy gave students, teachers, parents and sponsors a say in all educational decisions and the right of anyone to establish and maintain a school. Membership of the party is restricted to those aged between 16–35, but people over the age limit are able to stand for it at elections; and it is reportedly advised by two major opposition figures of an older generation — András Kovács and György Bence.

Affiliations. Links are claimed with most liberal and some social democratic parties of Europe.

For a Provincial Hungary Party
Vidéki Magyarországért Párt

Founded on Nov. 20, 1989 in Tiszaderzs; nothing is known of the party's activities except that it succeeded in getting Dr Dezső Herédy onto the ballot in Jász-Nagykun-Szolnok county's eighth district. He received 690 votes, 60 fewer than the number needed to get him onto the ballot in the first place.

Freedom Party
Szabadságpárt

Founded in Hungary on July 12, 1989 following its re-foundation in New Brunswick, USA on May 28, 1989, the party was originally founded by Dezső Sulyok in 1946 after he had been excluded from the ISP (under pressure from the communist-dominated Left-Wing Block) for his right-wing views. The party lists two presidents — Ernő Hóka in the USA and Gyula Gueth in Hungary. It participated in the draw for party political broadcast slots in January 1990, received two million forints state support in 1990, with a further 300,000 forints specifically for the elections, and forwarded five candidates (including the Hungarian President), sufficient to make the regional list in Somogy and Zala counties. It achieved only 0.06 per cent of the total vote, however, failing to qualify for state support in 1991, and closed 1990 with a surplus of 500 forints (less than £4), having spent most of the state money on three issues of their paper "Hungarian Tomorrow" (*Magyar Holnap*). Nothing is known of its subsequent activities. It is at the nationalist christian end of the political spectrum.

Generations Party, Party of Pensioners and those with Families
Nemzedékek Pártja, Nyugdíjasok és Családosok Pártja

Address. Budapest XIII, Kresz Géza utca 6.

Leadership. Vilmos Mihaletzky (pres.)

Founded on December 20, 1989 the party received two million forints state support in 1990 but none specifically for the elections. It participated in the draw for party political broadcast radio and TV slots and got one candidate (Dr Kornélia Kelemen Csekéné) onto the ballot in Hajdú-Bihar county. She was not elected. It closed 1990 with a surplus of almost one million forints (approximately £7,300). Nothing more is known of its structure or activities.

Happiness Party
Boldogság Párt

Founder. Gyula Hernádi (a writer who worked with the film-director Miklós Jancsó).

Leadership. Alfred Szűcs (g.s.)

Address. 1399 Budapest, pf 701/579.

Telephone. (1) 113 0607, extension 17.

Founded in the spring of 1991, its aim is reported to be that of freeing society from dry, day-to-day politics.

Holy Crown Association
Szent Korona Társaság

The Association is one of the many extreme right-wing organizations grouped around László Romhányi, president of the Jurta Theatre where the right-wing National Alliance of Hungarians (*Magyarok Nemzeti Szövetsége*) holds what it terms a National Forum of extra-parliamentary parties. It participated in the draw for party political broadcast slots on radio and television in January 1990, received 100,000 forints state support for the election and fielded a candidate each in Vas and Szabolcs-Szatmár-Bereg counties, although it failed to get on either regional list. In September 1990, it helped organize an attempt to re-erect the Irredentist Memorial, on which figured a quotation from Mussolini to the effect that no borders are permanent. By the spring of 1991, Romhányi and two other prominent names associated with the association were being prosecuted for incitement to public disorder for their anti-semitic and anti-Romanian statements. The precise relationship between the association and the *Szent Korona* (Holy Crown) newspaper, which claims to be the paper of the Hungarian National Party, the Christian National Union electoral alliance, and the National Alliance of Hungarians is unclear. Romhányi is not officially listed as a leader of any of them, but simply as the president of the Jurta Theatre. The details of the Holy Crown Association listed in the register of political parties are incorrect and refer to a body devoted to heraldry.

Homeland Party
Haza Párt

Address. Budapest V, Eötvös utca 10, H-1053.

Telephone. (1) 117 5911.

Foundation. May 7, 1989.

Membership. 200 members claimed in November 1989.

Leadership. a governing committee made up of: Dr Istvan Utasi (pres.); Dr Miklós Udvaros and István Győr (dep. pres.); Márta Hetési (g.s.)

History. Following its foundation, the party put forward a presidential candidate in October 1989 when it seemed likely that a presidential election would precede the parliamentary ones, and in January 1990 it took part in the draw for party political broadcast time-slots. It ran no candidates in the parliamentary elections, however, and its activity since the elections is unknown.

Programme. Its primary long-term aim is given as preventing the Hungarian nation from dying out. In the shorter term it advocates improving the material and spiritual condition of the individual, the family, and the nation; creating a state based on national traditions and the principles of christian morality, on western European values. It also supports military neutrality, the reduction of taxes, a convertible forint, and cancelling existing foreign debts. More controversially, it advocates peacefully re-examining the historical injustices Hungary has suffered over the past 70 years.

Hungarian Allied National Party
Magyar Szövetségi Nemzeti Párt

Founded in January 1990 and registered on Feb. 19, 1990 in Székesfehérvár with Károly Gábris as president. Nothing further is known about the party or its activities.

Hungarian Democratic Christian Party
Magyar Demokrata Keresztény Párt

The party was registered in Miskolc on Jan. 15, 1990, having been established in October 1989 out of the Christian Wing of the HDF. Its president is listed as Pál Vörös, and the party received two million forints (approximately £14,500) state support in 1990. It followed the HDF in advocating a boycott of the November 1989 referendum, but its activities since then are unknown.

Hungarian Democratic Forum (HDF), Democratic Forum
Magyar Demokrata Fórum (MDF), Demokrata Fórum

Contact. Imre Furmann, tel: (1) 115 4006.

Address. Budapest II, Bem tér 3, H-1027.

Telephone. (1) 115 9690, 115 9697, 115 9698, 115 9699, 115 0896.

Foundation. Sept. 27, 1987.

Membership. 37,500 (May 1991).

Leadership. József Antall (pres.); Balázs Horváth (executive dep. pres.); Imre Furmann (general dep. pres.); Gabriella Farkas, Tamás Szabó, István Csurka, Iván Szabó (dep.

pres.); National Executive: József Antall, István Bethlen, Sándor Csoóri (youth policy); István Csurka, Gabriella Farkas (trade unions and interest groups); Imre Furmann (party organization and internal party affairs); Lajos Für, István Grezsa, Balázs Horváth, Géza Jeszenszky, Imre Kónya, Sándor Lezsák, László Medgyasszay (agriculture policy); Péter Nahimi, Gábor Rozsik, György Szabad, Iván Szabó (economic policy); Tamás Szabó, Gábor Széles (enterprise); Gyula Zacsek. Leader in parliament: Dr Imre Kónya.

History. The first Lakitelep meeting at which the party was founded was a meeting of populist writers (five of its nine founding members were writers or poets) and reform communists. By the spring of 1989 its support base had broadened and christian democratic and liberal elements could also be found under its umbrella. It began as a "movement" and many members were reluctant to transform it into a party. When this change took place, the balance within the party also changed. The "populist" tradition which emphasized the uniqueness of Hungary's past and postulated the possibility of a "Third Way", neither capitalism nor socialism, was marginalized. The party found itself a new guard of economic experts, many of them associated with the planning office, but also including Gábor Széles, president of one of Hungary's most dynamic private companies.

By February 1990, József Antall, who was appointed party president at the Second National Conference (after he had turned down leading roles in the CDPP and ISP) publicly rejected "Third Way"-ism. Having marginalized the populists (using only their nationalism verging on anti-semitism to bolster its popular appeal), in its electoral campaign it sought to distance itself from the reform communists by vying with the AFD to prove its anti-communist credentials. The party received 15 million forints-worth of state support in 1989, a further 15 million in 1990 in addition to 9.6 million specifically for the elections. It fielded 174 candidates and achieved a total of 165 seats, on the basis of which it qualified for 158.4 million forints for 1991. Despite significant domestic and foreign support, the party ended 1990 with a 16.3 million forint (approximately £117,000) deficit. An independent Forum Foundation has been established with the aim of supporting the party's electoral campaign, and leading party figures established Forum plc in June 1989, with an initial capital of 31.5 million forints (approximately £230,000).

Since the elections, the HDF's nationalist-christian orientation has been confirmed and both populist and liberal strands continue to be isolated. At the Third Congress in June 1990, the populist wing was particularly upset by the pact with the AFD and capitulation on the issue of a directly elected President. Perhaps most characteristic of the governing party's policy since coming to power is its authoritarianism. Antall has his representatives in every ministry, and ISP leaders complain bitterly of his intervention into their affairs. When Kiss of the liberal wing of the party resigned from the leadership at the Fourth Congress in December 1990, he cited the excessively presidentialist running of the party as a reason.

Organization. Delegates from local organizations meet at least annually in a National Assembly to appoint an 88-member Greater National Committee and the National Executive listed above. A Smaller National Committee is made up of the executive bodies of the county party organizations, its work being co-ordinated by a six-person executive committee from the National Executive.

Programme. In its election manifesto, the HDF was a self-conscious advocate of the slower route to privatization, refusing to set targets for the privatization process. In its proposals, health care was to be funded by minimum compulsory and additional voluntary contributions to private health associations. Other policies included recognizing the calling of motherhood so that women should not be obliged to work outside the home and relieving doctors of the obligation to perform abortions if it were against their ethical code. Its agricultural policy, unlike that of the ISP which it had to represent in government, advocated leaving it to collective farm membership to decide whether to farm collective land jointly or singly, or whether to rent it to an outside party. It made no mention of reparations. The party is publicly neither openly anti-semitic nor anti-gypsy; but it has singularly failed to muzzle István Csurka, one of the founder members who is aggressively nationalistic and openly anti-semitic.

Since coming to power, its predilection towards authoritarianism and economic interventionism has been manifest in policies such as putting the State Property Agency under government rather than parliamentary control, introducing Republican Representatives (the equivalent of the French *préfet*) into each county, and insisting on keeping government control over the media. Within the party it is reflected in the appointment of former Minister of the Interior, Balázs Horváth, as executive deputy president.

Affiliations. It claims links with the European Democratic Union, the European Democratic Union, and the Centre Group of the Nordic Council (CENTERN), together with most conservative and christian democratic parties of Europe.

Hungarian Freedom Party Alliance
Magyar Szabadságpárti Szövetség

The Alliance registered as a party on Dec. 14, 1989 as a Hungarian continuation of the Hungarian Freedom Party (*Magyar Szabadságpárt*) which had been formed on April 10, 1946, but which had not been a major force in politics and which had gone into emigration in the United States. It received two million forints state support in 1990 and participated in the draw for party political radio and television slots. No candidates reached the ballot under the alliance banner. (But see Freedom Party.)

Hungarian Health Party
Magyar Egészség Párt

The party was founded on Aug. 24, 1989 out of the Temperate Life Health and Family Protection National Alliance. The original president was Mihály Gergely, who in 1990 was part of the provisional leadership which also included Dr László Berzsenyi, Ilona Bognár, Tibor Dezse, János Attila Eötvös, Dr Frigyes Funk and László Róbert. The party was originally based in Törökbálint, a village near Budapest, with its headquarters in a member's house. At some point István Kajtár became the new president; and by the spring of 1991 the party had an address in Budapest (Budapest VI, Andrássy út 124) which it did not occupy, although someone occasionally came to collect the mail. The party was sufficiently active in early 1990 to take part in the draw for party political broadcast radio and television slots, but did not get any candidates onto the ballot. Its programme emphasized the moral as well as political crisis occasioned by socialism, and placed great stress on the role of good health, social security, and the defence of the environment in this process. At a more mundane level it criticized the employer's 43 per cent national insurance contribution.

Hungarian Humanists' Party
Magyar Humanisták Pártja

Address. Kaposvár, Arany János utca 9, H-7400.

Contact names. László Landek, István Stier.

Founded in December 1989 in Kaposvár out of the Association of Hungarian Humanists, itself formed in June 1988. It received two million forints of state support in 1990, and closed the year with most of it (1.7 million, approximately £12,000) intact. Its activities since the election are unknown, and letters to its office are returned to sender.

Hungarian Independence Party
Magyar Függetlenségi Párt

Address. Budapest XIII, Frangepán utca 50–56, H-1135.

Telephone. (1) 111 0893.

Foundation. January 1989.

Leadership. Tibor Hornyák (pres.); Ferenc Forgács (dep. pres.); executive members: Dr Zoltán Tóth, Ferenc Czibula, Dr Attila Monostori, Mária Wittner Agárdi, Lajos Czinege.

History. The party claims continuity with the party of the same name founded in August 1947 (which won 13.4 per cent of the vote in the 1947 elections) and briefly re-founded in 1956. In October 1989 it announced the republication of its paper *Ellenzék*, which was still being published in January 1990, but has since folded. It received four million forints of state support in 1989, and a further four million in 1990, in addition to 200,000 for the elections, which it entered as part of the National Alliance of Parties of the Centre. It ran four candidates and gained least support of all the parties which got onto the regional list, a mere 0.04 per cent of the total vote, all recorded in Tolna county. The president abolished the party at the end of 1990, but other members of the National Committee excluded him from the party and in May 1991 were reported to have appealed to the Budapest courts to have the process to abolish the party set aside.

Programme. The party is on the nationalist-christian end of the Hungarian political spectrum, propounding christian values and stoutly defending the Hungarian minority in Transylvania. It is stronger on rhetoric — punctuating documents with slogans calling for God, Homeland, Freedom — and criticizing the former regime than on propounding new policies. In addition to calling for the re-establishment of private property and the abolition of monopolies, it advocated returning property to the basis of Oct. 6, 1944, when "foreign armies" first entered Hungary. This must refer to Soviet troops, since German troops occupied Hungary in March 1944. But this policy is then contradicted in the discussion of agricultural policy which implies returning land to the holding structure effective after the 1945 land reform. In health care it advocated a voucher system, and in education the introduction of optional religious education. It favoured military neutrality and the peaceful settlement of all disputes with its neighbours.

Hungarian Industrial Unity Party
Magyar Ipari Egység Párt

Registered on Feb. 12, 1990 with Tibor Novák as president. Nothing more is known about its activities or structure.

Hungarian Liberal Party
Magyar Liberális Párt

Address. 1363 Budapest, pf 57.

Contact. Dr Vilmos Mészáros (pres.), tel: (1) 111 6543.

The party was founded on Oct. 20, 1989, and received two million forints state support in 1990. It entered the elections as part of the Christian National Union, but did not succeed in getting candidates onto the ballot. It closed 1990 with a surplus of 400,000 forints (approximately £3,000). It is in favour of human rights, economic freedoms, privatization, agricultural banks, free basic social provision, improved health care, recreating the true family and home-creating role of mothers, and long-term membership of the European Community, together with permanent military neutrality.

Hungarian Liberal People's Party
Magyar Liberális Néppárt

The party was founded at the end of June 1989 with Sándor Sz. Nagy as president. It received two million forints state support in 1989 and four million in 1990. Despite taking part in the draw for party political broadcast radio and television slots, it failed to field any candidates in the parliamentary elections and nothing is known of its activities since then.

Hungarian National Christian Workers' Party
Magyar Nemzeti Keresztény Munkáspárt

The party was reportedly founded on May 4, 1989, and in 1989 it received 200,000 forints (approximately £1,400) state support. Other sources report that the party never existed, and there is certainly no record of its activities or structure.

Hungarian National Party
Magyar Nemzeti Párt

Address. Budapest X, Népliget út 4.

HUNGARY

Telephone. (1) 113 1280.

Leadership. Dr Ferenc Barthal (pres.)

History. The party received two million forints state support for 1990 and figured in the draw for party political broadcast radio and television slots. It entered the elections as part of the Christian National Union which, soon after he gave an infamous anti-semitic radio address, called for István Csurka to be brought into government. It failed, however, to get any candidates on the ballot. The address and telephone number above are those of the Jurta Theatre. By spring 1991 there was no trace of the party at either.

Programme. The party is hard to track down as a physical entity, but it lets its name be associated with extreme right-wing positions. The views presented in *Szent Korona* (Holy Crown), a newspaper published by László Romhányi, president of the Jurta Theatre, which prints the party's name underneath the title, reject every aspect of the former system and accuse other parties of having fifth columnists from the communist party in their ranks, a line continued even after the elections, with crypto-communists being unearthed in all areas of life. In the early spring of 1991 the paper called for signatories to a petition demanding new elections. It describes the mainstream press as "liberal bolshevik". In a television interview, Romhányi publicly identified himself with statements suggesting that the Jews were responsible for communism and for the Trianon treaty.

Hungarian October Party
Magyar Október Párt

Address. Budapest VI, Izabella utca 81. (The flat of Hujter-Kovács.)

Telephone. None.

Foundation. June 27, 1989.

History. The party is very much associated with one man (György Krassó), a student leader in 1956, who figured prominently in all its activities. Nevertheless it appears to have survived Krassó's death in early 1991. The party finally accepted two million forints state support in 1990, took part in the draw for party political broadcast radio and television slots, but received no additional support for the elections which it entered as the only member of the Christian National Centre (Keresztény Nemzeti Centrum). The party was very critical of the hurdles that had to be overcome to get candidates onto the ballot. Although four of its 21 prospective candidates received sufficient nominations to have qualified for the ballot, as a gesture of opposition to what they saw as an unfair system, the party burned the papers and returned their ashes instead to the electoral authorities.

Programme. The party considers itself the only truly revolutionary party and the party of the streets. Its primary aim is to realize, by means of the will of the people, with the weapon of telling the truth against its enemies (violence, misery and falsehood), the aims (as it saw them) of the 1956 revolution: true people's power, freedom, prosperity, neutrality. It opposed the Opposition Round Table negotiations because it did not recognize the legitimacy of the HSWP. Immediately after the parliamentary elections it erected a tent on the grass in front of the parliament buildings, planning to remain there for four years as a further protest against the electoral law. It also organized a petition to bring the criminals of 1956 to justice; appointed George Bush an honorary party member; organized soup kitchens for the poor; and was a primary mover in campaigns to get street names with communist associations changed back to their original form. The most unusual of the party's early demands was that Hungarians living in the West should share equal rights with Hungarians living in Hungary, and hence not be subject to visa regulations. The party's prospective candidate for the presidential elections, which did not take place, was Sándor Rácz, leader of the Greater Budapest Workers' Council in 1956.

Hungarian People's Party (HPP), Hungarian People's Party — National Peasant Party
Magyar Néppárt (MNP), Magyar Néppárt — Nemzeti Parasztpárt

Address. Budapest VIII, Baross utca 61.

Telephone. (1) 134 1509.

Foundation. March 8, 1989.

Membership. No figures released in 1991; 30,000 were claimed in the August of 1989.

Leadership. Gyula Fekete (pres.), Deputy presidents: Dr Mihály Töröcsik (agricultural policy); Dr Károly Dobszay (educational policy); Sámuel Benedekfi (party organization); Dr János Skultéti; Executive members: Pál Ballai, László Bihari, Bertalan Fábián, Dr József Kanyar, Dr Zoltán Koltay, Győző Libisch, Dr János Márton, Lajos Nemes, Dr Árpád Olajos, Piroska Pandor, György Páles, László S. Hegedűs, Ferenc S. Szabó.

History. The party sees itself as a continuation of the National Peasant Party, established in December 1944 following its initial formation in 1939, which operated under the name Petőfi Party in 1956. Its immediate predecessor was the Péter Veres Association.

It was a significant enough party in the spring of 1989 to be invited to take part in the Opposition Round Table negotiations. It interpreted the November 1989 referendum as an attack on the Opposition Round Table, however, and adhered to the government line. It received 10 million forints (approximately £73,000) in 1989, a further 10 million in 1990, and an additional 4.8 million for the elections. It ran only 45 candidates, despite claims in May 1989 to have organizations in every town and village in Hungary. Although this was sufficient for the party to figure on most regional lists and the national list, its total share of the vote (0.75 per cent) fell well below the 4 per cent barrier for entry into parliament. It qualified for no further funds following this poor electoral showing, and closed 1990 with a cumulated surplus of 1.3 million forints (approximately £9,500).

Organization. A Greater Council of 100 members made up of representatives from local organizations appoints an 18-member National Executive.

Programme. It is one of the few parties to keep a reference to the "Third Way" and Hungary's own way in its manifesto, which focuses on agricultural and rural issues such as local government reform and a new land law. It sees itself as the party that understands the provincial "silent majority", and openly calls for a return to the situation at the beginning of the decade when agriculture was supported by the government.

HUNGARY

The party's decline was the result of two factors. First, since the summer of 1989, when the HDF abandoned the notion, there was much less discussion nationally of the "Third Way". The HPP was left holding an idea whose time had passed. Second, the growth of the Agrarian Alliance and Hungary's Co-operative and Agrarian Party siphoned off some of the collective farm, village establishment constituency.

Affiliations. None claimed.

Hungarian Radical Party
Magyar Radikális Párt

Address. Budapest VII, Dózsa György u. 80/a, fsz 5, H-1071.

Leadership. Mihály Rózsa (pres.); István Siba (sec.); Zsolt Pál Kovács.

Founded on March 3, 1989 as a continuation of the party of the same name which was established in December 1944 but which received tiny shares of the popular vote in the 1945 and 1947 elections (0.2 per cent and 1.7 per cent respectively). The party received 1.3 million forints state support in 1989, 6.8 million in 1990, but none specifically for the elections, despite its participation in the draw for party political broadcast slots on radio and television. It failed to get any candidates onto the ballot, although it announced that it was entering the elections as part of the National Alliance of Parties of the Centre. Its programme called for "economic self-regulating pluralism", a social policy which prevented all from falling below the subsistence minimum, neutrality, and family-centred policies to help large families. Its activities since the elections are unknown. The address given was current in 1989.

Hungarian Realist Movement
Magyar Realista Mozgalom

Registered as a party on Feb. 19, 1990. Nothing further is known about its structure or activities.

Hungarian Republican Party, Győr Branch
Magyar Republikánus Párt Győri Szervezete

Although not registered as a party and nothing more is known of its structure or activities, the organization is listed as having received two million forints state support in 1990.

Hungarian Royalist Party
Magyar Legitimista Párt

Founded on Jan. 11, 1990 with László Pálos as president. It participated in the January 1990 draw for party political broadcast radio and TV slots, but nothing more is known of its structure or activities.

Hungarian Socialist Party (HSP)
Magyar Szocialista Párt (MSP)

Address. Budapest VIII, Köztársaság tér 26.

Telephone. (1) 113 4846, 144 4706.

Foundation. Oct. 7, 1989.

Membership. 35,000 (May 1991).

Leadership. Gyula Horn (pres.); Imre Szekeres (executive dep. pres., economic policy); György Jánosi (dep. pres., education). Spokespersons: Sándor Csintalan (social policy and the trade union movement); László Kovács (foreign policy, security policy); András Tóth (party organization, internal party affairs, local government affairs). Executive members: Ferenc Baja (youth policy); Zoltán Gál, József Géczi (enterprise and land affairs); Ferenc Kósa (arts and culture); György Marosán jnr (finance); Lajos Mátyás Szabó, Ildikó Kerékgyártó Vargáné. Leader in parliament: Zoltán Gál.

History. The party is the direct descendant of the Hungarian Communist Party, which went through a number of guises during the war, merged with the HSDP in 1948 to form the Hungarian Workers Party and, following the revolution of 1956 rechristened itself the Hungarian Socialist Workers' Party. Its history is virtually synonymous with Hungarian history until the XIV Party Congress in October 1989 when it changed its name and accepted that it would relinquish its privileged "leading role". Former foreign minister Horn took over from "father of economic reform" Rezső Nyers as party president in May 1990. It lost one of its key figures in November 1990 when Pozsgay resigned his membership. State support for the party was 919.6 million forints in 1989, 15 million in 1990 with an additional 9.5 million for the elections. It fielded 172 candidates and won a total of 32 seats, on the basis of which it received 84 million (approximately £613,000) for 1991. It closed 1990 with a surplus of almost 91,000 forints.

Organization. At the local level, the party consists of party communities, party organizations and regional associations. Delegates from the party organizations attend a congress which appoints a national committee with 73 members. The latter appoints the national executive listed above.

Programme. Since the change of name at the October 1989 Party Congress, the party has adopted social democratic policies and a commitment to mixed forms of property and the social market economy. It has inherited a number of private companies and foundations as a result of its past involvement in all aspects of Hungarian life.

At its Siófok congress in November 1990 it opposed all reprivatization, but called for an acceleration of privatization, a version of privatization that permitted the maximum number of owners, an open economy, and job creation measures. It also stated that what existed in Hungary between 1948 and 1956 and from 1956 to 1989 was not socialism, although its judgement of the period, especially since 1963, was not entirely negative. The party accepts the principles and policies of the Socialist International. It strives for a western European-type modern market economy and democratic society in which economic democracy does not oppose but is rather linked to private and public property. It also advocates solidarity and social justice and equality of opportunity. It opposes the government's christian-nationalist conservatism, and calls for the right to be able to represent left-wing and social democratic values. It also champions closer co-operation with the European Community, with associate status of the Community as its immediate goal. Consistent with its emphasis on institutional and public ownership, it encourages local authority ownership and employee ownership schemes.

Affiliations. It has applied for membership of the Socialist International and links are claimed with most socialist parties of Europe, the Socialist Group of the European Parliament, and the Confederation of the Socialist Party of the European Community. Links are retained with the Communist Party of the Soviet Union.

Hungarian Socialist Workers' Party (HSWP), Workers Party
Magyar Szocialista Munkáspárt (MSZMP), Munkáspárt

Contact name. Dr Miklós Tóth, tel: (1) 118 3100 extension 63.

Address. Budapest IX, Köztelek utca 8.

Telephone. (1) 118 3100, 118 3572, 118 3834.

Foundation. Dec. 17, 1989.

Membership. No figures published, although 82,000 claimed in January 1990.

Leadership. Gyula Thürmer (pres.); Sándor Nyiró (party organization), Attila Pozsonyi (economic policy) (vice-presidents).

History. The party consists of the rump of the former HSWP which refused to go along with the party's change of name to the Hungarian Socialist Party in October 1989 and its metamorphosis into a social democratic party. At its founding congress (which it viewed as a continuation of the XIVth) Gyula Thürmer, foreign policy adviser to the former leader, Károly Grósz, was appointed president. The Central Committee retained many prominent hard-liners such as János Berecz and the publicity-seeking stalinist Róbert Ribánszki. The party received 15 million forints state support in 1989, a further 7.6 million for the elections, and 15.9 million (approximately £110,000) for 1991. In the parliamentary elections it fielded 96 candidates and, with 3.68 per cent of the vote, came top of the list of parties which failed to cross the 4 per cent threshold. In the local elections it fared slightly worse. It closed 1990 with a 12,000 forint (approximately £88) profit. It has bitterly criticized the HSP for "taking our assets and leaving us Marx". The party is optimistic that as the economic crisis bites its popularity will grow. By January 1991 it had adopted the name Workers' Party (*Munkáspárt*).

Organization. A congress of delegates from local organizations appoints an 89-member central committee.

Programme. Despite being made up of the old guard of the party, its programme would have been considered radical and reformist under the old regime, encapsulated in the statement: "This HSWP is not that HSWP". It is committed to Kádárist reformism, and wants to carry it further in areas such as restoring national traditions. It does not oppose privatization and the introduction of foreign capital; and mention is even made of the "social market economy", although public (not state) ownership is advocated in preference to private. It remains explicitly a party primarily of the working class, based on the intellectual foundation of Marx. A XVth Party Congress will be held in 1991 at which its approach to property relations, land, and the trade unions will be determined. Despite its commitment to the Kádár tradition, however, a key speaker at its founding congress was György Marosán (a consistent opponent of Kádárist reform); and the party condemned its own 1962 critical comments concerning Marosán, despite the fact that these criticisms had been inspired by Kádár. The party is critical of moves to restore church property and reprivatize agricultural land. As part of a left-wing movement, it feels it must build itself from below and seek co-operation with the trade unions, the HSP and the Agrarian Alliance.

Affiliations. Links are maintained exclusively with communist parties of Eastern and Western Europe.

Hungarian Veterans' Party
Magyar Veteránok Pártja

Although the party was never officially registered and nothing is known of its activities, it is listed as having participated in the January 1990 draw for party political broadcast slots on radio and TV.

Hungarian Workers' Democratic Centre Party
Magyar Dolgozók Demokratikus Centrum Párt

The party was registered on Feb. 14, 1990, but nothing is known about its policies, history or leadership. It ran one candidate in the parliamentary elections (Tibor Majoros in Pest county) who received fewer than 1,000 votes.

Hungarian Workers' Party
Magyar Munkás Párt

The party was not registered but its formation was announced on Oct. 16, 1989 as a successor to the HSWP following the XIV Party Congress at which it transformed itself into the HSP. Nothing more is known of the party. Names associated with it are János Batyánsky, János Gyurkó and Mihály Bankó.

Hungary's Communists' Party
Magyarországi Kommunisták Pártja

Founded on Dec. 8, 1989, with István Salga as provisional president, claiming to be a left-wing party "from below". Nothing is known of its structure and activities.

HUNGARY

Hungary's Co-operative and Agrarian Party
Magyarországi Szövetkezeti és Agrárpárt

Founded on Nov. 24, 1989, in Gyöngyös with János Nyilas as president, this is a self-styled left-wing party of the countryside. It received two million forints state support in 1990 together with a further 300,000 forints for the elections, and closed 1990 with a surplus of 1.5 million forints. It took part in the draw in January 1990 for party political broadcast radio and television slots. It fielded five candidates, and made the Heves county regional list, where Gyöngyös is located, with an overall 0.1 per cent of the vote. This electoral showing was insufficient for it to qualify for state funds in 1991.

Hungary's Green Party
Magyarországi Zöld Párt

Contact. Erzsébet Schmuok, tel: (1) 156 2133.

Address. Budapest III, Kiskorona utca 3.

Telephone. (1) 168 8800.

Foundation. Nov. 8, 1989.

Membership. 1,500 (May 1991).

Leadership. Dr László Brezovits (pres.); Dr György Ilosvay, Dr Iván Gyulai, Zoltán Medveczik (associate pres.)

History. The party emerged out of the large number of environmental groups (such as the Danube Circle, the Tisza Circle, the Green Circle, the Hungarian Nature Conservancy Alliance) which were instrumental in the political collapse of the old regime. Some of the regional branches are separately registered, and the Debrecen branch claims parentage in a Hungary's Regional Green Party (*Magyarországi Regionális Zöld Párt*). Many of the prominent figures of the environmental movement joined the AFD or FIDESZ when it came to expressing party allegiance. At the time of the parliamentary election it considered entering an alliance with the Hungarian Health Party and Voks Humana. It ran 14 candidates, figured on a number of regional lists, but not the national one. It received 0.36 per cent of the total vote, concentrated in four counties, insufficient to qualify it for state support in 1991, although it received two million forints in 1989 and 1990, and a further 800,000 forints (approximately £6,000) for the elections. It closed 1990 with a surplus of almost two million forints. The party fielded more candidates than expected for the local elections, but was no more successful in them. Its Fourth Congress in January 1991 brought back into membership six founding members who had been suspended in June 1990.

Organization. A congress of delegates from local organizations elects a 40-member Green Representation which elects an executive.

Programme. It favours a society based on ecological principles and local level democracy, a non-violent society in which all minority rights are guaranteed. More specifically, it advocates environmental taxation and supports animal rights.

Affiliations. Links are claimed with the Austrian Green Party.

Hungary's Party of Transylvanian Hungarians
Erdély Magyarok Magyarországi Pártja

The party was registered on Jan. 15, 1990, in the provincial town of Miskolc, and founded in either late November or early December 1989. Its president is registered as Vilmos Kakuszi, but further details about its structure and activities are unknown.

Hungary's Social Democratic Party (HSDP)
Magyarországi Sociáldemokrata Párt (MSZDP)

Contact name. Ernő Ormándlaky.

Address. Budapest VII, Dohány utca 76.

Telephone. (1) 142 2385.

Foundation. Jan. 9, 1989.

Membership. 23,000 (May 1991).

Leadership. Dr Anna Petrasovits (pres.); Ernő Ormándlaky (g.s.); Dr Endre Borbély (dep. pres., home affairs). Executive: Tibor Baranyai (press); Sándor Bácskai (Budapest party organization); Dr Gábor Bordács (trade unions and interest groups); Dr János Szilágyi (education); Ilona György (foreign affairs); Dr János Grád (economic policy); Béla Nyitray (provincial party organization).

History. Hungary's Social Democratic Party (HSDP) was first formed on Dec. 7, 1890, was reorganized on Dec. 21, 1944, merged with the Communists on June 12, 1948, existed briefly again as an independent party in 1956 and was re-founded finally on Jan. 9, 1989. The party has been plagued with internal conflicts around personalities rather than policies. Despite spending the summer and autumn of 1989 papering over the cracks, it finally split at its conference on Nov. 6, 1989 when the Independent Social Democratic Party and the Social Democratic Party were formed. Attempts to resurrect the party's paper *Sociáldemokrata Népszava* were unsuccessful, although some trial issues appeared. The party received active encouragement from Europe's social democratic parties, and figured on most regional lists together with the national one. It fielded 76 candidates, but none was elected. It received 15 million forints in government support in 1989, 10 million in 1990, with a further 6.7 million for the elections, and 18 million in 1991 on the basis of its electoral performance. Despite this, and seven million forints from the Social Democratic Foundation, the party closed 1990 with a 22 million forint (approximately £160,000) deficit. Following the party's poor electoral showing, there were rumours that Petrasovits had attempted suicide.

The personality of the president was seen in May 1991 as the biggest barrier to unity amongst the various social democratic parties and factions (reportedly numbering seven by the spring of 1991). Rumours circulated that foreign sympathizers were attempting to organize an American scholarship for her to ease her from the scene.

Organization. A congress of delegates from local organizations appoints a committee with 101 members and a 27-member national leadership.

Programme. The party has very much the sort of programme to be expected from a European social democratic party: a mixed economy, but with social provision provided on a non-market basis. A distinctive Hungarian feature is its claim that the "'Third Way' would lead to the Third World". It favours radical property reform, but not in transport, communications or education, and advocates worker share-ownership schemes. Party programme statements are rarely more detailed that reiterating the principles of social democracy.

Affiliations. Links are claimed with the Socialist International and socialist parties of Europe and the rest of the world.

Independent Christian Democratic Party
Független Kereszténydemokrata Párt

Reported as having been formed by the time of the parliamentary elections in March–April 1990, although not officially registered. It has disappeared from the scene, and nothing is known about its structure or activities.

Independent Environmental Labour Party
Független Környézetvédő Munkapárt

Founded on April 29, 1989 in the town of Hévíz which suffers particular environmental problems. The party's president is listed as Zoltán Nagy. It has disappeared from the scene, and nothing is known about its structure or activities.

Independent Hungarian Democratic Party
Független Magyar Demokrata Párt (FMDP)

Address. Budapest XIV, Kolumbus utca 11.

Telephone. (1) 183 6706; *Fax*: (1) 183 7191.

Foundation. May 5, 1989.

Leadership. An executive committee made up of Sándor Ambrus, Ervin Böröczky, Gyula Kovár, István Neff and József Németh.

History. The party is a re-foundation of the party of the same name led by Father Balogh that operated between June 1947 and 1951. In the November 1989 referendum it supported the anti-government line. It received six million forints of state support in 1989 and seven million in 1990, with a further 200,000 for the elections, which it entered in association with the National Alliance of Parties of the Centre. It ran three candidates, but received only 0.06 per cent of the vote however (all votes coming from Komáron-Esztergom county where it figured on the regional list), so excluding it from parliament and from further state funding. Its activities since the elections are unknown. At its height, it was publishing a

Sunday paper entitled *Magyar Vasárnap* (Hungarian Sunday), edited by Sándor Ambrus; but by the spring of 1991 the newspaper had folded and the party did not give out information to enquirers.

Programme. Agriculture figured prominently in its programme, with calls for a market in land, agrarian banks, the disbanding of bureaucratic bodies associated with collectivized agriculture, higher pensions and an improved infrastructure. More generally it called for tax concessions for investors, an ending to technical backwardness, new property relations, an independent banking system, democratic education free from party interference, and freedom of religion.

Independent Hungarian Workers' Party, Székesfehérvár
Független Magyar Munkáspárt, Székesfehérvár

The party is registered as having been founded on Oct. 27, 1989, out of the Solidarity Trade Union Workers' Alliance (*Szolidaritás Szakszervezeti Munkászövetség*), which was founded on Feb. 25, 1989 and based in Budapest. Its address is a PO Box in Székesfehérvár (Székesfehérvár, pf 8001/206) and the president is listed as Tibor Rajna. Although its predecessor (Solidarity) was active in the independent trade union movement in 1989 and produced a magazine entitled (*Szolidaritás*) (Solidarity), the party is listed as having intended to enter the elections in association with the predominantly right-wing Christian National Union. In January 1990 it published a statement in the right-wing *Szent Korona* (Holy Crown) calling for an immediate 50 per cent increase in real wages and pensions. It was unable to generate sufficient support to register candidates, however, and its activities since the parliamentary elections are unknown.

Independent Republic Party
Független Köztársasági Párt

Registered on Feb. 7, 1990, in Kaposvár in south-western Hungary. The president is listed as Jenő Tóth and, although the party received two million forints (approximately £14,000) state support in 1990, it did not participate in the parliamentary and local elections and there have been no reports of subsequent activities. By the spring of 1991 it had a Budapest address (Budapest XIV, Kolumbus utca 11) but could not be found there.

Independent Smallholder, Land Labourer and Citizens' Party (ISP), Smallholders' Party
Független Kisgazda, Földmunkás és Polgári Párt (FKgP), Kisgazda Párt

Contact name. Omolnár Miklós, tel. (1) 111 1400.

Address. Budapest XII, Szoboszlai utca 2/4.

Telephone. (1) 155 5333.

Foundation. October 1930, Oct. 28, 1956, Nov. 12, 1988 in Szentendre; Nov. 18, 1988 in Budapest.

HUNGARY

Membership. 60,000 (May 1991).

Leadership. Ferenc József Nagy (pres.); Sándor Oláh (Sec.-gen.); Béla Németh (1st vice-pres.); Sándor Cseh, Pál Dragon, Antal Kocsenda, Gyula Kis (vice-pres.); Miklós Omolnar, Antal Bélafi jnr (deputy secretaries general); Dr Ferenc Bartal (party attorney general); Dr Gyula Pásztor (leader in parliament).

History. The party has suffered from much schism and factional fighting. In February 1989 it expelled four members, in March it allowed them back in again, and in April it declared itself to have got over its childhood illnesses; but just before the elections the National Smallholders' Party split away. The party received 15 million forints in state support in 1989, and a further 15 million in 1990, with an additional 9.3 million for the elections. It fielded 163 candidates and won a total of 44 seats, on the basis of which it received 87.7 million forints (approximately £640,000) for 1991. Like the other major parties, it has a foundation and public limited company closely associated with members of the leadership — the ISP Electoral Foundation and Hangya plc.

Factionalism continued after the parliamentary elections, the central issue being how radical a reparations policy to support. The summer was spent persuading the government to introduce the party's central policy goal: the return of land to its owners of 1947 or their heirs. The fact that before it could be passed, the Bill to achieve this was ruled unconstitutional played into the radicals' hands. The Constitutional Court ruling effectively stated that all property should be treated alike. The radical supporters of reparations therefore called for compensation for all property lost, not just land. Seven months later, in May 1991, the Court made a similar ruling about the compromise bill which granted some, but not full, or equal, reparations for all forms of property, leaving the issues and the factional struggle unresolved. Meanwhile, József Torgyán, demagogic leader of the party in parliament until the spring of 1991, caused a furore by getting himself elected (at a possibly inquorate meeting) joint president of the party. The leadership crisis this occasioned is due for solution at a special committee meeting on June 29, 1991. Adversaries have stated that Torgyán's confirmation as president would split the party.

Organization. A national committee, made up of delegates from the local organizations, appoints a political committee of 20 members plus the leadership listed above as *ex officio* members. The party also has a number of specialist secretariats whose leaders are as follows: Géza Varga (environment); László Kerékgyartó (culture); Attila Benke (economy and agriculture); Teréz Kovács (social); István Prepeliczay (education); István Rónaháti (transport).

Programme. Its commitment to the reprivatization of land on the basis of 1947 apart, the electoral programme stressed adherence to christian values and advocated rapid privatization, although with barriers against foreign ownership, low taxation to encourage entrepreneurship (a three-banded personal income tax with a maximum limit of 35 per cent, a maximum of 20 per cent value-added tax, and a maximum 30 per cent corporation tax, a maximum 20 per cent national insurance contribution, and a 10 per cent contribution to the pension fund), and negotiations to ease the conditions of foreign debt. The most important element in educational policy was seen as recreating moral values, with compulsory religious education in schools.

Affiliations. Links are claimed with various European christian democratic and people's parties and the European Union of Christian Democrats.

Independent Social Democratic Party
Független Szociáldemokrata Párt

The party was formed on Nov. 6, 1990, when a group of about 50 walked out of the congress of the HSDP in a blaze of publicity. The group was led by György Ruttner, who had figured in the early days of the re-founded party (as a member of a delegation of new parties visiting the USA for example), but was never part of the party leadership and considered too left-wing. There were suspicions at the time that the split had been engineered by the HSP which mistakenly saw the HSDP as a serious rival. The party received two million forints (approximately £14,000) in state support in 1990, and a further 100,000 forints for the elections. Although it took part in the draw for party political broadcast time-slots, it fielded only five candidates in the elections and did not qualify for either the regional or national lists. The party has since disbanded, to be replaced by the Social Democrat Alliance (*Szociáldemokrata Szövetség*).

Left-Wing Revision Party
Baloldali Revízío Pártja

Address. Budapest VII, Izabella utca 40, földszint 5.

Telephone. (1) 141 7136.

Foundation. January 1991.

Membership. 13.

Organization. Dr István Punyi (pres.); László Molnár (dep. pres.)

With a membership of 13, the party is not a force in Hungarian politics. However, it was prominent enough in January 1990 to participate in the draw for television and radio slots for party political broadcasts, and it took itself sufficiently seriously to register its 1990 accounts: a deficit of 3,362 forints (approximately £25). The address and telephone number given are those of the president's flat.

National Association of Those Not in Parties, Party of Those Not in Parties
Pártonkívüliek Országos Egyesülete, Pártonkívüliek Partja

Although not registered as a party, it is reported to have been founded at the end of October 1989 with András Bihari as president. One source lists it as having participated in the draw for party political radio and TV slots in January 1990. Its activities and structure are unknown.

National Reconstruction Party
Nemzeti Újjáépítés Partja

Nothing is known of this party other than that it was registered on Feb. 20, 1990.

HUNGARY

National Smallholder and Bourgeois Party
Nemzeti Kisgazda és Polgári Párt

Established in Szeged on Dec. 29, 1989, resulting from a split within the ISP. The split was not ideologically inspired, although the new party was accused of being "left-wing". It participated in the ballot for party political broadcast radio and television slots, received four million forints state support in 1990, with a further 700,000 forints specifically for the elections. It entered the elections as a member of the National Electoral Alliance, fielded 13 candidates, sufficient to get onto the regional list in Heves, Csongrád and Nógrád counties, but achieved only 0.2 per cent of the vote. It claimed, in January 1991, to be going onto the offensive, despite newspaper reports that its office address was being used by a local painter to run a sexual services business. It followed the mainstream ISP line on its most distinctive policy, returning land ownership to its 1947 basis.

New Hungarians' Justice Party, Party of Hungarian Gypsies
Újmagyarok Igazság Pártja, Magyar Cigányok Pártja

Founded on Oct. 18, 1989, as a successor to the Party of Hungarian Gypsies. Its president is listed as Albert Horváth, and it received seven million forints (approximately £51,000) state support in 1990. It fielded no candidates however and nothing is known of its structure and activities.

Party of Republican Youth
Republikánus Fiatalok Pártja

Nothing is known about this party other than that it was registered on Feb. 20, 1990.

Patriotic Electoral Coalition, Patriotic Party, Democratic Coalition
Hazafias Választási Koalíció (HVK), Hazafias Párt, Demokrata Koalíció

Operating between Nov. 21 and Dec. 21, 1989, as the Patriotic Party (*Hazafias Párt*), the Coalition was a vehicle for "movement" bodies of the old system closely associated with the Patriotic People's Front to fight the elections. On Aug. 4, 1990, its name was changed to the Democratic Coalition. State support for the Patriotic People's Front in 1989 was 247 million forints (approximately £1.8 million). The Electoral Coalition received two million forints in 1990 and 8.4 million for the election. On the basis of its electoral showing it qualified for 14.2 million forints (approximately £103,000) state support in 1991. It figured on both regional and national lists, but did not cross the 4 per cent hurdle.

Peasant and Worker Party (Debrecen), Hungarian Peasant-Worker Alliance Party
Paraszt-és Munkáspárt (Debrecen), Paraszt-Munkás Szövetség Párt

Founded on Aug. 12, 1989, out of the Hajdú-Bihar county Hungarian Peasant, Worker Alliance Party (*Magyar Paraszt, Munkás Szövetségi Párt*) and Hungarian Peasant Alliance

(*Magyar Parasztszövetség*) which had been formed a month previously. Nothing more is known of the party, except that its president was László Baki.

People of the East Party Christian Democrats
Kelet Népe Párt Kereszténydemokraták

Address. Budapest VII, Péterffy Sándor utca 42.

Telephone. (1) 141 5437.

Membership. 10,000 claimed (implausibly; May, 1991).

Leadership. Frigyes Tamási (party president and president of the policy body); András Ambrus (g.s.); József Németh (dep. g.s.)

History. Although the party received four million forints (approximately £29,000) state support in 1990, it received no funds for the elections and successfully fielded only one candidate (István Bukovics) who received votes from less than half the number of people who had nominated him. Subsequent activities are unknown.

Organization. An executive committee made up of leaders of local organizations. The Policy Body is the leading intellectual body of the party.

Programme. The party is at the nationalist end of the spectrum, with specific policies for Transylvania. It advocates: an independent and free Hungary which achieves a moderately democratic bourgeois democracy; a bicameral constitutional monarchy, an independent Transylvania built on the union of the three nations, autonomy for areas inhabited by Hungarians which were formerly parts of Hungary, a national economy based on radical property relations, a 35-hour week, and education in the spirit of christian and Hungarian values. No foreign or domestic affiliations are listed.

People's Will Party
NépAkarat (sic) Párt (NAP)

This party is not registered and nothing is known of its activities or structure, other than that the president's name is János Maczó. Nevertheless it filed accounts for 1990 showing a deficit of 46,173 forints (approximately £340) on the basis of a total income, mainly from membership fees, of 5,900 forints (approximately £43).

Regional Democratic Youth Organization, Felegyhazi Democratic Youth Organization
Területi Demokratikus Ifjúsági Szervezet, TEDISZ, Félegyházi Demokratikus Ifjúsági Szervezet, FÉDISZ

This joint organization does not figure as a registered party and it received no government support for the elections. TEDISZ was based in Kiskunmajsa and FÉDISZ in Kiskunfélegyháza. They were essentially a continuation of the local Young Communist organization, the inspiration of a local young doctor, and ran a single candidate, unsuccessfully, in the Bács-Kiskun county fifth district.

HUNGARY

Republican National Party
Republikánus Nemzeti Párt

Founded on Oct. 21, 1989, with Dr József Bánovics as president and giving its address as György Mihalovics's private address. Nothing more is known about the party, other than a newspaper report that it opposed government measures in November 1989 to introduce foreign currency controls.

Romany Parliament
Roma Parlament

Address. Budapest VIII, Tavaszmező utca 6.

Telephone. (1) 184 2917.

Leader. Jenő Zsigó.

Although not registered as a political party, this body was reportedly created out of a number of smaller gypsy parties and interest groups. It cannot be traced at the address given above.

Small Pensioners' Party
Kisnyugdíjasok Pártja

The party was registered on Feb. 1, 1990, with Dr József Buzás as president. Its structure and activities are unknown.

Social Democratic Party of Hungary's Gypsies
Magyarországi Cigányok Szociáldemokrata Pártja

Founded on Oct. 1, 1989, with Pál Farkas as president as an off-shoot from Hungary's Social Democratic party, it received 10 million forints state aid in 1990. It got one candidate onto the ballot for the parliamentary election (Elemér Csemer in Nógrad county) who received fewer votes than the number of signatures necessary necessary to nominate him. The party was a signatory to a petition to the German ambassador in Hungary in November 1990, but by the spring of 1991 it was believed to have disbanded or to have merged into the Romany Parliament.

Social Democratic Party
Szociáldemokrata Párt

Address. Budapest VIII, Baross utca 61.

Telephone. (1) 133 7983, 113 7662.

Membership. 5,000 (May 1991).

Leadership. Imre Takács (pres. and spokesperson). Executive: five members whose names are not published.

Organization. A committee of local organizations appoints a 15-member national leadership.

History. The party was originally founded in Diósd on Nov. 6, 1989 as a breakaway from Hungary's Social Democratic Party. It received seven million forints state support in 1990, but none for the parliamentary elections and none subsequently. It entered the elections as part of the National Alliance of Centre Parties and participated in the draw for party political broadcast radio and TV slots, but did not succeed in getting any candidates onto the ballot and closed 1990 with a surplus of four million forints (approximately £29,000). It claims links with all the socialist and social democratic parties of Europe, but none of them are official.

Somogy Christian Coalition
Somogyi Keresztény Koalíció

The organization does not figure on the list of 65 registered parties at the time of the election. Nevertheless, its candidates managed to get onto the ballot in three Somogy county constituencies, giving it 5.9 per cent of the county vote and a national share of 0.12 per cent. None of its candidates was elected.

Transnational Radical Party (European Group of the European Radical Party)
Transznacionális Radikális Párt (Európai Radikális Párt Magyar Csoportja)

Founded on Feb. 2, 1989, at about the time the Transnational Radical Party held a congress in Budapest. Nothing is known of its structure or subsequent activities.

Voks Humana, Voks Humana Movement, Biosphere Party
Voks Humana Mozgalom, Bioszféra Párt

Address. Budapest VIII, Köztársaság tér 27.

Telephone. (1) 133 5390, extension 170.

Leadership. János Sebeők (pres.)

The party is the vehicle of its eccentric president. Its propaganda materials border on the incomprehensible. It claims to be more radical than the environmentalists and to trancsend their technocratic principles. It calls for "life's right to life". Its concrete aim is "the construction of a Hungarian and international living space network by which the living world can survive us as an environment". It received two million forints (approximately £14,000) state support in 1990.

Workers' Marxist–Leninist Party, Hungary's Party of Communists
Munkások Marxista–Leninista Pártja, Kommunisták Magyarországi Pártja

The party was never officially registered but its formation was announced on Aug. 25, 1989, with Sándor Petres as president. The party was originally to have been called

HUNGARY

Hungary's Party of Communists (one of the historic variants used by the Hungarian Communist Party), but it is not clear whether this made it the same party as the elusive Party of Hungarian Communists (Leninist) reported in January 1989. It claimed to have former members of the HSWP Central Committee amongst its membership, and expected a membership of over 250,000. Petres stated at the time of its foundation that its existence would not be necessary if the HSWP returned to a "normal path". It did not, but nothing more was heard of the Workers' Marxist–Leninist Party.

LATVIA

Stephen White

Socialist rule was established in Latvia in 1917 but was overthrown in 1919. Under the secret protocol to the 1939 Nazi-Soviet Pact Latvia was assigned to the Soviet sphere of influence, and in 1940 it was formally incorporated into the USSR. Nationalists won a majority in the republican parliament in elections in 1990, and declared the republic independent on the basis of its pre-war constitution. This declaration was not accepted by the Soviet authorities but, after a continuing process of negotiation, Latvia became an independent state on Sept. 6, 1991, following a decision to that effect by the USSR State Council and recognition by most western countries.

Latvia has an area of 63,700 sq km and had a 1989 census population of 2,681,000.

Directory of Parties

Communist Party

As from January 1991 the republican CPSU organization had seven urban bodies, 30 district bodies and 2,829 branches. Following a split in 1990, it became effectively a party of the republic's large Russian-speaking population. Its First Secretary, elected in April 1990, is Alfreds Petrovich Rubiks, a Latvian national born in 1935. He became a member of the CPSU Central Committee and Politburo in July 1990. In August 1991, following the attempted coup, Rubiks was arrested and the Party's activities were suspended.

Democratic Labour Party of Latvia

Following the split in the republican Communist Party in 1990 an Independent Communist Party of Latvia was formed at a congress in April 1990. At its second congress, in September 1990, it renamed itself the Democratic Labour Party of Latvia. The main declared aim of the Democratic Labour Party is the establishment of a free, independent and law-based Latvian state based upon democracy and social justice. It publishes the paper *Neatkariba Tsinya* (Independence Struggle).

Latvian Liberal Party

Its establishment was announced in January 1990 at a congress of co-operative members; it places individual human values in the highest place, and favours the rights of private ownership.

Latvian Party of Renewal

Founded in April 1989 in Riga. Its declared aim is the establishment of a free and democratic Latvian state, which is combined in practice with firm opposition to the Communist Party and socialism. It publishes the newspaper *Yunda* (Dawn).

Latvian Popular Front

Founded in October 1988 in Riga as a "mass sociopolitical organization" whose purpose was to "support fundamental restructuring in Latvia on the basis of democratic socialism and humanism". A rather different programme was adopted at the Front's Second Congress in October 1989, which defined the Front's objective as the "restoration of the state independence of Latvia [and] the creation of a democratic parliamentary republic continuing the traditions of the Latvian Republic [of 1920–40]." Candidates supported by the Front won 130 of the 200 seats in the republican parliament in March 1990; the Front published the Latvian-language newspaper *Atmoda* (Renaissance) and the Russian-language *Baltiiskoe vremya*.

Latvian Social-Democratic Workers' Party

Formed — or more accurately, re-established — in December 1989, continuing the work of a party first established in 1904 which had been based abroad during the period of communist rule. Its declared aim is the establishment of a democratic, civilized society in a free and independent Latvian state. The Party publishes the newspaper *Social-Democrat* and the monthly *Narod i vlast'* (People and Power). In 1990 a split occurred in the Party, following which — in April 1990 — the Riga organization with its supporters established a Latvian Social-Democratic Party; a party of the "democratic centre", it publishes *Nedelyas Lapa* (Weekly Bulletin) and *Men'shevik* (for its Russian-speaking members).

LITHUANIA

Stephen White

The socialist republic of Lithuania was declared in December 1918 following the withdrawal of German forces, which was itself overthrown in 1919. Under the secret protocol to the Nazi-Soviet Pact of 1939 the greater part of Lithuania was assigned to the Soviet sphere of influence; following this the republic was incorporated into the USSR in 1940. In parliamentary elections in 1990 nationalist candidates won a majority of seats and declared the republic independent on the basis of its pre-war constitution. This declaration was regarded as invalid by the Soviet authorities, but on Sept. 6, 1991, following a decision by the USSR State Council and recognition by most western countries, Lithuania became an independent state.

Lithuania has an area of 65,200 sq km and had a census population in 1989 of 3,690,000.

Directory of Parties

Christian-Democratic Party of Lithuania

Founded at a conference in January 1990, the Party seeks the restoration of an independent and democratic Lithuania based on Christian teachings. Three of its candidates were elected to the Lithuanian Supreme Soviet in 1990. The Party publishes *Apzhvalga* (Review).

Communist Party

In December 1989 the republican Communist Party organization voted to secede from the

CPSU. A minority, consisting disproportionately of Russian speakers, remained affiliated to the CPSU. As from January 1991 this organization had nine urban bodies, 46 district bodies and 1,065 branches. Its First Secretary, Mikolas Martinovich Burokyavichus, a Lithuanian national born in 1927, was elected to this position in April 1990. He became a member of the CPSU Central Committee and Politburo in July 1990. However, Burokyavichus was arrested and the party itself suspended in the aftermath of the attempted coup in August 1991.

Democratic Labour Party of Lithuania

Founded in December 1990 following a split in the republican CPSU organization. Its chairman is A. K. Brazauskas, formerly the republican CPSU first secretary. The Party's declared aims include the state independence of Lithuania, social justice and democracy; it publishes the newspaper *Tiesa* and the journal *Politika*.

Democratic Party of Lithuania

Founded in July 1989; in 1991 had about 2,000 members. The Party continues the policies of the Democratic Party of Lithuania, which existed between 1902 and 1940. Its main declared aim is the restoration of a free, independent and democratic Lithuanian state, and it works closely with Sajudis in this connection. The Party publishes *Visario 16* (16 February).

Green Party of Lithuania

Founded in 1990, its purposes are predominantly ecological and environmental ones; it also favours the restoration of Lithuanian sovereignty and secession from the USSR. In the 1990 elections it secured three parliamentary seats.

Lithuanian Independence Party

Founded in Vilnius in October 1990. The Party broadly supports the policies of Sajudis; its structure is of a "club" character and it is concerned purely with parliamentary activities.

Lithuanian Social-Democratic Party

Founded in August 1989 on the basis of the party of this name that had been established in 1896. The Party's declared aim is to "restore the independence of Lithuania and, uniting the energies of the nation, to begin to create a democratic state". It has close relations with the Socialist International and other social democratic parties abroad, and publishes the paper *Sotsial-Demokrat Litvy*.

LITHUANIA

Sajudis

Founded in October 1988 in Vilnius; its first chairman was Vytautas Landsbergis, a professor at Vilnius Conservatory. Originally a civic movement whose purpose was to further the reconstruction of socialist society on the basis of democracy and humanism, *Sajudis* also sought to promote the "state, economic and cultural sovereignty of the Lithuanian SSR" and a "socialist rule-of-law state". *Sajudis* enjoyed substantial success at the USSR-wide elections of 1989, and in the February–March 1990 republican elections its candidates obtained 100 of the 133 seats in the republican parliament. On March 11 the parliament, having elected Landbergis its president, adopted a declaration on independence; *Sajudis* became an increasingly party-like organization and became increasingly insistent upon a fully independent status, although some internal differences emerged within its ranks. *Sajudis* publishes *Atgimimas* (Renaissance) and (for Russian speakers) *Soglasie*.

POLAND

George Sanford

Interwar Poland, after regaining independence in 1918, went through a democratic phase to 1926. The 1921 constitution, closely modelled on the French Third Republic, was marked by a weak President elected by both parliamentary chambers, the *Sejm* and the Senate, which were accorded the full plenitude of democratic legitimacy and power. The electoral system, proportional representation by party list, allowed the exceptionally wide range of regional, historical, political, economic, religious and national minority differences which independent Poland inherited from the 19th century partition period by her three neighbours to be reflected in full in an extremely fragmented party system. About 90 parties existed and many contested the democratic elections up till the late 1920s. There were usually between 16 to 20 separate political clubs in the *Sejm*. The most successful (*Piast* Peasant Party and the National Popular Union) rarely got as much as 20 per cent of the vote; only another two or three parties hovered around the 10 per cent mark. About 80–90 of the 444 *Sejm* Deputies represented national minority parties. The communists gained between two and six seats although they had a good result in 1928 (about 19 seats with allies). Whether a fully democratic parliamentary system with such an extremely fragmented multi-party system could survive in a hostile international environment has been much debated. It certainly did not last long enough to make more than a start on socioeconomic modernization and nation-building.

Marshal Piłsudski seized power in May 1926 and maintained a loose form of guided authoritarianism until his death in 1935. His ruling *Sanacja* (Moral Renewal) camp maintained its hegemony until the outbreak of war in September 1939. Parties, although increasingly repressed, especially from 1930 onwards, were not formally banned for the most part except for some revolutionary communist and national minority terrorist formations. As often happens in fragmented multi-party systems attempts were made to form larger conglomerate coalitions at various times, usually for electoral purposes. *Sanacja* formed the BBWR (Non-Party Bloc for Collaboration with the Government) in 1928 and OZON (the Camp of National Unity) in 1936. Their main National Democrat opponents formed the OWP (Camp of Greater Poland) in the late 1920s. The democratic opposition socialist, peasant and christian democrat parties launched a *Centrolew* alliance in 1929. General Sikorski, ex-Premier Paderewski and the peasant leader, Wincenty Witos, attempted to unite the democratic opposition forces abroad in the Morges Front of 1936. The corollary of fragmented multi-partyism was therefore both electoral coalition formation and attempts to mount conglomerate political camps.

The main parties of the interwar period deserve to be mentioned because of the exceptional strength of historical traditions and memories in Poland. Historic parties have reappeared in post-communist Poland but, like elsewhere in Eastern Europe, they have not, as such, been particularly successful. One cannot stress sufficiently, though, that names and recurring behavioural patterns have a strongly historical basis of explanation in Poland. That is why so many of the new forces have claimed lines of traditional continuity by cloaking themselves in old historical forms.

The main families of political parties belonged ideologically to the workers'-socialist, peasant, christian democrat, conservative and nationalist camps. To these should be added numerous parties representing national minorities, which made up about a third of Poland's interwar population, such as the Ukrainians, White Russians, Germans and Jews; the left-wing *Bund* (General Jewish Workers' Alliance) was particularly significant for the latter although it competed with Zionist and conservative religious groups. One should note the following parties, listed from Left to Right politically, with foundation dates.

Communist Party of Poland (*Komunistyczna Partia Polski* — KPP, originally KPRP, 1919), dissolved by the Comintern on Stalin's orders in 1938. Developed out of the Social Democracy of the Kingdom of Poland and Lithuania — SDKPiL (1893).

Polish Socialist Party (*Polska Partia Socjalistyczna* — PPS, 1892).

Polish Peasant Party (*Polskie Stronnictwo Ludowe* — PSL). Existed in two main forms; PSL-Piast, led by Wincenty Witos, was very strong in Galicia; while PSL-Liberation (Wyzwolenie) was more radical.

National Democratic Party (*Narodowa Demokracja* — ND, popularly known as the *Endecja*, formed in the 1890s); an anti-German and integral radical-nationalist party inspired by Piłsudski's lifelong opponent, Roman Dmowski, in the interwar period.

The Polish Workers' Party (*Polska Partia Robotnicza* — PPR), formed in 1942, became the dominant force in Poland at the end of World War II because of Soviet occupation and support. Anti-communist forces within the PPS and the PSL were gradually subordinated. By 1948 the PPS was forced to fuse with the PPR in the Polish United Workers' Party (*Polska Zjednoczona Partia Robotnicza* — PZPR). A similar fate had befallen the PSL which was forced to amalgamate with the pro-communist SL as the new United Peasant Party (*Zjednoczone Stronnictwo Ludowe* — ZSL).

The PZPR became the hegemonic political force in communist Poland and maintained its leading role until 1989; it formally dissolved itself in January 1990. The ZSL was allowed a maximum membership of 500,000 and between 90 and 118 *Sejm* seats. It developed a considerable influence in the countryside. The Democratic Party (*Stronnictwo Demokratyczne* — SD), formed in 1938, was allowed to represent small handicrafts and intellectual circles with a maximum membership of 130,000 and about 25 to 39 *Sejm* seats. Apart from these two minor parties a number of Catholic associations were also licensed. They were granted between three to eight Deputies apiece at various times who formed political clubs or circles in the *Sejm*. The regime established PAX, an organization of "patriotic priests" led by the notorious right-winger, Bolesław Piasecki. The much weaker UChS (*Unia Chrześcijańsko-Społeczna* — Christian Social Union) tried to balance between the regime and the Catholic hierarchy. The really significant body though was *Znak*, formed in 1957 and reorganized in the mid-1970s as a result of splits as the PZKS (*Polski Związek Katolicko-Społeczny* — Polish Catholic Social Union). This association was the nearest equivalent to a licensed opposition in any communist system. It produced major leaders such as Jerzy Zawieyski, Stanisław Stomma and Tadeusz Mazowiecki and was allowed a weekly *Słowo Powszechne* and a monthly *Więź*. Unlike historic parties like the PPS or PSL, parties of the communist period can therefore be described as ex-satellite minor parties if they remain largely unchanged as with the SD. On the other hand, they can be dubbed "successor parties" if they claim only partial continuity as in the SdRP's relationship to the PZPR.

Communist Poland was a most peculiar hybrid. It diverged from the Soviet totalitarian model in increasingly basic respects as a result of the confrontations between state and society in 1956, 1970 and 1980. The latter crisis produced Solidarity and free trade unions. Jaruzelski's system gained a lease of life for the remainder of the 1980s through martial law in December 1981, but communist-led reform proved neither consistent nor determined enough to be successful. The result was economic paralysis, political blockage and social alienation. Gorbachev's promotion of *Perestroika* within the USSR and the communist *bloc*, however, gave the regime a renewed reform impetus.

Strikes in spring–summer 1988 moved the PZPR leadership to the crucial August 1988 decision to negotiate with the pragmatic Wałęsa-Bujak wing of Solidarity which had re-established a semi-open Provisional Committee in 1986. The regime's aim was to incorporate moderate opposition within a novel system of PZPR hegemony. Political and trade union pluralism would be allowed within the Patriotic Front of National Rebirth (PRON). The erstwhile opposition would be granted minority representation in the *Sejm* on a single electoral list. Social support would thus be gained for the further hardships involved in restructuring the command economy in a market direction. The negotiations stalled during the remainder of 1988 because of the magnitude and complexity of the issues involved. The formation of Wałęsa's Civic Committee in December 1988 and the determination of PZPR First Secretary Jaruzelski, Prime Minister Rakowski and Minister of the Interior Kiszczak to widen the original terms of reference in January 1989, however, cleared the way for the Round Table negotiations of Feb. 6 to April 5, 1989. This inevitably was an agreement between élites, the PZPR reformers and the Solidarity-opposition pragmatists, to undercut social discontent through what was envisaged as a gradual four-year transition towards political democracy and a market system. The communists abandoned their original premises concerning Solidarity's systemic incorporation within PRON. They agreed to the opposition's legalization subject to a number of informal, gradualist and no-victimization understandings which have continued to dominate the Polish political scene right up to, and even after, Wałęsa's election as President.

The main mechanisms of transition and the basic planks of the new "mixed" system were that the opposition would be allowed to contest all 100 seats in the newly established Senate and 35 per cent of the *Sejm* seats. The PZPR would not have an overall majority in the *Sejm* and would thus depend upon its ZSL and SD minor party allies. In exchange, Solidarity would support Jaruzelski's election as the new executive President in charge of the Army and the police and relations with communist allies. The latter point was not formally written into the Round Table agreement but was subsequently adhered to loyally by Wałęsa. Other provisions regulated the independence of the judiciary, access to the mass media and the ending of censorship, autonomous local government, the conditions for pluralism and above all the complex issues involved in economic marketization and its social consequences.

The June 1989 elections proved an overwhelming victory for the Solidarity Civic Committee. It won 99 out of the 100 freely contested Senate seats and all the 161 *Sejm* seats which it was allowed to run for. Its representatives also gained high percentages of electoral support whereas communist and allied candidates were elected with low votes on low turnouts. The regime was humiliated by the failure of its national list to gain election. Jaruzelski himself was barely elected as President a little later. All this created the conditions for the ZSL and SD to ditch Kiszczak's nomination as Prime Minister by changing alliances. The Solidarity-led government of Tadeusz Mazowiecki thus emerged in August although communists retained control of the Interior and Defence ministries until the following summer.

The subsequent collapse of communist rule in the rest of Eastern Europe and the challenge of the Republics to central Soviet rule in the USSR then swept away the remaining constraints on the Mazowiecki government. It went ahead and dismantled the political framework of the communist state very rapidly. The IMF-backed Balcerowicz programme made a similar start in the economic field. The premises of the Round Table deal had therefore become obsolete by the time the PZPR dissolved itself in January 1990. But the novelty of the Polish "Negotiated Revolution" remained that the Solidarity experience of the 1980s had produced a broad-based counter-élite which took over power legally from the communists. Elite agreement on the systemic transformation to parliamentary democracy and to a market economy determined that this process should take place in a gradual and legal-bureaucratic manner without bloodshed and reprisals. The replacement of the communist *nomenklatura* was also slow and moderate, working down from the top.

The above realities were only partially changed by the split within the Solidarity camp caused by Wałęsa's demand from spring 1990 that President Jaruzelski should resign and that the "decommunization" process should be "accelerated". This started the train of events leading to Wałęsa's election as President by universal suffrage in December 1990. The new Bielecki government which he sponsored then got caught up in the complex political manoeuvring between the Wałęsa camp and the old *Sejm* during 1991. The inter-related conflicts were over the new constitution and the definition of executive-legislative relations, the type of new electoral law which would inevitably determine the character of the new parliament and the new party system and the speed of industrial restructuring and privatization. The political game was, however, overshadowed, as it had been since the 1976 Radom riots, by the élite's fear of uncontrollable outbursts of socioeconomic discontent signalled by growing industrial discontent from early 1990 onwards. The race was on to produce political mechanisms for legitimation, participation and interest articulation which might prevent this. The realization spread that democratic electoral-parliamentary mechanisms were ideologically neutral in post-communist systems; that is why the communist élite had agreed to them at the Round Table. Their purpose was to decide the character of the new social and economic systems, even though it might have seemed that the Balcerowicz strategy had foreclosed the latter issue; Poland had been embarked on the path of wholesale integration in a peripherally weak and dependent way in the capitalist world economy in a manner which might, after 20 years of exhaustive effort, get the country to the current level of Portugal. The emergence of new political parties and of a new post-communist party system from spring 1990 onwards outlined below should therefore be set within the above context. This early period was also dominated by the national unity rhetoric and illusions of the late 1980s. The very idea of a structured party system with a government majority-opposition minority relationship still had not taken a decisive hold.

Poland has a rich constitutional tradition which is deeply embedded in the national psyche because of the historical struggle for independence. The constitutions of May 3, 1791, of March 17, 1921 and even the "Little Constitution" of Feb. 19, 1947 are to this day revered both as symbols and as models for democracy and sovereignty. Public opinion contrasts them with the authoritarian constitutions of April 23, 1935 and July 22, 1952. One of the most striking features of Poland's "Negotiated Revolution" was therefore the gradual and wholly legal process by which systemic transformation was registered in successive amendments to the "communist" 1952 constitution which had provided the legal framework for the Polish People's Republic. The old communist system and its legal order was adapted piecemeal. Elite-led transition from the dictatorship of the proletariat to parliamentary democracy was achieved gradually during 1989–90. The move towards a market economy presided over by deputy-Premier and Finance Minister Leszek Balcerowicz was, however, much more divisive and contested. The process of political transformation was facilitated by the simplicity of the procedure, used 16 times before 1989, for changing the constitution in Poland. The *Sejm* passes a law by a two-thirds majority with at least half the Deputies voting.

The constitutional amendment of April 7, 1989 gave immediate legal expression to the Round Table agreement. It established the new offices of the Senate, the State President and a national council to ensure the independence of the judiciary. The *Sejm* also passed the revised electoral laws and legalized opposition, including Solidarity, in a new law on associations. Residual control over the creation of political parties was retained by the obligation that associations were to have their founding statutes registered by the Warsaw provincial court. The sweeping away of the domestic and international constraints which had made this balanced compromise arrangement for a gradual four-year shift to democracy possible then allowed the Mazowiecki government to dismantle the institutions of the communist state wholesale by parliamentary and judicial means in late 1989 and early 1990. Judges, procurators, secret and ordinary policemen and some types of bureaucrats were verified and where necessary dismissed. These institutions along with the Army were reorganized and de-politicized.

Communism's downfall was registered in the fundamental constitutional amendment of December 1989. The country became the "Polish Republic", a "democratic law-based state implementing the principles of social justice". Pre-communist national symbols were restored, all references to the socialist character of society and the economy were expunged while the notorious article three, enshrining the PZPR's leading role, was abolished. The constitution guaranteed the free formation of political parties, subject to the legal registration of their founding statutes. It granted them full legal equality and defined their role as that of influencing state policy through democratic means. These provisions were confirmed in the Law on Political Parties which came into force after much dispute in August 1990. As in Germany, parties whose aims or methods are held to be unconstitutional by the Constitutional Tribunal can be banned.

The legal framework for parliamentary democracy had thus been established. But the fundamental problem on the Polish agenda from 1990 onwards was how to use this democratic mechanism to decide the pace of transformation and the character of the social and economic systems as well as the final shape of institutions and the balance between them in the political system. The course of events already described, however, caused an embarrassing lack of synchronization between political and constitutional developments. The constitutional amendment of Sept. 27, 1990 laid down only the procedure for the election of the President by universal suffrage, leaving open the question of his powers. Wałęsa's election as President if anything pre-empted the possibility of the rapid election, widely envisaged for spring 1991, of a fully democratic and representative Constituent *Sejm* to pass the new constitution. It fuelled the suspicion that the Wałęsa camp was emulating Fifth French Republic Gaullist practice. Presidential influence on political practice would be used to determine the future shape of the political system and the new constitution and to mobilize an electoral majority to support the President in the *Sejm*.

Both the *Sejm* and the Senate established extraordinary committees to draft the new constitution in mid-1990. Their work was delayed repeatedly by the internal divisions which reflected the wider political scene, although a draft electoral law was passed in September 1990. The split between the Wałęsa and Mazowiecki wings of Solidarity then postponed any serious work until after the presidential election. The residual non-democratically elected ex-communist and minor party rump was then in a position to spike Wałęsa's plans for a May 1991 *Sejm* election. They voted to postpone it until the end of October. The net effect of all this was that a completely new constitution was not promulgated on the two hundredth anniversary of the constitution of May 3, 1791, as had been widely hoped and expected. Instead the parliamentary committees and the *Sejm* and Senate dragged out their bitter disputes over the new constitution for almost a year. The final draft compromise therefore developed organically through modification of the 1952 text. Wałęsa, at first in early May 1991, intimated his readiness to sign the constitution at the same time as the draft April electoral laws. He then reacted bitterly to the postponement of the election to October. Confused political manoeuvring then took place between the *Sejm* and the Presidential Office during summer 1991; the latter, as in Piłsudski's interwar case, came to be known as the Belvedere (*Belweder*) camp after the name of the official residence in Warsaw.

The democratic electoral law to replace the June 1989 arrangement was the subject of acrimonious and continuing dispute from spring 1990 onwards. The Senate wanted a continuation for itself of the simple majority 1989 law, of two Senators per province apart from three for Warsaw and Katowice. The *Sejm* constitutional committee wanted a mixed system with one Senator to be elected by each of the 49 provinces and 51 by proportional representation. The Senate submitted its agreed draft on March 15, 1991 and little interest was aroused at its first reading by the *Sejm* on March 22. But the *Sejm* constitutional committee voted decisively on April 19 for the mixed proportional-majority law. It maintained its standpoint despite Senate opposition but finally backed down on May 10. The controversial majority vote section was only passed by 142 votes to 141, although relations between the two houses were mollified by the 172 to 63 vote favouring the Senate electoral law as a whole.

The initial starting-off point in July 1990 on the *Sejm* electoral law was that the ex-communist coalition parties wanted it to be based solely on proportional representation. This would assure them some representation. The idea was therefore largely forced through with the support of such new parties as the ZCh-N (Christian National Union). The OKP (Solidarity Civic Parliamentary Club), fearing a fragmented party system with large numbers of parties having to be incorporated in necessarily unstable coalition government majorities, wanted a mixed system. Half could be proportional, based on regional lists, but the other half, a single-member constituency first-past-the-post system, would have then allowed the Solidarity camp to utilize its plebiscitary systemic change appeal to gain a comfortable *Sejm* majority. As what eventually turned into the September 1990 draft was unacceptable, the Wałęsa camp decided to ensure their leader's election as President before public feeling turned against him. Hence the absurdity of the democratic election of a President before the election of a democratic

Sejm required to promulgate a new constitution defining his powers within the new political system.

The final *Sejm* version of its electoral law, after long drawn-out haggling, moved more towards proportional representation at both regional and national levels, as had been practised in Hungary in 1990, than the autumn 1990 draft. The 460 Deputies were to be elected as follows: it was proposed that 246 would be elected on regional lists in 35 electoral districts and 115 in single-member sub-constituencies. Each voter was therefore to have two votes. Election in the single-member constituencies was to be by simple majority, although a minimum 10 per cent threshold was required for election. The votes in single-member constituencies were to be added to the regional list vote and this would thus produce the first category of 391 Deputies. The remaining 69 Deputies were to be elected by proportional representation from a single national list. A candidate for a single-member constituency would need 1,500 nominations, while a regional list would require 5,000 nominations. The registration of five regional lists by a party would be sufficient for it to put up regional lists elsewhere without further formalities. The *Sejm* passed its electoral law overwhelmingly on May 10, 1991 by 249 votes to 22 with 40 abstentions. The constitutional committee's draft passed unchanged in essentials, although two amendments were forced through: the party label was to be added to the candidate's name on ballot papers and the allocation system was modified to favour small parties rather more in the division of winning seats on the regional lists. On the other hand, 18 other floor amendments were rejected, including the controversial proposal that the Ministry of the Interior should reveal whether a *Sejm* candidate had collaborated with the communist secret police and that election expenses should be limited.

The above law was vetoed by Wałęsa in June 1991, ostensibly because of its complicated character, because it banned electoral activity in churches and because it would lead to political fragmentation. In reality the Belvedere camp panicked at being abandoned by the Democratic Union and most residual OKP Deputies by their compromise on this issue. Wałęsa feared that he would fail to gain a "presidential" majority under this electoral law. The veto was also a form of bargaining pressure on the Rump *Sejm* supporting Wałęsa's simultaneous demand for emergency economic decree powers for a year for the increasingly unpopular Bielecki government to unblock the legislative logjam. The *Sejm* just failed by a mere seven votes to muster a two-thirds majority to break Wałęsa's veto (257 votes to 123, the latter mainly residual OKP, PAX, PZKS and PSL-Bąk, with 16 abstentions). The constitutional committee revised the electoral law and the *Sejm* agreed to it (by 222 to 57 with 47 abstentions) within two days of its failure to break the veto in order to ensure that the election would be held in autumn 1991 as originally envisaged. Contrary to some expectations, the number of directly elected constituencies were not only not increased but this category was abolished completely. The bans on electoral activity in churches and on Poles abroad voting were also lifted. The *Sejm* proposed an open list system which would have allowed voters to choose between individual candidates on it. This did not satisfy the Belvedere camp who, having blown up such a storm over apparently minor issues, continued to do so with the demand, supported by the Senate, that the lists should be closed ones in order to strengthen party discipline and large parties. The *Sejm* on June 21 then rejected the Senate amendments by over a two-thirds majority in all four cases. Whether all this was a simulated Presidential-*Sejm* conflict designed to justify a Gaullist type of dissolution remained to be seen. The jockeying for political advantage in Wałęsa's attempt to gain a favourable *Sejm* majority and to dominate the emerging party system thus continued to be linked to the perennial post-1980 manoeuvring by Polish politicians to avoid explosions of socio-economic discontent and to throw responsibility for economic hardship and disappointment upon rivals.

It is impossible to be precise but it would seem that at least 100 political parties or organizations now exist and that around 70 have been registered. Most have small memberships of barely a few dozens or hundreds and very weak organizational structures, few of which even begin to cover the country as a whole. The characterization of the post-communist party system is therefore no easy task. Duverger's classic distinctions between mass membership and notables or electoral committee-type parties does not take one very far at the moment. Likewise, taxonomies according to programmatic aims, which is currently often the strongest developed dimension, tells us something about their location on the Left–Right spectrum and possible alliances but not very much about their type and degree of social support and extent of organizational development. As Poland still has not had a fully free national election one can only speculate about which parties are likely to have significant electoral support and therefore a political future, and which are going to wither away due to the fact that they are largely composed of would-be chiefs with no indians to back them up. The main issue, though, is whether the forces of systemic transformation and national independence of the late 1980s will be able to simultaneously complete this function while turning themselves into modern political parties carrying out the latters' normal range of functions. By this one means that they will be able to marry ideological-programmatic appeal with membership and electoral support and produce the leadership and structures which one associates with modern parties. Other associated issues are whether the most successful will emerge solely out of the political legitimacy of systemic transformation gained by the Solidarity conglomerate; or is there some political future for the historic, successor and ex-satellite parties and their traditions?

Taking Solidarity first, it was quite clear from public opinion polls and general observation that the civic committees and the OKP swept all before them between the summers of 1989 and 1990. It then seemed that the personality and tactical differences which divided the Wałęsa and Mazowiecki wings would produce two poles which would dominate the new party system. The case of Eire, where little real ideological or political differences divided Fine Gael from Fianna Fáil, suggests that purely historical factors and events can produce permanent organizational splits in movements of systemic transformation and national independence. Such a model was further supported by the apparently more christian democratic and workers' slant of the Wałęsa camp and ROAD's (Democratic Action Civic Movement) more social democratic and intelligentsia inclinations.

What has happened since then is that the Wałęsa camp, which organized the PC (Centre Agreement) in May 1990 to support their leader's drive for the Presidency, now seems to accept that this probably cannot become the dominant electoral force on its own. Its transformation into the Centre Party in March 1991, however, revealed the ambition that it should become a distinctive centre-right force controlling that part of the electorate while using Wałęsa's historical charisma to appeal across the whole length of the political spectrum. A whole range of political organizations also emerged to cover other sectors. The KLD (Liberal Democratic Congress) competes for the secular centre ground with the SD, the PSL-Solidarity and Solidarity RI (Private Farmers' Union) for the rural and peasant vote, and a large number of christian democratic forces exist both in autonomous alliance with the PC and as factions within it. Only political circumstances, particularly the composition of the fully democratically elected new parliamentary chambers, will decide whether other conservative and nationalist parties such as the ZCh-N will have a co-operative or competitive relationship with the PC. The evidence of the 1990 elections in Hungary and Czechoslovakia is that the first post-communist election in a sense founds the new party system by indicating which groupings will use their electoral success to incorporate or eliminate unsuccessful competitors. Poland has a more "Gaullist" aspect in that Wałęsa is clearly aiming to build a "presidential" majority around the PC which he intends to give a centre-right and moderate nationalist character. Whether this will produce a similar process of political aggregation as with the Gaullist parties of the Fifth Republic still remains to be seen.

The main opposition to the above formation is likely to crystallize out of ROAD and Mazowiecki's presidential election support. The problem here is that the UD (Democratic Union) which emerged subsequently seems to be competing for the same political ground as the Wałęsa camp because of Mazowiecki's christian democratic inclinations and background. This caused Bujak to form the RDS (Democratic Social Movement) in April 1991 for the ROAD section which refused to incorporate into the UD and which wanted to highlight its social democratic preferences. Either way, however, the UD and the RDS will inevitably be forced into close electoral alliance. Whether the latter will also be able to act as a bridge to Labour Solidarity, the PPS-Reborn and even the SdRP on the Left remains problematic. The PUS (Polish Social Democratic Union), if it survives, is likely to form the left-wing outrider of the Wałęsa camp as long as Fiszbach controls it.

The First Solidarity of 1980–81 was primarily a trade union federation and a social movement. Wałęsa remained as chairman of the former, being re-elected by the Second Congress in April 1990, but naturally had to resign on becoming State President. He then lost control of the body in early 1991; his supporters, Lech Kaczyński and Bogdan Borusiewicz, were defeated by Marian Krzaklewski. The latter and the Mazowsze chairman, Maciej Jankowski, voiced the growing economic discontent of their members. They distanced the union from both Solidarity political camps and the Bielecki government. They even threatened to run their own candidates in the parliamentary election in order to prevent the loss of ground to the OPZZ and the RLP which it has sponsored. The social movement side, the civic committees, run by the ex-Radio Free Europe director, Zdzisław Najder, ensured Wałęsa's election as President. Their long-term future in relation to the political parties emerging out of the Solidarity conglomerate is unclear, but they have largely supported the PC and its pro-Wałęsa allies.

The one generalization one can make about the complex and incessant to-ing and fro-ing of the peasant parties is that a single party, as evidenced by Bartoszcze's poor presidential election performance, will not be able to dominate the vote of this social group. Its loyalties are likely to be divided amongst the various political camps which are emerging. The detailed evolution is traced out in the directory section below, but one can note the following main trends here. The ZSL turned into the PSL which first split into PSL-Rebirth and PSL-Wilanów and then reunited in May 1990. The disputes between its successor-minor party and independent wings, symbolized by the Bartoszcze–Jagieliński conflict, continued to tear it apart right up to the moment of writing. PSL-Solidarity and Solidarity RI moved into the Wałęsa camp while PSL-Bąk did not commit itself to either wing, although it opposed the main PSL very bitterly.

The Left was discredited politically because of the systemic failure of Marxism–Leninism, but it remained quite strong organizationally as the SdRP, the PZPR's successor. The historic PPS split and divided at the slightest excuse of ideological or personality dispute but seems to have come together for the moment. Whether the SdRP, the PPS and Labour Solidarity either can, or want to, make permanent common electoral and political alliances of the Left between themselves and with the OPZZ-backed RLP remains unclear. Other left-wing organizations, like the ZKP "Proletariat", seem fated to remain no more than sects composed of aged activists who will die out in time.

Poland has a strong conservative, Catholic and integral nationalist tradition associated historically with the National Democrats. The signs are that this force is likely to be marginalized by the competition of the two Solidarity successor camps and the ZCh-N. It might become more significant in periods of anti-systemic reaction against the costs of building capitalism during the next two decades. Many of the national independence groupings of the 1980s are also likely to join the Wałęsa camp more because of his Piłsudski-like posturing than the historic type of nationalist parties.

One of the major problems in discussing the Polish party system at this time is that fully free elections still have not been held which would give a real picture of national support for the political groupings. The Round Table agreement was that there should be fully free elections only for the newly established Senate second chamber. The opposition was only allowed to contest 35 per cent of the *Sejm* seats with the minor ZSL, SD and catholic parties holding the balance in the *Sejm*.

This electoral contract was adhered to in the election held in two ballots on June 4 and 18, 1989 whose results are difficult to tabulate because of the foregoing circumstances. Civic committee (CC) Solidarity-backed candidates won 99 of the Senate seats, 92 on the first ballot as they received over 50 per cent of the votes. The remaining seat went to an independent, an ex-communist businessman in Piła province.

Although *Sejm* Deputies were elected in multi-member constituencies the system was not proportional representation. Each individual seat was assigned either to what had been the opposition-Solidarity or the government-coalition side at the Round Table; in the latter case it was further allocated to one of its constituent parties. CC *Sejm* candidates won all the 161 seats which they were allowed to contest against other opposition candidates, no less than 160 on the first ballot. On average they would seem to have been supported by about 70 per cent of the voters which, on a 62 per cent turnout, signified that the CC was backed by about 40 per cent of all adult Poles eligible to vote. The government-coalition side won all the remaining seats, totalling 299, with low votes on a low turnout on the second ballot, as allocated by the PZPR leadership, 173 PZPR, 76 ZSL, 27 SD and 23 Catholic and other associations. The matter was complicated by the failure of all bar two of the notables on the communist-proposed national list of 35 to secure election by gaining half the votes cast. They were replaced, arbitrarily, by new nominees elected in the constituencies on the second ballot to maintain the proportions agreed at the Round Table. The government-coalition ran numerous candidates for each of its seats but some of them, especially in the ZSL and SD, were nominated by membership and grassroots meetings against central leadership sponsored candidates. About 50 of these elected to the *Sejm* owed their election to CC endorsement on the second ballot and either joined or collaborated with the OKP subsequently. The actual composition of the *Sejm* elected in June 1989, unlike the 1990 elections elsewhere in Eastern Europe, therefore only reflects the Round Table contract, not popular feeling. The subsequent movement of Deputies away from their original affiliations in the *Sejm*'s political clubs is, however, a highly significant political indicator.

POLAND

While the composition of both the *Sejm* and the Senate is no reliable indicator of national levels of support it is also very difficult to estimate the percentage of the vote cast for individual formations. The best estimates are as follows; about 14,000,000 Poles voted on the first ballot for CC *Sejm* candidates, about 10,000,000 crossed off the names of all government-coalition candidates, around the same number voted for CC Senate candidates while about 9,000,000 voted against the national list. Taking the free Senate vote as the best indicator it would appear that CC support was regionally very differentiated. It ranged from a high of about 80 per cent in Kraków, Rzeszów, Nowy Sącz and rural-catholic areas of Little Poland (southern and eastern parts of the country) right down to 40 per cent in Piła; it was generally below its national average in most northern and western regions.

Post-communist Poland's first fully free election was held at the local government level on May 27, 1990. A single-member constituency, simple majority first-past-the-post system was adopted in communes with less than 40,000 population. In larger urban communes, a single list was submitted for multi-member constituencies. Seats were distributed on the basis of preferential proportional representation as practised in Norway. In both cases nomination procedures were simple; about 80 political parties and 240 local and other types of groupings submitted lists or individual nominations. Civic committees, which had replaced communist *aktyws* as the dominant political cores, submitted about 24 per cent of individual nominations and 21 per cent of the lists. Supporters of the old communist order still retained influence in local government. They attempted to survive under new political labels, including the SdRP, which proposed about 4 per cent of the lists and half a per

Local councils election May 27, 1990 (percentage of seats gained)

Civic committees	41.5	
Non-party candidates	39.5	
PSL	5.8	
Solidarity RI	3.25	
SD	0.58	(Claimed 1.2 with unofficial supporters)
SdRP	0.22	(Claimed 8.95 with camouflaged sympathizers)

Presidential election 1990 (percentage of votes gained)

First ballot, Nov. 25 (62 per cent turnout)	
Lech Wałęsa (PC and others)	39.96
Stanisław Tymiński (Independent)	23.1
Tadeusz Mazowiecki (ROAD and others)	18.8
Włodzimierz Cimoszewicz (SdRP)	9.2
Roman Bartoszcze (PSL)	7.15
Leszek Moczulski (KPN)	2.5
Second ballot, Dec. 9 (53.4 per cent turnout)	
Lech Wałęsa	74.75
Stanisław Tymiński	25.25

cent of the individual nominations. The ex-satellite parties still retained sufficient organization and membership to play a more significant role than new formations. The PSL and SD put up 8.3 per cent and 1.7 per cent of the individual nominations, and 5.1 per cent and 8.6 per cent of the lists respectively. The actual voting was a CC victory, but hardly an overwhelming one, given the lack of political organization and the local character of the election, particularly in small and rural communes. The low 42 per cent turnout was also an indicator of growing socioeconomic discontent and political demobilization after the excitement of 1989.

Directory of Parties

Byelorussian Democratic Union (BDU)
Białoruskie Zjednoczenie Demokratyczne (BZD)

Address. 15–062 Białystok, Warszawska 11.

Telephone. 31–118.

Foundation. Feb. 10, 1990.

Leadership. Sokrat Janowicz (main board ch.); Wiktor Stachwiuk (national board co-ordinator).

Programme. The first national minority party established in Poland. Its aims are to defend the rights of the Byelorussian minority by gaining access to the mass media. Does not demand autonomy so much as bilinguality of offices and place names.

Centre Agreement (CA)
Porozumienie Centrum (PC); Partia Centrum, March 1991

Address. 02–58 Warsaw, Puławska 41.

Telephone. 49–82–34; *Fax*. 38–89–81.

Foundation. May 12, 1990.

Membership. 10–20,000 (summer 1990 estimate) rising to an optimistic 30–35,000 by the autumn; the bulk coming from the civic committees (*Komitety Obywatelskie*) which the Centre dominated. Also drew support from membership of other centre and right parties. First congress method of delegate election suggested an extremely inflated figure of 68,000 (March 1991).

Leadership. First congress elected Senator Jarosław Kaczyński as president as well as a supreme political council. The latter elected a main board immediately afterwards with Jacek Maziarski as chair and Premysław Hniedziewicz, Marcin Przybyłowice and Adam Glapiński as deputy chairs.

History. Origins go back to autumn 1989 when Wałęsa imposed his closest supporter,

Jarosław Kaczyński, as editor of *Tygodnik Solidarność* (Solidarity Weekly). The group inspired by him started forming a christian democratic strand within the civic committees in opposition to the previously dominant Solidarity Left. The process was completed by the appointment of ex-Radio Free Europe director, Zdzisław Najder, as chairman. The PC was formed to support the call for President Jaruzelski's early resignation and Wałęsa's campaign for the Presidency. It produced a loose alliance of christian democrats, liberals and peasants with its demand for an "acceleration" of the processes of removing the communist *nomenklatura*, economic privatization and Polish independence. The PC was the driving force behind Wałęsa's election as President in December 1990. But it failed to achieve the early fully democratic parliamentary elections which it wanted held by spring 1991 and the passing of the new constitution was delayed by the "Rump *Sejm*". It also did not gain control of the OKP until mid-November 1990 when Bronisław Geremek was forced to resign as chairman and Mieczysław Gil was elected in his place. Its first congress in March 1991 brought together 38 Deputies and Senators, over 70 PC founder members and about 400 additional delegates elected in the provinces on the basis of one per 170 members. Thirteen parties and organizations dissolved themselves and joined the PC directly at this point being granted 30 per cent of the delegates. The PC had three ministers (Glapiński at Building, Eysmont at the Central Planning Office and Żabiński as Head of the cabinet office — URM — in the Bielecki government). Congress gave Bielecki a critical reception. It considered that he was continuing Mazowiecki's unpopular policies and tactically wanted him to shoulder the responsibility for mounting socioeconomic discontent. The PC was particularly strong in the Presidential Office with Jarosław Kaczyński, Sławomir Siwek, Teresa Liszcz and Jacek Maziarski amongst Wałęsa's closest advisers. Kaczyński demanded early parliamentary elections as the economy could only get worse, encouraging social discontent and the weakening of support for Solidarity's heirs. He continued the Wałęsa camp's tactic of blaming Poland's problems on the insufficiencies of the Round Table Agreement and the élitist policies of the Mazowiecki and Bielecki governments which had hampered the drive towards full pluralism, democracy and economic and national freedom promised by the PC. He envisaged the PC as a strong centre-right party of "ordinary Poles". His strategy was to squeeze out the ZCh-N which he disliked and to incorporate the KLD. He envisaged alliances with PSL-Solidarity which was represented at congress by the influential Jacek Szymanderski. Another congress guest, ChDSP leader Siła–Nowicki, denied however that the Roman Catholic hierarchy had endorsed the PC as Poland's christian democratic party. Kaczyński won the Presidency by 368 votes to 40 for Janusz Andruszkiewicz. The latter was a hawkish doctor from Gdańsk who wanted 26-year sentences for abortionists and 10-year bans on office-holding for ex-communists. The resolution supporting the proposed law banning abortion was not voted on and congress only passed a general motion on the subject. The indications were that the PC was being set up as the main political force supporting Wałęsa's Presidency in the forthcoming parliamentary elections. It stood a good chance of becoming the largest, although it was unlikely to become the majority, party. An unreliable June 1991 OBOP poll showed that it was the first preference of only 3.5 per cent and the most disliked by 6.1 per cent of those polled. Despite this, Kaczyński seemed slated as a probable Prime Ministerial candidate.

Organization. Developed rapidly and by September 1990 had branches in 35 provinces. In the year before the first congress the secretariat based in Warsaw was headed by

Przemysław Hniedziewicz (g.s. for organizational questions) supported by Stanisław Rojek and Piotr Skorzyński as secretaries and Maciej Zalewski as press bureau head. Around 29 Deputies and nine Senators usually belonged to its parliamentary circle within the OKP. It established policy groups on culture, economy, environment and foreign affairs. Numerous groupings such as the Christian Democratic Forum, made up of 18 christian democratic parties and groups, were set up within it.

Programme. Amorphous democratic and pro-capitalist, moderately conservative-nationalist but also married to social catholicism. The new Centre Party was described as "a political party modelled on Western Christian Democracy" (Uncensored Poland News Bulletin No 1/91, p.3).

Affiliations. Closest to PSL-Solidarity. Likely to have competitive electoral but government-coalition relationships with the ZCh-N and ChDSP. The following 13 independent parties and groups are formally affiliated to it: CD, UD "Baza", KLD, ChDSP, Young Christian Democrats (MChD), ChD, Democracy 90 SD, FDM, ZWD, civic committees (KO), "Rola", PSL–Wilanów and PSL-Solidarity.

Christian Democracy (CD)
Chrześcijańska Demokracja (ChD)

Address. Rynek Podgórski 9, 30–518 Kraków.

Phone. 56–52–53.

Foundation. March 7, 1990.

Leadership. Kazimierz Barczyk (council ch.)

History. A Christian Democratic Forum was set up within the Centre Agreement by a national conference of 18 christian democratic organizations on July 28, 1990. Barczyk became co-chair of the Forum's provisional council. (Among local based CD parties a founding congress of Christian Democrats in Poznań in January 1991 elected Senator Krzysztof Pawłowski as main board chair.) The christian democratic congress meeting in Warsaw on May 25, 1991, made up of representatives of eight christian democratic groups, supported the CD Wilanów electoral pact and set up a co-ordinating council. The christian civic movement (CRO) pushed most strongly for this and for others to work like it within the PC. A congress in late June 1991 established the Polish Christian Democratic Forum (PFChD — Polskie Forum Chrześcijańsko-Demokratyczne) with Maciej Wrzeszcz as chair. This body supported Wałęsa in his conflict with the *Sejm* and wanted the Church to play an active part in Polish public life.

Programme. Although it favours reprivatization and a market economy, it also wants strong anti-monopolistic measures, agricultural protectionism and a social welfare net.

Christian Democratic Labour Party (CDLP)
Chrześcijańsko-Demokratyczne Stronnictwo Pracy (ChDSP)

Address. Warsaw, Bagatella 10 m.7.

POLAND

Telephone. 29–16–11.

Foundation. Feb. 12, 1989.

Membership. About 2,000 in summer 1990, falling to a few hundred by end 1990.

Leadership. Władysław Siła–Nowicki (pres.); Kazimierz Świtoń (main council ch.); Stanisław Gebhardt (g.s.)

History. The party considers itself a continuation of the Labour Party (Stronnictwo Pracy — SP) founded in 1937 and suspended in July 1946. It grew again out of a Catholic intellectuals' club (KIK) set up in 1988. Led by Siła–Nowicki, who had become an indispensable mediator between Solidarity and the Jaruzelski regime in the mid-late 1980s. Siła quarrelled with Wałęsa; he and three supporters stood independently but were massacred electorally by civic committee candidates in the June 1989 elections. Marek Rusakiewicz (*Sejm*) and Walerian Piotrowski (Senate) were however more pro-Wałęsa and were elected on his ticket. The ChDSP supported the Mazowiecki government from the outside. It then split as it originally decided to support Wałęsa's Presidential candidature. The main council, however, backed Siła–Nowicki's bid to gain nomination as a candidate. When he failed to raise the required 100,000 signatures the leadership decided to support Bartoszcze (PSL). This led to a major secession by the pro-Wałęsa faction in mid December 1990.

Programme. Traditional christian democratic values favouring human rights, the family, the rights of the human embryo and the restoration of private enterprise. The ChDSP supports parliamentary democracy but also demands social welfare and justice, full employment and price stability. It is extremely pro-European and favours rapid integration within the EC.

Affiliations. Has established contacts with the international christian democratic movement. Competes with the ZCh-N which it considers extremist in terms of social and moral policy. Piotrowski's faction joined the PC but the bulk of the party remained outside. Collaborates with the PSL and the KPN in the Assembly for Democracy.

Christian Labour Party (CLP)
Chrześcijańska Partia Pracy (ChPP)

Established on March 31, 1990 as a Christian centrist group representing private enterprise, especially small businesses. As such, it wants a dominant private sector and a state with limited social functions which positively encourages small trade and handicrafts. Józef Hermanowicz (ch.); Piotr Karkowski, Henryk Rospara and Jan Zioberski (dep.-ch.); Maciej Łętowski (g.s.)

Christian National Union (CNU)
Zjednoczenie Chrześcijańsko-Narodowe (ZCh-N)

Address. Warsaw, Al. Krajowej Rady Narodowej 28.

Telephone. 20–18–00.

Foundation. Sept. 21, 1989.

Membership. 4,000 (late 1990 claim).

Leadership. January 1991 congress re-elected KUL (Catholic University of Lublin) Prof. Wiesław Chrzanowski as main board chair; Antoni Macierewicz and Marek Jurek are deputy chairs. Other prominent board members are Jerzy Kropownicki, Grzegorz Pałka and Deputies Jan Łopuszański and Stefan Niesołowski.

History. Formed out of political clubs such as *Ład i Wolność* (Order and Freedom) which campaigned against abortion, moral permissiveness and social laxity. Chrzanowski and Andrzej Tymowski were members of Wałęsa's civic committee. The ZCh-N has three Senators and three Deputies within the OKP led by the firebrand Jan Łopuszczański who criticized the Mazowiecki government. Other members include the long-time dissident, Antoni Macierewicz, and the Historic 1980–81 Leftist-Solidarity Łódź Chieftains, Andrzej Słowik and Grzegorz Pałka. The ZCh-N's attempt to compete with the PC by providing an ideological conservative-catholic national alternative, the Agreement for Democracy and Pluralism, proved a damp squib. The Christian Civic Movement (ChRO) gained more credit in supporting Wałęsa's Presidential campaign; this may have gained Chrzanowski the Ministry of Justice in the Bielecki government, a crucial post for influencing social and moral issues. His virulent personal views, especially over the punishment of abortion, soon aroused much controversy and opposition.

Organization. Branches in about 30 provinces, the strongest being Warsaw, Łódź, Poznań, Radom, Gdańsk, Wrocław, Szczecin, Lublin, Gorzów, Konin and Siedlce. The party won about 200 seats in the 1990 local elections. Its greatest success was in Łódź, where a ZCh-N-led coalition elected Grzegorz Pałka as city president. Its candidate, supported by the PSL, Solidarity RI and ChDSP, won 49 per cent of the vote in the Senate by-election in Lublin in June 1990.

Programme. The party takes a strongly conservative-national authoritarian view of Catholicism. It emphasizes the central importance of the family and private property and the need to limit the role and power of the state in all sectors. Strongly supported the reintroduction of religious instruction in schools and the proposed ban on abortion. It is unclear how it reconciles its proclaimed toleration for minorities with the assertion of what it considers majority identity and values.

Christian Social Union (CSU)
Unia Chrześcijańsko-Społeczna (UChS)

Address. 00–950 Warsaw, Marszałkowska 4.

Telephone. 29–70–56 and 29–92–51.

Leadership. Kazimierz Morawski (ch.). Tadeusz Nowacki is chair of the eight-strong *Sejm* Deputies Club.

Foundation. Established in 1957 as the Christian Social Association. Renamed at the 15th congress in January 1989.

History. One of the three associations licensed by communist regimes to represent

Catholics in the *Sejm*. An interesting radical social catholic strand, independent of the Vatican, its attempts to steer a middle course displeased both the Roman Catholic hierarchy and communist leaders. Failing to win much intellectual influence or popular support it was reduced to supporting Wałęsa in the Presidential election and to attempting to survive on his coat-tails.

Civic Agreement for Democracy and Pluralism (CADP)
Porozumienie Obywatelskie na Rzecz Demokracji i Pluralizmu (PORDiP)

Established on June 16, 1990, on the initiative of civic committees and political associations from Radom and Łódź. It was intended as forming a broad umbrella group for the Right and Centre to promote traditional Catholic and national values and to oppose the Left's hold on all walks of public life. It supported Wałęsa's candidacy for the Presidency calling for the confiscation of all communist assets, the hastened dismantling of the remnants of communist structures and influence, the reintroduction of religious instruction in schools, a ban on abortion and the withdrawal of all Soviet forces and influence from Poland. Backed by the ZCh-N, UPR and ChDPP.

Club August 80
Klub Sierpień 80

Contact name. Jerzy Pomin.

Address. Poznań, os. Kosmonautów 9c m.28.

Leadership. Paweł Łączkowski (dep. ch.)

History. A local club of christian democratic leanings founded by Solidarity and other opposition activists in 1989. Publishes the daily *Dzisiaj*.

Confederation for an Independent Poland (CIP)
Konfederacja Polski Niepodległej (KPN)

Address. 00–373 Warsaw, Nowy Świat 18.m.20.

Telephone. 26–10–43; 26–54–01 ext. 570 and 571.

Foundation. Sept. 1, 1979.

Membership. Unrealistic claim of 30,000 supporters (late 1990).

Leadership. Leszek Moczulski has been chair from the outset. Political council members include Antoni Lenkiewicz, Krzysztof Król, Andrzej Ostoja-Owsiany, Adam Słomka and Dariusz Wójcik.

History. Originally formed to oppose communism by radical nationalist and conservative dissidents dissatisfied with KOR. Its leaders, particularly Moczulski, were extremists both in terms of policy and means and this led to continuous legal repression during the 1980s. The KPN boycotted the Round Table and opposed the agreement as a tardy and incomplete compromise with communist power in Poland and its Soviet patron. The KPN stood independently in the June 1989 election (23 candidates) failing to win any *Sejm* seats, but civic committee approval ensured the election of Andrzej Fenrych to the Senate. Foremost in opposing the Mazowiecki government as a sell-out. Its well-seasoned cadres of some hundreds, steeled by a decade of opposition activity, had an influence out of all proportion to their actual numbers and gained the support of disillusioned workers through their extremism and dynamism. This enabled Moczulski to raise the 100,000 signatures required for nomination and to gain 2.5 per cent of the vote on the first ballot of the 1990 Presidential election. A Democratic Faction led by Ryszard Bocian broke away on Aug. 20, 1990, criticizing Moczulski's authoritarian running of the KPN. It supported Wałęsa for the Presidency from the outset as it was won over by his call for the removal of the Soviet garrison from Poland. The KPN rallied to Wałęsa on the second ballot.

Organization. Twelve regions and 40 districts. Strongest influence on the young especially in Warsaw, Kraków, Katowice, Lublin, Łódź and Toruń provinces. The KPN won about 60 of the 52,000 seats in the 1990 local election. Ostaja-Owsiany became Łódź municipal council chair. Publishes the weekly *Opinia*.

Programme. Virulently nationalist, it demands a strongly anti-Soviet policy and the dismantling of all remaining political and economic links with the USSR. It favours Lithuanian independence and the break-up of the USSR. Moczulski regards himself as belonging to the Piłsudski tradition. He therefore opposes the pro-Slav National Democratic Right and views the ZCh-N and even the PPS as potential allies. The KPN demands rapid marketization and privatization and an accelerated and far-reaching purge of officials associated with the communist era. It favours direct action, such as sit-ins in public buildings, and organizes often violent public protests to support its demands.

Conservative Club in Łódź
Klub Konserwatywny w Łodzi

Contact name. Jacek Bartyzel (Club Pres.)

Address. Łódź, Tatrzańska 70 m.72.

Telephone. 43–94–83.

Founded. April 1989. Co-signatory of the Łódź Civic Agreement. Considers that private property should be the dominant base of the economy. Business should be free of state control whose role should be limited to essential health and education services.

Conservative-Monarchist Club (CMC)
Klub Zachowawczo-Monarchistyczny (KZ-M)

Address. 02–643 Warsaw, Etiudy Rewolucyjnej 46 m.16.

Telephone. 48–11–08.

Leadership. Artur Górski (main council ch.)

Founded. March 7, 1988, in Warsaw. Registered Jan. 10, 1990.

POLAND

Affiliations. With the ideologically kindred Conservative Club in Łódź and the Count Aleksander Fredro Conservative Club in Wrocław.

Conservative Party (CP)
Partia Konserwatywna (PK)

Address. Warsaw, Poznańska 5 m.115.

Telephone. 20–67–28.

Foundation. Feb. 27, 1990.

Leadership. Stanisław Plewako (ch. of the organizing committee).

Programme. National independence and sovereignty, a strong executive power and a free market, private enterprise economy.

Conservative Party in Opole
Partia Konserwatywna (Opole)

Contact name. Zbigniew Kowalewski.

Address. 46–053 Suchy Bór, Sosnowa 14.

Telephone. Opole 60–97–26.

Count Aleksander Fredro Conservative Club
Klub Konserwatystow im. Aleksander hr. Fredry

Contact name. Aleksander Popiel.

Address. 51–140 Wrocław, Piętaka 9.

Telephone. 57–47–45.

Democratic Action Civic Movement — Democratic Social Movement (DACM-DSM)
Ruch Obywatelski Akcja Demokratyczna (ROAD) — Ruch Demokratyczno Społeczny (RDS)

Address. 00–714 Warsaw, Czerniakowska 34 m.18.

Telephone. 40–02–31 and 20–02–11 ext. 2724.

Foundation. ROAD founded on July 16, 1990 (registered December 1990); RDS set up in April 1991.

Membership. Claimed 4,000 (July 1990).

Leadership. ROAD was founded and led by Zbigniew Bujak and Władysław Frasyniuk. Other prominent figures included Deputies Jacek Kuroń, Adam Michnik, Jan Rokita and Henryk Wujec, and Senators Andrzej Celiński, Zofia Kuratowska, Jerzy Regulski, Andrzej Szczypiorski, Andrzej Wajda and Andrzej Wielowiejski. Bujak is chair of RDS.

History. ROAD was established to oppose Wałęsa's drive for the Presidency and to support Mazowiecki's candidacy. It remained as the largest circle within the OKP during 1990 (Michnik resigned December 1990). Bujak and Michnik, who were secular-leftist Historic Chieftains of the 1980–81 period, opposed Wałęsa's growing centre-right orientation and his hold over the civic committees. Following Mazowiecki's defeat and resignation as Premier, ROAD split. The Road congress in January 1991, claiming 5,000 members, declared itself for its own statute, leadership and organization and postponed unification with the UD. It elected Frasyniuk as chair. Bujak and his mainly Warsaw-based supporters wanted to maintain an independent centre-left force to compete in the parliamentary elections. They broke away and organized the RDS for this purpose in April 1991. Bujak claimed that the party would find natural allies in defending workers' interests in the PPS and Labour Solidarity. The remainder supported Mazowiecki's idea of a broader more centre-right formation, incorporating the FDP, and joined his UD.

Programme. ROAD's leaders stressed its roots in the Solidarity inheritance in terms of civil rights, legal parliamentary methods and protection for socially disadvantaged groups during the process of establishing market capitalism. It distrusted Wałęsa's demagogic populism and the authoritarian implications of the cult of his personality. It saw itself as providing the political core for the evolution of a broad social democratic party emerging out of Solidarity's legitimacy. As such, it divided between those who wanted to emphasize this identity in the RDS and those who favoured Mazowiecki's conception of a broad social-to-christian-democratic conglomerate.

Organization. ROAD had local branches in over 37 provinces.

Democratic Centre (DC)
Centrum Demokratyczne (CD)

Contact name. Adam Lipski (ch.)

Address. Wrocław, Rynek Ratusz 13/14 m.3.

Contact name. Adam Strug (Warsaw branch ch.)

Address. 05–511 Warsaw, Nowogrodzka 16, room 18.

Telephone. 28–96–37.

Foundation. April 23, 1989. Registered in Wrocław in July 1989.

History. A current within the PC with its strongest pockets of strength in Warsaw and Silesia.

Democratic Forum "Mazowia" (DF "M")
Forum Demokratyczne "Mazowsze" (FD "M")

Foundation. May 8, 1990.

Leadership. FDM signatories included Krzysztof Czabański, Jerzy Dyner, Jarosław Kaczyński, Jacek Maziarski, Marcin Przybyłowicz and Andrzej Wieczorek.

History. Formed by activists mainly from Solidarity, the civic committees and associated groups. Its aims were to influence the Warsaw municipal authorities in favour of "acceleration" and to support Wałęsa's drive for the Presidency at this local level.

Democratic Party (DP)
Stronnictwo Demokratyczne (SD)

Contact name. Tadeusz Kozłowski (SD central committee spokesman), tel. 27–23–75.

Address. Main office 00–021 Warsaw, Rutkowskiego 9.

Telephone. 26–10–01.

Foundation. Formed in spring 1939 on the basis of Democratic Clubs established in 1937.

Membership. Oscillated between 140,000 in 1948, 35,000 in 1955, rising to a peak of 130,000 by 1989. Mainly represented University-educated and white-collar professionals; also small private tradesmen and handicraftsmen. Its support from the communist period has been whittled down by defections to the PC, KLD, SP and ZCh-N, but the remaining hardcore has assured its survival although it is clearly well below the notional 100,000 claimed as late as summer 1990.

Leadership. Party chair changed rapidly in the 1980s (Edward Kowalczyk, Tadeusz Witold Młyńczak and Jerzy Jóźwiak). Aleksander Mackiewicz, Minister of Domestic Trade in the Mazowiecki government became chair in March 1990, re-elected by the April 1991 congress.

History. Originally formed in late 1930s by liberal-democratic intellectual clubs opposed to authoritarianism. The SD survived postwar as a minor party subordinated to communist hegemony. Its liberal-democratic strand re-emerged in reformist periods, notably 1945–47, 1955–57, 1980–81 and again after 1987 when pro-communist leaders and policies were changed. Its September 1988 theses demanded a curtailment of the PZPR's leading role and a genuine coalition form of power-sharing, parliamentary and pluralist democracy and a rejection of the command economy in favour of the equal and competitive character of various forms of ownership. At the Round Table the SD was particularly influential in the debate on establishing the new Presidential office and the revised electoral law and in supporting judicial autonomy and the freedom of the mass media. In the June 1989 elections the SD failed to win a single Senate seat; in the 27 *Sejm* seats assigned to it by the PZPR civic committee, support ensured the victory of about a third of their winning candidates. The pro-Solidarity SD parliamentary club was thus able to dominate the official leadership and to effect the SD's change of alliance in August 1989. In the Mazowiecki government it held the portfolios of deputy-premier and scientific-technical development as well as domestic trade and communications. It only retained the latter (Jerzy Slezak) in the Bielecki cabinet having supported Wałęsa for the Presidency. It suffered from its association with the communist period and was deprived of some of its assets. Once its 1988 postulates for systemic transformation towards democracy and a market economy had been fulfilled it was unable to produce a clear political profile. The SD underwent rapid and continuing leadership change and numerous splits and secessions linked to the programmatic dispute over whether it should become a right-wing, centre or centre-left party. It is now beaming its electoral appeal at its traditional lower middle-class and civil rights pockets of support. The Democracy 90 faction, led by Tadeusz Bień, was founded on Jan. 24, 1991, by pro-Solidarity SD Deputies and seceded in May 1991.

Organization. Almost entirely urban, based mainly on the intelligentsia and petit bourgeoisie. Its daily *Kurier Polski* was a critical force during reform periods and it also had a weekly *Tygodnik Demokratyczny.* At end-1987 it had 4,303 circles. The SD won about 1.5 per cent of the vote and 860 seats in the 1990 local elections, scoring best in Bielsko-Biała, Bydgoszcz, Elbląg and Jelenia Góra provinces. It did very badly in the large cities but held its own in small-to-medium towns.

Programme. Liberal and mainly secular principles of pluralist and parliamentary democracy, individual rights and the rule of law, decentralization and the development of a privately owned market economy. Disputes over the direction of political orientation, the degree of state economic interventionism and social welfare and alliance strategy led to various secessions during 1991. Its alliance offers have been shunned by its new liberal-democratic competitors.

Democratic Union (DU)
Unia Demokratyczna (UD)

Membership. Estimated 12–13,000 (May 1991). Inherited about 10,000 from old ROAD/UD, 140 from FDP.

History. Mazowiecki's presidential election committees set up the UD core on Dec. 2, 1991, and a nine-strong foundation committee with representatives from ROAD and the FPD (Forum of the democratic Right) on Dec. 15 (Mazowiecki, ch.; Piotr Nowina-Konopka, g.s.). A new PKUD parliamentary club (Parlamentarny Klub Unia Demokratyczna), claiming 43 Deputies and 27 Senators emerged, which elected Geremek as chair. A dispute followed whether to form a single party or a broader electoral coalition. Bujak and Hall favoured the latter. Mazowiecki wanted a compromise as he claimed that the UD was now recruiting support outside its original intelligentsia base and that polls were showing it to be the strongest party in Katowice and the second in Gdańsk. Over 600 delegates attended the UD's unification congress on May 11–12, 1991, which brought together the UD, FDP and ROAD. Mazowiecki was elected chair (556 votes) and Władysław Frasyniuk (555 votes), Jacek Kuroń (518 votes) and Aleksander Hall (511 votes) became deputy chairs. Congress, chaired by Geremek, also elected a council, audit board and comrades' court and passed a compromise programme and a statute which allowed factions. The ROAD Social-Liberal Faction, led by Zofia Kuratowska, and the Faction of the Democratic Right, led by Aleksander Hall, had already been established to dispute whether the party should go in a centre-left or centre-right direction. Although a two-thirds majority of the FDP voted to dissolve itself, the Poznań-based minority led by Michał Wojtczak left the congress. "The Agreement for Poland" programme called for the regaining of democratic support for the continuation of reform. It held that a balance should be struck between satisfying current social and economic demands and building the future common good. Congress papered over cracks on the issue of whether the UD should be a CD or SD party. A UD council meeting in late May 1991 appointed Piotr Nowina-Konopka as general secretary and Jacek Kuroń as electoral committee head. A new UD-Green Faction, chaired by Radosław Gawlik, emerged at this time.

Forum of the Democratic Right (FDR)
Forum Prawicy Demokratycznej (FPD)

Contact name. Tomasz Wołek, tel. Warsaw 20–79–19.

Address. Warsaw, Wspólna 41 m.73.

Telephone. 29–63–93.

Foundation. June 27, 1990.

Membership. Some hundreds. (Unrealistic four-figure claims.)

Leadership. Aleksander Hall elected as main board chair on resigning from the Mazowiecki government in November 1990. Notables include Tomasz Wołek, Michał Chaloński, Stanisław Stomma, Tadeusz Syryjczyk, Michał Wojtczak and Henryk Woźniakowski.

History. Supported Mazowiecki government and worked within the Agreement for Democracy. Its informal guiding light, Aleksander Hall, Mazowiecki's minister for collaboration with political parties, had animated a similar grouping during the late 1980s. It joined the UD in May 1991 as a centre-right counterpoise.

Organization. A broad group bringing together conservatives, liberals and christian democrats. Strongest in Warsaw, Poznań, Kraków, and Kielce. Formed FPDUD (Fraction of the Democratic Right within the Democratic Union) on June 30, 1991.

Programme. Supports a law-based state. The free market economy should be based on private property and a massive transfer of shares to citizens. Favours a strong Presidency and the idea that the state should carry out the socioeconomic functions outside the individual's capacities. Strongly in favour of international political and economic co-operation.

Freedom Party (FP)
Partia Wolności (PW)

Foundation. June 7, 1990.

Membership. 200 (est.)

Leadership. Kornel Morawiecki (ch.)

History. The political wing of Fighting Solidarity which split away from Solidarity in June 1982 and produced extremist left-wing underground opposition to the communist system.

It opposed Wałęsa's control over the mainstream Solidarity movement and the Round Table, which it considered an élitist deal. It maintained the tradition of radical, often violent, grass-roots protest against the Mazowiecki government, especially Balcerowicz' policies and in the call for President Jaruzelski's resignation in spring–summer 1990. Morawiecki just failed to collect the 100,000 required signatures to stand in the 1990 Presidential election, which led to a judicial appeal which was rejected.

Programme. Based on the 1987 Fighting Solidarity demands for a fully independent and democratic non-communist Poland with a free market economy. Its post-communist demands centred on the speed and extent of the dismantling of the communist system at home and the withdrawal from the Warsaw Pact and Comecon abroad. It opposes the Balcerowicz plan and stands for a more socially motivated and self-managing Third Way successor system to communism. Supports East European federalism.

Affiliations. Leans towards Solidarity 1980, PPS, Labour Solidarity.

Freedom and Peace (F & P)
Wolność i Pokój (WiP)

Originally established in 1984 in Kraków to fight for the rights of conscientious objection and alternatives to military service. On the achievement of these aims in 1988 the pressure group, which mustered a hard core of some hundred activists, broadened out into such issues as the environment, human rights, disarmament and later opposition to religious education in schools and the proposed ban on abortion. Blended with other direct action, mainly youth, groups such as Intercity Anarchism (*Międzymiastówka Anarchistyczna*) in opposition to the Round Table, the 1989 elections, Balcerowicz' economic policies and the Presidential election, and took part in street protests demanding the withdrawal of the Soviet garrison.

Green Union (GU)
Unia Zielonych (UZ)

Address. 78–200 Białogard, Sawickiej 15/16.

Foundation. June 8, 1990.

Leadership. Jan Prochowski (pres.)

Programme. All aspects of environmental protection. Competes with the Polish Green Party.

Independence Party "Solidarity" (IP-S)
Niepodległościowa Partia "Solidarność" (NP-S)

Contact name. Krzysztof Wolf.

Telephone. Warsaw 35-85-04.

POLAND

Labour Party "Solidarity"
Partia Pracy "Solidarność"

Contact name. Andrzej Zieliński.

Address. 30–039 Kraków, Jozefitów 4 m.5.

Labour Solidarity
Solidarność Pracy (SP)

Contact name. Ryszard Bugaj.

Address. 05–807 Podkowa Leśna, Szpaków 6.

Telephone. Warsaw 58–52–63.

Foundation. Aug. 4, 1990.

Leadership. Main figures are Deputy Ryszard Bugaj, Senator Karol Modzelewski, Jan Jósef Lipski, Wojciech Lamentowicz, Piotr Marciniak and Jan Mujzel.

History. Developed out of the Group for the Defence of Employees' Interests made up by a number of OKP Deputies and Senators.

Programme. Aims to defend the interests of employees and to develop the left-wing strands of the Solidarity inheritance.

Liberal-Democratic Congress (LDC)
Kongres Liberalno-Demokratyczny (KLD)

Address. Gdańsk, Grunwaldzka 8.

Telephone. 41–82–23.

Foundation. Feb. 15, 1990.

Membership. A few hundred, rising to 2,000 (May 1991).

Leadership. Premier Jan Krzysztof Bielecki is political council chair with Deputy Andrzej Arendarski, Janusz Lewandowski and Zbigniew Rokicki as deputy chairs. Donald Tusk (a dynamic 34-year-old Gdańsk journalist) replaced Janusz Lewandowski as main board chair (May 1991).

History. Grew out of the December 1988 Gdańsk, and then National, Congress of Liberals animated by Donald Tusk. The party recruits most strongly amongst the white-collar and private business sectors. Apart from Prime Minister Bielecki it provided three other members of his cabinet (Adam Glapiński at housing, Janusz Lewandowski at ownership transformation and Adam Zawiślak at industry). The second KLD national conference, meeting in May 1991 with 150 delegates, strengthened the position of local branches and abolished the institutions of presidium and treasurer. Congress also decided, on Jacek Merkel's motion, that the KLD circle would leave the OKP and become a full parliamentary club.

Organization. Strongest in the Gdańsk, Gdynia, Sopot Tri-City, where it elected eight local councillors in 1990. Also has branches in Warsaw, Bydgoszcz and Kraków. The daily *Gazeta Gdańska* and the *Przegląd Polityczny* support the KLD.

Programme. The KLD favours the rapid rebuilding of a capitalist free market especially in labour, the lifting of restrictions on entrepreneurial activity and the accelerated privatization of state industry including the state farms (PGRs). It calls for the complete abolition of subsidies and the unrestricted sale of land in agriculture. A pragmatic liberal-individualist, somewhat secular, although moderately Catholic-based party appealing to specific interests rather than vague values.

Affiliations. It collaborates with the PC, although apart from Arendarski, it has not formally joined. It is highly likely to form an essential component of President Wałęsa's *Sejm* support after the 1991 election. It has a strong hold on the Independent Students' Union (NZS).

Liberal-Democratic Party "Independence" (LDP "I")
Liberalno-Demokratyczna Partia "Niepodległość" (LDP "N")

Contact name. Sławomir Mikołajczyk.

Address. Poznań, Wroniecka 17 m.7a.

Founded. Nov. 11, 1984.

Leadership. Four-strong political council.

Programme. Its original aims were the regaining of national independence and the breaking up of both the communist bloc and the USSR. It now favours the establishment of democratic capitalism and the establishment of a Central European alliance, if not federation.

Organization. Mainly Poznań-based, it publishes *Orientacje na Prawo*.

Modern Liberalism Club (MLC)
Klub Nowoczesnego Liberalizmu (KNL)

Contact name. Jan Szczepański.

Address. 00–543 Warsaw, Mokotowska 46a m.23.

Telephone. 28–21–93.

Foundation. Jan. 4, 1990. Co-founders included intellectuals like the sociology professor Szczepański, the Canadian politics professor Adam Bromke and ex-Deputy Premier Zdzisław Sadowski.

Programme. Favours a mixed economy and state intervention to correct the excesses of the market especially in the social, cultural and environmental fields.

Movement of Free Democrats
Ruch Wolnych Demokratów (RWD)

Contact name. Karol Głogowski (ch.)

Address. 93–031 Łódź, Senacka 24 m.61.

Telephone. 84–62–10.

Foundation. Established in mid-1970s by activists who had belonged to the short-lived Union of Democratic Youth of 1956–57.

Membership. Supporters mainly in Łódź, Wrocław and Warsaw.

Programme. Liberal-democratic, opposed to the extreme forms of capitalism. It calls for the equality of all economic sectors and territorial and working self-management.

Movement of the Working People (MWP)
Ruch Ludzi Pracy (RLP)

Contact name. Ewa Spychalska.

Address. OPZZ, 00–924 Warsaw, Kopernika 36 m.40.

Telephone. 26–02–31.

Foundation. December 1990 congress.

History. Grew out of the Agreement of the Working People (*Porozumienie Ludzi Pracy*) established on July 22, 1990, by a 120-strong group of ex-communists, including Mieczysław Mieczczańkowski, Norbert Michta, Bożena Krzywobłocka, Edward Osóbka-Morawski and Mieczysław Krajewski. The RLP is clearly the political arm of the OPZZ, whose chair Miodowicz and deputy chair Ewa Spychalska became members of its national committee.

Programme. The RLP statute declares that it is "a political platform for the activity of working people". Its aim "is to influence state policy in favour of the social and economic interests of working people" and to develop workplace self-management.

National Party (NP)
Stronnictwo Narodowe (SN)

Address. 00–264 Warsaw, Piekarska 6 m.19.

Telephone. 31–63–51 and 29–24–23.

Foundation. July 8, 1989.

Leadership. Bronisław Ekert (supreme council ch.)

Membership. 2,000.

History. The SN continues the traditions and values of the Polish national movement which goes back to the 1890s, and the ideas of Roman Dmowski which were incorporated in the interwar SN. It works on the basis of the 1935 statute as the "Seniors" like Ekert and Adam Krajewski, who re-established the party in 1989, were elderly survivors of the historic party. The SN allied itself with PSL-Rebirth in the May 1990 local elections and supported Wałęsa somewhat critically for the Presidency. A whole series of splits have occurred, mainly for personality reasons, amongst its elderly ranks. Stefan Jarzębski moulded National Democracy (*Narodowa Demokracja*) in August 1990 out of three currents which had split away earlier (Union of National Democrats, National Party-Piast and National Organization of Women). There is a plethora of competing SN labels, but the Seniors are not to be confused with other competing parties of the same name including a minor, more Catholic, body led by Marian Barański.

Organization. Branches in 11 provinces.

Programme. Its values are those of Church, nation and family. It considers them threatened by the contemporary moral and social ills of alcoholism, pornography, prostitution and cosmopolitanism. Like all SN parties it fears Germany, advocates a Russian alliance and a Slav union and wants Poland to have an "independent" foreign policy.

National Party (NP)
Stronnictwo Narodowe (SN)

Contact name. Janusz Leonard Majewski.

Address. 00–772 Warsaw, Sady Żoliborskie 7a m.2.

Telephone. 38–12–57.

National Rebirth of Poland Party (NRPP)
Narodowe Odrodzenie Polski (NOP)

Contact name. Bogdan Byrzykowski, spokesman.

Continues pre-war National Democratic domestic values of extreme anti-communism and anti-Leftism with a fear of the German threat which leads to a pro-Soviet foreign policy slant. An integral Polish nationalist and Catholic formation. Its mouthpiece is *Jestem Polakiem* (I am a Pole).

National Workers' Party
Narodowa Partia Robotnicza (NPR)

Address. 00–629 Warsaw, Partyzantów 3 m.12.

Telephone. 25–04–12.

POLAND

Foundation. In Warsaw on May 12, 1990.

Leadership. Marek Łukaniuk (ch. of a five-strong organizing committee).

Party of Fidelity to the Republic
Stronnictwo Wierności Rzeczpospolitej

Address. 00–264 Warsaw, Sady Żoliborskie 7a m.2.

Telephone. 39-71-46.

Foundation. Dec. 31, 1989.

Leadership. The long-time nationalist dissident Wojciech Ziembiński is the party's leader.

History. An extremist nationalist independence grouping which developed out of the Congress of National Solidarity (*Kongres Solidarności Narodu*).

Party "X"
Partia "X"

Address. 00–029 Warsaw, Nowy Świat 29 m.35.

Telephone. 26-66-74.

Founded. Party registered March 1991.

Membership. Claimed 40,000 membership declarations at above. First congress claimed 5,500.

Leadership. Stanisław Tymiński (pres.)

History. Tymiński announced his intention of forming his own party after his good showing in the Presidential election. The party, launched by 280 members and 80 sympathizers, at its first congress held in Warsaw on May 11–12, 1991, unanimously elected Tymiński as leader. Józef Ciurus, a building engineer and ex-PZPR member, became deputy-leader. Józef Dudziński, a presidium member of the committee in defence of the unemployed, co-founder of *Grunwald* and representative of an Italian firm in Poland, became the party's senior director. The statute retained the original name of X (as in Ten Commandments and 10 centuries of Polish history, according to the congress chair). Congress resolutions called for Balcerowicz to be impeached before the Constitutional Tribunal for losing Poland her economic and state sovereignty and for Wałęsa to learn how to maintain the dignity of the presidential office. Congress also protested against the measure, aimed at Tymiński, depriving Polish citizens who had not spent the previous five years in Poland of their right to election. The party gained a spokesman in the *Sejm* through the adherence of the Deputy for Oświęcim,

Stefan Bibrzycki, an electrician who had belonged to the PZPR until its dissolution and to the KLD after that.

Organization. Ad hoc, based on Tymiński's financial resources. Shares office space with the chauvinist *Grunwald* association, but whether this is politically significant is unclear.

Programme. First congress passed a 22-point programme which favoured the building of a market economy out of Poland's own domestic resources. Industry, handicrafts and agriculture should be protected and steps taken to reduce unemployment. Equality of access should be guaranteed to ideologically and religiously neutral schools and state institutions. Tymiński has been accused of demagogic populism and of appealing to ex-communists but his real political programme, apart from gaining power, remains hazy.

PAX Association
Stowarzyszenie PAX

Contact name. Michał Kołodzieczyk (press spokesman), tel. Warsaw 29–72–62.

Address. Main office: 00–551 Warsaw, Mokotowska 43.

Telephone. 28–60–11.

Foundation. 1952.

Leadership. Maciej Wrzeszcz (ch.).

History. The communist regime established PAX as an association of patriotic priests led by Bolesław Piasecki from 1952–79 to undermine the Roman Catholic hierarchy. PAX, under Ryszard Reiff's leadership, attempted to reform itself during 1980–81 and became an important support of the Jaruzelski leadership during the 1980s. PAX was guaranteed 10 *Sejm* seats in the 1989 election. This political influence would seem to be short-term and the organization has an uncertain future.

Organization. Publishes the daily *Słowo Powszechne*. It has considerable resources from a successful publishing house and the sale of devotional objects.

Polish Catholic-Social Union (PCSU)
Polski Związek Katolicko-Społeczny (PZKS)

Address. 00–513 Warsaw, Nowogrodzka 4 m.3.

Telephone. 29–21–63 and 21–52–96.

Foundation. Jan. 31, 1981.

History. The PZKS is a continuation of the Centre for Documentation and Social Studies (*Ośrodek Dokumentacji i Studiów Społecznych* — ODiSS); itself a successor to *Znak* which dissolved itself in 1976 as a result of the complex interplay between internal divisions and Gierek regime pressure in 1976. Mazowiecki was connected with these very influential groups who were licensed by communist regimes to express moderate Catholic opinion and to act as links with the Roman Catholic hierarchy.

Leadership. The influential Janusz Zabłocki was president until 1984. The current incumbent is Wiesław Gwiżdż. Ryszard Gajewski chairs the five-strong PZKS *Sejm* Deputies Club.

Programme. To promote the social teaching of the Roman Catholic Church and to influence Poland's political, social and cultural life in this direction.

Affiliations. Ideologically closest to the ChDSP and ZCh-N, although less extreme and strident than the latter. Whether this will result in a co-operative or a competitive relationship remains to be seen.

Polish Christian Right (PCR)
Polska Prawica Chrześcijańska (PPCh)

Address. Warsaw, Pańska 5 m.107.

Telephone. 20–60–56.

Foundation. May 3, 1990 in Warsaw.

Leadership. Witold Jazwiński headed a 10-strong founding committee.

Programme. Based on the social teaching of the Roman Catholic Church and the experience of the Solidarity Movement.

Polish Economic Party (PEC)
Polska Partia Gospodarcza (PPG)

Address. 60–247 Poznań, Nehringa 7.

Telephone. 66–43–71 and 66–10–41.

Foundation. Feb. 9, 1990.

Leadership. Wojciech Kronowski (ch.; also ch. of All-Poland Association of Managers).

History. A political club for managers which has established groups in Poznań, Gdańsk, Katowice, Łódź, Warsaw and Wrocław.

Programme. Campaigns for support for small businesses, trade and services and the training of Polish managers. Favours economic efficiency, supply-side economics and a management style of running enterprises excluding self-management.

Polish Green Party (PGP) (sometimes referred to as Polish Ecology Party)
Polska Partia Zielonych (PPZ)

Contact name. Janusz Bryczkowski.

Address. 02–051 Warsaw, Wawelska 78 m.30.

Telephone. 659–22–53 and 659–22–53; *Telex.* 814385 and 817530; *Fax.* 23–11–55.

Other contacts. Henryk Sobański, 31–140 Kraków, Łobzowska 24a m.14, tel: 34–24–61; Zygmunt Fura, 30–960 Kraków, PO Box 783, tel: 55–10–98.

Membership. Claims 16,000 members and sympathizers.

Foundation. At Kraków congress on Dec. 10, 1988.

History. Origins go back to the Polish Environmental Club of 1981. It assumed its contemporary form with a 26-point programme in late 1988. The main pro-ecology force in Poland, it has always been a fissiparous federation of autonomous grouplets. It split up into three factions led by Bryczkowski, Sobański and Fura in 1989. Steps towards reunification were taken by the establishment of the Polish Green Alliance at Szklarska Poręba in August 1990 and the holding of the Green's congress later in 1990. These divisions prevented Bryczkowski from raising the 100,000 signatures required for nomination as a Presidential candidate especially as the Fura faction supported Wałęsa from the start. Greens won some local council seats in 1989; one of their members became municipal President in their Kraków stronghold.

Programme. As well as the usual ecological and anti-nuclear power concerns the PPZ, like its French counterpart, is marked by a reaction against strong centralized state power. It opposed the concept of a strong popularly elected President even though Bryczkowski tried to gain publicity for the cause by attempting to gain Presidential nomination. The PPZ favours direct democracy in the form of national and local referenda, the right of legislative initiative for citizens and a participatory form of local government.

Affiliations. A member of the Green International.

Polish Handicrafts Party (PHP)
Partia Rzemiosła Polskiego (PRP)

Contact name. Ryszard Szylman or Andrzej Stysiak.

Address. Bydgoszcz, Piotrowskiego 11.

Telephone. 39–53–20.

Polish Independence Party (PIP)
Polska Partia Niepodległości (PPN)

Contact name. Romuald Szeremietiew.

Telephone. Warsaw 17–12–86.

Established on Jan. 22, 1985, by the secession from the KPN of activists led by Tadeusz Jandziszak, Tadeusz Stański and Romuald Szeremietiew who disliked Moczulski's authoritarian style. The general objectives of Poland's independence and national self-determination remained the same.

POLAND

Polish National Front (PNF)
Polski Front Narodowy (PFN)

Contact name. Andrzej Wylotek.

Address. 01–843 Warsaw, Grodeckiego 4 m.37.

Polish National Commonwealth — Polish National Party (PNW-PNP)
Polska Wspólnota Narodowa — Polskie Stronnictwo Narodowe (PWN-PSN)

Contact name. Bolesław Tejkowski.

Address. 00–521 Warsaw, Hoża 25 m.13.

Telephone. 29–36–06.

Foundation. Late 1989.

Membership. 7,000.

Leadership. Bolesław Tejkowski (ch.)

History. Tejkowski brought together the two title groups, the former established clandestinely in 1955 and the latter in 1989. The party is anti-democratic, radical Right and virulently anti-communist, based on integral nationalist values of God, nation and family. A real historical throwback, its anti-communism and anti-capitalism renders it both anti-Soviet and anti-American. Its frothy anti-Semitic rhetoric even makes it criticize the alleged influence of International Jewry on the Roman Catholic Church. It favours economic protectionism for "Real Poles" and a ban on land sales to foreigners. Tejkowski claimed to have collected about 60,000 signatures during his unsuccessful bid for nomination as a Presidential candidate.

Organization. Publishes the monthly *Narodowa Myśl Polska* (Polish National Thought).

Polish Party of the Friends of Beer (PPFB)
Polska Partia Przyjaciół Piwa (PPPP)

Registered Dec. 28, 1990. Popularly known as the Four Ps. Its first congress and an artistic festival with free beer was held in the Warsaw congress hall on April 20, 1991. Elected 49-year-old Janusz Rzewiński, an actor and satirist, as chair and a 10-strong supreme bench. Claimed 4,000 members then and 6,500 in May 1991 and hoped to win 20 seats in the 1991 parliamentary elections. Programme favoured toleration and the use of beer for mutual confidence-building in society. Opposed to the use of strong spirits, especially vodka, which it considers a dangerous poison. Rejected offers of collaboration from Polish Party of Friends of Whisky (PPPW).

Polish Party of World Citizens
Polska Partia Obywateli Świata (PPOS)

Address. 40–954 Katowice, Młyńska 21/23, room 19.

Telephone. Katowice 53–95–08.

Leadership. Józef Rogowski (main council ch.)

Polish Peasant Party (PPP)
Polskie Stronnictwo Ludowe (PSL)

Address. 00–131 Warsaw, Grzybowska 4.

Telephone. 20–02–51 and 20–60–20.

Foundation. May 5, 1990.

Membership. PSL-Rebirth claimed 300,000 and PSL-Wilanów 30,000 members in spring 1990 just before their merger. The PSL gained 7 per cent of the seats in the May 1990 local elections with its strongest performance in Chełm, Ciechanów and Kielce provinces.

Leadership. Roman Bartoszcze, President, and Roman Jagieliński, supreme council ch. till the Extraordinary congress on June 30, 1991, which replaced the former with 32-year-old Deputy Waldemar Pawlak and the latter with Deputy Józef Zych (53 years old, supreme council deputy chair).

History. The PSL was formed from the merger of PSL-Rebirth (PSL-Odrodzenie) with PSL-Wilanów (PSL-Wilanowskie). PSL-Rebirth developed largely out of the United Peasant Party (ZSL) of the communist era which had been a considerable force in the Polish countryside. The new party, founded on Nov. 26, 1989, on the ZSL's dissolution, attempted to gain credibility by developing an independent peasant new course and by allying on the interwar model with SN "Seniors". Its leaders were Kazimierz Oleśniak, a minister in the Rakowski government, and Józef Zych, their parliamentary club chair. PSL-Wilanów was set up on Sept. 19, 1989 by democratic peasant activists led by General Józef Kamiński. It harked back to the traditions of Witos' interwar peasant party and of the immediate postwar party of Stanisław Mikołajczyk. Their deputies left the OKP and formed their own club led by Bartoszcze in late 1989. Quarrelsome negotiations then led to the May 1990 unification, but this only papered over the continuing disputes over policies and basic direction.

The new PSL went into formal opposition to Mazowiecki's government over its agricultural policies in September 1990. Bartoszcze, however, won only 7.15 per cent of the vote in the Presidential election and failed to make significant inroads in even the most rural areas (over 15 per cent in only five provinces). This made a mockery of the PSL ambition to become Poland's third major party alongside the Solidarity PC and ROAD. The PSL voted for the Bielecki government but remained in opposition. The PSL Deputies Club voted for the unification of all peasant parties and the three peasant parties signed an electoral agreement in spring 1991. The conflict between ex-ZSL activists and those who wanted a wholesale purge of everyone connected with the communist period, however, continued to cause rifts between the parties and within the parties themselves. The PSL found itself in a complete impasse between Jagieliński's support of the former option and Bartoszcze's backing of the latter. Bartoszcze refused to accept Jagieliński's offer to stand down together with him in April 1991. There was at first an insufficient quorum for the calling of a congress to break the deadlock. This was eventually held in late June and Bartoszcze, who had been suspended and physically removed from his bureau, was supported by a mere 30 delegates out of 500. The PSL also passed a new programme and ideological declaration. It decided to extend its electoral alliance with PSL-Solidarity and Solidarity RI to include the League of Rural Youth (ZMW) and the National Union of Agricultural Circles (KZRKiOR).

Programme. The PSL has a largely agrarian programme concerned with the problems and interests of small farmers and the rural population. It opposes the plan to transform the existing small plots into large-scale capitalist units on the American model. The deflationary aspects of Balcerowicz' policy hit the countryside very hard, driving the PSL into opposition. It produced its own food policy and supported a whole range of protests including a sit-in in the Ministry of Agriculture in Warsaw. The PSL favours parliamentary democracy, but considers that the second chamber should represent self-managing interests. The party harks back to interwar traditions by calling for Poland to federate with other East European countries. It also favours an alliance with Russia because of the potential Russian market and its suspicion of West European capitalism and the united German threat.

Polish Peasant Party (Bąk Faction — PPP-Bąk)
Polskie Stronnictwo Ludowe (Grupa Henryka Bąka — PSL-Bąk). Also termed "Mikołajczykowska"

Address. Warsaw, Rakowiecka 26/30, room 307.

Telephone. 49–06–13.

Made up of those PSL-Wilanów members led by Henryk Bąk (former supreme council deputy chair) who refused to merge with PSL-Rebirth. The party has a four-strong Deputies Club and collaborates with the PC. Publishes the daily *Gazeta Ludowa*.

Polish Peasant Party — Solidarity (PPP-S)
Polskie Stronnictwo Ludowe "Solidarność" (PSL-S)

Address. 00–020 Warsaw, Rutkowskiego 42 m.1.

Telephone. 26–26–14 and 27–07–82.

Foundation. Sept. 21, 1989.

Membership. It has a parliamentary circle of around 22 members affiliated to the OKP. The party has pockets of strength in Nowy Sącz, Rzeszów, Lublin, Konin and Gdańsk provinces.

Leadership. Senator Józef Ślisz (ch.). Notables include ex-Minister Artur Balasz and Jacek Szymanderski.

History. It grew out of Solidarity RI (Peasant Farmers' Union) and was established when Ślisz lost control of the former to Gabriel Janowski, who favoured a trade union revindication model for its activities. Developed in reaction to the ZSL which it considered too tainted by its association with communism. It therefore rejected General

Kamiński's offers of unification with PSL-Rebirth in spring 1990 and remained hostile to PSL-Wilanów. On the other hand, Bąk rejected Ślisz offer of the deputy-chairmanship of a united party. The likelihood is that it will ally with the PC and other successor-Solidarity forces and possibly the ZCH-N and ChDSP rather than with other peasant parties.

Programme. Attempts to blend the Solidarity and Catholic ethos with the traditions of the pre-communist Polish peasant movement. It calls for the abolition of remaining restrictions to the development of a full market system in agriculture and for state support for rural areas. Demanded President Jaruzelski's resignation and supported Wałęsa's Presidential campaign.

Polish Republican Club
Polski Klub Republikański (PKR)

Founded. May 8, 1990.

Leadership. Co-founders included four Senators; B. Kołodziej, Z. Nowicki, S. Obertaniec and Aleksander Paszyński (housing minister in the Mazowiecki government).

Programme. To provide a platform for participation by private entrepreneurs in political life.

Polish Social Democratic Party (PSDP)
Polska Partia Socjaldemokratyczna (PPSd)

Contact name. Juliusz Garztecki 05–074 Halinów, Sienkiewicza 43; Czeslaw Seniuch, tel. Warsaw 20–12–25.

Polish Social Democratic Union (PSDU)
Polska Unia Socjaldemokratyczna (PUS)

Address. Sejm of the Republic of Poland, 00–902 Warsaw, Wiejska 6, room 149.

Telephone. 28–41–12 and 694–20–07.

Foundation. Jan. 28, 1990 (dissolved July 1991).

Membership. 3,500 (April 1990).

Leadership. Tadeusz Fiszbach (national council ch.). Its deputy chairs are Wiesława Ziółkowska, Jacek Wódz (programme questions) and Kazimierz Kik (organizational questions).

History. Constituted by 89 delegates (out of 1,633) who refused to join the SdRP when the PZPR dissolved itself in January 1990. Led by the pro-Wałęsa *Sejm* vice-marshal and 1980–81 PZPR Gdańsk First Secretary Tadeusz Fiszbach. The Social Democratic Union (originally US) was backed by 25 *Sejm* Deputies at the outset rising to 43 in April 1990. It was much more strident than the SdRP in condemning and distancing itself from the PZPR inheritance. The rejection of democratic centralism produced an emphasis on spontaneous local initiatives and groupings which developed in about a third of the provinces. PUS supported Wałęsa against Cimoszewicz for the Presidency, but its influence on the post-communist élites, especially in the *Sejm*, has proved transitory although Deputies Ziółkowska, Krzysztof Komornicki and Andrzej Bratkowski have played influential roles. The *Sejm* elected its parliamentary club chair, Wiesława Ziółkowska, chair of the Supreme Control Chamber (NIK) in February 1991 but the Senate refused to ratify the appointment. By May 1991 there was strong speculation that PUS would dissolve itself with most of its members joining the PPS and that Wałęsa would reward Fiszbach with some appointment.

Organization. Has about 14 branches, the main ones being in Warsaw, Gdańsk, Katowice, Leszno and Poznań provinces. PUS claimed to have won about 40 seats in the 1990 local election. Publishes the fortnightly *Gazeta Wspólna*. PUS is supported by Union of Young Socialdemocrats (Unia Młodych Socjaldemokratów).

Programme. PUS is made up largely of ex-communists who reject the PZPR heritage in its entirety and who refused to take over its assets. It wants to build a law-based state, a parliamentary democracy and a civil society gradually by using social democratic policies to protect the poorest sections of society. It has collaborated with both the Mazowiecki and the Wałęsa wings of Solidarity and aims to act as a bridge between social democracy and Roman Catholic social teaching.

Polish Socialist Party (PSP)
Polska Partia Socjalistyczna (PPS)

Contact name. Adrian Stankowski (PPS spokesman), tel. Warsaw 24–17–24.

Address. PPS Bureau Warsaw, Krakowskie Przedmieście 6.

Telephone. 26–20–54.

Foundation. Nov. 15, 1988 as a continuation of the PPS (formed in 1892) which was forcibly integrated with the Polish Workers' Party (PPR) into the PZPR. The unification of the PPS strands mentioned in the entries below with the London PPS took place in October 1990 after which it became known as PPS-Reborn (PPS-Odrodzona).

Membership. About 1,500.

Leadership. Jan Józef Lipski, who gets a good press in the West because of his earlier dissident activities, resigned as chair in March 1991 in protest at left-wing tendencies in the socialist press, but was prevailed upon to continue. The Łódź region chair, Edward Jendrys, was elected deputy chair in June 1991 prior to the congress planned for July 20. Other prominent executive figures include Deputies Kazimierz Błaszczyk and Henryk Michalak, Senator Kazimierz Brzeziński, Władysław Kunicki-Goldfinger and Andrzej Malanowski.

History. The PPS suffered from a large number of splits although the secessionists generally expressed their desire to work for reunification which was achieved in October 1990. The party supported the Round Table and four of its candidates, including Lipski, were allowed to run and gain election on the civic committee label. The party remained aloof during the Presidential campaign although there was some informal support for Cimoszewicz.

Organization. Groups in Warsaw, Kielce, Kraków, Poznań, Toruń, Szczecin, Wrocław and in Silesia.

Programme. Stands for democratic socialism and its value system of social justice and equality as opposed to dictatorial Marxist-Leninism. It supports the right to employment, workers' shareholding and a comprehensively high level of state social security. The PPS, as a strongly secular party, opposed the introduction of religious teaching in schools. It considered that the new constitution should be passed by a new fully democratically elected parliament.

Polish Socialist Party — Democratic Revolution (PPS-DR)
Polska Partia Socjalistyczna — Rewolucja Demokratyczna (PPS-RD)

Contact name. Piotr Ikonowicz.

Address. Warsaw, Piękna 43.

Telephone. 28–40–35.

Foundation. Dec. 19, 1988.

Membership. A fluid 500–1,500, mainly young workers and students.

Leadership. Piotr Ikonowicz (ch.). Main council members include Czesław Borowczyk, Zuzana Dąbrowska and Cezary Miżejewski.

History. Formed by the most radical secessionists from the PPS. Only agreed to unification when Józef Pinior's Wrocław-based Trotskyists split away.

Organization. Groups in Warsaw, Katowice, Kraków, Wałbrzych, Przemyśl and Białystok.

Programme. The March 1990 "Self-Managing Alternative" called for the Senate to be transformed into a Yugoslav type of self-management chamber, for local government to be decentralized right up to the provincial level and for workplace self-management and co-operative farms to be encouraged. It demanded social control over the mass media, army and police and the retention of a universal and obligatory social security system.

Polish Socialist Party (Provisional National Committee — PPS-PNC)
Polska Partia Socjalistyczna (Tymczasowy Komitet Krajowy — PPS-TKK)

Address. Warsaw, Archiwalna 3 m.7.

Telephone. 47–27–23.

Foundation. May 27, 1989.

Leadership. Grzegorz Ilka (ch.)

Membership. Brought in about 700 on unification.

History. Formed by a combination of secessionists from the PPS-RD (Ilka's group) and the PPS (Janusz Pawłowicz' group).

Organization. Branches in Warsaw, Gdańsk, Kraków, Lublin, Płock, Rzeszów, Siedlce and the Silesian region.

Programme. This faction always declared its readiness to work for the unification of all PPS currents. It stressed individual and group rights, particularly self-management and social security. It wanted an economy owned and run on social lines and for the state to promote equality. In foreign policy it demanded the withdrawal of Soviet troops from Poland and stood for Poland's economic independence from Germany, the USSR and the IMF.

Polish Socialist Party (Independent)
Polska Partia Socjalistyczna (Niezależna — PPS-N)

Contact name. Mieczysław Krajewski (ch.)

Address. 03–982 Warsaw, Bartosika 3 m.4.

Telephone. 13–72–28.

Foundation. Feb. 21, 1990 as the successor to the Polish Socialist Labour Party (*Polska Socjalistyczna Partia Pracy* — PSPP).

Leadership. Mieczysław Krajewski (ch.); Tadeusz Bilewicz (g.s.)

Not to be confused with the Independent PPS (NPPS) which splintered away from the London PPS in 1975 under Tadeusz Prokopowicz' leadership.

Polish Socialist Party (Rebirth — PSP-R)
Polska Partia Socjalistyczna (Odrodzona — PPS-O)

Contact name. Edward Osóbka-Morawski (PPS Prime Minister of Poland 1945–47).

Address. 02–534 Warsaw, Falata 2 m.4.

Telephone. 49–02–35.

Foundation. March 1990.

Leadership. Edward Osóbka-Morawski (ch. of nine-strong central committee); Stanisław Szwalbe (ch. of 24-strong main council).

Programme. The party is led by elderly 1940s activists who hark back to interwar PPS values. Wishes to collaborate with all other socialist political and trade union organizations.

"Reform and Democracy" Association
Stowarzyszenie "Reforma i Demokracja"

Address. 01–684 Warsaw, Klaudyny 14 m.54.

Telephone. 33-53-36.

Foundation. Established autumn 1987, registered November 1989.

Leadership. Prof. Jerzy Szacki, (ch.)

Membership. About 60, mainly intellectuals, including Ryszard Bugaj, Andrzej Friszke, Krystyna Kersten, Szymon Jakubowicz and Tadeusz Kowalik.

Republican Party — Polish Republican Society (RP-PRS)
Partia Republikańska — Towarzystwo Republikańskie Polskie (PR-TRP)

Address. 01-684 Warsaw, Klaudyny 32 m.299.

Telephone. 33-40-52.

Foundation. In Warsaw on April 12, 1990.

Leadership. Ewa Anna Malewska (pres.)

History. A locally based centre-right party.

"Rola" Peasant Agrarian Movement
Ruch Opcja Ludowa-Agrarna "Rola"

Foundation. July 21, 1990.

Leadership. Piotr Baumgart (national organizer).

History. Formed by a Solidarity RI conference in Koszalin attended by branches from West Pomerania. The movement supports the PC.

Social Democracy of the Polish Republic (SDPR)
Socjaldemokracja Rzeczpospolitej Polskiej (SdRP)

Address. Warsaw, Rozbrat 44a.

Telephone. 21-03-41.

Foundation. Jan. 28, 1990.

Membership. Claimed 60,000 (April 1990 and again in May 1991).

Leadership. In January 1990 the founding congress elected 36-year-old Aleksander Kwaśniewski as supreme council chair, Leszek Miller as general secretary and a 147-strong council. Włodzimierz Cimoszewicz became chair of the SdRP parliamentary club (PKLD). Kwaśniewski and Miller were re-elected by the first national SdRP convention on May 18, 1991 which carried out some changes to the supreme council. The latter elected a 17-strong presidium for the first time.

History. Formed directly out of the dissolution of the PZPR. The new party was marked by the victory of the social democratic Movement of the Eighth of July over doctrinal

Marxist-Leninism. The difficulty of establishing social credibility in its separateness from the post-Stalinist legacy was exacerbated by its sharp but losing conflict with the government over the confiscation of PZPR assets, notably its offices and the huge RSW publishing conglomerate. The SdRP claims to respect parliamentary democratic principles. It aims to establish itself as a pragmatic party capable of winning power at the ballot box. It therefore opposed Balcerowicz' socioeconomic measures. Mazowiecki was, however, preferred to the more authoritarian and right-wing Wałęsa in the Presidential election. Its candidate, Cimoszewicz, polled a very creditable 9.2 per cent on the first ballot. The SdRP called for early *Sejm* elections and was very active in proposing an electoral alliance of the Left aimed at the PPS, Labour Solidarity, the OPZZ and Solidarity left-wingers in spring 1991. Its first national convention in May 1991 criticized right-wing national values, clericalism and the Bielecki-Balcerowicz programme of building peripheral capitalism. Divided assessments of the achievements and the failures of communist Poland led to the establishment of a historical commission to prepare a report on the subject in collaboration with its Kelles-Krauze Foundation Organization. It included 2,587 local circles in May 1991. Membership was about a third white-collar, another third pensioners, 18 per cent workers and 12 per cent peasants. The number of Deputies belonging to its PKLD parliamentary club has fluctuated around 20 (23 in May 1991). It claimed to have won 784 seats in the 1990 local elections (and also claimed that another 4,000 councillors were covert sympathizers) doing best in the Łódź, Warsaw, Wrocław and Koszalin provinces. Publishes the daily *Trybuna* (successor to the PZPR daily *Trybuna Ludu*).

Programme. The April 1991 socioeconomic programme had a "Third Way" character. It emphasized the role of the state in maintaining social services and in alleviating the harmful consequences of Balcerowicz' marketization, notably unemployment and de-industrialization. It wanted to limit the extent of privatization and proclaimed itself in favour of workers' self-management, decentralized local government and a coherent food policy within a mixed economy. The SdRP opposed the draft anti-abortion bill most strongly and appealed to the Constitutional Tribunal against religious instruction in schools.

Affiliations. Has attempted to join the Second International. Proposed an Electoral Alliance of the Left in its 13-point March 1991 Appeal. Seems most inclined to collaborate with the PPS and Labour Solidarity as well as to win back PUS supporters.

"Truth and Justice" Political Association
Stowarzyszenie Polityczne "Prawda i Sprawiedliwość" (SPPiS)

Contact name. Stefan Pastuszewski (board ch.)

Address. Bydgoszcz, Jar Czynu Społecznego 4.

Telephone. 61–23–64.

Foundation. In Bydgoszcz on Feb. 21, 1989.

Affiliations. Associated with ChDSP.

Union of Communists of the Polish Republic "Proletariat" (UCPR-"P")
Związek Komunistów Polskich "Proletariat" (ZKP-"Proletariat")

Contact name. Jan Zieliński (ch.)

Address. 41–200 Sosnowiec, Jastrzębia 13. Also 00–910 UPT Warsaw 72, poste restante box 37.

Founded. In Katowice in January 1990. Now legally registered.

Leadership. A founding group headed by Zieliński. Bolesław Jaszczuk (dep. ch.; PZPR politburo member and economic supremo from the late Gomułka period).

Organization. Claims branches in Zabrze, Racibórz, Sosnowiec and Ruda Śląska. Collaborates with SdRP, PPS, RLP, ZSMP and DUK. A residual group of non-Stalinist Marxist-Leninists who oppose what its members call right-wing nationalist-conservative "Stalinization" and Balcerowicz' headlong flight into capitalism and national impoverishment. They promise economic rejuvenation through modern mixed methods of state action and basic social equality and security.

Union of Free Co-operatives (UFC)
Unia Wolnych Spółdzielców (UWS)

Contact name. Michał Sandowicz (ch.)

Address. 03–932 Warsaw, Dąbrowiecka 12 m.1.

Telephone. 44-31-70 and 44-40-22.

Foundation. June 8, 1990.

Leadership. Sandowicz heads a six-strong board.

Programme. Considers that co-operatives are the best form of socialized means of production and that the state should encourage their widespread formation.

Union of Real Politics (URP)
Unia Polityki Realnej (UPR)

Address. Warsaw, Nowy Świat 41.

Foundation. Nov. 14, 1987 as Movement for Real Politics. Registered under its present name on April 7, 1989.

Membership. About 2,000, mostly in Warsaw and Lower Silesia.

Leader. Janusz Korwin-Mikke (ch.; survived an attempt to displace him because of his unsuccessful bid to achieve presidential nomination). Influential figures include Krzysztof Bąkowski, Tomasz Gabiś, Stefan Kisielewski, Aleksander Popiel and Stanisław Michałkiewicz.

History. Critical of the Round Table Agreement and of the Mazowiecki government's continuation of what it regarded as wasteful socialist economic policies. It wants accelerated privatization and the return of resources to their rightful owners, massive cuts in taxes and social security and the emasculation of trade unions. A conservative-liberal party prone to right-wing laissez-faire and extremist views, especially by its somewhat eccentric and unbalanced leader. Korwin-Mikke, for example, declared that Tymiński's Party X would gain 40 per cent of the vote in the forthcoming general election and his own party 5 per cent.

Organization. Its support is mainly in Warsaw and Lower Silesia. Publishes the weekly *Najwyższy Czas.* Put up about 200 candidates in the 1990 local elections without much success.

Programme. The UPR favours a minimal state with the government subject to independent judicial control. It wants rapid and thoroughgoing privatization so that the state can withdraw from all economic activity. It has an unclear, somewhat mechanical, view of a political system governed by stable and natural laws with priority being given to the individual and the family before the state.

Universal Party of Slavs and Allied Nations (UPSAN)
Powszechna Partia Słowian i Narodów Sprzymierzonych (PPSiNS)

Contact name. Kazimierz Abramski.

Address. 80–345 Gdańsk-Oliwa, Pomorska 82c m.31.

Telephone. 53–18–13.

The PPSiN organized a two-day conference of six independent "sofa parties" (*partii kanapowych*) in Gdańsk in mid-April 1991.

ROMANIA

Bogdan Szajkowski

In Romania the elimination of multi-party politics in the postwar period took place between 1944 and 1948 through the familiar Soviet process used for the purposes of establishing a Leninist system. This involved the communists, under the watchful eye of the Soviet military, gaining control of key ministries (Interior, Information, and Justice); the penetration, internal splitting and eventual incorporation of rival parties and other mass organizations; and the extensive use of terror and annihilation of the opposition. In August 1947 two "historical" parties, the National Peasant Party and the National Liberal Party, were banned. The process of creation of a communist party system was completed in February 1948 with the merger of the communist and Social Democratic parties. The disappearance of the third "historical" party established the communist monopoly of power.

Although for the next two decades Romania followed closely the Soviet pattern of social, political and economic development under the leadership of Gheorghe Gheorghiu-Dej, towards the end of his rule an increasing emphasis was placed on the merger of Romanian nationalism and communism. The "re-Romanization" campaign which stressed the separateness of the political processes in the country from that of the Soviet Union and other Eastern European States became a centrepiece of the rule of Nicolae Ceaușescu. He succeeded Gheorghiu-Dej as the Secretary-General of the Romanian Communist Party in 1965 and in 1974 also assumed the post of President. Initially regarded as a reformer, because of his opposition to the Warsaw Pact invasion of Czechoslovakia in 1968, Ceaușescu in fact headed an increasingly authoritarian and nespotic regime. Throughout his 24 years' rule Ceaușescu managed successfully to present his policies to the outside world as anti-Russian. Little attention was paid to his bizarre version of nationalism and the use of extensive terror in order to emasculate even the slightest manifestation of dissent and opposition. After his trip to China and North Korea in 1971, apparently impressed by social engineering in both countries, Ceaușescu embarked on a similar process in Romania. The stated aim of the so-called "systematization" policy was the elimination of differences between towns and the countryside. It involved the reduction of the number of 13,000 villages by half through the forcible re-location of people into new concrete housing blocks with communal facilities and communities and the destruction of old individual dwellings. More precisely, however, this process was an attempt to increase further the state's control over the population. Closer scrutiny over individuals and families could be exercised more effectively in a communal environment. The "systematization" policy formed a part of a larger process of homogenization of social and political life which has been the hallmark of Ceaușescu's rule. The extensive use of the *Securitate* (secret police), and the placement of his and his wife Elena's family members in important government and party positions, also became a characteristic of the Ceauşescu regime over the years.

The Romanian dictator paid little attention to the changes taking place in the Soviet Union and the rest of Central and Eastern Europe. In the summer of 1989 he even suggested that the other Warsaw Pact countries should invade Poland in order to prevent the Solidarity-led government from taking office.

The eventual fall of the Ceauşescu regime was precipitated by mass protests in the Transylvanian town of Timişoara. On Dec. 17, 1989, the security forces fired on demonstrators protesting against attempts to remove from the town an outspoken Lutheran pastor, László Tökes. As news of the carnage in Timişoara spread to Bucharest and other parts of Romania, what began as a local incident led to a popular uprising against the dictatorship. Ceauşescu, to demonstrate that he was firmly in control, staged a mass rally in Bucharest on Dec. 21. Although several hundred thousand people gathered in the centre of Bucharest the crowd turned against him and his address was interrupted by shouts and demands for resignation. As Ceauşescu and his wife Elena fled by helicopter from the roof of the Palace of the Republic crowds began attacking the building. The rally in support of the regime turned into anti-Ceauşescu demonstrations. The fate of the regime was sealed during the night of Dec. 21–22 when the army changed sides and joined the uprising. Nicolae and Elena Ceauşescu were captured, brought before a hastily convened court, sentenced to death, and executed by firing squad on Dec. 25. The shooting of the Ceauşescus weakened the resistance of the *Securitate*, who attempted to mount resistance to the revolution by staging indiscriminate attacks on civilians and army units.

Within hours after the fleeing of the Ceauşescus the National Salvation Front (NSF) announced that it had taken power as a provisional government. The list of the 39 original members of the NSF Council released on Dec. 22, 1989 included: Ion Iliescu, Petre Roman, Silviu Brucan, Corneliu Manescu, Gen. Victor Stanculescu, Alexandru Birladeanu, and Dan Martian, all former communists. Other members included intellectuals known for their opposition to the Ceauşescu regime, army officers and students who joined the anti-communist revolt. On the same date the NSF issued its 10-point programme. It stipulated the introduction of a democratic, pluralistic form of government and the abolition of the leading role of a single party; the holding of free elections; the separation of powers; the elimination of centralized economic management and the promotion of initiative and skills in all economic sectors; the restructuring of agriculture and the promotion of small-scale production; the reorganization of education; the observance of the rights and freedoms of ethnic minorities and the guarantee that these minorities enjoy full equality with ethnic Romanians; the reorganization of trade and halting of food exports; and the conduct of foreign policy "in the interest of the people".

The programme formed the core of the programmatic decree issued on Dec. 27 which renamed the country Romania (previously Socialist Republic of Romania). The decree abrogated most of the provisions of the 1965 constitution and dissolved all power structures of the deposed dictatorial regime.

Within days, the membership of the NSF Council was increased to 145 persons to include prominent writers, artists, scientists and academics, but the real power remained in the hands of the initial core members headed by Ion Iliescu as Chairman of the Council and interim President of the republic, and Petre Roman as Prime Minister of an interim government. The Council quickly consolidated its position by taking over the old structures of the communist party in the setting up, as early as Dec. 29, of committees of the NSF in workplaces and at the level of each county, municipality, town and commune. An instruction issued on Jan. 12 by the NSF Council and signed by Ion Iliescu stipulated that these bodies at the central and territorial level "function as bodies of state power".

Following the Council's decision to outlaw the leading role of one single party, several political organizations soon emerged. By Jan. 18, 1990, 13 were registered with the Municipal Court in Bucharest, including the three "historical" parties having a direct lineage to pre-war parties. The National Liberal Party evoked nationalist sentiments with a strong commitment to a free-market economy. Its leader, Radu Campeanu, staunch anti-communist, imprisoned during the 1950s, had lived in exile in France since 1975 and returned to Romania in December. The National Peasant's Party was reactivated by Corneliu Coposu who led the party immediately after the war. The Social Democratic Party, which between the wars held the loyalty of Romania's small industrial working class, re-emerged under the leadership of Sergiu Cunescu and Dr Adrian Dimitriu.

During the first weeks after the revolution the NSF still maintained that it was not a political party and that its creation "was a spontaneous act, the fruit of those days". However, as it continued to increase its hold on power, the NSF Council began to advocate that the Front should turn into a movement independent of other political parties and should nominate its candidates for the forthcoming elections. The Front's increased control over the political spectrum, its style and method of government reminiscent of the old regime, and the fact that the inner core of the NSF Council was dominated by former prominent members of the communist party inevitably brought accusations of crypto-communism. As opposition to the Council grew, protesters set up a tent city on the University Square and declared it a "communist free zone". At the same time opposition parties openly branded the Front's leadership as a group of "reformist communists". They argued that the revolution was being taken over by an anti-Ceauşescu, but not anti-communist, group inclined towards a Romanian variant of *perestroika*.

In Romania, perhaps more than in any of the Eastern European countries, the question of previous political affiliations played an important factor in the transition process. Ion Iliescu had done little to disguise his communist roots. Even during the historic television broadcast in December 1989, when he announced the arrest of Nicolae Ceauşescu, he addressed his fellow revolutionaries as "comrades".

He had joined the Union of Communist Youth at the age of 14, was educated in Moscow for five years, and for 10 years was a non-voting member of the Political Bureau during the Ceauşescu regime. He fell out with Ceauşescu over the issue that settled Romania's fate — the copying of Chinese and North Korean techniques after the Ceauşescus' visit to Asia in 1971. Iliescu, who accompanied them, disagreed and was demoted. Petre Roman revealed on Jan. 7 that he had broken with the party a few days before the revolution when he learned what happened in Timişoara, but he still held Marxist views.

The past association of the prominent leaders of the NSF infuriates students and intellectuals who make up the majority of supporters of the main opposition parties, but has done little to disturb the blue-collar workers who form the bulk of supporters of the Front. Many leaders of the main opposition parties suffered torture, imprisonment and exile at communist hands. They suspect that their old enemies are hiding in the NSF. The subject of past membership of the communist party is a complex one. As the RCP exploded into thin air within days of the Ceauşescus' fall it had proved impossible to distinguish those who were party members out of self-interest (the majority) from committed activists. In addition the reality, in Romania more perhaps than elsewhere in Central and Eastern

Europe, was and will continue to be for some time, that everyone of consequence — from university professors to civil servants and factory managers — had to be members of the communist party to survive. Much of the country's infrastructure depends on the expertise of this vast army of complacent fellow travellers. At the level of senior administration and command, only committed party members know how the nation functions. Reconciling the desire for multi-party democracy and the realization that, in many sectors, communists hold the key, is and will remain for some years one of the most delicate tasks of the government.

The prospect of parliamentary and presidential elections, scheduled for April 1990, intensified another controversy that had dominated Romania's party politics during the first few months after the revolution — namely NSF participation in the elections.

On Jan. 23 the Front's Council declared that it would take part in the election as an organization. Ion Iliescu explained at that time that the decision was made as a result of "pressure from the bottom". "It is not only parties that can take part in the elections", he said. "The notion of the party as a narrow concept of a group or the interests of a certain category of people . . . is an obsolete notion. It seems to me that the notion of the Front as a broad organization, made up of people with different positions and opinions who gather around a platform of broad national unity on the major interests of Romanian society, is fully justified and is entitled to assume responsibilities before the country. In the discussion", he continued, "we had with numerous workers, with miners in the Jiu Valley, in Maramures, with workers in large works in the capital, with representatives of local organizations of the Front, of free trade unions, of youth organizations as well as of some parties that adhere to the Front's platform, the Front as such was requested to declare openly that it would participate in the elections."

The response from the opposition parties was predictable. They charged the Front with overt intentions of consolidating its grip further and prolonging it beyond the elections. On Jan. 23 the leaders of the three "historical" parties in a joint statement maintained that the Council's decision was in flagrant contradiction of its earlier promises and intentions expressed in the December programme. "Through this decision", read the statement, "the NSF has lost its neutrality and capacity of provisional administrator of power and its credibility before the public opinion. There can be no free elections and equitable conditions for all political formations when the NSF has the monopoly in a clearly totalitarian way on all state levers". The National Liberal, Romanian Social Democratic and National Christian Democratic Peasants' parties demanded that the NSF should withdraw from state and administration and instead a provisional government consisting of representatives of the active political parties and prominent personalities should be established. Such a government should be also invested with legislative power until the election of a new parliament.

Under mounting pressure the Front's Council agreed to hold round-table negotiations with all 30 political parties registered at that time. The negotiations resulted in a compromise that cleared away some of the obstacles to elections and peaceful transition. The NSF Council was reconstructed as a Provisional Council of National Unity, to operate as a legislative body until the elections, and included three representatives of each of the political parties present at the talks. They comprised half of the new Council's membership. The other 50 per cent of its 180 members represented the NSF and included "active participants" of the revolution, prominent scientists and intellectuals, personalities from the world of culture, workers, peasants, students, young people and representatives of national communities. The agreement also stipulated that the National Salvation Front should become a "political formation" with its own structure and platform, eligible to take part in the forthcoming elections on equal terms with other political forces.

A great deal of controversy also surrounded the formulation and provision of the electoral law. Its initial version devised by the NSF Council on Jan. 17 was opposed and required prolonged negotiations. The final version agreed on Feb. 21 was issued as a decree from the Provisional Council of National Unity on March 14. According to this, until the adoption of a new constitution, legislative power is vested in a bicameral Parliament comprised of the Assembly of Deputies (387 members) and the Senate (119 senators). It divided the country into 41 constituencies. Political parties and other organizations put forward their list of candidates in each of the constituencies. The voters are to express their preferences for a political party and not for an individual candidate. The Law also stipulated that organizations representing national minorities registered until March 14 which do not receive the required number of votes for a seat in the Assembly of Deputies would be entitled to a seat *ex officio*. The Assembly of Deputies and the Senate form *de jure* the Constituent Assembly which is to adopt the new constitution within 18 months. New elections are to be held within a year after the new constitution has come into force. The Law also defined the procedures of electing the president, by absolute majority vote in the first ballot, or simple majority if the election has to go to a second round. It prohibited the president from being a member of any political party or grouping.

Responding to the demands from opposition parties for the postponement of elections, the NSF agreed to changed the date from April to May 20.

Controversy dogged the election campaign from the start with the opposition parties alleging violence and intimidation by supporters of the NSF. In the remoter regions of the country the Front made it almost impossible for the two main opposition parties, the National Liberal Party and the National Peasants' Party, to campaign. Candidates opposing the NSF were prevented from entering some of the villages because of the hostility of local Front's officials. At the beginning of May the USA recalled its ambassador from Bucharest in protest over intimidation by supporters of the NSF against political opponents. Despite the agreement reached in February the campaign was conducted in a tense and bitter atmosphere of intimidation and sometimes violence, and was still dominated by the issue of NSF participation in the election, its disproportionately large and unfair use of mass media and other electoral resources, and the issue of cripto-communism. Opponents of the National Salvation Front demanded from the outset of the campaign that all former communist party activists be excluded from standing for office for 10 years.

Apart from the NSF virtually all other political parties consisted at that time of only small initiative committees, having an inconsequential membership and presenting a barely improvised declaration of political intentions. The appeal of the two historic parties, the Liberals and Peasants', was clearly limited. Both sought support from an older constituency, small in terms of numbers, that could remember and associate with their past political performance.

Among the eight presidential candidates the race was between Ion Iliescu for the NSF, Radu Campeanu for the Liberals and Ion Ratiu for the Peasants' Party. Campeanu (66) and Ratiu (72), both elderly men, hoped to revive old loyalties among the generation which remembered the pre-communist era. They failed largely because of the skilful tactics employed by the NSF which was able to divide their opponents. The Front managed to present Ion Ratiu as a wealthy émigré, as a reincarnation of the hoary old capitalist stereotype. Ratiu, albeit an untainted anti-communist, was probably wrong to allow his name to go forward. As an exile, he was certain to provoke mixed feelings in a country which has suffered as much as Romania did under Ceauşescu. As far as Radu Campeanu was concerned, the Front alternated between physical intimidation, which apparently terrified him sufficiently to deter him from leaving the capital in the latter stages of the campaign, and friendly overtures designed to compromise the Liberals with their supporters who demonstrated against the government in the squares of Bucharest and Timişoara.

Some 75 political parties and organizations took part in the elections. The results (see Table 1) reflected closely opinion polls conducted by Western organizations prior to and on election day. Some 400 foreign observers representing the European Parliament, the Council of Europe, the International Helsinki Human Rights Federation and the National

Table 1: Election results, May 1990

	% of total	Vote total	Seats
Presidential election			
Ion Iliescu (National Salvation Front)	85.1	12,232,498	–
Radu Campeanu (Liberal)	10.2	1,529,188	–
Ion Ratiu (Peasants)	4.3	617,007	–
Lower House of Parliament (Assembly of Deputies)			
National Salvation Front	66.3	9,089,659	263
Hungarian Democratic Union of Romania	7.2	991,601	29
National Liberal Party	6.4	879,290	29
Romanian Ecological Movement	2.6	358,864	12
National Peasants' Party	2.6	351,357	12
Romanian Unity Alliance — RUA	2.1	290,875	9
Agragian Democratic Party	1.8	250,403	9
Romanian Ecological Party	1.7	232,212	8
Socialist Democratic Party	1.1	143,393	5
Other votes split among more than 64 parties			(20)
Upper House (Senate) of Parliament			
National Salvation Front	67.0	9,353,006	92
Hungarian Democratic Union of Romania	7.2	1,004,353	12
National Liberal Party	7.1	985,094	9
National Peasants' Party	2.5	348,687	1
Romanian Ecological Movement	2.15	341,478	2
Romanian Unity Alliance — RUA	2.45	300,473	1
Romanian Ecological Party	1.4	192,574	1
Other votes split among more than 68 parties			(1)

Source: Rompres, May 25 1990.

Democratic Institute for International Affairs, among others, which monitored the election around the country, found few irregularities. They reported that although the electoral process had its flaws, they found no indication of systematic fraud.

The National Salvation Front won a convincing victory both in the Assembly of Deputies and the Senate. Ion Iliescu also surpassed by a wide margin his Liberal and Peasant opponents. The opposition protested at the results, demanding new elections.

Despite their crushing defeat in the polls, anti-Front activists continued their occupation of Bucharest's University Square, which began again in April, demanding the removal of Iliescu and all former communists from power. Claiming that the Front's opponents were attempting to stage a "fascist coup", on June 13 Iliescu appealed to the population to come to the rescue of the authorities. On June 14 around 7–10,000 miners from the Jiu Valley arrived by trains and buses and embarked on a rampage throughout the capital, ransacking the offices of opposition parties and the independent press. The tent city on the University Square, a symbol of resistance to the NSF, was brutally dismantled. In the process six people were killed and several hundred injured. The miners' rampage, which badly damaged the country's image in the outside world and the credibility of its leaders, has never been properly explained despite the setting up of a parliamentary commission of enquiry. In its wake several countries suspended aid to Romania. Alarmed by the international repercussions the Prime Minister Petre Roman sent letters to the governments of European countries, the USA, Canada, Japan, China and Australia, the United Nations, UNESCO, the European Parliament, and the Parliamentary Assembly of the Council of Europe, giving assurance that the Romanian government would continue to consolidate the process of the country's democratization with a view to ensuring the full observance of human rights. Despite this, sporadic protests, strikes and demonstrations continued from June 1990, demanding the resignation of the country's leadership.

The new government proceeded with an impressive legislative programme. A draft of a new constitution was presented to the parliament in February 1991 and is expected to be ready for approval in December 1991. However, on March 21, five main opposition parties, the Liberal, Peasants', Social Democratic, Ecologist and the Hungarian Democratic Union issued a message to the nation presenting an alternative opposition political and economic programme. It called for the replacement of the NSF government with a "responsible government enjoying the nations' confidence" and capable of introducing "real changes" into the country's political life.

During 1991 there has been mounting evidence that the support for the National Salvation Front has declined substantially with various Front spokesmen acknowledging the rapidly declining membership. The Front, after numerous postponements, held its national conference in March 1991, and despite clear divisions among the 1,119 delegates did not split into smaller groups, retaining its overall structural unity. However, several often contradictory political tendencies became apparent during the conference proceeding, suggesting that formal divisions of the Front are likely to occur in the future. In March 1991 one splinter group created the Social-Democratic National Salvation Front.

Since the May 1990 elections some parties active at that time have disappeared or merged with others. At the same time other parties have been created. However, as a result of what appears to be a peculiar trend of suspicion and distaste for openness, most of the parties active in Romania, with a few exceptions, have been more than reluctant to give their membership figures, details of their political programmes and in some cases even leadership. The Directory that follows provides details of political parties and organizations primarily based on Romanian media reports and registered since December 1989 until August 1991.

Directory of Parties

Agrarian Democratic Party of Romania
Partidul Democrat Agrar din România

Address. 71273 Bucharest, Aleea Alexandru 45.

Telephone. 33 58 10.

Leadership. Dr Dumitru Teaci (ch.)

Programme. The party aims to give the land back to those who work on it, to give farmers long-term credits to buy animals, farm machinery, implements, fertilizers etc., to encourage animal farming, to help young people resettle in the countryside and to pay all experts who work in the countryside higher salaries. The party also wants to develop agricultural education; research and design; to protect, conserve and increase the fertility of the land, forests and waters through development projects; to give subsidies to farmers in mountainous areas to increase soil fertility and to develop agriculture and tourism; to support every measure conducive to village life revival and modernization, to expand and modernize rural roads and to guarantee old-age pensions to agricultural workers that they may live a decent life.

Alliance for Democracy Party
Partidul Alianta Pentru Democraţie

Address. 70256 Bucharest, Bd. Dacia 43.

Telephone. 13 22 95.

Affiliations. Centre-Left (Social Democratic) Alliance.

ROMANIA

Association of the December 1989 Revolution Fighters, Wounded, Invalids and Descendants of the Fallen
Asociatia Luptătorilor Revolutiei din Decembrie 1989, Răniţi, Invalizi si Urmaşii Eroilor Căzuţi

Address. 70623 Bucharest, Str. Anghel Saligny 8.

Association of Former Political Detainees and Victims of the Dictatorship
Asociaţia Foştilor Deţinuţi Politici şi Victime Ale Dictaturii

Address. 70387 Bucharest, Str. Mintuleasa 10.

Brătianu Liberal Union
Partidul "Uniunea Liberală Brătianu"

Address. 70176 Bucharest, Calea Victoriei 95–97.

Telephone. 59 44 87.

Foundation. 27, March 1990.

Leadership. Ion I. Bratianu (pres.)

History. The Union emerged as a result of a split with the National Liberal Party. The split followed personal differences between Ion I. Bratianu and the leader of the NLP, Radu Campeanu, each accusing the other of "personal ambitions".

Programme. To find a Liberal and responsible solution to the problems confronting the state and society.

Centre-Left (Social Democratic) Alliance

Formed in July 1990, this grouping includes the following organizations: Alliance for Democracy Party, Co-operative Party, Democratic Labour Party, Romanian New Society Party, and the Socialist Justice Party.

Christian Democratic Union of Romania
Partidul Uniunea Creştin-Democrată din România

Address. 1900 Timişoara, Splaiul Titulescu 2.

Telephone. (961) 403 50.

Christian Democratic Union (CDU)
Uniunea Democrat Creştină

Address. 70174 Bucharest, Piaţa Amzei 13.

Telephone. 50 24 10.

Leadership. Mihai Grama (pres.); Octavian Voinea (first dep. pres.)

Programme. The Christian Democratic Union is a centre-left Christian party, which intends to improve morally Romanian society after 45 years of communist dictatorship, in the spirit of the Christian faith. The party does not only promote the spirit of Romanian Orthodoxy but also seeks a rapprochement among all denominations in Romania. As for foreign policy, the CDU pursues a concerted action for the unification of Europe, the achievement of the so-called "common house", to reach accords supporting the development of Romanian economy and allowing for Romania's participation in European civilization and culture.

Affiliations. Christian Democratic International.

Christian Human Rights and Freedom Party
Partidul Creştin al Libertăţii şi Drepturilor Omului

Address. 70718 Bucharest, Str. Şipotul Fîntînilor 4.

Telephone. 16 77 70.

Christian Republican Party
Partidul Republican Creştin

Address. 70781 Bucharest, Str. Berzei 46.

Telephone. 15 30 59.

Leadership. Gheorge Popilean (ch.)

Cluj-Napoca Civic Forum
Forumul Cetăţenesc Cluj-Napoca

Address. 3400 Cluj-Napoca, Str. Motilor 18.

Co-operative Party
Partidul Cooperatist

Address. 70328 Bucharest, Str. Ienăchiţă Văcărescu 20.

Telephone. 13 61 19.

Affiliations. Centre-Left (Social Democratic) Alliance.

December 21 Association
Asociata "21 Decembrie"

Address. 70131 Bucharest, Str. Batistei 22–24.

Telephone. 16 62 23.

ROMANIA

Democratic Agricultural, Industrial and Intellectual Workers' Party
Partidul Democrat al Muncii Agricole, Industriale şi Intelectuale

Address. 71133 Bucharest, Şos. Ştefan cel Mare 2.

Democratic Ecological Party
Partidul Democrat Ecologist

Address. 3350 Turda, Piata Republici 11.

Democratic Future of the Homeland Party
Partidul "Vitorul Democrat al Partiei"

Address. 78209 Bucharest, Bd 1 Mai 33.

Telephone. 66 54 06.

Democratic Labour Party
Partidul Democrat al Muncii

Address. 70317 Bucharest, Str. Olari 12.

Telephone. 35 13 75.

Foundation. March 1990.

Programme. The party is in favour of a republican, multi-party, democratic regime, the separation of powers, freedom of action by the opposition, the fundamental rights of individuals and professional, religious and ethnic groups, guaranteed under the constitution. it supports the building of a mixed economy that should harmonize social ownership with free individual or group initiative, the decentralization of economic management, the differentiation of incomes according to the quality of work performed, averting unemployment and inflation, improving living conditions, a five-day working week, free medical assistance and the right to strike. In agriculture, it is campaigning for diversification in the forms of ownership of land. It also advocates the constitutional guarantee of the rights of national minorities, individual and collective rights.

Publications. Fapta (The Deed), weekly, began its publication on March 27, 1990.

Affiliations. Centre-Left (Social Democratic) Alliance.

Democratic Party
Partidul Democrat

Address. 3400 Cluj-Napoca, Str. Moţilor 18.

Telephone. (951) 15301.

Leadership. Vigil Vata (pres.)

Affiliations. Democratic Union.

NEW POLITICAL PARTIES OF EASTERN EUROPE AND THE SOVIET UNION

Democratic Party of Free Romanis
Partidul Democratic al Romilor Liberi

Address. 4000 Sfintu Gehorghe, Str. Garoafei 2.

Democratic Party of Romania
Partidul Democrat din România

Address. 70118 Bucharest, Str. 13 Decembrie 4.

Telephone. 14 34 48.

Foundation. Dec. 27, 1989.

Leadership. Liviu Tereties (ch.); Mihai Tipac, Viorel Coiziu (dep. ch.)

Programme. The initial programme formulated at the end of December 1989 included among other things: eradicating from the constitution the article stipulating the Romanian Communist Party's leading role; free general elections; political pluralism; the setting up of free and independent trade unions; the representation in government of all minorities regardless of religious or political creed; the election through a secret vote of the country's president for one or two mandates depending on the period of time set by parliament; the right to practise a profession or trade at the same time in the state and private sectors; free initiative in the arts, culture and sports fields; the alteration of the social security system in order to create a fair framework both in the state and private sectors; Romania's membership of the Warsaw Treaty Organization while at the same time working for a united European home.

At the time of its registration (Jan. 16), the party presented the following programme: Romania should become a constitutional republic; political pluralism; the separation of power in state; depolitization of the armed forces, prosecutor's office, judicial bodies, police and national mass media; the President of the country should exercise power for one term only; Romania's economy should be decentralized, with state, joint and private property; the orientation of the economy towards joint ventures with shareholders, with Romanian and foreign capital; the gradual privatization of small industries, trade and tourism; the reorganization of agriculture with the dissolution of the producer co-operatives and the maintenance of the state farming and animal-breeding enterprises; the appropriation of peasants and of other citizens who want to till the land individually or in associations; the reorganization of machinery and tractor stations as service units in agriculture; freedom of movement of people and ideas, freedom of religion and religious traditions; every citizen's right to do additional work in his leisure time in various trades or arts; the assistance of the family as the cell of society by granting credits to newly-weds; paid leave for mothers to raise their children; urgent and efficient measures to re-establish ecological equilibrium; the gradual replacement, at all levels, of the managerial staff in the economy and superstructure compromised, professionally and morally, during the old regime; the erection of memorials to the martyrs who died for freedom and democracy and the declaration of the day of Dec. 22 as the national day of Romania.

ROMANIA

Democratic Union
Uniunea Democratica

Foundation. July 17, 1990.

Organization. The Union is an umbrella organization for eight political parties: Democratic Unity Party, Liberal Socialist Party, Democratic Party of Cluj, Progressive Democratic Party, the Romanians' Union Republican Party, Christian Democratic Socialist Party, Free Democratic Party, and the Party to Honour the Revolution's Heroes and for National Salvation.

Democratic Unity Party (DUP)
Partidul Unităţii Democratice

Address. 71261 Bucharest, Piaţa Aviatorilor 3.

Telephone. 17 48 12.

Foundation. January 1990.

Leadership. Nicu Stancescu (pres.)

Programme. The DUP describes itself as an anti-totalitarian party fighting against totalitarianism of all kinds, in favour of a multi-party, democratic system endorsed by free democratic elections.

Affiliations. Democratic Union.

Democratic Unity Party of Moldova
Partidul Unităţii Democratice din Moldova

Address. 6600 Iaşi, Str. Stefan cel Mare 15.

Telephone. (981) 350 60.

Federation of the Jewish Communities of Romania
Federatia Comunităţilor Evreieşti din România

Address. 70478 Bucharest, Str. Lapusna 9–11.

Telephone. 15 50 90.

Free Change Party
Partidul Liber Schimbist

Address. 70778 Bucharest, Str. Transilvaniei 12.

Telephone. 13 62 94.

Free Democratic Party
Partidul Liber Democrat

Address. 70602 Bucharest, Bd. Mihail Kogălniceanu 25.

Telephone. 14 12 35.

Leadership. Leon Nica (pres.)

Affiliations. Democratic Union.

Free Democratic Social Justice Party
Partidul Dreptăţii Sociale Liber Democrat

Address. 75166 Bucharest, Str Cuza Voda 158.

Free Democratic Union of Romanis in Romania
Uniunea Leberă Democratică a Romilor din România

Address. 3400 Cluj-Napoca, Str. Maramuresului 187.

Free Democratic Youth Party
Partidul Tineretului Liber Democrat

Address. 4000 Sfintu Gheorghe, Piata Libertatii.

Telephone. (923) 147 30.

Free Trade Union Organization
Sindicatul Muncitorilor Liber

Address. 14 Modrogan Alley sect. 1, Bucharest.

Publication. Romania Muncitoare (Working Romania), daily newspaper.

Free Youth Association of Romania
Asociatia Tineretului Liber din România

Address. 70119 Bucharest, Str. Onesti 46.

Freedom and Democracy Party
Partidul Libertatii si Democratiei Romane

Address. 1100 Craiova, Cartier Rovine, Bloc A-62.

Telephone. (941) 329 366.

ROMANIA

German Democratic Forum of Romania
Forumul Democrat al Germanilor din România

Address. 2400 Sibiu, Str. General Magheru 1–3.

Telephone. (924) 181 45.

Human Rights League
Liga Apărării Drepturilor Omului

Address. 70119 Bucharest, Str. Onesti 11.

Telephone. 13 71 90.

Humanist Ecological Party
Partidul Ecologist Umanist

Address. 29 Arad, Str. Tribunul Dobra 11.

Humanitarian Peace Party
Partidul Umanitar al Păcii

Address. 70461 Bucharest, Bd. George Cosbuc 1.

Telephone. 81 38 39.

Hungarian Christian Democratic Party of Romania
Partidul Crestin Democrat Maghiar din România

Address. 3400 Cluj-Napoca, Paita Libertatii 16.

Telephone. (951) 110 89.

Foundation. February 1990.

Leadership. Gyoergy Loerincz (pres.)

Hungarian Democratic Union of Romania (HDUR)
Uniunea Democrată Maghiară din România

Address. 71297 Bucharest Str. Herastrau 13.

Telephone. 33 35 69.

Foundation. Dec. 21, 1989.

Leadership. Geza Domokos (pres.); Geza Szocs (vice-pres.)

Programme. The HDUR aims to be an active political force in the building of a free, democratic Romania in which all citizens should enjoy full equality without distinction as to nationality, political or philosophical beliefs, race or sex. The organization sets out to achieve the rights of the Hungarian with due respect for the territorial integrity and sovereignty of free and democratic Romania. It wants a sincere dialogue on interethnic relations with all parties, organizations and social clubs which assume responsibility for setting them on a new basis.

It sees a need for mutual confidence, objectivity and tolerance, realization of the fact that a future society cannot be built by simply correcting and amending the relations compromised by the Ceauşescu dictatorship between Romanians and the national minorities, and that a new vision is required — a new approach based on reality. The Union's aims also include the development of an educational system guaranteeing minority language instruction at every level, the re-establishment of the independent Hungarian University in Cluj, the introduction of mandatory biligualism in Transylvania, with administrative and judicial proceedings being conducted in the Romanian and Hungarian languages, and the creation of the Ministry of Nationalities.

Affiliations. National Convention for Democracy.

Hungarian Independent Party
Partidul Independent Maghiar

Address. 4300 Tirgu Mureş, Str. Memoranduli 4.

Telephone. (954) 274 20.

Foundation. Jan. 29, 1990.

Membership. 300,000 in 17 counties.

Programme. Dialogue with every Romanian party and organization in the interest of guaranteeing nationality rights.

Hungarian Smallholders' Party in Romania
Partidul Gospodarilor Maghiari din România

Address. 4100 Miercurea Ciuc, Str. Spicului, Bloc D-37.

Telephone. (958) 1666 52.

Foundation. February 1990.

Leadership. Zoltan Eltes (pres.)

Independent National Christian Party
Partidul Naţional Creştin Independent

Address. 73986 Bucharest, Str. Popa Sapca 19.

Telephone. 55 46 95.

ROMANIA

Labour Party
Partidul Muncii

Address. 732229 Bucharest, Str. Fluierului 21 A.

Telephone. 48 00 91.

Labour and Social Justice Party of Romania
Partidul Muncii şi Dreptătii Sociale din România

Address. 70141 Bucharest, Str. Cosmonauţilor 9.

Liberal Party of Romania
Partidul Liberal din România

Address. 70461 Bucharest, Bd. George Coşbuc 1.

Telephone. 31 00 55.

Liberal Socialist Party
Partidul Socialist Liberal

Address. 71101 Bucharest, Calea Victoriei 176.

Telephone. 50 47 19.

Leadership. Nicolae Cerveni (pres.)

Affiliations. Democratic Union.

Libertatea — Anti-communist and Anti-fascist Workers' Alliance
Alianta Muncitorească "Libertatea" Anticomunistă şi Antifascistă

Address. 7437 Bucharest, Str. Romulus 36.

Telephone. 21 36 50.

Lippovans' Community of Romania
Comunitatea Lipovenilor din România

Address. 70461 Bucharest, Bd. Georfe Cosbuc 1.

Modern Democracy Movement
Partidul Mişcarea Democratia Moderňa

Address. 1100 Craiova, Str. Nicolae Titulescu 7.

Telephone. (941) 181 16.

Muslim Turkish Democratic Union of Romania
Uniunea Democratâ Turcâ Musulmană din România

Address. 75251 Bucharest, Str. Constantin Manescu 4.

Telephone. 59 62 54.

National Christian Democratic Peasants' Party
Partidul Naţional Tărănesc-Creştin şi Democrat

Address. 70334 Bucharest, Bd. Republicii 34.

Telephone. 11 54 40, 15 45 33.

Contact name. Valentin Gabrielescu.

Foundation. 1869, re-founded on Dec 26, 1989.

Leadership. Corneliu Coposu (pres.); Ion Diaconescu (vice-pres.); Ion Lup (gen. sec.)

Membership. 800,000.

History. Originally founded in 1869 and re-founded in 1895. During the interwar period it was one of the strongest parties in the country. It was banned by the communist regime and all its property confiscated in 1947.

Programme. Pluralist democracy, a state *de jure* with the strict observance of laws, a return to the market economy and the restoration of peasant property, a society characterized by the priority of the work of farmers and workers, the reorganization of education, the promotion of academic autonomy, national rebirth in the spirit of Christian morals, the separation of powers in the state, free election of management bodies in all areas of society, equality of all nationalities and religious beliefs in the spirit of the proclamation of Alba Iulia of Dec 1, 1918. The programme also stipulates the introduction of a new constitution whose provisions would include strict observance of human rights, as enshrined in the Helsinki convention, the dissolution of democratic centralism, introduction of market economy, the dissolution of producer co-operative farms and giving of land to the people, the resettlement of all farmers (who are to receive two hectares per family), the dissolution of military blocs, the reconstruction of cultural and historic edifices destroyed by the dictatorship, the granting of pensions to all former political detainees. Citizens in all social strata, including those who were members of the Communist Party – with the exception of individuals who held important offices in that party or committed abuses – are admitted to the party.

Publication. Dreptatea (Justice), daily.

National Convention for Democracy

The Convention is an umbrella organization for the following parties: National Liberal Party, Ecological Movement, Ecological Party, Hungarian Democratic Union of Romania, and the Romanian Social Democratic Party.

ROMANIA

National Democratic Party (NDP)
Partidul National Democrat

Address. 70208 Bucharest, Str. Aaron Florian 1.

Telephone. 11 04 79

Contact name. Nicolae Costel.

Foundation. January 1990

Leadership. Cristian Butusiu (pres.)

History. On July 6, 1990, the NDP merged with the National Unity and Dignity Party.

Programme. The party advocates the gradual privatization of the national economy and the setting up of joint companies with foreign and local capital. It wants land controlled by the state to be returned to the peasants without any payment. The party aims to represent workers, peasants and intellectuals alike. The programme would avoid any rigid ideology, and would take into consideration the proven experience of other political organizations worldwide.

Publication. Oblio, weekly review.

National Liberal Party (NLP)
Partidul National Liberal

Address. 70112 Bucharest, Bd. Nicolae Bălcescu 21.

Telephone. 15 73 10.

Foundation. 1876, reactivated Dec 30, 1989.

Leadership. Radu Campeanu (gen. sec.); I. V. Sandulescu, Nae Bedros.

Membership. 600,000.

History. Originally founded in 1876, the party was disbanded in 1948. After the overthrow of Ceauşescu the party refused to take part in the National Salvation Front administration. Two members of the NLP became ministers in the Petre Roman government appointed in January 1990 despite the NLP objection. Mihnea Marmeliuc served as Minister of Labour, and Nicolae Gavriliescu was a counsellor to the Prime Minister. The National Liberal Party denied that they represented the party and in a statement issued on Jan. 27, 1990 stressed that "these two figures were appointed by the leadership of the government and the National Salvation Front". During 1990 several fractures have occurred within the NLP. The first split on March 27, 1990, gave rise to the Liberal Union. Another break in July 1990 brought about the expulsion from its ranks of Gelu Netea, the editor of the party's newspaper *Viitorul*. The same month a Youth Wing and an Initiative Committee for the Reform of the NLP was created. Both criticized the "authoritarian and undemocratic spirit of the party's leadership", which was "monopolized by a restricted group unconnected with contemporary Romanian realities". On July 5 four leading members of the Executive Secretariat of the NLP were expelled from the party.

Programme. Guarantees of individual freedom, the separation of powers in the state, the establishment of democracy, freedom of expression and dissemination of opinion, the freedom of the press and the liquidation of censorship, the guarantee of the freedom of all religious denominations and the restoration of the Greek Catholic Church to its rights, the strict observance of the equal rights of all minorities, the abolition of collectivization and nationalization in agriculture and the creation of propitious conditions for agricultural property to go to those willing to have it, the gradual privatization of enterprises and their restructuring according to principles of profitability, as part of a market economy, the guarantee of the freedom of trade unions and of the right to strike, the gradual involvement of workers in the administration of enterprises and their sharing of profit. The party stresses that current power structures should not depart from the aims of the revolution of December 1988. A tough communist regime should not be replaced by a "milder" one. Major economic targets are the establishment of private property and the gradual privatization of economic units based on profitability. According to the NLP, the privatization of the industrial aggregate can be achieved in three ways: productive units bought by some investors, enterprises bought by the employees and limited societies. In case of competition between investors, of equal offers, the employees of the respective unit will be given priority and they will also make the major decisions.

Affiliations. National Convention for Democracy.

Publications. Viitorul (The Future), daily, first appeared on March 27, 1990. *Liberalul* (The Liberal), a weekly organ.

National Progress Party
Partidul National Progresist

Address. 74406 Bucharest, Str. Constantin Brancusi 11.

Programme. Strongly nationalist, advocating a return to traditional cultural and religious values of Romanian society.

National Reconstruction Party
Partidul Pentru Reconstrucţia Naţională

Address. 4800 Baia Mare, Str. Crisan 17.

Telephone. (994) 130 88.

National Reconstruction Party of Romania
Partidul Reconstrucţie Nationale din România

Address. 70461 Bucharest, Bd. George Cosbuc 1.

Telephone. 81 55 88.

ROMANIA

National Republican Party
Partidul National Republican

Address. 3400 Cluj-Napoca, Bd. 22 Decembrie 54–56.

Telephone. (951) 179 63.

National Salvation Front (NSF)
Frontul Salvării Nationale

Address. 71274 Bucharest, Aleea Modrogan 22.

Telephone. 13 78 87.

Foundation. Dec. 22, 1989.

Leadership. Petre Roman (1.); Ion Aurel Stoica (executive ch. of the Steering Council)

Membership. 1,000,000 claimed in April 1990, rapidly declining since.

History. The NSF emerged on Dec. 22, 1989, within hours after the toppling of the Ceauşescu regime, as a provisional government, an "alliance of all patriotic and democratic forces opposing dictatorship in Romania". The list of the 39 original members of the NSF Council released on Dec. 22, 1989 included: Ion Iliescu, Petre Roman, Silviu Brucan, Corneliu Manescu, Gen. Victor Stanculescu, Alexandru Birladeanu, and Dan Martian, all former communists. Other members included intellectuals known for their opposition to the Ceauşescu regime, army officers and students who joined the anti-communist revolt. Within a week the Council's membership had grown to some 150 persons; however, the real power was in fact exercised by the few original core members. It leaders maintained that the Front was a broad mass movement embracing diverse political tendencies. The Front had initially limited its mandate to administering the country until free elections and pledged to dissolve itself after the new parliament was chosen by the population. The Front's leadership has often been accused of crypto-communism. It responded by emphasizing that it was a broad mass movement with a centre-left orientation. Iliescu and Roman compared the NSF to the Solidarity movement in Poland, the Civic Forum in Czechoslovakia and the New Forum in East Germany. On Jan. 23, 1990 the NSF Council declared that the Front would take part in the election on a par with other political parties. The NSF was officially registered on Feb. 6, 1990. Its first conference took place on April 8, 1990 in Bucharest in order to launch preparations for the June parliamentary elections which it won with 66.3 per cent of the votes, but against a background of accusations of intimidation of voters and manipulation of procedures and results. Serious conflicts with the Front began to be mentioned by the Romanian press as early as March 1990. The parliamentary elections, rather than boost its standing within Romanian society and increase support for it, have in fact undermined its credibility. The Front's membership began to decline rapidly in the aftermath of the elections. The independent weekly *Cuvintul* published in Bucharest noted on Sept. 24, 1990 that "the Front has leaders and power, but no members". After numerous postponements, the NSF's first national convention, attended by 1,119 delegates, took place in Bucharest between March 16 and 17, 1991. Contrary to expectations that the NSF would become a political party and change its name, no adjustments were made.

The conference, however, redefined the NSF as a centre-leftist party of social-democratic orientation. Political divisions within the Front have accelerated during 1991. The NSF daily newspaper *Azi* on Feb. 28, 1991, identified five different political streams: a centrist or orthodox one; a liberal, reformist, and pro-governmental wing; a centrist-left grouping (supporting an increased social welfare system); a left wing (opposing the speeding up of economic reforms); and a radical group calling for rapid and substantial political and economic reforms. In March 1991 a splinter group emerged from the NSF and created the Social-Democratic National Salvation Front.

Publication. Azi (Today), daily newspaper.

National Unity and Democracy Forum of Romania
Forumul Democraţiei şi Unităţii Nationale din România

Address. 72112 Bucharest, Str. Mihail Eminescu 142.

Telephone. 10 86 98.

National Unity Party of Romanians in Transylvania
Partidul de Uniune Naţională a Românilor din Transilvania

Address. 2200 Brasov, Str Crisan 7 A.

Telephone. (921) 163 92.

Foundation. March 19, 1990.

New Democracy Social Justice Party
Partidul Dreptăţii Sociale (Nuova Democratie)

Address. 3700 Oradea, Str Abacului 23.

Telephone. (991) 727 44.

Orthodox Christian Union
Partidul Uniunea Creştin Ortodoxă

Address. 70526 Bucharest, Aleea Marii Adunari Nationale 11.

Party to Honour the Revolution's Heroes and for National Salvation

Leadership. Ioan Antonescu (pres.)

Party of Private Enterprises of Romania

Foundation. March 4, 1991.

Leadership. Alexandru Constatinovici (pres.)

ROMANIA

Programme. To build wide in scope and social base a political movement that should offer a solid alternative to the country's rulers.

People's Party of Romania
Partidul Poporului din România

Address. 1100 Craiova, Str. Lotru 4.

Progressive Party
Partidul Progresist

Address. 4800 Baia Mare, Str Oituz 6 A.

Leadership. Vasile Priale (pres.)

Programme. The Progressive Party describes itself as a moderate, centre party, whose aims are to promote genuine, uncompromised human values and to help the recovery of the country. The party does not admit activists and members of the bureaus and committees of the former Communist Party, former security people or collaborators of the security service.

Progressive Democratic Party
Partidul Democrat Progresist

Address. 71131 Bucharest, Calea Dorobantilor 39.

Telephone. 82 47 78.

Leadership. Ion Uta (pres.)

Affiliations. Democratic Union.

Radical Democratic Party
Partidul Radical Democrat

Address. 77617 Bucharest, Bd Pacii 186.

Republican Party
Partidul Republican

Address. 70222 Bucharest, Str. Popa Rusu 28.

Telephone. 11 00 49.

Foundation. April 2, 1991.

Leadership. Ion Minzatu (ch.); Adrian Chisalita (dep. ch.)

History. The party was formed as a result of a merger on April 2, 1991 of the Republic Party and the National Republican Party.

Republican Peasants' Party

Leadership. Gheorghe Pantea (pres.)

Republican Union Party
Partidul Uniunea Republicană

Address. 70461 Bucharest, Bd. George Cosbus 1.

Telephone. 81 32 90.

Republican Unity Party of Romania
Partidul Republican de Unitate a Românilor

Address. 70461 Bucharest, Bd. George Coşbuc 1.

Leadership. Pavel Ghiban (pres.)

Affiliations. Democratic Union.

Romani of Romania Party
Partidul Ţiganilor din România

Address. 2400 Sibiu, Str. Stefan cel Mare 8.

Telephone. (924) 335 46.

Romanian Anti-totalitarian Forum
Forumul Antitotalitar Român

Address. 70700 Bucharest, POB 1–78.

Romanian Christian Social Democratic Party
Partidul Social Democrat Creştin Român

Address. 8700 Constanta, Str. Grivitei 18.

Telephone. (916) 157 24.

Romanian Communist Party (RCP)
Partidul Communist Roman

Membership. 3,800,000 (December 1989).

History. On Jan. 12, 1990, the Executive Bureau of the National Salvation Front issued a decree outlawing the RCP. The declaration read: "on this day of national mourning, 12 January 1990, considering the fact that the Romanian Communist Party was confiscated by the dictatorship and became the instrument of political demagoguery and lies as methods of government used by that dictatorship against the people, together with the people of good faith throughout the country, the council of the National Salvation Front decrees: The Romanian Communist Party is outlawed, the position of this party being regarded as against the national spirit and the ancestral law." This decree was to be subject of a national referendum on Jan. 28. However, the decree was annulled by the Council of the NSF on Jan. 17, 1990. A communiqué issued by the Council described the earlier decision as "an inadmissible political mistake". "Outlawing any party is a political and legal issue with wide implications. This is anti-democratic measure, which runs counter to the NSF principles of building a democratic and pluralistic society in Romania, in which all political parties and groupings are permitted to organize and function, except for the fascist ones." On Jan 17, 1990 the assets of the RCP were transferred to state ownership. These included 21 properties in and around Bucharest, 41 palaces and houses and 20 hunting lodges. In addition the assets comprised the Carpati Economic Office with 60 industrial enterprises with an annual commodity production of 16 billion lei and an annual profit of two billion lei from domestic production and 220,000 dollars from exports. Moreover, the RCP also had 55,000 hectares of agricultural land on which it employed 18,000 workers organized into 45 agro-industrial units. All the assets became formally the property of the state on March 31, 1991. The total value of the assets was 43,825.2 million lei.

Romanian Democratic Front
Frontul Democrat Român

Address. 1900 Timisoara, Str. Mihail Eminescu 5.

Telephone. (961) 331 77.

Romanian Ecological Movement
Miscarea Ecologistă din România

Address. 70259 Bucharest, Str Olga Bancic 11.

Telephone. 11 29 43.

Foundation. Jan. 5, 1990.

Leadership. Toma George Maiorescu (ch.)

Membership. 100,000 members in numerous groups and factions throughout the country.

Programme. Slogan, "A clean man in a clean world". It calls on all countries to ensure a positive co-operation aimed at regenerating and preserving the ecological base.

The Movement reflects a broad trend of opinion and social action which is independent, democratic, pacifist and humanistic in character. Its targets include: environmental protection, ecological administration of the territory and protection from any kind of pollution. It also fights against the degradation and destruction of nature and of historical and cultural monuments and the degradation of Romanian ethos, and for placing of human beings at the core of all activities.

The Movement is a pacifist, democratic, humanist, non-violent movement which gathers scientists, artists and writers. This movement has in view the working out of a national economic programme with ecological considerations. To this end the movement is working on an ecological map of Romania indicating the sources of pollution, on setting priorities and underscoring palpable measures. The Ecological Movement of Romania will work for the observance of human rights, for a state of law, for democracy, pluralism, freedom and the establishment of civilized relations among people.

Affiliations. National Convention for Democracy.

Romanian Ecological Party
Partidul Ecologist Român

Address. 70461 Bucharest, Bd. George Coşbuc 1.

Telephone. 31 23 50.

Foundation. December 1989.

Leadership. Iustin Draghici (pres.); Raluca Marinescu, (vice-pres.)

Programme. To increase ecological awareness among the public; to lobby for the establishment of a national environmental monitoring system and a Ministry for Environmental Protection and for joint action with neighbouring countries to preserve the environment.

Affiliations. National Convention for Democracy.

Romanian Home of Democratic Europe
Casa Româna a Europei Democrate

Address. 75576 Bucharest, Bd. Metalurgiei 2 bis.

Romanian National Party
Partidul National Român

Address. 7012 Bucharest, Bd. Nicolae Bălcescu 26.

Telephone. 16 60 54.

Romanian New Society Party
Partidul Român Pentru Noua Societate

Address. 71341 Bucharest, Piata Presei Libere 1.

Telephone. 17 60 10.

Affiliations. Centre-Left (Social Democratic) Alliance.

ROMANIA

Romanian Peasants' Party
Partidul Tărănesc Român

Address. 70407 Bucharest, Str. Smirdan 15.

Telephone. 15 77 24.

Foundation. January 1990.

Programme. The party aims to represent and defend the interests of agricultural co-operative members, and of small-scale agricultural producers in conformity with the requirements of the process of renewal and democratization in Romania. In the process of restructuring agriculture on a democratic basis, the party aims to ensure the economic independence of owners, the development of agricultural production in accordance with zones of the country, and the sale of products through trade outlets and under efficient conditions; the reconsideration of the role and place of small-scale farms; an increase in privately-owned plots of land and those for construction purposes, and plots of land used to ensure the development of farmers' households; the production of vegetables and fruits, and the breeding of an increasingly greater number of animals and poultry; an improvement in the standard of living of the peasantry, and the prosperity of the Romanian state. Moreover it stresses the need to ensure the diversification of the forms of association of peasants, including those within the framework of agricultural production co-operatives, the development of small-scale industry and services to the rural population, and the processing and industrialization of certain agricultural produce and its direct utilization by consumers. It advocates the cancellation of debts created as a result of the unjust policy of prices and tariffs for agricultural co-operative units, the creation of its own bank which will ensure credits, finance and aid for units and the peasantry, broadening the aid system and material base of units both in money and in kind. Financial management control should be carried out by the bodies of the agricultural co-operative units and by their unions. It seeks the radical improvement of the pension system and the establishment of social security at the same level as that of workers in the state agricultural units. It aims at taking over from the Ministry of Labour the activities and funds designed for granting pensions and other rights to the peasantry and setting up an autonomous system of pensions for the peasantry as was the case formerly, the operation of nurseries and kindergartens in all agricultural co-operative units for the children of co-operative members and of other village residents, and the development and diversification of the activity of units in charge of treatment in health resorts and of the creation of co-operative members, which should benefit the entire free peasantry in Romania.

Publications. Atitudinea (Attitude), weekly magazine.

Romanian People's Front
Frontful Popular Român

Address. 6600 Iaşi, Str 23 August 19.

Telephone. (981) 174 30.

Romanian Social Democratic Party (SDP)
Partidul Social Democrat Român

Address. 70119 Bucharest, Str. Oneşti 9.

Telephone. 16 47 21.

Foundation. 1893, reactivated Dec. 24, 1989.

Leadership. Sergiu Cunescu (pres.); Dr Adrian Dimitriu, (hon. ch.); Prof. Traian Greavu (first vice-pres.); Constantin Avramescu, Nicolae Strachinaru, Victor Vaum, Traian Novac (vice-presidents); Alexandur Meissner, Nicolae Bildea, Variu Arbore, Corneliu Vlad Diaconescu, Radu Dimitrescu (secretaries)

Membership. Several thousand.

History. one of Romania's three historical parties, the SDP was originally founded in 1893 as the Social Democratic Party of Romania's Workers. The party was forced to merge with the RCP in February 1948. At that time it had some 260,000 members. In September 1990 the SDP proposed the creation of an Anti-totalitarian Confederation to bring together all the democratic forces in Romania and to co-ordinate their activities. The party has been under a considerable pressure from the NSF to merge with it. All advances, however, have been so far firmly repulsed. On March 8 and 9, 1991, the party held its national congress in Bucharest which reasserted its separate indentity.

Programme. Full restoration of civil liberties, free trade union activities and the right to strike, an economic policy balancing market forces and state intervention, co-operation with Social Democratic Parties in Western Europe, encouragement of Western capital and investment, close links with the European Community leading to Romania's full membership of the EC.

Affiliations. National Convention for Democracy.

Romanian Socialist Democratic Party
Partidul Socialist Democratic Român

Address. 76212 Bucharest, Str. Obedenaru 33.

Telephone. 81 45 80.

Foundation. January 1990.

Leadership. Cornel Nica.

History. The party is one of the strongest supporters of the National Salvation Front and is often referred to as the Front's satellite. It held its first national congress in Braila on April 9, 1990 during which it identified itself fully with the Front's policies. The party's first chairman, Marian Circiumaru, was dismissed in August 1990 and accused of embezzlement, leading an immoral life and political recklessness.

Programme. Published on Jan. 16, 1990, in the newspaper *Adevarul*, the programme called for support for the activity of the National Salvation Front with a view to normalizing the socioeconomic situation, abrogation of all laws that violated human rights, a mixed economy set on profitability, adherence to the Socialist International and the inclusion of a party representative to the National Front Council.

Romanian's Democratic Constitutional Party
Partidul Democrat Constitutional din Romania

Address. 70602 Bucharest, Bd. Mikhail Kogalniceanu 25.

Telephone. 14 12 35.

Serbian Democratic Union of Romania
Uniunea Democrată a Sîrbilor din România

Address. 1900 Timişoara, Bd. 23 August 8.

Telephone. (961) 115 47.

Foundation. Feb. 22, 1990.

Social-Democratic National Salvation Front

Foundation. March 18, 1991.

Leadership. Velicu Radina (pres.); Nicolae Dide, Gheorge Petu, Eugen Zainea (vice-presidents); Traian Duica (sec.)

History. The Front emerged from the NSF in the aftermath of its first national convention held in March 1991. It claims that its creation is the result of dissension within the NSF dating back to the summer of 1990 when the government's economic reform programme signalled a deviation from the NSF's December 1989 platform. It maintains that the NSF had shifted from social-democratic leanings to a liberal right-wing position.

Socialist Justice Party — Independent
Partidul Socialist al Dreptăţii

Address. 71102 Bucharest, Calea Victoriei 151.

Telephone. 59 48 69.

Affiliations. Centre-Left (Social Democratic) Alliance.

Socialist Labour Party (SLP)

Foundation. Nov. 18, 1990.

Leadership. Ilie Verdet (ch.)

History. The formation of the SLP follows a merger of groups from the Democratic Labour Party, the Socialist Party and remains of the Romanian Communist Party. The creation of the party has been seen as a continuation of the Romanian Communist Party. Its chairman, Ilie Verdet, is Nicolae Ceaşescu's brother-in-law, and a former member of the Permanent Bureau of the RCP and Prime Minister in the early 1980s.

Programme. To ensure the continuity of the valuable progressive traditions of the working-class, socialist and democratic movement in Romania.

Ţara Ouşului Democratic Union
Uniunea Democratică "Ţara Oaşului"

Address. 3919 Negreşti-Oaş, Str. Victoriei 95.

Telephone. (998) 511 13.

Timişoara Society
Societatea Timişoara

Address. 1900 Timişoara, Str. Mihai Eminescu 5.

Telephone. (961) 324 53.

Traditional Social Democratic Party

Foundation. May 10, 1991.

Leadership. Lucian Cornescu (pres.)

Membership. 297.

Union of Armenians in Romania
Uniunea Armenilor din România

Address. 70334 Bucharest, Str. Armeneasca 9.

Telephone. 14 02 08.

Union of Hungarian Youth Organizations

Address. Sfintu Gheorghe.

Foundation. April 1, 1990.

United Democratic Party of the Romani, Fiddlers and Woodworkers of Romania
Partidul Unit Democrat al Romilor, Lăutarilor şi Rudarilor din România

Address. 1000 Rimnicu Vilcea, Cartier Goranu 889.

ROMANIA

Vatra Românească Union (VR)
Uniunea Vatra Românească

Address. 70172 Bucharest, Str. Biserica Amzei 5–7.

Foundation. Feb. 1, 1990.

History. Vatra Romaneasca (Romanian Hearth) was formed against the background of the growth of importance of the Hungarian minority in Transylvania. The NSF decision in January 1990 to restore Hungarian language radio broadcasts and to allocate four hours of national television broadcasting time to programmes in Hungarian was followed on Jan. 20, 1990, by the reorganization of primary and secondary schools by the Ministry of Education with a view of guaranteeing the minorities education in their native languages. Also on Jan. 15 the NSF issued an instruction for the reopening later that year of the Hungarian Bolyai University in Cluj, closed by the communist regime in 1959. The efficiency and speed with which the Hungarian minority rights were asserted have aroused suspicion and resentment among the Romanians in Transylvania. They fear that granting concessions to the Hungarians would encourage the two million Hungarians in Transylvania to seek greater autonomy and closer association with Hungary. Since its formation the VR has been accused of fomenting organized riots and individual attacks on Hungarians in Transylvania.

Programme. Vatra Romaneasca describes itself as an organization of the Romanian spirituality of Transylvania and the expression of the identity of all those who feel and speak Romanian in that part of the country. The union is against any manifestation of separatism, chauvinism and nationalism. It protests against attempts at harming state unity and the culture of the Romanian people, opposes the creation of administrative-territorial and cultural enclaves, asking that the historic rights of the Romanian population that has been living in Transylvania from time immemorial be observed. It demands the use of the Romanian language as the only official language throughout the country's territory. The VR bases its intra-national relations on the loyalty of all the country's citizens, no matter what their mother tongue, faith, political allegiance or race, to the Romanian people and to Romania.

Workers' and Peasants' Brotherhood Political Trade Union of Romania
Sindicatul Politic Fraternitatea Muncitorilor şi Ţăranilor din România

Address. 1900 Timişoara, Str. Cermena 10.

Telephone. (961) 394 69.

UNION OF SOVIET SOCIALIST REPUBLICS

(Soviet Union)

Stephen White

Soviet rule in the USSR was established on Nov. 7, 1917, when a Military-Revolutionary Committee under the control of the Bolshevik party arrested the Provisional Government which had ruled since earlier in the year and transferred power to the second all-Russian Congress of Soviets. This in turn elected a new Soviet government, headed by Lenin; power in fact belonged to the Bolshevik party, the more radical wing of the Russian Social Democratic Labour Party, within which Lenin had earlier established his ascendancy. In July 1918 a constitution was adopted for the Russian Soviet Federal Socialist Republic (RSFSR), which was the first regime of its kind to be established. In the course of the civil war other Soviet republics were established in the Ukraine, Belorussia and Transcaucasia; these formally combined in December 1922 to form the Union of Soviet Socialist Republics. In 1924 the Uzbek and Turkmen republics and in 1929 the Tadzhik republic became constituent members of the USSR, with the status of union republics. At the 8th Congress of Soviets in December 1936 a new constitution was adopted, at which the Transcaucasian republic was separated into Georgian, Armenian and Azerbaidzhani union republics, which also became constituent members of the USSR. The Kazakh and Kirgiz republics, previously autonomous republics within the RSFSR, became full union republics at the same time. The changes that took place during World War II led to the incorporation, under a secret protocol to the Nazi-Soviet Pact of 1939, of the three Baltic republics. Moldavia became a Soviet republic at the same time and under the same circumstances.

After an acknowledged retreat into a mixed economy — the New Economic Policy — during the 1920s, a decision was taken at the end of the 1920s to industrialize on the basis of centralized state planning. The first Five Year Plan was introduced in 1928 and pronounced achieved "ahead of time" at the end of 1932. It is probably fair to say that there has been no more significant development in the post-revolutionary period, and this pattern of centralized state direction of the economy has persisted, with minor variations, up to the present. At the same time agriculture was collectivized, "voluntarily" but in fact with great loss of life, and all other spheres of Soviet life, from the family to sport and recreation, were placed under the detailed direction of the state. Initially very successful (even the most "revisionist" recalculations of economic growth after 1928 show Soviet rates exceeding those of the developed capitalist nations), this system became steadily less effective as a means of directing social and economic development, and the post-Stalin period has essentially consisted of an attempt to devise a substitute for what has come to be known as the "command-administrative system" developed during these years. Stalinism had a still greater direct bearing upon political liberties and the development of democracy based upon the elected soviets; by the late 1930s, if not earlier, any elements of pluralism that still remained within the party and the state had been eliminated, and large numbers of political opponents had been arrested and in many cases shot on groundless charges.

With all its faults it was widely believed that this was a system that had "won the war" with Nazi Germany, although the costs of doing so were horrendous, and for an older generation of Soviet leaders there is still much to be said for this centralized, state-directed form of social direction, modified in various respects but not abandoned in principle. The post-Stalin years have nonetheless seen a continuous search for an alternative, socialist (in the sense of being based on public ownership) but also democratic, in a way that (it was argued) the Soviet system had been during its early Leninist years. The first Soviet leader to make a determined effort to cleanse the Soviet system of its Stalinist deformations while yet retaining its healthy Leninist essence was Nikita Khrushchev, particularly through his "secret speech" to the 20th Congress of the CPSU in 1956. There followed an attempt to develop a new legal system based on "socialist legality", and a more responsive political system based upon "Leninist norms of party life" such as collectivism and rank-and-file initiative. Many of these reforms, however, were ill-considered and hastily implemented, and when Khrushchev was compelled to resign in October 1964 there was a widespread wish (and certainly in the party and state leadership) to avoid any more of the "hare-brained schemes" with which he was associated. The Brezhnev years developed, in part, as a reaction to the hectic pace of change under Khrushchev; they in turn became years of immobilism and "stagnation", and the task that Gorbachev inherited on becoming party leader in 1985 was to resume the reformist programme, defined once again as an attempt to eliminate the bureaucracy, corruption and inertia of the Brezhnev and Stalin years and to return to healthy Leninist foundations.

The advent of a new general secretary has normally meant a significant change in the direction of Soviet public policy, although any change of course has usually taken some time to establish itself as the new leader marginalizes his opponents and co-opts his supporters on to the Politburo and Secretariat. At the outset of his administration Gorbachev's objectives, and indeed his personal background, were still fairly obscure even at leading levels of the party. Gorbachev, unlike his two main rivals, had not addressed a party congress, and he had still no published collection of writings to his name. He had made only a couple of important visits abroad, to Canada in 1983 and to the United Kingdom in late 1984, on both occasions as the head of a delegation of Soviet parliamentarians. Andrei Gromyko, proposing Gorbachev's candidacy to the Central Committee, explained what had convinced him personally that Gorbachev would be a suitable general secretary: Gorbachev, he indicated, had chaired meetings of the Politburo in the absence of Konstantin Chernenko and had done so "brilliantly, without any exaggeration". Gorbachev himself, in his acceptance speech, paid tribute to the late general secretary and then pledged himself to continue the policy of his two predecessors, which he defined as "acceleration of socio-economic development and the perfection of all aspects of social life". Relatively quickly, however, the new general secretary began to develop a more distinctly reformist agenda of his own.

Of all the policies that were promoted by the Gorbachev leadership, *glasnost* was perhaps the most distinctive and the one that had been pressed furthest by the early

1990s. *Glasnost*, usually translated as openness or publicity, was not the same as freedom of the press or the right to information; nor was it original to Gorbachev. It did, however, reflect the new general secretary's belief that without a greater awareness of the real state of affairs and of the considerations that had led to particular decisions there would be no willingness on the part of the Soviet people to commit themselves to his programme of *perestroika*. "The better people are informed", Gorbachev told the Central Committee meeting that elected him, "the more consciously they act, the more actively they support the party, its plans and programmatic objectives". Existing policies were in any case ineffectual, counterproductive and much resented. The newspaper *Sovetskaya Rossiya*, for instance, reported the case of Mr Polyakov of Kaluga, a well-read man who followed the central and local press and never missed the evening TV news. He knew a lot about what was happening in various African countries, Polyakov complained, but he had "only a very rough idea what was happening in his own city". Nor was this an isolated case. In October 1985, another reader complained to the same paper, there had been a major earthquake in Tadzhikistan in Soviet Central Asia, but no details were made known other than that "lives had been lost". At about the same time there had been an earthquake in Mexico and a volcanic eruption in Colombia. Both had been covered extensively with on-the-spot reports and full details of the casualties that had been suffered. Was Tadzhikistan really further from Moscow than Latin America?

Influenced by considerations such as these, the Gorbachev leadership made steady and sometimes dramatic progress in removing taboos from the discussion of public affairs and exposing both the Soviet past and the Soviet present to critical scrutiny. The Brezhnev era was one of the earliest targets. It had been a time, Gorbachev told the 27th Party Congress in 1986, when a "curious psychology — how to change things without really changing anything" had been dominant. A number of its leading representatives had been openly corrupt, and some (such as Brezhnev's son-in-law, Yuri Churbanov) were brought to trial and imprisoned. More generally, it had been a period of "stagnation", of wasted opportunities, when party and government leaders had lagged behind the needs of the times. The Stalin question, however, was clearly the most critical one, as it had been for all Soviet reformers. Gorbachev, to begin with, was reluctant even to concede there was a question. Stalinism, he told the French press in 1986, was a "notion made up by enemies of communism"; the 20th Party Congress in 1956 had condemned Stalin's "cult of personality" and drawn the necessary conclusions. By early 1987, however, Gorbachev was insisting that there must be "no forgotten names, no blank spots" in Soviet literature and history, and by November of that year, when he came to give his address on the 70th anniversary of the revolution, he was ready to condemn the "wanton repressive measures" of the 1930s, "real crimes" in which "many thousands of people inside and outside the party" had suffered.

In the course of his speech Gorbachev announced that a Politburo commission had been set up to investigate the political repression of the Stalinist years, and this led to the rehabilitation of many prominent figures from the party's past (and thousands of others). The most important figure to be restored to full respectability in this way was the former *Pravda* editor Nikolai Bukharin, whose sentence was posthumously quashed in February 1988 (later in the year his expulsions from the party and the Academy of Sciences were both reversed). Two other old Bolsheviks, Grigorii Zinoviev and Lev Kamenev, were rehabilitated in July 1988. Trotsky had not been sentenced by a Soviet court and there was therefore no judgement to be quashed; but his personal qualities began to receive some recognition in the Soviet press, and from 1989 onwards his writings began to appear in mass-circulation as well as scholarly journals. An extended discussion took place about the numbers that Stalin had condemned to death: for some it was about a million by the end of the 1930s, but for others (such as the historian and deputy Roy Medvedev) it was at least 12 million, with a further 38 million repressed in other ways. Perhaps still more significant, a number of mass graves of victims of the Stalin period began to be uncovered, the most extensive of which were in the Kuropaty forest near Minsk. This, and the other mass graves that began to be discovered in the late 1980s and early 1990s, was an indictment of Stalinism still more powerful than anything the historians and writers could muster.

The "democratization" of Soviet political life, of which *glasnost* was a part, was also intended to release the human energies that, for Gorbachev, had been choked off by the bureaucratic centralism of the recent past. The Soviet Union, he told the 19th Party Conference in the summer of 1988, had pioneered the idea of a workers' state and of workers' control, the right to work and equality of rights for women and all national groups. The political system established by the October revolution, however, had undergone "serious deformations", leading to the development of a "command-administrative system" which had extinguished the democratic potential of the elected soviets. The role of party and state officialdom had increased out of all proportion, and this "bloated administrative apparatus" had begun to dictate its will in political and economic matters. Nearly a third of the adult population were regularly elected to the soviets and other bodies, but most of them had little influence over the conduct of state and public affairs. Social life as a whole had become unduly "governmentalized", and ordinary working people had become "alienated" from the system that was supposed to rule in their name. It was this "ossified system of government, with its command-and-pressure mechanism", that was now the main obstacle to *perestroika*.

The Conference duly approved the notion of a "radical reform" of the political system, and this led to a series of constitutional and other changes from 1988 onwards. An entirely new electoral law, for instance, approved in December 1988, broke new ground in providing for (though not specifically requiring) a choice of candidate at elections to local and national-level authorities. A new state structure was established, incorporating a relatively small working parliament for the first time in modern Soviet political history. A constitutional review committee, staffed by lawyers and political scientists, was set up as part of a move to what Gorbachev called a "socialist system of checks and balances" (the new union treaty, approved in principle in 1991, envisaged a full-fledged Supreme Court). Judges were to be elected for longer periods of time, and given greater guarantees of independence in their work. And the CPSU itself was to be "democratized", although in practice the changes were less dramatic than in other parts of the political system (see below). Leading officials, it was agreed, should be elected by competitive ballot for a maximum of two consecutive terms; members of the Central Committee should be involved much more directly in the work of the leadership; and there should be much more information about all aspects of the party's work, from its finances to the operation of its decision-making bodies.

For all the importance of individual changes of personnel and policy, it was the establishment of a qualitatively different representative system that was perhaps the single most important political development of the late 1980s. Under the previous electoral system, which was governed by the 1936 and then the 1977 constitutions, there was no choice of candidate and very little opportunity, in practice, to reject the single nominee. Only one party, the Communist Party (CPSU), had a legal standing, and it either nominated candidates directly or arranged for its preferred nominations to be made by the other bodies that enjoyed this right, such as the trade unions and the *Komsomol* (Young Communist League). No candidate at the national level, since the introduction of this system in 1937, had ever been defeated, and the reported turnout had never fallen below 99 per cent (at the last national elections under this system, in 1984, it achieved the record level of 99.99 per cent).

A limited experiment, in local elections in 1987, saw the nomination of more candidates than seats available in a small number of specially enlarged constituencies (about 1 per cent of the total). Under constitutional amendments and an entirely new electoral law approved in December 1988 these more competitive arrangements became universal. A choice of candidate was to become normal (although not obligatory). Candidates were to live in the areas they represented, they were required to put forward election manifestos, and had the right to appoint campaign staff to assist them. Deputies could not simultaneously hold governmental office, as they could hardly be expected to hold themselves to account. The voters themselves were to pass through screened-off booths before casting their vote, ending the earlier practice by which they had been discouraged from voting against the single candidate by the need to make use of the booth to do so. The forthcoming elections, set for March 1989, would be "unlike all those that had preceded them", the Central Committee promised at its meeting in November 1988; probably few inside or outside the USSR realized quite how different they would be.

Under the new arrangements, candidates were to be nominated and then approved by a selection conference; in the second stage they would compete with each other for the support of their respective electorates, who would then cast their decisive ballots. There had been some resistance, in the discussion of the constitutional amendments, to these somewhat elaborate provisions. Selection conferences came in for particular criticism, with some letters to the press asking who needed these "elections before elections". There was also some hostility to the most novel feature of the revised arrangements by which a wide range of public bodies, from the CPSU and the trade unions to stamp collectors and film fans, had the right to elect specified numbers of deputies to the new Congress. Was not this a violation of the principle "one person one vote", it was asked, and what, in any case, had stamp collecting to do with affairs of state? The new arrangements, notwithstanding these criticisms, were approved almost unanimously by the outgoing Supreme Soviet and they served as the basis of the first-ever elections to the USSR Congress of People's Deputies on March 26, 1989 (see Table 1).

In both the public bodies and ordinary constituencies the electoral process took a variety of forms. A number of public bodies, in the end, approved no more candidates than the seats available: the CPSU itself was one of these, agreeing to nominate just 100 candidates for the 100 seats it had been accorded under the constitutional amendments. In the vote, at a special plenary meeting of the Central Committee on March 15, 52 candidates were elected unanimously; 12 votes were cast against Gorbachev but 78, the largest number, against the prominent "conservative", Yegor Ligachev. The elections in the Academy of Sciences were much more vigorously contested. A number of leading reformers, among them the physicist Andrei Sakharov and the space scientist Roald Sagdeev, were not originally selected as nominees for the Academy's 20 seats. In the elections that followed only eight of the 23 nominees secured the necessary majority, and further elections had to

Table 1: The USSR General Election, March 1989

The final results, as made public by the Central Electoral Commission, were as follows:

	Turnout (percentages)
Armenia	71.9
Azerbaidzhan	98.5
Belorussia	92.4
Estonia	87.1
Georgia	97.0
Kazakhstan	93.7
Kirgizia	97.0
Latvia	86.9
Lithuania	82.5
Moldavia	90.5
Russian Republic	87.0
Tadzhikistan	93.9
Turkmenia	96.1
Ukraine	93.4
Uzbekistan	95.8
USSR as a whole	89.8

The deputies

Altogether 1,958 of 2,250 USSR People's Deputies were elected, which left 292 deputies still to be chosen at subsequent by-elections. The elected deputies included 334 women (17.1 per cent); 1,624 men (82.9 per cent); 365 workers (18.6 per cent); and 219 collective farmers (11.2 per cent). The total of workers and collective farmers was 584 (29.8 per cent). Among the deputies 1,176 (87.6 per cent of the total) were CPSU members or candidates; 242 (12.4 per cent) were non-Party candidates; and 114 (5.8 per cent) were members of the *Komsomol* or Young Communist League. Altogether 60 different nationalities were represented among the deputies.

Source: *Izvestiya*, April 5, 1989, p.1.

be held at which Sakharov, Sagdeev and other reformers were successful (Sakharov, who went on to become an outspoken and controversial parliamentarian, died the following December). Practices in the constituencies varied still more widely, some constituencies dispensing with selection conferences and approving up to 12 nominations for a single seat, while others, particularly in the southern republics, much more frequently approved a single candidate in the traditional manner.

In the end, 2,884 candidates were selected to contest the 1,500 constituency seats; in 384 of them, despite the intentions of the new law, there was just a single nomination. The first and in some ways most significant result was the turnout. The election legislation and official commentaries had made it plain that the abuses of earlier years would not be tolerated, and voting took place over a slightly shorter period than usual. In the circumstances a reported turnout of 89.8 per cent, although well down on previous recorded levels, suggested that the new arrangements had succeeded in their primary task, to engage the interest and involvement of the Soviet mass public. More remarkable, however, were the results themselves. The Communist Party, in fact, increased its representation: 87.6 per cent of the new deputies were members, a considerable increase on the outgoing assembly. Many of its leading officials, however, suffered sensational defeats. At least 38 regional first secretaries were defeated, even though in some cases they had stood as the single candidate. The former Moscow party leader, Boris Yeltsin, enjoyed a spectacular success in the capital's no. 1 national-territorial seat, where he secured 89.4 per cent of the vote despite attempts by the central party apparatus to hinder his campaign. The most striking series of defeats occurred in Leningrad, where the list of casualties included the regional party first secretary (a candidate member of the Politburo), the regional second secretary, the chairman of the city soviet and his deputy, the chairman of the regional soviet and the city party secretary. Gorbachev, addressing the Central Committee a month later, professed to see the elections as a victory for *perestroika* on the grounds that the victims had been predominantly conservative officials who were less than fully committed to its success. The results were nonetheless difficult to interpret as other than a humiliating snub to the Communist Party, and in some respects, such as the sweeping victories achieved by nationalist candidates in the Baltic republics, they appeared to prejudice the unity of the Soviet state itself.

The 28th Congress of the Communist Party of the Soviet Union (CPSU) took place in July 1990. By the time it convened the party had already lost a substantial part of the authority it once commanded. The most important single development in this connection was the decision taken by the Central Committee in February 1990 to relinquish the guarantee of its "leading role" contained in Article 6 of the 1977 constitution. Gorbachev, who had resisted a challenge to Article 6 at the Congress of People's Deputies the previous December, argued that the leading role had already been overtaken by events, in particular the establishment of a wide range of independent political groupings. The party, however, should seek to retain a position of "political leadership" through the electoral process. The constitution was amended accordingly by the Third Congress of People's Deputies in March; henceforth, the new Article 6 suggested, the Communist Party would share the task of forming and administering public policy with other parties and social movements.

The formal loss of its leading position was only one of the ways in which the CPSU saw its formerly unchallengeable position erode over the late 1980s and early 1990s. The party, for instance, began to lose members: about three million of them (14 per cent) during 1990 alone, of whom a large proportion had simply resigned. The existing membership became increasingly divided, despite the formal prohibition of "factions" within its ranks. The two groupings that secured the widest attention in the run-up to the Congress were the "Democratic Platform", whose members called for the CPSU to abandon its Leninism in favour of a purely parliamentary role, and the "Marxist Platform", whose members called for a party based more closely on the interests and participation of the industrial working class. The party press lost circulation: *Pravda*, for instance, had only 30 per cent of its 1990 subscribers in 1991. Members and whole branches began to withhold their dues, and party income as a whole fell by about half. The party's public standing, as measured by opinion polls, declined sharply. Perhaps (for its leaders) most alarming of all, the party began to fragment as a national organization. In December 1989 the Lithuanian party organization seceded; in March and April 1990 the Latvian and Estonian party organizations split into pro-Moscow and independent factions; and in December 1990 the Georgian party organization followed the Lithuanians by opting for full independence.

The 28th Party Congress, which met in Moscow from July 2–13, 1990, was accordingly a very different gathering from the congresses that had preceded it. It was the first to meet against a background of demonstrators shouting "Down with the red fascists!" It was the first congress, for many years at least, at which members of the leadership rendered individual account. It was the first congress at any time at which there was a direct contest for the party leadership: Gorbachev originally faced nine challengers and had to be content with three-quarters of the vote in the final choice between himself and a district party secretary. It was the first congress since the late 1920s that adopted no "Guidelines" for the forthcoming five-year plan, reflecting the view that this was the responsibility of government alone. An entirely new set of Party Rules was adopted, and a new "Programmatic Declaration" which was meant to guide the party's activities until a new Party Programme could be adopted. There were calls for the party to drop the word "Communist" from its title, and the *Internationale* as its anthem. The Congress concluded by electing its first-ever deputy leader and a newly constituted Politburo, including the party first secretaries of the 15 republics.

Gorbachev, in his opening address, described the process of *perestroika* as one by which a "Stalinist model of socialism" had been replaced by a "civil society of free men and women". The political system, more particularly, had been "radically transformed" with the establishment of "genuine democracy" based upon free elections, a multi-party system, human rights and popular self-government. An atmosphere of "ideological domineering" had been replaced by one of freedom of thought. The crimes of the past had been "resolutely condemned". There had been a "real revolution in people's thinking"; life had become fuller and richer, the "absurd bans" of the Stalinist years had been removed, and scientists and intellectuals had been given a much more prominent place in the party's decision-making processes. And new opportunities had opened up for the development of culture, literature and the arts, or what Gorbachev rather grandly called the "ecology of the soul".

The Congress adopted a formal position on these and other matters with its approval of a declaration entitled "Towards a humane, democratic socialism". The declaration made it clear that, for the party at least, the origins of Soviet difficulties lay in deformations of socialism rather than the socialist project itself. Party dictatorship had led to popular alienation and lawlessness; nature had been plundered without restraint; and dogmatism had reigned supreme in the world of culture. *Perestroika* meant a "radical turn towards a policy aimed at the country's renovation"; the CPSU itself was presented as a party of the "socialist choice and communist perspective", seen as a natural stage in the advance of civilization. The declaration incorporated a set of "urgent anti-crisis measures", including a new union treaty and normalization of the consumer market. Longer-term measures included strengthened civil liberties, a "stage-by-stage transition to a market system" international co-operation and democratization of the party itself. The declaration was to serve, in effect, as the party's Programme until a new Programme could be adopted at a conference or congress in the first half of 1992.

Gorbachev discussed democratization of the party in his opening address, noting that the party's own organization and role required constant reappraisal. For many years, he suggested, the party had served as an extension of the command-administrative system, leading to serious mistakes in its choice of personnel and policies. Millions of party members had been removed from direct control over its affairs, and the result had been a "climate of indifference, apathy and passivity" in party branches. What would an "updated CPSU", freed of these defects, look like? It would, Gorbachev suggested, be a party of the "socialist choice and communist perspective", committed at the same time to the common ideals of humanity. It would be a party "freed of its ideological blinkers", promoting its policies through dialogue and co-operation with other progressive social and political forces. It would be a tolerant party, based on a recognition of minority rights and "total freedom of debate". It would be a "vanguard" as well as a parliamentary party, organizing in the workplace and armed forces as well as in residential areas. And it would be a self-managing party, based upon the freedom of action of branches and the independence of republican party organizations within a common programme and statute.

The Congress formalized its decisions on these matters with the adoption of an entirely new set of Party Rules, which introduced some quite significant changes as compared with drafts published earlier in the year and still more so the Rules that had been adopted at the previous congress in 1986. The important principle of democratic centralism was retained, after some discussion, in the final version. There was much more emphasis, however, upon the rights of ordinary members, who were given greater access to information about party committees at all levels and the right to "evaluate" their work. Branches were to be allowed to express their views on particularly contentious issues before they were considered by the Central Committee, and had the right to retain up to half of their membership income. The changes as compared with the Rules of 1986 were still more dramatic, including the explicit right to form "platforms" if not organized factions, greater respect for the rights of the minority, and official endorsement of "horizontal" structures such as political clubs and seminars of a kind that had hitherto been regarded as incompatible with democratic centralism. It was nonetheless unclear, after the Congress, if these and other changes would be sufficient to encourage the degree of commitment from party members that would be necessary if it was to retain the dominant position it had enjoyed for more than 70 years.

The experience of partly competitive national elections in March 1989 led to further consideration of the system under which they had been conducted. There was strong support, in the discussion, for dispensing with some of the arrangements that had given rise at the time to the greatest number of objections, particularly selection conferences and the representation of social organizations, and both of these provisions were altered in the revisions of the electoral law that took place in October 1989. Speaking to the Supreme Soviet, its chairman Anatolii Luk'yanov explained that general procedures had been reconsidered and that there would also be a greater tolerance of local variation in practices and institutions. Russia and the Ukraine, for instance, both intended to convene Congresses of People's Deputies from which a working Supreme Soviet would be elected; the other republics intended to elect a Supreme Soviet by direct and popular vote. Some republics proposed to retain the representation of social organizations, and others to abandon it. Different views had similarly been expressed about the idea of selection conferences, and this would be left to the republics to decide (in the end, four Central Asian republics retained a provision of this kind). Equal conditions should be created for all candidates — "far from all" had competed under such circumstances in the election earlier in the year. On the question of electoral choice, finally, the existing constitutional provisions would be left unchanged, allowing but not requiring the nomination of more candidates than seats available. This, thought Luk'yanov, was "more democratic".

These and other changes were passed into law at the Second Congress of People's Deputies in December 1989. Congresses of People's Deputies, it was made clear, would not be obligatory at the republican level (Art. 91); there had been some objection to arrangements of this kind from the Baltic republics at the time of their original adoption, and in the event only the Russian Republic introduced the complicated two-level parliamentary institution that remained in existence at the national level. It was decided to make no reference at all to the representation of social organizations in the USSR constitution; the Congress of People's Deputies, Luk'yanov explained, would continue to be composed in the same way, but republics would be free to make their own arrangements. In the event, two of them — Kazakhstan (where a quarter of the seats were allocated on this basis) and Belorussia (where handicapped and veterans' organizations were given 50 of the 360 seats — decided to retain such representation in their republican parliaments). The reference to selection conferences, equally, was dropped from the constitution, allowing republics to make their own decisions. Despite further suggestions for a change, finally, the number of candidates that were to be nominated remained as before: there could be any number, leaving the decision (at least in principle) to the electorate.

The republican and local elections that took place upon the basis of this amended law were held over a period of months and often on different dates — a further deviation from established practice, which left republican parliaments in some cases to vote themselves an extended period of office. The elections in the Baltic were among the first: in Estonia, for instance, elections to local Soviets took place in December 1989 and to the republican Supreme Soviet in March 1990. More than 20 organized groups took part in the elections to the republican parliament; the Communist Party took 55 of the 105 seats, but it was the Popular Front, with 46 seats and allies in other groups, that headed the largest group of deputies and provided the new prime minister. The outcomes in the other Baltic states were broadly similar, with sweeping successes for nationalist candidates. This was particularly true of Lithuania, where 90 of the 141 seats in the elections of February 1990 went to supporters of Sajudis; the Communist Party's leading role had been removed from the republican constitution the previous December and these were, in effect, the first genuinely competitive elections in Soviet history. Latvia, like Estonia, held its local elections in December 1989 and its parliamentary elections the following March; here again the Popular Front was overwhelmingly successful, although more so in the countryside than in the largely Russian-speaking capital. Candidates claiming membership of the Popular Front took 111 of the 210 seats, and allies brought the total to 131 — close to the two-thirds majority needed for constitutional change.

The Slavic republics voted in early March 1990. Over 6,700 candidates competed for the 1,068 seats that were available in the Russian Republic, with up to 28 nominations for a single seat. The turnout was 77 per cent, substantially lower than the corresponding figure a year earlier; it was lower still in Moscow and Leningrad, and less than half in a Noril'sk constituency where no valid result could be declared. Only 121 seats could be filled after the first round of voting; among them, once again, was Boris Yeltsin, chosen by over 80 per cent of the electorate in his home town of Sverdlovsk. In the second round, later in the month, turnout was down to about 70 per cent and a "whole series" of seats could not be filled because the turnout fell below 50 per cent. The "Democratic Russia" bloc of candidates (see below) enjoyed considerable success, taking 20–23 per cent of the vote in the republic as a whole and a considerably larger share in the cities, and after several inconclusive votes its candidate, the former Moscow party secretary Boris Yeltsin, was elected to the chairmanship of the republican Supreme Soviet on May 29, 1990 (and to a newly-established Russian Presidency in June 1991). Another radical, the economist Gavriil Popov, became mayor of Moscow, and a law professor, Anatolii Sobchak, became head of the city administration in Leningrad; both were re-elected by a direct popular ballot in June 1991. All three, meanwhile, had left the Communist Party.

In the Ukraine only 112 of the 450 constituencies were able to declare a result after the first round of voting, although turnout was relatively high at 85 per cent. In one Kiev constituency there were as many as 33 candidates; the republican average was seven. Large numbers of seats were won by candidates associated with the nationalist movement *Rukh* and the Greens; *Rukh*, for instance, took control of Kiev and of much of the west of the republic (a nationalist heartland). In the L'vov region, in the western Ukraine, voters elected not the first secretary of the regional party committee but the Goryn brothers, who had spent many years in prison for their "anti-Soviet activities". Another of the successful candidates was the Metropolitan of Vinnitsa and Bratslav; the Ukrainian head of state, Valentina Shevchenko, withdrew from the electoral contest "because of a number of circumstances" when its outcome began to seem doubtful. In the third Slavic republic, Belorussia, 1,473 candidates fought it out for 310 seats, only 20 of which were uncontested. There was an 87 per cent turnout, but (as elsewhere) only a minority of seats were filled on the first ballot. In one particularly outstanding case a journalist defeated a member of the Belorussian Central Committee Secretariat; *Pravda* described the result as "sensational".

Elections in the other republics took place at various times: in Armenia, for instance, in May 1990, and in Georgia the date was first postponed and then set for November 1990. In Armenia the turnout, already the lowest in 1989, was lower still — "just over 60 per cent"; nationalist candidates enjoyed considerable success and a member of the Karabakh committee, Levon Ter-Petrosyan, was elected president in early August. In Georgia, the elections which finally took place at the end of October led to the clear victory of a nationalist coalition, Round Table/Free Georgia, which took 54 per cent of the vote as compared with the Communists' 29.6 per cent. Shortly afterwards the veteran dissident Zviad Gamsakhurdia was elected republican president on a programme of transition to full independence; in May 1991 he was re-elected by a direct popular ballot. As before, there was least competition in Central Asia. In Uzbekistan, for instance, about a third of seats in the February 1990 elections had only one candidate, and more than half of all the candidates were managers or executives. Elections to the 250 places in the Kirgiz parliament also took place in February 1990; so too did the elections to the Tadzhik parliament, where 1,035 candidates completed for the 230 seats available. The turnout here was close to the Central Asian norm, at 91.2 per cent.

The republican elections in the spring and autumn of 1990 had a number of common characteristics. In the first place, turnout levels were down on those that had been recorded a year earlier, particularly in the later rounds of voting and in the towns as compared with the countryside. Turnout levels, as in March 1989, were higher in Central Asia than in the other republics; Armenia, on both occasions, recorded the lowest figures. Secondly, there was a greater degree of electoral choice than in the elections to the Congress of People's Deputies, although the level of competition remained much lower in Central Asia and in the elections to local rather than republican levels of government. As a result, larger numbers of seats remained unfilled after the first round of balloting than ever before;

the whole exercise became a lengthier and, inevitably, a more expensive one (Estonia, the only republic to employ the single transferable vote system, was able to avoid most of these difficulties). The candidates, in the third place, remained overwhelmingly CPSU members, but a greater share of seats than ever before went to managers, executives, academics and clerics, and the representation of workers, collective farmers, women and young people declined even further (Moscow and Leningrad, for instance, each returned a single worker). And finally, there was a significantly higher level of party or organized group activity, with the beginnings of co-ordinated platforms across or within republics. This was particularly true of the Baltic and the major cities.

The formation of new political parties, by the early 1990s, was still at a rudimentary level, with no clear association between a candidate's programme, his organizational affiliation and his subsequent behaviour in the legislature. There were, however, at least 20 parties in operation on an all-union basis by this time, with a membership ranging from a few dozen to some tens of thousands. In addition, about 500 parties were active at the republican level. Membership figures were difficult to establish: some of the parties kept no central register of members or regarded them as confidential, and almost all of them exaggerated their own numbers considerably. The new parties fell into two main types: "vanguard parties" (which had adopted some of the organizational forms of the CPSU) and "movement parties" (which were similar to the broadly based popular coalitions that had been formed in Eastern Europe in the late 1980s). The Democratic Party, an example of the first of these, based itself on democratic centralism and exercised strict discipline over the activities of its members; the Democratic Union, which fell into the second category, did not impose the decisions of its leadership upon the mass membership and allowed the formation of organized factions (even of communists) within its ranks. All of these parties operated within the framework of a Law on Public Associations, approved in October 1990, which laid the formal basis of a Soviet multi-party system.

According to the Law, the right of association was an "inalienable human and civil right", embodied already in the Universal Declaration of Human Rights and the USSR constitution, and guaranteed to all Soviet citizens. The Law covered public associations of all kinds, including trade unions, women's and veterans' associations, sporting societies and creative unions as well as political parties. Associations could be created for a variety of purposes, including the "exercise and protection of civil, political, economic, social and cultural rights and liberties", provided that their objectives did not extend to the "overthrow of or violent change in the constitutional system or the forcible violation of the unity of the territory of the USSR, the union and autonomous republics or other autonomous formations; propaganda of war, violence or cruelty; the stirring up of social discord, including class as well as racial, national or religious discord; or the commission of other criminally punishable acts". The creation of military associations or formations was also prohibited, and associations whose activities were detrimental to the health, morality, rights or interests of other citizens were liable to prosecution. All associations had to operate within the framework of the constitution and Soviet law.

At least 10 citizens were required to establish an association under the Law; they were then required to hold a founding congress or conference at which their statutes were adopted and executive bodies elected. An all-union party or trade union had to have a minimum of 5,000 members. The statutes of an association had then to be registered, with supporting documentation and a fee, with the USSR Ministry of Justice or its counterparts at other levels of government. Registration could be refused, if (for instance) the objectives of the association appeared to conflict with the Law, but this decision could in turn be appealed against up to the Supreme Court. Political parties, in particular, were supposed to have the basic goal of participation in bodies of state power and administration; they had programme documents, which were to be published for general information, and had the right to nominate candidates for election, to campaign on their behalf and to form organized groups in the bodies to which their candidates were elected. They were not, however, allowed to receive financial or other material assistance from foreign states, organizations or citizens, and bore legal liability for their actions including (in specified circumstances) their possible abolition. The registration of new and existing parties, including the CPSU, began on this basis in 1991.

At the "bourgeois-liberal" end of the new spectrum, at least from the perspective of the Communist Party, was "Democratic Russia", whose founding congress was held in Moscow in October 1990. A loosely structured coalition of political forces originally formed to contest the republican elections, Democratic Russia nonetheless shared a number of distinctive positions: a refusal to co-operate with the CPSU or with groups that were associated with it; a rejection of the economic policies of the central government and a demand that it resign (to be achieved, among other means, by a campaign of mass disobedience); the depoliticization of law enforcement; transfer of CPSU property to the people; the early holding of general elections for the presidency of Russia; and full sovereignty for the Russian Republic outside the framework of the USSR. Each collective member retained its own independence, but Democratic Russia was explicitly an organization opposed to the CPSU and it became the vehicle through which massive demonstrations were organized in support of Yeltsin and in opposition to the party and state authorities. Its demonstration in Moscow on the opening of the Russian Congress of People's Deputies in March 1991, at least half-a-million strong, took place even though it had been declared illegal by the central government.

About 20 different parties and movements constituted the "centre" of the political spectrum, including a Liberal Democratic Party, the Russian Popular Front, and the Democratic Party of Russia. The Democratic Party, led by former CPSU member Nikolai Travkin, was the largest of these, and according to most estimates the largest of all the new parties with 25–30,000 members in the early 1990s. Founded in May 1990, the Democratic Party declared its aim to be the restoration of an independent Russian democratic state within a voluntary union of republics. State power was to be decentralized, and a "society of equal opportunities" was to be created on the basis of market relations and equality of all forms of property. Science, culture and education were to be "deideologized", and a pluralistic political system established. Although a party based on "unity of will and action", the Democratic Party was committed to peaceful methods of struggle and aimed to secure the earliest possible holding of multi-party elections on the grounds that the existing soviets no longer reflected the popular mood. Travkin, a national and republican deputy, was the party's most prominent public spokesman; another was the chess player Gary Kasparov, who was elected one of its deputy chairmen at the party's founding congress but subsequently resigned his position (many of the new parties were prone to personality clashes of this kind).

Finally, there was a "left democratic" grouping based upon the Socialist and Social Democratic parties, the Greens, and an anarcho-syndicalist confederation. These groups were joined in November 1990 by the Republican Party of the Russian Federation, a "left centrist party of the parliamentary type", which occupied an intermediate position between the CPSU and the Democratic Party. The Republican Party consisted largely of former members of the CPSU who had been members of the Democratic Platform, a group that had been active in pressing for party democratization before the 28th Congress. Led by Vyacheslav Shostakovsky, former rector of the Higher Party School, the new party declared its intention of merging ultimately with the Social Democratic Party. Estimates suggested that this was, by the early 1990s, the second largest of the new parties with about 20,000 members; the Social Democrats and Christian Democrats had an estimated 10,000 members each, and other parties significantly less. Gorbachev, speaking to US Senators in 1990, described the USSR as the "most politicized society in the contemporary world"; but party memberships and identities were still very fluid and it would clearly be some time before the USSR became a system with competing, nationally organized parties that were capable of providing a coherent alternative to the CPSU.

The converse of this process of pluralization, party formation and republican assertiveness, was a strengthening of central authority, above all through the establishment of an executive presidency in 1990. The creation of the new presidency had been among the radical proposals announced by Gorbachev at the Central Committee plenum in February 1990 at which the constitutionally guaranteed "leading role" had been relinquished. The idea of presidential government, it appears, was under discussion in Gorbachev's immediate circle from late 1987 onwards as a means of circumventing the central party bureaucracy, which was seen as the main obstacle to reform. There was some uncertainty in the discussion as to whether the chief executive should be popularly elected or not, and Gorbachev's own intentions remained unclear. The idea of a Soviet presidency, in fact, was a good deal older than this. It had been under discussion at the time of the adoption of the 1936 constitution (Stalin, however, had opposed it and the idea made no further progress), and had also been considered in 1964 during preparatory work for the constitution eventually adopted in 1977. The idea of presidential government surfaced once again in 1989, when it was suggested in the press and was formally proposed to the First Congress of People's Deputies — provided the choice was made by direct and competitive elections — by Andrei Sakharov.

The introduction of a presidential system of this kind, for which there was no obvious precedent in Soviet or Russian political practice, was justified by Gorbachev as a means of ensuring that swift executive action could be taken in circumstances that required it, particularly where the economy, ethnic relations and public order were concerned. Anatolii Luk'yanov, who presented the proposals to an extraordinary Congress of People's Deputies in March 1990, argued that an institution of this kind would facilitate dialogue among the sociopolitical movements that had been brought into being by democratization and decentralization, and that in turn it would strengthen consensus and mutual understanding. The President could act quickly in the event of wars, disasters, social disorders or other circumstances, and he could help to resolve the impasse that had developed between the Soviet government and the Congress and Supreme Soviet. Nor, he went on, was there any reason to fear that the new presidency would lead to a new form of authoritarian rule; there were several safeguards against this, including limits on age and tenure and the ability of Congress — if a sufficiently large majority decided accordingly — to recall the President and overrule his decisions. What they needed, and what the law provided, was "authoritative legislative organs, and a powerful President, and an energetic government, and an independent legal system".

Gorbachev was duly elected to the new post on March 5, although he received no more than 59 per cent of the votes of all the members of the Congress (or 71 per cent of those who took part) in an uncontested ballot. Any citizen aged between 35 and 65, under the Law, could be elected to the Presidency for a maximum of two five-year terms. The President was normally to be elected by universal, equal and direct suffrage, although in the difficult circumstances that obtained it was agreed that Gorbachev — exceptionally — would be elected by the Congress itself. The President, under the terms of the legislation, was to report annually to the Congress of People's Deputies and would brief the Supreme Soviet on the "most important questions of the USSR's domestic and foreign policy". He would propose candidates for the premiership and other leading state positions; he had a suspensory veto over legislation; and he could dissolve the government and suspend its directives. He could also declare a state of emergency, and introduce direct presidential rule. The President headed a new Council of the Federation, consisting of the presidents of the 15 union republics, with responsibility for inter-ethnic and inter-republican issues; he also headed a new Presidential Council, which was responsible for the "main directions of the USSR's foreign and domestic policy".

In September 1990 these already impressive powers were extended by parliamentary vote, giving Gorbachev the right to institute emergency measures to "stabilize the country's sociopolitical life" for a period of 18 months. Several further changes were made by the Fourth Congress of People's Deputies in December 1990, completing the move to a fully presidential administration. The Council of Ministers was replaced by a more limited "Cabinet", headed by a prime minister who — together with his colleagues — would be nominated by the President and accountable to him (the former finance minister, Valentin Pavlov, was elected to this position in January 1991). The President became head of a new Security Council with overall responsibility for defence and public order (he himself appointed its other members). He also appointed a new Vice-President, responsible for carrying out the functions that were entrusted to him. The Presidential Council, formed the previous March, disappeared entirely, and a reconstituted Council of the Federation headed by the President became, in effect, the supreme state decision-making body.

There was some concern among Soviet liberals that these extensive powers, greater even than Stalin had commanded, could open the way to a new dictatorship. There were, in fact, considerable limitations upon the powers of the new President, extensive though they undoubtedly were. He could be impeached by a two-thirds vote of the Congress of People's Deputies; his ministerial nominations required the approval of the Supreme Soviet, which could force the resignation of the Cabinet as a whole if it voted accordingly; and he had himself to report annually to the Congress of People's Deputies upon the exercise of his responsibilities. In any case, as Gorbachev told a gathering of miners in April 1991, he had voluntarily surrendered the extraordinary powers of the General Secretary of the CPSU, powers which at that time were greater than those of any other world leader. Would he have done so if he had been seeking unlimited personal authority? Gorbachev, taking his oath as President in March 1990, made it clear that he would represent the interests of all citizens, not just of party members; and in the June 1991 elections to the Russian Presidency (see Table 2) he refrained, for this reason, from publicly endorsing any of the candidates. It was clear that in the future the Soviet President would deal mainly with the heads of state of the various republics, many of whom would not be CPSU members, and that the Soviet government he appointed would have to reflect the wide diversity of political forces that had come into legal existence by the early 1990s.

Soviet politics, however, were thrown into some confusion by the launching of a

Table 2: The Russian Presidential Election, June 16, 1991

The final results, as made public by the Central Electoral Commission on June 19, 1991, were as follows (percentages):

Bakatin, Vadim Viktorovich	3.42
Makashov, Albert Mikhailovich	3.74
Ryzhkov, Nikolai Ivanovich	16.85
Tuleev, Aman-Geldy Moldagazyevich	6.81
Yeltsin, Boris Nikolaevich	57.30
Zhirinovsky, Eladimir Volfovich	7.81

In accordance with Article 15 of the Law of the RSFSR on the election of the President of the RSFSR, the following was elected President of the RSFSR: Boris Nikolaevich Yeltsin.

Alexander Vladimirovich Rutskoi, chairman of the RSFSR Supreme Soviet Committee on the affairs of invalids, veterans of war and labour, social support of military servicemen and their families, was considered elected Vice-President of the RSFSR.

Source: *Izvestiya*, June 20, 1991, p.1.

---

quasi-military coup on Aug. 19, 1991, when a self-styled National Emergency Committee announced that President Gorbachev was "unwell" and that his functions were being transferred to Vice-President Yanaev. The Committee banned the activity of political parties, other than those that supported the state of emergency, and suspended publication of all newspapers and journals other than a small number of a broadly conservative character. Yanaev announced, at a hastily-convened press conference, that Gorbachev might be able to resume his duties when his health had recovered, but it subsequently became known that the Soviet President had been imprisoned at his holiday home in the Crimea and that he had refused to authorise the seizure of power. The coup, which appeared to have been poorly planned, collapsed rapidly when the armed forces refused to obey orders and storm the Russian parliament, where Boris Yeltsin became a potent focus of resistance. After just three days the coup collapsed ignominiously; its leaders were arrested, except for Interior Minister Pugo who committed suicide, and their decisions were declared invalid. President Gorbachev, evidently shaken, returned to Moscow on Aug. 21 and addressed a crowded press conference; he expressed support for the Communist Party as an organization, but on Aug. 24, more fully aware of the extent to which its leadership had supported the coup, he resigned as General Secretary and called upon the Central Committee to dissolve itself.

On Aug. 26 the Supreme Soviet took matters further by voting to suspend the activity of the party throughout the Soviet Union (it had already been suspended or banned in several of the republics). It seemed clear that the CPSU as such would not survive its suspension (Gorbachev spoke of the possibility of a newly constituted party of the left, and indicated his commitment to European social democracy as professed by Willy Brandt and his Swedish counterparts). Moves towards a very different party system were thereby accelerated, and the survival of the Soviet state in any form became doubtful as most of the republics (including Ukraine) voted in favour of a fully independent status. In September 1991 the Congress of People's Deputies began to place these developments into the context of legislation, providing for the formation of a loose confederation of states (under a new name, for the time being referred to as the Union of Sovereign Republics) and for a broader network of economic links involving all the former Soviet republics. Elections, for both the Presidency and the Soviet parliament, were announced for 1992; it was expected that Gorbachev, with Yeltsin's support, would remain as a (much reduced) President but that radical and democratic parties would enormously increase their political representation at the centre (if there was a Soviet parliament at all) and in the various states that made up the new union.

Directory of Parties

The listing that follows concentrates upon those political parties or movements that were organized on a union-wide basis in the early 1990s, other than the CPSU whose recent development is discussed above.

Confederation of Anarcho-Syndicalists (CAS)
Konfederatsiya anarkho-sindikalistov

Foundation. The Confederation of Anarcho-Syndicalists was founded at a Congress in May 1988 of clubs and organizations from 30 cities. It did not elect a leading organ; the CAS is led by A. Isaev, A. Shubin and V. Gurbolikov. In their Organizational Agreement the CAS declares that it is an independent organization of a non-party type which does not intend to seek political power.

Programme. The CAS seeks a decentralization which would include the deconstruction of the economy and the elevation of the status of local self-government and the formation of a stateless society. In this stateless structure, the means of production would be transferred to workers and state organization would be changed to a federation of self-managing autonomous entities. It also seeks to restructure the organs of representative democracy and the bureaucratic apparatus as organs of self-government. Its political objectives include the elimination of parties and party *blocs*, the abolition of the death penalty, the replacement of criminal punishment by social education, and changing the standing army and militia into a universal army of the people based in work collectives and on territorial divisions retaining only limited contingents of military specialists, all of which would be conducted on a voluntary basis. The Confederation's social policy encompasses social support for those who are unable to work and for the victims of "competition". During the period of *perestroika* CAS proposes more autonomy and self-management in production and the reform of the ministries as bodies with guiding and consultative functions. It also advocates the introduction of free, direct elections to representative organs, the elimination of *nomenklatura* privileges, the introduction of trial by jury and reform of the KGB as an organ for combating political violence and terror.

Organization. Membership of CAS is open to those who accept the aims of its Programme, support the activities of other CAS organizations, and participate in the group's activities. Members who are in the minority on the resolution of a question are not obliged to work for its realization, but must not work or agitate against it. The CAS has an anti-discriminatory policy.

Publications. KAS produces the publications *Obshchina* (Commune), *Vol'ya* (Will), *Zdravyi smysl'* (Common Sense), *Nabat* (Alarm Bell, published in Khar'kov), and other independent local press organs.

Confederation of Labour (CL)
Konfederatsiya truda

Foundation. The Confederation of Labour was established as the result of an all-union congress of independent workers' movements and organizations by delegates who were from workers' clubs, work and strike committees and representatives of the scientific intelligentsia. The Confederation is co-chaired by Yu. Gerol'd, V. Golikov and M. Sobol'. It declares itself a sociopolitical organization based on confederative principles; it associates itself in its activities with supporters of political, economic and social reforms more generally and seeks to eliminate any element of monopoly in the development of society.

Programme. The Confederation states that it is necessary to participate in the political struggle to defend workers' incomes, to establish rights in the workplace and unemployment assistance, to create a flexible work system that will allow for extra training of staff under the aegis of independent trade unions and organizations, the elevation of the consumer sector and the lowering of government expenditures on costly projects, the implementation of a significant positive change in the socioeconomic condition of workers, the liquidation of destitution and exploitation by the state, technocracy and other forces and the transition to a democratic political system. It states that its most important task is to become engaged in a struggle that will facilitate the liquidation of the CPSU, its apparatus and its monopolies in state departments, the bureaucracy and economic administration. The Confederation also seeks to end disinformation in official propaganda, to depoliticize the KGB, army, courts, procuracy and other state organs, to remove party committees from enterprises, develop market relations and the economic independence of enterprises, defend the rights and freedoms of servicemen, establish links with the democratic intelligentsia and form local organs of self-government.

Organization. Members of the Confederation may belong to other organizations as long as their aims do not contradict the Rules and Declaration of the Confederation.

Constitutional Democratic Party (Party of Popular Freedom)
Konstitutsionno-demokraticheskaya partiya (Partiya narodnoi svobody)

Foundation. The Party of Popular Freedom emerged in May 1990 as the result of a referendum among sociopolitical groups and associations that supported the notion of constitutional democracy. Organs and groups that participated were from the Ukraine, Belorussia, Uzbekistan, the Bashkir, Kalmytsk, Tatar and Udmurt ASSRs, Krasnodar *krai* and Voronezh, Gorky (now Nizhnyi Novgorod), Leningrad, Moscow, Novosibirsk, Orenburg, Omsk, Perm, Sverdlovsk, Tambov, Chelyabinsk and Yaroslavl regions. According to the referendum, the Constitutional Democratic Party (Party of Popular Freedom), banned on Dec. 11, 1917, would be regarded as renewed on May 15, 1990. Its leaders include a five-member Central Committee which comprises: V. Vitt, G. Deryagin (chairperson), D. Efimov (secretary), A. Ostrovsky and N. Solov'ev.

Programme. The Constitutional Democratic Party seeks to establish a constitutional democracy based on organized popular sovereignty and a state structure regulated by law. In order to facilitate the construction of a constitutional democratic state, they propose the primacy of individual rights, the inadmissibility of the rights of one individual violating the rights of another, the inadmissibility of state discrimination based on an individual's social group, a state guarantee of inalienable personal and civil rights, and equality for all forms of political, economic and spiritual life for the individual and society.

Publication. The Constitutional Democratic Party publishes the bulletin *Ka-Det* (Cadet).

Democratic Party (DP)
Demokraticheskaya partiya

Foundation: The Democratic Party was formed at a congress in November 1989 at which it elected its Central Co-ordinating Committee (21 members) and Secretariat (seven members). The party chairperson is R. Semonov.

Programme. The aim of the DP is the "liquidation of the totalitarian order and the formation of a democratic society based on the foundations of a multi-party system and pluralism of opinions, economic and spiritual freedoms". To promote legal reform it advocates the supremacy of law over all spheres of social life and to raise the quality of law-creating activities with a special emphasis on human and individual rights and an improvement of judicial activity. The DP propose pluralism of all forms of property in the economic sphere and the adoption of wage labour; freedom of private enterprise; the transfer of land to the peasants on the basis of lease holding and private property; a transition to a market economy and an abolition of state monopolies over foreign trade, manufacturing, wine and vodka producing industries. Its suggestions for political reform include the adoption of a multi-party system; independent creation of media and trade unions; guarantees of civil rights; abolition of the passport system; freedom of entry into and exit from the country; reform of the KGB and MVD; the elimination of compulsory military service and the establishment of a professional army.

In the foreign policy arena DP advocates the establishment of social control over international relations; a guarantee of full openness on the questions of economic assistance to movements and countries and the withdrawal of armed forces from foreign soil. Its nationality policies advance the notion of the reform of the USSR on the basis of a democratic confederation, the elevation of the status of autonomous territorial divisions, and the redrawing of the country's administrative boundaries in accordance with actual population distributions. In order to facilitate social security and health care the DP advocates reduced military expenditures and the construction of a national assistance fund, and intends to de-ideologize education by eliminating censorship, granting the opposition media a status parallel to the government's, and permitting the religious education of children.

Democratic Union (DU)
Demokraticheskii soyuz

Foundation. The initial congress of the Democratic Union was held in Moscow in May 1988 and was attended by nearly 100 representatives from 15 cities. A second congress was conducted in Riga in January 1989 at which the representatives adopted the Provisional Draft Programme of the DU. The third congress, convened in Tallinn in January 1990, was attended by 99 delegates (59 of whom had voting status) from 50 cities. The congress adopted a resolution to boycott the elections to republican and local soviets of people's deputies. Its leading organ is the Party Council of the Democratic Union. The DU is led by V. Novodvorskaya, I. Tsar'kov, A. Eliovich and others.

Programme. The Democratic Union stands for the non-violent change of the country's political system with the aim of constructing a representative parliamentary democracy at all levels. It advocates a primacy of equality and pluralism of all political forces. Its attitudes to the organs of security include the dissolution of the KGB; the abolition of the political departments of the MVD; the assurance that the MVD is fully subordinated to the elected organs of power; and the introduction of partial electability of local militia leaders. The Democratic Union seeks to reduce the armed forces; form a professional army; eliminate the military-patriotic education of young people; eliminate arms exports; eliminate military transportation throughout the country's territory; and abolish the Warsaw Pact and NATO. On national politics, the DU advocates full freedom and self-determination of each union republic; the rights of indigenous national state formations to a state language; the acknowledgement of law over cultural-national autonomy for peoples living in foreign nationality areas; the right of each national republic to form its own state army and separate military sub-divisions; and the establishment of the USSR as a democratic confederation.

So far as legal reform is concerned, the Democratic Union proposes an independent judiciary, the introduction of trial by jury, the elimination of the death penalty, the release and rehabilitation of all victims of Soviet bureaucracy, the elimination of the *propiska* and passport systems, and the freedom to leave the USSR and to return to it. Socioeconomically, the Democratic Union proposes a mixed economy, defence of workers

— including the right to form independent trade unions, and work to introduce equality to the country's economic sectors — state, collective and private. In agriculture, it suggests that the land should belong to whose who work it; and to reduce the shortage of goods and services, it would reduce military expenditures. It would also establish a national assistance fund. The Democratic Union proposes that children begin specialized education in their teens and that the study of Marxism-Leninism in schools be eliminated. It proposes the return of property to religious organizations and churches.

Publications. The Democratic Union published a *Bulletin* and the weekly newspaper, *Svobodnoe slovo* (Free Word).

Liberal-Democratic Party of the Soviet Union (LDP)
Liberal'no-demokraticheskaya partiya Sovetskogo Soyuza

Foundation. The Liberal-Democratic Party of the Soviet Union was formed at a Congress in Moscow in March 1990 which was attended by 215 delegates. The congress elected its leading organ, a 13-member Central Committee, and adopted its Rules and Programme. The LDP is led by V. Zhirinovsky and V. Bogachev.

Programme. The LDP promotes the formation of a "rule-of-law state" (*pravovoe gosudarstvo*) headed by a president elected for a five-year term by secret ballot, restricted to no more than two consecutive terms and in charge of a highest executive power, the Cabinet of ministers, and the establishment of a market economy. It proposes, as the highest executive organ, a State Assembly (*Gosudarstvennoe sobranie*) to be comprised of 500–700 delegates who are professional politicians elected to five-year terms. In the economic sphere the Liberal Democratic Party advocates equality among all types of property with identical constitutional guarantees, full freedom of enterprise and purely co-ordinating and informational roles for economic departments and ministries. To implement a social security programme the Party proposes the establishment of a social fund and that social benefits should be distributed according to wage labour.

So far as politics is concerned, the LDP seeks a multi-party system in which parties do not interfere in economic and cultural life. The LDP proposes a Declaration defining inhabitants of the USSR as citizens of the Soviet state, but not requiring them to claim nationality. It advocates that institutions of national culture should be established based on cost-accounting principles. The Party would declare a stance of neutrality for the Soviet state; withdraw from all military blocs; and conduct its foreign policy, trade and cultural relations regardless of the political orientations of other regimes. It would propose guaranteed human rights based on a law on the inviolability of the person and work to eliminate the residence permit (*propiska*), and allow freedom to emigrate. The LDP's other policies include the de-ideologization of social life; it opposes the supremacy of party monopoly, dogmatism, and wage-levelling; and it would eliminate the concept of class struggle, party art and the revolutionary war. The Liberal Democratic Party considers itself a "party of all strata of society open to membership for all citizens without recommendations and decisions of meetings of primary party organizations".

Organization. According to the party Rules, the LDP is "a mass political organization which is built primarily on a territorial basis". Its main organs include an annual Congress (convened in April) and an All-Union Party Conference (convened in October). Among its chief personnel are a chairperson, a chief co-ordinator, and a secretary. There are also members of a Central Committee and Central Auditing Commission who are elected to three-year terms. At the lower levels, the party elects regional committees, headed by regional secretaries. Party dues are collected from 1 per cent of members' wages and there is a 5-ruble registration fee. Students and pensioners are absolved from financial obligations.

Publication. The LDP's press organ is the newspaper *Liberal*, which has a circulation of 15,000.

Party of Islamic Rebirth (PIR)
Partiya islamskogo vozrozhdeniya

Foundation. The party was established at a congress in Astrakhan attended by 143 members. The Congress elected the party's highest organ, the Council, which is comprised of chairperson A. Akhmedkady (Dagestan ASSR), deputy chairperson S. Ibragim (Tadzhikistan), and 11 council members representing Moscow, Azerbaidzhan, Tadzhikistan, the Dagestan ASSR, Chechen-Ingush ASSR and Astrakhan region.

Publication. The PIR publishes the newspaper of the independent information centre, *Taykhid*.

Peasant Union of the USSR
Krest'yanskii soyuz SSSR

Foundation. The Peasant Union of the USSR held its inaugural congress in Moscow in June 1990. The Congress was attended by 1,718 delegates who represented collective and state farmers, state farm employees, agro-industrial workers, leaseholders, academics and the agricultural intelligentsia from nine republics. The congress elected its highest leading organ, the Central Council, which is chaired by V. Starodubstev, the chairman of the Agro-industrial Association *Novomoskovskoe* (New Moscow) in Tula region.

Programme. The Union operates to promote and defend the socioeconomic, collective and individual rights of its members in state organs, economic, social and co-operative organizations. It seeks to promote the equal and free development of various forms of economic property and management, and to establish peasants as the masters of their land and production. In order to facilitate these objectives the Union seeks to direct a mass sociopolitical movement aimed at large-scale reconstruction in agricultural economics. The Union also seeks to foster the spiritual rebirth of the peasantry and to improve the living and working conditions of workers in the agro-industrial complex. The Union provides organizational, economic and legal assistance to its members, defends their interests and establishes ties with other national and international organizations — including those in foreign countries — that have mutual interests in the agricultural sector. The Union, where appropriate, exercises the right of legislative initiative, participates in the formation of organs of state power and management, and promotes its aims through elected deputies and other representatives.

UNION OF SOVIET SOCIALIST REPUBLICS

Organization. Membership of the Union is on an individual and collective basis. Primary organizations are formed in work collectives on a voluntary basis. These are organized in a territorial association of unions, established on a district, regional, territorial and republican basis. Its highest organ is the Congress, which for the first five years of the union's existence is designated to meet annually; and thereafter at five-yearly intervals. Sittings of a Central Council are scheduled to take place no less than twice yearly, and meetings of its Presidium are intended to be initiated at the behest of the chairperson. However, these shall take place no fewer than four times yearly. Funding is derived from admission charges, annual membership dues, deductions from the profits of union enterprises, and associations (as determined by the Union). The Union has created a charity fund from donations of citizens, enterprises and organizations.

Radical Association for Peace and Freedom
Radikal'naya assotsiatsiya za mir i svobodu

Foundation. The Radical Association for Peace and Freedom was formed in May 1989 and elected a 13-member Council of the Association which includes E. Debryanskaya, O. Lipovskaya, E. Podol'tseva, A. Proznin, D. Starostin, N. Khramov and V. Yarmenko. According to its Memorandum, the Association considers itself "part of the Transnational Radical Party, a party of citizen activists whose aim is the attainment of a more humanitarian and just social and economic order and having departments in several foreign countries". It includes participants in the "anti-imperialist struggle" who consider the maintenance of the Soviet empire the main cause of the political, cultural and ideological division of Europe and the Soviet system as a burden on civilization and one that cannot change its "anti-social" nature.

Programme. The Association has a new vision of Europe which will be formed on the basis of a unitary system of economic administration and through universal intellectual and spiritual values. Several requirements — freedom of economic choice, the introduction of market initiatives and the elimination of trade barriers and quotas and tariffs — will help facilitate the "New Europe". It also proposes the adoption of a Law on All-European Citizenship and the elimination of national armies, and advocates civic mobilization against unpopular governments by waging non-violent and political boycotts against the activities of its policies.

The Association's programme includes sections on anti-militarism, which calls for the elimination of weapons of mass destruction, the liquidation of the army and KGB and the disbandment of military-patriotic clubs and associations; legal reform, which advocates a universal amnesty, the repeal of the death penalty, the rehabilitation of political prisoners, the adoption of new humanitarian laws and their integration with European laws, the abolition of the passport system, unrestricted travel across the planet, and the right to choose a place of residence; and the formation of a new system of uncensored media. There is also a section on economics, which focuses on the utilization of "moral economics" taking into account ecological considerations and consumer interests, the introduction of a locally co-ordinated market system, decentralization of the state economy, rights for invalids and pensioners and grants for orphaned children. The Association is committed to an anti-nuclear policy, the breakup of the Soviet empire and the construction of a confederation of free self-governing units organized on national, economic, territorial and other lines with the right to leave the confederation.

On education, the Association proposes the ending of compulsory state education and the introduction of alternative methods. On religion, the Association would grant churches the status of autonomous social institutions, and absolute equality for all beliefs. So far as drugs are concerned, the Association advocates the legalization of narcotics and the elimination of state monopolies over tobacco and spirits. On sexual politics, the Association advocates freedom of sexual relations and the right to complain in court on matters of sexual discrimination. According to the Association's Rules, these stances are not only applicable to the USSR but to all countries where legislation affects their members.

Organization. The highest organ is the Congress which is held annually and is attended by all members. There is also an elected Council which performs co-ordinating functions, and which meets once every two months. The Association has an anti-discriminatory membership policy. Funds are generated through registration fees, membership dues and donations from individual and non-state organizations. Supplemental income is derived from press, co-operatives, lectures and concerts.

Divisions in the Party in May–June 1990 led to the formation of the *Radikal'naya partiya* (Radical Party), headed by N. Khramov and A. Proznin, and the *Libertarianskaya partiya* (Libertarian Party), led by E. Debryanskaya.

Scientific-Industrial Union of the USSR
Nauchno-promyshlennyi soyuz SSSR

Foundation. The Union was established on June 16, 1990, in Moscow, by a group of USSR People's Deputies who proposed its formation in an address to industrial, scientific, economic associations and organizations, enterprise directors, academics, engineer specialists and workers. Its president is A. Vol'sky; the Chairperson of the Executive Committee Governing Board is A. Vladislavlev, Secretary of the Governing Board of the Union of Scientific and Engineering Societies of the USSR.

Programme. The Union claims to be an independent, self-governing social organization which has, as a main task, the defence of the rights and the advancement of the interests of domestic industry and its scientific basis in conditions of multiple forms of property and the development of the market. It is a voluntary association of individuals, scientific, financial and economic associations as well as enterprise directors, entrepreneurs, engineers and specialists. The Union is independent of party, departmental, territorial and national influences. It supports private enterprise, business partnerships and the strengthening of the export potential of domestic industry and its position on the world market. Its main tasks include the introduction of anti-monopolistic legislation, the establishment of norms of friendly competition, the advocacy of consumer rights and the raising of the qualifications of various institutions and individuals.

Organization. Membership is available on both an individual and a collective basis and is open to foreigners as well as to Soviet citizens. The Governing Board approves all memberships; this body and the Control Commission are elected by the Congress for four-year terms. The President and Vice-President are elected for three-year terms and may not serve more than two successive terms of office. The Union is established on a regional basis. Each unit registers with the local organs of power and is granted the status of a juridical person which allows financial independence.

Socialist Party
Sotsialisticheskaya partiya

Foundation. A political group, the New Socialists, were formed in June 1989 in Moscow and by July–August of the same year had established contacts with strike committees in the Kuzbass and Karganda. By October these ties had been extended to strike committees in Vorkuta. A conference organized by L. Volovik, O. Voronïn, A. Voronov, B. Kagarlitsky, M. Malyutin, E. Ostrovsky and L. Sherova was held in Moscow in June 1989 for social groups and organizations which resulted in the formation of the *Vserossiiskii komitet Sotsialisticheskoi partii* — VKSP (the All-Union Committee of the Socialist Party).

Programme. The Socialist Party seeks to build democratic, self-managed socialism in a *bloc* with all leftist forces: social democrats, democratic-minded Communists, representatives of workers' movements and national fronts. According to its programme, it is striving to change the attitude of society so that it will be possible to adopt a more discriminating approach towards the revolutionary past of the USSR and towards the utopia. In its view, the 1917 Revolution ushered in a socialist ideal, but it did not bring with it socialism in practice. The political objectives of the Socialist Party include: democracy; judicial reform and freedom of the press; strong local government with broad economic independence; opposition to all forms of monopoly economics — either state or private; workers' self-management in production; the transfer of the means of production to the soviets at all levels; the acceptance of foreign capital, provided it is subject to the control of strong unions and legislation that defends the economic independence of the country and workers' rights; the improvement of various forms of property; and the formation of a society with a strategy for development. The Socialist Party's stance on social policies strives to guarantee full employment, curb the inflation rate without impeding technical progress, the implementation of a standardized work week that does not exceed 40 hours, the elevation of the position of women in Soviet society, reform of the health and education systems, guaranteed housing and a redistribution of wealth from the prosperous elements of society to raise the living conditions of the poor.

The Party proposes, in particular, the transfer of resources, trade and capital investment to the soviets; implementation of state orders that guarantee attainment of the most important economic demands of the country; the granting of more power to the local soviets; giving workers and engineers the right to choose and remove enterprise officials; and the establishment of a framework which will compel administrative personnel to work for the collective. It seeks to establish a series of rights: a genuinely equal and universal suffrage; pluralism of political, professional and social organizations; the elimination of media censorship; the guarantee of workers' rights to strike, and the inviolability of home and individual. In order to achieve these goals, the Party seeks to co-operate with organizations and groups that are also based on general democratic principles.

The Socialist Party claims that "socialists of the USSR are part of the international democratic and socialist movement striving towards the international solidarity of leftist forces in the struggle for a new world and social economic order and for the triumph of democracy in national and international politics".

Publication. The Socialist Party publishes the journal *Levyi povorot* (Left Turn), which has a circulation of 3,000.

Union of Constitutional Democrats/Party of Constitutional Democrats (UCD)
Soyuz konstitutsionnykh demokratov/partiya konstitutsionnykh demokratov

Foundation. The Union of Constitutional Democrats held its first conference in Moscow. It was attended by nearly 100 delegates from 26 cities in the RSFSR, the Ukraine, Latvia, Georgia, Moldavia and Kazakhstan. The conference adopted provisional Rules, a Political Declaration and a Declaration on Economic Questions, in which the party proposes to liquidate state property, distribute the national wealth, grant the juridical status of a "person" to each citizen, and grant individuals the right to choose their preferred form of property and occupation. In order to achieve these goals, it claims, it is first necessary to institute renewal as a democratic state. It publishes the weekly newspaper, *Grazhdanskoe dostoinstvo* (Civil Dignity). In March–April 1990 V. Zolotarev, G. Deryagin and D. Grugin co-authored a draft Rules of the Party of Constitutional Democrats.

Programme. The Constitutional Democrats seek to eliminate force from the attaining of political aims, to determine human rights on the basis of the Universal Declaration of Human Rights and other legal acts, and to observe laws insofar as they do not contradict each other or violate state and national obligations. According to the draft preamble to its Programme, the Constitutional Democratic Party was formed as a political organization of citizens and associations aspiring to continue and develop the best traditions of Russian liberalism and to establish in Russia the constitutional-democratic movement previously embodied in the Party of Constitutional Democrats (*Kadets*), the largest non-socialist party in pre-revolutionary Russia. Sections of the draft version of the Political Programme of the Party of Constitutional Democrats include chapters on human rights, state formation, state organization and the national question, education and culture, and social security.

Organization. The party is administered territorially in regional divisions. Regional activities are determined and instituted by a Political Committee. The Congress elects a chairperson, the Political Committee, a Control Council and the party's other working organs. There are two types of membership in the Constitutional Democrats, associate and active. Members with associate status may attain active status by involvement in party work.

Supporters of the idea of constitutional democracy of the past left the party in May 1990 and revived the Constitutional Democratic Party (Party of Popular Freedom) (see separate entry).

United Front of Workers of the USSR (UFW)
Ob"edinennyi front trudyashchikhsya SSSR

Foundation. The United Front of Workers of the USSR was established at a congress held on June 15–16 1989, attended by 83 delegates of six union republics at which it elected its Co-ordinating Council, comprised of A. Zolotov, I. Malyarov and Yu. Rakov. The

UFW also has affiliated organizations throughout the country such as the UFW RSFSR (established in September 1989 in Sverdlovsk), the UFW Leningrad (established in June 1989), and the UFW Moscow (established in July 1989). The international movements of Moldavia and the Baltics are also included in the UFW.

Programme. The UFW seeks to guarantee the conditions for people of all nationalities in the struggle for the communist reorientation of the reconstruction of society and for the improvement of the lives of the people. It is critical of the CPSU's handling of *perestroika*, stating that it has not produced the desired results but has rather facilitated the growth of social inequality, deepened the economic crisis and further complicated the country's economic conditions, weakened discipline, fostered increases in transgressions of the law and sharpened inter-nationality tensions. The Front states that part of the CPSU membership speaks from an "anti-Soviet" position and has brought the Party to the point of a split; this section of the CPSU (in the view of the UFW) propagates bourgeois values and contradicts those of the workers.

Among its political tasks the UFW seeks to implement a Leninist view of the rights of workers and exploited peoples. It seeks to strengthen social unity based on socialist interests and the communist aims of the working class, the establishment of friendship among peoples, the development of socialist democracy, worker participation in management, the holding of elections of people's deputies in industrial enterprises, full openness in all spheres of life and workers' control over the media. It is also in favour of an increase in the role of working people in public life, and against pornography, violence and "immorality" in the media.

Its social and economic policy includes the employment of ecological experts to advise on all work activities, improving the conditions of life, labour and leisure, social security for all workers — primarily women, the young and servicemen and their families. The UFW claims that society must be made free from "socialist millionaires" and corrupt elements and seeks the elimination of the privileges of high-ranking officials. Greater control from below, it states, can be achieved through elections, the elimination of the propagandistic press, support for the initiatives of the movement's participants and the struggle for the interests of labour in conjunction with other sociopolitical organizations.

Its other goals include support for those who are seeking to change the social nature of the CPSU and to rebuild the party as an organization of the working class. It also upholds the "socialist fatherland" and strengthens the multi-national union on the principles of socialist internationalism.

Organization. The UFW offers collective membership which is accepted by the Co-ordinating Council and activated by the Congress. Members are expelled from the UFW for violating its Rules and engaging in activities that do not correspond with its goals and decisions of the Congress. Its Rules establish the UFW as a territorially-based organization founded upon the principles of democratic centralism. The highest organ is the Congress which must meet no less than once every three years. A Political Commission, formed by the Co-ordinating Council, verifies the upholding of collective membership by enforcing responsibilities and studying members' appeals. An Auditing Commission controls the Front's financial and economic matters. Funds are apportioned to councils of enterprise work collectives, and to the institutional and organizational collectives that promote the Front's aims. It accepts donations from individuals and collectives.

The Republics

ARMENIA

Proclaimed a Soviet Socialist Republic in 1920. From 1922 to 1936 a part of the Transcaucasian Soviet Federal Republic, and from 1936 a constituent republic of the USSR. Under nationalist administration since 1990, and committed to ultimate independence. Area 29,800 sq km; population (1989 census), 3,283,000.

Communist Party

As from January 1991, organized in four urban and 47 district bodies, with 5,873 branches. First Secretary, elected in November 1990, was Stepan Karapetovich Pogosyan, an Armenian national, born in 1932. He joined the CPSU Central Committee in July 1990 and the Politburo in December 1990. The Party's activities were suspended in August 1991.

Karabakh Committee

The principal nationalist organization, banned during 1988–89. Its representative, Levon Ter-Petrosyan, was elected Armenian president in October 1990.

AZERBAIDZHAN

Declared independent in 1918, Azerbaidzhan became a Soviet Socialist Republic in 1920. From 1922, together with Georgia and Armenia, it constituted the Transcaucasian Soviet Socialist Republic. In 1936 it assumed the status of one of the union republics of the USSR. Since 1988 in dispute with Armenia over the enclave of Nagorno-Karabakh, whose population is overwhelmingly Armenian. The republic adopted a declaration of independence in August 1991. Area 86,600 sq km; population (1989 census), 7,029,000.

Communist Party

As from January 1991 the republican party organization included two regional bodies (for the Nachichevan autonomous republic and the Nagorno-Karabakh autonomous region), 10 urban bodies, 75 district bodies and 11,166 branches. The First Secretary, elected in January 1990, was Azya Niyazi ogly Mutalibov, an Azerbaidzhani national born in 1938.

From 1989 to 1990 chairman of the republican Council of Ministers, Mutalibov became President of the republic in May 1990 and a member of the CPSU Central Committee and Politburo in July 1990. In August 1991 the Party's activities were officially suspended.

BELORUSSIA

The Belorussian Soviet Socialist Republic was established in 1919 and is one of the original members of the USSR, as established in 1922. In August 1991, following the collapse of the attempted coup, the republic declared in favour of independence. The republic's area is 207,600 sq km; its population is 10,200.000 (1989 census).

Belorussian Peasant Party

Founded in February 1991 as a "peasant oppositional parliamentary party on a centrist platform".

Belorussian Popular Front

Founded in June 1989 in Vilnius. Originally in favour of Belorussian sovereignty on the basis of the Belorussian constitution, from 1990 the Popular Front adopted a more explicitly anti-communist position and sought to restore the fully independent status that had been lost — in the Front's view, illegally — in 1922. Its chairman, re-elected at its Second Congress in March 1991, is Z. Poznyak, an historian by profession; its published organ is *Naviny BNF* (Belorussian Popular Front News).

Communist Party

As of Jan. 1 1991, the republican party organization had six regional bodies, 33 urban bodies, 113 district bodies and 14,650 branches. Its First Secretary, elected in November 1990, was Anatolii Aleksandrovich Malofeev, a Belorussian national born in 1933. A member of the CPSU Central Committee since 1986, he became a member of the Politburo in December 1990. Party activities were suspended in August 1991 following the collapse of the attempted coup.

Democratic Party

Founded in June 1990 in Grodno. Its manifesto, adopted at the founding congress, calls for the establishment of an "independent, democratic Belorussian republic" and for the realization in Belorussia of the Universal Declaration of Human Rights and other international legal norms.

National-Democratic Party of Belorussia

Founded in June 1990 in Minsk. A cultural-political organization, whose aim is the "national renaissance, democratization, political, economic and cultural independence of the Belorussian people". Its membership is limited to those who speak Belorussian and declare themselves to be Belorussians.

Social-Democratic Party of Belorussia

Founded in March 1991; its objective is a pluralist society on the Western European model. Since August 1990 has issued the bulletin *Sotsial-Demokrat Belorussii*. In March 1991, a related organization, the Belorussian Social-Democratic Gromada, was founded in Minsk as a political party of the centre-left. It publishes the newspaper *Gromada*.

United Democratic Party of Belorussia

In October 1989 the Democratic Party of Belorussia was founded in Minsk; in March 1989 the political club "Communists for *Perestroika*" was formed in the republican capital; and in May 1990 the Republican Party of Belorussia was founded in Brest. In November 1990 these parties merged to form the United Democratic Party of Belorussia, whose agreed objective is the establishment of a "democratic society" in the republic.

GEORGIA

Declared independent in 1918 and recognized as such by the Soviet government in 1920, Georgia was subsequently occupied by the Red Army and declared a Soviet republic in February 1921. In 1922 Georgia, together with Armenia and Azerbaidzhan, formed the Transcaucasian Federal Socialist Republic as a member of the USSR. In 1936 Georgia became a Soviet socialist republic and a member of the USSR in its own right. In 1990 nationalists, organized in a coalition entitled "Free Georgia/Round Table", secured a parliamentary majority and their representative, Zviad Gamsakhurdia, was elected republican President in 1991. The republic declared for ultimate independence in 1990 and put this decision into effect, following a republic-wide vote, in 1991. Area, 69,700 sq km; population (1989 census), 5, 449,000.

Communist Party

As of January 1991 the Georgian party organization had three regional bodies, 15 urban bodies, 73 district bodies and 10,177 branches. Its First Secretary, elected in April 1989, was Givi Grigor'evich Gumbaridze, a Georgian national born in 1945; he became a member of the CPSU Central Committee and Politburo in July 1990. His resignation was announced in 1991, and the Party itself was suspended later in the year following the failure of the attempted coup in Moscow.

Democratic Party

Established in May 1990 and a close ally of the National Democratic Party (see below). In contrast to the National Democratic Party, it rejects the idea of a theocratic democracy and puts a decentralized administrative structure based on municipal councils at the heart of its programme. It has also campaigned on social issues and has taken up prisoners' rights. Its membership stood at 700 in June 1990; its newspapers, such as *Tavisupleba* (Freedom), are among the most widely available unofficial publications.

Georgian Popular Front

Established in 1989 following extended discussion among oppositional intellectuals. Its ultimate goal is the "creation of a free and democratic society and the restoration of Georgia's complete state independence". Nodar Natadze, a philosopher, was elected its first chairman. At its peak the Front has claimed a membership of 15,000.

Georgian Social Democratic Party

Formally established at its first conference in February 1990, the Party was based upon the work of an organizing committee established the previous September. The Party was led by a professor at the Communist Party Higher School, Guram Muchaidze, and many of its founder members were also ex-communists. The Party was recognized in November 1989 by the remnants of the pre-Soviet Social-Democratic (Menshevik) Party in exile, and it was accepted as an observer at the Social Democratic Association which united many of the new social democratic parties in the Soviet Union. The Party took a moderate line on independence and in March 1990 publicly supported the creation of a new union of independent states; the association of the Party with the failure to defend the independent Georgian state in 1921, however, meant that it did not attract a widespread following. It publishes a newspaper, *Ertoba* (Unity).

Green Party

Established in 1988 as a section of the nationalist cultural association, the Rustaveli Society. Its leader is Zurab Zhvania; the Party's publication, from 1990, is *Deda Mitsa* (Mother Earth).

Monarchist-Conservative Party

Launched in December 1989 by Temur Zhorzholiani, but with no clear strategy for the restoration of a Georgian monarchy in the absence of a widely accepted claimant. The Party, which claimed 780 members in the spring of 1990, split later in the year.

National Democratic Party

Founded in 1988 by Giogi Chanturia, the NDP claimed to be the legitimate successor of a pre-Soviet party of the same name. The Party aims to re-establish Georgian independence, and it has a nationalist-Christian orientation. Its claimed membership is 4,000. With its ally, the Democratic Party (see above), it took 32.6 per cent of the vote in the republican elections of 1990.

National Independence Party

Founded in 1988 by Iraklii Tsereteli and Iraklii Batiashvili. The Party favours a democratic Georgia within the framework of NATO, and it took 35.6 per cent of the vote in the republican elections of 1990.

KAZAKHSTAN

In 1920 the Kirgiz (in 1925 renamed Kazakh) Autonomous Soviet Socialist Republic was formed within the Russian Republic. It became a constituent republic of the USSR in December 1936. Next in size to the RSFSR among the Soviet republics, its area is 2.7 million sq km; its population (1989 census) is 16,538,000.

Communist Party

As from January 1991 the Kazakh republican party organization had 19 regional bodies; 45 urban bodies, 225 district bodies and 21,377 branches. Its First Secretary, elected in 1989, was Nursultan Abishevich Nazarbaev, who in April 1990 additionally became the republic's President. A member of the CPSU Central Committee from 1986, Nazarbaev became a member of the Politburo in July 1990. In August 1991 the Party's activities were officially suspended; Nazarbaev, who resigned from the Politburo and Central Committee of the CPSU itself, indicated that he would be seeking to take the Kazakh party outside the framework of the CPSU and it was subsequently renamed the Socialist Party.

KIRGIZIA

After the establishment of the Soviet regime in Russia, Kirgizia became part of Soviet Turkestan, which itself became an Autonomous Soviet Socialist Republic within the RSFSR in April 1921. In 1924, when Central Asia was reorganized territorially on a national basis, Kirgizia was separated from Turkestan and formed into an autonomous region within the RSFSR. In 1926 Kirgizia became an Autonomous Soviet Socialist Republic within the RSFSR, and finally in December 1936 it became one of the constituent republics of the USSR. In August 1991 its parliament voted in favour of independence. The republic's area is 198,500 sq km; its population, in the 1989 census, was 4,291,000.

Communist Party

The republican party organization, in January 1991, included two regional bodies, 14 urban bodies, 45 district bodies and 5,370 branches. Its First Secretary until 1991 was Absamat Masalievich Masaliev, a Kirgiz national who was born in 1933. He became First Secretary of the republican party in November 1985 and in April 1990 additionally became chairman of the republican Supreme Soviet. A member of the CPSU Central Committee from 1986, he became a member of the Politburo in July 1990. In April 1991 Masaliev was replaced by Dzhumgalbek Beksultanovich Amanbaev, a Kirgiz national born in 1945; in the same month Amanbaev became a member of the CPSU Central Committee and a member of the Politburo. In August 1991 the party's activities were suspended following the attempted coup.

MOLDAVIA (MOLDOVA)

The Moldavian Soviet Socialist Republic was formed by the union of part of the former Moldavian Soviet Socialist Republic (established in 1924), formerly included in the Ukrainian Soviet Socialist Republic, and areas of Bessarabia (ceded to the USSR by Romania in 1940) with a mainly Moldavian population. In August 1991, following the collapse of the attempted coup against President Gorbachev, its parliament voted in favour of a wholly independent status. The republic's area is 33,700 sq km and in 1989 its census population was 4,341,000.

Communist Party

As from January 1991 the republican party organization had five urban bodies, 44 district bodies and 4,689 branches. Its First Secretary, elected February 1991, was Grigorii Isidorovich Eremei, a Moldavian national born in 1935. A member of the CPSU Central Committee from July 1990, he became a member of the Politburo in April 1991. The party's activities were suspended in August 1991.

Democratic Party of the Gagauz

Founded in July 1990. Based in the main upon members of the Gagauz intelligentsia and students. Its chairman is G. Savostin. According to its programme the party "supports and deepens the processes of *perestroika* that have been begun on the basis of democracy and humanism"; more particularly the party stands for the "restoration of historical justice" with regard to the Gagauz people.

Democratic Platform in the Communist Party of Moldova/Independent Communist Party of Moldova

Formed in Kishinev in July 1990 and headed by USSR People's Deputy A. Gradzhieru, A. Gavrilov and A. Muntyanu. A part of the Democratic Platform within the national CPSU, the party constituted itself as an Independent Communist Party in July 1991.

National-Christian Party of Moldova

The foundation of this party was announced in October 1990; its aims centre upon the restoration of the Moldovan cultural heritage.

People's Front of Moldova

Founded in Kishinev in May 1989. Its first chairman was I. Khadyrke; he was succeeded in the autumn of 1990 by Yu. Roshka. Originally a "voluntary sociopolitical movement" whose aim was support of the "new political course of the CPSU for the restructuring of all aspects of social life", the Front from 1990 sought the "achievement of complete sovereignty" and believed that this aim could be achieved only by replacing the "communist regime" by a "Romanian Republic of Moldova". The Front publishes *Tsara* (Country).

Social-Democratic Party of Moldova

Founded in May 1990 in Kishinev. According to its programme, the party seeks to restore the independence and sovereignty of Moldova based upon the equality of all national groups. An agreement has been signed with the Romanian Social-Democratic Party (Historic), providing for co-ordination of the efforts of both parties. Publishes the bulletin *Respublika*.

Union of Peasants of Moldova/Peasant-Democratic Party of Moldova

Founded in Kishinev in January 1989. Its original membership consisted of scholars specializing in rural problems, together with peasants wishing to farm individually. Its director is Kh. Andreev, a USSR people's deputy. The Union is committed to a radical reform of agriculture involving a pluralism of forms of property and management. The Union was reconstituted as the Peasant-Democratic Party in October 1990.

UNION OF SOVIET SOCIALIST REPUBLICS

THE RUSSIAN REPUBLIC (RSFSR)

The RSFSR is by far the largest of the Soviet republics, accounting for 76 per cent of the total area of the USSR. Its population is overwhelmingly (83 per cent) of Russian nationality, and the great majority (82 per cent) of Russians live in this republic. The Russian Republic includes 16 autonomous republics, including several — such as the Bashkir and Tatar — that are as large and populous as union republics elsewhere in the USSR. The Russian Republic had its own Communist Party organization, re-established in 1990, but government is in the hands of Boris Yeltsin, the former Moscow party secretary, who was elected chairman of the RSFSR Supreme Soviet in May 1990 and then President of the RSFSR by a direct popular ballot in June 1991. Although it can scarcely secede from the USSR, the Russian Republic adopted a declaration of sovereignty in June 1990 and has generally favoured the greatest possible devolution of power to the republics. Under a decree promulgated by President Yeltsin in August 1991 the activities of the Communist Party within the territory of the republic were suspended and its buildings were transferred to the state. The republic's area is 17,075,000 sq km, and its 1989 census population was 147,386,000.

Christian-Democratic Union of Russia (CDUR)
Khristiansko-demokraticheskii soyuz Rossii

Foundation. The Christian-Democratic Union of Russia was established in August 1989 during a conference of 80 representatives of political groups and organizations. The CDUR is on the Co-ordinating Committee of Christian Democrats of the USSR along with the National Democratic Party of Georgia, the Armenian movement *Prkutyun* (Salvation), the Christian-Democratic parties of Lithuania and Estonia. The CDUR's chairperson is A. Ogorodnikov. At a second conference, held in September 1989, the party adopted its rules.

Programme. The CDUR claims to be "a political party of associated Christians of various denominations who set as their aim, the spiritual and economic renewal of Russia and the formation of a democratic rule of law state based on the principles of Christian democracy over its territory". Its pre-election goals included the formation of a *bloc* with all the country's democratic parties and organizations. It also seeks to defend the rights and interests of believers, to adopt a new law on freedom of association in accordance with international legal norms, to involve young people in the spiritual rebirth of society and to form a Christian-Democratic youth organization.

Organization. Membership of the CDUR is open to any person, 16 years of age or older, who accepts Jesus Christ as his or her Lord and Saviour, accepts the Programme and Basic Principles of the CDUR and actively participates in the work of primary organizations. Members may not belong to another party or organization that has goals in contradiction with those of the CDUR. The simplest party structure is the primary organization, which is based in cities and other population points, enterprises and parishes.

Democratic Party of Russia (DPR)
Demokraticheskaya partiya Rossii

Foundation. The Democratic Party of Russia was established in Moscow in May 1990 at a conference attended by 600 participants (310 of whom had voting status). Participants at the conference elected a 24-member Governing Board and chairperson (USSR people's deputy Nikolai Travkin); it also adopted a Declaration and Programme Theses. The party claims in its Declaration that "communist ideology and planning are to blame for the crisis in Soviet society". The Democratic Party of Russia declares itself a party of "a parliamentary type" promoting "the consolidation of all democratic forces on the basis of a struggle for the constitutional overthrow of the CPSU apparat through elections and in the Congress, Supreme and local soviets of people's deputies".

Programme. The Democratic Party of Russia advocates the reconstruction of Russia as an independent democratic state that is an equal member of a voluntary association of republics, the adoption of a new Russian constitution, the decentralization of state management and the creation of an "equal opportunity society" based upon the principles of freedom of enterprise, equality of all forms of property and the development of market relations without lowering the population's standard of living. In the economic sphere, the DRP proposes to stimulate unrestricted agricultural labour and the transfer of property and production to peasants, the integration of republican economies into the world economic system and the attraction of foreign capital. The DPR favours the de-ideologization of science, education and cultural institutions; the Party seeks to consolidate society on the basis of universal human and individual rights underpinned by the factual equality of nations, and the creation of a developed, unified market and the right to private property. It claims that it is willing to join a united *bloc* with all democratic parties, social and workers' movements and independent trade unions.

Organization. The DPR is based on a federative principle. It conducts relations with parties at home and abroad that support independence, equality and non-intervention in each other's affairs, that reject nationalism and chauvinism, and that respect individual rights. Membership takes place on both an individual and collective basis. Primary party structures are allowed to form vertical, horizontal and provisional organs based on professional, creative and other interests such as cells, organizations and clubs. Party organs are established in administrative-territorial units; military, law enforcement and state institution workers belonging to the DPR belong to the corresponding territorial party structure. Members have the right to form factions, and members who are in the minority when a party decision is taken may appeal against the decision at party meetings and conferences. The highest organ is the Congress, which convenes once every three years. There is also an All-Russian Conference convened at least yearly and for the most important questions of party policy, referenda are conducted. People's deputies in elected bodies form fractions, and are accountable, first of all, to their voters. In order to achieve its goals the Democratic Party of Russia advocates the establishment of enterprises, economic, commercial and social organization, and it receives additional funding from membership dues and donations from foreign citizens, unions, foreign and international organizations and workplaces.

UNION OF SOVIET SOCIALIST REPUBLICS

Publication. The DPR publishes the newspaper *Demokraticheskaya Rossiya* (Democratic Russia), which has a circulation of 25,000.

Order Union of Orthodox Monarchists
Pravoslavnyi monarkhicheskii orden-soyuz

Foundation. The Order had its initial Congress in Moscow on May 19, 1990, at which it elected its leading organ, the Synod. Its leader is Marshal of the Order Union, S. Engel'gardt-Yurkov.

Programme. The Order's objectives include non-violence, the re-establishment of the Romanov dynasty, the re-establishment of gentry lands and the opening of parishes and monasteries on Russian soil.

Organization. Members of other parties are excluded from the Order. There is a youth organization for Orthodox youth aged 16–22.

Russian Christian-Democratic Movement (RCDM)
Rossiiskoe khristianskoe-demokraticheskoe dvizhenie

Foundation. The Russian Christian-Democratic Movement was established at a conference in Moscow in April 1990 in which 215 delegates participated and elected the highest organ, the 15-member *Duma* of the Russian Christian Democratic Movement, and three co-chairpersons, clergyman V. Polosin, V. Aksyuchits and G. Anishchenko. According to the Rules of the RCDM, it is a "sociopolitical organization (party) of associated supporters of a radical reconstruction in all spheres of life in the country based on the norms of Christian morality".

Programme. Among the policies promoted by the RCDM are the holding of an Assembly of the Land (*Zemskii sobor*) as a governing body, the full abolition of communist and state ideology from state institutions, enterprises, the army and law enforcement agencies. It also seeks the formation of a professional army with the institution of a military clergy established therein. The RCDM aims to introduce trial by jury and to bring back the old Russian national state symbols. The party's stance on human rights includes a choice of residence, the abolition of the passport system, the return of churches and monasteries to believers and the elimination of governmental intervention at all levels from religious affairs. In the economic sphere, the RCDM proposes the decentralization of management, the transition to a market economy based on private property and Christian justice, equality for all forms of property and enforcement of this through legislation. Its social policies include a guaranteed minimum standard of living, permission to form independent trade unions, improvements in conditions of labour and recreation, open private and communal hospitals, and the formation of Christian charity organizations and institutions. In science and education the RCDM will institute a law which will increase private research, support the creation of private funds, museums, libraries, concert halls and galleries; eliminate the *Komsomol* and similar organizations; and stimulate the opening of state, private and parochial schools.

Organization. Membership is open on an individual or collective basis to people who are 16 years of age or older.

Publication. The RCDM publishes the bulletin, *Vestnik Khristianskogo informatsionnogo tsentra* (Bulletin of the Christian Information Centre).

Social Democratic Party of the Russian Federation (SDPR)
Sotsialdemokraticheskaya partiya Rossiiskoi Federatsii

Foundation. The Social Democratic Party of the Russian Federation was formed after a breakaway from the Social Democratic Association (SDA). The SDA was inaugurated in May 1989 as a confederation of clubs from various cities. Its founding congress took place in January 1990 and was attended by members from more than 100 socialist and social-democratic organizations. At this Congress, the delegates adopted a Declaration of Principles; elected the leading organs and co-chairpersons, O. Rumantsev, N. Tutov and V. Saatpalu and an Executive Committee; and established commissions. The SDA considers itself a confederation with an orientation towards social democracy, pluralism of social and economic relations, the establishment of a multi-party system and a confederation state structure.

Those elements of the SDA that broke away to form the SDPR held a founding congress from May 4–6, 1990, in Moscow. Participants in the Congress included 237 delegates from 104 organizations based in 94 cities. Documents adopted at the Congress included a Manifesto on Foundations of the SDPR and Rules, and Basic Principles of the SDPR.

Programme. The SDPR promotes its principles of parliamentarianism through municipal power and elected authorities and seeks to abolish all forms of dictatorship, over-powerful leadership (*vozhdizm*) and violence. It seeks to work for a social partnership with various social groups and does not proclaim itself to be the party of a single class. The SDPR seeks to build humanitarian internationalism through working for a civil world and trying to establish international agreement. Among its "spiritual criteria", the SDPR includes the using the best parts of Russian social democracy; utilizing the tradition of the democratic movement in the country; implementing the theoretical and practical legacy of international social-reformism; and using the legacy of peaceful humanitarianism. The SDPR considers itself part of the international and all-union movements for freedom. Their views differ from those of the SDA on the principles of the Universal Declaration of Human Rights, the Declaration of the Principles of the Socialist International and its Declaration of Principle. Included in their programme are the de-ideologization of culture, education, the state apparatus, the armed forces, the KGB (state security) and MVD (internal security forces), and judicial organs. They seek to promote a broad range of policies, grass-roots politics and state sovereignty for Russia and the other union republics. The main goal of the SDPR is the establishment of a "civil society".

Organization. Party membership is open to citizens of the RSFSR who are at least 16 years of age and who accept the party's programme and rules. The elected organs of the SDPR include a 40-member Governing Board, a three-member Presidium, to which were elected A. Obolensky, O. Rumyantsev and P. Kudyukin, and a 10-member Control Commission.

Publication. The SDPR publishes the newspaper *Sotsialdemokrat* (Social Democrat), which has a circulation of nearly 5,000 copies per issue.

UNION OF SOVIET SOCIALIST REPUBLICS

TADZHIKISTAN

The Tadzhik Soviet Socialist Republic was formed from those regions of Bokhara and Turkestan where the population consisted mainly of Tadzhiks. It was admitted as a constituent republic of the USSR in December 1929. As of mid-1991 it remained under communist administration. Area, 143,100 sq km; population (1989 census), 5,112,000.

Communist Party

The republican party organization, in January 1991, had three regional bodies, 15 urban bodies, 42 district bodies and 5,765 branches. Its First Secretary, elected in 1985, was Kakhar Makhkamov, a Tadzhik national born in 1932. A member of the CPSU Central Committee from 1986, he became a member of the Politburo in July 1990. The Party itself was suspended in August 1991.

TURKMENIA

The Turkmen Soviet Socialist Republic was formed in October 1924. In 1925 it entered the USSR as one of its constituent republics. In mid-1991 the republic remained under communist administration. The republic's area is 488,100 sq km, and in 1989 its census population was 3,534,000.

Communist Party

The republican party organization, in January 1991, had three regional bodies, nine urban bodies, 44 district bodies and 5,222 branches. Its First Secretary, elected in December 1985, was Saparmurad Ataevich Niyazov, a Turkmen born in 1940. A member of the CPSU Central Committee since 1986, Niyazov became a member of the Politburo in July 1990. In August 1991, following the attempted coup, the Party's activities were officially suspended.

UKRAINE

The Ukrainian Soviet Socialist Republic was proclaimed in December 1917 and was finally established in December 1919. From December 1922 it was a constituent republic of the USSR. In 1990 the republic adopted a declaration of sovereignty affirming the primacy of its own laws over those of the USSR. In August 1991, following the attempted coup, the Ukrainian parliament voted in favour of independence. Area, 603,700 sq km; population (1989 census), 51,704,000.

Communist Party

As from January 1991 the Ukrainian party organization had 25 regional bodies, 140 urban bodies, 521 district bodies and 71,658 branches. After the Russian party organization, it was the largest republican section of the CPSU. Its First Secretary, elected in June 1990, was Stanislav Ivanovich Gurenko, a Ukrainian national born in 1936. A member of the CPSU Central Committee from July 1990, Gurenko was a member of the Politburo since the same date. The party's activities were formally suspended in August 1991.

Democratic Party of the Ukraine

Founded in Kiev in December 1990 with about 2,500 members. Its declared aim is the achievement of the "national independence of the Ukraine and the construction within it of a democratic and humane society"; towards this end the Party seeks the removal from power of the CPSU and Ukrainian secession from the USSR. It publishes the paper *Golos*.

Green Party of the Ukraine

Founded in Kiev in October 1990, the Party calls for ecology to have priority over economics and for individual rights to have priority over those of the state. Its leader is the publicist Yuri Shcherbak and the Party publishes the paper *Zelenyi mir*.

Liberal-Democratic Party of the Ukraine

Founded in Kiev in November 1990. According to the Party, "socialism is incompatible with humanism and democracy" and it calls for the withdrawal of the Ukraine from the USSR together with legislation in support of private enterprise. It publishes the paper *Polslovo*.

Party of the Democratic Renaissance of the Ukraine

Founded in December 1990 with about 2,500 members; about three-quarters of its members were formerly in the CPSU and the Party is based upon the "Democratic Platform" grouping then active within the republican Communist Party. Its declared aim is, with other democratic forces, to convert the Ukraine into a "democratic independent state with an effective market economy and social security for its citizens". It publishes the bulletin *Demokraticheskii vybor*.

Party of Slavonic Renaissance

The initiative to establish this Party was taken in August 1990; its principal aim is the establishment of the complete independence of the republic.

People's Party of the Ukraine

Founded in Dnepropetrovsk in September 1990, the Party aims to establish an "independent parliamentary republic" with particular emphasis upon the support of less prosperous citizens affected by the transition to market relations. It publishes the paper *Olimo*.

Rukh

Founded as a "Popular Movement of the Ukraine for *Perestroika*", it took its origins from the Union of Writers and the Institute of Literature in the republic and was formally established in September 1989 in Kiev. The aims of *Rukh*, as defined at this time, centred on the creation of a "democratic and humane society" in the republic. The Second Congress took place in Kiev in October 1990, at which the writer Ivan Drach was re-elected its chairman. The programme of *Rukh*, as amended at this time, called for the establishment of political and economic pluralism in the republic and called for the establishment of the "state independence of the Ukraine" and the formation of a "democratic parliamentary republic". *Rukh* publishes the paper *Narodnaya gazeta*.

Social-Democratic Party of the Ukraine

Formed in May 1990; essentially a right-wing split from the United Social-Democratic Party of the Ukraine. The Party publishes *Sotsial-Demokrat Ukrainy*.

Ukrainian Christian-Democratic Party

Formed on the basis of the Ukrainian Christian-Democratic Front established in 1989, the Party was founded in April 1990 with the objectives of eliminating totalitarianism in all its forms and the restoration of full republican sovereignty, together with the "full and absolute restoration of religion in our society".

Ukrainian National Party

Founded in L'vov in October 1989, the Party aims at the withdrawal of Soviet "occupying" forces from the republic and the establishment of full independence. It maintains a youth section, and publishes the journal *Ukrainskii chas* and the paper *Prizyv natsii*.

Ukrainian Peasant-Democratic Party

Founded in Kiev in June 1990, the Party aims to represent all sections of society but gives priority to agrarian problems. It favours private land ownership and publishes the paper

Zemlya i volya.

Ukrainian Popular-Democratic Party

Founded in Kiev in June 1990, the Party favours republican independence and a free market economy. It publishes the paper *Nezavisimost'*.

Ukrainian Republican Party

It was decided to form the Party at a congress of the Ukrainian Helsinki Union in April 1990; in June 1990 the Party had about 2,000 members. The Party's declared aim is a "parliamentary republic, in which all political parties and organizations have a constitutionally guaranteed freedom of activity". The Party has a youth movement, and publishes the paper *Golos vozrozhdeniya* and the journal *Ukrainskii vestnik*.

United Social-Democratic Party of the Ukraine

A left-wing section of the Ukrainian social democrats, favouring democratic socialism as understood by social democratic parties in other countries.

UZBEKISTAN

Soviet rule was established in Uzbekistan in 1917 and gradually extended into the semi-independent khanates of Khiva and Bokhara during the early 1920s. The Uzbek Soviet Socialist Republic was formed in 1924 and the following year it became a constituent republic of the USSR. In August 1991 the republican parliament voted in favour of a fully independent status. Its area is 447,400 and its 1989 census population was 19,906,000.

Birlik

Established in 1988, *Birlik* has organized demonstrations against cotton monoculture and in favour of the declaration of Uzbek as the republican state language.

Communist Party

As of January 1991 the republican party organization included 12 regional bodies, 29 urban bodies, 162 district bodies and 21,709 branches. Its First Secretary, elected in June 1989, was Islam Abduganievich Karimov, an Uzbek born in 1938 who from March 1990 has also been President of the republic. He became a member of the CPSU Central Committee and of the Politburo in July 1990. In August 1991, following the attempted coup, the Party's activities were formally suspended.

YUGOSLAVIA

John B. Allcock

The distinctive features of the contemporary Yugoslav political scene are rooted in a long and complex past which can only be suggested in this context. History provides the substratum upon which rest the characteristics of rule by the Communist Party of Yugoslavia (later renamed the League of Communists) since 1945, the more recent struggle for the realization of new democratic political forms, and the currently anticipated collapse of the entire federation.

Of primary importance in this respect is the location of Yugoslavia across the principal historical fault-lines of Europe. The boundaries between the Roman and Greek traditions of Christianity, between Christianity and Islam (in particular, between the Austro-Hungarian and Turkish Empires), between the Mediterranean world and that of the Slav cultures and peoples, all have divided in one way or another the South Slav peoples, who in 1918 came together in the Kingdom of the Serbs, Croats and Slovenes.

This complex cross-cutting of lines of cultural identity and strategic orientation has left the Yugoslav peoples in many respects without natural and positive forces of cohesion. Consequently many observers have seen in the Yugoslav state an entirely artificial creation imposed upon the region, which suits the interests of powerful outsiders rather than serves the real needs and ambitions of its peoples. Yugoslavia has been described as a creature of the Versailles Conference, the inherent weakness of which was testified to by the collapse of that state (renamed "Yugoslavia" by King Alexander, in 1929) under the impact of invasion by the Axis powers in April 1941. In February 1945, however, the conference of the Great Powers at Yalta reaffirmed the perceived necessity of a unified Yugoslav state, but recognized its position of marginality, in the celebrated Stalin-Churchill "50/50" formula, which acknowledged the joint legitimate interest in Yugoslavia of both the western powers and the Soviet Union. Those who take this view of Yugoslavia are able to ask, with some point, why else do we now apparently face the prospect of a second (and possibly definitive) failure of the Yugoslav experiment?

To pose this question in this way, however, is to neglect a very important though negative factor. The "Balkanization" of the region has meant that its component parts are not only extremely diverse and even disparate, from the point of view of language, religion, political culture and level of economic development, but also that these parts are themselves typically too small to stand as viable independent units in a world increasingly shaped by large states, trans-state groupings and international corporations. It can therefore be argued that the Yugoslav peoples need each other if for no other reason than to provide an institutional means of protecting their diverse individuality in a world in which far more powerful groupings could consume them all. In this view the existence of Yugoslavia is not seen as any kind of historical necessity: merely as sound common sense in the kind of world we now confront.

There is no requirement in this context that an attempt be made either to argue the case for the existence of Yugoslavia, or to predict its future. At the time of writing, the future possibilities for a Yugoslav state are far from clear. One thing can be said with confidence, however, and that is that the condition of "balkanization" is not the exclusive property of the state called Yugoslavia, whose disintegration could somehow replace disorder and division with stability. "Balkanization" afflicts also its component parts. Consequently, if in the near future that state does disintegrate, to be replaced by a nest of smaller ones, they will each replicate on a smaller scale the self-same processes which characterize Yugoslavia itself, which have given rise to the features of our present day political scene, and which explain the political processes documented in this chapter.

One significant feature sets off Yugoslavia from the majority of other states in eastern and central Europe. When Yugoslavia emerged from war in 1945, the victorious partisan movement, led by Josip Broz "Tito" had earned a valuable capital fund of legitimacy which only in recent years has shown signs of exhaustion. This is not to deny the importance of the complex civil war between the communist forces, the Serbian royalist "chetniks", and several brands of domestic collaborationist forces, as a continuing source of bitterness within historical memory. Nor does its recognition mean that one is prepared to ignore the brutal way in which the superficial trappings of democracy devised by the Tito-Šubašić agreement on 1945 were swept aside within a year, to be replaced by communist authoritarianism. The partisan experience, even so, endowed the regime in Yugoslavia with both a legitimating mythology (which has allowed its rule to sit relatively lightly upon its citizens) and a tremendous source of *esprit de corps* (which has reinforced its own solidarity and conviction of its right to rule).

That wartime experience continues to have a lively impact upon the current political scene in three ways. First of all, it intensifies the difficulties of political change. The ousting of communism in Yugoslavia is not invariably experienced as the sloughing off of an unnatural and foreign system of domination, and a return to "normality". We are witnessing a real and intense crisis of Yugoslav political culture. This is reflected, at the very least, in the continuing vigour with which the various successors to the League of Communists cling to political life, and indeed, have earned a significant measure of electoral success. Communism has not even been definitely "deposed" throughout the Yugoslav federation, let alone "eliminated" as a political force.

Secondly, the manner in which communist revolution was intertwined both with a "war of national liberation" and an inter-ethnic civil war in the period 1941–45 has meant that the formation of present-day political groupings is burdened with a history of peculiar and bitter emotional intensity, which makes the containment of political struggle within a framework of democratic politics extremely difficult. In addition, there is a tradition of political violence among the Yugoslavs (far older than the wartime experience, but reinforced by it) which to a greater or lesser extent in every republic lurks beneath the surface of newly devised forms of democratic party politics. The *prima facie* illegitimacy of political violence cannot be taken for granted in Yugoslavia in the way in which it can in many other European countries.

This ties in closely with the third sense in which the experience of the war is relevant to the contemporary scene. Since 1945 the armed forces have enjoyed a particularly privileged position within the Yugoslav system. It is no exaggeration to say that their importance as a political force has been comparable to that of any one of the individual republics. Within the Praesidium of the League of Communists, the armed forces were represented on exactly the same level as were the republican delegations; and although excluded from the federal collective presidency, the Yugoslav National Army (YNA) has always had an effective voice in the conduct of affairs.

More significantly, the Yugoslav military has always been consistently committed to a particular vision of the nature of Yugoslavia. This ideological standpoint is most strongly identified, not so much with the economic characteristics of the communist system, nor even with a specifically "bolshevik" view of the nature of the Party, as with the central dogmas regarding the nature of federation, and above all the nature of the relationship between nations and nationalities within that federation. The old wartime Titoist slogan of *bratstvo i jedinstvo* (brotherhood and unity) provides the key to this. (The fact that "brotherhood and unity" can act as ideological screens behind which to hide particular interests, especially national interests, is beside the point in the present context.) Consequently, although it has always been indeed highly politicized, the YNA has seen itself as the principal guardian of "the system" not defined by reference to any specific set of economic or even political institutions, but rather by reference to the sacrosanct status of the federation itself. The armed forces have seen in the adamant defence of the federation the only effective defence against a return to the horrors of the civil war.

A further important general characteristic of the communist experience has a direct bearing upon the recent development of multi-party politics in Yugoslavia. It is fundamentally mistaken to equate communism in the country with a monolithic political orthodoxy, which is to be contrasted with the diversity and debate which are the supposed characteristics of democracy. The communist movement has a long and highly fraught tradition of *internal* dissent in Yugoslavia. Party discipline has been a precarious achievement throughout the greater part of its history. When Josip Broz was nominated to the post of Secretary General of the Yugoslav Communist Party in 1937 it was quite specifically with the remit of "tidying up" the Cold Comfort Farm of political factionalism for which the party had become a by-word. National divisions were especially problematic from the beginning; but internal conflict was by no means confined to these.

The story of internal dissent continues strongly into the postwar period. In many ways the regime set up in 1946 was a model of communist orthodoxy, and the Tito regime was regarded by the West as particularly obdurate. The expulsion of Yugoslavia from the Cominform in 1948, as a consequence of the refusal of the Yugoslav leadership to accept discipline from Moscow, came as a shock to all observers. The dispute also placed the most enormous strains on *internal* party discipline, and in the years which followed there was a protracted struggle to root out the *ibeovci* (supporters of the *Informbiro*), the marks of which are still carried by sections of the communist movement to this day, especially in Montenegro.

Party discipline was strained further by the campaign of the forced collectivization of agriculture upon which Yugoslavia embarked the following year, partly as a means of demonstrating the socialist credentials of the regime; partly with the intention of subordinating agriculture to the already agreed policy of rapid industrialization. For a variety of reasons this attempt collapsed, and was definitively abandoned in 1953. In 1950, again to some extent as a direct response to the dispute with the Soviet Union, the first steps were taken in the creation of Yugoslavia's celebrated system of "workers' self-management" (*radničko samoupravljenje*). The accommodation of this ideological novelty was one of the reasons behind the constitutional reform enacted in 1953. These events brought with them the most intense intra-party discussion over the characteristics of socialism, the nature of the real political possibilities open to Yugoslavia, and above all over the nature of the Party itself.

The severity of these divisions became briefly apparent in 1953–54, when the vice-president of the Party, and one of its leading ideologists, Milovan Djilas, broke ranks with the publication of a series of highly critical articles in the party paper *Borba*. These pieces, together with his subsequently published book *The New Class*, mounted a thoroughgoing moral and political critique of the emergent leadership stratum, and ensured his political disgrace and imprisonment. Djilas became a *cause célèbre* as a "dissident": but the attention paid in the west to his personal dissent has diverted attention from the deeper and more widespread party disunity which his gesture both expressed and precipitated.

During the same period Tito also led Yugoslavia into its prolonged involvement with the Non-Aligned Movement (NAM). In the inevitable period of revaluation which has followed Tito's death in 1980 there has been a tendency to dismiss the NAM as a quirky personal obsession of the Marshal, and no more than evidence of his tendency to seek personal aggrandisement. This is, to say the least, partly misplaced as a judgement on Yugoslavia's relationship to the NAM. It is vital to acknowledge also the part which this foreign policy stance played in relation to Yugoslav domestic politics. The Communist Party had been compelled to come to terms with the delicacy of the problems posed by the ethnic diversity of the region early in the war. It moved rapidly from the mainstream CP line of denigrating nationality as a bourgeois distraction from the essential unity of the working class, and particularly under the influence of the Slovene ideologist, Edvard Kardelj, came to build recognition of national diversity into the main frame of the ideological and political structure of the country. As early as the first meeting of AVNOJ (the Anti-fascist Council for the National Liberation of Yugoslavia), in November 1942, the need for a federal solution to the problems of political order in any postwar settlement was accepted. Indeed, the Yugoslav state came to be defined as an association of nations, in which respect the communist predelection for collectivist concepts in politics was extended and not challenged. The putative unity of the "working people" of the country was legitimately qualified by their division into *nations*, without being undermined by any recognition of their diversity as individual *citizens*.

This capacity to incorporate a recognition of the central importance of nationality into the ideological orthodoxy of Yugoslav communism thus simultaneously added to the effectiveness of its legitimacy, while sowing the seeds of future national conflicts. It is to the first of these purposes that involvement in the NAM centrally relates. The policy of using a world platform to insist upon the right to self-determination of peoples, and the significance of the anti-colonial struggle, not only underlined publicly the determination of the Yugoslav party to maintain its independence from Moscow: it also entrenched at the domestic level the primary political importance of the nation. Non-alignment provided an ideological parable on the international plane of the correctness of the regime's stance with respect to national identity within Yugoslavia.

The central features of the "Yugoslav road to socialism" — workers' self-management, decentralization and adhesion to the NAM — laid down in the '50s therefore worked in two directions. They served to buttress the communist regime; but they also at least potentially served to legitimate particular potential forms of dissent, in relation to both the nature of a socialist polity and the importance of nationality.

The mounting economic problems faced by Yugoslavia during the early '60s added to the pressures for diversity within the country's politics. The steps taken to extend regional decentralization and to introduce "market socialism", in the form of the new constitutional law of 1963, and the economic reform package of 1965, brought with them new conflicts. The severity of these is suggested by the dramatic dismissal of Aleksandar Ranković from his position as head of the internal security services, in 1966, accused of abuse of his powers.

In many respects the reform programme was a resounding success. The late '60s were a period of unrivalled prosperity for most Yugoslavs; and this new economic freedom was accompanied by a measure of political liberalization. This was expressed in publications as diverse as the Catholic paper *Glas Concila* and the philosophical journal *Praxis*, as well as in much more open political debate within the League of Communists itself. Public acknowledgement of this new toleration was marked by the change of the name of the former Communist Party of Yugoslavia to the League of Communists of Yugoslavia (LCY).

These halcyon days were relatively short-lived. By the turn of the decade the return of severe economic difficulties found the regime feeling exposed and threatened once again by outspoken dissent, and the participation of Yugoslav students in the international movement of unrest during 1968 was met with a very heavy-handed response. When reaction to the country's economic problems began to take the form not only of demand for radical economic liberalization, but linked this to the demand for a massive extension of national independence, the result was a vigorously enforced return to centralized political control, by a variety of means.

The most widely reported and dramatic of these movements of dissent was the MASPOK (*masovni prokret* — mass movement) in Croatia during 1971–72. The party replied with the suppression of the cultural organization *Matica Hrvatska*, which had been revived in 1967, and which had become increasingly significant as the medium of expression of Croat nationalism. It also led to a thorough purge of the Croatian LCY, and most notably to the expulsion from the party of its republican secretary Savka Dabčević-Kučar, and the prime minister Mika Tripalo. (The former has recently returned to active political life, and now heads the Croatian People's Party.)

Whereas press and academic attention were caught by the events in Zagreb, the same process was repeated at a more discreet level throughout the federation. In Slovenia, for example, the pro-reform Kavčić was also removed, and in Macedonia the Milosavljevski faction was ousted on similar grounds.

The disturbed period of 1968–72 did produce "reform" in the Yugoslav system, but in the form of a retrenchment of stalinism. This was concealed for some time by the externalities of the reform process, and in particular by the new constitution introduced in 1974, and the now infamous Law on Associated Labour (typically known by its Yugoslav acronym, ZUR — *Zakon o udruženom radu*). The former created an outward show of radical democratization and decentralization. The new constitution thus apparently conceded the Croatian case, by devolving a far greater measure of responsibility to republics and municipalities, and by involving citizens in the complex set of institutional mechanisms known as the "delegate system" (*delegatski sistem*). The latter supposedly elaborated and developed the existing system of self-management. It gradually became apparent, however, that behind the screen of these radical measures lay the reaffirmation of control by the LCY (even if at the cost of reducing the party itself to a federation of republican parties). There followed a *de facto* repoliticization of the economy, the relative marginalization of technical and managerial expertise, a reduction in inner-party democracy and the recapture of the political system by representatives of the partisan generation and their nominees — a return to *nomenklatura*. There was a perceptible enhancement at the same time of the position of the military in politics. These measures together heralded the arrival of the "leaden years" (*olovne godine*) in Yugoslav political life, which featured a reduction in the diversity of opinion and the freedom of its expression both within the party and more generally.

Institutional controls of this kind turned out to be ineffective in Yugoslavia (as elsewhere) as a means of containing the pressures created by the country's real complexity. The situation was exacerbated in 1979 by the effects of the first "oil shock" upon the Yugoslav economy, which began to expose serious weaknesses. While it was possible to some extent to contain conflict during the lifetime of Josip Broz — for all the demystification which has been set in motion since the death of "Tito", there is no denying the real political force of his personal hold on politics — the continued imposition of political cohesion became rapidly impossible after his death in May 1980. By 1983 it emerged that Yugoslavia was in very acute economic difficulties. These had been concealed behind heavy foreign borrowing, but unwisely this had not been used to fund modernization or restructuring, and consequently had not resulted in compensating gains in productive capacity or corresponding growth in exports. The retrenchment of political interests within the economy had in fact exacerbated the problems of economic irrationality. Yugoslavia was not paying its way on a massive scale. The seriousness of this state of affairs was not publicly known until the assistance of the IMF was sought in the management of the country's US$20 billion external debt, in 1983.

Throughout the '80s successive governments struggled to manoeuvre the country towards at first "stabilization" and then economic restructuring, in the face of the determined resistance of a large section of the Communist political establishment, and hampered by the sometimes extreme conflicts of regional interest, to which the new emphasis on the power of the republics gave free rein. Things finally came to a head in December 1988, when the government of Branko Mikulić resigned over its failure to secure acceptance of a reform package. This was the first resignation of any government in postwar Yugoslavia, and is significant if for no other reason in that it raised the possibility that governments could be held accountable for their performance, and needed to generate their own legitimacy. Mikulić was succeeded by Ante Marković, who has been distinguished not only by the way in which his own economic reform programme has attracted both domestic and foreign respect, but by the way in which he has seen the necessity of linking economic reform to the creation of democratic politics, as a means of relegitimating the political system.

The debate about the economy, the need to move away from various forms of politicization and towards the creation of proper markets for all the factors of production, fiscal reform and monetary responsibility, has been complicated by equally important conflicts over the proper character of Yugoslavia's political structure. The most intractable issue here has been that of nationality. It has already been suggested that the roots of this problem lie deep within the history of Yugoslavia. The problems do not stem simply from the facts of the ethnic diversity of the country, but more particularly from the features of a political system which insists that the unit of political account is *the nation* and not the citizen. (The commitment of the communists to the centrality of the nation in politics is underscored by the fact that three new "nations" have virtually been created under the auspices of the LCY — the Macedonians, the Montenegrins and the Muslims.) The collectivist straight jacket of Yugoslav ideology has rendered the entire problem of political rights and the relationship between ethnic groups in terms of the need to protect or balance the rights and claims of *nations*; and the federal structure of the country has made matters particularly intractable through its tendency to identify the full recognition of national identity with control of a national quasi-state.

Two problems have been persistently difficult in this regard, both touching upon the position of Serbia and of Serbs within the federation. As the largest of Yugoslavia's constituent ethnic groups, with 8.4 million of the Yugoslav population of 23.9 million in the census of 1991, the Serbs make up 35 per cent of the total. Only 6.3 million of these (75 per cent) live within the republic of Serbia itself. A quarter of all Serbs in Yugoslavia are resident in other republics, particularly in Croatia (where somewhat more than half a million of them make up 11 per cent of the republic's population) and in Bosnia and Hercegovina (where 1.4 million of the republic's 4.5 million inhabitants are Serbs). In addition to this, the republic of Serbia is itself the host to substantial national minorities. The largest of these is the Albanians, whose 1.7 million represent about 11 per cent of the population of the republic. These are largely concentrated in the former Autonomous Province of Kosovo, bordering Albania itself, in the south-west of Serbia. There are also some 370,000 Magyars, generally located in the north, in the former Autonomous Province of the Vojvodina. The status of Autonomous Provinces granted to these ethnically distinctive areas, before the imposition of the revised Serbian constitution in 1990, was fiercely resented by Serbs.

The position of Serbs was thus doubly problematic. A quarter of Serbs increasingly regarded themselves as second-class citizens within other republics, dominated by other nations within Yugoslavia; and at the same time the privileged status of the Autonomous Provinces meant that they felt that they even lacked standing within significant areas of "their own" republic. Attempts to extend the arm of the Serbian state into other republics where there were substantial Serb minorities naturally aroused hostility there — especially in Croatia. On the other hand, the attempt to enforce Serb control within the Autonomous Provinces created its own problems; and correspondingly, the efforts of the Albanians to enhance their own situation by transforming the Province in which they constituted more than 80 per cent of the population into a fully-fledged republic were met with aggressive Serb resistance. After the outburst of Albanian unrest in Kosovo in 1981 the area has remained under a state of virtually permanent armed occupation by either federal or republican security forces, with particularly serious disorder breaking out in 1987 and 1989.

The debates about the economic future of Yugoslavia have intersected with the debate about nationality in important ways. In particular, the sometimes extreme differences in levels of economic development between the republics have led to sharp differences in their views about economic structure and policy. The economically more advanced and wealthier republics of Slovenia and Croatia have come to look with greater favour upon competition, the market and the depoliticization of economic life. The economically less advanced and poorer areas have remained attached to socialist concepts of economic solidarity and *dirigisme*. These contrasts have tended to become identified with the differences between the interests of the various nationalities which inhabit these regions. Consequently the defence of economic interest has come to be expressed through demands for greater republican autonomy, even to the point of secession from the Yugoslav federation.

So powerful were these fissiparous tendencies that they affected the League of Communists itself. Following the constitutional reform of 1974 the LCY gradually decomposed to the point where it was itself no more than a federation of eight loosely allied parties. At the XIVth Congress of the party in Belgrade in January 1990 it collapsed altogether.

In the light of these developments, it is clear that it cannot be said in any meaningful sense that the LCY "permitted" the growth of political diversity. It was itself caught up in political processes making for pluralism which it was powerless to resist. It was to an appreciable extent the victim of devices which it created with the intention of perpetuating its own hegemony. The simultaneous need to both enact and to legitimate drastic processes of economic reform, and to cope with the consequences of the disintegration of the ruling League of Communists, left little room for alternatives to a rapid movement towards multi-party democracy in 1990.

In the struggle to secure the elections to the republican Assemblies, in the pattern of party activity which was created surrounding that electoral contest, and in the results which they produced, can be traced not only the postwar (and even pre-war) history of dissent *against* communist rule, but also the complex story of the internal struggles of the LCY itself.

Furthermore, it is clear that the process of political differentiation in Yugoslavia has not been confined to the development of a multi-party system. Possibly even more important than this has been the process of the "republicanization" of politics, by which the federation has gradually decomposed into a number of barely-related sub-systems. This is plainly reflected in the pattern of party organization, in that only Marković's Alliance of Reform Forces among the principal parties makes any pretence of operating across the entire federation.

The depth of this disintegrative process is indicated by the referenda conducted in Slovenia and Croatia, which led to declarations of their secession from the federation (Slovenia) or their intention to move in that direction (Croatia), on June 26, 1991. The subsequent intervention of the YNA in Slovenia in the attempt to overrule that move underlines two central features of the Yugoslav situation — the collapse of effective control by the federal government, and that fact that the future of the Yugoslav peoples has not been decided, at least in the short term, through the ballot box.

Although the federal constitution of Yugoslavia enacted in 1974 suggests a wide variety of freedoms which are at the disposition of its citizens, in effect these excluded the freedom to form competing political parties. Among those things which constitute the "inviolable foundation of the position and role of man" are found "democratic political relations, which enable man to realize his interests" (*Ustav SFRJ*, Basic principles, II, 1974). Article 153 insists that "the freedom and rights of man and citizen are limited only by the equal freedom and rights of others and by the constitutionally affirmed interests of the social community". These general declarations were both counter-balanced by others and circumscribed in practice, precisely by the statement that:

YUGOSLAVIA

> The League of Communists of Yugoslavia . . . has become the organized leader of the ideal and political powers of the working class in the building of socialism and in the realization of the solidarity of working people and of the brotherhood and unity of the nations and nationalities of Yugoslavia.
>
> (Basic principles, VIII)

In spite of the much-publicized unique features of "the Yugoslav way", the League of Communists of Yugoslavia secured for itself the same privileged position, on the basis of its claim to play a "leading role", as did communist parties elsewhere in eastern Europe.

Within the criminal code of the federation the delineation of offences such as "counter-revolutionary activity" (Article 114), the commission of "hostile propaganda" (Article 118), and especially "association for the purposes of hostile activity" (Article 136), gave ample scope for interpretation in such a way as to suppress any attempt at the organization of opposition. These laws were even used in order to suppress relatively innocuous groups, such as the *Praxis* group of philosophers. Article 133, which made possible prosecution for "verbal delicts", was particularly effective as an instrument for silencing opposition, and regularly earned for Yugoslavia the opprobrium of civil rights organizations. Internal party discipline, of course, regularly sanctioned those within the ranks of the LCY who were regarded as subversive of party order.

Elections have been a standard feature of the Yugoslav political scene throughout the postwar period, and under the 1974 constitution provision was made for a complex array of electoral choices at neighbourhood (*mjesna zajednica*), municipality (*općina*) and republican levels. The possibility that elections might be contested by more candidates than there are seats available, within the complex Yugoslav system of "delegations", antedates the formation of competing parties. Furthermore, it was not uncommon for candidates both to compete and be elected (certainly at the lower levels of government) who were not party members. (See Amendment XXVI to the federal constitution, enacted in 1988.) The absence of legitimate organized competition within elections, however, meant that the system could at best be described as a form of "managed democracy".

The first steps towards the creation of new parties were taken *within* the framework of the 1974 constitution, when the Slovene Peasant League registered as an "association" within the Socialist Alliance of Slovenia, in May 1988. In January the following year Dimitrij Rupel's Slovene Democratic League was launched on a similar basis, and in February the Zagreb-based Association for a Yugoslav Democratic Initiative was set up under the same provisions. This practice was declared "unconstitutional" by the Praesidium of the Socialist Alliance, but their judgement was never put to the test of the courts.

The Marković government began the process of institutional reform in earnest by announcing its intention to make possible multi-party elections, following its nomination in May 1989, by which time the League of Communists was faced with a rash of emerging "associations". Significant progress towards liberalization with respect to the expression of opinion was made when Article 133 of the Criminal Code was abolished in December 1989; nevertheless, legislation to facilitate the creation of competing political parties was first enacted at the republican rather than the federal level. The Slovenes once again jumped the federal gun by passing their own new Law on Political Associations, on Dec. 27, 1989.

On Jan. 20, 1990, the League of Communists finally began its ill-fated and long deferred XIVth Congress. The proposal that there should be reform of the law relating to political association was approved, although several other Slovene proposals for political reform were rejected. This led immediately to the withdrawal of the Slovenes from the LC, and its rapid collapse. The failure of the reconvened Congress of the LCY later in March both confirmed its fate, and underlined the absolute necessity for reform. Legislation in the other republics followed in anticipation of any unifying federal legislative framework, the Croatian Assembly leading the way on April 25. The process of legitimation was not underwritten at the federal level until July 25, 1990, with the passage of the Law on the Association of Citizens. The last of the republics to pass appropriate legislation was Serbia, in September. (The texts of all relevant laws, federal and republican, are collected in *Stranke u Jugoslaviji*, TANJUG, Belgrade, 1990.)

The round of elections to republican Assemblies under the new laws was initiated by the Slovenes in April 1990, and concluded in December by the Serbs, Montenegrins and Macedonians. Multi-party elections have yet to take place to the federal Assembly, and at the time of writing the unstable condition of the country must place a question-mark over the possibility of their being held at all in advance of a completely new constitutional settlement.

The new federal law declares that "citizens may freely and voluntarily join together for the purposes of founding associations, social organizations and political organizations within the territory of the SFRY" (Article 1). It is specifically forbidden that such bodies should take as their aim the overthrow of the constitutional order, the threatening of the territorial integrity or independence of the country, or the infringement of the constitutionally guaranteed freedoms of citizens. Neither is it permitted to organize for purposes of inciting national, racial or religious hatred (Article 2). Otherwise no limits are placed upon the legitimate purposes of associations within the meaning of the act. Secret organizations are forbidden, as it is necessary for them to be registered. Article 6 defines the basic provisions which must be made in the statute of all associations (the statement of their purposes; nature and responsibility of their administrative organs; duties of their officers and arrangements for the disposition of property, and so on).

The most important restrictions placed upon political assocations are of a formal kind. They must be constituted by a minimum of 10 citizens who are eligible to vote (Article 9); registration must be undertaken in accordance with certain specified particulars (Articles 11–13); and it is possible for associations to be excluded from the register for infractions of procedure (Article 14). Provisions are outlined for the winding up of associations (Articles 18–21): especially important to note here is the fact that they are obliged to adhere to their stated and registered purposes (Article 20). The remaining articles detail penalties which may be exacted in the event of infraction of the provisions of the law.

Although enacted over the period of a year, occasionally in advance of the passage of federal legislation, and by individual republican Assemblies, the several republican laws are remarkably similar in form and provisions. Typically they spell out in a more long-winded way the variety of purposes for which citizens may wish to associate, and the procedures involved in registration. There are, however, some interesting features upon which it is appropriate to comment.

The law in Bosnia and Hercegovina, for example, outlaws "association on the basis of national or religious membership" where these are not already governed by the law on religious bodies; and provisions of this kind are typical. Although the letter of this is respected in the republic it has not prevented the major parties there from forming in practice precisely along national or religious lines. The intentions of the law in this respect are clear. The key to its demonstrable failure lies in the fact that the restriction is applied to the *statement of the aims* of political associations and not to their *conduct*. The abolition of the law on verbal delicts now makes it possible for political figures to engage in all kinds of racial, ethnic or religious abuse or incitement on the hustings, but provided that these things are not contained in the statement of their party's *aims*, they can not be prosecuted.

The procedure governing registration is variably complex, but invariably spelled out in detail, and adhesion to these provisions is a strict precondition for permission to operate. Whereas only 10 suitably qualified adults are required to found an association in Montenegro (as in federal law), 20 are required in Slovenia, 30 in Bosnia and Hercegovina and 100 in Serbia! Several of the republics express particular caution with respect to the registration of associations which have links with organizations outside the country. Slovene legislation particularly specifies financial links in this regard, but ensures that measures are taken by appropriate municipal authorities for the support of political organizations representing Italian and Magyar minorities within the republic. Several republics require that either the registered founders or the nominated officials of associations should not be convicted criminals or accused of criminal offences. Several exercise particular care over ensuring the financial probity of associations.

The particular differences are less interesting here than is the fact that registration procedures of one kind or another are required by law, and it is possible that associations which are deemed not to meet the requirements of the law for one reason or another may be fined, or in extreme cases, prohibited. The general declarations of freedom of association with which both federal and republican laws open, therefore, may turn out to be qualified significantly in practice.

Provisions for the conduct of elections are also worthy of comment in this context. Elections were an established element of the Yugoslav system even within the single party order. Amendment XXVI to the federal constitution specifies that these must be "direct, universal and secret". The handling of elections has historically been one of the prerogatives of the Socialist Alliance. Under the system of multi-party elections, however, this task is delegated to "electoral commissions" which are set up in each republic upon the announcement of an election to the Assembly. Although managed by republican officials, these commissions are composed of representatives of the parties themselves, who take on routine tasks such as the staffing of polling stations and the telling of votes. (This is in contrast with the British system, for example, where the volunteers who run the electoral process are generally recruited from the ranks of professional civil servants.)

Arrangements for the republican Assembly elections of 1990 appear to have worked fairly well, and the majority of problems which have been reported stemmed from inexperience, and in theory could be remedied with ease. The most serious problems resulted from the fact that not all republics had verified electoral registers in advance of the elections. Polling cards were sent out to voters, the presentation of which was intended to be the prerequisite of voting. Since it was rapidly recognized that the lists according to which these were issued were seriously defective, it was announced that electors would be permitted to vote on production of either a valid passport or an identity card. Not altogether surprisingly, significant numbers of citizens in some areas rapidly grasped the opportunity which these problems offered to engage in multiple voting. The issue was particularly serious in some areas of Macedonia.

Allegations have also been made about the failure to make adequate provision in some areas to protect the secrecy of the vote, through proper screening of the booths. This is a relevant concern where the members of the electoral commissions who staff the polling booths are themselves active members of the parties contesting the election. Evidence relating to this is, however, anecdotal, as are the occasional stories of intimidation.

A feature of the electoral system adopted throughout Yugoslavia, which is essential to an understanding of the development of party politics there, is the adoption of the simple majority principle. Provision varies to some extent between republics, but the general outline appears to be uniform. Parties present separate lists of candidates constituency by constituency. In other words, named representatives are elected for each and every consituency, and not selected in proportion to the party's vote from a list offered to the republic as a whole. Voting takes place over several rounds. If any candidate secures an absolute majority of votes cast within a constituency in the first round, there is no need for further rounds. If no candidate has the necessary absolute majority, a second round is run in which the leading candidate in the first round stands again, but may be contested by only one other candidate. The second candidate may be simply the one with the second largest number of votes, or may be decided by agreement among several of the losing candidates in the first round.

An important consequence of this system, of course, is that the victorious candidate in each case has always received the votes of more than half of the electorate in the constituency. That person is not necessarily the first choice of the majority of voters, however, since the candidate with the largest number of votes after the first round may be defeated in the second round by a candidate who is a lower-ranking choice for the majority of those who cast their votes in the second round, but is nevertheless acceptable as a compromise candidate. Analysis of the operation of this system of multiple rounds in Yugoslavia could yield interesting insights, although it has yet to be undertaken systematically. It does suggest, for example, that the support base for Vuk Drašković's Movement for Serbian Renewal may be even more shaky than is indicated by its relatively weak showing at the polls, as *none* of the party's candidates secured seats in the first round.

The practical process of establishing political parties outside of the ruling League of Communists of Yugoslavia was managed at first through the device of setting up "political associations", which were registered within the Socialist Alliance of the Working People of Yugoslavia. This body was a classic popular front organization which operated throughout the federation, providing a vehicle through which communist influence could be assured within a number of "democratically" elected bodies, the agency through which the process of "delegation" was handled, and an all-purpose medium of agitation and mass mobilization.

By these means the first independent body with expressly political aims in postwar Yugoslavia, the Slovene Peasant League, was set up by Ivan Oman (together with its associated youth organization) in May 1988. In a similar manner a group of academics from Zagreb and elsewhere created the Association for a Yugoslav Democratic Initiative, under the leadership of the eminent Zagreb economist, Branko Horvat, in the spring of 1989. Whereas the aims of the Slovene organization were limited to the advancement of agricultural interest within the republic, the Democratic Initiative set out explicitly to work for the realization of a democratic multi-party system throughout the whole Yugoslav federation. Its well connected and articulate support has had an influence far greater than its minimal electoral success might suggest. It provided both a forum within which ideas about the future development of the system could be aired and examined, and the seed-bed out of which a number of other independent parties of a variety of kinds were subsequently to emerge.

The device of using the Socialist Alliance as a stalking horse for the creation of political parties explains the fact that so many of them now trace their origins to this organization. Former association with the SA has turned out to have remarkable benefits in many cases, in that those parties which are able to count themselves among its legatees often find themselves far better endowed than the majority of their competitors with accommodation and the other material prerequisites of effective party organization.

The process of party formation in recent years in Yugoslavia is also illuminated by brief reference to older patterns of political activity in the region. It is important to acknowledge that for some areas of Yugoslavia the experience of multi-party politics is entirely novel, whereas for others the task of party formation and organization is able to draw upon older models. The regions of Yugoslavia which were formerly incorporated into the Austro-Hungarian Empire — Slovenia, Croatia, and the Vojvodina — have historical experience of the election of representatives to the Diets of either Vienna or Budapest. The former kingdom of Serbia also had its own *Skupština*, around which parties were formed during the last quarter of the 19th century. The greater part of southern Yugoslavia — namely Bosnia and Hercegovina, Macedonia, the Sandžak of Novi Pazar, Kosovo and Montenegro — had no proper acquaintance with modern party politics until after the formation of Yugoslavia in 1918. The flowering of freely competitive party life was even then rather brief. The royal dictatorship which King Alexander imposed in 1929 terminated that freedom, and the elections of 1935 and 1938 were orchestrated as a highly artificial competition between a "Yugoslav National Party" and a "United Opposition". The short period of nominal return to party pluralism in 1945–46, before the realities of communist hegemony became fully apparent, have contributed little to qualifying that pattern.

These early years have left a direct legacy to contemporary political actors in several ways. First of all, several of the parties now on the stage can trace either direct or symbolic continuity with earlier bodies. The most important of these, of course, are the continuing legatees of the communist movement. Even before the formation of Yugoslavia, communist parties were quite successful in Macedonia and Montenegro. The first interwar parliament contained 58 communist deputies. Communism does have very long indigenous roots in this part of the Balkans, so that it can in no way be dismissed as some kind of exogenous imposition on the region, which is likely to disappear under conditions of a presumed non-communist "normality". In every one of the Republics can still be found a significant communist party. Each went through a process of refurbishment between 1989 and 1991 which has varied in its impact from the more or less cosmetic (Serbia) to the dramatic and thorough (Croatia). Communist parties, thus reconditioned, form the republican governments in Serbia and Montenegro, and provide the major oppositional force in Bosnia and Hercegovina, Macedonia, Croatia and Slovenia.

The interwar period also saw in Yugoslavia the rise of vigorous populist movements of a markedly nationalistic character. These have returned dramatically onto the contemporary stage, although not always in the same dress. The Croatian Peasant Party, which dominated Croatian politics after World War II, still functions in Zagreb after 45 years in Canadian exile. Both metaphorically and literally senilized, the CPP is no longer a force in Croatian politics, nor does it stand a chance of becoming one; but its spirit of romantic nationalistic collectivism still flourishes in Tudjman's Croatian Democratic Union. Although the mantle of Serbian nationalism is now worn by Milošević's Serbian Socialist Party, and not by the resuscitated Radical Party of Nikola Pašić (now the National Radical Party), much of the former Radical rhetoric still functions, and the methods adopted by the SSP owe as much to Pašić as they do to the communists. Macedonia's IMRO (Internal Macedonian Revolutionary Organization) is in many respects a bird of similar feather.

The most remarkable continuity in party life across the hiatus of the war is, indeed, the persisting importance of *nationality* as the dominant organizing principle of Yugoslav politics, either explicitly or implicitly. Thus the Bosnian Party of Democratic Action takes over almost exactly where the pre-war Muslim Organization left off; the Democratic League in Kosovo carries on the work of the former *Džemijet*, and the DEMOS (Democratic Opposition) coalition in Slovenia has continued to carry the banner of Mgr Korošec's Slovene People's Party. Very few of the parties currently in contention for power are not, in effect, national parties, and only Ante Marković's Alliance of Reform Forces makes any attempt to operate consistently across the whole federation. (Even the ARF is organized as a network of republican parties, and in any case may have suffered beyond recovery following the attempt by the Yugoslav National Army to reimpose federal unity, in July 1991.)

Nationality is, even so, not the only significant point of division between parties in Yugoslavia. The observer can not fail to be bewildered, and possibly even amused, by the sheer number of parties which "sprang up like mushrooms after rain" following the liberalization of the law on freedom of association in Yugoslavia in 1989. More than 200 separate political organizations are listed in the following directories. "Rates of fragmentation" vary, with the Slovenes being content to field a mere dozen parties in the proper sense of the term, whereas the Serbs find that they need more than 60! Perhaps the record for the entire eastern European region is held by the Montenegrins, whose 649,000 inhabitants were offered a choice of no fewer than 22 parties in the elections of 1990. Of course there is some truth in the humorous response to this of many — including the Yugoslavs themselves — who explain this political cornucopia by reference to the novelty of the electoral process. One frequently hears it said that "three men in a *bife* are a political party".

The reasons for acute fragmentation are more serious than this, however, and merit attention here. The growth of a multiplicity of parties reflects the cross-cutting of a multiplicity of possible principles of organization within Yugoslav politics. Political life within each of the republics is fissured by a series of lines of cleavage which do not reinforce but cut across each other. Consequently, even *within* each of the nationalist camps there is invariably a cleavage between what might be called "modernist" and "traditionalist" stances. Croation nationalism (to take just one example) is not entirely encapsulated within Tudjman's CDU, which is counterposed by the "modernist" Croatian People's Party, led by Savka Dabčević-Kučar. Within those republics in which the Roman Catholic church is strong, the anti-communist forces are acutely divided between clericals and anti-clericals. Thus within Slovenia's DEMOS coalition this is a very active fault line, separating groups such as the Slovene Christian Democrats (where clerical influence is strong) from the secular intellectuals who dominate Dimitrij Rupel's Slovene Democratic League. Montenegrin politics is splintered into groups representing varying shades of opinion regarding the relationship of Montenegro to Serbia. This issue has been reflected in the vocabulary of Montenegrin politics, which distinguishes between *zelenaši* (those who favour greater autonomy from the Serb state) and *bijelaši* (those who wish to tie Montenegro more closely to Serbia). Identically, attitudes towards union with the Albanian republic cut through Kosovar politics.

The rural/urban divide is still the focus of important clashes of interest throughout Yugoslavia, and every republic has at least one peasant party. The significance of locality as a focus of political identity is witnessed both by the relatively large number of parties which operate within very circumscribed areas, and by the remarkably large number of independent candidates who stood for election. These might be said to represent a metropolitan/local split — which is not the same as the rural/urban division. Although several of the independent candidates were successful in the elections of 1990, inspection of the election results does not really reveal the importance of this phenomenon. The directories of parties below, however, include mention of the place of registration of every organization. It is worth noting that in Bosnia and Hercegovina, to take just one example, of the 23 minor parties which did not send representatives to the republican Assembly, only five were registered in the capital, Sarajevo.

If one takes all of these observed lines of political cleavage — communist/anticommunist; nationalist/non-nationalist; modernist/traditionalist; secular/clerical; rural/urban; local/metropolitican — one is faced with a theoretical matrix which is capable of generating without difficulty the kind of hyper-plurality of parties which we now find in Yugoslavia.

Partly as a consequence of this acute fragmentation a further central characteristic of the party scene in Yugoslavia is its acute instability. Depending upon the particular axis which dominates party debate at any one time, the grouping of allies can shift radically. One illustration of this is the DEMOS coalition of six parties which ousted the communists in the Slovene elections, which at the time of writing is dead on its feet. (For results of the elections of 1990, see Tables 2 to 7 in the republic sections.) The two principal pillars upon which this coalition was built were the defeat of the communists and the achievement of Slovene independence. The first of these was enabled by the elections. Although the second of these is by no means secure, its apparently immediate prospect allowed deep divisions to appear between the partners to DEMOS during the months leading to the declaration of independence on June 26, 1991. A succession of important policy and legislative questions, especially the Slovene citizenship bill, the question of abortion and, above all, matters relating to economic policy, revealed its fragility and suggested alternative possible party groupings. These divisions can only have been temporarily suppressed by the armed intervention of the federation at the end of June 1991.

Another example of this instability is the drastic regrouping of parties which followed almost immediately upon the Montenegrin elections in December 1990. Three left-oriented parties with a broadly modernizing stance which had contested the elections independently, the Liberal Alliance, the Socialist Party and the Party of Socialists, united under the banner of Marković's Alliance of Reform Forces — which had not previously existed in the republic. At the same time five of the smaller parties representing national minorities within Montenegro underwent a complex series of accommodations to create the Democratic Coalition.

Another dimension of instability is the instability of public commitment to specific parties. Possibly the most dramatic illustration of this is found in Macedonia, where MAAK (the Movement for Pan-Macedonian Action), which was hailed both within

Yugoslavia and abroad as the respectable voice of moderate Macedonian nationalism, suddenly found itself completely eclipsed at the polls by the plebian IMRO.

Such polling of public opinion which has taken place since the elections suggests that these upheavals were not artefacts of the campaign itself. Tudjman's CDU would be highly unlikely to repeat its landslide if the ballot of 1990 was to be rerun — indeed there are indications of severe splits within the party itself. The *apparent* massive homogeneity of the Croat political consensus hinges almost entirely upon the fact that the issue of republican autonomy has been foregrounded to the extent that not only is political dissent within the CDU suspended, but also several other parties hostile to Tudjman are prepared to back him on this one issue. Should the current Croat government ever be seriously challenged upon a major issue which falls outside of that area of consensus, the appearance of unanimity would rapidly evaporate.

The stranglehold which Milošević's SSP has on Serbia would also, in all probability, be far less secure had it to submit to the test of the electorate its performance following the elections. That insecurity is partly based upon the very restricted geographical base upon which Milošević's victory was based. Analysis of the results in Serbia shows that the Serbian Socialist Party made little headway in Belgrade, where it was largely beaten by the Mićunović's Democratic Party and Drašković's Serbian Movement for Renewal. The Sandžak fell to the Muslim parties, principally the Sarajevo-based PDA. Kosovo would have been lost in its entirety had the Albanian parties not boycotted the election. The Vojvodina was a patchwork composed of seats taken by ethnic parties such as the Democratic League of Magyars of Vojvodina, or by explicitly cross-ethnic parties such as the ARF. Independent candidates also thrived in the northern province. Support for the SSP is effectively confined to "Serbia Proper"; so that an effective challenge mounted there could be fatal. This is the heartland of Serbian nationalism; and it can hardly have escaped the notice of either Milošević or his opponents that there are in the field parties whose nationalistic credentials are at least as sharply highlighted as his own.

It is widely believed that many of the organizations listed in this directory, which fielded candidates in the contest of 1990, have failed to survive their electoral defeat, so that the fact that they are chronicled here is of purely historical interest. This is a fairly safe bet in view of the fact that the principal item in the platform of many of the smaller parties was the appeal for parliamentary democracy. Should the system (even if only at a republican level) survive into a second election, their rationale will have been largely removed. On the other hand, the conspicuous failure of *any* of the republican political establishments to secure results in the wake of their mandates will, no doubt, provide justification for the sprouting of a crop of novel parties on the eve of any future contest.

In short; although the material presented here will provide a good indication of the broad shape of electoral politics within the Yugoslav republics over the next few years, very little of the detail of the political process will be suggested by the state of affairs as it was following the elections of 1990.

The fragmentation and instability of current Yugoslav party politics have very significant consequences for the extent to which, and the sense in which, it might be possible to talk of the emergence of political "pluralism" in the Balkans. Above all, it is not very useful to define "pluralism" solely in terms of a multiplicity of parties. There must also be a plurality of *effective political forces*. In the majority of cases, when we examine the scene republic by republic, what we generally observe is a series of one-party states. Ruling parties with massive majorities are opposed by relatively small and highly fragmented oppositions in their respective legislatures. This is certainly the position in Croatia, Montenegro and Serbia. Table 1 suggests the relative strengths of government and opposition in each case. Slovenia and Macedonia escape this pattern, with Bosnia and Hercegovina presenting a rather special case.

In Slovenia, acknowledging the long-term irrelevance of DEMOS, there will probably be a fairly stable configuration of choice between a conservative, nationalistic clericalism (the Slovene Christian Democrats, with or without the support of several small business groups, such as the Slovene Peasant League); a socialist party (the Party of Democratic Changes, with or without the support of other socialist factions), and the modernizing and secular, but non-Communist, Liberal Democratic Party.

The possible configurations in Macedonia are less clear. The populism of IMRO is probably here to stay, and there is a strong assurance of a continuing and effective socialist movement, in one form or another. On present showing, neither of these groupings could govern alone, and yet the strong showing of ethnic minority parties (especially the Albanian Party of Democratic Prosperity) makes the formation of stable coalition governments highly problematic.

The republic of Bosnia and Hercegovina is run by a coterie of parties (an agreement, not a coalition) which reflects its ethnic composition. It is widely acknowledged within the republic and elsewhere that consensus among all three is an essential but precarious precondition for the stability of the republic. At the time of writing, the Serbian Democratic Party has effectively blocked the parliamentary process through its unwillingness to compromise. Arithmetically and politically speaking, a number of possible coalition governments are conceivable which exclude the Serbs. Even setting aside the likely long-term repercussions upon the republic of the federal armed intervention in Slovenia in June 1991, any attempted solution of this kind would precipitate an internal crisis and the breakdown of parliamentary government. The sense in which this fractured stalemate can be described usefully as "pluralism" is not immediately evident. Perhaps it is more accurate to define Bosnia and Hercegovina as a "necessary hegemony of fragments" rather than an example of "pluralism".

The focus of discussion of the electoral process in Yugoslavia must remain, at least for the present, at the republican level. There have been no freely contested elections to the federal Assembly. This lack is one of the contributing factors to the deteriorating

Table 1: **Government and opposition in the elected Assemblies of the Yugoslav Republics**

Republic	Seats held by the governing party (%)		Seats held by the largest opposition party (%)	
Bosnia & Hercegovina	(PDA/SDP/CDU)	84	PDC	8
Croatia	(CDU)	60	PDC	21
Macedonia	(IMRO)	32	PDC	26
Montenegro	(LCM)	66	ARF	14
Serbia	(SSP)	78	MSR	8
Slovenia	(DEMOS)	53	LDP	15

situation in the country, in that the principal decision-making body at federal level lacks proper legitimation. It can be dismissed as an anachronistic residue of an old order. The federal Assembly has no proper control over the federation's collective presidency, the members of which individually look over their shoulders to their home republics where questions of their accountability do arise, rather than to an elected body. The negotiations concerning the future of federation during May and June 1991, following the blocking of the nomination of the Croatian Stipe Mesić to the chair of the collective presidency, were undertaken by the presidents of the republics, not by the presidency itself.

The most vivid illustration of this is the dismissal of the Croatian representative on the presidency, Stipe Šuvar, in August 1990, because of his alleged lack of vigour in defending Croat interests in relation to the formation of a breakaway Serb enclave of "*Krajina*" from the Croatian republic. He was replaced by Stipe Mesić, who was nominated from the Croatian Assembly. A similar situation developed in May–June 1991, in connection with the controversy over the blocking of Mesić's election to the chair of the presidency, by the Serbs and their allies. The Montenegrin Assembly was able to remove its existing delegate to the presidency (Bogić Bogičević) and replace his with a new nominee (Branko Kostić).

In the light of the rapid deterioration of the Yugoslav political situation during late June and July 1991, however, it become increasingly questionable that there could ever be a revival of the Yugoslav federation under any circumstances. In which case, if the material collected here continues to be relevant at all, it will only be so with respect to some aspects of the conduct of politics *within* each of the individual republics.

There are, in effect, no federal parties in Yugoslavia. The vast majority of the more than 200 parties of which there are records, around and subsequent to the period of the 1990 elections, confine both their potential appeal and their activity to specific republics. Where they do aspire to a more general representation (most notably in the case of the Alliance of Reform Forces) they are organized typically into separate republican associations, and do not function as single organizational entities across the entire federation. It seems most sensible in these circumstances to divide the entries which follow along republican lines.

It should be noted that the vernacular names of organizations are usually given in both the language appropriate to their own membership, and in the dominant language of the republic. This means specifically that the names of parties in Slovenia and Macedonia are not recorded here in Serbo-Croatian, although the name of (for example) an Albanian party operating in Macedonia may be given in both an Albanian and a Macedonian variant.

Because of the republican fractionalization of the party scene, there are parties operating in more than one republic with identical names (e.g. *Liberalna Stranka*). No common programme or organizational link can be deduced from the identity of names. The directory entries only include regional qualifiers were these are a part of the vernacular title.

Because there are synonyms in Serbo-Croatian for the word "party" (*stranka* and *partija*) it is possible that confusion can arise between parties which seem to have identical titles in English, but which are distinguishable in the vernacular. Furthermore, the word *savez* can be translated either as "league" or "alliance". The practice adopted here is to use the form suggested by local sources. This does mean that other commentators on the Yugoslav political scene may legitimately decide to use translations of the names of parties which differ from those used here.

Information about the size of membership of parties in Yugoslavia is thoroughly untrustworthy. There is no possibility of objective verification of the claims made by parties, and these are often obviously inflated. The figures reported here are mainly those given by the parties themselves when they registered, and should be treated with vigorous scepticism in most cases. Where greater confidence seems merited, this is suggested in the entry.

The information upon which this directory is based has been gathered during visits to the republican capitals in question during May and June 1991, and in many cases verified by direct contact with the party in question. This degree of care has only been possible for the principal parties; and in any case, the political situation in Yugoslavia is extremely fluid. In particular, the effects upon party structure and life of the military intervention at the end of June 1991 cannot be judged at the time of writing.

Detailed entries have not been attempted for all known political organizations. All organizations with elected representatives in the republican Assemblies are included here, together with those which local reports indicate to be significant in spite of their lack of electoral success in 1990. Entries have also been included for a number of bodies which should not be regarded as "parties" in the strict sense of the word, but which are probably better described as "movements". Their inclusion is based upon an assessment of their importance in regional political processes. An account of the political situation in Kosovo in particular would be grossly incomplete without reference to movements of this kind. Abbreviated reference is made to other groups of lesser importance.

BOSNIA AND HERCEGOVINA

Formerly a part of the Ottoman Empire, Bosnia and Hercegovina were occupied by the Austrians in 1878, formally annexed in 1908, and united into the newly formed Kingdom of Serbs, Croats and Slovenes in 1918 (renamed "Yugoslavia" in 1929). During World War II the area was incorporated into the "Independent State of Croatia", under joint Italian/German military control, but reconstituted as a republic within Yugoslavia following liberation in 1945. With a surface area of 51,129 sq km, the Republic of Bosnia and Hercegovina is the third largest of the six republics of the federation (20 per cent of the total). Population (census of 1991) is 4,542,014 (19 per cent of the total). The most numerous (and the most rapidly growing) ethnic group in the republic are the Muslims, with 41 per cent of the population, followed by Serbs, with 30.7 per cent, and Croats, with 18.1 per cent. No single group has an absolute majority, although particular areas of the republic may be dominated by any one of these three. Generally speaking, Serbs are most heavily concentrated in the north-west and in eastern Hercegovina, Croats in the south-west, and Muslims in the central and eastern regions, although no clear territorial segregation along ethnic lines is possible. More than 8 per cent of the population of Bosnia and Hercegovina refused to declare their identity in national terms to the census, suggesting the sensitivity of this issue in the republic. Eight per cent of the population declared themselves to be "Yugoslavs".

Table 2: The presidential election of 1990 in Bosnia and Hercegovina

Ethnic group	Candidate	Party	% of vote[1]
Muslim	Fikret Abdić	Party of Democratic Action (SDA)	44
	Alija Izetbegović	Party of Democratic Action (SDA)	37
Serb[2]	Nikola Koljević	Serbian Democratic Party	25
	Biljana Plavšić	Serbian Democratic Party	24
Croat	Stjepan Kljuić	Croatian Democratic Union	21
	Franjo Boras	Croatian Democratic Union	19
Other (Yugoslav)	Ejup Ganić	Party of Democratic Action (SDA)	

[1] Votes at the second round, Dec. 2, 1990.
[2] A third Serb (Nenad Kecmanović) stood for the Alliance of Reform Forces, but secured only 21 per cent of the vote.

Table 3: Elections of November 1990 to the Assembly of Bosnia and Hercegovina

Parties in the Chamber of Citizens	(130 seats)
Party of Democratic Action	43
Serbian Democratic Party	34
Croatian Democratic Union	21
Party of Democratic Changes (LCBH)	15
Alliance of Reform Forces for BH	12
Muslim-Bosnian Organization	2
Democratic Socialist Party	1
Democratic League of Greens — EKO	1
Liberal Party	1

Parties in the Chamber of Municipalities	(110 seats)
Party of Democratic Action	43
Serbian Democratic Party	38
Croatian Democratic Union	23
Party of Democratic Changes (LCBH)	4
Democratic Socialist Party	1
Serbian Movement for Renewal	1

Source: Ministry of Information, Republic of Bosnia and Hercegovina.

In Bosnia and Hercegovina the electoral process and its results necessarily reflect the ethnic diversity of the republic — indeed, at the presidential level they are explicitly designed to do so. The three principal ethnic groups in the republic, the Muslims, the Serbs, and the Croats, are required by the republican constitution to be equally represented within a collective presidency of seven members, with the seventh member representing the other nationalities within the population. Voting in this necessarily extremely complex process, in which 28 candidates stood, took place over two rounds, on Nov. 18 and Dec. 2, 1990. The results are presented in Table 2.

The elections to the Assembly (*Skupština*) itself also produced a result which reflects the ethnic mix fairly closely. The principal Muslim party (Party of Democratic Action) secured 34 per cent of the seats; the Serbs (Serbian Democratic Party) 30 per cent, and the Croats (Croatian Democratic Union) 18 per cent (see Table 3). Taking all the parties into consideration, the ethnic composition of the Assembly was: Muslims, 41.25 per cent; Serbs, 35.41 per cent; Croats, 20.41 per cent; others, 2.93 per cent.

This apparently satisfactory result in fact bodes ill for effective government. An "agreement" between the three largest parties to put together a multi-ethnic administration has turned out to be almost totally ineffective, and outside of this block the opposition is too weak and too divided to do anything about it, until its members themselves decide that it is time for a change. (Together the block has 202 of the 240 seats in the bicameral Assembly.)

Directory of Parties (Bosnia and Hercegovina — BH)

Alliance of Reform Forces of Yugoslavia for Bosnia and Hercegovina (ARFYBH)
Savez Reformskih Snaga Jugoslavije za Bosnu i Hercegovinu (SRSJ BiH)

Contact. See "Leadership".

Address. Rektorat Univerziteta u Sarajevu, 71000, Sarajevo.

Telephone. (071) 211–729.

Foundation. Sept. 15, 1990.

Membership. Claims 420,000.

Leadership. Dr Nenad Kecmanović (pres.); Dr Džemal Sokolović (vice-pres.)

History. In the late summer of 1990 the president of the Executive Council (Prime Minister) of the federal government, Ante Marković, decided that he would contest the coming elections through his own party. In deliberately setting out to create an image of a party free from specific ethnic loyalties, Marković chose to launch the new Alliance in Bosnia — ethnically the most diverse of the republics. The ARF later spread throughout the federation, but its heartland and one of its greatest electoral successes have been in BH.

Organization. At the time of the election, 76 branch organizations were in being. In spite of its late launch, the party secured the election of 12 candidates to the Assembly.

Programme. The ARF seeks the establishment of full parliamentary democracy, and the replacement of various forms of collectivism (class, nation and religion) with a society of free citizens. It advocates the modernization of the state and the legal system, and the complete reconstruction of the economic order in terms of its regulation through market mechanisms. It proposes corresponding reform of the systems of banking, taxation, education, communication and social security. A central consideration in relation to all of these projects is the harmonization of Yugoslav institutions with those in other European countries.

Affiliations. Although they carry the same name, the republican organizations of the ARF are in fact independent, but maintain regular contact. The principal link is through personal loyalty to Ante Marković and faith in his leadership.

Croatian Democratic Union of Bosnia and Hercegovina (CDUBH)
Hrvatska Demokratska Zajednica Bosne i Hercegovine (HDZ BiH)

Contact. Ivan Markezić.

Address. Maršala Tita 7a, 71000, Sarajevo.

Telephone. (071) 517–576 or 277–168.

Foundation. Aug. 18, 1990.

Membership. Claims 300,000.

Leadership. Franjo Boras (member of the Presidency of BH); Mariofil Ljubić (vice-pres. of Assembly of BH); Jure Pelivan (pres. of government of BH). CDU members hold four other ministerial positions within the republic.

History. It appears that the initiative for its foundation came from the parent body in Croatia.

Organization. The party contested seats in 65 constituencies in the elections of 1990, where there were substantial numbers of Croats. With 18 per cent of the vote, it secured a total of 44 seats in both chambers of the Assembly, and is the smallest partner of the three-party ethnically balanced coalition which forms the government of the republic of BH.

Programme. See the entry in the section on Croatia. The party declares that it defends the sovereign independence of the republic of BH (i.e. it does not support the "cantonization" of Bosnia along ethnic lines, nor its absorption by other republics). It sees itself explicitly as the defender of the interests of the Croat population of the republic.

Affiliations. The CDU in BH is in effect a branch of the main party in Croatia.

Democratic Party of Socialists (DPS)
Demokratska Stranka Socijalista (DSS)
formerly Demokratski Socijalistički Savez Bosne i Hercegovine (DSS BiH)

Contact. Prof. Ismet Grbo (sec.)

YUGOSLAVIA

Address. Maršala Tita 7a, 71000, Sarajevo.

Telephone. (071) 36–365.

Foundation. June 30, 1990.

Membership. Claims 100,000.

Leadership. Dr Mirko Pejanović (pres.)

History. The party is an adaptation of the former Communist popular front organization, the Socialist Alliance, to the new conditions of party pluralism.

Organization. Out of 109 communes in the republic, there are DSS branches in 92. The party is represented in the republican Assembly.

Programme. Presents itself as preserving the "best values of the European and Soviet socialist movements". While advocating the development of a "modern democratic state" it refers also to the major symbols of Yugoslavia's past — AVNOJ and the war of liberation. Expects that its programme will take BH "out of the circle of undeveloped republics"; but its programme, while high on images, is low on specific proposals. In short, its programme is more "communist" than the Communists!

Affiliations. The DSS collaborates closely with representatives of other small left-oriented parties in the Assembly. Discussions are under way regarding the merger of the DSS with the former League of Communists, now PDC, which would make them a significant partner in any future coalition governments.

League of Communists of Bosnia and Hercegovina — Party of Democratic Changes (LCBH-PDC)
Savez Komunista Bosne i Hercegovine — Stranka Demokratskih Promjena (SK BiH-SDP)

Contact. Zlatko Lagodžija; Adil Kolenović.

Address. Djure Djakovića 41, 71000, Sarajevo.

Telephone. (071) 218–169 or 216–644; *Fax.* (071) 215–747.

Foundation. November 1948.

Membership. 350,000.

Leadership. Dr Nijaz Duraković (pres.)

History. Continues the work of the former League of Communists of BH.

Organization. As with most other communist parties in Yugoslavia, the PDC in BH has inherited the apparatus of the former LC, with branches throughout the 110 communes of the republic. It was able to contest only 14 seats successfully on its own account, and another five in association with other socialist groups. Regrouping after this setback, the PDC is now managing to emerge as the focus of a more consolidated socialist force in the republic.

Programme. Describes itself as a "modern party of left orientation", which specifically disavows association with any particular nationality. While emphasizing the continuing importance of the Yugoslav federation, the DPS calls for the integrity of the republic's borders and its sovereignty. Seeks the development of a modern market economy, including reform of the taxation system, but several points presuppose the continuing active economic intervention of the state — compensation for the former "neo-colonial" situation of the republic; an active programme of infrastructure development; housing reform. Advocates return of formerly confiscated land to the peasantry.

Affiliations. It is not known to what extent the collapse of the LCY has been followed by any reconstitution of links between the various republican organizations.

Muslim-Bosnian Organization (MBO)
Muslimanska-Bošnjačka Organizacija (MBO)

Contact. Mujo Kafedžić (sec.)

Address. Vase Miskina 12, 71000, Sarajevo.

Telephone. (071) 276–320.

Foundation. Oct. 19, 1990.

Leadership. Adil Zulfikarpašić (pres.); Muhamed Filipović; Hamza Mujagić.

History. The MBO broke with the Party of Democratic Action in September 1990, objecting to its alleged "clericalism", and attempting to secure a platform for the electoral representation of all "Bosnians".

Organization. Although a relatively late creation, on the eve of the elections, the MBO secured two seats in the republican Assembly. The party claims to be growing quickly: at the time of the elections they were represented in 19 communes, but now have branches in more than 50, controlling the local Assemblies in three. The MBO is regarded as very much the personal following of Zulfikarpašić (a very wealthy businessman who has made his fortune outside the country) who provides its finance, and Filipović, who provides its ideology.

Programme. The MBO presents itself as the voice of distinctively Bosnian (*Bošnjak*) nationality — "all who belong to the three great cultural-religious traditions of Bosnia and Hercegovina and who consider this to be their homeland". In spite of its name it seeks the dissociation of regional identity from any specific religious connotation. Bosnia for the Bosnians! A great deal of its programme and related publications relate to questions of the nature and means of developing Bosnian cultural identity. Yugoslavia is the "optimal space" in which these aims can be achieved. It stresses the autonomy of institutions from the state, especially the law and education; the subordination of administration and the police to the law. Its most specific proposals lie in the area of the polity — reform of parliament and of local government. Beyond generalizations about modernization and the development of a market economy its economic programme is far less specific.

YUGOSLAVIA

Party of Democratic Action (PDA)
Stranka Demokratske Akcije (SDA)

Contact. Sidik Spasić.

Address. Maršala Tita 7a, 71000, Sarajevo.

Telephone. (071) 518–967 or 36–771.

Foundation. May 26, 1990.

Membership. Claims 650,000.

Leadership. Alija Izetbegović (pres. of party and pres. of Presidency of BH); Fikret Abdić (member of Presidency of BH); Muhamad Ćengić (vice-pres. of government of BH). PDA members hold eight other ministerial positions within the republic.

Organization. Although this fact is not acknowledged in its title, the PDA is a self-consciously nationalist organization representing Bosnian Muslims. Consequently it only contested 65 seats in the elections within BH, where Muslims were a substantial element of the population. With 36 per cent of the popular vote, the party secured 86 seats in the two-chamber republican Assembly, where it forms the largest party.

Programme. The PDA's programme presents it primarily as the party of Yugoslav Muslims. It gives central place to demands for parliamentary democracy and the defence of human rights and the rights of ethnic or religious minority groups, specifically insisting that the Kosovo problem can not be resolved by the use of force. In the economic field it is content to give support to the Marković programme. Its manifesto gives a prominent place to the defence of the family.

Affiliations. The party also successfully contested elections in the Sandžak area of Serbia, and has offices in Novi Pazar (see section on Serbia). It is alleged to have links with several Arab countries, but nothing is known for certain about these.

Serbian Democratic Party of Bosnia and Hercegovina (SDPBH)
Srpska Demokratska Stranka Bosne i Hercegovine (SDS BiH)

Contact. Dr Radovan Karadžić (pres.)

Address. Djure Djakovića 45, 71000, Sarajevo.

Telephone. (071) 270–572.

Foundation. July 12, 1990.

Membership. Claims 450,000.

Leadership. Dr Radovan Karadžić and Dr Biljana Plavšić (members of Presidency of BH); Dr Miodrag Simović (vice-pres. of government of BH); seven other members of the SDP hold ministerial positions within the republic.

Organization. With the support of around 30 per cent of the vote in the 1990 elections, drawn from those areas with substantial Serb settlement, the party won 72 seats in the bicameral Assembly of BH.

Programme. The SDP is explicitly the political voice of Serbs living in BH. It advocates the development of multi-party democracy, toleration and respect for the rights of minorities, and legality in the conduct of the affairs of the state. Its programme has little to say about economic affairs beyond the abolition of a maximum size for landholdings. It defends the Serbian position in Kosovo; and seeks to protect and develop Serbian cultural institutions, especially the Orthodox church.

Affiliations. The SDP has close relations with similarly-named parties in both Serbia and Croatia. It has acquired notoriety because of its involvement in the illicit arms trade in Hercegovina.

Three other parties secured representation in the Assembly in the elections of 1990, although very little is known about them, and they appear to operate in practice in close association with other groups to an extent which suggests their ultimate merger into larger and more stable configurations.

Democratic League of Greens — EKO (DLG-EKO)
Demokratski Savez Zelena — EKO (DSZ-EKO)

Contact. Dražen Petrović, elected as member of the Assembly of BH. There is no known contact address, and no published programme or other details of the party.

Liberal Party (LP)
Liberalna Stranka (LS)
formerly Savez Socijalističkih Omladina-Demokratski Savez Bosne i Hercegovine (SSO-DS BiH)

Contact. Rasim Kadić (pres.)

Address. Danijela Ozme 7, 71000, Sarajevo.

Telephone. (071) 218-320; *Fax.* (071) 219-866.

Secured the election of one member to the Assembly. Like the Slovene equivalent of the same name, the party is an outgrowth of the former official communist youth organization.

Serbian Movement for Renewal (SMR)
Srpski Pokret Obnove (SPO)

Contact. Milan Trivunčić

Address. Nemanje Vlatkovića 21, Šipovo, 70000.

Telephone. (070) 71-350.

This is a branch in Bosnia of Serbian movement led by Vuk Drašković, and supports his programme. It sends one representative to the republican Assembly.

The following minor parties also registered within the republic of Bosnia and Hercegovina at the time of the 1990 elections: Association for a Yugoslav Democratic Initiative — AYDI (*Udruženje za Jugoslovensku Demokratsku Inicijativu* — UJDI; is a branch of the Belgrade-based organization of the same name, in Mostar, and reported under Serbia); Bosnian Democratic Party — BDP (*Bosanska Demokratska Stranka* — BDS; registered in Bihać); Democratic Party — DP (*Demokratska Stranka* — DS; parties with this title are registered in Bosanski Brod, Mostar and Tuzla, although it is not known whether they are branches of the Belgrade party of the same name); Democratic Party of Freedom — DPF (*Demokratska Stranka Slobode* — DSS; registered in Mostar); Democratic Union of Bosnia and Hercegovina — DUBH (*Demokratska Zajednica Bosne i Hercegovine* — DZBiH; registered in Bosanski Šamac); Hercegovina Democratic Union — HDU (*Hercegovačka Demokratska Zajednica* — HDZ; registered in Čitluk; the initials make it sound suspiciously like a spoiling party against the Croatian Democratic Union); National Council for the Defence of the Peoples of Bosnia and Hercegovina — NCDPBH (*Narodno Vijeće za Zaštitu Naroda Bosne i Hercegovine* — NVZN BiH; registered in Gradačac); National Party of Bosnia — NPB (*Narodna Stranka Bosne* — NSB; registered in Sarajevo); Party for Democracy and a Just State — PDJS (*Stranka za Demokratiju i Pravnu Državu* — SDPD; registered in Nevesinje); Party of Democratic Agreement — PDA (*Stranka Demokratskog Dogovora* — SDD; registered in Bosanski Brod); Party of Democratic Reforms of Bosnia and Hercegovina — PDRBH (*Stranka Demokratskih Reforma Bosne i Hercegovine* — SDR BiH; registered in Banja Luka); Party of Private Initiative — PPI (*Stranka Privatne Inicijative* — SPI; registered in Doboj); Party of Progressively Oriented Yugoslavs — PPOY (*Stranka Progresivno Orijentisanih Jugoslovena* — SPOJ; registered in Teslić); Party of Yugoslavs for Bosnia and Hercegovina — PYBH (*Stranka Jugoslovena za Bosnu i Hercegovinu* — SJ BiH; is presumably a regional organization of the party registered in Zagreb, and reported under Croatia; registered in Sarajevo); Peasant-Workers' Party — PWP (*Seljačko-Radnička Stranka* — SRS; registered in Bosanska Dubica); Peasant Yugoslav Party — PYP (*Seljačka Jugoslavenska Stranka* — SJS; registered in Bosanska Gradiška); Republican Party of Bosnia and Hercegovina — RPBH (*Republička Stranka Bosne i Hercegovine* — RSBiH; registered in Sarajevo); The Social-Democratic League of Bosnia and Hercegovina — SDLBH (*Socijaldemokratski Savez Bosne i Hercegovine* — SDS BiH; this is understood to be a branch of the Belgrade-based Yugoslav Social-Democratic Party, in Mostar); United Socialist Party of Yugoslavia — USPY (*Jedinstvena Socijalistička Partija Jugoslavije* — JSPJ; registered in Jajce); Yugoslav Democratic Party — YDP (*Jugoslovenska Demokratska Stranka* — JDS; registered in Banja Luka); Yugoslav Democratic Party "Fatherland Front" — YDPFF (*Jugoslovenska Demokratska Stranka "Otadžbinski Front"* — JDSOF; registered in Kukulje kod Srpca); Workers' Democratic Party — Party of Federalists — WDP-PF (*Radnička Demokratska Stranka — Stranka Federalista* — RDS-SF; registered in Sarajevo).

CROATIA

The area historically known as Croatia since the 12th century has had a chequered history, in which the greater part was associated with the Hungarian crown (principally Slavonia and central Croatia); the larger part of Dalmatia was attached to Austria, but parts remained Italian territory. These were only reunited in the settlement of 1918 (although Istria and parts of Dalmatia remained Italian). As the result of sustained nationalist agitation, a semi-autonomous *banovina* of Croatia (which incorporated some areas now in Bosnia and Hercegovina) was established in 1938. Following the attack by the Axis powers in 1941, an "Independent State of Croatia" was formed, governed by the indigenous fascist *Ustaša* movement, but under the military control of Italy/Germany. Croatia was returned

Table 4: Elections of May 1990 to the Croatian Assembly

Parties in the Social-Political Chamber	(78 seats)
Croatian Democratic Union	54
Party of Democratic Changes (LCC)	16
Socialist Party of Croatia	1
Green Action, Split/Party of Democratic Changes*	1
Croatian Christian Democratic Party	1
Croatian Democratic Party	1
Croatian People's Party	1
Serbian Democratic Party	1
Independents	2

Parties in the Chamber of Associated Labour	(156 seats)
Croatian Democratic Union	84
Party of Democratic Changes (LCC)	36
Croatian Democratic Party	5
Croatian People's Party	4
Party of Democratic Changes/Socialist Party of Croatia*	4
Croatian Social-Liberal Party	3
Croatian Peasant Party	2
Socialist Party of Croatia	1
Croatian Christian Democratic Party	1
Serbian Democratic Party	1
League of Socialist Youth of Croatia	1
Independents	14

Parties in the Chamber of Municipalities	(115 seats)
Croatian Democratic Union	70
Party of Democratic Changes (LCC)	23
Party of Democratic Changes/Socialist Part of Croatia*	11
Croatian Democratic Party	3
Serbian Democratic Party	3
Socialist Party of Croatia	1
League of Socialist Youth of Croatia	1
Social Democratic Party of Croatia	1
Croatian Christian Democratic Party	1
Croatian Social-Liberal Party	1

* Joint Candidates
Source: Ministry of Information, Republic of Croatia.

to Yugoslavia (with additional territories ceded from Italy) in 1945. With a surface area of 56,538 sq km the Republic of Croatia is the second largest of the six republics of the federation (22 per cent of the total). Its population (census of 1991) is 4,688,507 (20 per cent of the total). The most numerous ethnic group in the republic are the Croats, with 74.6 per cent of the population, followed by the Serbs, with 11.3 per cent. There are small, locally significant minorities of Muslims, Slovenes, Magyars, Italians and Czechs. The largest concentrations of Serbs are found in the areas south of Zagreb, known as Kordun and Banija, and along the western border of Bosnia, especially in the region of Lika. This latter, containing about a half of Croatia's Serb minority, in 1990 declared itself to be independent of the Croatian republic as an autonomous *Krajina* (border area) associated with Serbia, centred on the town of Knin. There are also estimated to be around 100,000 Serbs living in Zagreb itself. Nine-and-a-half per cent of the population of Croatia (the highest proportion in the whole federation) refused to declare their nationality to the census of 1991. Nine per cent of the population declared themselves to be "Yugoslavs" — the highest proportion to do so in the federation.

The election to the presidency of the republic was concluded in the first round, on April 22, 1990, with an overwhelming victory for Franjo Tudjman of the Croatian Democratic Union. He was opposed by two other candidates, Ivica Račan of the former Communist party (Party of Democratic Changes), and Ivo Družić, representing an *ad hoc* grouping of parties with a non-ethnic base, the Coalition of National Agreement.

The presidency is a personal and not a collective office in Croatia; and Tudjman has exploited this to the full since his election. There is already a developed "cult of personality", and it is widely reported in Croatia that he resents the growing success and popularity of Stipe Mesić, the Croatian member and president of the federal Presidency.

The elections to the tricameral republican Assembly (*Sabor*) also resulted in a landslide victory for the CDU, with huge majorities in all three chambers (see Table 4). Opposition is acutely divided, with the communist PDC coming a slow second in each case. Many observers of the Croatian situation express grave concern over the extent to which the republic may have replaced one single-party system by another. Tudjman's cult of personality is only one feature of his methods which lend credibility to these fears. It is possible that these may be exaggerated; as on the essential points relating to the enhancement of republican independence there is a broad political consensus which extends beyond the CDU itself. Even the communists recommended that their supporters vote "Yes" in the referendum on independence held on May 19, 1991. On matters of economic policy, however, there is no such consensus; and indeed there are quite deep divisions within the CDU itself.

Directory of Parties (Croatia)

Alliance of Reform Forces of Yugoslavia for Croatia (ARFYC)
Savez Reformskih Snaga Jugoslavije za Hrvatsku (SRSJH)

Contact. Bora Djordjević (press sec.)

Address. Trg V. Vlahovića 1/I, 41000, Zagreb.

Blatine 58, 58000, Split.

Telephone. (041) 561–333 or (058) 516–147.

Leadership. Emil Kajganić (pres.)

Organization. The relatively late foundation of the Alliance in Croatia (after the completion of the republican elections) means that it is not represented in the Assembly. It has developed a fairly extensive network of local branches. Opinion polls suggest that it is to be taken seriously as a factor in the political process in the republic.

Programme. See entry in section on Bosnia and Hercegovina.

Affiliations. Linked with other republican associations of the ARFY. There is also a separate organization for the ARFY in Pula.

Croatian Christian Democratic Party (CCDP)
Hrvatska Kršćanska Demokratska Stranka (HKDS)

Contact. See "Leadership".

Address. Park V. Vlahovića 2, 41000, Zagreb.

Telephone. (041) 327–233 and 313; *Fax.* (041) 325–190.

Foundation. Oct. 15 1989.

Membership. 100,000.

Leadership. Ivan Cesar (pres.)

Organization. Claims around 100 branches throughout the republic. Has two representatives in the Assembly.

Programme. The party claims to be based upon the Christian principles of faith, hope and love. A good part of its programme is devoted to the exposition of very general ideals of an ethical nature. More specifically, it envisages the separation of Croatia from the Yugoslav federation, based upon its "inalienable right". It demands the depoliticization of the organs of administration and justice; the creation of a market economy based upon private property and the encouragement of Croat emigrants to return to Croatia. A substantial part of its manifesto is concerned with specific ethical issues, such as abortion, suicide and euthanasia.

Affiliations. The CCDP claims to co-operate with all other Christian Democratic parties, but it is unclear to what extent there is any real collaboration.

Croatian Democratic Party (CDP)
Hrvatska Demokratska Stranka (HDS)

Contact. Anto Kovačević (press sec.)

Address. Tkalčevića 4, 41000, Zagreb.

YUGOSLAVIA

Telephone. (041) 422–494 or 422–062; *Fax.* (041) 421–969.

Foundation. Nov. 4, 1989

Membership. Claimed 100,000 at the time of the elections. Now claims to be the strongest party in Croatia.

Leadership. Marko Veselica (pres.); Josip Cvitan (vice-pres.)

History. The CDP was formed as a split from the CDU, which they regard as too compromised with communism and too ready to make accommodations with respect to Yugoslavia.

Organization. At the time of the election the party was active in 48 communes, but claims to be greatly expanded. A number of former émigrés are in leading positions in the party. Has nine members in the republican Assembly.

Programme. Although it declares that membership is open to all regardless of religion, language, social position etc., the CDP is a strongly nationalistic Croatian party. While demanding political and civil rights for all individuals, it insists that "every attempt to combine or identify the Croatian nation with any other nation is contrary to the natural aspirations . . . of the Croatian nation". Hence it is vigorously opposed to all "Yugoslavism", and distinguishes itself from the CDU principally because it regards the latter as too willing to compromise on constitutional questions. It is staunchly committed to the capitalist system, and also regards the CDU as too compromised with socialism. The manifesto expresses concern over the danger that the "Croatian nation is in danger of dying out", and is in favour of measures supportive of the family and the rearing of children. Croatia is "not a land of free immigration", although Croats are to be encouraged to return. Resettlement is to be encouraged in those areas of the republic where Croats are now in a minority. Policies, such as the support for agriculture, are linked to these aims.

Croatian Democratic Union (CDU)
Hrvatska Demokratska Zajednica (HDZ)

Contact. Ante Beljo (g.s.)

Address. Trg Hrvatskih Velikana 4, 41000, Zagreb.

Telephone. (041) 450–338 or 450–466; *Fax.* (041) 435–314.

Foundation. June 17, 1989.

Membership. At one time claimed a million members. This figure must be preposterous, even allowing for the inclusion here of members in Bosnia and Hercegovina. It is even questionable if one accepts the possibility of a large overseas membership.

Leadership. Franjo Tudjman, pres. of party and of the Croatian Republic. The CDU has a massive majority in all three chambers of the Croatian Assembly, and forms the government of the republic. All ministries are therefore filled by party nominees. Stijepan Mesić is the party's nominee for the federal collective presidency.

Organization. At the time of the elections the CDU claimed to be active in 117 communes, and more than 80 per cent of the republic's neighbourhoods. It is the principal political organization of Croats in BH as well as Croatia, and has an extensive and effective network of fund-raisers abroad.

Programme. The CDU is an explicitly anti-communist expression of Croatian nationality. It envisages a pluralistic transformation of the state, and the institutionalization of civil and human rights, including the freedom of labour organization. The problems of the federation can only be resolved by consensus. It insists upon the "full sovereignty" of the Croatian state, but does not preclude the creation of forms of association between the republics of Yugoslavia. Curiously, a section of its manifesto is devoted to criticism of Serbian policy in Kosovo. Concern is expressed about the decline of the Croatian population, and this is related to a range of policies including the stimulation of return migration and pro-natality measures. The rather brief treatment of economic issues centres more on processes of modernization of the economy than on issues of property, accepting a mixed economy.

Croatian Peasant Party (CPP)
Hrvatska Seljačka Stranka (HSS)

Contact. Mirko Dreta (sec.)

Address. Gundulićeva 21a, 41000, Zagreb.

Telephone. (041) 433–830 or 423–888.

Foundation. Originally founded by the brothers Radić in 1904. Re-established in Croatia, Nov. 20, 1989.

Membership. 20,000.

Leadership. Drago Stipac (pres.)

History. The party is the oldest in Yugoslavia. It is the only party currently in operation which can legitimately claim continuity with a pre-war organization. Founded in 1904, it became during the interwar years the principal political expression of Croatian nationalism. Its leaders were interned by the fascists during the last war, and after the war fled to Canada, where the party was kept in being. Returned to register in Zagreb when party pluralism was again permitted in 1989.

Organization. The CPP claims to have around 200 branches, but as this exceeds the number of communes in Croatia, the figure probably includes affiliates abroad. In addition to the conventional apparatus of the party, discussions are afoot to recreate the network of co-operatives and related organizations which were the strength of the party in the pre-war years. It has two representatives in the republican Assembly.

Programme. The CPP stresses the continuity of its links with the party of Maček and the brothers Radić — it is still distributing copies of their speeches, and led the celebrations in 1991 of the bicentenary of the birth of Stjepan Radić. In this respect it sees itself as offering a vision of Croatian society as much as a programme, which combines radical libertarianism, pacifism and a commitment to localism and mutual co-operation. The CPP advocates complete privatization and reprivatization of economic resources, but combines this economic individualism with a sense of local solidarity in the provision of comprehensive welfare.

Croatian People's Party (CPP)
Hrvatska Narodna Stranka (HNS)

Contact. Ivica Vrkić (sec.)

Address. Gajeva 12/II, 41000, Zagreb.

Telephone. (041) 425–335; *Fax* (041) 425–332.

Foundation. Jan. 30, 1991.

Leadership. Savka Dabčević-Kučar (pres.); Krešimir Džeba (vice-pres.)

History. The leadership core dates back to the Croatian party struggles of 1971–72 as a relatively coherent political clique. The party in its present form is a very new phenomenon.

Organization. Has five representatives in the republican Assembly, through the "conversion" of members elected under other party labels. A recent *Danas* opinion poll suggested very rapid growth of the CPP, under its rather celebrated leadership. Consequently organizationally things are in flux.

Programme. Although clearly "nationalistic", in that it sets its sights upon the creation of a "sovereign, independent and democratic" Croatia, the key concept in the programme of the CPP is probably "modernity". Its individualism is therefore presented not in "right/left" terms, but as a distancing from traditionalistic collectivisms of various kinds (by implication also from socialism). The creation of strong private enterprise in the economy is only one dimension of a wider project of building a vigorous "civil society". To this end also the party is outspoken in its demands for a free press, and for regionalism. The role of the state is seen as regulatory rather than operative. The CPP probably has the fullest and most elaborated analysis of any of the parties of the nature and needs of Croatian society, but makes few concrete legislative proposals.

Croatian Social-Liberal Party (CSLP)
Hrvatska Socijalno-Liberalna Stranka (HSLS)

Contact. Vlado Bogdanić (g.s.)

Address. Šubićeva 29, 41000, Zagreb.

Telephone. (041) 417–093 (also Fax).

Foundation. May 20, 1989.

Membership. 8,000.

Leadership. Dražen Budiša (pres.)

Organization. Claims more then 70 branches. Has four representatives in the Assembly.

Programme. In many ways the CSLP can be described as a 19th century Liberal party. It emphasizes the "democratic and European tradition and orientation of Croatia", in which it expects to find its place in a confederal Yugoslavia. In one way or another the European context features prominently in the party's literature, although rhetorically rather than in relation to concrete proposals.

Green Action — Split (GA-S)
Zelena Akcija (ZA-S)

Contact. See "Leadership".

Address. Žrtava Fašizma 8, 58000, Split.

Telephone. (058) 44–421 or 45–677.

Foundation. Dec. 22, 1989.

Membership. 600.

Leadership. Zoran Pokrovac (pres.)

Organization. The Greens in Split claim to have four branches. They have succeeded in electing a member to the republican Assembly.

Programme. The concerns of this group spring very directly from the particular conditions in the Kaštelet-Split area, and from the impact of its spatially concentrated industrial development. Its literature therefore presents not only general demands for such measures as the control of smoke emissions, but raises specific issues regarding given industrial plants which are regarded as ecologically damaging.

Affiliations. Although not a single party, there are also "Green Action" groups in Rijeka, Šibenik and Zagreb. Contact can be made through the Split organization.

League of Socialist Youth of Croatia (LSYC)
Savez Socijalističkih Omladina Hrvatske (SSOH)

The organization has two seats in the Assembly. It is reputed to have changed its name to the Liberal Party, as in the case of the Slovene organization of the same name, to share a similar programme, and indeed to have close links with it. The party has been formed from the former official Communist youth organization, Klub Poslanika SSOH, Sabor Republike Hrvatske, 41000, Zagreb.

Party of Democratic Changes (PDC)
Stranka Demokratskih Promjena (SDP)
formerly Savez Komunista Hrvatske — Stranka Demokratskih Promjena

Contact. Prof. Branko Caratan.

Address. Šetalište Karla Marxa 14, 41000, Zagreb.

Telephone. (041) 517–000 or 234–201; *Fax* (041) 518–249.

YUGOSLAVIA

Foundation. Aug. 1, 1937.

Membership. 46,000.

Leadership. Ivica Račan (pres.)

History. The Croatian Communist Party, in one form or another, has been in continuous existence ever since its reorganization in 1937 by Josip Broz "Tito". It has also been characterized by a succession of important attempts to liberalize and reform the party.

Organization. The PDC has suffered enormously from the rise of the CDU, losing an estimated 100,000 to the CDU bandwagon. It does retain intact the republic-wide network of the organization, however, even though this is undergoing a comprehensive shake-up. The PDC remains by far the largest party in all three chambers of the Assembly, after the CDU.

Programme. The party describes itself as a "contemporary political organization of the left in Croatia, European in its orientation, which is committed to political democracy and a market economy". As with other such parties in Yugoslavia, it attempts to hold together the imperatives of economic modernization with a strong emphasis on "solidarity" — the defence of welfare state measures. While deferring to the dominant nationalism, and acknowledging that Croatia is the "national state of the Croatian people", the party stresses the need to accommodate other groups for whom the republic is a "historic homeland". This requires a "new historical agreement" about the nature of the Yugoslav state. A surprisingly large amount of the published programme is devoted to settling ideological and political accounts with the past, rather than addressing the future character of Croatian society.

Affiliations. As with other former LC organizations, it is unclear to what extent an effective federal network of links remains in existence.

Serbian Democratic Party (SDP)
Srpska Demokratska Stranka (SDS)

Contact. Dragan Pribićević (sec.)

Address. Preradovićeva 18/I, 41000, Zagreb.

Jove Miodragovića 22, 59000, Knin.

Telephone. (041) 423–583 or (059) 22–499 or 22–750.

Foundation. Feb. 17, 1990.

Membership. 150,000.

Leadership. Jovan Rašković (pres.)

Organization. The party has a rather unusual organizational form, in that a good deal of its coverage of the territory is on a regional rather than a municipal basis. This is the direct result of its aspiration to represent Serbs resident outside of Serbia, who in many cases are rather dispersed. It is the moving spirit behind the separatist enclave of *Krajina*, which encompasses about 12 communes within Croatia, along the border with Bosnia and

Hercegovina, hence its offices in Knin. Because of its association with the "Krajina", the Zagreb offices have been the repeated target of Croat terrorist attacks, and the leaders are compelled to live in Belgrade. The SDP publishes its own paper, *Zbilja*, in Knin and Karlovac.

Programme. The party advocates the development of pluralistic, democratic party politics. As the representative of the Serb minority in Croatia, a good deal of its manifesto is devoted to the defence of the rights of national minorities within the Yugoslav republics. "Nations can not be identified with their home units in the federation." A place has to be found for the expression of their language and culture wherever they are resident. The regionalization of Croatia (of which the creation of the "Krajina" is seen as one case) is an attempt to answer this need.

Affiliations. The SDP has sought some links with the Democratic Party in Belgrade (Mićunović), although they are organizationally distinct. Affiliates of the Party also operate in Bosnia.

Social-Democratic Party of Croatia (SDPC)
Socijaldemokratska Stranka Hrvatske (SDSH)

Contact. Zoran Abramović (sec.)

Address. Šetalište Karla Marxa 14, 41000, Zagreb.

Telephone. (041) 537–604 or 517–000; *Fax*. (041) 534–432.

Foundation. Dec. 16, 1989.

Membership. 7,000.

Leadership. Antun Vujić (pres.)

Organization. Claims 50 local branches. Elected one representative to the Assembly.

Programme. The SDPC is a centre-left grouping which emerged from the reorganization of the former Socialist Alliance in Croatia. It stands within the Croatian nationalist consensus in representing Yugoslavia as an "association of states" whose rights to self-determination extend to and include separation, but on the whole its programme does not make much of the constitutional issue. Its programme offers the prospect of a democratic welfare state with a mixed economy. As with other socialist fractions, it balances the creation of freedom of individual economic initiative with a public concern for equality.

Socialist Party of Croatia (SPC)
Socijalistička Stranka Hrvatske (SSH)

Contact. Jadran Vilović (sec.)

Address. Kruge 48, 41000, Zagreb.

Telephone. (041) 517–835; *Fax*. (041) 510–422.

Foundation. June 2, 1990.

YUGOSLAVIA

Membership. 50,000.

Leadership. Željko Mažar (pres.)

History. The SPC is one of the successor organizations to the former Socialist Alliance in Croatia.

Organization. The party operates in around 70 communes, distributed between six regional co-ordinating committees. It has representation in the republican Assembly.

Programme. There is little to distinguish the programme of the SPC from those of the PDC and the SDPC with respect to its main objectives and values. If it has distinctiveness this lies in the nuances, in that the SPC gives greater prominence to the defence of the disadvantaged, and appears to be more positive about the role of the state in the economy. It supports "flexible and selective reprivatization". It gives greater prominence than do the other socialist groups to agriculture and to questions of regional development. If anything, it can be said to be more positive also about the importance of the continuation of the Yugoslav federation as the guarantor of the defence of the interests of national minorities.

In addition to these parties with established electoral success, four others merit detailed mention, either because of the size of their following or their impact on political debate.

Croatian Muslim Democratic Party (CMDP)
Hrvatska Muslimanska Demokratska Stranka (HMDS) (sometimes known simply as the MDS)

Contact. Hasan Bosnić (acting pres.)

Address. Voćarska 40, 41000, Zagreb.

Telephone. (041) 445–597 or 277–216.

Membership. 35,000.

Leadership. See "Contact"; Azis Mikić.

Programme. The programme of the party makes it clear that it is a "Muslim" party in the national and not the religious sense. It expresses "full confidence" in the federal order of Yugoslavia, and within that order seeks to defend the cultural, economic and social interests of Muslims resident in Croatia. It sees these aims as best served within a multi-party democracy and a mixed economy. The party is expressly opposed to the tyranny of majorities.

Croatian Party of Rights (CPR)
Hrvatska Stranka Prava (HSP)

Contact. Dobroslav Paraga (pres.)

Address. Šenoina 13, 41000, Zagreb.

Telephone. (041) 424–368 or 426–310; *Fax.* (041) 423–929.

Foundation. Feb. 25, 1990.

Membership. Claims around 3,500 in Croatia and Bosnia and Hercegovina, and 8,500 abroad.

Leadership. See "Contact".

History. It is not known to what extent its claimed descent from the party of the same name which existed before the war is justified. This may well be the case, as it has certainly a highly active following outside Croatia — more so than in the republic.

Organization. Claims 10 branches in Croatia, and 20 overseas.

Programme. The published programme of the party makes it difficult to distinguish it from other nationalistic, centre-right groupings in Croatia, such as the Croatian Democratic Party, or even the CDU. It does have a reputation, however, for extreme nationalism. Possibly this is hinted at in its concern for "Croatian national-state sovereignty throughout the whole of its historical and ethnic space", which could be taken as indicating territorial ambitions extending well beyond the borders of the republic.

Affiliations. These are unclear, although it does have a reputation for links with terroristic groups.

Democratic League of Albanians of Croatia (DLAC)
Demokratski Savez Albanaca Hrvatske (DSAH)

Contact. Tom Berisha (pres.)

Address. Park V. Vlahovića 2, 41000, Zagreb.

Telephone. (041) 324–192 or 526–845; *Fax.* (041) 234–192.

Foundation. Jan. 13, 1990.

Membership. 30,000.

Leadership. See "Contact".

Organization, programme, affiliations. The League is a republican branch of the *Lidnja Demokratike* based in Kosovo. See section on Serbia.

Party of Yugoslavs (PY)
Stranka Jugoslovena (SJ)

Contact. Mirko Franceschi (pres.)

Address. Galovićeva 8, 41000, Zagreb.

Telephone. (041) 217–495 or 217–185.

Foundation. Feb. 21, 1990.

Membership. 600,000 throughout the whole federation.

Leadership. See "Contact".

Organization. Claims roughly 120 branches throughout the federation.

Programme. The party seeks the creation of a "democratic federal Yugoslavia". It aspires to be a movement of all citizens who want a "new and modern Yugoslavia", and not only of those who claim "Yugoslav" nationality in the terms of the census. Through the creation of institutions of democratic participation and the market, it seeks to create a measure of integration, which will be a part of wider processes of European integration.

The following minor parties were either registered in Croatia at the time of the elections of 1990, or have appeared since then: Albanian Christian Democratic Party — ACDP (*Albanska Demokršćanska Stranka* — ADS; registered in Zagreb; it is not known whether this is in fact a branch of the Kosovo party of the same name, representing principally Catholic Albanians); Bosnian Democratic Party — BDP (*Bosanska Demokratska Stranka* — BDS; registered in Zagreb); Croatian Liberal Movement — CLM (*Hrvatski Liberalni Pokret* — HLP; registered in Zagreb); Croatian Republican Party — CRP (*Hrvatska Republikanska Stranka* — HRS; registered in Zagreb); Croatian Party — CP (*Hrvatska Stranka* — HS; registered in Zagreb); Croatian Peace Movement — CPM (*Hrvatski Mirotvorni Pokret* — HMP; registered in Split); Dalmatian Action — DA (*Dalmatinska Akcija* — DA; registered in Split); Democratic Action of Croatia — DAC (*Demokratska Akcija Hrvatske* — DAH; registered in Osijek); Democratic Union of Muslims of Croatia — DUMC (*Demokratska Zajednica Muslimana Hrvatske* — DZMH; registered in Osijek); Civic Party — CP (*Gradjanska Stranka* — GS; registered in Split); Istrian Democratic Assembly — IDA (*Istarska Demokratska Sabor* — IDS); *Sieta Democratica Istriana* — SDI; registered in Pula; evidently an Italian ethnic party; Istrian Independent Party — IIP (*Istarska Nezavisna Stranka* — INS; registered in Rovinj); Istrian Popular Party — IPP (*Istarska Pučka Stranka* — IPS; registered in Pula); League of Social Democrats — LSD (*Liga Socijalnih Demokrata* — LSD; registered in Zagreb); List for Osijek — LO (*Lista za Osijek* — LO; registered in Osijek); Magyar People's Party of Croatia — MPPC (*Madžarska Narodna Stranka Hrvatske* — MNSH); *Horvatorszagi Magyar Neppart* — HMN; registered in Zmajevac. Movement for Confederation — MC (*Pokret za Konfederaciju* — PK; registered in Zagreb); New Party — NP (*Nova Stranka* — NS; registered in Velika Gorica); Party of Democratic Action — PDA (*Stranka Demokratske Akcije* — SDA; registered in Zagreb, but a Croatian branch of the Sarajevo-based party of Bosnian Muslims); Party of Independent Democracy — PID (*Stranka Nezavisne Demokracije* — SND; registered in Rijeka); Party of Romanies in Croatia — PRC (*Stranka Roma u Hrvatskoj* — SRH; Registered in Bjelovar); Rijeka Democratic League — RDL (*Riječki Demokratski Savez* — RDS; registered in Rijeka); Serbian National Party — SNP (*Srpska Narodna Stranka* — SNS; registered in Zagreb); Socialist Party of Croatia — Party of Yugoslav Orientation — SPC-PYO (*Socijalistička Partija Hrvatske-Partija Jugoslovenske Orijentacije* — SPH-PJO; registered in Petrinja); Transnational Radical Party — TRP (*Transnacionalna Radikalna Stranka* — TRS; registered in Zagreb); Union of Progressive Workers of Yugoslavia — UPWY (*Zajednica Radnika Progresista Jugoslavije* — ZRPJ; registered in Zagreb); Yugoslav Independent Democratic Party — YIDP (*Jugoslavenska Samostalna Demokratska Stranka* — JSDS; registered in Zagreb).

MACEDONIA

Macedonia was only freed from Turkish rule following the Balkan Wars, in 1913, when it was divided between Serbia, Greece and Bulgaria. The Macedonian territories included in Serbia were brought into the Kingdom of Serbs, Croats and Slovenes in 1918 (renamed Yugoslavia in 1929). Following partition under Axis occupation in 1941, Yugoslav Macedonia was occupied principally by the Bulgarians, with the western part allocated to the Italian client state of Albania. Following liberation in 1945 a Macedonian republic was created within the Yugoslav federation. With a surface area of 25,713 sq km the Republic of Macedonia is the fourth largest of the six republics of the federation

(10 per cent of the total). Its population (census of 1991) is 2,147,090 (9 per cent of the total). The most numerous ethnic group in the republic are the Macedonians, with 64.8 per cent of the population, followed by the Albanians, with 21.5 per cent. There are small, locally significant minorities of Muslims, Romanies, Serbs and Turks. The majority of the Albanians are concentrated in a triangular area in the north-west of the republic and adjacent to the border with Albania, although the capital, Skopje, also has a substantial Albanian minority.

The situation in Macedonia is extremely complex. Because of massive irregularities in the conduct of the first round of the elections on Nov. 9, 1990, it was necessary to declare the first round void in 176 voting districts. This was re-run on Nov. 25, and a second round proper concluded on Dec. 9, 1990.

Because of the difficulty experienced in ensuring that a high enough turnout was achieved (the successful candidate must receive votes equivalent to 51 per cent of the *electorate*) it was at one stage feared that the republic would be unable to elect a president. In the end Kiro Gligorov, the candidate of the communist Party of Democratic Changes was elected.

No single party is able to form a majority within the single chamber of the Macedonian Assembly (*Sobranie*). The Internal Macedonian Revolutionary Organization is the largest single party, with 38 of the 120 seats (see Table 5). As the principal party of Macedonian nationalism, it is opposed both by the less nationalistic communists (PDC), and by parties representing other national interests, especially by the Albanian Party of Democratic Prosperity, which draws its support largely from western Macedonia.

Table 5:   Elections of December 1990 to the Macedonian Assembly[1]

Parties in the Assembly	*(120 seats)*
Internal Macedonian Revolutionary Organization/Democratic Party for Macedonian National Unity	38
Party of Democratic Change (LCM)	31
Party for Democratic Prosperity	17
Alliance of Reformed Forces of Macedonia/Young Democratic Progressive Party[2]	6
Party for Democratic Prosperity/National Democratic Party[2]	5
Socialist Party of Macedonia	4
Party of Yugoslavs in Macedonia	2
National Democratic Party	1
Socialist Party of Macedonia/Alliance of Reform forces of Macedonia/Young Democratic Progressive Party[2]	1
Socialist Party of Macedonia/Party for the Full Emancipation of Romanies[2]	1
Independents	3

[1] The Macedonian Assembly has only one Chamber.
[2] Joint candidates.

Source: Secretariat for Information, Republic of Macedonia.

YUGOSLAVIA

Both Vasil Tupurkovski, the republic's representative on the federal presidency, and the newly elected Gligorov, have played very active roles in the attempt to break the political deadlock at the federal level.

Within the republic itself the actual government relies heavily upon ministers recruited from outside the parties themselves, on the basis of their expertise. (This does not express adhesion to some constitutional principle, but rather to the fact that the largely working-class, populist IMRO is unable to provide nominees of appropriate experience and qualification from within its own ranks.) The lack of a clear majority held by one ruling party has not perceptibly obstructed the relatively smooth transition to an effective democratically elected order in Macedonia. Nevertheless, it is impossible to predict any stable future pattern on the basis of these electoral results.

Directory of Parties (Macedonia)

Alliance of Reform Forces of Macedonia (ARFM)
Sojuz na Reformskite Sili na Makedonija (SRSM)

Contact. Zoran Krstevski.

Address. (temporary) Ilindenska bb., 91000, Skopje.

Telephone. (091) 213–034 or 237–840.

Leadership. Stojan Andov (pres.)

History. The ARF in Macedonia is a relatively late creation, and its representatives in the Assembly were elected in the second round in association with other parties. There is some evidence that it made ground in the post-election period in terms of both its general popularity and organizational development.

Organization. The ARF does not have a complete territorial coverage of the republic, with its main strength in the cities.

Programme. As outlined in the entry for Bosnia and Hercegovina.

Affiliations. Linked with other republican organizations of the ARF.

Internal Macedonian Revolutionary Organization-Democratic Party for Macedonian National Unity (IMRO-DPMNU)
Vnatrešna Makedonska Revolucionerna Organizacija-Demokratska Partija za Makedonsko Nacionalno Edinstvo (VMRO-DPMNE)

Contact. Boris Zmejkovski (sec.)

Address. Gornovranovska 122, 91000, Skopje.

Telephone. (091) 421–585 or 228–145.

Foundation. June 17, 1990.

Membership. Claims 100,000.

Leadership. Prof. Ljupčo Georgievski (pres.); the minister for urban development and construction, Aleksandar Lepavcov.

History. The name of IMRO is traced back to the revolutionary organization which fought for independence from the Turks at the end of the 19th century, founded by Goce Delčev in 1893. There is no direct link with the present party. It was refounded in Skopje, and then merged with the DPMNU, which was founded by Macedonian migrant workers in Sweden.

Organization. The party has more than 30 branches. With 38 seats in the republican Assembly it is the largest parliamentary party in Macedonia. It is distinguished by the solid base of its support among the manual working class.

Programme. The party seeks the creation of an independent Macedonian state linked to a loose Yugoslav confederation. It aspires to the unification of Macedonia, but rejects the use of force to that end. Macedonian cultural identity should be affirmed more strongly both within Yugoslavia and through respresentation abroad, and there should be greater resistance to Serbianization. Expresses concern about the Albanian "demographic explosion". Calling itself a party of the "democratic centre", IMRO recognizes the need for a market economy and for the stimulation of foreign private investment. It proposes the building of a main international rail link from Durrës and Tirana through Skopje and Sophia to Istanbul.

National Democratic Party (NDP)
Partis Demokratis Populore (PDP)

Contact. Isuf Rexepi (pres.)

Address. Cvetan Dimov 7, 94000, Tetovo.

Foundation. July 23, 1990.

Leadership. Ilijas Halini (pres.)

Organization. Active in six communes with large Albanian populations. Secured election of one representative to the republican Assembly.

Programme. It is unclear how this Albanian language organization differs from the PDP. It demands parliamentary democracy and the defence of human rights within a "federal or confederal" Yugoslavia.

Party for Democratic Prosperity in Macedonia (PDP)
Partija za Demokratski Prosperitet vo Makedonija (PDP)

Contact. Midhat Edimi (sec.)

Address. Dojče Stojčevski 14-a, 94000, Tetovo.

Telephone. (094) 21–380 or 28–792 or (091) 231–148.

Foundation. May 25, 1990.

Leadership. Prof. Halili Nevzat (pres.); Prof. Sami Ibrahimi (vice-pres.)

Organization. Although this is clear neither from its name or even its programme, the party in effect operates as the principal political vehicle for Albanian opinion within Macedonia. It operates only in 17 communes with large Albanian populations, in each of which it secured a seat in the Assembly.

Programme. The party's programme (as does its title) specifically denies its attachment to a specific ethnic group. The party makes no challenge to the federal or republican boundaries of Yugoslavia. It demands the depoliticization of the judiciary and the military, and a state which is specifically not associated with the interests of any ethnic group. In economic affairs it is in favour of a radical programme of the privatization of social property and the expansion of private investment, both indigenous and foreign.

Party of Yugoslavs in Macedonia (PYM)
Stranka na Jugosloveni vo Makedonija (SJM)

Contact. Prof. Milan Durčinov (pres.)

Address. Ženevska 6/2–6, 91000, Skopje.

Telephone. (091) 234–681 or 245–961.

Foundation. June 26, 1990.

Membership. 5,000.

Leadership. See "Contact".

Organization. Branches in nine larger towns in the republic. Has two representatives in the republican Assembly.

Programme. The PYM aspires to represent all those who consider themselves to be of Yugoslav nationality. It advocates the reintegration of Yugoslavia as a modern federation, with a democratic political system and a market economy. It seeks the protection and enhancement of human and civil rights, mentioning those of women and minors as well as ethnic minorities, the freedom of the press and an independent judiciary. It describes itself as a "centre-left" party.

Affiliations. Linked to similar organizations in other republics, the main centre being located in Zagreb.

Social-Democratic League of Macedonia (SDLM)
Socijaldemokratski Sojuz na Makedonija (SDSM)
formerly **League of Communists of Macedonia — Party of Democratic Change (LCM-PDC); Sojuz na Komunistite na Makedonija — Partija za Demokratska Preobrazba (SKM-PDP)**

NB Not to be confused with the Social-Democratic Party of Macedonia

Contact. Erol Hajretin.

Address. Ilindenska bb., 91000, Skopje.

Telephone. (091) 231–371 or 226–700.

Foundation. The Communist Party of Macedonia was founded in 1943. The reformed party (LCM-PDC) was set up in 1989, after the collapse of the LCY. The title SDLM was adopted in 1991.

Membership. 30,000 is a reliable figure.

Leadership. Petar Gošev (pres.); Kiro Gligorov is the Macedonian member of the federal presidency. Ministers in Macedonia are not chosen explicitly because of party attachment, but Jovan Andonov is a vice-pres. of the government.

Organization. The party has inherited the organization and the real-estate of the former LC, and is therefore operationally and materially well-endowed. With 31 representatives it is the second largest party in the Assembly.

Programme. In its reformed state the party now describes itself as standing in the "European democratic tradition". It is in favour of economic reform, an "effective" market economy and the "transformation" of property relations, democratic socialism, social freedoms, rights and solidarity. The SDLM is specifically non-national. It looks for the creation of a "sovereign and independent" Macedonia within a confederal Yugoslavia.

Affiliations. The nature and extent of links between former LCs is unknown.

Socialist Party of Macedonia (SPM)
Socijalistička Partija na Makedonija (SPM)
formerly **Socijalistički Sojuz-Socijalistička Partija na Makedonija (SS-SPM)**

Contact. Zejnel Begović (sec.)

Address. Ilindenska bb., 91000, Skopje.

Telephone. (091) 231–255 or 228–015.

Foundation. Sept. 28 1990.

Leadership. Kiro Popovski (pres.)

History. The party grew out of the former "Socialist Alliance" within the republic.

Organization. Represented in every commune within the republic, with a good network of branches at neighbourhood level. Has four representatives, and several joint representatives, in the republican Assembly.

Programme. The SPM identifies itself specifically with the socialist traditions of "Macedonia, Yugoslavia and Europe". It demands the speedy creation of a "politically free, economically effective, ecologically responsible and socially just state". The key to this project it sees as the creation of a parliamentary democracy, the organs of which will control institutions, in place of "the bureaucracy". Several specific projects are mentioned, including fiscal reform, the need to improve the social security situation of the agricultural population and the improvement of water supplies.

In addition to the parties with established electoral success, three other parties merit detailed mention, either because of the size of their following of their impact on political debate.

Movement for Pan-Macedonian Action (MAAK)
Dviženje za Semakedonska Akcija (MAAK)

Contact. Branko Josifovski.

Address. Dame Gruev 3, 91000, Skopje.

Telephone. (091) 227–037 or 226–363.

Foundation. March 11, 1990.

Membership. 50,000.

Leadership. Ante Popovski.

History. Founded under the leadership of the poet Gane Todorovski, but he was replaced after the disastrous showing of the movement in the election. Began as a spectacular national movement, but its exclusively intellectual leadership was out of touch with popular responses, and it was soon overtaken by IMRO as the principal vehicle for popular nationalism. Now largely in eclipse.

Organization. Branches in every commune in the republic.

Programme. MAAK seeks the creation of a democratic political order based upon the "inviolable sovereignty of the people". Although its programme does touch briefly upon economic issues, including the "radical transformation" of agriculture, by far the greater part of its concerns have to do with "the Macedonian question" — the cultural heritage and prestige of the Macedonian people, and the question of the relationship between the republic and neighbouring states in which Macedonians are resident. The most concrete implications of this are seen to lie in the improvement of transport links and in problems of population policy.

Social-Democratic Party of Macedonia (SDPM)
Socijaldemokratska Partija na Makedonija (SDPM)

Contact. Prof. Slavko Milosavljevski (pres.)

Address. J.H. Konstantinov 20, 91000, Skopje.

Telephone. (091) 205–907.

Foundation. March 18, 1990.

Leadership. See "Contact"; also, Dragoljub Budomovski, Dževdet Vejseli and Tihomir Jovanovski.

History. Milosavljevski is one of the principal figures in the history of postwar dissent in Macedonia, being dismissed from the party in 1972 for his liberalism.

Organization. Has branches in every commune in Macedonia.

Programme. The party is distinguished by its openly non-nationalistic stance — "the Republic of Macedonia is the common fatherland and state of all of the people who live in it". It seeks a secular, modern state with a depoliticized administration and judiciary, and the expansion of civic freedoms — including that of free trade union organization. In the "tradition of western European social democracy" it aspires to combine "economic democracy" with a market economy. It expresses particular concern for the development of small enterprises, and for the economic development of the more mountainous areas of the republic. As with other Macedonian parties, attention is given to the situation of Macedonia in relation to its Balkan neighbours.

Young Democratic Progressive Party of Macedonia (YDPPM)
Mlada Demokratsko-Progresivna Stranka na Makedonija (MDPSM)

The party which contested the elections under this title was the reformed version of the former official Communist youth organization. It gained one seat in the republican Assembly. Since then it has merged with the ARFM.

The following minor parties either contested the elections of 1990 or have appeared since then: Christian-Democratic Party of Macedonia — CDPM (*Demohrščanska Partija na Makedonija* — DPM; registered in Ohrid); Democratic Alliance-Party of Cultivators of Macedonia — DA-PCM (*Demokratski Sojuz-Zemjodelska Partija na Makedonija* — DS-ZPM; registered in Skopje; interesting particularly as a rare example of a party explicitly oriented towards small business as well as simply farmers); Democratic League of Turks in Macedonia — DLTM (*Demokratski Sojuz na Turcite vo Makedonija*; specifically defines itself as a "league for political action" rather than a party, but the significance of the distinction is unclear); Democratic Macedonian Workers' Association — DMWA (*Demokratsko Makedonsko Rabotničko Obedinuvanje* — DMRO; registered in Prilep, and apparently based upon the tobacco industry there); League for Democracy — LD (*Liga za Demokratija* — LD; the Macedonian branch of the major Kosovo Albanian Party; registered in Skopje); Party for the Complete Emancipation of Romanies — PCER (*Partija za Celosna Emancipacija na Romite* — PCER; registered in Skopje; collaborated with the SPM to secure the election of a member to the republican Assembly); Party of Human Rights of Macedonia — PHRM (*Partija Ljudskih Prava Makedonije* — PLPM; Macedonian title not known; registered in Strumica); People's Party of Macedonia — PPM (*Narodna Partija na Makedonija* — NPM; registered in Skopje); Political Party of the Unemployed of Macedonia — PPUM (*Politička Partija Nezaposlenih Makedonije* — PPNM; Macedonian title not known; registered in Prilep); Workers'-Cultivators' Party — WCP (*Rabotničko-Zemjodelska Partija* — RZP; registered in Skopje); Workers' Party of Macedonia — WPM (*Rabotnička Partija na Makedonija* — RPM; registered in Skopje).

Incidental reference has been encountered to four other, recently formed parties; but full information is lacking even regarding their proper titles and location: IMRO-Democratic Party (an extremist nationalist split from IMRO-DPMNU); Party of Progress; Party of United Macedonians; Party of Direct Action.

MONTENEGRO

This small semi-independent state survived the general Ottoman occupation of the Balkan peninsula, and sustained intermittent armed resistance against Turkish hegemony since the 15th century. Ruled from the end of the 17th century by a dynasty of prince/bishops, Montenegro became a Kingdom in 1851. Throughout the 19th century there were several accretions of territory, at Turkish expense. The monarchy was abolished in 1918 when Montenegro joined the Kingdom of Serbs, Croats and Slovenes (renamed Yugoslavia in 1929). Montenegro was placed under an Italian governor after the invasion of 1941, and became a republic within the Yugoslav federation in 1945. With a surface area of 13,812 sq km the Republic of Montenegro is the smallest of the six republics of the federation (only 5.4 per cent of the total). Population (census of 1991) is 648,483 (2.1 per cent of the total). The most numerous ethnic group in the republic are the Montenegrins, with 61.8 per cent of the population, followed by Muslims, with 13.9 per cent, Albanians, with 6.2 per cent, and Serbs, with 3.5 per cent. The Muslims are generally concentrated in the west and south-west of the republic, and the Albanians in the south. These form continuous areas of Muslim settlement with the Sandžak of Novi Pazar, in neighbouring Serbia, and of Albanian settlement with the former Autonomous Province of Kosovo and with Albania itself. The proportion of Montenegrins in the population at the census of 1981 was 68.5 per cent, and the decline relative to various Muslim groups has become something of a political issue in the republic. Nearly 6 per cent of the population declared themselves to be "Yugoslav".

In Montenegro, the first round of the elections was held on Dec. 9 and the second concluded on the Dec. 23, 1990. It was necessary to take the presidential election to a second round, although the candidate from the League of Communists of Montenegro (Momir Bulatović) secured a clear majority. He failed in the first round to secure the requisite 51 per cent of the votes of the electorate. His victory over Ljubiša Stanković (for the Alliance of Reform Forces) and Novak Kilibarda (for the National Party) was secured with 76 per cent of the votes cast.

In the republican Assembly (*Skupština*) the LCM has a very substantial majority, with 83 of the 125 seats (two-thirds of the total). Montenegro therefore provides a case of a Communist party governing following success in freely contested open elections (see Table 6).

The principal problems within the republic, from an electoral point of view, lie in the fragmented and relatively ineffective nature of the opposition, which includes

Table 6: Elections of December 1990 to the Montenegrin Assembly[1]

Parties in the Assembly	(125 seats)
League of Communists of Montenegro	83
Alliance of Reform Forces[2]	17
Democratic Coalition[3]	13
National Party	12

[1] The Montenegrin Assembly has only one Chamber.
[2] The Alliance of Reform Forces in Montenegro was created through a coalition of three parties; the Liberal Alliance; the Socialist Party and the Party of Socialists.
[3] The Democratic Coalition was created through a coalition of the Party of Democratic Action, the Democratic League and the Party of Equality (itself a fusion of three small parties).

Source: Secretariat for Information, Republic of Montenegro.

representatives of minority ethnic groups (principally Albanian, within the Democratic Coalition), non-communist modernizers, such as the ARF, and conservative Montenegrin nationalists, such as Kilibarda's NP.

In Montenegro more than anywhere else the significance of the possession by the Communists of their inherited assets of real estate and equipment becomes apparent. The physical and organizational machinery of the old order have all been appropriated by the LCM, leaving all opposition groups at a dreadful disadvantage. The ARF is run largely from Stanković's office at the University, and Kilibarda operates from a room in a Titograd hotel.

Although it was not successful in the elections themselves, the lately organized Democratic Party should be watched for the future. It appears to be well organized and financed, with its own paper (*Demokratska Riječ*).

Directory of Parties (Montenegro)

The party scene in Montenegro is complicated by the fact that since the elections of 1990 there has been a series of party mergers, simplifying the structure very considerably. Principal entries here are confined to the parties which are currently operating. For the sake of historical interest, minor entries only are given for the original parties which contested the elections.

Alliance of Reform Forces for Montenegro (ARFM)
Savez Reformskih Snaga za Crnu Goru (SRSCG)

Contact. Dr Ljubiša Stanković (pres.)

YUGOSLAVIA

Address. Elektrotehnički fakultet, Univerzitet "Veljko Vlahović", 81000, Titograd.

Telephone. (081) 13–797.

Foundation. Formed after the elections of December 1990 by the merger of three parties: the Liberal Alliance of Montenegro; the Socialist Party and the Party of Socialists of Montenegro.

Membership. Before the elections the three parties taken separately were claiming a total of 21,500 members.

Leadership. See "Contact"; Srdjan Darmanović.

History. Several of the opposition parties emerged in Montenegro through a Democratic Forum set up towards the end of 1989, including those which now comprise the ARFM.

Organization. The ARF is represented in 17 of the 20 communes in the republic. It has 17 members in the Assembly. The Alliance is strongest in the coastal towns and Titograd; weakest in country areas and Cetinje.

Programme. See the entry under Bosnia and Hercegovina.

Affiliations. Linked with other republican organizations of the ARF.

Democratic Coalition (DC)
Demokratska Koalicija (DK)

Contact. Lekë Lulgjuraj (sec.)

Address. Klub poslanika DK, Skupština SROG, 81000, Titograd.

Telephone. (081) 36–513.

Foundation. Formed after the elections of December 1990 through the collaboration of three parties: the Party of Democratic Action; the Party of Equality; the Democratic League.

Leadership. See "Contact"; also Mehmet Bardhi and Asim Dečević.

Organization. The party has 13 representatives in the republican Assembly. It is not clear to what extent the Coalition entails the subordination of the specific aims of its individual components. Explicitly it remains a coalition, and is not a new party.

Programme. It is possible to identify the platform of the new Coalition in relation to its formerly independent components. All expressed strong concern for the building of a "legal state", a market economy and a pluralistic democracy. All were especially firm about the protection of human and civil rights. All were vocal on issues of the position of national minorities. All accepted the "AVNOJ idea" of federation. Nevertheless, each in different ways, explicitly or implicitly, addressed problems of the inadequate political representation of the interests of Muslim or Albanian citizens in the republic.

Affiliations. The Party of Democratic Action is the principal Muslim party in Bosnia and Hercegovina. The Democratic League is an important Albanian political organization based in Kosovo.

Democratic Party (DP)
Demokratska Stranka (DS)

Contact. Dr Bogoljub Šijaković.

Address. Ljubljanska 4, 81400, Nikšić.

Telephone. (083) 41–193 or (081) 812–647.

Foundation. Sept. 20 1990.

Membership. 5,000 (fairly reliable figure).

Leadership. See "Contact", who also edits the party's paper; also Žarko Stanovčić (pres.); Savo Laušević.

History. The leadership group contains a number of prominent non-communists; Stanovčić was the first postwar non-Communist mayor of Herceg Novi.

Organization. The relatively late emergence of the DP meant that it secured no seats in the election, but it has been making steady progress in coverage and support since then. An important resource is its paper, *Demokratska Riječ*.

Programme. The Democrats appear to offer a specifically non-communist alternative which holds the middle ground between those groups who indentify uncritically with Serbia and those who can be regarded as Montenegrin nationalists. How they differ from the ARF is unclear.

League of Communists of Montenegro (LCM)
Savez Komunista Crne Gore (SKCG)

(A proposal is to be considered regarding the change of name of the party during the summer of 1991.)

Contact. Sanja Mihailović (press sec.)

Address. Jovana Tomasevića bb., 81000, Titograd.

Telephone. (081) 52–833.

Foundation. July 1948 — the date of its first Congress. Registered under the present law, July 24 1990.

Membership. Claims 68,000.

Leadership. Momir Bulatović (pres. of the party and of the republic); Milo Dukanović (g.s.); Jugoslav Kostić (represents Montenegro in the federal presidency). As the ruling party in the republic, all ministers are appointed by the party.

Organization. The apparatus of communist party organization is very much intact in Montenegro, and the LCM retains in its hands the real estate and other resources appropriate to its former position as the sole party.

Programme. As with the other reformed Communist parties, the LCM presents itself as standing in the "European tradition of democratic socialism", fighting for the "humanistic ideas of socialism". Its programme stresses very much the unification of all interests, of gender, nationality, religion, and region. It accepts a mixed economy and pluralistic democracy. The party is probably distinguished among Yugoslav parties for the abstraction of its rhetoric and the poverty of its concrete proposals.

Affiliations. It is not known to what extent there remain effective links between the several republican communist organizations in their reformed mode.

National Party (NP)
Narodna Stranka (NS)

Contact. Miodrag Dubina (press sec.)

Address. Poštanski fah 306, 81000, Titograd.

    Located at: Hotel "Podgorica".

Telephone. (081) 45–952.

Foundation. May 12, 1990.

Membership. 20,000.

Leadership. Prof. Novak Kilibarda (pres.)

Organization. The party has 12 seats in the Assembly.

Programme. The National Party is probably the most uncompromisingly Serbian of the parties in Montenegro. It is aggressively and explicitly in favour of the "Great Serb" ideal, seeing Montenegrins simply as one branch of the Serbian people. In many respects, including its anti-Communism, the NP resembles Drašković's MSR in Serbia itself.

The following minor parties either contested the elections in 1990 or have appeared since then: Association for a Yugoslav Democratic Initiative — AYDI (*Udruženje za Jugoslovensku Demokratsku Inicijativu* — UJDI; should be considered a movement rather than a party; see principal entry under Serbia); Association for the Advancement of Democratic Processes — AADP (*Udruženje za Unapredjenje Demokratiskih Procesa* — UUDP; should be considered a movement rather than a party; registered in Nikšić); Democratic Alternative — DA (*Demokratska Alternativa* — DA; registered in Titograd; did not contest the elections of 1990); Democratic League — DL (*Demokratski Savez* — DS; this is a branch of the principal Albanian political organization, based in Kosovo; works within the Democratic Coalition following the elections of 1990; for additional information see the entry under Kosovo); Democratic Socialist League — DSL (*Demokratski Socijalistički Savez* — DSS; another fraction to emerge from the "Socialist Alliance"; registered in Titograd); Ecological Movement of Montenegro — EMM (*Ekološki Pokret Crne Gore* — EPCG; the Montenegrin version of the Greens; registered in Titograd); Independent Organization of Communists — IOC (*Nezavisna Organizacija Komunista* — NOK; registered in Bar); Liberal Alliance of Montenegro — LAM (*Liberalni Savez Crne Gore* — LSCG; merged with the ARF following the elections of 1990; registered in Cetinje); Montenegrin Federalist Movement — MFM (*Crnogorski Federalistički Pokret* — CFP; registered in Cetinje); Party of Democratic

Action — PDA; this is a branch of the principal Muslim Party in Bosnia and Hercegovina; works within the Democratic Coalition, following the election of 1990); Party of Equality — PE (*Stranka Ravnopravnosti* — SR; merged with the Democratic Coalition following the election of 1990; registered in Titograd); Party of National Equality — PNE (*Stranka Nacionalne Ravnopravnosti* — SNR; registered in Titograd); Party of Socialists of Montenegro — PSM (*Partija Socijalista Crne Gore* — PSCG; another fraction to emerge from the "Socialist Alliance"; merged with the ARF after the elections of 1990; registered in Titograd); Socialist Party — SP (*Socijalistička Partija* — SP; merged with the ARF following the elections of 1990; registered in Titograd); Social-Democratic Party of Montenegro — SDPM; *Socijaldemokratska Stranka Crne Gore* — SDSCG; registered in Titograd); Yugoslav National Party — YNP (*Jugoslovenska Narodna Stranka* — JNS; registered in Titograd).

SERBIA

A semi-independent principality of Serbia was created from Ottoman territory following a successful rebellion by the Serbs in 1813, which underwent a series of enlargements throughout the 19th century. The most substantial of these were the gains made as a result of the Balkan wars, when the Sandžak of Novi Pazar, Kosovo and Macedonia were acquired. (Serbia was effectively fully independent as a Kingdom after 1868.) After World War I Serbia joined the new Kingdom of Serbs, Croats and Slovenes (renamed Yugoslavia in 1929), which was ruled by the Serbian Karadjordjević dynasty. At this time also the territories known as Bačka and the Banat, north of the Danube and formerly part of Hungary, but settled largely by Serbs, were also acquired. Following the invasion by the Axis powers in 1941 Serbia was dismembered, with large areas in the south under Bulgarian occupation (including Macedonia) and those areas with predominantly Albanian populations being attached to the Italian client state of Albania. A truncated Serbian state was set up, nominally still under the monarchy, but under an indigenous military governor, backed by German occupation forces. Bačka was annexed by Hungary, and the Banat (with its large German minority) directly by the German Reich. Following the reunification of Yugoslavia in 1945 a Serbian republic was created, but containing an "Autonomous Province" of the Vojvodina, which included Bačka, the Banat and Srem (formerly regarded as a part of Croatia). The largely Albanian areas of the south-west, "Kosmet" (a neologism combining Kosovo and Metohija) were an "Autonomous region" until 1968, when as "Kosovo" they were granted the same status as the Vojvodina. The autonomy of both of these Provinces was abrogated in the revised Serbian consitution of 1990. With a surface area of 88,361 sq km the Republic of Serbia is the largest of the six republics of the federation (34.5 per cent of the total). Population (census of 1991) is 9,916,068 (41.5 per cent of the total). The most numerous ethnic group in the republic are the Serbs, (63.7 per cent), followed by the Albanians (estimated 11.2 per cent) the Magyars (3.1 per cent) and the Muslims (2.6 per cent). There are also locally significant minorities of Croats, Montenegrins and Romanies. The ethnic structure of the republic was reflected before 1990 in the creation of two Autonomous Provinces within the republic. Kosovo, in the south-west and adjacent to Albania, covered 10,887 sq km (about 12 per cent of the territory of the republic); the Vojvodina in the north covered 21,506 sq km (about 24 per cent). Containing nearly 1.7 million of the 2.2 million Albanians resident in Yugoslavia, Kosovo is thought to be nearly 85 per cent Albanian in its population. (The Albanians boycotted the census of April 1991, and these figures are estimates.) With a rate of increase of roughly 30 per cent over the decade 1981–91, the Albanian population in Serbia is the fastest growing demographic group in Yugoslavia. The Vojvodina contained the majority of Yugoslavia's Magyar minority, who are especially numerous in the area known as Bačka. Their numbers declined at an accelerating rate over the intercensal period, as have the numbers of Croats living in Serbia. Numbers of national minorities in the republic generally fell in this interval, with the exception of Albanians, Muslims and Romanies. The presence of all of these is politically sensitive in Serbia.

The electoral process in Serbia delivered the anticipated majority for Slobodan Milošević's Serbian Socialist Party (the former League of Communists of Serbia), although by a larger margin than expected. The apparently strong showing made by Vuk Drašković and the Movement for Serbian Renewal during the electoral campaign was contradicted at the polls. In the presidential contest, which was concluded in the first round on Dec. 9, Drašković himself secured only 17 per cent of the vote. Milošević romped home with 65 per cent. No fewer than 32 candidates competed.

The elections to the Assembly of the republic (*Skupština*) went to a second round on Dec. 23, and here too the SPS swept the board, gaining 194 of the 250 seats (77.6 per cent) in the single chamber (see Table 7).

One clear feature to emerge from the electoral results, although these have yet to be analyzed in detail, is the pattern of regional differences in party support. A very important

Table 7: Elections of December 1990 to the Serbian Assembly*

Parties in the Assembly	*(250 seats)*
Socialist Party of Serbia (LCS)	194
Serbian Movement for Renewal	19
Democratic Union of Magyars of Vojvodina	8
Democratic Party	7
Party of Democratic Action (SDA)	3
Alliance of Peasants of Serbia	2
Alliance of Reform Forces of Vojvodina	2
Party of Yugoslavs	1
Democratic Reform Party of Muslims	1
National Peasant Party	1
Serbian Democratic Party	1
Association for a Yugoslav Democratic Initiative	1
Party of Democratic Action (PDD)	1
Democratic League of Croats in Vojvodina	1
Independents	8

* The Serbian Assembly has only one Chamber.
Source: *Politika* Dec. 26, 1990, pp.1, 5 and 6.

feature of the Serbian elections is the fact that the Albanian parties in Kosovo boycotted the entire process in protest against the abrogation of the Provincial Assembly, in the revision of the republic's constitution enacted in September 1990. This contributed in no small measure to Milošević's victory, but helps to mask the local scale of his real support. If this point is valid for the SPS, it can be made even more forcefully with respect to Drašković's MSR. The latter gained not a single seat in the first round of voting; and its gains in the second were confined to the north-east of "Serbia proper" (Belgrade, Kragujevac and Užice) and to southern and central Vojvodina (Novi Sad and Zemun) — in short, to large urban centres principally within 50 miles of Belgrade. Both Drašković himself and other observers were blinded by the massive success of his rallies in the capital itself to the actual limitations of his following throughout the republic as a whole.

Directory of Parties (Serbia)

Because of the specific political conditions prevailing within the former Autonomous Province of Kosovo, entries relating to parties and groups whose primary sphere of activity lies in that region are grouped in a separate section following the main entries for Serbia.

Alliance of Reform Forces of Vojvodina (ARFV)
Savez Reformskih Snaga Vojvodine (SRSV)

Contact. Dr Dragoslav Petrović.

Address. Bulevar 23 Oktober 94, 21000, Novi Sad.

Leadership. See "Contact".

Organization. The ARF in Serbia has been most successful in the Vojvodina, where it secured the election of two representatives to the republican Assembly for seats in Novi Sad and Zrenjanin.

Programme. See entry for Bosnia and Hercegovina.

Affiliations. Linked to the ARF in Belgrade, and Alliances in other republics.

Alliance of Reform Forces of Yugoslavia (ARFY)
Savez Reformskih Snaga Jugoslavije (SRSJ)

Contact. Dr Vojin Dimitrijević.

Address. Bulevar Lenjina 2, 11000, Belgrade.

Telephone. (011) 635–836.

Membership. The ARF as a whole claimed over two million throughout Yugoslavia at the time of the 1990 election. It is not known what proportion of this support was specific to Serbia.

YUGOSLAVIA

Leadership. Dr Ante Marković (pres., and pres. of the Federal Executive Council of Yugoslavia); Mirjana Popović (co-ordinator).

Organization. An association of republican Alliances, for which individual entries are given in each republic section, including specific entry for the Vojvodina.

Programme. See entry for Bosnia and Hercegovina.

Association for a Yugoslav Democratic Initiative (AYDI)
Udruženje za Jugoslovensku Demokratsku Inicijativu (UJDI)

Contact. Prof. Nebojša Popov (pres.)

Address. Aberdareva 1, 11000, Belgrade.

Telephone. (011) 332–982.

Foundation. November 1989.

Leadership. See "Contact"; Prof. Žarko Puhovski.

History. Initially the Association saw itself as a movement, the function of which was to promote the process of democratization. In the early phase of its development it operated as an approved organization within the "Socialist Alliance". The extent to which it later evolved into a party in the more conventional sense is still unclear.

Organization. There are branches of the Association in several republics, for which entries are recorded here separately. One representative of the movement was elected to the Serbian Assembly in the elections of 1990, and there was close collaboration with the ARF in the election of several others in Serbia.

Programme. AYDI seeks the reconstitution of Yugoslavia as a federation of fully democratic, multi-party democracies, with direct elections to all levels of government, and the effective legal protection of human rights.

Affiliations. Branches of the Association in each republic are linked through a central Association.

Democratic Community of Magyars of Vojvodina (DCMV)
Demokratska Zajednica Vojvodjanskih Madžara (DZVM)

(Magyar title of the party not known)

Contact. Agoston Andraš (pres.)

Address. Draga Spasića 9, 21000, Novi Sad.

Trg Oslobodjenja 11, 21100, Ada.

Telephone. (021) 611–300 or (021) 1369–255.

Foundation. March 31, 1990.

Membership. Claims 12,000.

Leadership. See "Contact"; Janoš Vekaš (vice-pres.)

Organization. As its title suggests, the party is concerned to represent the interests of the Magyar population of the Vojvodina, and has secured the election of eight of its members to the republican Assembly, all for seats in that region. No information is available about the internal organization of the party.

Programme. The party's programme stresses the protection of individual and collective rights, and especially those which have a bearing upon cultural and linguistic minorities.

Democratic League of Croats in the Vojvodina (DLCV)
Demokratski Savez Hrvata u Vojvodini (DSHV)

Contact. Bela Tonković (pres.)

Address. Čapajeva 33, 24000, Subotica.

Telephone. (024) 39–459.

Foundation. July 15, 1990.

Membership. ca. 9,000; these are drawn especially from Croat minorities known as *Bunjevci* and *Šokci*.

Leadership. See "Contact".

Organization. The party secured the election of one of its representatives to the republican Assembly for the Subotica area, with the support of the DCMV.

Programme. The DLCV advocates the protection of individual rights, and those of all national and religious minorities, especially rights to linguistic and literary expression. It supports the creation of multi-party parliamentary democracy, and the reform of the judicial and educational systems. It gives a strong emphasis to private enterprise in the economic sphere.

Affiliations. No formal affiliations, but in fact works closely with the ARFV, the DCMV, the NPP and the Social Democrats.

Democratic Party (DP)
Demokratska Stranka (DS)

Contact. Radoslav Stojanović (press sec.)

Address. Nušićeva 6/IV, 11000, Belgrade.

Telephone. (011) 338–078.

Foundation. Feb. 3, 1990.

Membership. Claims 10,000.

Leadership. Dragoljub Mićunović (pres.). The level of popular respect for Mićunović considerably outweighs the representation of his party in the Assembly. Z. Djindjić.

Organization. The party had about 80 local committees at the time of the elections of 1990, and secured seven seats in the republican Assembly. There are several indications of the growth in effectiveness and popularity of the party since the end of 1990.

Programme. The Democrats advocate the creation of full, multi-party democracy, the freedom of the press, and respect for human rights, and the rights of national minorities. In particular, they demand the creation of a more independent judiciary, the protection of individual property rights, and the abolition of maximum landholding. They envisage constitutional reform along confederal lines, but emphasize that this must be reached by agreement. They give an important place to issues of foreign policy — European integration, Yugoslav participation in regional and other international organizations, and respect for international law. There are acute divisions within the party between the Mićunović and Djindjić factions which threaten a split in the party, but the extent to which these are rooted in programmatic rather than personality differences is unclear.

Democratic Reform Party of Muslims (DRPM)
Demokratska Reformska Stranka Muslimana (DRSM)

Contact. Azar Zulji (pres.)

Address. Koritnik 3, 29000, Prizren.

Telephone. (029) 22–322 or 31–281.

Leadership. See "Contact".

Organization. The party secured the election of one member to the republican Assembly in December 1990. The extent to which it is able to function effectively beyond its base in Prizren, and its programme, are not known.

National Peasant Party (NPP)
Narodna Seljačka Stranka (NSS)

Contact. Dragan Veselinov (pres.)

Address. Nušićeva 17, 11000, Belgrade.

Telephone. (011) 327–791 or Pančevo (013) 2537.

Foundation. May 20, 1990.

Membership. No data.

Leadership. See "Contact".

Organization. The extent to which this party operates beyond its base in Pančevo is unknown. It did secure the election of one member for Pančevo in the elections of 1990.

Programme. The NPP declares itself strongly in favour of the continuation of the Yugoslav federation, roughly in its postwar form. Nevertheless, the principal concerns of the party are economic. Here it advocates very emphatically the defence of private property and the free movement of private capital, although within a mixed economy. It has a special concern for agriculture, and advocates the payment of reparations to those who suffered under the collectivization and nationalization programmes. Several specific reforms are advocated, in the area of social security and working conditions, including the development of free trade unions. In foreign affairs the party expects Yugoslavia to move much closer to the European Community.

Party of the Alliance of Peasants of Serbia (PAPS)
Stranka Saveza Seljaka Srbije (StSSljS)

Contact. Milomir Babić (pres.)

Address. Maršala Tita 81, Višnjica, 11000, Belgrade.

Telephone. (011) 789–235.

No information is available about this party other than the fact that they secured two seats in the elections to the republican Assembly.

Party of Democratic Action (PDA)
Partija Demokratsko Delovanje (PDD)

NB This Party is not to be confused with the principal party of Bosnian Muslims, the English title of which is the same.

Contact. Riza Haljimi (pres.)

Address. 15 Novembra 74, Preševo.

Membership. Claims 3,000.

Leadership. See "Contact".

Organization. The PDA appears to operate exclusively in the area of Preševo-Bujanovac-Medveda, in the extreme south of Serbia, where they succeeded in electing a member to the republican Assembly in the election of 1990. The population of the area is largely Albanian.

Programme. The programme of the PDA starts out from the observation that its home area is among the poorest in Yugoslavia. It sees parliamentary democracy as a way out of the extreme "degradation" of Albanian culture, which is a victim of the "arbitrariness" of the state in Yugoslavia, and towards respect for national minorities. Advocates the continuation of the Yugoslav federation. While strongly pursuing the defence of Albanian culture, its programme expresses concern for the position of women, and demands the "complete rooting-out of blood-revenge".

Party of Democratic Action (PDA)
Stranka Demokratske Akcije (SDA)

NB This is not to be confused with the similarly-named party above.

Contact. Dr Sulejman Ugljanin (pres.)

Address. E. Redžepagića 54, Novi Pazar.

Foundation. Aug. 11, 1990.

Leadership. See "Contact".

Organization. The party secured the election of three representatives to the republican Assembly in the elections of 1990, all from the Sandžak region. It is clearly a Serbian branch of the principal party of Bosnian Moslems, reported under Bosnia. The extent to which it functions independently of the parent organization is unknown.

Programme. Whereas in general the programme of the party in Serbia repeats that of its parent in Bosnia, it does give greater place to the expression of concern over the rights of minorities, and in particular includes advocacy of the "complete cultural autonomy of the Sandžak".

Party of Yugoslavs (PY)
Stranka Jugoslovena (SJ)

Contact. Zaharije Trnavčević (pres.)

Address. Prote Mateje 36, 11000, Belgrade.

Foundation. No data for Serbia; but see entry under Croatia.

Membership. No data for Serbia; but see entry under Croatia.

Leadership. See "Contact".

Organization. The party secured the election of one representative for a constituency in Novi Beograd, in the Assembly elections of 1990. No additional specific data are available for its operations in Serbia.

Serbian Democratic Party (SDP)
Srpska Demokratska Stranka (SDS)

Contact. Miodrag Dobrić (sec.)

Address. Kolarčeva 9, 11000, Belgrade.

Telephone. (011) 320–659.

Membership. Claims 45,000.

Leadership. See "Contact"; Momčilo Kosović (pres.)

Organization. The party succeeded in securing the election of one candidate in the Vojvodina (Stara Pazova), although the extent to which it is generally more effective is unclear.

Programme. The SDP claims to be a party of "the Serbian people wherever they may live". In spite of its explicit adherence to the notions of federation and of national autonomy as inscribed in the "AVNOJ" declarations, it is clear that the party is a vocal advocate of the "Great Serb" ideal, seeking "to realize the political union of the greater part of its members in the boundaries of one state". In this respect, the SPD regards as entirely artificial creations the Macedonian, Montenegrin and Muslim "nations". Its programme is almost entirely limited to the exposition of these and closely related issues.

Affiliations. Although the party is registered separately in Serbia it is linked with similarly-named parties in Croatia and Bosnia and Hercegovina. The precise nature of these links is unclear. It is regarded by outsiders as having involvement in the supply of illegal weapons to Serbian minorities in other republics.

Serbian Movement for Renewal (SMR)
Srpski Pokret Obnove (SPO)

Contact. Milan Komnenić (pres. of exec. board)

Address. Nušićeva 8/III, 11000, Belgrade.

Telephone. (011) 342–918.

Membership. Claims 700,000, but this is acknowledged to include supporters outside of Serbia itself.

Leadership. Vuk Drašković (pres.); Slobodan Rakitić (head of the parliamentary group).

History. The party emerged during 1989 largely as the personal following of Drašković, a charismatic figure who made his name as a writer and poet of a highly emotional and nationalistic colour.

Organization. The SMR is represented in the majority of the republic's communes, and also has branches in other republics of Yugoslavia as well as among the Serb diaspora abroad. The extent of this network is unknown, but is certainly large. The party secured the election of 19 members to the republican Assembly in the elections of 1990.

Programme. The SMR is a highly vocal advocate of the "Great Serb" ideal. It is hard to distinguish it on a policy basis from the SDP, with the exception of the greater specificity with which it spells out demands for the maintenance of what it considers to be the historic rights of the Serb people, and the methods by which these are to be secured. If Slovenia and Croatia do secede from the federation, large areas of the latter which are considered to be either "historically" Serbian, or which are now inhabited by a majority of Serbs, should remain with Serbia (i.e. the rest of Yugoslavia). A plan for the "cantonization" of Bosnia and Hercegovina is advanced. The party demands the restoration of the monarchy, the defence of the cyrillic script and other symbols of the Serbian past. Its programme includes the consolidation of Serbian domination in Kosovo (by various means, including the massive ejection of Albanians) and in Macedonia. Anti-Islamic and Anti-Papal invective is prominent.

Affiliations. Central member of the ASDO.

YUGOSLAVIA

Socialist Party of Serbia (SPS)
Socijalistička Partija Srbije (SPS)

Contact. Petar Škundrić (g.s.)

Address. Bulevar Lenjina 6, 11000, Belgrade.

Telephone. (011) 627–084.

Foundation. July 16–17, 1990.

Membership. Claims 350,000.

Leadership. Slobodan Milošević (pres. of the republic of Serbia); Mihailo Marković (vice-pres. of republic). Since the party is the governing party of the republic all ministers are party nominees.

History. The SPS is a renamed "League of Communists of Serbia", which as the Communist Party of Serbia has been in existence at least since the war.

Organization. The party is effectively organized at local and municipal levels throughout the republic. It has massive real estate and other resources. It also continues to exercise the kinds of informal control of other organizations — especially the press — which have been associated with Communist Party practice for a long time. With 194 of the 250 members of the republican Assembly, the SPS exercises an effectively unchallenged control over the legislative process within the republic.

Programme. While acknowledging the importance of its links with the Communist movement in the past, the programme of the SPS stresses that this is not "given forever, and must be constantly subjected to critical re-examination". In this respect, it emphasizes the importance of the democratic electoral process, and the independence of the press and the judiciary. The party advocates a "democratic socialism", which excludes racial, religious or national hatred, and indicates its willingness to co-operate with other groups of a "left orientation". While giving place to the need to create markets for all factors of production, it sees there being a continuing role for the state in the economy, is opposed to unregulated "enrichment" and privatization, and advocates solidarity, participation and the defence of the system of social security. Although emphasizing its opposition to the idea that the Autonomous Provinces in Serbia could ever be states, it advocates a new constitution which would involve the setting up of other such provinces throughout Yugoslavia. The significance of this proposal is illuminated by the claim that "the party will constantly follow the living conditions and development of those parts of the Serbian people in other republics and abroad . . .".

Affiliations. The extent to which real co-operation between former republican organizations of the LCY is sustained under present circumstances is unknown.

In addition to these parties with established electoral success, five others merit detailed mention, either because of the size of their following or their impact on political debate.

Associated Serbian Democratic Opposition (ASDO)
Udružena Srpska Demokratska Opozicija (USDO)

Not strictly a party, but a loose association of four centre-right opposition parties within Serbia, which may evolve into a closer association through merger. The group includes (centrally) the SMR of Vuk Drašković, but also the the New Democracy (led by Dušan Mihailović), the Serbian Liberal Party (led by Nikola Milošević) and the Democratic Forum. Launched at a press conference on May 23 1991, it appears to be of growing importance, although no concrete data are available regarding its location and internal organization.

League of Communists — Movement for Yugoslavia (LC-MY)
Savez Komunista — Pokret za Jugoslaviju (SK-PJ)

This group, often known as the "party of the generals" is a fragment of the former LCY which is devoted to a relatively hard-line communism linked to a strong affirmation of the integrity of the 1974 constitution. If and when necessary, these aims are to be furthered by the appropriate use of military force. It is reputed to be centred around a number of mainly retired senior officers (especially former defence chief Admiral Branko Mamula) and the have the backing of a substantial section of the Veterans' Association. The extent to which it can be regarded as a "party", and not an informal clique, is unclear, as it is not registered with the authorities in Belgrade. Recognition of its significance is based upon the frequency with which its existence has been cited since the elections as clear evidence of the active political aspirations of the military and the continuing likelihood of a military coup. Why the military should need such an outfit if they do in fact have such aspirations is never made clear.

New Democracy-Movement for Serbia (ND)
Nova Demokratija-Pokret za Srbiju (ND)

The party is the legal heir of the former official Socialist Youth Organization in Serbia. Led by Dušan Mihajlović. Participates in the ASDO. Registered in New Belgrade.

Serbian Liberal Party (SLP)
Srpska Liberalna Stranka (SLS)

No indication that this is associated with other Liberal groups elsewhere in the federation. A newly founded group believed to be quite distinct from the LP. Led by Dr Nikola Milošević and Dr Kosta Čavoški. Participates in the ASDO.

Serbian Radical Party (SRP)
Srpska Radikalna Stranka (SRS)

NB To be distinguished from the NRP, see below.

Contact. Vojislav Šešelj (pres.)

YUGOSLAVIA

Address. Milutina Bojića 4, 11000 Belgrade.

Telephone. (011) 332–852.

Foundation. January 1990.

Membership. Claims 25,000 members of the party and 15,000 members of its paramilitary četnik movement.

Leadership. See "Contact".

Organization. The relationship between the party and the armed units is unclear. Successfully contested a by-election to the Serbian Assembly in June 1991. The majority of its efforts appear to be devoted to extra-parliamentary action. The organization is very heavily centred upon the person of its "leader" (*vodj*) — Šešelj — in the classic fascist manner.

Programme. The SRP is among the most vociferous and aggressive advocates of a "Great Serbia" — which its literature indicates is intended to encompass all of the Yugoslav federation without Slovenia. All other policy considerations are either subordinated to or eclipsed by that goal. The movement is known to be engaged in terrorism and arms-running on a large scale.

The following minor parties either contested the elections of 1990 or have appeared since then: Alliance of All Serbs of the World — AASW (*Savez Svih Srba Sveta* — SSSS; note the way in which two parties have chosen to play on the monogram included in the Serbian coat of arms; registered in Belgrade); All-Nation Democratic Front of Vojvodina — ANDFV (Serbo-Croat title not confirmed; registered in Novi-Sad); All-Serbian National Movement — ASNM (Serbo-Croat title not confirmed; registered in Novi-Sad); Belgraders' Party — BP (Serbo-Croat title not confirmed; registered in Belgrade); Big Rock 'n Roll Party (the Yugoslav equivalent of "Screaming Lord" Sutch! registered in Belgrade); Communist Party of Yugoslavia — Party of Freedom — CPY-PF (*Komunistička Partija Jugoslavije* — *Partija Slobode* — KPJ-PS; registered in Belgrade); Democratic Forum — DF (*Demokratski Forum* — DF; participates in the ASDO; registered in Belgrade); Democratic Party — DP (*Davidović-Grol* — DS (D-G): *Demokratska Stranka* (*Davidović-Grol*) — DS (D-G); the reference here is to the Democratic Party of pre-war years, which was allowed to function briefly after the war in the "popular front" period; registered in Belgrade); Democratic Party of Liberty — DPL (*Demokratska Stranka Slobode* — DSS; registered in Belgrade); Democratic Political Party of Romanies of Kragujevac — DPPRK (*Demokratska Politička Partija Roma Kragujevca* — DPPRK; registered in Kragujevac); Democratic Union of Bulgarians in Yugoslavia — DUBY (vernacular title not confirmed; registered in Niš); Democratic Women's Movement — DWM (Serbo-Croat title not confirmed; registered in Kragujevac); Green Party — GS (*Zelena Stranka* — ZS; sometimes also referred to as the "Ecological Party"; it is not known to what extent this may be linked with other Green organizations elsewhere in the federation; registered in Belgrade); Independent Political Community — IPC (*Samostalna Politička Zajednica* — SPZ; a small business party; registered in Belgrade); League for Pančevo — Party for Moderate Progress — LP-PMP (Serbo-Croat title not confirmed; registered in Pančevo); League of Social Democrats of Vojvodina — LSDV (Serbo-Croat title not confirmed; registered in Novi Sad); Liberal Party — SLP (*Liberalna Stranka* — LS; no indication that this is associated with other Liberal groups elsewhere in the federation; believed to be quite distinct from the SLP; registered in Valjevo); Movement for the Protection of Human Rights in Yugoslavia — MPHRY (*Pokret za Zaštitu Ljudskih Prava u Jugoslaviji* — PZLjPJ; registered in Belgrade); Movement for the Unification of Serbia and Montenegro — MUSM (*Pokret za Ujedinjenje Srbije i Crne Gore* — PUSCG; registered in Belgrade); National Radical Party — NRP (*Narodna Radikalna Stranka* — NRS; claims to be the direct inheritor of the mantle of the party of Nikola Pašić, from before the war; registered in Belgrade); Old Radical Party — ORP (*Stara Radikalna Stranka* — SRS; registered in Belgrade); Party of Independent Businessmen — PIB (Serbo-Croat title not confirmed; registered in Belgrade); Party of Independent Democrats of Serbia — PIDS (Serbo-Croat title not confirmed; registered in Niš); Party of National Concord — PNC (*Stranka Narodnog Dogovora* — SND; registered in Belgrade); Party of Social Justice — PSJ (*Stranka Socijalne Pravde* — SSP; registered in Belgrade); Peasant Labour Party of Serbia — PLPS — (Serbo-Croat title not confirmed; registered in Belgrade); People's Independent Party of Vlahs — PIPV (Serbo-Croat title not confirmed; registered in Kladovo); People's Party — PP (*Narodna Stranka* — NS; registered in Novi Sad); Republican Party — RP (*Republikanska Stranka* — RS; registered in Arandjelovac); School Youth Party of Serbia — SYPS (Serbo-Croat title not confirmed; registered in Kragujevac); Serbian National Revival — SNR (*Srpska Narodna Obnova* — SNO; not to be confused with the SMR of Drašković; registered in Nova Pazova); Serbian Party of St Sava — SPSS (*Srpska Svetosavska Stranka* — SSSS; registered in Belgrade); Serbian Royalist Block — SRB (Serbo-Croat title not confirmed; registered in Belgrade); Social-Democratic Party of Romanies in Serbia — SDPRS (*Socijaldemokratska Stranka Roma u Srbiji* — SDSRS; registered in Belgrade); Social-Democratic Party of Yugoslavia — SDPY (*Socijaldemokratska Partija Jugoslavije* — SDPJ; not to be confused with the YSDP — see below; registered in Belgrade); Socialist Party of Yugoslavia — SPY (*Socijalistička Stranka Jugoslavije* — SSJ; registered in Belgrade); Užice Movement — UM (Serbo-Croat title not confirmed; registered in Belgrade); Women's Party — WP (Serbo-Croat title not confirmed; registerd in Belgrade); Workers' Party of Yugoslavia — WPY (*Radnička Partija Jugoslavije* — RPJ; registered in Belgrade); Yugoslav Socialist Democratic Party — (YSDP (*Jugoslavenska Socijalistička Demokratska Stranka* — JSDS (not to be confused with the SDPY — see above; registered in Belgrade).

KOSOVO (former Autonomous Province)

Political conditions in the former Autonomous Province of Kosovo are very different from those which obtain elsewhere in the Republic. Electoral success is no guide to political significance, since the Albanian parties boycotted the electoral process. Milošević's SPS completely dominated the electoral process there, and no single opposition candidate was returned from a constituency in the province. No candidate of the major opposition party, the SMR, survived into the second round. The principal Serb parties are reviewed above. Among the locally based parties it is possible to make an informed distinction between those groups which are relatively more important or interesting.

Albanian Christian-Democratic Party (ACDP)
Partia Shqiptare Demokristiane (PSD)

Founded September 1990. Estimated to have 100,000 members. Paradoxically most of these are believed to be Muslims, although the party was founded specifically among the Catholics of Peć. Its policy stance tends towards the internationalization of the Kosovo problem, although the extent to which it has real links with Christian-Democrat organizations elsewhere is unknown.

"Božur"

This is nominally a cultural association of Serbs rather than a party, but it has considerable political impact as a vehicle for Serb nationalism. It is based in Kosovo Polje. Its president is Bogdan Kecman. Very closely linked to Milošević and the SPS.

YUGOSLAVIA

Democratic League of Kosovo (DLK)
Lidhja Demokratike e Kosovës (LDK)

Contact. Isuf Buxhovi (g.s.)

Address. Beogradska bb., 38000, Priština.

Telephone. (038) 24–234.

Foundation. December 1989.

Membership. Claims 700,000 in Kosovo alone, with up to one million including branches elsewhere.

Leadership. Ibrahim Rugova (pres.)

History. Following the formation of AYDI in 1989 as a forum for more general democratic discussion in Yugoslavia, a Council for Civil Rights was formed in Kosovo. This was a direct response both to the immediate past history of violent protest against Serb rule in the province, and to the prospect of a changed Serbian constitution, abolishing the Autonomous Provinces. The League rapidly emerged as the principal political expression of Kosovo Albanians.

Organization. Although primarily based in Kosovo, the League has a total of 28 branches, some of which are in other republics.

Programme. The DLK identifies the basic cause of the problem of Kosovo as economic backwardness, and proposes that the most effective way out of this is via the creation of a market economy. The League would accept either a federal or confederal solution to the constitutional problems of Yugoslavia (i.e. it does not espouse Albanian separatism). Nevertheless, it "affirms the individuality of Kosovo as a unit" — in other words, is opposed to the abolition of the Autonomous Provinces in Serbia. The programme is, however, unspecific as to whether recognition of that "individuality" demands *republican* status. It advocates multi-party democracy with the full equality of all citizens before the law, the abolition of restrictions on the press and other civil rights, and the abandonment of all forms of "nationalistic and bureaucratic manipulation of the nationality problem", believing that it is possible for all nationalities resident in Kosovo to live together peaceably.

Affiliations. It is known that the League has extensive links with the Albanian diaspora in Western Europe (especially Switzerland) and the USA. These are a vitally important source of funding. It is believed that there are strong links with political groups in the republic of Albania, but nothing definite is known about the nature of these or their significance.

Parliamentary Party of Kosovo (PPK)
Recently changed to **Liberal Party of Kosovo (LPK)**
Partia Parlamentare e Kosovës

Founded summer 1990. Led by Veton Surroi (pres.). Publishes its own paper, *Koha* (Time). Contact address, Sunčani Breg, Lamela 10, Priština. Tel. (038) 49–236 or

43–999. Described as a party of the "modern European centre", it has links with Liberal organizations elsewhere in Yugoslavia.

Serbian Democratic Forum of Kosovo and Metohija (SDF)
Srpski Demokratski Forum Kosova i Metohije (SDF)

This organization was set up after the 1990 elections, specifically in order to counter the political monopolization of the region by the SPS. Although like "Božur" it describes itself as "an independent and non-party association", it specifically distinguishes itself from "Božur", which it accuses of allowing responsibility to be taken out of the hands of local people by Belgrade. SDF was founded by a group of Priština intellectuals, led by Dušan Čelić.

Social-Democratic Party (SDP)
Partia Socialdemokrate (PSD)

Led by Shkëlzen Maliqi. The party insists that it is not a specifically Albanian organization. It is not known to what extent it is linked with other social-democratic groups elsewhere in Yugoslavia. Contact address, Miladin Popović 27, Priština. Tel. (038) 35–678. Founded January–February, 1990. A group of western-oriented intellectuals provides its core. Maliqi in particular is known as a moderate and effective communicator of the Albanian case outside of Kosovo.

Among the less significant or less well-reported political organizations in the province are the following: Albanian Democratic Unification Party — ADUP (*Partia e Bashkimit Demokratik Shqiptar* — PBDS; founded May 1991); Democratic Community of Croats in Kosovo and Metohija — DCCKM (Serbo-Croat title unconfirmed; registered in Janjevo); Democratic League of Turks — DLT (*Demokratski Savez Turaka* — DST; registered in Prizren); Independent Democratic Association — IDA (*Nezavisno Demokratsko Udruženje* — NDU; Albanian title unknown; believed to be a principally Albanian party, although this is not recognized in its programme; registered in Preševo); National Unity Party — NUP (*Partia Unitetit Kombëtar* — PUK; founded May 1991); Peasant Party of Kosovo — PPK (*Partia Fshatare e Kosovës* — PFK; founded January–February, 1990); Republican Party of Kosovo — RPK (*Partia Republikane e Kosovës* — RPK; founded May 1991).

SLOVENIA

Historically, Slovene settlement was dispersed over four parts of the Austrian monarchy — Styria, Carniola and Carinthia and Gorizia. Following the dismemberment of the Austro-Hungarian monarchy in 1918, the first two of these, and southern Carinthia, joined the newly founded Kingdom of Serbs Croats and Slovenes (renamed Yugoslavia in 1929), together with small Slovene-speaking parts of Hungary — Prekmurje and

Medjugurje). Partly because of their linguistic identity, the Slovenes within Yugoslavia were able to develop an appreciable degree of *de facto* autonomy between the wars. The division of Yugoslavia after the Axis invasion of 1941 awarded Carinthia to Italy, Styria was absorbed into the German Reich, and the eastern territories returned to Hungary. In the peace settlement of 1945 a Slovene republic was established within the reconstituted Yugoslavia. To the areas which were part of the 1918 settlement were added eastern Gorizia. Areas including large numbers of Slovene speakers remained outside of Yugoslavia in western Gorizia — including Trieste — and (following a referendum) northern Carinthia. With a surface area of 20,251 sq km the Republic of Slovenia is the fifth largest of the six republics of the federation (7.9 per cent of the total). The most numerous ethnic group in the republic are the Slovenes, with 89 per cent of the total, followed by the Croats, with 3.2 per cent, and the Serbs, with 2.6 per cent. There is a small but locally significant minority of Magyars in the far north-western (Prekmurje) area, although both these and the Italians in the west have declined steadily over the postwar period.

In Slovenia the elections produced an interesting and potentially important contradiction. In the first round, on April 8, the presidential contest was fought by four candidates (Milan Kučan for the Communists, 44.5 per cent; Jože Pučnik for DEMOS, 26.2 per cent; Josip Kramberger, a wealthy and idiosyncratic ex-patriot competing on an independent ticket, 18.9 per cent and Marko Demsar, for the Liberal Democrats, 10.5 per cent. The second round play-off between Kučan and Pučnik, on April 22, gave the victory to Kučan and the Party of Democratic Reform (58.4 per cent against 41.7 per cent). Slovenia thus produced a communist president elected in a free and open ballot.

In the elections to the Assembly itself, however, things turned out somewhat differently. The DEMOS coalition of six parties, grouped around the joining of forces of the Christian Democrats and the Slovene Peasant League, clearly held a dominant position in all three chambers. It was thought likely from the outset, however, that this grouping would be unstable; and within a year the divisions within its ranks had become sufficiently acute for its members to be talking openly of the inevitability of its demise. It had served its purpose, and was coming to be perceived as a burden by its more ambitious and successful partners. It was only by virtue of the coalition, however, that its members were able to participate in government. Although the communist PDR did not secure the largest number of representatives of any individual party in the Assembly as a whole, with 14 seats they were the principal force in the Socio-Political Chamber; but overall (in all three chambers) they were out-performed by their former youth organization, the Liberal Democratic Party. Both of these parties were more strongly represented than any of the separate components of the DEMOS group.

The military takeover in Slovenia, following its declaration of independence on June 26, 1991, clearly introduced a new factor into Slovene politics. The outcome of this can not be forseen at the time of writing. Whatever the political future for the republic, however, as in Macedonia a variety of possible scenarios can be deduced from the election results alone, including the possibility of a future return to socialist-led elected government.

Table 8: Elections of April 1990 to the Slovene Assembly

Parties in the Social-Political Chamber	(80 seats)
Party of Democratic Reform (LCS)	14
Liberal Democratic Party	12
Slovene Christian Democrats	11[1]
Slovene Peasant League	11[1]
Slovene Democratic League	8[1]
Greens of Slovenia	8[1]
Social Democratic League	6[1]
Socialist Party	5
Slovene League of Craftsmen	3[1]
Italian and Magyar national minorities[2]	2

Parties in the Chamber of Associated Labour	(80 seats)
DEMOS Coalition	29
Liberal Democratic Party	9
Slovene Trade Unions	7
Slovene Chamber of Trade	7
Party of Democratic Reform (LCS)	5
Socialist Party	3
Other individual organizations, enterprises incl. the Yugoslav National Army	20

Parties in the Chamber of Municipalities	(80 seats)
DEMOS Coalition	51
Liberal Democratic Party	16
Party of Democratic Reform (LCS)	5
Socialist Party	5
Italian and Magyar national minorities[2]	2
Independent	1

[1] Member of the DEMOS Coalition.
[2] Seats reserved for candidates representing these groups.

Source: Tanjug, *Stranke u Jugoslaviji*, Belgrade, 1990, p. 241.

YUGOSLAVIA

Directory of Parties (Slovenia)

Greens of Slovenia (GS)
Zeleni Slovenije (ZS)

Contact. Prof. Petar Jamnikar (pres. of the executive committee)

Address. Komenskega 11, 61000, Ljubljana.

Telephone. (061) 312–368; *Fax.* (061) 311–629.

Foundation. In its present form, June 11, 1989.

Membership. ca. 2,000.

Leadership. Bojan Brumen (pres.); Dušan Plut (member of republican presidency); Vane Gosnik (vice-pres. of the Assembly); Leo Seserko, Petar Tancig and Miha Jazbinšek all have ministerial posts.

History. The Greens have a 20-year history in Slovenia of activity in informal, non-political groups directed to specific environmental issues, such as the nuclear plant at Krško. The movement acquired a more connected form during the middle and late '80s. The party was created with the change of the law.

Organization. The movement still has a strong sense of local identity. There are groups in about 40 of Slovenia's 65 communes; each is represented in the party's assembly. The Greens have eight members in the republican Assembly.

Programme. Although ostensibly an environmental party, a surprising amount of its literature stresses the secession of Slovenia from the federation. The link between "Green" concerns and strident nationalism is the issue of demilitarization. The party is strongly pacifist. This point makes intelligible its active role within DEMOS, as does the emphasis in its economic policy on the stimulation of smaller businesses and the development of agriculture. The programme of the Greens probably contains the greatest number of specific legislative proposals of any of the parties, covering economic social security and welfare and cultural life. The general tone of its approach is highly collectivistic and interventionist.

Affiliations. Participates in DEMOS. There are loose links with other Green groups in other Yugoslav republics, and indeed in other European countries.

Liberal Democratic Party (LDP)
Liberalna Demokratična Stranka (LDS)
Formerly **ZSMS-Liberalna Stranka**

NB Not to be confused with the Liberal Party

Contact. Roman Lavtar (sec.)

Address. Dalmatinova 4, 61000, Ljubljana.

Telephone. (061) 312–659.

Foundation. Nov. 10 1990.

Membership. 8–9,000.

Leadership. Jožef Školč (pres.); prominent in the leadership group (presidential candidate in 1990) is Marko Demsar.

History. The party emerged from the former official Communist youth organization, the Federation of Socialist Youth of Slovenia. The party literature makes deferential reference to the pre-war Liberal Party, but there is no evidence of a direct relationship. In effect it has been an independent party with respect to the LCS for some time, and certainly since the growth of interest in "civil society" in the early 1980s. A key event in the crystallization of that distinctive status was the case of the "Ljubljana 4" in 1988.

Organization. A key organizational feature of the LDP is its use of non-party expert "think tanks" in relation to policy formation. A strong support for regionalism is reflected in party organization.

Programme. The party supports the "essential liberal values" of individual rights and liberties. It proposes constitutional reform, introducing regional government and strengthening local government. It advocates demilitarization and the reduction of the coercive power of the state. Equality of opportunity is to be pursued at a variety of levels, especially gender. Its most specific proposals relate to the creation of a market economy, and the details of the process by which privatization should be undertaken. The Liberal Democrats are explicitly and staunchly secular.

Affiliations. There is no formal affiliation, but the Liberal Democrats do have links with the Hungarian FIDESZ, the Danish Radical Party and with several English New Right intellectuals.

Liberal Party (LP)
Liberalna Stranka (LS)
Formerly **Slovenačka Zanatska Stranka.**

NB Not to be confused with the Liberal Democratic Party

Contact. Franc Golija, (pres.)

Address. Poštna ulica 3, Kranj.

Telephone. (061) 22–985.

Foundation. Jan. 22, 1990.

Membership. ca. 800.

Leadership. See "Contact".

Organization. Branches in 16 communes in the republic, with three representatives elected to the Assembly in the elections of 1990.

Programme. In programmatic terms there appears to be little to distinguish the Liberals from the Liberal Democrats. Both emphasize individual liberty, the rule of law and the primary importance of the market within economic life. The more significant distinguishing factors are the small business social base of the Liberals, and the metropolitian orientation of the Liberal Democrats.

Party of Democratic Renewal (PDR)
Stranka Demokratične Prenove (SDP)

The party was formerly known as the ZKS-SDP, indicating its origins in the former League of Communists of Slovenia — *Zveza Komunista Slovenije*.

Contact. Prof. Sonja Lokar.

Address. Tomšičeva 5, 61000, Ljubljana.

Telephone. (061) 215–916.

Foundation. In its present form, Feb. 7, 1990.

Membership. 30,000 after crash from its established status. Now growing again.

Leadership. Dr Ciril Ribičič (pres.); Milan Kučan was elected to the republican presidency on the party ticket; Dr Matjaž Kmecl is a member of the collective presidency. Although the party is not in the DEMOS coalition, Dr Franc Bucer, Jožica Pher, Miha Tomšič and Franc Godesa all have junior government posts.

History. The new orientation of Slovene Communists dates from around 1986, especially the election of Kučan to the party leadership. Figures such as Ribičič still remain from the past, but on the whole the party has striven to create a new image, the success of which is reflected in its recent recovery of membership.

Organization. The party retains much of the old structure — and property — of the former LCS. Has branches in all communes and most neighbourhoods. Has developed a bimodal structure of support, with strength among the manual workers and professional and managerial groups. Remains a substantial electoral force, with 24 seats in the various chambers of the Assembly.

Programme. The Slovene communists have a long history of the advocacy of both internal party democracy and wider political pluralism. The party presents itself as a party of reconciliation between diverse social interests, seeing it as especially important to recognize and deal with the divisions remaining from the wartime period. In this respect it continues the socialist tradition of solidarity. It describes itself as "Eurocommunist" and as embodying the "left current of neoliberalism". Regarding the constitutional position of Slovenia, it declared itself in favour of a continuing "confederal" association with Yugoslavia. Probably the only Yugoslav party to use the term "stagflation" in its manifesto! The greater part of its specific proposals are concerned with the enhancement of social security and welfare legislation — the creation of a Slovene welfare state.

Affiliations. It is not known to what extent former republican organizations of the League of Communists might still retain active links.

Slovene Christian Democrats (SCD)
Slovenska Krščanski Demokrati (SKD)
Formerly **Slovensko Krščansko Socialno Gibanje**

Contact. Peter Reberc (g.s.)

Address. Beethovnova 4, 61000, Ljubljana.

Telephone. (061) 222–522 or 210–135; *Fax.* (061) 210–076.

Foundation. March 10, 1989.

Membership. ca. 40,500 members, with ca. 4,000 in its youth movement.

Leadership. Alojz Peterle (pres. of party and prime minister of the republic); Franc Miklavčič (vice-pres.); Isidor Rejc (pres. of Council); Ivan Bizjak (pres. of Chamber of Municipalities); five other representatives have ministerial positions in the republican government.

History. Claims links to the pre-war Ljudska Stranka, but these appear to be largely sentimental. Christian Democracy does not have a strong tradition in Slovenia. The movement is largely the creation of non-clerical Catholic intellectuals. Although the movement was founded in March, it was not registered as a party until November 1989.

Organization. Has a network of branches in just about every commune. There are 12 local mayors from the party. With 11 representatives in the Assembly, the party is the largest member of DEMOS.

Programme. Central concerns of the Christian Democrats are the protection of human and civil rights, the defence of the "full sovereignty of Slovenia", and the protection of Slovene minorities elsewhere. "Moral renewal" is seen as necessary, which is to be achieved through legislation relating to the family as well as through the building of parliamentary democracy. Advocates a market economy, but with an "ecological and social filter". Among its economic concerns the party lists the problems of regional under-development within the republic.

Slovene Democratic League (SDL)
Slovenska Demokratična Zveza (SDZ)

Contact. Tone Peršak (acting sec.)

Address. Komenskega 11, 61000, Ljubljana.

Telephone. (061) 312–548 or 314–538; *Fax.* (061) 305–340 or 314–538.

Foundation. Jan. 11, 1989, although not registered until March 1990.

Membership. In excess of 4,000.

Leadership. Dimitrij Rupel (pres. of the party and foreign minister of the republic); Prof. Jože Mencinger was vice-pres. of the government before resigning over economic policy in May 1991; Janez Janša, Igor Bavčar and Rajko Pirnat have ministerial positions.

History. The idea of the League was launched by the sociologist Rupel at a meeting of cultural workers on June 2, 1988. Initially it was seen as a loose association of intellectuals rather than a party, and still tends to be dominated by them, together with members of the business and professional élite.

Organization. Well represented in 52 of the 65 communes of the republic. The leadership is aware of the long gap which separates the local activist from the party centre, and is working towards the creation of a regional structure. Note the importance of MLIN (*Mlada Inicijativa*), its youth organization, which is very active as a forum for ideas. Has six representatives in the Assembly.

Programme. The party claims to articulate the "political interests of the Slovene people", which include the creation of an independent political system — it is probably the most outspokenly separatist of the principal parties. The enhancement of the political self-consciousness of Slovenes and the building of a specifically Slovene "system" are given the highest priority, but without particular indication of the legislative form which this programme might take. Slovenes who have migrated overseas are to be encouraged to take an active part in the building of the new order.

Affiliations. A member of the DEMOS coalition.

Slovene Peasant League (SPL)
Slovenska Kmečka Zveza (SKZ)

Contact. Ivan Oman (pres.)

Address. Sternenova 8, 61000, Ljubljana.

Telephone. (061) 551–107.

Foundation. Registered Jan. 25, 1990, but founded earlier.

Membership. Claims 33,000.

Leadership. See. "Contact".

History. The League was founded as a non-political association, serving the interests of cultivators, on May 12, 1988. As such it is one of the oldest of the postwar political organizations in Yugoslavia.

Organization. Branches in most rural communes of the republic. The League also has an associated youth organization. Eleven members represent the SPL in the republican Assembly.

Programme. The party advocates the building of the family enterprise as "the most effective and rational form of economic activity in agriculture". This is to be supported by a co-operative movement and a favourable taxation regime. Formerly expropriated land is to be reprivatized. A competitive market economy is to be established (concern is expressed about the dangers of monopoly); questions of regional development are recognized as important, as is the reorganization of local government. The social security system should be reorganized. The educational system should not be "ideologically burdened". Military service should be shortened. The programme is one of the most concrete of all those proposed by Slovene parties.

Affiliations. Participates in DEMOS.

Social-Democratic Party of Slovenia (SDPS)
Socialdemokratična Stranka Slovenije (SDSS)

Contact. Erik Modic (g.s.)

Address. Komenskega 11, 61000, Ljubljana.

Telephone. (061) 311–086; *Fax.* (061) 313–065.

Foundation. Feb. 16, 1989.

Membership. ca. 5,000.

Leadership. Jože Pučnik (pres., also pres. of DEMOS); Vitograd Pukl, (vice-pres. of the Assembly); Dr Katija Boh has a ministerial post.

History. Emerged from the "Litostroj" factory, in February 1987, and grew within the "Socialist Alliance", from which it separated two years later. Largely the inspiration of Franc Tomšič, who has now left to set up an independent Trade Union.

Organization. Has a branch organization throughout Slovenia. Participates in DEMOS, and would be the principal loser should that organization collapse. Has six representatives in the republican Assembly.

Programme. The party presents itself as a "social-democratic party in the traditions of European democracy and the social state". Its centrally expressed concerns are the overcoming of social and economic inequalities, and in this respect it looks for an enhanced democratization within the economy as well as in the creation of parliamentary forms. The manifesto makes much of the historical links to the Austro-marxists. The Social Democrats claim to be the only genuinely working class party. Many outsiders see their specifically class concerns as overlaid in practice by an aggressive populist nationalism.

Affiliations. Applied to join the Socialist International, but was turned down as being too nationalistic.

Socialist Party of Slovenia (SSS)
Socialistična Stranka Slovenije (SSS)

Contact. Prof. Primož Hainz (sec.)

Address. Komenskega 11, 61000, Ljubljana.

Telephone. (061) 312–221; *Fax.* (061) 313–065.

Foundation. June 9, 1990.

Membership. 39,000.

Leadership. Viktor Žakelj (pres.); Ciril Zlobec represents the party within the republic's collective presidency.

History. The party grew out of the former "Socialist Alliance", and traces its links with former communist organizations back to 1911. The leadership are a group of intellectuals who felt the full weight of the "leaden years" following the fall of Kavčič. The beginnings of party independence are traced back to 1986.

YUGOSLAVIA

Organization. The party has inherited a good deal of the apparatus and property of the former SA. There are branches in 58 of the republic's 65 communes. The party holds 10 presidencies of communes, and returned 10 members in the Assembly elections of April 1990.

Programme. The Socialists see "a system of pluralist parliamentary democracy as the basis for a civilized standard of living": parliamentary democracy is necessarily linked to the development of a welfare state. Political reform must go beyond the forms of party pluralism and include genuine protection of human and civil rights. The Socialists participate in the general consensus about the need for an "independent and sovereign" Slovenia. The party is opposed to "real-socialist egalitarianism", and in favour of equality of opportunity. There must be room for private initiative and innovation in a mixed economy.

Affiliations. Informal links are reported both with socialist groups in Croatia, and with Italian and Austrian groups.

The following minor parties were registered at the time of the elections of 1990.

Democratic League of Kosovo (DLK)
Lidhja Demokratike e Kosovës (LDK)

This is a branch of the Albanian organization based in Kosovo, and reported in full in the Section on Serbia.

Grey Panthers — Pensioners' Party of Slovenia (GP)
Sijedi Panteri — Stranka Upokjencev Slovenije (SP)

Was associated with DEMOS at the time of the election, but did not present its own candidates, urging voters to support the DEMOS coalition. In fact it is a pressure group for pensioners' interests. Claims links with the American organization of the same name, and with groups in Switzerland and Austria. Registered in Maribor.

Movement for a Culture of Peace and Non-violence (MCPN)
Gibanje za Kulturu Mira i Nenasilja (GKMN)

Specifically insists that it is a movement and not a party. Did not seek election in April 1990, but is concerned to promote awareness of the possibility of non-violent solutions to political issues. Its leader, Marko Hren, is a well-known and vocal figure in Slovene politics. Registered in Ljubljana.

Party of Citizens' Equality (PCE)
Stranka za Enakopravnost Občanov (SEO)

Registered in Ljubljana. Although it claimed a membership of 20,000 at the time of the election, it secured no places in the Assembly.

Progressive People's Party of the Centre (PPPC)

No confirmed Slovene title. A specifically anti-clerical party. Registered in Ljubljana.

Slovene Craftsmen's and Tradesmen's Party (LCTP)
Slovenska Obrinopodjetniška Stranka (SOS)

Not to be confused with the former name of the Liberal Party. Did not contest the elections of April 1990, but has one representative in the Chamber of Associated Labour. Has support in several areas at municipal level.

Contact. Emil Kandrič.

Address. Linhartova 13, 61000, Ljubljana.

INDEX

A

A Few Words 56
AB Beszelo kft 138
Abdic Fikret 317
Abramovic Zoran 328
Abramski Kazimierz 217
Action Alliance United Left 104, 126
Adamec Ladislav 57
Adevarul 246
Adler Helga 122
Adzharov Elisaveta 37
Adzharov Konstantin 37
Agardi Wittner Maria 149
Agrarian Alliance (ASZ) 137, 153
Agrarian Banner 29
Agrarian Democratic Party of Romania 226
Agrarian Progress 7
Agrarian Reform Circles Movement 137
Agrarian Youth League 28
Agraszovetseg (ASZ) 137
Agreement for Democracy and Pluralism 190
Agreement for Poland 196
Agreement Guaranteeing a Peaceful Transition to Democratic Society 25
Agreement of the Working People 201
Agro-industrial Association Novomoskovskoe 272
Akhmedkady A. 272
Aksyuchits V. 287
Alarm Bell 268
Albania 307, 308, 331, 332, 344, 357
Albanian Academy of Sciences 8
Albanian Agrarian Party (AAP) 1, 3, 5, 6, 7
Albanian Christian-Democratic Party (ACDP) 331, 356
Albanian Communist Party (ACP) 13
Albanian Democratic Front (ADF) 4, 5, 6, 8
Albanian Democratic Party (ADP) 1, 2, 3, 4, 6, 7, 8, 9, 11, 12, 14, 15
Albanian Democratic Unification Party (ADUP) 358
Albanian Ecology Party (AEP) 3, 5, 10
Albanian National Unity Party (ANUP) 3, 10, 11, 358
Albanian Party of Democratic Prosperity (APDP) 9, 309, 332
Albanian Party of Labour (APL) 1, 2, 3, 4, 5, 6, 7, 8, 9, 16, 17, 18

Albanian People's Army (APA) 14
Albanian Republican Party (ARP) 1, 3, 5, 7, 11
Albanian Socialist Party (ASP) 1, 2, 3, 7, 12, 13, 14, 15
Albanian Workers' Party (AWP) 1, 2, 3, 4, 5, 6, 7, 8, 9, 16, 17, 18
Albanians 299, 332, 334, 335, 339, 341, 344, 345, 350
Albanska Demokrscanska Stranka (ADS) 331
Aleko Haxhi 16, 17
Alev 51
Alia Ramiz 1, 2, 3, 6, 7, 12, 13, 14, 16
Alianta Muncitoreasca "Libertatea" Anticomunista si Alidema Halil 11
All-Nation Democratic Front of Vojvodina (ANDFV) 355
All-Poland Association of Managers 205
All-Russian Congress of Soviets 251
All-Serbian National Movement (ASNM) 355
All-Union Committee of the Socialist Party 275
Alliance 90 13, 98, 99, 103, 108, 115, 117, 120, 122
Alliance for Democracy Party 226, 227
Alliance for Germany 103, 107, 109, 113, 114
Alliance for the Village and the Countryside 137
Alliance of All Serbs of the World (AASW) 355
Alliance of Christian Democrats 138
Alliance of Farmers and the Countryside 85
Alliance of Free Democrats (AFD) 130, 131, 132, 133, 137, 140, 143, 147, 157
Alliance of Hungarian Political Prisoners 139, 140
Alliance of Hungarian Revolutionary Socialists 140
Alliance of Nature and Society Conservers 140
Alliance of Reform Forces (ARF) 300, 306, 307, 308, 310, 313, 314
Alliance of Reform Forces of Macedonia (ARFM) 333, 334, 338
Alliance of Reform Forces of Montenegro (ARFM) 339, 340, 341, 342
Alliance of Reform Forces of Vojvodina (ARFV) 346, 348
Alliance of Reform Forces of Yugoslavia (ARFY) 346, 347
Alliance of Reform Forces of Yugoslavia for Bosnia and Hercegovina (ARFYBH) 313, 314

Alliance of Reform Forces of Yugoslavia for Croatia (ARFYC) 321, 322
Alliance of the Poor and Defenceless 140
Alliance of Young Democrats (FIDESZ) 130, 131, 132, 133, 138
Allianz fur Deutschland 103
Alternative Forum 51
Alternative Jugendliste (AJL) 103
Alternative Movement of Those Resettled from Aegean, Vardar and Pirin Macedonias 52
Alternative Social-Liberal Party (ASP) 28
Alternative Socialist Association (ASA) 28, 29, 36
Alternative Socialist Organization (ASO) 22, 36
Alternative Socialist Party 50
Alternative Women's Union
Alternative Youth List (AJL) 103
Alternativen Forum 51
Alternativna Sotsialiberlna Partiya 28
Alternativo Sotsialistichesko Obedinenie (ASO) 28, 29
Amanbaev Dzhumgalbek Beksultanovich 283
Ambarev Ivan 32
Ambrus Abdras 164
Ambrus Sandor 159, 160
Ananieva Nora 40
Andonov Jovan 336
Andov Stojan 333, 336
Andras Agoston 347
Andreev Kh. 284
Angelov Dimitar Todorov 37
Anishchenko G. 287
Annus Lembit El'marovich 94
Antall Jozsef 146, 147
Anti-fascist Council for the National Liberation of Yugoslavia (AVNOJ) 296, 315, 341, 352
Antifascista 235
Anti-totalitarian Confederation 246
Antonescu Ioan 240
Apostoli Gaqo 16
Apzhvalga 171
Arbore Variu 246
Arendarski Andrzej 199
Ark Network 126
Armenia 251, 261, 278, 280
Arnandov Dimitur 42
Arnaudov Dimitar 46
Aron Marton Society 141
Asociace socialnich demokratu (ASD) 77, 78
Asociata 21 Decembrie 228
Asociata Tineretului din Romania 232
Asociatia Fostilor Detinuti Politici si Victime Ale Dictaturii 227
Asocitia Luptatorilor Revolutiei din Decembrie 1989, Raniti, Invalizi si Urmasii Eroilor Cazuti 227
Assembly for Democracy 189
Assembly of Deputies 223, 225
Assembly of the Land 287

Associated Serbian Democratic Opposition (ASDO) 352, 354
Association for a Yugoslav Democratic Initiative (AYDI) 301, 304, 319, 343, 347, 557
Association for the Advancement of Democratic Processes (AADP) 343
Association for the Republic — the Republican Party of Czechoslovakia 69, 71
Association of Agrarian Reform Circles 137
Association of Czechoslovak Businessmen 84
Association of Former Political Detainees and Victims of the Dictatorship 227
Association of Former Political Prisoners and Detainees (Albania) 8
Association of Hungarian Humanists 149
Association of Private Farmers 84
Association of Saxon Werewolves 127
Association of Social Democrats 77, 78, 80, 81, 85, 86
Association of the December 1989 Revolution Fighters, Wounded, Invalids and Descendants of the Fallen 227
Association of Working Groups for Employee Politics and Democracy (VAA) 104
Atanasov Georgi 22
Atanasov Petar 47
Atgimimas 173
Atituinea 245
Atmoda 170
Attitude 245
Aurich Eberhard 103
Australia 225
Austria 96, 130, 139, 319, 367
Austrian Empire 67
Austrian Green Party 158
Austro-Hungarian Empire 305
Autonomous Provinces 299
Avramescu Constantin 246
Avramov Georgi 41
Aytos 24
Azerbaidzhan 251, 272, 278, 279, 280
Azi 240

B

Baba maa 94
Babic Milomir 350
Backa 344, 345
Bacskai Sandor 158
Baden-Wurttemberg 124
Baja Ferenc 154
Bajraktari Agim 15
Bak Henryk 210
Bakalov Dimitur 38
Bakalov Zdravko 34
Bakardzhiev Mladenov Yuli 51
Baker James 8
Baki Laszlo 164
Bakowski Krzysztof 216

INDEX

Balasz Artur 209
Balasz Peter 141
Balcerowicz Leszek 178, 179, 198, 203, 209
Balkanization 293, 294
Balkans 2, 6
Ballai Pal 152
Balogh Gabor 141
Baloladali Revizio Prtja 162
Baltic republics 251, 257, 260, 262, 278
Baltiiskoe vremya 170
Banat 344
Bangladesh 2
Banko Mihaly 156
Bankos Andrea 143
Banovics Jozsef 165
Barankovics Foundation 141
Baranski Marian 202
Baranyai Tibor 158
Barczyk Kazimierz 188
Bardhi Hysen 17
Bardhi Mehmet 341
Bardhi Reshat Baba 11
Barka Panajat 15
Barta Boleslav 86
Bartal Ferenc 161
Barthal Ferenc 151
Bartoncik Josef 83
Bartoszyce Roman 183, 189, 208
Bartscher Rainer 104
Bartyzel Jacek 192
Bashkimi i Sindikatave te Paravura Shqiperise (BSPS) 1, 2, 3, 6, 13, 15, 17, 18
Bashkir 269, 285
Bashkurti Isen 15, 17
Battek Rudolf 77, 84, 85
Batiashvili Iraklii 282
Batyansky Janos 156
Baumgart Piotr 214
Bavaria 124
Bavcar Ogor 364
Becher Bernhard 123
Bedros Nae 237
Begari Shkelqin 12
Begovic Zejnel 336
Bek XXI 48
Beki Gabriella 138
Bektashi 11
Belafi Antal jnr. 161
Beljo Ante 323
Belorussia 260, 261, 269, 279, 280
Belorussian Peasant Party 279
Belorussian Popular Front 279
Belorussian Popular Front News 279
Belorussian Social-Democratic Gromada 280
Belvedere camp 180, 181
Bencze Gyorgy B. 143
Benda Vaclav 59, 78
Benedekfi Samuel 152
Benelux 73

Benke Attila 161
Beqiri Iaajet 11
Berecz Janos 155
Berenyi Ferenc 142
Bergmann Pavel 77
Berisha Sali 3, 8, 9
Berisha Tom 330
Berlin House of Representatives 106
Berlin Wall 95, 130
Beron Petar 24
Berzsenyi Laszlo 148
Bessarabia 283
Beszelo 130
Bethlen Istvan 146
Bialoruskie Zjednoczenie Demokratyczne (BZD) 186
Bibrzycki Stefan 204
Bielecki Jan Krzysztof 178, 181, 183, 187, 190, 195, 199
Big Rock 'n Roll Party 355
Bihari Andras 162
Bihari Laszlo 152
Bijelasi 307
Bildea Nicolae 246
Bilewicz Tadeusz 213
Billa Llambo 7
Biosphere Party 166
Bioszfera Part 166
Birlandeanu Alexandru 220, 239
Birlik 292
Bizjak Ivan 364
Blass Petra 117
Blaszczyk Kazimierz 211
Blessing Karlheinz 14
Board of Commissioners 68
Bocian Ryszard 192
Bogachev V. 271
Bogdanovic Vlado 325
Bogicevic Bogic 310
Bognar Ilona 148
Boh Katija 366
Bohdan Dvorak 72
Bohemia 53, 67, 68, 76, 77, 80, 81, 84, 87
Bohlen Manifesto 126
Bohley Barbel 119, 122
Bohm Tatjana 116, 117
Bohme Ibrahim 124, 125
Boldogsag Part 145
Bolshevik Party 251
Boras Franjo 314
Borba 296
Borbely Endre 158
Bordacs Gabor 158
Borner Rainer 122
Boroczky Ervin 159
Borowczyk Czeslaw 212
Borusiewic Bogdan 183
Bosanska Demokratska Stranka (BDS) 319, 331
Bosnia and Hercegovina 9, 299, 302, 303, 305,

307, 309, 313–319, 323, 327, 330, 333, 341, 347, 351, 352
Bosnian Democratic Party (BDP)   319, 331
Bosnian Party of Democratic Action   306, 313, 316
Bosnic Hasan   329
Bosnjak   316
Bozur   356, 358
Braband Jutta   126
Brandt Willy   124, 125, 266
Brankov Dimitur   33
Bratianu Ion I.   227
Bratianu Liberal Union   227, 237
Bratinka Pavel   79
Bratkowski Andrzej   211
Brazauskas A.K.   172
Brezhnev Leonid   55, 252, 253
Brezovits Laszlo   157
Brie Andre   121
Broxhi Arben   6
Brucan Silviu   220, 239
Brumen Bojan   361
Bryczkowski Janusz   205
Brzezinski Kazimierz   211
Bucer Franc   363
Buchkov Nikolai   32
Budisa Drazen   325
Budomovski Dragoljub   338
Bufi Ylli   1, 2, 3, 7, 11, 12, 13
Bugaj Ryszard   199, 214
Bujak Zbigniew   177, 183, 193, 194
Bukharin Nikolai   253
Bukovics Istvan   164
Bulatovic Moir   339
Bulatovic Momir   342
Bulgaria   331, 344
Bulgarian Agrarian National Union (BANU)   23, 24, 25, 28, 29, 31
Bulgarian Agrarian National Union — Nikola Petkov (BANU-NP)   21, 28, 29, 30, 50
Bulgarian Business Bloc (BBB)   30
Bulgarian Business Party   30
Bulgarian Communist Party   31
Bulgarian Communist Party (BCP)   19, 20, 22, 28, 29, 30, 31, 35, 36, 39, 41, 42, 47, 51, 52
Bulgarian Communist Party (BCP) factions   22
Bulgarian Communist Party (Marxist)   31
Bulgarian Communist Party (Revolutionary)   31, 32
Bulgarian Democratic-Constitutional Party   32
Bulgarian Democratic Forum   32, 50
Bulgarian Democratic Party   32
Bulgarian Democratic Youth Federation   32, 41
Bulgarian Democratichna Mladezh   32
Bulgarian Labour Social-Democratic Party   33
Bulgarian Liberal Party   33
Bulgarian National Democratic Party   33
Bulgarian National Democratic Union (BNDU)   33
Bulgarian National Party   33
Bulgarian National Radical Party   33, 34
Bulgarian National Union   19
Bulgarian People's Party (BPP)   34
Bulgarian Revolutionary Youth Party   32
Bulgarian Road to Europe   22, 36
Bulgarian Social Democratic Party   34, 50
Bulgarian Social Democratic Party (BSDP)   21, 29, 30, 34, 35
Bulgarian Socialist Party (BSP)   22, 23, 24, 25, 26, 28, 31, 34, 35, 36, 46, 52
Bulgarian Voice   34
Bulgarisation   20, 21, 43, 46, 47
Bulgarska Biznes Partiya   30
Bulgarska Demokrat-Konstitucionna Partiya   32
Bulgarska Demokraticheska Partiya   32
Bulgarska Komunisticheska Partiya (BKP)   30, 31
Bulgarska Komunisticheska Partiya (Marksismu)   31
Bulgarska Komunisticheska Partiya (Revoliucionna)   31
Bulgarska Liberalna Partiya   33
Bulgarska Narodna Partiya   33
Bulgarska Narodna Partiya (BNP)   34
Bulgarska Nasionalna Demokraticheska Partiya   33
Bulgarska Natsionalna Radikalna Partiya   33, 34
Bulgarska Rabotnicheska Sotsialdemokraticheska Partiya   33
Bulgarska Sotsialdemokraticheska Partiya   34
Bulgarska Sotsial-demokraticheska Partiya (BSDP)   34, 35
Bulgarska Sotsialisticheska Partiya (BSP)   22, 23, 24, 25, 26, 28, 31, 34, 35, 36
Bulgarski Biznes Blok   30
Bulgarski Demokraticheski Forum   32
Bulgarski Glas   34
Bulgarski Natsionalen Demokraticheski Sayuz (BNDS)   33
Bulgarski Zemedelski Naroden Sayuz (BZNS)   29
Bulgarski Zemedelski Naroden Sayuz — Nikola Petkov (BZNS-NP)   29, 30
Bulletin of the Christian Information Centre   288
Bund Freier Demokraten (BFD)   98, 112, 113, 117, 118, 119
Bund-General Jewish Workers' Alliance   176
Bund Sozialistischer Arbeiter (BSA)   117
Bundestag   97, 99, 103, 106, 108, 110, 112, 114, 115, 116, 121, 122, 123, 124, 126
Bundnis 2000   108, 123
Bundnis 90   98, 99, 103
Bunjevci   348
Buresova Dagmar   65
Burokyavichus Mikolas Martinovich   172
Bush George   69, 152
Butusiu Cristian   237
Buxhovi Isuf   357

INDEX

Buzas Jozsef 165
Byelorussian Democratic Union (BDU) 186
Byelorussians 186
Byrzykowski Bogdan 202

C

Cabinet (Soviet Union) 265
Cadet 269
Calfa Marian 57, 91
Cameria-Vatra Amtare 11
Camp of Greater Poland (OWP) 175
Camp on National Unity (OZON) 175
Campeanu Radu 221, 223, 224, 227, 237
Canada 225, 252, 305, 324
Caratan Branko 326
Carinthia 358, 359
Carnations 104, 108, 126
Carniola 358
Carnogursky Jan 88
Carpati Economic Office 243
Casa Romana a Europei Democrate 244
Catholic associations 176
Catholic opposition 88
Catholic People's Party 140
Catholic University of Lublin — KUL 190
Ceausescu Elena 220
Ceausescu Nicolae 2, 14, 219, 220, 221, 224, 234, 237, 238, 248
Cech Vladimir 75
Celic Dusan 358
Celinski Andrzej 194
Cengic Muhamad 317
Central Asia 261
Central Council of Albanian Trade Unions (CCATU) 3, 17, 18
Central Electoral Commission (Czechoslovakia) 59
Centre Agreement (CA) 182, 183, 186, 188
Centre for Documentation and Social Studies 204
Centre Group of the Nordic Council (CENTERN) 148
Centre-Left (Social Democratic) Alliance 226, 227, 228, 229, 244, 247
Centre Party 182
Centrolew 175
Centrum Demokratyczne (CD) 194
Cermak Petr 80
Cerveni Nicolae 235
Cesar Ivan 322
Ceskoslovenska socialni demokracie (CSSD) 53, 75, 84, 85
Ceskoslovenska strana lidova (CSL) 53, 57, 59, 61, 78, 83, 84
Ceskoslovenska strana socialisticka (CSS) 53, 59, 61, 69, 74
Ceskoslovenske demokraticke forum (CSDF) 74
Chalonski Michal 197

Chanturia Giogi 281
Charter 77 55, 56, 59, 80, 81, 84
Chaushev Dimitar 51
Chechen-Ingush 272
Chernenko Konstantin 252
Cherpokov Aleksandur 30
Chetniks 294
China 219, 221, 225
Chisalita Adrian 241
Christian and Democratic Union 59, 61, 78, 83
Christian Civic Movement (ChRO) 190
Christian Democracy (CD) 188
Christian Democratic Community 51
Christian Democratic Forum 188
Christian Democratic Front 36, 37, 50
Christian Democratic International 106
Christian Democratic International 228
Christian Democratic Labour Party (CDLP) 188, 189
Christian Democratic Movement 59, 61, 66, 78, 87, 88, 89, 91
Christian Democratic Party 59, 61, 63, 69, 78, 84, 86
Christian Democratic People's Party (CDPP) 130, 131, 132
Christian Democratic People's Party (CDPP) 140, 141, 147
Christian Democratic Social Union (CDSU) 104, 114
Christian Democratic Socialist Party 231
Christian Democratic Union (CDU) 227
Christian Democratic Union (CDU) 96, 97, 98, 99, 103, 105, 106, 109, 110, 114, 121, 125
Christian Democratic Union Coalition 84, 88
Christian Democratic Union of Romania 227
Christian Democratic Union of Russia 264
Christian Democrats (Bulgaria) 41
Christian Democrats of the USSR 285
Christian Human Rights and Freedom Party 228
Christian Labour Party (CLP) 189
Christian League 107
Christian National Centre 150
Christian National Union (CNU) 180, 183, 184, 187, 188, 189, 190
Christian National Union 145, 150, 151, 160
Christian Radicals (Bulgaria) 41
Christian Republican Party 228
Christian Republican Party (CRP) 37, 45
Christian Social Association 107, 114
Christian Social Association 190
Christian Social Party of Germany (CSPD) 107, 114
Christian Social Union (Bulgaria) 49
Christian Social Union (CSU) (Germany) 97, 99, 106, 107, 113, 114
Christian Social Union (CSU) (Poland) 176, 190, 191
Christian-Democratic Party of Estonia 93, 260, 285

Christian-Democratic Party of Lithuania   171, 285
Christian-Democratic Party of Macedonia (CDPM)   338
Christian-Democratic Union of Russia (CDUR)   285
Christlich-Demokratische Soziale Union (CDSU)   104
Christlich-Demokratische Union Deutschlands (CDU)   96, 97, 98, 99, 103, 104, 105, 106, 109, 110, 114, 121, 125
Christlich-Soziale Partei Deutschlands (CSPD)   107
Christlich-Soziale Union (CSU)   97, 99, 106, 107, 113, 114
Christlich-Soziale Vereinigung   107, 114
Christliche Liga   107
Chrzanowski Wieslaw   190
Chrzescijanska Demokracja (ChD)   188
Chrzescijanska Partia Pracy (ChPP)   189
Chrzescijansko-Demokratyczne Stronnictwo Pracy (ChDSP)   188, 189, 190, 205, 210, 215
Church from below   126
Churchill Winston   293
Circiumaru Marian   246
Citizens' Initiative (CI)   20, 21, 37, 50
Citizens' Movement for the Republic   132
Citizens' Party (ISP)   130, 131, 132, 133, 137, 144, 147, 148, 160, 161, 163
Ciurus Jozef   203
Civic Agreement for Democracy and Pluralism (CADP)   191
Civic Committee (CC) (Poland)   177, 184, 185
Civic Democratic Alliance   60, 65, 69, 72, 79, 80, 81, 86
Civic Democratic Party   65, 66, 67, 72, 73, 77, 78, 79, 80, 82, 86, 91
Civic Forum   239
Civic Forum   57 58, 59, 60, 61, 63, 64, 65, 66, 67, 69, 75, 76, 77, 78, 79, 80, 81, 84, 85, 86, 91
Civic Forum Club of Social Democrats   77, 81
Civic Forum Liberal Club   65, 82
Civic Movement   65, 77, 80, 81, 82, 85
Civic Party (CP) (Croatia)   331
Civil Dignity   276
Club August 80   191
Club Communities for Perestroika   280
Club for the Victims of Repression after 1945   21, 37, 38, 50
Club of Committed Non-Party Members (KAN)   72, 79
Club of Friends of Jesus Christ   47
Club of Social Democrats   60, 84, 85
Club of the Democratic Right   81
Club to Support Glasnost and Perestroika   20, 42
Cluj-Napoca Civic Forum   228
Co-operative Party   227, 228
Coalition for the Turnovo Constitution   49

Coalition of National Agreement   321
Coalition of the All-People's Democratic Party   61
Cob'ani Hysen   12
Coexistence   69, 72, 87, 89
Coiziu Viorel   230
Colombia   253
Combat Sport Group Peipe   127
Cominform   295
Comintern   13, 176
Committee 273   37
Committee for Religious Rights and Spiritual Values   50
Committee for Religious Rights, Freedom of Conscience, and Spiritual Values   20, 21, 38
Committee for the Defence of the Unjustly Prosecuted (VONS)   80
Committee for the Defence of Workers (KOR)   191
Committee of Ruse   41
Common Sense   268
Commune   268
Communist Party of Bohemia and Moravia   66, 72, 73, 82, 83
Communist Party of Czechoslovakia (CPCS-CPCz)   53, 54, 55, 57, 58, 61, 63, 66, 67, 68, 69, 72, 73, 74, 80, 90
Communist Party of Estonia   93, 94, 258
Communist Party of Germany (KPD)   95, 107, 108, 121, 124, 125
Communist Party of Poland (CPP)   176
Communist Party of Slovakia — Party of the Democratic Left   66, 72, 90
Communist Party of the Soviet Union (CPSU)   54, 155, 252, 253, 254, 255, 257, 258, 259, 261, 262, 263, 264, 265, 266, 268, 278, 282, 284, 286, 289, 290, 291, 292
Communist Party of the Soviet Union (CPSU) (Armenia)   278
Communist Party of the Soviet Union (CPSU) (Azerbaidzhan)   278, 279
Communist Party of the Soviet Union (CPSU) (Belorussia)   279
Communist Party of the Soviet Union (CPSU) (Estonia)   93, 94, 258
Communist Party of the Soviet Union (CPSU) (Georgia)   280
Communist Party of the Soviet Union (CPSU) (Kazakhstan)   282
Communist Party of the Soviet Union (CPSU) (Kirgizia)   283
Communist Party of the Soviet Union (CPSU) (Latvia)   169, 170, 258
Communist Party of the Soviet Union (CPSU) (Lithuania)   171, 172, 257
Communist Party of the Soviet Union (CPSU) (Moldavia) (Moldova)   283
Communist Party of the Soviet Union (CPSU) (Russia)   285

INDEX

Communist Party of the Soviet Union (CPSU) (Tadzhikistan) 289
Communist Party of the Soviet Union (CPSU) (Turkmenia) 289
Communist Party of the Soviet Union (CPSU) (Ukraine) 290
Communist Party of the Soviet Union (CPSU) (Uzbekistan) 292
Communist Party of Yugoslavia (CPY) 293, 295, 296
Communist Party of Yugoslavia — Party of Freedom (CPY-PF) 355
Communist Youth League (Bulgaria) 19, 22
Comunitatea Lipovenilor din Romania 235
Conservative Party (Great Britain) 79
Confederation for an Independent Poland (CIP) 191, 192
Confederation of Anarcho-Syndicalists (CAS) 267, 268
Confederation of Independent Syndicates in Bulgaria 51
Confederation of Independent Trade Unions (Bulgaria) 51
Confederation of Labour (CL) 268, 269
Confederation of Social Democratic Parties of Central and Eastern Europe 17
Confederation of Socialist Parties of the European Community 126, 155
Conference on Security and Co-operation in Europe (CSCE) 9, 21, 41, 43
Congress of Co-operative Farmers 59
Congress of National Solidarity 203
Congress of People's Deputies (Russia) 263
Congress of People's Deputies (Soviet Union) 255, 257, 259, 260, 261, 264, 265, 267
Conservative Club in Lodz 192
Conservative Party (CP) 193
Conservative Party (Bulgaria) 38
Conservative Party (Czechoslovakia) 66
Conservative Party — the Free Bloc 73, 80
Conservative Party in Opole 193
Conservative-Monarchist Club (CMC) 192, 193
Constantinovici Alexandru 240
Constituent Assembly (Romania) 223
Constituent National Assembly 53
Constitution (Soviet Union) 257
Constitution of May 3 178, 180
Constitutional Alliance 38, 39
Constitutional Court (Hungary) 130, 161
Constitutional Democratic Party (Party of Popular Freedom) 269, 276
Constitutional Tribunal 179
Coposu Corneliu 221, 236
Cornescu Lucian 248
Costel Nicolae 237
Council of Europe 224
Council of Federation 265
Count Aleksander Fredro Conservative Club 193
Country 284

Court of Registration 132
Crnogorski Federalisticki Pokret (CFP) 343
Croatia 297, 299, 300, 305, 308, 309, 310, 314, 318, 319–331, 352
Croatian Assembly 302
Croatian Christian Democratic Party (CCDP) 322
Croatian Democratic Party (CDP) 322, 323, 330
Croatian Democratic Union (CDU) 306, 308, 313, 321, 323, 324, 330
Croatian Democratic Union of Bosnia and Hercegovina (CDUBH) 314
Croatian League of the Communists of Yugoslavia 297
Croatian Liberal Movement (CLM) 331
Croatian Muslim Democratic Party (CMDP) 329
Croatian Party (CP) 331
Croatian Party of Rights (CPR) 329, 330
Croatian Peace Movement (CPM) 331
Croatian Peasant Party (CPP) 324, 325
Croatian People's Party (CPP) 297, 305, 306, 325
Croatian Republican Party (CRP) 331
Croatian Social-Liberal Party (CLP) 325, 326
Croats 293, 311, 313, 314, 321, 344, 345, 359
Crypto-communism 221, 223
Csaszar Terezia 141
Csefko Ferenc 137
Cseh Sandor 161
Csekene Kornelia Kelemen 144
Csemer Elemer 165
Csikos Csaba 142
Csintalan Sandor 154
Csoori Sandor 147
Csurka Istvan 146, 147, 148, 151
Cunescu Sergiu 221, 246
Cuvintul 239
Cvitan Josip 323
Czabanski Krzysztof 195
Czech and Slovak Federative Republic 68
Czech National Council 57, 58, 61, 65, 69, 76, 84, 86
Czech Republic 58, 60, 63, 65, 66, 67, 69, 72, 73, 74, 75, 77–87
Czech Socialist Republic 68
Czechoslovak Democratic Forum 61, 74
Czechoslovak Democratic Initiative 59, 60, 65, 81, 85
Czechoslovak Farmers' Party 59, 74
Czechoslovak National Socialist Party 86
Czechoslovak News Agency — CTK 85
Czechoslovak People's Party 53, 57, 59, 61, 78, 83, 84, 84
Czechoslovak Social Democracy 53, 61, 75, 84, 85, 85
Czechoslovak Socialist Party 53, 57, 59, 61, 69, 74, 85, 86
Czechoslovak Socialist Republic 68
Czechoslovakia 129, 183, 219, 239

Czechs 61, 68, 75, 77, 87, 321
Czibula Ferenc 149
Czinege Lajos 149
Czollek Michael 104

D

Dabcevic-Kucar Savka 297, 306, 325
Dabrowska Zuzana 212
Dagestan 272
Dalmatia 319
Dalmatian Action (DA) 331
Dalmatinska Akcija (DA) 331
Danube Circle 157
Darakchiev Plamen 44
Darmanovic Srdjan 341
Daubler-Gmelin Herta 14
Dawn 170
de Maiziere Lothar 97, 98, 103, 104, 105, 106, 109, 114, 117, 125
Debrecen Democratic Club 142
Debryanskaya E. 273, 274
Decevic Asim 341
Deda Mitsa 281
Delia Pal 11
Demba Judith 115
Democracy 90, 188
Democracy Now (DJ) 103, 108, 120, 122, 123
Democratic Action Civic Movement — Democratic Social Movement (DACM-DSM) 182, 183, 193, 194
Democratic Action Movement (ROAD) 182, 183, 193
Democratic Action of Croatia (DAC) 331
Democratic Agricultural, Industrial and Intellectual Workers' Party 229
Democratic Alliance — Party of Cultivators of Macedonia (DDA-PCM) 338
Democratic Alternative (DA) 343
Democratic Association GDR 40 109
Democratic Awakening 103, 106, 109, 110, 114
Democratic Block 96, 103, 105, 110, 111, 118, 119
Democratic centralism 22
Democratic Centre (DC) 194
Democratic Coalition 163
Democratic Coalition 307
Democratic Coalition (DC) 341, 344
Democratic Community of Croats in Kosovo and Metohija 358
Democratic Community of Magyars of Vojvodina (DCMVV) 347, 348
Democratic Constitutional Party
Democratic Departure (DA) 103, 106, 109, 110, 114, 126, 127
Democratic Ecological Party 229
Democratic Farmers' Party of Germany (DBD) 96, 97, 98, 106, 110, 119
Democratic Forum (Bulgaria) 36, 39

Democratic Forum (Hungary) 130, 131, 132, 133, 139, 146, 147, 153
Democratic Forum (Montenegro) 341
Democratic Forum (Serbia) 354, 355
Democratic Forum Mazowia (DF M) 194, 195
Democratic Future of the Homeland Party 229
Democratic Labour Party 227, 229, 247
Democratic Labour Party of Latvia 170
Democratic Labour Party of Lithuania 172
Democratic League (DL) 343
Democratic League (Kosovo) 306
Democratic League (Montenegro) 341
Democratic League for the Defence of Human Rights 39
Democratic League of Albanians of Croatia (DLAC) 330
Democratic League of Croats in the Vojvodina (DLCV) 348
Democratic League of Greens — EKO (DLG-EKO) 318
Democratic League of Kosovo (DLK) 357, 367
Democratic League of Magyars of Vojvodina 308
Democratic League of Turks (DLT) 358
Democratic League of Turks in Macedonia (DLTM) 338
Democratic Macedonian Workers' Association (DMWA) 338
Democratic Monarchist Party (DMP)
Democratic Movement for Constitutional Monarchy 39, 40
Democratic Party (Belorussia) 279
Democratic Party (DP) (Bosnia and Hercegovina) 319
Democratic Party (DP) (Bulgaria) 40
Democratic Party (DP) (Croatia) 348, 349
Democratic Party (Czechoslovakia) 57, 59, 87
Democratic Party (Georgia) 281, 282
Democratic Party (DP) (Montenegro) 342
Democratic Party (DP) (Poland) 176, 177, 178, 182, 184, 186, 195, 196
Democratic Party (Romania) 229
Democratic Party (Serbia) 308
Democratic Party (Slovakia) 88, 89
Democratic Party (DP) (Soviet Union) 262, 269, 270
Democratic Party — DP (Davidovic-Grol — DS (DG) 355
Democratic Party in Bulgaria 40, 50
Democratic Party of Cluj 231
Democratic Party of Free Romanis 230
Democratic Party of Freedom (DPF) 319
Democratic Party of Liberty (DLP) 355
Democratic Party of Lithuania 172
Democratic Party of Romania 230
Democratic Party of Romanies of Kragujevac (DPPRK) 355
Democratic Party of Russia (DPR) 263, 286

INDEX

Democratic Party of Socialists (DPS)   314, 315, 316
Democratic Party of the Gagauz   283
Democratic Party of the Ukraine   290
Democratic Pensioners' Party   141
Democratic Platform   257, 264, 284, 290
Democratic Platform in the Communist Party of Moldova/Independent Communist Party of Moldova   284
Democratic Political Cultural Foundation   143
Democratic Russia   260, 263, 287
Democratic Social Movement (RDS)   183
Democratic Socialist League (DSL)   343
Democratic Union   229, 231, 232, 241
Democratic Union of Bosnia and Hercegovina (DUBH)   319
Democratic Union of Bulgarians in Yugoslavia (DUBY)   355
Democratic Union of Muslims of Croatia (DUMC)   331
Democratic Union of the Greek Minority (OMONIA)   1, 3, 5, 6, 11, 15, 16
Democratic Union (DU) (Poland)   181, 196, 196
Democratic Union (DU) (Soviet Union)   262, 270, 271
Democratic unity   22
Democratic Unity Party (DUP)   231
Democratic Women's League of Germany (DFD)   111, 116
Democratic Women's Movement (Bulgaria)   40
Democratic Women's Movement (Serbia)   355
Democratic-Republican Coalition   61
Democraticher Aufbruch (DA)   103, 106, 109, 110, 114, 126
Democratic Reform Party of Muslims (DRPM)   349
Demohrscanska Partija na Makedonija (DPM)   338
Demokrata Forum   130, 131, 132, 133, 139, 146, 147, 153
Demokrata Kalicio   163
Demokrata Nyugdijasok Partja   141
Demokratichen Forum   39
Demokratichen Sayuz Zhenite   40
Demokraticheska Monarhistka Partiya
Demokraticheska Partiya (DP)   40
Demokraticheska Partiya v Bulgaria   40
Demokraticheskaya partiya   269, 270
Demokraticheskaya partiya Rossii   286
Demokraticheskaya Rossiya   287
Demokraticheskii soyuz   270, 271
Demokraticheskii vybor   291
Demokratichnata Liga za Zashtita na Pravata na Choveka   39
Demokratichno Dvizhenie za Konstytucjonalna Monarhia   39, 40
Demokraticka strana (DS)   88, 89
Demokratie Jetzt (DJ)   103, 108, 120, 122, 123

Demokratische Bauernpartei Deutschlands (DBD)   96, 97, 98, 106, 110, 119
Demokratische Vereinigung DDR 40   109
Demokratischer Frauenbund Deutschlands (DFD)   111
Demokratsija   50
Demokratska Akcija Hrvatske (DAH)   331
Demokratska Alternativa (DA)   343
Demokratska Koalicja (DK)   341
Demokratska Politicka Partija Roma Kragujevca (DPPRK)   355
Demokratska Reformska Stranka Muslimana (DRSM)   349
Demokratska Rijec   340, 342
Demokratska Stranka (Davidovic-Grol — DS (D-G)   355
Demokratska Stranka (DS)   319
Demokratska Stranka (DS) (Croatia)   348, 349
Demokratska Stranka (DS) (Montenegro)   342
Demokratska Stranka Slobode (DSS)   319, 355
Demokratska Stranka Socijalista (DSS)   314, 315
Demokratska Zajednica Bosne i Hercegovine (DZBiH)   319
Demokratska Zajednica Muslimana Hrvatske (DZMH)   331
Demokratska Zajednica Vojvodjanskih Madzara (DZVM)   347, 348
Demokratski Forum (DF)   355
Demokratski Savez (DS)   343
Demokratski Savez Albanaca Hrvatske (DSAH)   330
Demokratski Savez Hrvata u Vojvodini (DSHV)   348
Demokratski Savez Turaka (DST)   358
Demokratski Savez Zelena — EKO (DSZ-EKO)   318
Demokratski Socijalisticki Saves Bosne i Hercegovine (DSS BiH)   314, 315
Demokratski Socijalisticki Savez (DSS)   343
Demokratski Sojuz na Turcite vo Makedonija   338
Demokratski Sojuz-Zemjodelska Partija na Makedonija (DS-ZPM)   338
Demokratsko Makedonsko Rabotnicko Obedinuvanje (DMRO)   338
DEMOS (Democratic Opposition)   306, 307, 309, 359, 361, 363, 364, 365, 366, 367
Demsar Marko   359, 362
Deneke Marlies   121
Depolitization Act   24
Dertliev Peter   24, 34
Deryagin G.   269, 276
Deutsche Forumpartei (DFP)   113, 117, 118
Deutsche Freiheitsunion   113
Deutsche Soziale Union (DSU)   98, 103, 105, 107, 109, 111, 113, 114, 119, 123, 124, 125
Deutsche Wiedervereinigungspartei   113
Dezse Tibor   148
Diaconescu Corneliu Vlad   246

Diaconescu Ion 236
Dide Nicolae 247
Die Andere 120
Die Nelken 104, 108, 126
Die Republikaner (REPs) 123, 124
Dienstbier Jiri 55, 65, 82
Diestel Peter-Michael 114
Dimitrescu Radu 246
Dimitrijevic Vojin 346
Dimitriu Adrian 221, 246
Dimitrov Apostol 35
Dimitrov Communist Youth League 32, 40, 41
Dimitrov Filip 50
Dimitrov Mahol 33
Dimitrovski Komunisticheski Mladezhki Sayuz 32, 40, 41
Djilas Milovan 296
Djordjevic Bora 321
Dlouhy Vladimir 57, 65, 79
Dmowski Roman 176, 202
Dobranyi Zsuzsa 141
Dobric Miograd 351
Dobrudzka All-Bulgarian Union 52
Dobszay Karoly 152
Dogan Ahmet 46
Dolev Aleksandru 32
Domokos Geza 233
Drach Ivan 291
Draganov Dragomir 39
Draghici Iustin 244
Dragon Pal 161
Drahos Peter 143
Draskovic Vuk 304, 308, 318, 343, 345, 346, 352, 354
Dreeptatea 236
Drenchev Mihan 50
Drenchev Milan 29
Dreta Mirko 324
Drita 8
Drundarov Stoyan 52
Druzic Ivo 321
Dtarostin D. 273
Dubcek Alexander 54, 55, 56, 57, 91
Dubina Miodrag 343
Dudzinski Jozef 203
Duica Traian 247
Dukanovic Milo 342
Durakovic Nijaz 315
Duray Miklos 72
Durcinov Milan 335
Duris Ivan 76
Duverger Maurice 182
Dvizenje za Semakedonska Akcija (MAAK) 337
Dvizhenie za Prava i Svobodi (DPS) 23, 24, 46
Dvizhenie za Razvitie na Marksizma i Obnovlenie na Sotsializma 51
Dvorak Ladislav 74
Dyner Jerzy 195
Dzeba Kresimir 325

Dzemijet 306
Dzhadzhev Ivan 42
Dzisiaj 191
Dzurov Dobri 21

E

East Germany 56, 130
Ebeling Fred 109
Ebeling Hans-Wilhelm 113, 114
Ecoforum for Peace Association 52
Ecoglasnost 20, 21, 41, 43, 50
Ecological Movement 236
Ecological Movement of Montenegro (EMM) 343
Ecological Party (Serbia) 355
Eco-Voice 41
Edimi Midhat 334
Edinen Front za Preustroistvo i Zashtita na Sotzialisma 51
Edinstvo-Dvizhenie za Sotsialistichesko Vazrazhdane 51
Edisonov Ivan 38
Efimov D. 269
Egyutteles; Spoluzitie; Wspolnota; Suzitie; Coexistence 72
Einheit Jetzt 127
Eire 182
Ekert Bronislaw 202
Ekoloski Pokret Crne Gore (EPCG) 343
Electoral Coalition 163
Electoral Foundation 161
Electoral Law (Albania) 4
Electoral Law (Bulgaria) 22, 23
Electoral Law (Czechoslovakia) 58
Electoral Law (Poland) 180, 181
Electoral Law (Romania) 223
Electoral Law (Soviet Union) 254, 255, 262
Eliovich A. 270
Ellenzek 149
Eltes Zoltan 234
Endecja 176
Engel'gardt-Yurkov S. 287
Engholm Bjorn 124
Enterpreneurs' Party 142
Enterpreneurs' Party of Estonia 94
Eotvos Janos Attila 148
Eppelmann Rainer 109, 110
Erdely Magyarok Magyarorszagi Partja 158
Eremei Grigorii Isidorovich 283
Erster Weiblicher Aufbruch (EWA) 116
Ertoba 281
Estonia 260, 262
Estonian Democratic Labour Party 94
Estonian Independent Social-Democratic Party 94
Eurocommunism 363
Eurocommunists 61
Europa-Union der DDR 111
Europai Radikalis Part Magyar Csoportja 166

INDEX

Europaische Foderalistische Partei — Europa Partei 111
Europe Union of the GDR 111
European Christian Democratic Union 107
European Communities 36, 88, 150, 246, 350
European Democrat Union 106, 148
European Group of the European Radical Party 166
European House Party 127
European Parliament 124, 224, 225
European People's Party 106
European Union of Christian Democrats 161
Evlogiev Ivan 32

F

Fabian Bertalan 152
Fapta 229
Farago Miklos Hanko 138
Farkas Gabriella 146, 147
Farkas Geza 141
Farkas Pal 165
Farkas Peter 141
Farmers' Party 85
Fatherland Front 19
Fatherland Party of Labour 42
February 16 172
Federal Assembly 57, 58, 61, 65, 68, 69, 72, 86, 89, 91
Federal Association of Greens 115
Federatia Comunitatilor Evreiesti din Romania 231
Federation of Christian Parties and Movements 41
Federation of Clubs for Glasnost and Democracy 42, 50
Federation of Independent Students' Associations 47
Federation of Independent Students' Societies 21, 42, 43, 50
Federation of Liberal, Democratic and Reform Parties of the European Community 112
Federation of the Jewish Communities of Romania 231
Federatsiya na Klubove za Glasnost i Demokratsiya 42
Federatsiya na Nezavisimi Studentski Druzhestva 42, 43
FEDISZ 164
Fekete Gyuala 152
Felegyhazi Democratic Youth Organization 164
Felegyhazi Demokratikus Ifjusagi Szrvezet 164
Fenrych Andrzej 192
Ferenc Munnich Society 142, 143
Fianna Fail 182
Fico Ltd 143
FIDESZ, Alliance of Young Democrats 130, 131, 132, 133, 138, 143, 144, 362
FIDESZ, Fiatal Demokratak Szovetsege 130, 131, 132, 133, 138, 143, 144, 362

Fighting Solidarity 197
Filipovic Muhamed 316
Fine Gael 182
First Female Departure (EWA) 116
Fischbek Hans-Jurgen 108
Fiszbach Tadeusz 210, 211
Five Year Plan 251
Fodor Gabor 143
Fonay Jeno 139
For a Provincial Hungary Party 144
For Democratic Slovakia 66
Forgacs Ferenc 149
Fortschrittliche Volkspartei (FVP) 114, 123
Forum 6 Septemvri 49
Forum Demokratyczne Mazowsze (FD M) 194, 195
Forum Foundation 147
Forum of Free Democrats 52
Forum of the Democratic Right (FDR) 197
Forum Party of Thuringia 111, 114
Forum Prawicy Demokratycznej (FPD) 197
Forumspartei Thuringen 111
Forumul Antitotalitar Roman 242
Forumul Cetatenesc Cluj-Napoca 228
Forumul Democrat al Germanilor din Romania 233
Forumul Democratiei si Unitatii Nationale din Romania 240
Foundation for a European Hungary 138
Fourth (Trotskyist) International 117
Fraction of the Democratic Right within the Democratic Union (FPDUD)
France 2, 139
Franceschi Mirko 330
Frasyniuk Wladyslaw 193, 196
Frauen fur den Frieden 116
Free Bloc 59, 63, 66, 69, 76
Free Change Party 231
Free Democratic Party 52
Free Democratic Party 231
Free Democratic Party (FDP) 97, 99, 106, 111, 112, 113, 117, 118, 138
Free Democratic Social Justice Party 232
Free Democratic Union of Germany (FDUD) 112, 114
Free Democratic Union of Romanis in Romania 232
Free Democratic Youth Party 232
Free Democrats 130, 131, 132, 133, 137, 140, 143, 147, 157
Free Georgia — Round Table 261, 280
Free German Youth 103, 104, 114
Free Land 94
Free Peasants' Party 84
Free People 35
Free Trade Union Organization 232
Free Word 271
Free Youth Association of Romania 232
Freedom 281

379

Freedom 49
Freedom and Democracy Party 232
Freedom and Peace (F & P) 198
Freedom Party (Czechoslovakia) 53, 89
Freedom Party (Hungary) 144
Freedom Party (Poland) 197, 198
Freie Demokratische Partei (FDP) 97, 99, 106, 111, 112, 113, 117, 118
Freie Demokratische Union Deutschlands (FDUD) 112
Freie Deutsche Jugend (FDJ) 103, 104
Friends of Beer Party 60
Friszke Andrzej 214
Frontul Democrat Roman 243
Frontul Popular Roman 245
Frontul Salvarii Nationale 220, 221, 222, 223, 224, 225, 237, 239, 240, 242, 243, 246, 247, 249
Fuggetlen Keresztenydemokrata Part 159
Fuggetlen Kissgazda, Foldmunkas es Polgari Part (FKgP) 130, 131, 132, 133, 137, 144, 147, 148, 160, 161, 163
Fuggetlen Kornyezetvedo Munkapart 159
Fuggetlen Koztarsasagi Part 160
Fuggetlen Magyar Demokrata Part (FMDP) 159, 160
Fuggetlen Magyar Munkaspart 160
Fuggetlen Szocialdemokrata Part 162
Funk Frigyes 148
Fur Lajos 147
Fura Zygmunt 206
Furjes Balazs 143
Furmann Imre 146, 147
Fuzessy Tibor 141

G

Gabis Tomasz 216
Gabrielescu Valentin 236
Gabris Karoly 146
Gagalov Todor 44
Gagauz 283
Gajewski Ryszard 205
Gal Zoltan 154
Galicia 176
Gambeta Vangjush 12
Gamsakhurdia Zviad 261, 280
Ganev Stoyan 51
Ganti Tibor 140
Garelov Kamen 46
Garztecki Juliusz 210
Gavriliescu Nicoale 237
Gavrilov A. 284
Gawlik Radoslaw 197
Gazeta Gdanska 200
Gazeta Ludowa 209
Gazeta Wspolna 211
Gebhardt Stanislaw 189
Geczi Jozsef 154
Gegenstimmen 126

Gehrcke Wolfgang 120
Genchev Nikolay 33
General Assembly of the Union of Economic Leaders 52
Generations Party 144, 145
Genov Georgi 33
Genscher Hans-Dietrich 82, 98, 99
Georgia 251, 261, 276, 278, 280, 281, 282
Georgian Communist Party 258
Georgian Popular Front 281
Georgian Social Democratic Party 281
Georgiev Konstantin 40
Georgiev Pavel 52
Georgiev Rumen 36
Georgievski Ljupco 334
Geremek Bronislaw 187, 196
Gergely Mihaly 148
Gerlach Manfred 110, 118
German Alternative 124
German Beer Drinkers' Union (DBU) 113
German Communist Party (DKP)
German Democratic Forum of Romania 233
German Democratic Republic (GDR) 21
German Forum Party (DFP) 112, 117, 118
German Free Democrats 82
German Freedom Union 113, 114
German Marxist Party 108
German People's Party 127
German People's Union (DVU) 99, 114
German Reunification Party 113
German Social Union (DSU) 98, 103, 105, 107, 109, 111, 113, 114, 119, 123, 124, 125
Germans 68, 77, 176
Germany 58, 76, 139, 165, 344
Gerol'd Yu. 268
Gerzfall 122
Gheg 6, 9, 11, 17
Gheorghiu-Dej Gheorghe 219
Ghiban Pavel 242
Gibanje za Kulturu Mira i Nenasilja (GKMN) 367
Gil Mieczyslaw 187
Gjanushi Skendir 16
Gjoleka Meno 7
Gjoni Xhelil 1, 13
Glapinski Adam 186, 187
Glas Concila 297
Glaser Wolfgang 119
Glasnost 252, 253, 254
Gligorov Kiro 332, 333, 336
Glogowski Karol 201
Godesa Franc 363
Godo Sabri 12
Gogov Licho 33
Golija Franc 362
Golikov V. 268
Golos 290
Golos vozrozhdeniya 292
Goncz Arpad 131, 139, 140

INDEX

Gorbachev Mikhail   21, 55, 56, 96, 129, 177, 252, 253, 254, 257, 258, 259, 264, 265, 266, 267
Gorev Vangel   38
Gorizia   358, 359
Gorski Artur   192
Gosev Petar   336
Gosnik Vane   361
Gotting Gerald   105
Gottwald Klement   53, 54
Government of National Responsibility   96, 108
Government of National Understanding   57, 81, 88
Grad Janos   158
Gradjanska Stranka (GS)   331
Gradzhieru D.   284
Grama Mihai   228
Grand National Assembly   19, 22, 23, 24, 25, 26, 46, 50
Grazhdanska Initsiativa (GI)   37
Grazhdanskoe dostoinstvo   276
Grbo Ismet   314
Greater Albania   2, 6
Greater Budapest Workers' Council   152
Greavu Traian   246
Grebencik Miroslav   72
Greece   2, 6, 15, 331
Greek Catholic Church   238
Greek Orthodox Church   16
Green Action — Split (GA-S)   326
Green Circle   157
Green International   206
Green League (Germany)   97, 99, 103, 114, 115, 116, 117
Green Movement   10
Green Party (Bulgaria)   43, 50
Green Party (Czechoslovakia)   59, 61, 69, 75, 85
Green Party (Georgia)   281
Green Party (Germany)   97, 99, 103, 114, 115, 116, 117
Green Party (GP) (Serbia)   355
Green Party of Lithuania   172
Green Party of the Ukraine   261, 290
Green Union (GU)   198
Green Youth   103
Greens of Slovenia (GS)   361
Grey Panthers — Pensioners's Party of Slovenia (GP)   367
Grezsa Isstvan   147
Grigasi Laszlo   141
Gromada   280
Gromyko Andrei   252
Grosz Karoly   155
Grugin D.   276
Grune Liga   97, 99, 103, 114, 115, 116
Grune Partei   97, 99, 103, 114, 115, 116
Grunwald   203, 204
Gueth Gyula   144
Gulf War   106
Gumbaridze Givi Grigo'evich   280

Gurbolikov V.   267
Gurenko Stanislav Ivanovich   290
Gwizdz Wieslaw   205
Gyor Branch   153
Gyor Istvan   146
Gyorgy Ilona   158
Gypsies   24, 60, 68, 76, 77, 87
Gysi Gregor   98, 121, 122
Gyulai Ivan   157
Gyurko Janos   156

H

Hack Peter   138
Hainz Primoz   366
Hajretin Erol   336
Halachev Konstantin   39
Halini Ilijas   334
Haljimi Riza   350
Hall Aleksander   196, 197
Hangya plc.   161
Happiness Party   145
Haramiev Kiril   46
Haraszti Miklos   138
Hare-Niemeyer procedure   96
Hartmann Gunter   119
Hasznos Miklos   141
Havel Vaclav   55, 56, 57, 68, 80, 81, 86
Haza Part   145, 146
Hazafias Part   163
Hazafias Valasztasi Koalicio (HVK)   163
Hegedus Laszlo S.   152
Heilmann Friedrich   115
Heiner Ferenc   142
Heinrich Rold   119
Hercegovacka Demokratska Zajednica (HDZ)   319
Hercegovina Democratic Union (HDU)   319
Heredy Dezso   144
Hermanowicz Jozef   189
Hernadi Gyula   145
Hetesi Marta   146
Hniedziewicz Przemyslaw   186, 188
Hnuti ceskoslovenskeho porozumeni (HCP)   75
Hnuti za samospravnou demokracii — Spolecnost pro Moravu a Slezsko (HSD-SMS)   59, 61, 63, 77, 86
Hnutie za demokraticke Slovensko (HZDS)   66, 67, 87, 89, 90
Hoka Erno   144
Holcik Jan   88
Holy Crown   160
Holy Crown Association   145, 151
Homann Heinrich   119
Homeland Party   145, 146
Homogenization   219
Honecker Erich   56, 95, 96, 98, 104, 121
Horak Jiri   84
Hornyak Tibor   149
Horvat Branko   304

Horvath Albert   163
Horvath Balazs   146, 147, 148
Horvatorszagi Magyar Neppart (HMN)   331
House of the Nations   58, 61, 88, 92
House of the People   58, 61, 88, 92
Hoxha Enver   1, 4, 9, 13, 14, 15, 16
Hoxha Hafiz Salih Terhat   11
Hoxha Nexhmije   4
Hren Marko   367
Hristiyan-Demokraticheska Fronta   36, 37
Hristiyan-Republikanska Partiya (HRP)   37
Hrvatska Demokratska Zajednica (HDZ)   323, 324
Hrvatska Demokratska Zajednica Bosne i Hercegovine (HDZ BiH)   314
Hrvatska Krscanska Demokratska Stranka (HKDS)   322
Hrvatska Narodna Stranka (HNS)   325
Hrvatska Republikanska Stranka (HRS)   331
Hrvatska Seljacka Stranka (HSS)   324, 325
Hrvatska Socijalno-Liberalna Stranka (HSLS)   325, 326
Hrvatska Stranka (HS)   331
Hrvatska Stranka Prava (HSP)   329, 330
Hrvatski Liberalni Pokret (HLP)   331
Hrvatski Mirotvorni Pokret (HMP)   331
Human Rights Forum (HRF) (Albania)   3, 8
Human Rights League   233
Humanist Ecological Party   233
Humanitarian Peace Party   233
Hungarian Allied National Party   146
Hungarian Bolyai University   249
Hungarian Centre Alliance   132
Hungarian Christian Democratic Movement   59, 72, 87, 89
Hungarian Christian Democratic Party of Romania   225, 233, 234, 236
Hungarian Co-operative and Agrarian Party   153
Hungarian Communist Party   154, 158, 167
Hungarian Democratic Christian Party   146
Hungarian Democratic Forum (HDF)   130, 131, 132, 133, 139, 146, 147, 153
Hungarian Democratic Union of Romania (HDUR)   225, 233, 234, 236
Hungarian Freedom Party   148
Hungarian Freedom Party Alliance   148
Hungarian Health Party   148, 149, 157
Hungarian Humanists' Party   149
Hungarian Independence Party   149, 150
Hungarian Independent Initiative   88
Hungarian Independent Party   234
Hungarian Industrial Unity Party   150
Hungarian Liberal Party   150
Hungarian Liberal People's Party   150
Hungarian National Christian Workers' Party   150
Hungarian National Party   145, 150, 151
Hungarian Nature Conservancy Alliance   157
Hungarian October Party   151, 152

Hungarian Peasant Alliance   163
Hungarian Peasant, Worker Alliance Party   163
Hungarian Peasant-Worker Alliance Party   163, 164
Hungarian People's Party (HPP)   133, 152, 153
Hungarian People's Party — National Peasant Party   133, 152, 153
Hungarian Radical Party   153
Hungarian Realist Movement   153
Hungarian Republican Party   153
Hungarian Royalist Party   153
Hungarian Smallholders' Party in Romania   234
Hungarian Socialist Party (HSP)   130, 131, 133, 143, 153, 154, 155, 156, 162
Hungarian Socialist Workers' Party (HSWP)   129, 130, 137, 142, 143, 151, 155, 156, 167
Hungarian Sunday   160
Hungarian Tomorrow   144
Hungarian Trotskyist Party   140
Hungarian Veterans' Party   156
Hungarian Workers' Party   154, 156
Hungarian Workers' Democratic Centre Party   156
Hungarians   59, 63, 68, 69, 72, 87, 92
Hungary   21, 22, 67, 96, 181, 183, 344, 358
Hungary's Co-operative and Agrarian Party   157
Hungary's Communist Party   156
Hungary's Green Party   157, 158
Hungary's Party of Communists   166, 167
Hungary's Party of Transylvanian Hungarians   158
Hungary's Regional Green Party   157
Hungary's Social Democratic Party (HSDP)   130, 131, 133, 158, 159, 162, 165, 166
Hunniapack Ltd   141
Husak Gustav   54, 55, 56, 57
Huti Namik   10
Hvatska Demokratska Stranka (HDS)   322, 323

I

Ibragim S.   272
Ibrahimi Sami   335
Ikonowicz Piotr   212
Iliescu Ion   220, 221, 222, 223, 225, 239
Iliev Vasil   40
Ilinden   52
Ilka Grzegorz   212, 213
Ilosvay Gyorgy   157
IMRO-Democratic Party   339
Independence Party Solidarity (IP-S)   198
Independence Struggle   170
Independent 19 November Club   52
Independent Association for the Defence of Human Rights   20, 21, 37, 50
Independent Association for the Defence of Human Rights in Bulgaria   43, 44
Independent Christian Democratic Party   159
Independent Communist Party of Latvia   170

INDEX

Independent Communist Party of Moldova 284
Independent Democratic Association (IDA) (Kosovo) 358
Independent Environmental Labour Party 159
Independent Hungarian Democratic Party (FMDP) 159, 160
Independent Hungarian Workers' Party 160
Independent Miners' Union (IMU) 17, 18
Independent National Christian Party 234
Independent Organization of Communists (IOC) 343
Independent People's Party (UVP) 116
Independent Political Community (IPC) 355
Independent Republic Party 160
Independent Smallholder, Land Labourer and Citizens' Party (ISP), Smallholders' Party 160, 161
Inotai Ferenc 141
Independent Social Democratic Party (Hungary) 158, 162
Independent Social Democratic Party of Germany (USPD) 116
Independent State of Croatia 319
Independent Students' Union (NZS) (Poland) 200
Independent Trade Union Federation Podkrepa 20, 21, 22, 25, 44, 50
Independent Women's Association (UFV) 115, 116, 117, 126
Initiative Committee for the Reform of the NLP 237
Initiative Frieden und Menschenrechte (IFM) 108, 120, 122, 123
Intercity Anarchism 198
Internal Macedonian Revolutionary Organization (IMRO) 306, 308, 309, 332, 333, 337
Internal Macedonian Revolutionary Organization-Democratic Party for Macedonian National Unity (IMRO-DPMNU) 333, 334
International Confederation of Trade Unions 44
International Democrat Union 106
International Helsinki Federation for Human Rights 8
International Helsinki Human Rights Federation 224
International Monetary Fund (IMF) 178, 213, 298
Interparliamentary Club of the Democratic Right 65
Irredentist Memorial 145
Isaev A. 267
Iskenderov Sabri 39
Islam 42
Istarska Demokratska Sabor (IDS) 331
Istarska Nezavisna Stranka (INS) 331
Istarska Pucka Stranka (IPS) 331
Istrian Democratic Assembly (IDA) 331
Istrian Independent Party (IIP) 331
Istrian Popular Front (IPF) 331

Italian Republican Party (IRP) 12
Italians 303, 321
Italy 2, 12, 344, 367
Ivanov Lyubomir 43
Ivanov Vasil 51
Ivanovna Olga 48
Izetbegovic Alija 317

J

Jagielinski Roman 183, 208
Jakes Milos 56, 83
Jakubowicz Szymon 214
Jamnikar Petar 361
Jancso Miklos 145
Jani Jani 15
Jankowski Maciej 183
Janosi Gyorgy 154
Janovski Tihomir 338
Janowicz Sokrat 186
Jansa Janez 364
Japan 225
Jaruzelski Wojciech 177, 178, 187, 198, 210
Jaszczuk Boleslaw 216
Jaworski Gabriel 209
Jazbinsek Miha 361
Jazwinski Witold 205
Jedinstvena Socijalisticka Partija Jugoslavije (JSPJ) 319
Jestem Polakiem 202
Jeszenszky Geza 147
Jews 99, 151, 176
Jezek Tomas 79
Joachymstal Vratislav 72
John Paul II 20
Josifovski Branko 337
Jozwiak Jerzy 195
Jugoslavenska Samostalna Demokratska Stranka (JSDS) 331
Jugoslavenska Socijalisticka Demokratska Stranka (JSDS) 356
Jugoslovenska Demokratska Stranka (JDS) 319
Jugoslovenska Demokratska Stranka Otadzbinski Front (JDSOF) 319
Jugoslovenska Narodna Stranka (JNS) 344
Junge Union (JU) 127
Jurek Marek 190
Jurta Theatre 130, 145, 151
Justice 236

K

Kaczynski Jaroslaw 186, 187, 195
Kaczynski Lech 183
Kadar Janos 129, 130, 155, 156
Kadare Ismail 4, 8, 9
Ka-Det 269
Kadets 276
Kadic Rasim 318
Kafedzic Mujo 316
Kagarlitsky B. 275

NEW POLITICAL PARTIES OF EASTERN EUROPE AND THE SOVIET UNION

Kahlwald Brigitte 104
Kajganic Emil 322
Kajtar Istvan 148
Kakas Sandor 137
Kakuzi Vilmos 158
Kalmytsk 269
Kalvoda Jan 65
Kamenev Lev 253
KAN in Slovakia 72
KAN na Slovensku 72
Kandric Emil 368
Kanis Pavol 72
Kanyar Jozsef 152
Kapuvar Union of Private Enterpreneurs 142
Karabakh Committee 261, 278
Karadimov Rosen 32
Karadzic Radovan 317
Karaivanov Tako 38
Karakachanov Aleksander 43
Kardelj Edvard 296
Kareco Teodor 12
Karimov Islam Abduganievich 292
Karkowski Piotr 189
Kasparov Gary 263
Katolikus Neppart 140
Katov Asen 48, 51
Kavaldzhiev Todor 38
Kazakhstan 251, 260, 276, 282
Kecman Bogdan 356
Kecmanovic Nenad 313
Kejval Miloslav 75
Kelet Nepe Part Kereszstenydemokratak 164
Keller Reinhard 113, 114
Kerekgyarto Laszlo 161
Kereszteny Nemzeti Centrum 151
Keresztenydemokrata Neppart (KDNP) 140, 141
Keresztenydemokratak Szovetsege 138
Kersten Krystyna 214
Keshilli Qendror i Bashkimeve Profesionale te Shqiperise (KQBPS) 17
KGB 268, 269, 270, 273, 288
Khadyrke I. 284
Khaskovo 24
Khramov N. 273, 274
Khristiansko-demokraticheskii soyuz Rossii 285
Khrushchev Nikita 54, 252
Kik Kazimierz 210
Kilibarda Novak 339, 340, 343
Kingdom of Serbs, Croats and Slovenes 293, 331, 339, 344, 358
Kirche von unten 126
Kirchner Martin 105
Kirgizia 251, 261, 282, 282, 283
Kirimov Vielin 29
Kis Gyula 161
Kis Janos 138
Kisgazda Part 130, 131, 132, 133, 137, 144, 147, 148, 160, 161, 163
Kisielewski Stefan 216

Kisnyugdijasok Partja 165
Kiszczak Czeslaw 177, 178
Klaus Vaclav 65, 80, 81, 82
Klein Thomas 126
Klimovic Igor 76
Klub angazovanych nestraniku (KAN) 72, 79
Klub Konserwatystow im. Aleksandra hr. Fredry 193
Klub Konserwatywny w Lodzi 192
Klub na Represiranite sled 1945 Godina 37, 38
Klub Nowoczesnego Liberalizmu (KNL) 200, 201
Klub Poslanika SSOH 326
Klub Sierpien 80 191
Klub Zachowawczo-Monarchistyczny (KZ-M) 192, 193
Kmecl Matjaz 363
Kocev Lyulian 44
Kocollari Sotir 17
Kocsenda Antal 161
Koha 357
Kohl Helmut 98, 99, 105, 106, 107, 112, 118
Kolenovic Adil 315
Kolodziejczyk Michal 204
Koltay Zoltan 152
Komarek Valtr 57
Komitet Obrony Robotnikow (KOR) 191
Komitet obywatelski 186
Komitet za Zashtita na Religioznite Prava Svobodata na Savestta i Duhonite Tsenosti 20, 21, 38
Kommunistak Magyarorszagi Partja 166, 167
Kommunistische Partei Deutschlands (KPD) 95, 107, 108, 121, 124, 125
Komnenic Milan 352
Komornicki Krzysztof 211
Komsomol (Bulgaria) 19, 22, 29
Komsomol (Soviet Union) 255
Komunisticka Partija Jugoslavije-Partija Slobode (KPJ-PS) 355
Komunistyczna Partia Polski (KPP) 176
Konfederacja Polski Niepodleglej (KPN) 189, 191, 192
Konfederatsiya anarkho-sindikalistov 267, 268
Konfederatsiya truda 268, 269
Kongres Liberalno-Democratyczny (KLD) 182, 187, 188, 199, 200
Konserwatiwna Partyia 38
Konstantinova Elka 48
Konstitucionen Sayuz 38, 39
Konstitutsionno-demokraticheskaya partia (Partiya narodnoi svobody) 269
Konya Imre 147
Konzervativni strana — Svobodny blok (KS SB) 73
Korea (North) 219, 221
Korosec 306
Korwin-Mikke Janusz 216, 217
Kosa Ferenc 154

INDEX

Kosmet 344
Kosovo 2, 3, 11, 17, 18, 299, 305, 307, 308, 317, 318, 324, 339, 341, 344, 346, 356–358
Kosovo Democratic Association (KDA) 9
Kospartov Stefan 38
Kostic Branko 310
Kostic Jugoslav 342
Kotas Jiri V. 66, 73
Kovacevic Anto 322
Kovacs Laszlo 154
Kovacs Terez 161
Kovacs Zsolt Pal 153
Kovar Gyula 159
Kowalczyk Edward 195
Kowalewski Zbigniew 193
Kowalik Tadeusz 214
Kozlowski Tadeusz 195
Krajewski Adam 201
Krajewski Mieczyslaw 213
Krajina 321
Kramberger Josip 359
Krasso Gyorgy 151
Krause Gunther 106
Krctev Ivan 34
Krenz Egon 95, 104, 118, 121
Krestanska a demokraticka unie (KDU) 59, 61, 78
Krestanskodemokraticka strana (KDS) 59, 61, 63, 69, 78
Krestanskodemokraticke hnutie (KDH) 59, 61, 66, 78, 87, 88
Krest'yanskii soyuz SSSR 272, 273
Kresz Zoltan 142
Krol Krzysztof 191
Kronowski Wojciech 205
Kropownicki Jerzy 190
Kroupa Daniel 79
Krstevski Zoran 333
Kruzlics Istvan 141
Krycer Jan 86
Krzaklewski Marian 183
Krzywobocka Bozena 201
Kubat Bohumil 79
Kucan Milan 359, 363
Kucerak Jozef 91
Kudyukin P. 288
Kulteti Janos 152
Kumunisticka strana Cech a Moravy (KSCM) 66, 72, 73, 82, 83
Kumunisticka strana Ceskoslovenska (KSCS-KSC) 53, 54, 55, 57, 58, 61, 63, 66, 67, 68, 69, 72, 73
Kunicki-Goldfinger Wladyslaw 211
Kupcsok Lajos 142
Kuratowska Zofia 194, 196
Kurdzhali 24
Kurier Polski 196
Kuron Jacek 193, 196, 197
Kutsarov Stoyan 51

Kwasniewski Aleksander 214
Kyuranov Chavdov 24

L

La Malfa Giorgio 12
Labour and Social Justice Party of Romania 235
Labour Party (SP) (Poland) 189
Labour Party (Romania) 235
Labour Party Solidarity 199
Labour Solidarity 183, 184, 198, 199
Laczkowski Pawel 191
Lad i Wolnosc 190
Lafontaine Oskar 98, 124
Lambsdorff Otto Graf 112
Lamentowicz Wojciech 199
Landek Laszlo 149
Landsbergis Vytautas 173
Laso Teodor 16, 17
Latin America 253
Latvia 260, 276
Latvian Communist Party 258
Latvian Liberal Party 170
Latvian Party of Renewal 170
Latvian Popular Front 170, 260
Latvian Social-Democratic Party 170
Latvian Social-Democratic Workers' Party 170
Lauristin M. 94
Lausevic Savo 342
Lavtar Roman 361
Law on Associated Labour 297
Law on Association of Citizens 302
Law on Political Associations (Yugoslavia) 301
Law on Political Parties (Bulgaria) 22, 23
Law on Political Parties (Czechoslovakia) 59, 65, 80, 81
Law on Political Parties (GDR) 96
Law on Political Parties (Poland) 179
Law on Political Parties (Soviet Union) 262, 263
Law on Political Parties (Yugoslavia) 301
Law on Public Associations 262
Law on the Main Constitutional Provisions (Albania) 4
Leagua of Social Democrats (LSD) 331
League for Democracy (LD) (Macedonia) 338
League for Pancevo — Party for Moderate Progress (LP-PMP) 355
League of Communists — Movement for Yugoslavia (LC-MY) 354
League of Communists of Bosnia and Hercegovina — Party of Democratic Changes (LCBH-PDC) 315, 316
League of Communists of Bosnia and Hercegovina 315
League of Communists of Macedonia — Party of Democratic Change (LCM-PDC) 335
League of Communists of Montenegro (LCM) 339, 340, 342, 343
League of Communists of Serbia 345, 353
League of Communists of Slovenia 363

League of Communists of Yugoslavia
  (LCY)   293, 294, 295, 297, 298, 299, 300, 301,
  302, 304, 315, 316, 353, 354
League of Free Democrats (BFD)   98, 112, 113,
  117, 118, 119
League of Rural Youth (ZMW)   209
League of Social Democrats of Vojvodina
  (LSDV)   355
League of Socialist Workers (BSA)   117
League of Socialist Youth of Croatia
  (LSYC)   326
Left Alternative   60, 65, 81, 85
Left list   122
Left Turn   276
Left-Wing Block   144
Left-Wing Revision Party   162
Leibknecht Karl   104
Leka I of the Albanians   12
Lenin Vladimir I.   251, 252
Leninism   22, 252, 257, 277
Lenkiewicz Antoni   191
Lepavcov Aleksandar   334
Letowski Maciej   189
Leva alternativa (LA)   60, 65, 81, 85
Levyi povorot   276
Lewandowski Janusz   199
Lezsak Sandor   147
Liberal   272
Liberal Alliance of Montenegro (LAM)   307,
  341, 343
Liberal Bourgeois Alliance   142
Liberal Club (Czechoslovakia)   65, 81
Liberal Congress Party   44
Liberal-Democratic Congress (LDC)
  (Poland)   182, 199, 200
Liberal Democratic Party (LDP)   45
Liberal Democratic Party (Czechoslovakia)   65,
  80, 81, 85, 86, 86
Liberal Democratic Party (LDP) (Slovenia)   309,
  359, 361, 362
Liberal-Democratic Party in Bulgaria   45
Liberal-Democratic Party Independence (LDP
  I)   200
Liberal Democratic Party of Germany (LDP)   96,
  97, 110, 112, 117, 118, 119
Liberal-Democratic Party of the Soviet Union
  (LDP)   271, 272
Liberal-Democratic Party of the Ukraine   290
Liberal-Demokratische Partei (LDP)   96, 97, 110,
  112, 117, 118, 119
Liberal International   112, 139
Liberal Party (LP) (Bosnia and
  Hercegovina)   318
Liberal Party (Bulgaria)   45
Liberal Party (LP) (Serbia)   355
Liberal Party (LP) (Slovenia)   362, 363
Liberal Party of Kosovo (LPK)   357
Liberal Party of Romania   235
Liberal Social Union (Czechoslovakia)   74, 85

Liberal Socialist Party   231, 235
Liberal-Socialist People's Party   127
Liberal Union (Bulgaria)   45, 49
Liberalis Polgari Szovetseg   142
Liberalna Demokraticna Stranka (LDS)   361, 362
Liberalna Partiya (Bulgaria)   45
Liberalna Stranka (LS) (Bosnia and
  Hercegovina)   318
Liberalna Stranka (LS) (Serbia)   355
Liberalna Stranka (LS) (Slovenia)   362, 363
Liberalne demokraticka strana (LDS)   65, 80, 81,
  85, 86
Liberalne socialni unie   74, 85
Liberalni Savez Crne Gore (LSCG)   343
Liberalno-Demokraticheska Partiya (LDP)   45
Liberalno-Demokraticheska Partiya v
  Bulgaria   45
Liberal'no-demokraticheskaya partiya Sovetskogo
  Soyuza   271, 272
Liberalno-Demokratyczna Partia Niepodleglosc
  (LDP N)   200
Liberalnyi Sayuz (Bulgaria)   45
Liberalul   238
Libertarian Party   274
Libertarianskaya partiya   274
Libertatea — Anti-communist and Anti-fascist
  Workers' Alliance   235
Libisch Gyozi   152
Lidhja Demokratike e Kosoves (LDK)   357, 367
Lidnja Demokratike   330
Liebrenz Viktor   115
Liga Apararii Drepturilor Omului   233
Liga Socijalnih Demokrata (LSD)   331
Liga za Demokratija (LD)   338
Ligachev Yegor   255
Lila offensive (LILO)   116
Lilac Offensive (LILO)   116
Lilov Aleksandur   22, 35
Linke liste   12
Lipovskaya O.   273
Lippai Pal Gabor   143
Lippovans' Community of Romania   235
Lipski Adam   194, 211
Lipski Jan Jozef   199
Liszcz Teresa   187
Lithuania   260
Lithuanian Communist Party   257, 258, 260
Lithuanian Independence Party   172
Lithuanian Social-Democratic Party   172
Litostroj   366
Little Constitution (Poland)   178
Ljubic Mariofil   314
Loerincz Gyoergy   233
Logodzija Zlatko   315
Lokar Sonja   363
Lopuszczanski Jan   190
Lukacs Miklos   141

INDEX

Lukaniuk Marek 203
Lukanov Andrei 25, 29, 35, 42, 44
Luk'yanov Anatolii 259, 260, 264
Lulgjuraj Leke 341
Lup Ion 236
Lux Josef 83
Luxemburg Rosa 104

M

Macedonia 9, 11, 303, 305, 307, 309, 310, 331–339, 344
Macedonians 52, 299, 302, 352
Macek Miroslav 80
Machalik Jiri 83
Macierewicz Antoni 190
Mackiewicz Aleksander 195
Maclarova Emilia 40
Maczo Janos 164
Madarska Narodna Stranka Hrvatske (MNSH) 331
Madarska nezavisla iniciativa 88
Madarske krestansko-demokraticke hnutie (MKDH) 59, 72, 87, 89
Magyar Balint 138
Magyar Ciganyok Partja 163
Magyar Demokrata Forum (MDF) 130, 131, 132, 133, 139, 146, 147, 153
Magyar Demokrata Kereszteny Part 146
Magyar Dolgozok Demokratikus Centrum Part 156
Magyar Egeszseg Part 148, 149
Magyar Foradalmi Szocialistak Szovetsege 140
Magyar Fuggetlensegi Part 149, 150
Magyar Holnap 144
Magyar Humanistak Partja 149
Magyar Ipari Egyseg Part 150
Magyar Legitimista Part 153
Magyar Liberalis Neppart 150
Magyar Liberalis Part 150
Magyar Munkas Part 156
Magyar Nemzeti Kereszteny Munkaspart 150
Magyar Nemzeti Part 150, 151
Magyar Neppart (MNP) 133, 152, 153
Magyar Neppart — Nemzeti Parasztpart 133, 152, 153
Magyar Oktober Part 151, 152
Magyar Paraszt, Munkas Szovetsegi Part 163
Magyar Parasztszvetseg 164
Magyar People's Party of Croatia (MPPC) 331
Magyar Politikai Foglyok Szovetsege (POFOSZ) 139, 140
Magyar Radikalis Part 153
Magyar Realista Mozgalom 153
Magyar Republikanus Part Gyori Szervezete 153
Magyar Szabadsagpart 148
Magyar Szabadsaparti Szovetseg 148
Magyar Szocialista Munkaspart (MSZMP) 129, 130, 137, 142, 143, 151, 155, 156, 167
Magyar Szocialista Part (MSP) 130, 131, 133, 143, 153, 154, 155, 156, 162
Magyar Szovetsegi Nemzeti Part 146
Magyar Trockista Part 140
Magyar Vasarnap 160
Magyar Veternok Partja 156
Magyarok Nemzeti Szovetsege 145
Magyarorszagi Ciganyok Szocialdemokrata Partja 165
Magyarorszagi Kommunistak Partja 156
Magyarorszagi Regionalis Zold Part 157
Magyarorszagi Socialdemokrata Part (MSZDP) 130, 131, 133, 158, 159, 162, 165, 166
Magyarorszagi Szovetkezeti es Agrarpart 157
Magyarorszagi Zold Part 157, 158
Magyars 67, 303, 321, 344, 345, 348, 359
Maiorescu Toma George 243
Majewski Janusz Leonard 202
Majus 1 Tarsasag 142, 143
Makhkamov Kakhar 289
Makkai Laszlo 138
Malanowski Andrzej 211
Maleuda Gunter 110
Malewska Ewa Anna 214
Maliqi Shkelzen 358
Malofeev Anatolii Aleksandrovich 279
Malyarov I. 276
Malyatin M. 275
Mamula Branko 354
Mandler Emanuel 85
Manescu Corneliu 220, 239
Marciniak Piotr 199
Marinescu Raluca 244
Marinova Klara 35
Markezic Ivan 314
Markov Georgi 40
Markovic Ante 313, 317, 347
Marmeliuc Mihnea 237
Marosan Gyorgy 154, 156
Martian Dan 220, 239
Marton Janis 152
Marxism 35, 52, 83
Marxism-Leninism 4, 13, 22, 26, 31, 32, 34, 120, 183, 212, 215, 216
Marxist Alternative Movement 36
Marxist Platform 257
Marxist Youth Association 103
Masaliev Absamat Masalievich 283
Masaryk Democratic Movement 84
Masarykovo demokraticke hnuti 84
MASPOK 297
Maternal Hearth 11
Matica Hrvatska 297
Matica slovenska 68
May 1st Society 142, 143
Mazar Zeljko 329
Maziarski Jacek 186, 187, 195

Mazowiecki Tadeusz   176, 178, 179, 180, 182,
  183, 187, 189, 190, 192, 195, 196, 197, 198, 208
Meciar Vladimir   66, 87, 88, 89, 91
Meckel Markus   124, 125
Mecs Imre   138
Medgyasszay Laszlo   147
Medgyesy Balazs   143
Medjumurje   359
Medveczik Zoltan   157
Medvedev Roy   254
Meissner Alexandur   246
Melazi Hyqmet   17
Mencinger Joze   364
Men'shevik   170
Menzel Bruno   112
Merkel Angela   106
Merkel Ina   116
Merkel Jacek   200
Mesic Stijepan   310, 323
Meszaros Vilmos   150
Metaniev Hristo   39
Metohija   344
Metropolitan of Vinnitsa and Bratslav   261
Mexico   253
Michalak Henryk   211
Michalkiewicz Stanislaw   216
Michnik Adam   193
Michta Norbert   201
Micunovic Dragoljub   308, 348, 349
Middle East   9, 11, 18
Mieczankowski Mieczyslaw   201
Miedzymiastowka Anarchistyczna   198
Miejewski Cezary   212
Mihailo Markovic   353
Mihailov Mikhail   29
Mihailov Vasil   47
Mihailovic Dusan   354
Mihailovic Sanja   342
Mihaletzky Vilmos   144
Mikic Azis   329
Miklavcic Franc   364
Mikolajczyk Slawomir   200
Mikulic Branko   298
Military League-Zveno   31
Military-Revolutionary Committee   251
Miller Leszek   214
Milosavljevski Slavko   337, 338
Milosevic Nikola   354
Milosevic Slobodan   306, 308, 345, 346, 353, 356
Milusheva Bozhnka   39
Minchev Mincho   33, 46
Minev Ilya   43
Minkov Stroimir   33
Minzatu Ion   241
Miodowicz Witold   201
Miscarea Ecologista din Romania   243
Mlada Demokratsko-Progresivna Stranka na
  Makedonija (MDPSM)   338
Mladenov Petur   21, 22, 23, 24, 42

MLIN (Mlada Inicijativa)   365
Mlynczak Tadeusz Witold   195
Moczulski Leszek   191 192
Modern Democracy Movement   235
Modern Liberalism Club (MLC)   201
Modeva Rumiana   40
Modic Erik   366
Modos Marton   143
Modrow Hans   96, 98, 105, 108, 109, 117, 118,
  121, 122
Modzelewski Karol   199
Moldavia   251, 276, 277, 283, 283, 284
Moldova   283, 284
Mollov Valentin   30
Molnar Laszlo   162
Monarchic-Conservative Union   45
Monarchist Conservative Party (Georgia)   281
Monarhichsko-Konservativen Sayuz   45
Monolov Manol   28
Monostori Attila   149
Montenegrin Federalist Movement (MFM)   343
Montenegrins   299, 302, 339, 344, 352
Montenegro   295, 303, 305, 306, 307, 309, 310,
  339–344
Moravia   53, 59, 63, 67, 68, 76, 77, 80, 81, 84,
  86, 87
Moravian Civic Movement   84
Moravian National Party   77
Moravska narodni strana   77
Moravske obcanske hnuti   84
Morawiecki Kornel   197
Morawski Kazimierz   190
Moreth Peter   118
Moskov Atanas   34
Mosovni pokret (mass movement)   297
Mother Earth   281
Movement for a Culture of Peace and Non-
  violence (MCPN)   367
Movement for a Democratic Slovakia   66, 67, 87,
  89, 90
Movement for Civic Peace   52
Movement for Confederation (MC)   331
Movement for Czechoslovak Understanding   60,
  75 87
Movement for Democratic Socialism   22, 36
Movement for Developing Marxism and
  Renewing Socialism   51
Movement for Pan-Macedonian Action
  (MAAK)   307, 337
Movement for Radical Changes in the Socialist
  Party   36
Movement for Real Poltics   216
Movement for Self-Governing Democracy — the
  Society for Moravia and Silesia   59, 61, 63, 77,
  86
Movement for Serbian Renewal (MSR)   304,
  345, 346
Movement for the Defence of the Interest of the
  People and Homeland   15

INDEX

Movement for the Promotion of Marxism and the Renewal of Socialism 52
Movement for the Protection of Human Rights in Yugoslavia (MPHRY) 355
Movement for the Rights and Freedoms (MRF) 23, 24, 46
Movement for the Rights and Freedoms of the Turks and Muslims in Bulgaria 46
Movement for the Unification of Serbia and Montenegro (MUSM) 355
Movement of Free Democrats 201
Movement of the Working People (MWP) 201
Movement parties 262
Muchaidze Guram 281
Muco Kastrict 17
Mujagic Hamza 316
Mujzel Jan 199
Munkasok Marxista-Leninista Partja 166, 167
Munkaspart 155
Munnich Ferenc Tarsasag (MFT) 142, 143
Muntyanu A. 284
Muslim Organization 306
Muslim-Bosnian Organization (MBO) 316
Muslim Party in Bosnia and Hercegovina 344, 351
Muslim Party of Democratic Action (PDA) 9
Muslim Turkish Democratic Union of Romania 236
Muslimanska-Bosnjacka Organizacija (MBO) 316
Muslims 20, 21, 46, 51, 299, 311, 313, 317, 332, 339, 341, 344, 345, 352
Mutalibov Azya Niyazi ogly 278
MVD 270, 288

N

Nabat 268
Nachev Ventsislav 33
Nachichevan 278
Nadelchev Mikhail 49
Nagorno-Karabakh 278
Nagy Ferenc Jozsef 161
Nagy Sandor Sz. 150
Nagy Tamas 137
Nagy Zoltan 159
Nagy-Husszein Tibor 137
Nahimi Peter 147
Najder Zdzislaw 183, 187
Najwyzszy Czas 217
Nano Fatos 1, 3, 6, 7, 12, 13, 14, 16, 18
Naradno Zemedelsko Zname 30
Narod i vlast' 170
Naroden Sayuz Zveno 47
Narodna Partija na Makedonija (NPM) 338
Narodna Radikalna Stranka (NRS) (Serbia) 355
Narodna Seljacka Stranaka (NSS) 349, 350
Narodna Stranka (NS) (Montenegro) 343
Narodna Stranka (NS) (Serbia) 356
Narodna Stranka Bosne (NSB) 319
Narodnaliberalna Partyia Stafan Stambolov 47

Narodnaya gazeta 291
Narodne socialisticka strana 74
Narodne socialni strana (NSS) 74, 86
Narodno Vijece za Zastitu Naroda Bosne i Hercegovine (NVZN BiH) 319
Narodowa Demokracja (ND) 176
Narodowa Demokracja 202
Narodowa Mysl Polska 207
Narodowa Parta Robotnicza (NPR) 202, 203
Narodowe Odrodzenie Polski (NOP) 202
Natadze Nodar 281
National Agrarian Banner 30
National Alliance of Hungarians 145
National Alliance of Parties of the Centre 149, 153, 159, 166
National Association of Those Not in Parties 162
National Christian Democratic Peasants' Party 219, 221, 222, 223, 225, 36
National Christian Party of Moldova 284
National Committee for the Defence of National Interests 46, 47
National Convention for Democracy 234, 236, 238, 244
National Council for the Defence of the Peoples of Bosnia and Hercegovina (NCDPBH) 319
National Democracy 184, 202
National Democratic Forum 49
National Democratic Institute for International Affairs 225
National Democratic Party (NDP) (Georgia) 281, 282, 285
National Democratic Party (NDP) (Macedonia) 334
National Democratic Party (NDP) (Poland) 176
National Democratic Party (NDP) (Romania) 237
National-Democratic Party of Belorussia 280
National Democratic Party of Germany (NDPD) 96, 97, 98, 110, 117, 118, 119
National Democratic Party of Germany (NPD) 99, 120
National-Demokratische Partei Deutschlands (NDPD) 96, 97, 98, 110, 117, 118, 119
National Electoral Alliance 138, 140, 163
National Emergency Committee 266
National Forum 145
National Front (GDR) 105, 110, 118, 119
National Independence Party (Georgia) 282
National Liberal Party (NLP) 219, 221, 222, 223, 225, 227, 236, 237, 238
National Liberal Party Stefan Stambolov 47
National Liberation Front (NLF) 13
National Organization of Women 202
National Party (NP) (Montenegro) 343
National Party (NP) (Poland) 201, 202, 202
National Party of Bosnia (NPB) 319
National Party-Piast 202
National Peasant Party (NPP) (Croatia) 348, 349, 350

389

National Peasant Party (Hungary) 152
National People's Army (GDR) 109
National Popular Union 175
National Progress Party 238
National Radical Party (NRP) (Serbia) 306, 355
National Rebirth of Poland Party (NRPP) 202
National Reconstruction Party (Hungary) 162
National Reconstruction Party (Romania) 238
National Republican Party 239, 241
National Resistance of Germany 127
National Salvation Front (NSF) 220, 221, 222, 223, 224, 225, 237, 239, 240, 242, 243, 246, 247, 249
National Smallholders and Bourgeois Party 163
National Social Party 74, 86
National Socialist Party (Czechoslovakia) 74
National Union of Agricultural Circles (KZRKiOR) 209
National Union Zveno 47
National Unity and Democracy Forum of Romania 240
National Unity and Dignity Party 237
National Unity Party of Romanians in Transylvania 240
National Veterans' Committee (NVC) 5, 15
National Workers' Party 202, 203
National Youth Union 47
Nauchno-promyshlennyi soyuz SSSR 274, 275
Naviny BNF 279
Nazarbaev Nursultan Abishevich 282
Nazi Germany 252
Nazi-Soviet Pact 93, 169, 171, 251
Neatkariba Tsinya 170
Nedelchev Mikhail 48
Nedelyas Lapa 170
Neff Istvan 159
Negotiated Revolution 178, 179
Nemes Lajos 152
Nemeth Bela 161
Nemeth Jozsef 159, 164
Nemeth Laszlo Akos 143
Nemeth Zsolt 143
Nemzedekek Partja 144, 145
Nemzeti Kisgazda es Polgari Part 163
Nemzeti Ujjaepites Partja 162
NepAkarat Part (NAP) 164
Nessing-Stranz Dorrit 115
Netea Gelu 237
Network of Free Initiatives 130, 138
Netzwerk Arche 115
Neubert Jurgen 112
Neues Forum (NF) 103, 108, 113, 119, 120, 122, 126
Nevrokopski Ivan 38
Nevrokopski Krum 29
New Class 296
New Course (Bulgaria) 20
New Democracy (Serbia) 354
New Democracy-Movement for Serbia (ND) 354

New Democracy Social Justice Party 240
New Economic Mechanism 129
New Economic Policy 251
New Forum (NF) 103, 108, 113, 119, 120, 122, 126, 239
New Hungarians' Justice Party 163
New Party (NS) 331
New Right 362
New Social Democratic Party 47
New Socialists 275
Nezavisima Federatsiya na Truda Podkrepa 20, 21, 22, 25, 44, 50
Nezavisimo Druzhestvo za Zashtita na Choveshkite Prava v Bulgariya 43, 44
Nezavisimost 292
Nezavisna Organizaci ja Komunista (NOK) 343
Nezavisno Demokratsko Udruzenje (NDU) (Kosovo) 358
Nezvat Halili 335
Nica Leon 231
Niepodleglosciowa Partia Solidarnosc (NP-S) 198
Niesolowski Stefan 190
Nikola Petkov Agrarian Youth Union 47
Nikolov Ivan 36
Nikolov Zahari 42
Niyazov Saparmurad Ataevich 289
Noli Fan 4
nomenklatura 34, 178, 268, 298
Non-Aligned Movement (NAM) 296
Non-Party Bloc for Collaboration with Government (BBWR) 175
North America 9, 18
North Atlantic Treaty Organization (NATO) 270, 282
Nova Demokratija-Pokret za Srbiju (ND) 354
Nova Sotsialdemokraticheska Partiya 47
Nova Stranka (NS) 331
Novac Traian 246
Novak Tibor 150
Novak V. 82
Novakov Dimitri 43
Novi Pazar 305, 317, 339, 344
Novodvorskaya V. 270
Novotny Antonin 54
Nowacki Tadeusz 190
Nowina-Konopka Piotr 196, 197
Nuschke Otto 15
Nyers Rezso 154
Nyilas Janos 157
Nyiro Sandor 155
Nyitray Bela 158
Nyugdijasok es Csaladosok Partja 144, 145

O

Obcanska demokraticka aliance (ODA) 60, 65, 69, 72, 79
Obcanska demokraticka strana (ODS) 65, 66, 67, 72, 73, 77, 78, 79, 80

INDEX

Obcanske forum (OF)   57 58, 59, 60, 61, 63, 64, 65, 66, 67, 69, 75, 76, 77, 78, 80, 81
Obcanske hnuti (OH)   65, 77, 80, 81, 82
Ob'edinennyi front trudyashchikhsya SSSR   276, 277
Obolensky A.   288
Obroda (Reawakening) Club for Socialist Restructuring   59, 65, 75, 81, 84
Obroda Klub pro socalistickou prestavbu   59, 65, 75, 81, 84
Obshchina   268
Obshtestven Forum   51
Obshtonaroden Komitet za Zashtita na Natsionalnite Interesi   46, 47
Ogorodnikov A.   285
Olah Imre   142
Olah Vladimir   76
Olaj Sandor   161
Olajos Arpad   152
Old Radical Party (ORP)   355
Olimo   291
Oman Ivan   304, 365
Omolnar Miklos   160, 161
OMONIA Socio-Political Organization   1, 3, 5, 6, 11, 15, 16
Opinia   192
Opletal Jan   57
Orban Viktor   131, 143
Order and Freedom   190
Order Union of Orthodox Monarchists   287
Organization of Independent Romanians   59
Orientacje na Prawo   200
Ormandlaky Erno   158
Ormanliev Ali   39
Orthodox Christian Union   240
Orthodox Church   52, 318
Ortleb Rainer   112, 118
Osman Oktay   46
Osmani Resmi   7
Osobka-Morawski Edward   201, 213
Osrodek Dokumentacji i Studiow Spolecznych   204
Ostoja-Owsiany Andrzej   191
Ostrovsky A.   269
Ostrovsky E.   275

P

Paderewski Ignacy   175
Palach Jan   56
Pales Gyorgy   152
Palka Grzegorz   190
Palos Laszlo   153
Palos Miklos   141
Palyi Gyula   141
Palyushev Bozhidar   44
Pan-European Union   81
Pandor Piroska   152
Pantea Gheorghe   242
Paraga Dobroslav   329

Paraszt-es Munkaspart (Debrecen)   163, 164
Paraszt-Munkas Szovetseg Part   163, 164
Parlamentary Klub Unia Demokratyczna (PKUD)
Parliamentary Assembly of the Council of Europe   225
Parliamentary Party of Kosovo (PPK)   357, 358
Partei der Mitteldeutschen Nationaldemokraten   120
Partei des Demokratischen Sozialismus (PDS)   97, 98, 99, 103, 107, 112, 117, 120, 121, 122, 125
Partia Bashkimi Kombetarwe Shqiperise (PBKS)   3, 10, 11
Partia Centrum (PC)   182, 183, 186, 187, 189, 190, 208, 210
Partia Demokratike Shgiperise (PDS)   1, 2, 3, 4, 6, 7, 8, 9, 11, 12, 14, 15
Partia e Bashkimit Demokratik Shqiptar (PBDS)   358
Partia Ecologia Shuiperise (PES)   3, 5, 10
Partia Fshatare e Kosoves (PFK)   358
Partia Konserwatywna (Opole)   193
Partia Konserwatywna (PK)   193
Partia Parlamentare e Kosoves   357, 358
Partia Pracy Solidarnosc   199
Partia Republikanska Shqiperise (PRS)   1, 3, 5, 7, 11
Partia Republikanska — Towarzystwo Republikanskie Polskie (PR-TRP)   214
Partia Rzemiosla Polskiego (PRP)   206
Partia Shqiptare Demokristiane (PDS)   356
Partia Socialdemokrate (PDS) (Kosovo)   358
Partia Socialdemokratike e Shqiperise (PSDS)   1, 3, 16, 17
Partia Socialiste Shqiperise (PSS)   1, 2, 3, 7, 12, 13, 14, 15
Partia Wolnosci (PW)   197, 198
Partia X   203, 204
Partidul Alianta Pentru Democratie   226
Partidul Communist Roman   219, 221, 230, 241, 242, 243, 246, 247
Partidul Cooperatist   228
Partidul Crestin al Libertatii si Drepturilor Omului   228
Partidul Crestin Democrat Maghiar din Romania   233
Partidul de Uniune Nationala a Romanilor din Transilvania   240
Partidul Democrat   229
Partidul Democrat Agrar din Romania   226
Partidul Democrat al Muncii   229
Partidul Democrat al Muncii Agricole, Industriale si Intelectuale   229
Partidul Democrat Constitutional din Romania   247
Partidul Democrat din Romania   230
Partidul Democrat Ecologist   229
Partidul Democrat Progresist   241
Partidul Democratic al Romilor Liberi   23

Partidul Dreptatii Sociale Liber Democrat 232
Partidul Dreptatii Sociale (Nuova Democratie) 240
Partidul Ecologist Roman 244
Partidul Ecologist Umanist 233
Partidul Gospodarilor Maghiari din Romania 234
Partidul Independent Maghiar 234
Partidul Liber Democrat 231
Partidul Liber Schimbist 231
Partidul Liberal din Romania 235
Partidul Libertatii si Democratiei Romane 232
Partidul Miscarea Democratia Moderna 235
Partidul Muncii 235
Partidul Muncii si Dreptatii Sociale din Romania 235
Partidul National Crestin Independent 234
Partidul National Democrat 237
Partidul National Liberal 219, 221, 222, 223, 225, 227, 236, 237, 238
Partidul National Progresist 238
Partidul National Republican 239, 241
Partidul National Roman 244
Partidul National Taranesc-Crestin si Democrat 236
Partidul Pentru Reconstructia Nationala 238
Partidul Poporului din Romania 241
Partidul Progresist 241
Partidul Radical Democrat 241
Partidul Reconstructie Nationale din Romania 238
Partidul Republican 241
Partidul Republican Crestin 228
Partidul Republican de Unitate a Romanilor 242
Partidul Roman Pentru Noua Societate 244
Partidul Social Democrat Crestin Roman 242
Partidul Social Democrat Roman 219, 221, 222, 225, 236, 246
Partidul Socialist al Dreptatii 247
Partidul Socialist Democratic Roman 246
Partidul Socialist Liberal 235
Partidul Taranesc Roman 245
Partidul Tiganilor din Romania 242
Partidul Tineretului Liber Democrat 232
Partidul Umanitar al Pacii 233
Partidul Unit Democrat al Romilor, Lautarilor si Rudarilor din Romania 248
Partidul Unitatii Democratice 231
Partidul Unitatii Democratice din Moldova 231
Partidul Uniunea Crestin-Democrata din Romania 227
Partidul Uniunea Crestin Ortodoxa 240
Partidul Uniunea Liberala Bratianu 227
Partidul Uniunea Republicana 242
Partidul Vitorul Democrat al Partiei 229
Partie Agrar Shqiperise (PAS) 1, 3, 5, 6, 7
Partija Demokratsko Delovanje (PDD) 350
Partija Ljudskih Prava Makedonije (PLPM) 338
Partija Socijalista Crne Gore (PSCG) 344

Partija za Celosna Emancipacija na Romite (PCER) 338
Partija za Demokratski Prosperitet vo Makedonija (PDP) 334, 335
Partis Demokratis Populore (PDP) 334
Partiya islamskogo vozrozhdeniya 272
Partiya konstitutsionnykh demokratov 276
Partiya Liberalen Kongres 44
Partonkivuliek Orszagos Egyesulete 162
Partonkivuliek Partja 162
Party for Democracy and a Just State (PDJS) 319
Party for Democratic Prosperity in Macedonia (PDP) 334, 335
Party for the Complete Emancipation of Romanies (PCER) 338
Party of Central German National Democrats 120
Party of Citizens' Equality (PCE) 367
Party of Constitutional Democrats 276
Party of Constitutional Democracy 73
Party of Czechoslovak Neutrality 73
Party of Democratic Action (PDA) 308, 317, 331, 341, 344, 350, 351
Party of Democratic Agreement (PDA) 319
Party of Democratic Changes (PDC) 309, 315, 321, 327, 329, 332
Party of Democratic Reforms of Bosnia and Hercegovina (PDRBH) 319
Party of Democratic Renaissance of the Ukraine 290
Party of Democratic Renewal (PDR) 363
Party of Democratic Socialism (PDS) 97, 98, 99, 103, 107, 112, 117, 120, 121, 122, 125
Party of Direct Action 339
Party of Equality 341, 344
Party of Fidelity to the Republic 203
Party of Free Democrats 73
Party of Human Rights of Macedonia (PHRM) 338
Party of Hungarian Communists (Leninist) 167
Party of Hungarian Gypsies 163
Party of Independent Businessmen (PIB) 355
Party of Independent Democracy (PID) 331
Party of Independent Democrats of Serbia (PIDS) 356
Party of Islamic Rebirth (PIR) 272
Party of National Concord (PNC) 356
Party of National Equality (PNE) 344
Party of National Independence of Estonia 94
Party of Pensioners and those with Families 144, 145
Party of Popular Freedom 269
Party of Private Enterprises of Romania 240
Party of Private Initiative (PPI) 319
Party of Progress (Macedonia) 339
Party of Progressively Oriented Yugoslavs (PPOY) 319
Party of Republican Youth 163

INDEX

Party of Romanies in Croatia (PRC) 331
Party of Slavonic Renaissance 291
Party of Slovak Renewal 53, 57, 89
Party of Social Justice (PSJ) 356
Party of Socialists of Montenegro (PSM) 307, 341, 344
Party of the Alliance of Peasants of Serbia (PAPS) 350
Party of the Centre 127
Party of the Democratic Left 90
Party of the Working People 31
Party of Those not in Parties 162
Party of United Macedonians 339
Party of Yugoslavs (PY) 330, 331, 351
Party of Yugoslavs for Bosnia and Hercegovina (PYBH) 319
Party of Yugoslavs in Macedonia (PYM) 335
Party to Honour the Revolution's Heroes and for National Salvation 231, 240
Party X 203, 204
Pashko Gramoz 3, 8, 9
Pasic Nikola 306, 355
Pastuszewski Stefan 215
Pasztor Gyula 161
Patriotic Electoral Coalition 163
Patriotic Front of National Rebith (PRON) 177
Patriotic Party 163
Patriotic People's Front 163
Pavlov Lyubomir 51
Pavlov Valentin 265
Pawlowicz Janusz 213
Pawlowski Krzysztof 188
PAX Association 176, 181, 204
Peace and Human Initiative 103
Peace and Human Rights Initiative (IFM) 108, 120, 122, 123
Peasant and Worker Party (Debrecen) 163, 164
Peasant-Democratic Party of Moldova 284
Peasant Farmers' Union
Peasant Labour Party of Serbia (PLPS) 356
Peasant Party of Kosovo (PPK) 358
Peasant Union of the USSR 272, 273
Peasant-Workers' Party (PWP) 319
Peasant Yugoslav Party (PYP) 319
Peev Hristo 37
Peicheva Vera 47
Pejanovic Mirko 315
Pelivan Jure 314
People and Power 170
People of the East Party Christian Democrats 164
People's Union 123
People's Assembly (Albania) 4, 6, 15
People's Chamber 95
People's Committee for Defending National Interests 42
People's Front of Moldova 284
People's Independent Party of Vlahs (PIPV) 356
People's Party (PP) (Serbia) 356

People's Party of Macedonia (PPM) 338
People's Party of Romania 241
People's Party of the Ukraine 291
People's Republic of Albania 13
People's Republic of China 13
People's Socialist Republic of Albania 13
People's Will Party 164
People's Youth Union 41
Perestroika 56, 177, 221, 253, 254, 257, 258, 268, 283
Persak Tone 364
Personality cult 54
Peter Veres Association 152
Peterle Alojz 364
Petkanov Dimitar 37
Petkanova Ekaterina 37
Petkov Boris 31
Petkov Krustyn 51
Petkov Nikola 19, 30
Peto Ivan 138
Petofi Party 152
Petres Sandor 166
Petrik Jan 88
Petrov Boycho 48
Petrov Petar Kanev 38
Petrovic Dragoslav 346
Petrovic Drazen 318
Petu Gheorge 247
Pflugbeil Sebastian 119
Pher Jozica 363
Piasecki Boleslaw 176, 204
Piast Peasant Party 175
Pilsudski Jozef 175, 176, 180, 184
Piotrowski Walerian 189
Pirnat Rajko 364
Pithart Petr 57, 61, 65, 82
Pitra Frantisek 57
Plamen Minchev 28
Plavsic Biljana 317
Plewako Stanislaw 193
Plosiin V. 287
Plut Dustan 361
Podkrepa Independent Trade Union Federation 20, 21, 22, 25, 44, 50
Podol'tseva E. 273
Pogosyan Stefan Karapetovich 278
Pohl Wolfgang 121
Pokret za Konfederaciju (PK) 331
Pokret za Ujedinjenje Srbije i Crne Gore (PUSOG) 355
Pokret za Zastitu Ljudskih Prava u Jugoslaviji (PZLjPJ) 355
Pokrovac Zoran 326
Poland 21, 22, 96 220, 239
Poles 72, 77
Polish Catholic Social Union (PCSU) 176, 204, 205
Polish Christian Democratic Forum (PChDF) 188

Polish Christian Right (PCR) 205
Polish Ecology Party 205
Polish Economic Party (PEP) 205
Polish Green Alliance 206
Polish Green Party (PGP) 205, 206
Polish Handicrafts Party (PHP) 206
Polish Independence Party (PIP) 206
Polish National Commonwealth — Polish National Party (PNW-PNP) 207
Polish National Front (PNF) 207
Polish National Thought 207
Polish Party of Friends of Whisky (PPPW) 207
Polish Party of the Friends of Beer (PPFB) 207
Polish Party of World Citizens 207, 208
Polish Peasant Party (PPP) 176, 208, 209
Polish Peasant Party (Bak Faction — PPP-Bak) 209
Polish Peasant Party — Solidarity (PPP-S) 209, 210
Polish People's Republic 179
Polish Republic 179
Polish Republikan Club 210
Polish Social Democratic Party (PSDP) 210
Polish Social Democratic Union (PSDU) 183, 210, 211
Polish Socialist Party (PSP) 176, 184, 211, 212
Polish Socialist Party (Independent) 213
Polish Socialist Party (Provisional National Committee — PSP-PNC) 212, 213
Polish Socialist Party (Rebirth — PSP-R) 213
Polish Socialist Party — Democratic Revolution (PPS-DR) 212
Polish United Workers' Party (PUWP) 176, 177
Polish Workers' Party (PPR) 176, 211
Political Opposition Block (POB) 37, 45
Political Party of the Unemployed of Macedonia (PPUM) 338
Political Patriotic Association Cameria 11
Politicka Partija Nezaposlenih Makedonije (PPNM) 338
Politika 172
Polska Partia Gospodarcza (PPG) 205
Polska Partia Niepodleglosci (PPN) 206
Polska Partia Obywateli Swiata (PPOS) 207, 208
Polska Partia Przyjaciol Piwa (PPPP) 207
Polska Partia Robotnicza (PPR) 176
Polska Partia Socjaldemokratyczna (PPSd) 210
Polska Partia Socjalistyczna (PPS) 176, 211, 212
Polska Partia Socjalistyczna (Niezalezna — PPS-N) 213
Polska Partia Socjalistyczna (Odrodzona — PPS-O) 213
Polska Partia Socjalistyczna (Tymczasowy Komitet Krajowy — PPS-TKK) 212, 213
Polska Partia Socjalistyczna — Rewolucja Demokratyczna (PPS-RD) 212
Polska Partia Zielonych (PPZ) 205, 206
Polska Prawica Chrzescijanska (PPCh) 205
Polska Socjalistyczna Partia Pracy (PSPP)

Polska Unia Socjaldemokratyczna (PUS) 183, 210, 211
Polska Wspolnota Narodowa — Polskie Stronnictwo Narodowe (PWN-PN) 207
Polska Zjednoczona Partia Robotnicza (PZPR) 176, 177, 178, 179, 183, 184, 210, 211, 214
Polski Front Narodowy (PFN) 207
Polski Klub Republikanski (PKR) 210
Polski Zwiazek Katolicko-Spoleczny (PZKS) 176, 181, 204, 205
Polskie Forum Chrzescijansko-Demokratyczne 188
Polskie Stronnictwo Ludowe (Grupa Henryka Baka — PSL-Bak) 181, 183, 209
Polskie Stronnictwo Ludowe (PSL) 176, 186, 208, 209
Polskie Stronnictwo Ludowe-Piast (PSL-Piast) 176
Polskie Stronnictwo Ludowe Solidarnosc (PSL-S) 209, 210
Polskie Stronnictwo Ludowe-Wyzwolenie (PSL-Wyzwolenie) 176, 208
Polslovo 290
Pomian Jerzy 191
Poor Support Fund 138, 139
Popiel Aleksander 193, 216
Popov Aleksandur 48
Popov Dimitur 25, 29
Popov Gavriil 261
Popov Nebojsa 347
Popov Nikodim 29
Popovic Miladin 358
Popovic Mirjana 347
Popovski Ante 337
Popovski Kiro 336
Poppe Gerd 122
Poppe Ulrike 108
Popular Front (Estonia) 260
Popular Movement of the Ukraine for Perestroika 291
Porozumienie Ludzi Pracy 201
Porozumienie Obywatelskie na Rzecz Demokracji i Pluralizmu (PORDiP) 191
Portugal 178
Potentialist People's Party 127
Powszechna Partia Slowian i Narodow Sprzymierzonych (PPSiNS) 217
Poznyak Z. 279
Pozsgay Imre 130, 131, 132, 154
Pozsonyi Attila 155
Prague Spring 55, 56, 84, 90
Prava i Svobodi 46
Pravda 253, 257, 261
Pravoslavnyi monarkhicheskii order-soyuz 287
Praxis 297, 301
Premurje 358, 359
Prepeliczay Istvan 161
Presidency (Bulgaria) 23, 24

INDEX

Presidency (Poland)   177, 178, 179, 180, 181, 182, 187
Presidency (Russia)   261, 263, 265, 285
Presidency (Soviet Union)   264, 265, 267
Presidential Council   265
Priale Vasile   241
Pribicevic Dragan   327
Private Farmers' Union   182
Prizyv natsii   291
Prkutyun   285
Prochowski Jan   198
Programme of the Communist Party of the Soviet Union   258
Progresi Agrar   7
Progressive Democratic Party   231, 241
Progressive New Party   127
Progressive Party   241
Progressive People's Party   52, 114, 123
Progressive People's Party of the Centre (PPPC)   368
Prokes Jozef   91
Proletarian Youth Union   41
Provisional Committee   177
Provisional Council of National Unity   222, 223
Provisional Government   251
Proznin A.   273, 274
Przeglad Polityczny   200
Przybylowice Marcin   186, 195
PSL-Odrodzenie   183, 208, 210
PSL-Rebirth   183, 208, 210
PSL-Solidarity   182, 183, 187, 188, 209
PSL-Wilanow   183, 188, 208, 209
PSL-Wilanowskie   183, 188, 208, 209
Public Against Violence   57 58, 59, 60, 61, 63, 66, 67, 69, 75, 76, 80, 81, 87, 88, 89, 90, 91
Public Forum   51
Pucnik Joze   359, 366
Pugo   266
Puhovski Zarko   347
Pukl Vitograd   366
Pullaha Ruzhdi   16
Punyi Istvan   162
Puto Arben   8

R

Rabotnicheski Mladezhki Sayuz   41
Rabotnicka Partija na Makedonija (RPM)   339
Rabotnicko-Zemjodelska Partija (RZP)   338
Racan Ivica   321
Racz Sandor   152
Radic Stjepan   324
Radical Association for Peace and Freedom   273, 274
Radical Democratic Party (RDP) (Bulgaria)   48
Radical Democratic Party (Romania)   241
Radical Party (Denmark)   362
Radical Party (Serbia)   306
Radical Party (Soviet Union)   274
Radikalna Demokraticheska Partiya (RDP)   48

Radikal'naya assotsiatsiya za mir i svobodu   273, 274
Radikal'naya partiya   274
Radio Free Europe   183, 187
Radnicka Demokratska Stranka-Stranka Federalista (RDS-SF)   319
Radnicka Partija Jugoslavije (RPJ)   356
Rado Alban   10
Rajk Laszlo   138
Rajna Tibor   160
Rakitic Slobodan   352
Rakov Yu.   276
Rakowski Mieczyslaw   177
Ramin Lothar   113
Raskovic Jovan   327
Ratiu Ion   223, 224
Rau Johannes   124
Rauls Wolgang   119
Razgrad   24
Reberc Peter   364
Reform and Democracy Association   213, 214
Regeneration process   20
Regional Democratic Youth Organization   164
Regulski Jerzy   194
Reich Jens   119
Rejc Isidor   364
Renaissance (Latvia)   170
Renaissance (Lithuania)   173
Republic Party   241
Republican National Party   165
Republican Party (RP) (Bulgaria)   48, 50
Republican Party (Czechoslovakia)   61, 76
Republican Party (Romania)   241
Republican Party (Russia)   263, 264
Republican Party (RP) (Serbia)   356
Republican Party (United States)   60, 61
Republican Party — Polish Republican Society (RP-PRS)   214
Republican Party in Bulgaria   48
Republican Party of Bosnia and Hercegovina (RPBH)   319
Republican Party of Kosovo (RPK)   358
Republican Peasants' Party   242
Republican Union   60, 72, 73, 76
Republican Union Party   242
Republican Unity Party of Romania   242
Republicans (REPs)   123, 124
Republicka Stranka Bosne i Hercegovine (RSBiH)   319
Republikanska Partiya (RP)   48
Republikanska Partiya v Bulgaria   48
Republikanska strana (RS)   61, 76
Republikanska stranka (RS) (Serbia)   356
Republikanska unie (RU)   73, 76
Republikanus Fiatalok Partja   163
Republikanus Nemzeti Part   165
Respublika (Estonia)   94
Respublika (Moldova)   284
Rexepi Isuf   334

Rhineland-Palatinate   99, 106
Ribanszki Robert   155
Ribicic Ciril   363
Riha Vladimir   85
Rijecki Demokratski Savez (RDS)   331
Rijeka Democratic League (RDL)   331
Rilindja Demokratike   8
Rippert Ulrich   117
Robert Laszlo   148
Rogowski Jozef   208
Rojek Stanislaw   188
Rokicki Zbigniew   199
Rokita Jan   193
Rola Peasant Agrarian Movement   188, 214
Roma Parlament   165
Roman Catholic Church   187, 204, 205, 211, 306
Roman Petre   220, 221, 225, 237, 239
Romani of Romania Party   242
Romania   2, 14, 55, 203
Romania Muncitoare   232
Romanian Anti-totalitarian Forum   242
Romanian Christian Social Democratic Party   242
Romanian Communist Party   219, 221, 230, 241, 242, 243, 246, 247
Romanian Democratic Front   243
Romanian Ecological Movement   243
Romanian Ecological Party   225, 236, 244
Romanian Home of Democratic Europe   244
Romanian National Party   244
Romanian New Society Party   227, 244
Romanian Peasants' Party   245
Romanian People's Front   245
Romanian Republic of Moldova   284
Romanian Social Democratic Party (SDP)   219, 221, 222, 225, 236, 246, 284
Romanian Socialist Democratic Party   246
Romanian's Democratic Constitutional Party   247
Romanians' Union Republican Party   231
Romanies   77, 332, 344, 345
Romanov dynasty   287
Romany Civic Initiative   76
Romany National Congress   76, 77
Romany Parliament   165
Romhanyi Laszlo   145, 151
Romska obcanska iniciativa (ROI)   76
Romsky narodni kongres (RNK)   76, 77
Ronahati Istvan   161
Roshka Yu.   284
Rospara Henryk   189
Rossisloe khristianskoe-demokraticheskoe dvizhenie   287
Rott Nador   141
Round Table (Bulgaria)   22, 23,
Round Table (GDR)   96, 108, 109, 114, 115, 117, 122, 126
Round Table (Hungary)   130, 132, 133, 139, 143, 151, 152
Round Table (Poland)   177, 178, 179, 184, 187, 191, 195, 198, 211, 216

Round Table-Free Georgia   261
Roussanov Lenko   48
Rozsa Mihaly   153
Rozsik Gabor   147
Rubiks Alfred Petrovich   169
Ruch Akcja Ludowo-Agrarna Rola   214
Ruch Ludzi Pracy (RLP)   183, 184, 201
Ruch Obywatelski Akcja Demokratyczna (ROAD) — Ruch Demokratyczno Spoleczny (RDS)   208
Ruch Wolnych Demokratow (RWD)   201
Rugova Ibrahim   9, 357
Ruhe Volker   105
Ruhle Heide   115
Rukh   261, 291
Rules of the Communist Party of the Soviet Union   258, 259
Rumen Krumov   34
Rumyantsev O.   288
Rupel Dimitrij   301, 306, 364
Rusakiewicz Marek   189
Ruse   37
Russia   259, 260, 276, 277, 282, 285, 286, 287, 288
Russian Christian-Democratic Movement (RCDM)   287
Russian Popular Front   263
Russian Social Democratic Labour Party   251
Russian Social-Democratic Party of Estonia   94
Russian Soviet Federal Socialist Republic (RSFSR)   251
Rustaveli Society   281
Ruthenians   68, 72
Rutter Gyorgy   162
Rychetsky Pavel   65, 82

S

Saarland   98
Sabo Peter   75
Sabor Republika Hrvatska   326
Sadowski Zdzislaw   200
Sagdeev Roald   255, 256
Sajudis   172, 173, 260
Sakharov Andrei   255, 256, 264
Salga Istvan   156
Salvation   285
Samizdat   130, 138
Samostalna Politicka Zajednica (SPZ)   355
Sanacja   175
Sandowicz Michal   216
Sandulescu I. V.   237
Sandzak   305, 308, 317, 339, 344, 351
Santulov Hristo   45
Savez Komunista Bosne i Hercegovine — Stranka Demokratskih Promjena (SK BiH-SPD)   315, 316
Savez Komunista — Pokret za Jugoslaviju (SK-PJ)   354
Savez Komunista Crne Gore (SKCG)   342, 343

INDEX

Savez Komunista Hrvatsske-Stranka Demokratskih Promjena 326
Savez Reformskih Snaga Jugoslavi je za Bosnu i Hercegovinu (SRSJ BiH) 313, 314
Savez Reformskih Snaga Jugoslavije (SRSJ) 346, 347
Savez Reformskih Snaga Jugoslavije za Hrvatsku (SRSJH) 321, 322
Savez Reformskih Snaga Vojvodina (SRSV) 346
Savez Reformskih Snaga za Crnu Goru (SRSCG) 340, 341
Savez Socijalistickih Omladina-Demokratski Savez Bosne i Hercegovine (SSO-DSBiH) 318
Savez Socijalistickih Omladina Hrvatske (SSOH) 326
Savez Svih Srba Sveta (SSSS) 355
Savon Stefan 40
Savostin G. 283
Saxony 97, 98, 114
Sayuz na Demokratichni Myusyulmani 51
Sayuz na Demokratichni Sili (SDS) 21, 22, 23, 24, 25, 28, 29, 30, 32, 34, 35, 36, 37, 38, 40, 41, 42, 43, 44, 47, 48, 49, 50, 51
Sayuz na Narodna Mladezh 41
Sayuz za Grazhdanska Stopanska Initsiativa 49
Sbrzesny Klaus 107
Schabowski Gunter 121
Schenk Christina 117
Schmalz-Jacobsen Cornelia 111, 112
Schmieder Jurgen 113
Schmuok Erzsebet 157
Schnur Wolfgang 109
Schonhuber Franz 123, 124
School Youth Party of Serbia (SYPS) 356
Schorlemmer Friedrich 109
Schrammm Henry G. 115
Scientific-Industrial Union of the USSR 274, 275
Scuka Emil 76
Sdruzeni ceskoslovenskych podnikatelu 84
Sdruzeni pro republiku — republikanska strana Ceskoslovenska (SPR-RSC) 69, 71
Sdruzeni soukromych zemedelcu 84
Sebeok Janos 166
Securitate 2, 219, 220
Security Council (Soviet Union) 265
Seeling Marion 126
Sejdija Hajdin 9
Sejm 175, 176, 177, 178, 179, 180, 181, 184, 185, 188, 211
Selami Eduard 8
Seljacka Jugoslovenska Stranka (SJS) 319
Seljacko-Radnicka Stranka (SRS) 319
Semonov R. 269
Senate (Poland) 175, 177, 179, 180, 184, 185
Senate (Romania) 223, 225
Seniuch Czeslaw 210
September 6 Forum 49
Serbia 11, 299, 303, 305, 306, 307, 309, 310, 317, 318, 327, 331, 344–356

Serbian Democratic Forum of Kosovo and Metohija (SDF) 358
Serbian Democratic Party (SDP) 309, 313, 327, 328, 351, 352
Serbian Democratic Party of Bosnia and Hercegovina (SDPBH) 317, 318
Serbian Democratic Union of Romania 247
Serbian Liberal Party (SLP) 354
Serbian Movement for Renewal (SMR) 308, 318, 352, 354, 356
Serbian National Party (SNP) 331
Serbian National Revival (SNR) 356
Serbian Party of St Sava (SPSS) 356
Serbian Radical Party (SRP) 354, 355
Serbian Royalist Block (SRB) 356
Serbian Socialist Party (SSP) 306, 308, 345
Serbianization 334
Serbs 293, 294, 299, 302, 306, 311, 313, 318, 321, 327, 332, 339, 344, 359
Seselj Vojislav 354, 355
Seserko Leo 361
Shcherbak Yuri 290
Shehu Mehmet 14
Sherova L. 275
Shevchenko Valentina 261
Shostakovsky Vyacheslav 264
Shotlekov Ilian 28
Shubin A. 267
Shumen 24
Siba Istvan 153
Sieta Democratica Istriana (SDI) 331
Sigurimi 2, 3, 6, 14, 15
Sijakovic Boguljub 342
Sijedi Panteri — Stranka Upokjencev Slovenije (SP)
Sikorski Wladyslaw 175
Sila-Nowicki Wladyslaw 187, 189
Silesia 59, 68, 76, 77, 80, 86
Sillari Enn-Arno Augostovich 94
Simeon II of Turnovo 40
Simeonov Petko
Simovic Miodrag 317
Sindicatul Muncitorilor Liber 232
Sindicatul Politic Fraternitatea Muncitorilor si Taranilor din Romania 249
Siwek Slawomir 187
Skolc Jozef 362
Skorzynski Piotr 188
Skundric Petar 353
Skupstina 305
Slabakov Peter 41
Sladek Miroslav 69
Slansky Rudolf 54
Slavic republics 260
Slavonia 319
Slezak Jerzy 195
Slisz Jozef 209
Slomka Adam 191
Slovak Christian Democratic Movement 61, 78, 84

Slovak Freedom Party 57, 59
Slovak National Council 57, 58, 61, 68, 69, 75, 88, 89, 91, 92
Slovak National Party 59, 63, 68, 87, 91, 92
Slovak Socialist Republic 68
Slovakia 53, 58, 60, 61, 63, 66, 67, 68, 69, 72, 73, 75, 76, 78, 79, 80, 87–92
Slovaks 61, 68, 75, 77, 87
Slovenacka Zanatska Stranka 362
Slovene Christian Democrats (SCD) 306, 309, 359, 363, 364
Slovene Democratic League (SDL) 301, 306, 364, 365
Slovene Peasant League (SPL) 301, 304, 309, 359, 365
Slovene People's Party 306
Slovenes 293, 301, 302, 306, 321, 359, 365
Slovenia 17, 296, 297, 299, 300, 302, 303, 304, 305, 306, 307, 309, 310, 355, 358–368
Slovenska Demokraticna Zveza (SDZ) 364, 365
Slovenska Kmecka Zveza (SKZ) 365
Slovenska Krscanski Demokrati (SKD) 363, 364
Slovenska narodna strana (SNS) 59, 63, 68, 87, 91, 92
Slovenska Obrinopodjetniska Stranka (SOS) 368
Slovensko Krscansko Socialno Gibanje 363
Slowik Andrzej 190
Slowo Powszechne 176, 204
Small Pensioners' Party 165
Smallholders' Party 130, 131, 132, 133, 137, 144, 147, 148, 160, 161, 163
Smutny Pavel 74
Sobanski Henryk 206
Sobchak Anatolii 261
Sobol M. 268
Social Citizens' Union 114
Social Civic Union 124
Social Contract 130
Social Democracy of the Kingdom of Poland and Lithuania (SDKPiL) 176
Social Democracy of the Polish Republic (SDPR) 177, 183, 184, 185, 210, 214, 215
Social-Democrat 170
Social Democrat 289
Social Democrat Alliance 162
Social Democratic Association (SDA) 288
Social Democratic Foundation 158
Social-Democratic League of Bosnia and Hercegovina (SDLBH) 319
Social-Democratic League of Macedonia (SDLM) 335, 336
Social-Democratic (Menshevik) Party 281
Social-Democratic National Salvation Front 225, 240, 247
Social Democratic Party (Czechoslovakia) 59, 81
Social Democratic Party (Hungary) 165, 166
Social Democratic Party (SDP) (Kosovo) 358
Social Democratic Party (Non-Marxist) 44
Social Democratic Party (Soviet Union) 263, 264

Social Democratic Party in Slovakia 85, 92
Social Democratic Party of Albania (SDPA) 1, 3, 14, 16, 17
Social-Democratic Party of Belorussia 280
Social-Democratic Party of Croatia (SDPC) 328, 329
Social-Democratic Party of Estonia 94
Social Democratic Party of Germany (SPD) 95, 97, 98, 99, 105, 107, 109, 116, 121, 124, 125, 126
Social Democratic Party of Hungary's Gypsies 165
Social-Democratic Party of Macedonia (SDPM) 337, 338
Social-Democratic Party of Moldova 284
Social-Democratic Party of Montenegro (SDPM) 344
Social Democratic Party of Romania's Workers 246
Social-Democratic Party of Romanies in Serbia (SDPRS) 356
Social-Democratic Party of Slovenia (SDPS) 366
Social Democratic Party of the Russian Federation (SDPR) 288
Social-Democratic Party of the Ukraine 291
Social-Democratic Party of Yugoslavia (SDPY) 356
Socialdemokracja Rzeczypospolitej Polskiej (SdRP) 177, 183, 184, 185, 210, 214, 215
Socialdemokrata Nepszava 158
Socialdemokrata Part 165, 166
Socialdemokraticna Stranka Slovenije (SDSS) 366
Socialist Alliance of Croatia 328, 329
Socialist Alliance of Slovenia (SA) 301, 366, 367
Socialist Alliance of Working People of Yugoslavia (SAWPY) 301, 303, 304, 305, 315
Socialist Federal Republic of Yugoslavia (SFRY) 302
Socialist Group of the European Parliament 155
Socialist International 35, 94, 126, 154, 155, 159, 172, 366
Socialist Justice Party 227
Socialist Justice Party — Independent 247
Socialist Labour Party (SLP) 247
Socialist Party (SP) (Montenegro) 307, 341, 344
Socialist Party (Romania) 247
Socialist Party (Soviet Union) 263, 275, 276
Socialist Party of Croatia (SPC) 328, 329
Socialist Party of Croatia — Party of Yugoslav Orientation (SPC-PYO) 331
Socialist Party of Macedonia (SPM) 336, 337
Socialist Party of Serbia (SPS) 345, 346, 353, 356, 358
Socialist Party of Slovenia (SSS) 366, 367
Socialist Party of Yugoslavia (SPY) 356
Socialist Unity Party (SED) 95, 96, 98, 103, 104, 105, 107, 110, 118, 119, 121, 125, 126
Socialist Womens's Initiative (SOFI) 116

INDEX

Socialist Youth Union 49
Socialisticheski Maldezhki Sayuz 49
Socialisticna Stranka Slovenije (SSS) 366, 367
Socialne demokraticka strana na Slovensku (SDSS) 85, 92
Societatea Timisoara 248
Socijaldemokratska Partija Jugoslavije (SDPJ) 356
Socijaldemokratska Partija na Makedonija (SDPM) 337, 338
Socijaldemokratska Stranka Crne Gore (SDSCG) 344
Socijaldemokratska Stranka Hrvatske (SDSH) 328
Socijaldemokratska Stranka Roma u Srbji (SDSRS) 356
Socijaldemokratski Savez Bosne i Hercegovine (SDS BiH) 319
Socijaldemokratski Sojuz na Makedonija (SDSM) 335, 336
Socijalisticka Partija (SP) (Montenegro) 344
Socijalisticka Partija Hrvatske— Partija Jugoslovenske Orientacije (SPH-PJO) 331
Socijalisticka Partija na Makedonija (SPM) 336, 337
Socijalisticka Partija Srbije (SPS) 353
Socijalisticka Stranka Hrvatske (SSH) 328, 329
Socijalisticka Stranka Jugoslavije (SSJ) 356
Socijalisticki Sojuz-Socijalisticka Partija na Makedonija (SS-SPM) 336
Soglasie 173
Sojuz na Komuniste na Makedonija — Partija za Demokratska Preobrazba (SKM-PDP) 335
Sojuz na Reformskite Sili na Makedonija (SRSM) 333, 334
Sokci 348
Sokolovic Dzemal 313
Solidarity 160, 239
Solidarity 177, 178, 179, 180, 182, 183, 184
Solidarity Civic Parliamentary Club (OKP) 180, 181, 182, 184, 187
Solidarity RI (Rolnikow Indywidualnych) 182, 183, 190, 209
Solidarity Trade Union Workers' Alliance 160
Solidarity Weekly 187
Solidarity Women's Initiative 116
Solidarnosc Pracy (SP) 199
Solov'ev N. 269
Solt Ottilia 139
Somogy Christian Coalition 166
Somogyi Kereszteny Koalicio 166
Soos Karoly Attila 138
Soros-Hungarian Academy of Sciences Foundation 143
Sotirov Ivan 48
Sotsial-Democrat Belorussii 280
Sotsial-Demokrat Litvy 172
Sotsialdemokrat 289

Sotsialdemokraticheskaya partiya Rossiiskoi Federatsii 288
Sotsialisticheskaya partiya 275, 276
Sovetskaya Rossiya 253
Soviet Academy of Sciences 255
Soviet Central Asia 253
Soviet Military Administration 95
Soviet Union 20, 30, 55, 56, 93, 129, 171, 172, 173, 200, 293, 295
Soyuz konstitutsionnykh demokratov/partiya konstitutsionnykh demokratov 276
Sozialdemokratische Partei Deutschlands (SPD) 95, 97, 98, 99, 105, 107, 109, 116, 121, 124, 125, 126
Soziale Burgerliche Union 124
Sozialistische Einheitspartei Deutschlands (SED) 95, 96, 98, 103, 104, 105, 107, 110, 118, 119, 121, 125, 126
Sozialistische Frauen-Initiative (SOFI) 116
Spartacist Workers' Party of Germany (SpAD) 126
Spartakist-Arbeiterpartei Deutschlands (SpAD) 126
Spasic Didik 317
Spasov Ivan 31
Spectator 139
Spojenectvi zemedelcu a venkova 85
Spreme Control Chamber (NIK) 211
Spychalska Ewa 201
Srem 344
Srpska Demokratska Stranka (SDS) 327, 328, 351, 352
Srpska Demokratska Stranka Bosne i Hercegovine (SDS BiH) 317, 318
Srpska Liberalna Stranka (SLS) 354
Srpska Narodna Obnova (SNO) 331 356
Srpska Radikalna Stranka (SRS) 354, 355
Srpski Demokratski Forum Kosova i Metohije (SDF) 358
Srpski Pokret Obnove (SPO) 318, 352
SS-East 127
Sselj Vojislav 354
Stachwiuk Wiktor 186
Stalin 13, 20, 54, 176, 251, 252, 253, 254, 264, 265, 293
Stalinism 1, 4, 14, 35, 52, 53, 95, 253, 254, 258
Stambolov Stefan 47
Stanculescu Victor 220, 239
Stanescu Nicu 231
Stankovic Ljubisa 339, 340
Stanovic Zarko 342
Stara Radikalna Stranka (SRS) 355
Stara Zagora 45
Starodubstev V. 272
Stasi 105, 109, 114
State Assembly 271
State Property Agency 148
Staykov Zahari 49
Stier Istvan 149

NEW POLITICAL PARTIES OF EASTERN EUROPE AND THE SOVIET UNION

Stipac Drago   324
Stoichev Stlian   42
Stojanovic Radoslav   348
Stomma Stanislaw   176, 197
Stowarzyszenie PAX   204
Stowarzyszenie Reforma i Demokracja   213, 214
Stoyanov Lchezar   33
Strachinaru Nicolae   246
Strana ceskoslovenske neutrality   73
Strana demokratickej l'avice (SDL)   66, 72, 90
Strana slobody (SS)   53, 89
Strana svobodnych demokratu   73
Strana ustavni demokracie   73
Strana Zelenych (SZ)   75
Stranka Demokraticne Prenove (SDP)   363
Stranka Demokratske Akcije (SDA)   317, 331, 350, 351
Stranka Demokratskih Promjena (SDP)   326
Stranka Demokratskih Reforma Bosne i Hercegovine (SDR BiH)   319
Stranka Demokratskog Dogovora (SDD)   319
Stranka Jugoslovena (SJ)   330, 331, 351
Stranka Jugoslovena za Bosnu i Hercegovinu (SJ BiH)   319
Stranka na Jugosloveni vo Makedonija (SJM)   335
Stranka Nacionalne Ravnopravnosti (SNR)   344
Stranka Narodnog Dogovora (SND)   356
Stranka Nezavisne Demokracije (SND)   331
Stranka Privatne Inicijative (SPI)   319
Stranka Progresivno Orijentisanih Jugoslovena (SPOJ)   319
Stranka Ravnopravnosti (SR)   344
Stranka Roma u Hrvatskoj (SRH)   331
Stranka Saveza Seljaka Srbije (StSSljS)   350
Stranka Socijalne Pravde (SSP)   356
Stranka za Demokratiju i Prava Drzavu (SDPD)   319
Stranka za Enakopravnost Obcanov (SEO)   367
Stronnictwo Demokratyczne (SD)   176, 177, 178, 182, 184, 186, 195, 196
Stronnictwo Narodowe (SN)   201, 202, 202
Stronnictwo Pracy (SP)   189
Stronnictwo Wiernosci Rzeczypospolitej   203
Strug Adam   194
Stumbov Emil   37
Stworzyszenie Polityczne Prawda i Sprawieliwosc (SPPiS)   215
Stysiak Andrzej   206
Subev Hristofor   38, 50, 51
Sulyok Dezso   144
Supreme Court (Soviet Union)   263
Supreme Soviet   259, 261
Surjan Laszlo   141
Surroi Venton   357
Suvar Stipe   310
Svoboda Jiri   82
Svoboden Narod   35
Svobodna rolnicka strana   84

Svobodnoe slovo   271
Svodoba   49
Sweden   334
Switon Kazimierz   189
Switzerland   11, 357, 367
Syria   358, 359
Syryjczyk Tadeusz   197
Systematization   219
Szabad Demokratak Szovetsege (SZDSZ)   130, 131, 132, 133, 137, 138, 139, 140, 143, 147, 157
Szabad Gyorgy   147
Szabadsagpart   144
Szabo Ferenc S.   152
Szabo Ivan   146, 147
Szabo Lajos Matyas   154
Szabo Tamas   146, 147
Szacki Jerzy   214
Szakolczay Gyorgy   138
Szczepanski Jan   200
Szczypiorski Andrzej   194
Szegenyek es Kiszolgaltatottak Szovetsege   140
Szekeres Imre   154
Szekesfehervar   160
Szeles Gabor   147
Szent Korona   160
Szent Korona Tarsasag   145, 151
Szeremientiev Romuald   206
Szilagyi Janos   158
Szocialdemokrata Szovetseg   162
Szocs Geza   233
Szolidaritas   160
Szolidaritas Szakszervezeti Munkaszovetseg   160
Szovetseg a Faluert, Videkert   137
Szucs Alfred   145
Szwalbe Stanislaw   213
Szylman Ryszard   206
Szymanderski Jacek   187

T

Tadzhikistan   251, 253, 261, 272
Takacs Imre   165
Tamas Gaspar Miklos   139
Tamasi Frigyes   164
Tancig Petar   361
Tara Ousului Democratic Union   248
Tarkalanov Aleksandar   48
Tatars   269, 285
Tavisupleba   281
Taykhid   272
Teaci Dumitru   226
TEDISZ   164
Tejkowski Boleslaw   207
Temperate Life Health and Family Protection National Alliance   148
Templin Wolfgang   122
Ter-Petrosyan Levon   261, 278
Tereties Liviu   230
Termeszet es Tarsadalomvedok Szovetsege   140
Teruleti Demokratikus Ifjusagi Szrvezet   164

INDEX

The Deed 229
The Future 237, 238
The Liberal 238
The Other One 120
Thierse Wolfgang 124
Thietz Peter 112
Thomaskirche 114
Thuringia 98, 114, 115
Thurmer Gyula 155
Tiesa 172
Time 357
Timisoara Society 248
Tipac Mihai 230
Tirts Tamas 143
Tisza Circle 157
Tito Josip Broz 13, 294, 295, 296, 298
Tito-Subasic agreement 294
Todorovski Gane 337
Tokes Laszlo 220
Tolgyessy Peter 139
Tomov Aleksandur 35, 36
Tomov Dimitur 44
Tomsic Franc 366
Tomsic Miha 363
Tonkovic Bela 348
Torgyan Jozsef 161
Torkowsky Frank 103
Torocsik Mihaly 152
Tosk 6, 9, 11, 12, 15
Toth Andras 154
Toth Jeno 160
Toth Miklos 155
Toth Sandor 141
Toth Zoltan 149
Totov Totyu 37
Trade Union of Oil Workers 18
Trade Unions (Bulgaria) 19
Traditional Social Democratic Party 248
Transcaucasia 251, 278, 280
Transnacionalna Radikalna Stranka (TRS) 331
Transnational Radical Party (Hungary) 166
Transnational Radical Party (Soviet Union) 273
Transnational Radical Party (TRP) (Yugoslavia) 331
Transznacionalis Radikalis Part 166
Travkin Nikolai 263, 286
Trenchev Konstantin 44
Treuhandanstalt 105, 122
Tripalo Mika 297
Trivuncic Milan 318
Trnavcevic Zaharije 351
Trnka Frantisek 85
Trotsky Leon 253
Trotskyist Left Alternative
Trustee Agency 105, 122
Truth and Justice Political Association 215
Trybuna Ludu 215
Tsara 284
Tsar'kov I. 270

Tschiche Hans-Jochen 119
Tsereteli Iraklii 282
Tsonev Angel 31
Tudjman Franjo 306, 308, 321
Tupurkovski Vasil 333
Turkestan 282
Turkey 11, 24, 34 39
Turkmenia 251, 289
Turks 20, 21, 24, 34, 43, 46, 47, 51, 332
Turnabout and Reform 129
Tusk Donald 199
Tygodnik Demokratyczny 196
Tygodnik Solidarnosc 187
Tyminski Stanislaw 203, 204, 217

U

Udmurt 269
Udruzena Srpska Demokratska Opozicija (USDO) 354
Udruzenje za Jugoslovensku Demokratsku Inicjativu (UJDI) 319, 343, 347
Udruzenje za Unapredjenje Demokratiskih Procesa (UUDP) 343
Udvaros Miklos 146
Ugljanin Sulejman 351
Uhl Peter 85
Ujmagyarok Igazsag Partja 163
Ukraine 259, 261, 267, 269, 276, 283, 290, 291, 292
Ukrainian Christian-Democratic Front 291
Ukrainian Helsinki Union 292
Ukrainian National Party 291
Ukrainian Peasant-Democratic Party 291
Ukrainian Popular-Democratic Party 292
Ukrainian Republican Party 292
Ukrainians 68, 72, 87, 176
Ukrainskii chas 291
Ukrainskii vestnik 292
Ulbricht Walter 95, 121
Ullmann Wolfgang 108
Unabhangige Sozialdemokratische Partei Deutschlands (USPD) 116
Unabhangige Volkspartei (UVP) 116
Unabhangiger Frauenverband (UFV) 115, 116, 117, 126
UNESCO 225
Unia Chrzescijansko-Spoleczna (UChS) 176, 190, 191
Unia Demokratyczna (UD) 183, 196
Unia Polityki Realnej (UPR) 191, 216, 217
Unia Wolnych Spoldzielcow (UWS) 216
Unia Zielonych (UZ) 198
Union for Civic Economic Initiative 49
Union for Civil Society 52
Union for the Republic 61
Union of Albanian Writers and Artists 8
Union of Armenians in Romania 248
Union of Bulgarian National Legions 32

Union of Communists of the Polish Republic Proletariat (UCPR-P) 216
Union of Constitutional Democrats/Party of Constitutional Democrats (UCD) 276
Union of Democratic Forces (UDF) 21, 22, 23, 24, 25, 28, 29, 30, 32, 34, 35, 36, 37, 38, 40, 41, 42, 43, 44, 47, 48, 49, 50, 51, 52
Union of Democratic Muslims 51
Union of Democratic Youth (Poland) 201
Union of Free Co-operatives (UFC) 216
Union of Free Democrats 45, 52
Union of Hungarian Youth Organizations 248
Union of Independent Trade Unions of Albania (UITUA) 1, 2, 3, 6, 13, 15, 17, 18
Union of Labour Youth of Albania (ULYA) 5, 8, 14, 15
Union of Mutual Peasant Aid (VdgB) 110
Union of National Democrats 202
Union of Peasants of Moldova/Peasant-Democratic Party of Moldova 284
Union of Progressive Workers of Yugoslavia (UPWY) 331
Union of Real Politics (URP) 216, 217
Union of the Democratic Party 47
Union of Young Social Democrats (Bulgaria) 47
Union of Young Social Democrats (Poland) 211
United Democratic Centre 50, 51
United Democratic Party of Belorussia 280
United Democratic Party of the Romani, Fiddlers and Wood-Workers of Romania 248
United Front for the Restructuring and Defence of Socialism 51
United Front of Workers of the USSR (UFW) 276, 277
United Kingdom 20, 252
United Left (VL) 104, 108, 126
United Nations 225
United Opposition 305
United Peasant Party (UPP) 176 177, 178, 183, 184, 208, 209
United Peasant Party (ZSL) 176, 177, 178, 183, 184, 208, 209
United Republican Party 94
United Social-Democratic Party of the Ukraine 291, 292
United Socialist Party of Yugoslavia (USPY) 319
United States of America 9, 84, 144, 148, 162, 225, 357, 367
United Young Left 103
Unity 281
Unity Now 127
Unity-Movement for a Socialist Revival 51
Uniunea Armenilor din Romania 248
Uniunea Democrat Crestina 227
Uniunea Democrata a Sirbilor din Romania 247
Uniunea Democrata Maghiara din Romania 225, 233, 234
Uniunea Democrata Turca Musulmana din Romania 236

Uniunea Democratica 231
Uniunea Democratica Tara Oasului 248
Uniunea Lebera Democratica a Romilor din Romania 232
Uniunea Vatra Romaneasca 249
Universal Declaration of Human Rights 262, 279, 288
Universal Party of Slavs and Allied Nations (UPSAN) 217
USSR 95, 96
Ustasa 319
Uta Ion 241
Utasi Istvan 146
Uzbekistan 251, 261, 269, 292
Uzice Movement (UM) 356

V
Vallalkozok Partja 142
Vanguard parties 262
Varga Endre 140
Varga Geza 161
Varga Laszlo 141
Vargane Kerekgyarto Ildiko 154
Vas Jozsef 143
Vasilev Nikolay 28
Vata Vigil 229
Vatra Romaneasca Union (VR) 249
Vatsev Valentin 36
Vaum Victor 246
Vejseli Dzevdet 338
Vekas Janos 348
Veliko Turnovo 24, 38, 45, 47, 51
Velkov Ivan 35
Velvet revolution 53, 55, 85, 91
Verdet Ilie 247, 248
Vereinigte Linke (VL) 104, 108, 126
Vereinigung der Arbeitskreise fur Arbeitnehmerpolitik und Demokratie (VAA) 104
Vereinigung der gegenseitigen Bauernhilfe (VdgB) 110
Verejnost proti nasiliu (VPN)
Vergev Vlkan 33
Versailles Conference 293
Veselica Marko 323
Veselinov Dragan 349
Vestnik Khristianskogo informatsionnogo tsentra 288
Vestnik NFE 94
Vhurbanov Yuri 253
Videki Magyarorszaget Part 144
Vielinov Zafir 47
Viitorul 237, 238
Village Alliance 137
Vilovic Jadran 328
Visario 16, 172
Vitt V. 269
Vladislavlev A. 274
Vnatresna Makedonska Revolucionerna

INDEX

Organizacija-Demokratska Partija za Makedonsko Nacionalno Edinstvo (VMRO-DPMNE) 333, 334
Vodenicharov Rumen 44
Voice of the People 14
Voice of the Youth 8
Voinea Octavian 228
Vojvodina 299, 305, 308, 344, 346, 347, 348, 351
Voks Humana 157, 166
Voks Humana Movement 166
Voks Humana Mozgalom 166
Volkskammer 95, 96, 97, 98, 103, 104, 105, 107, 108, 109, 110, 111, 117
Volksunion 123
Volovik L. 275
Vol'sky A. 274
Vol'ya 268
Voronin O. 275
Voronov A. 275
Vrkic Ivica 325
Vserossiiskii komitet Sotsialisticheskoi partii (VKSP) 275
Vujic Antun 328
Vulkov Stefan 43
Vulkov Viktor 24, 29

W

Wagner Jozef 84
Waigel Theodor 113
Walesa Lech 177, 178 180, 181, 182, 183, 184, 186, 187, 188, 189, 190, 191, 194, 195, 198, 200, 203, 211, 215
Walther Hans-Joachim 113
Warsaw Pact 55, 73, 90, 219, 220, 230, 270
Weekly Bulletin 170
Weinholz Erhard 126
Weiske Christine 115
Weiss Konrad 108
Weiss Peter 90
Wekler Ferenc 138
West Berlin 95, 98, 99
Western Europe 9, 18
White Russians 176
Wieczorek Andrzej 195
Wielowieski Andrzej 194
Wiez 176
Will 268
Wisser Martin 112
Witos Wincenty 175, 176
Wodz Jacek 210
Wojcik Dariusz 191
Wojtczak Michal 196, 197
Wolek Tomasz 197
Wolf Janos 142
Wolf Krzysztof 198
Wolnosc i Pokoj (WiP) 198
Women for Peace 116
Women's Organization (Bulgaria) 19

Women's Party (WP) 356
Women's Union (WU) (Albania) 5, 15
Workers' and Peasants Brotherhood Political Trade Union of Romania 249
Workers'-Cultivators' Party (WCP) 338
Workers' Democratic Party-Party of Federalists (WDP-PF) 319
Workers' Marxist-Leninist Party 143, 166, 167
Workers' Militia 142
Workers' Party 30
Workers' Party 155
Workers' Party of Macedonia (WPM) 339
Workers' Party of Yugoslavia (WPY) 356
Workers' self-management 296
Workers' Social Democratic Party 30
Working Romania 232
World Confederation of Labour 44
World Council of Elders 11
Wozniakowski Henryk 197
Wrzeszcz Maciej 188, 204
Wujec Henryk 194
Wunsche Kurt 118
Wylotek Andrzej 207

X

Xheka Valer 17
Xibri Shyqri 17

Y

Yalta 293
Yanachkov Nikola 32
Yanaev 266
Yanchev Konstantin 29
Yanchev Mitriu 51
Yankov Mitryu 36
Yankov Yanko 44
Yankova Mariya 33
Yarmenko V. 273
Yeltsin Boris 257, 260, 261, 263, 266, 267, 285
Yonov Hristo 32
Yordanov Aleksander 48
Young Christian Democrats (MChD) 188
Young Communist League 255
Young Communist Organization 164
Young Democratic Progressive Party of Macedonia (YDPPM) 338
Young Union (JU) 114, 127
Yugoslav Communist Party (YCP) 13
Yugoslav Democratic Party (YDP) 319
Yugoslav Democratic Party Fatherland Front (YDPFF) 319
Yugoslav Independent Democratic Party (YIDP) 331
Yugoslav National Army (YNA) 295, 300, 306
Yugoslav National Party (YNP) 305, 344
Yugoslav Social-Democratic Party 319
Yugoslav Socialist Democratic Party (YSDP) 356

Yugoslavia   2, 6, 9, 11, 17, 18
Yumerov Mustafa   39
Yunda   170

Z

Zablocki Janusz   205
Zacsek Gyula   147
Zahareva Ekaterina   33
Zahariev Luko   33
Zainea Eugen   247
Zajednica Radnika Progresista Jugoslavije (ZRPJ)   331
Zakelj Viktor   366
Zala Boris   92
Zalewski Maciej   188
Zapotocky Antonin   54
Zawieyski Jerzy   176
Zawislak Adam   199
Zbilja   328
Zdravyi smysl   268
Zelena Akcija (ZA-S)   326
Zelena Partiya   43
Zelena Stranka (ZS) (Serbia)   355
Zelenasi   307
Zeleni Slovenije (ZS)   361
Zelenyi mir   290
Zeles Gabor   147
Zemedelska strana (ZS)   85
Zemedelski Mladezhki Sayuz   28
Zemedelsko Zname   29
Zemlya i volya   292
Zemskii sobor   287
Zeri i Popullit   12, 14
Zeri i Rinise   8
Zhelev Zhelyu   22, 24, 25, 42, 50, 52
Zhelyazka Bogdana   40
Zhirinovsky V.   271
Zhivkov Todor   20, 21, 22, 26, 29, 31, 32, 41, 47, 50
Zhivkov Vladimir   21
Zhorzholiani Temur   281
Zhurnalov Manol   38
Zhvania Zurab   281
Zielinski Andrzej   199
Zielinski Jan   216
Ziembinski Wojciech   203
Zinoviev Grigori   253
Zioberski Jan   189
Ziolkowska Wieslawa   210, 211
Zionist   176
Zjednoczenie Chrzescijansko-Narodowe (ZCh-N)   180, 183, 184, 187, 188, 189, 190, 190, 191, 205, 210
Zjednoczone Stronnictwo Ludowe (ZSL)
Zlatarov Vasil   32
Zlobec Ciril   366
Zmejkovski Boris   333
Znak   176, 204
Zolotarev V.   276
Zolotov A.   276
Zsigo Jeno   165
ZSMS-Liberalna Stranka   361
Zulfikarpasic Adil   316
Zulji Azar   349
Zveza Komunista Slovenije   363
Zwiazek Komunistow Polskich Proletariat (ZKP-Proletariat)   184, 216
Zych Jozef   208

LIBRARY USE ONLY
DOES NOT CIRCULATE